AUSTRALIA'S NORTH-WEST

AUSTRALIA'S NORTH-WEST

ALEX KERR

UNIVERSITY OF WESTERN AUSTRALIA PRESS

First published in 1967 by
University of Western Australia Press
Nedlands, Western Australia

268937

COPYRIGHT

Library of Congress Catalog Card Number 67-16100
Dewey Decimal Classification Number 919.43

Printed in Australia by
Imperial Printing Co. Pty. Ltd., Perth,
Western Australia
Registered at the G.P.O. Perth for transmission by post as a book

To Joan Ivy Kerr

FOREWORD

Dr. Alex Kerr's *Australia's North-West* provides an up to date account of the economy of a region within a state (Western Australia) within a federation (the Commonwealth of Australia). This region is remarkable for its great size, its pastoral and mineral wealth and its small population. At the dates covered – 1960 to 1965, with some reference also to 1966 – the region was expanding economically, and its population was increasing. Each major aspect of these changes is explained by Dr. Kerr, and the total picture is one of economic growth in many fields of activity.

Dr. Kerr's earlier study entitled *Northwestern Australia,* completed in 1962, raised implicitly the question 'how should the region be developed – if at all?' Now, after five years, some of the answers to this question have been found. Private investment, in conjunction with government enterprise, has already developed a part of the Ord river area, the fishing industry, and the great new mining areas. One development has led to another; common services such as transport and communications have been improved, at a far lower subsidized cost than would have been possible without simultaneous expansion on several fronts. But the question is still not fully answered.

In this latest study, Dr. Kerr has not only up-dated his information, but expanded the scope of his discussions. On each subject, he brings up some of the policy issues implied in plans for further growth or for even larger investments than have already taken place. This volume provides, therefore, an indispensable background to an understanding of the problems of the northern part of Western Australia, an important sector of Australia's north.

There have been failures in the region, as well as successes; mines have closed down as well as been opened, and industries have worked themselves out (whaling, for instance) as well as expanding. There have been reforms in pastoral practices, and some improvement in the stocks reared, but there is still plenty of room for further technological gains.

The study provides a further, and in many respects, more mature, analysis of the work done and still to be done. The pros and cons of policy are discussed at several points, providing a basis for any serious planning for the region's development.

The future of the region is bound up with, among other things, its chances of attracting further capital inflow, some of it almost necessarily from overseas, owing to the scarcity of Australian risk capital. Future investors will look to studies like Dr. Kerr's to give them a comprehensive account of the economy of their possible choice.

Regional economics is becoming more widely studied every year in all parts of the world. The reason for this seems to be that national economies rarely develop throughout at an even rate; some regions advance much faster than the average, while others lag. From this arises the need to consider particular regions as separate economic entities, in a word, to study regional economics. This special activity can be developed usefully in Western Australia, itself a region within a national economy, with distinct sub-regions within its boundaries.

Northwestern Australia is not a lagging, but is still in some respects, a precarious and an under-developed economy. A few decisions can so easily close down the economic basis of a whole area within it, but, as Dr. Kerr's study shows, there are now many strands of development, and a set-back in all simultaneously becomes less likely.

Another five years will see further changes in the area. Meanwhile, economic research and economic planning, as Dr. Kerr explains, may themselves make some contribution to growth. The upsurge in private investment has been a beneficial stimulus to growth, but many problems arise as this growth takes place. Dr. Kerr's book contributes to their early solution.

This book is to be produced quite rapidly after its completion, and this will enhance its topical value. Many organisations and industries, as Dr. Kerr acknowledges, have assisted the Department of Economics in its work on Western Australian economic problems, but the burden of putting together and interpreting facts on this region drawn from many sources has been entirely Dr. Kerr's.

Understanding the economic significance of multiple developments in so large an area must begin with descriptive assessment of trends, and some attempt to see what policies have been at work. Dr. Kerr's new book is an economist's contribution to a development which has political and social significance for Western Australia, and for Australia, as a whole, nor must it be overlooked that Australia is part of several international economic and political 'worlds' for which developments of this kind have an increasing rather than a diminishing importance.

IAN BOWEN

Department of Economics,
The University of Western Australia
January, 1967

PREFACE

The economy of Northwestern Australia has undergone such changes in the last five years that the book which appeared in 1962 under the title *Northwestern Australia* is now quite out of date and in many parts misleading. This book is intended as a successor to *Northwestern Australia* and to a limited extent makes use of some of the same material, in particular the historical sections of some of the chapters. In fact these are the only parts of the first book remaining untouched.

Hand in hand with a complete text revision has gone a fundamental change in layout. The survey of physical resources which constituted Chapters 1 and 4, now forms Appendixes 1 to 4, so that the body of the text is concentrated upon the region's economic resources. The order of chapters has also been changed and the lengths of chapters altered to give somewhat different emphases than previously. The number of statistical tables has been reduced and the statistics appearing in the text have been kept to a minimum. The number of maps has been increased and they have been modified and re-drawn.

By and large, the alterations that have been made take account of the changes occurring over the period 1960 to 1965 but in some cases it has been possible to extend the study to 1966, the year Australia introduced the decimal currency. This has sometimes raised problems when comparing values over time. Values are expressed in pounds when dealing with the period before the changeover in 1966, dollars when discussing the period since. The conversion rate of £1 equals $2 is simple enough to apply.

The book owes much to many people. It contains a great deal of statistical information which has been contributed by the officers of the Bureau of Census and Statistics and other government departments, both commonwealth and state, and many private companies. It also contains opinions gleaned from conversations in the region with people of all walks of life. Shire secretaries and councillors, businessmen and bank managers, graziers and agriculturalists, experts and laymen, airline pilots and ships' officers, drivers and drovers all contributed to the picture of the region which is built up in these pages.

In the preparation of the first book Mr. Michael Lightowler, B.A. (Hons.)

and Mr. Peter Rappolt, B.A. (Hons.) assisted with the gathering of statistical and other information and Mrs. Betty Willmott, B.Ed., assembled and
drafted the section on physical resources, including the maps. Draftsmen
from the state Public Works Department also assisted with the preparation
of some of the maps. Subsequently Mr. Charles Kuiper, B.Ec. (Hons.), and
Mrs. Catherine Chapman, B.Ec. (Hons.) assisted with the gathering of
material for this work and the original maps were re-drawn and others added
by Mr. G. N. Ward of the Department of Geography in the University of
Western Australia.

The technical data in the appendixes was checked for accuracy by the
Director of the Geological Survey of Western Australia, the Regional Direc-
tor of the Commonwealth Bureau of Meteorology, the former Government
Botanist, and the Professor of Soil Science in the University of Western
Australia. Other government experts checked various technical sections in
the body of the text.

Professor Ian Bowen, Head of the Department of Economics in the
University of Western Australia offered helpful advice on chapter drafts and
at all times encouraged the research. Likewise, encouragement and practical
assistance was given throughout by the Hon. C. W. M. Court, Minister for
the North-West, and his staff and by Mr. H. J. McGuigan, Administrator for
the North-West. Miss Jenny Yelverton patiently transformed masses of
sometimes confused manuscript into readable typescript.

My debt is great to all those mentioned, and their various contributions
have influenced the presentation of fact and opinion in these pages. At the
same time, of course, the responsibility for what follows is my own.

ALEX KERR

The University of Western Australia
July, 1966

CONTENTS

FIGURES

TABLES

CHAPTER 1

INTRODUCTION

By 1960 the industries of Northwestern Australia, which had lain virtually dormant in the period between the two world wars and then had begun to stir in the post-war period, were showing signs of rapid growth and change. Since then the pace of the region's economic development has accelerated considerably and its character has changed even further. This book attempts to tell the story of this metamorphosis.

The region has assumed an atmosphere of bustle, of change, of rapid growth, which has rubbed off on most of those who live and visit there and at the same time it has attracted, in the south of the state and in the other states of Australia and overseas, a greater interest in and awareness of what is happening there. Public interest has quickened because of the relatively large sums of public money being spent in the north on specific development projects and the even greater sums of private money flowing in, and because of the keenness with which some of the issues have been debated publicly, both within and outside the state. The fact that the development of Northwestern Australia is now seen, at least on the national front, as a facet of the much wider issue of northern development has also focussed many more eyes in that direction, for the northern development case has been argued with increasing vigour of late. The appointment of senior officers in commonwealth and state governments to positions created specifically for the purpose of considering problems of northern development, and the formation of study groups throughout Australia in universities and elsewhere with an orientation towards the north, have further stimulated interest in the region's development.

Since wise development can be achieved only if the characteristics and limitations of the region are fully known and appreciated, a survey of its physical and economic resources and their past and present development is a necessary first step. Once a picture of the region's economy in broad terms is obtained, the way is open to proceed to more intensive studies of particular aspects of it and to consider them in relation to the whole. Thus, for example, certain technical features of the development of irrigated agriculture on the Ord may be studied in a narrow setting while at the same time the project can be seen as a localized activity making a demand upon the limited public funds available for development within the region as a whole and thus competing with other localized development schemes else-where in the region. The careful husbanding of public resources demands that the authorities responsible for their allocation to various uses, and the general public as well, should know as much as possible about the economy.

Interest in possibilities for the investment of material and human re-sources in this area has been displayed by private individuals and companies, both Australian and overseas, as well as by state governments on both sides of the house. State government departments have, over the years, acquired accurate and detailed knowledge of certain parts of the region and its resources and certain facets of its productive activities, though gaps still remain. But as yet the potential private investor has no way of acquaint-ing himself in reasonable detail with all the main features of the region except in piecemeal fashion by obtaining literature from government departments, consulting journal articles, sifting newspaper files and so on. All of this involves the expenditure of a considerable amount of time and effort and leads to constant duplication, and there is an urgent need to assemble information of this sort under one cover and present a compre-hensive picture of the region as a whole to the interested observer, and this is what this book endeavours to do. Initial investigations were set in motion in 1955 when a visit was made by the author to all the northern ports and major inland centres, and discussions were held with road board members, local administrators, pastoralists and businessmen. The enquiry was taken up again in 1959 when a further visit was made to the area and more data gathered. In 1961, after a third visit, a preliminary report was drafted and the book *Northwestern Australia* appeared in 1962. Visits were made to the region again in 1962, 1963, 1965 and 1966, and the re-writings and re-arrangements effected, resulted in this book.

The first problem in 1955 was to define the region to be studied. The area vaguely referred to locally as the 'North-West' probably included, in most people's minds, the Kimberley Statistical Division, 162,000 square miles in extent and containing 5,668 persons in 1961, the Pilbara Statistical Division with 171,000 square miles and 3,243 persons, the North-West Statistical Division with 76,000 square miles and 4,563 persons and perhaps part of the Central Statistical Division with 167,000 square miles and 1,387 persons. In total this constituted an area of 576,814 square miles, and with a population of 14,861 it had a population density of 2.6 persons per 100 square miles in 1961. This area, bounded in the south by the twenty-sixth parallel and shown in Figure 1, was finally adopted as con-stituting Northwestern Australia, for the purposes of this study.

It is such a vast area that one might well point out that its geographical distribution of physical and economic resources is such that there may be expected to be few common characteristics running through the whole region. Why not, for instance, concentrate on the Kimberley alone or on the North-West Division, or on the Pilbara? Within this great area one can, of course, distinguish regions with distinctive physical and economic characteristics which would justify intensive individual study. To take but one example – conditions in the pastoral industry differ as between the Kimberley and the Pilbara. The major problems differ somewhat, the character of production varies slightly, the vermin menace has a different complexion, climatic conditions are not the same. Thus, it may be argued, while there are common threads running through the region, one cannot descend to the particular and must remain upon a certain level of generalization, and this is broadly true. There are, however, several reasons why the region should be studied as a whole.

In the first place, the area north of the twenty-sixth parallel is an administrative unit for the government of Western Australia. This is the area for which the Minister for the North-West is responsible, and it is the area over which the government's Administrator for the North-West has administrative and planning responsibilities. Within other government departments (for example Agriculture, Labour, Public Works) this area receives special attention and divisions have been set up to deal with it. Thus development proposals of all sorts relevant to this broad region compete with one another for limited capital resources, for limited research funds and personnel, and for limited administrative and operative personnel. Each proposal must, therefore, to a certain extent be considered in relation to others within the region so delineated. The commonwealth government also recognises specific differences between northern and southern areas within the greater Australian economy.

Second, certain taxation provisions relate to the area north of the twenty-sixth parallel and this, of course, affects the financial operations of companies and individuals. Various types of fare concessions, educational allowances, and living cost adjustments also recognize the parallel as a boundary. In toto, these constitute substantial adjustments to real incomes in the region, as pointed out in Chapter 2, even though many claim they are insufficient, and undoubtedly they represent income differentials that influence location decisions in some cases.

Third, and on the practical side, the distance and costs involved in travel from Perth to focal points in the area are so high that to carry out separate surveys of sub-regions, at least in the initial stages, would be too time-consuming and costly. The decision was made, therefore, to cover the whole area north of the twenty-sixth parallel in fairly general terms, leaving researchers to concentrate subsequently upon particular sub-regions or industries.

Thus was settled the question of what groups of shires should constitute 'Northwestern Australia'. The Kimberley, with its pastoral industry and mining, the North-West, with its fishing, agriculture and sheep industries, the Pilbara, with its grazing and mining, were obvious inclusions. But the Central Division presented some problems. It possessed a grazing industry which had certain factors in common with the other grazing industries in the region and it possessed a mining industry which was broadly similar to the mining of the Pilbara. In addition, the railhead of Meekatharra was the communications centre for small communities and for miners and pastoralists of parts of the Nullagine and Upper Gascoyne shires. As the Division extended to within 175 miles of Perth, only its two northern shires, Meekatharra and Wiluna, were extracted and included in the region. In 1955, therefore, Northwestern Australia comprised the shires of Wyndham, Broome, West Kimberley, Hall's Creek, Roebourne, Port Hedland, Marble Bar, Tableland, Nullagine, Ashburton, Gascoyne-Minilya, Upper Gascoyne, Shark Bay, Meekatharra and Wiluna and the Municipality of Carnarvon. Since 1961, the name of one shire has been changed, the Gascoyne-Minilya Shire and the Carnarvon Town Council have been amalgamated to form the Carnarvon Shire and a new shire, Exmouth, has been gazetted, but the area remains the same.

The information for this study has been gathered from many sources. The visits which have been made in the region over a period of years have enabled important on-the-spot information to be gathered. Talks have been held with local government bodies and individual local government officers, state government officials, private businessmen, farmers and commonwealth officers. Questionnaires have also been used at two-yearly intervals. These were designed to gather information which was not available from normal publication channels. Most of it is used in Chapter 8. Seminars were also held at the University during 1960 and 1961 to which were invited government officials and private businessmen who could claim considerable experience in the region in respect of the particular topics discussed. The exchange of information and the views expressed at these seminars were of great assistance in supplementing the information gathered from other sources for the first book. Extensive use has been made of published materials, both official and private, particularly where much of the information is of a technical nature. The bibliographies indicate the scope of the specialized studies, in various fields, relating to parts of the region and to particular subjects. Specially prepared maps have been used to supplement the text, and a considerable amount of statistical information in tabular form accompanies each chapter.

From many points of view it is unfortunate that the detailed figures of the 1966 census will not be available until after this book goes to press, but in some chapters, particularly in Chapter 2, census information for 1961 is given in considerable detail so that comparisons can be made by the interested reader when the results of the 1966 census are finally to hand. Nevertheless sufficient interim figures are available from the

Deputy Commonwealth Statistician and other sources to enable the post-1961 story to be told in its broadest aspects.

The appendices, which are somewhat technical in parts and which may be dry reading to the uninitiated, each have a summarizing section which is inserted for the purpose of providing a rather more brief and concise statement for those who do not wish to study the physical characteristics of the region in the detail given. The extensive footnotes, given in abbreviated form in the text but in fuller detail in the bibliography at the end of each appendix, are designed to serve two purposes : first, to document the statements made, and, second, to enable the reader to follow up particular avenues of enquiry which might interest him.

Taken as a whole, the appendices give an account of the physical resources of Northwestern Australia and the reader can gain from them an impression of the limitations which are imposed upon the character of the region's economic development by its physical resource endowment. In the industry surveys in the body of the text this point is brought home time and again – one thinks of the devastation resulting from the 1961 cyclone at Carnarvon, of the distance factor and other physical conditions which heavily influence the transport costs of manganese, of the way in which the forbidding barrier of the King Leopold Ranges stimulated the establishment of Air Beef, of road costs amounting to $36,000 a mile in some parts of the country, of vicious floods destroying bridges and communications, and so on. Within these limitations man has worked to achieve economic development. It is the story of how this has been done and is being done that forms the body of this text. As far as possible the physical and economic aspects are kept separate to avoid overlapping, though it cannot be avoided to a certain minor extent.

Each major industry is dealt with in a separate chapter, and the attempt has been made to examine past development, present characteristics and future prospects. Additional chapters deal with particular economic problems or characteristics of the region as a whole, and a concluding chapter attempts to synthesise the body of the work and suggest in broad terms what the future years may hold for the region.

There is the ever-present tendency to think of economic development as being somehow good in its own right and, while one may dismiss criticism of 'development for development's sake' on the grounds that not even a mediocre planner would think purely in these terms to the exclusion of other considerations, one has to admit the possibility of important issues – in particular sociological considerations – sometimes being submerged in the enthusiasm with which a new project is approached. Relating economic decisions to the accepted goals of society as expressed by successive Australian governments – full employment, stability and growth – one should inevitably come down to the individual, the citizen, and it is to emphasize this – to suggest that the region should be viewed as a collection not of cattle stations, dams, pearling luggers, and so on, but of stockmen, engineers, fishermen, and their wives and children – that Chapter 2 has been inserted before embarking upon a survey of the region's economy.

The repercussions of the big planning decisions taken in the region by private organizations and by government bodies will be felt ultimately in terms of human happiness or unhappiness. The great moves taking place in Northwestern Australia are discussed below. It is as well to remember that there are human beings behind all of these moves : the cotton farmer and his family at Kununurra, the pearler and his family at Broome, the miner and his family at Wittenoom, the cattle or sheep station manager and his family in the Kimberley, the aborigine and his family on the station or in the township, and the many single men with no ties moving from camp to camp, and the married men separated from their families for the purpose of earning money quickly.

The changing character of the region's population and workforce including aborigines, the problems of family living, general costs of living, and attempts to overcome these in order to bring some stability into the population and living pattern are also discussed in Chapter 2.

The region has always been associated in the minds of most people with primary industry. Beef cattle and sheep, whales and pearls, bananas and beans, iron, asbestos and manganese; all have symbolised the north and they have recently been extended to include oil and gas, prawns and scalefish, rice and cotton. Most of what little manufacturing activity there is exists to process the raw materials of primary industry, so that the region's primary industry including mining may be said to provide employment for about one half of the total workforce, a proportion more than twice as high as for the whole state. Even so, the tertiary workforce is increasing in relative importance at the expense of primary industry and this trend can be expected to continue as long as the period of brisk construction activity lasts in the region. This activity is linked to several industries : iron ore mining in the Pilbara, tertiary industry (communications) at North-West Cape, irrigated agriculture on the Ord, port construction for shipping are examples, and the demand for labour is likely to remain firm for some time.

Within the region's primary industry, pastoralism still remains dominant in terms of output values, though there is no doubt that it soon will have been surpassed by mining. The two main segments of the pastoral industry, beef cattle and sheep, together have constituted the backbone of the Northwestern economy in the past and still continue to do so. Their influence is spread throughout the region by means of the million-acre cattle properties of the East and West Kimberley and the half million-acre sheep stations further south. Both of these industries have seen hard times but are now showing signs of partial rejuvenation, though at different rates, and the story of their recent growth and the problems they face is given in Chapter 3.

The mining industry which is second in importance now but destined to be of overwhelming importance in the future was, like the pastoral industries, an early form of activity in the region. The state's first goldfield was gazetted in Northwestern Australia. Now it is iron ore, petroleum and natural gas, manganese and tin which have become the glamour minerals and their large-scale exploitation has brought a new dimension of development to the region. The story of the transition from small to large-scale research and development is told in Chapter 4 where current plans for future exploitation are also discussed, along with the price controversy and export argument over iron ore.

The fishing industry, again an early activity in the region, has been responsible in the past for assisting development at crucial periods. More recently, it has been changing its face, much like mining. The change has been one of techniques as well as of products, and the present character of the industry is vastly different from that of only a decade ago. The story of this metamorphosis is told in Chapter 5.

Irrigated agriculture is the youngest of the Northwestern primary industries, having been born in the 1930's at Carnarvon. There are now two other ventures in this field, at Camballin and Kununurra, and the newest, the Ord Scheme, has made as great an impact on the general Australian public in terms of public debate as the immense iron ore schemes further south. The historical development of these areas, the current technological and social and economic considerations determining their future prospects, and the public controversy surrounding both the Ord and the whole concept of northern development are discussed in Chapter 6.

The problem of water conservation rates a chapter to itself and this is really the second of the chapters devoted to specific aspects of the region's economy which are common to all industries. Since, however, it is more directly oriented to the agricultural industry than any other, by virtue of the large sums of money so far proposed for expenditure on irrigation, it follows Chapter 6. Proposals for the development of Kimberley water resources, for the provision of town water supplies, and for the utilization of ground and underground water throughout the region are examined, and the engineering features of the water control schemes proposed for the Ord and the Fitzroy are discussed, as well as the proposal to harness the tidal power resources, and the future of Carnarvon agriculture. The discussion of these issues is to be found in Chapter 7.

As mentioned above, tertiary industry is a large employer of labour in the region, as one would expect. Under normal circumstances the proportion of government employees in such a sparsely populated area would be higher than the average and the costs of government per head would be much higher still. This would normally be offset by a smaller than usual proportion of the workforce being engaged in commerce, retailing etc. But in the region at the moment are many thousands of construction workers following in the wake of the mineral and other exploitation projects. Fortunately, not all of these projects are scheduled to mature at the same time and they can, to a certain extent, be phased in with one another thus diminishing the maximum requirement of construction workers at any one time. Nevertheless the quickening of activity in the region which has continued now for some years has been sufficient to increase substantially the proportion of the workforce employed in tertiary industry. Associated with this has been increased government activity in the region and the demand has been great for an extension of such services as hospitals and schools. The character of the region's tertiary industry as it is revealed by official statistics and by supplementary information gathered through the medium of questionnaires to local government officers is discussed in Chapter 8.

One fact that stands out even to the casual observer is the high cost of living in Northwestern Australia, and one of the major factors responsible for this, in conjunction with high labour costs, is the heavy transport charges which help to inflate material costs. The reasons for this are varied and they are considered in Chapter 9 where the major transport modes in the region, land, air, sea and rail are examined separately and in relation to one another. This is the third of the chapters which deal with problems common to all parts of the region and all industries within it.

In the decade 1955 - 1965 the pattern of development in Northwestern Australia has been a dynamic one. The characteristics and methods of individual industries are different from those of the past, even in the long-established cattle industry, and in some cases the change has been both rapid and momentous. In particular in the mining industry but also in fishing and agriculture, horizons have altered discernibly in the short space of ten years and will, no doubt, alter again in the next ten. The forces that now have been set in motion will continue into the future and the challenge is to produce a pattern of development that will make the best use of the resources that can be allocated to the region from public and private sources. Administrative and planning aspects of the region's growth must be examined as well as the more general question of government versus private development. These issues are taken up in Chapter 10.

Northwestern Australia is not merely a collection of natural resources and basic primary industries coupled with service industries. It is a land of rivers and deserts, of mountains and plainlands, of floods and droughts, of rugged cliffs and sprawling white beaches, of vivid greens and reds and dull browns. It is a land of small communities separated by vast distances and linked by road, air, rail and sea routes which the elements sometimes close for brief periods. For the visitor from the south the region presents a completely different environment and way of life. Its rugged beauty compels and repels at the same time. The harshness and force of nature combine to produce devastation with creation, the struggle for life with a plethora of nature's bounties, natural beauty with stark ugliness. Its contrasts perhaps provide its greatest asset and very few who visit the area are not impressed and do not wish to return.

Living there and developing the land is, in itself, a challenge and one which was accepted by the early pioneers who were prepared to trade personal comfort and security for the opportunity to reap high returns. The

scene has changed greatly since those days but the element of personal discomfort, now much reduced, still remains to be contended with, and the
possibilities for high returns, again in some directions reduced, still exist.
In the last decade development of areas remote from the capital in Western
Australia (for instance at Esperance and Carnarvon) indicates fairly clearly
that where economic incentive and feasibility exist, there is no insuperable
shortage of personnel with sufficient spirit in them to open up new land,
and to form new communities.

Given essential minimum public support for development, Northwestern
Australia, as its resources are opened up and its potential is realized, may
be expected to attract immigrants from other parts of Australia and other
parts of the world without much difficulty.

CHAPTER 2

POPULATION, EMPLOYMENT AND LIVING CONDITIONS

Population estimates by shires for each year are available from the Deputy Commonwealth Statistician so that at any time one can ascertain approximately how many people are in the region or in each part of it. But detailed demographic information is available only from the census which is now conducted at five-yearly intervals. The most recent detailed information is that available from the 1961 census but before long the results of the 1966 census should be coming to hand, to throw more light upon the population and employment characteristics. So much change has taken place in the region in the inter-censal period that the 1961 figures are now useful mainly for comparative purposes. It should be noted that since the census is taken in June, a time of the year when activity in Northwestern Australia is brisk, its results can be misleading. Some of the information it reveals should be thought of as being representative of winter conditions and not necessarily of summer conditions.

1. POPULATION

Demographic Characteristics

At June, 1961, Northwestern Australia contained 14,861 persons. Current estimates put the figure at over 20,000 in 1965. Since the region covers some 577,000 square miles this gives it a population density in 1961 of 2.6 persons per 100 square miles and a density in 1965 of 3.5. Population increase between the census of 1947 and that of 1961 was 62 per cent, a compound rate of increase of 3.5 per cent annually, and the annual rate of increase between 1961 and 1966 will be considerably greater than this. It could be about 7.5 per cent.

The proportion of males to females in the region is, as one would expect, considerably greater than in the state as a whole, though it is slowly falling. Between 1947 and 1954 the ratio fell from 1.90 to 1.86 and in 1961 it was 1.76. For the state as a whole it was 1.04 in 1961.

The age distribution of the population in the region is again appreciably different from that of the state. The proportions of children under 15 and of persons over 65 were lower at the census dates of 1947, 1954 and 1961. Thus Northwestern Australia contains a higher proportion of persons in the active working-age group than the state as a whole, and a lower proportion of persons who could be classified generally as dependants.

Closely linked with age structures are the ratios of the workforce to total population. Again there is a wide disparity between the region and the state. The workforce comprised 58 per cent of the region's total population in 1947 and 59 per cent in 1954. The comparable figures for the state were 41 per cent and 40 per cent. In 1961 the ratios for the region had dropped to 56 per cent and 38 per cent respectively.

The region contains the bulk of the state's aboriginal population but accurate figures are difficult to obtain. Approximately three quarters of the state's full-blood aborigines are to be found north of the twenty-sixth parallel and almost one quarter of its part-aborigines. The proportion of children to adults in the native population is higher than in the non-native population. Altogether there are over 7,000 full-bloods in the region.

Population Growth

During the triple census period, 1947 - 1954 - 1961, the total population of Northwestern Australia grew from 9,197 to 11,880 to 14,861. Of the state's total population, 1.8 per cent was located in the region in 1947. In 1954 the figure was 1.9 per cent and in 1961 it was 2.0 per cent. Thus the region's population rose at a rate slightly faster than that for the state.

At the 1961 census there were fifteen shires and one municipality, and their fortunes in the preceding period 1947 to 1961, were partly reflected in their population growth rates. Tableland Shire recorded the greatest rate of increase (400 per cent) due to the development of the asbestos deposits at Wittenoom Gorge. Wyndham - East Kimberley and West Kimberley shires both recorded increases of more than 150 per cent, the former because of the Ord River irrigation development and the latter because of the development of the Yampi iron ore deposits and the activity associated with the Camballin irrigation project. Two other shires doubled their population in the period, namely Shark Bay, due to the expansion of fishing industry, and Port Hedland, where mining activity and other small industries, particularly transport, had stimulated population inflow.

Two shires recorded a decline. Wiluna had seen the closing down of several gold mines and suffered a population loss of 70 per cent, while Nullagine suffered a 16 per cent loss for the same reason. Both of these shires are land-locked and have a low and unreliable rainfall, and no other activity has sprung up to compensate for the population drift.

The fact that strikes one immediately, and merely serves to underline the diversity of activity in this vast region, is that the population movements in the various shires were due to several diverse activities – irrigated agriculture,

iron ore exploitation, asbestos mining, manganese mining, gold mining
and fishing.

As explained above, detailed results of the 1966 census are not yet to hand
at the time of writing but population estimates for 1965 throw some light
upon movements since 1961.

As might be expected recent population increases have been greatest in
the Pilbara Statistical Division. Roebourne Shire, with an increase of over
150 per cent, and Port Hedland Shire (over 75 per cent) and Nullagine
(almost 50 per cent) reflect the impact of the iron ore exploitation in this
period and the building of the ports and inland townships has caused a substantial population upsurge. The more recent census figures when they come
to hand, will show even greater increases. Again, the construction of the
United States naval communication establishment at Exmouth Gulf has
resulted in the creation of a new township and an increase of approximately
one thousand persons living in the area in the one year from June 1964 to
June 1965. The other substantial population increase recorded in this
four-year period has been almost 40 per cent in the Wyndham-East Kimberley
Shire, due to the further development of irrigated agriculture at Kununurra.
Overall, the total number of persons in Northwestern Australia increased
in four years, by an estimated 37 per cent, from 14,861 to 20,350, at an
annual rate of 8.2 per cent. An annual rate of increase of this magnitude
cannot be sustained indefinitely and the rapid build-up of population may
be expected to drop off fairly soon, but even so one may anticipate that rates
of population increase for the region will continue to outstrip those for the
state as a whole for some years to come.

2. LABOUR AND EMPLOYMENT

For a region to develop rapidly three main conditions must be satisfied.
It must have the basic natural resources for exploitation, it must have the
capital equipment with which to operate upon these resources, and it must
have an adequate labour force in terms of numbers and standards. There
is little doubt that Northwestern Australia has enough natural advantages
of one kind and another to allow rapid development for some time to come.
While shortage of capital is a perennial problem — in relation to all the
possible uses to which it may be put – it has flowed into the region in pro-
digious quantities in recent years. As regards labour, it can be said that
any lack of the right numbers and types has not yet constituted a serious
obstacle to the region's development. Provided living conditions are reasonably adequate and possibilities exist for deriving substantial weekly pay
cheques from extra work (and both of these conditions hold in the region
at the present time) men will go there to work. Questions of labour
availability and its quality will be discussed below.

Broadly, it may be said that the main characteristic of employment in the
region is its seasonal aspect which gives the area a large migratory labour

force. Employees of meat works, drovers, drivers, fishermen, shearing teams, public and private construction workers, transport workers, waterside workers and some miners all find their activities regulated in some way by the climate. For this reason, as pointed out earlier, census figures will always inflate figures of employment and population in the region since the month of June lies in the period of peak activity. This is also a period of peak tourist activity, again because of climatic factors.

Workforce Characteristics

In 1961 one-fifth of the region's total workforce was to be found in the grazing segment of primary industry, and 13 per cent was to be found in mining. Altogether primary industry accounted for 43 per cent of the region's workforce, in marked contrast to the figure of 18 per cent for the whole state. When the 1966 figures come to hand one can expect mining to have made some relative gains at the expense of the grazing industry but primary industry as a whole will probably not have changed much in its relative importance. In future years when construction workers move out of the mining areas and the permanent mining workforce establishes itself, one can expect primary industry to be even more predominant than it is now.

Tertiary industry in 1961 was more important than primary industry, occupying 49 per cent of the total regional workforce, but this figure, despite the large extent of government activity in the region, was well below the state figure of 64 per cent. One may expect the 1966 census figures to reflect the heavy preponderance of construction workers in the north which has become so marked recently as a result of the building of new townships and ports for the iron ore development. Even at the time of the 1961 census the numbers engaged in building and construction exceeded the next most important tertiary activity, transport and communications, by almost 100 per cent.

In 1961, all but 1.8 per cent of the workforce in the region were at work and by far the most important group, constituting 85 per cent of the whole, were employees on wage and salary. Employers and self-employed each constituted about six per cent of the total and unpaid helpers less than one per cent.

Several shires: Gascoyne-Minilya, Upper Gascoyne, Ashburton, Wiluna, Marble Bar, Roebourne, and Tableland, had virtually no manufacturing workforce at all in 1961 while others: Meekatharra, Shark Bay, Nullagine and Port Hedland, had less than 20. Broome, Derby and Wyndham, each with a meatworks, were the only towns to possess a manufacturing workforce of any substance.

Employment

Labour in the region is largely seasonal, and at the peak of the season there are great opportunities for earning attractive wages because of the fact that overtime work is plentiful since a time limit is imposed by the length of the season. For the individual who goes to a remote spot in the north there is generally little to provide diversion from work, anyhow, and the consequence is that otherwise spare time is occupied in overtime work at attractive rates. The result of this is that many southern workers return from the north at the finish of the season with large savings.

To the seasonal demand for labour, which is occasioned partly by the nature of the region's primary industry and partly by climatic conditions which place a limit upon movement and other activity at certain times of the year, may be added the strong demand over recent years for construction labour. First the development of the Ord River scheme and the Camballin scheme in the early sixties was followed by iron ore exploitation and its associated developments and then superimposed upon this was the construction programme for the $80 million United States naval communications base at Exmouth Gulf and the N.A.S.A. tracking station at Carnarvon. At the same time government activity, from port construction and road building to the erection of hospitals and houses, stepped up in pace and was accompanied by equally brisk activity in the private sector, from the construction of hotels and houses to the building of factories, offices, depots and other places of work.

This work did not have a seasonal urgency in the same sense as that deriving from the primary industries (e.g. killing, shearing, harvesting or weeding), although climatic factors did still impose limitations. On the other hand it did have urgency in the sense that the fulfilment of contracts depended upon early construction work proceeding on schedule. The end result, therefore, was the same in terms of the opportunities for working overtime at attractive rates. From the figures given in Table 11 it can be seen that average earnings for males in the region are more than 50 per cent higher than for the state as a whole whereas in the case of females, earnings are about the same.

The actual wages paid are a reflection of the state of demand for labour within the region. They also serve to give some indication of the higher costs involved for employers situated in the north. Of course, the earnings divergence of 50 per cent does not necessarily indicate that costs in the region are half as great again as they are in the rest of the state for, as well as indicating a better payment rate, the divergence is the result of greater than average working hours and thus greater than average production. On the other hand, certain non-monetary benefits mentioned below, must be taken into account and labour costs can be said to be considerably higher than elsewhere when all factors are considered.

There are, as suggested, many other indirect costs associated with the employment of labour in the north. Workers are flown to the job and flown back at the end of their employment provided they have served a minimum period. Leave conditions are usually liberal as they have to be to induce married men and their families into the area. Makeshift accommodation is no longer acceptable and amenities generally have to be the equal of those elsewhere, or even better. All of these elements, and many more, help to inflate labour costs.

Despite the disabilities of working north of the twenty-sixth parallel it may be said that so far no serious shortage of labour has been experienced, and this despite the large construction programmes undertaken. Earnings have been sufficient to draw the necessary workers to the region, sometimes at the expense of other parts of the state. Considerable pressure on available labour resources has been felt, for example, in the Perth metropolitan area and shortages have appeared in many trades. This has caused, on occasion, loss of contracts by Western Australian manufacturers unable to expand production sufficiently. The reasonably large and steady inflow into the state of workers from the eastern states, Adelaide in particular, has sometimes not been sufficient to compensate for the flow to the north.

Various means of alleviating this problem have been suggested including the temporary importation of labour for specific jobs, but generally this has been opposed by the unions. Mention is also made in Chapter 4 of the sponsoring of migrants from Britain and the Lebanon for work at Wittenoom Gorge to replace miners lost to construction projects elsewhere in the north. At Port Hedland a team of Japanese seamen works the giant dredge *Alameda*. Thus the region has so far been able to cope in general with its labour problems, at least for constructional and seasonal workers.

This is, of course, only one part of the problem and perhaps the most tractable. Of much greater significance for the future of the region is the question of how to attract and hold both the family man and his family as well. Indeed it may be said that one of the principal problems of northern development is that of increasing the stable or core element of the total population. This question is taken up below.

Actual earnings apart, many workers in the region in the employ of the state government get only one major concession as far as award rates of payment are concerned. Wages are determined on the same basis as in the Goldfields and other districts, and margins for skill are exactly the same as in Perth. The only form of loading applied to the northern areas is the district allowance. There are three broad areas in the region for the purposes of determining the district allowance: area 4, around Carnarvon (which had an allowance in 1930 of 15/-, now standing at 30/-), area 5, north of Carnarvon to Derby (30/- in 1930, now 60/-) and area 6, north and east of Derby (38/- in 1930, now 70/-). This allowance is nominally given to cover variations in the cost of living, and to compensate for isolation factors and climatic discomfort. It has not been changed for many years despite substantial cost increases. The Civil Service Association has estimated that in 1963 it cost a family unit of five persons £370 per year more to live in Wyndham than in the south of the state. This amount reduced progressively, as one moved further south, to a figure of £200 in the Carnarvon area.

The Arbitration Court of Western Australia makes trips into the region for the purpose of obtaining first-hand knowledge of working conditions and to take on-the-spot evidence. On such trips, matters affecting the stevedoring, mining, meat, building and construction industries and certain government employment are determined by the Court. The Conciliation Commissioner and the Industrial Registrar have also made a number of trips into the region for the purpose of settling disputes and holding boards of reference. The majority of trade union secretaries are domiciled in the metropolis, but it is a relatively simple procedure for the members of unions to obtain early redress of any grievance emanating from the region. In addition to this, the Australian Workers' Union has had a resident organizer in Port Hedland since 1965, and representatives of both the trade unions and the Employers' Federation make periodic visits to the region.

The Commonwealth Employment Service has an agency established at Carnarvon but employment matters in townships further north, for example, applications for unemployment benefits, are at present handled by the Perth office. This is undoubtedly a cumbersome and time-consuming procedure dictated by the fact that no townships in the region are yet big enough to justify the establishment of a district office. In time, with the growth of Port Hedland and other centres, it may be expected that the Employment Service will be better represented in the north.

Native Labour

At 30 June 1964 there were, as pointed out above, over 7,000 full-bloods and over 2,600 part-aborigines in Northwestern Australia according to estimates made by the Native Welfare Department. Of the full-bloods some two-thirds were in the Kimberley, and of the part-aborigines some two-thirds were in the more southerly parts of the region. It must be noted that these figures are not complete since nomadic tribes beyond the confines of civilization are not included in the count. More than three-quarters of the state's full-bloods are to be found in Northwestern Australia.

A glance at Table 10 will indicate that by far the most important avenue of employment for the native males is still the pastoral industry, with industrial workers (factory hands, labourers, fettlers, road workers, truck drivers, etc.) next in importance, followed by mining, self-employed (artefacts, firewood, etc.), fishing, and rural work (fencing, shearing, clearing, etc.) absorbing much smaller numbers. Of the 2,126 native males employed in 1964 (roughly two-thirds of the region's total) only 11 were employed as tradesmen and four were clerical workers. Most of the 973 females employed, roughly one-third of the total in the region, were domestics and 95 were in unskilled occupations. It is interesting to note, however, that 40 females in the region worked at occupations classed as skilled. There were 15 women in professional occupations(nursing, teaching, etc.) but no men. The natives are being taken into trade unions in some areas and this has sometimes raised problems connected with the payment of award rates. Natives in the ports who are union members receive award rates of pay without question but in some awards, in particular the important pastoral workers' award, natives are excluded. In the Northern Territory, native workers will receive award rates as from December 1968 as a result of a recent decision by the Conciliation and Arbitration Commission.

Generally speaking, conditions for the native workers are improving on stations throughout the region but most station managers in cattle areas are still reluctant to train their native labourers as skilled or semi-skilled workers, though there are exceptions to this. Because of this some natives have tended to leave the station properties and move to the towns where employment opportunities are increasing. A contributing factor to this movement has been a falling off in the station demand for native labour throughout the region, particularly in the Pilbara which is mainly sheep country. This is related to wage payments and to increasing mechanization in the transport of cattle in the northern area – droving is now well on the decline – and to mechanization in the operation of the station itself in the sheep areas. Northern pastoralists claim that the native has not proved to be adaptable in this regard but in the Pilbara those natives that are retained are fairly skilled with machinery, operating landrovers and trucks and other equipment.

Aborigines who move to the towns are taken into state and church schools and missions and into government trade schools but this move tended in the past to create greater problems than it solved. The native thus trained found it difficult to rejoin the tribe he had left whenever he wished to do so, for he no longer fitted into the integrated tribal system. Yet he came up against a resistance from many of the white population to employing him in preference to a white man. In this situation he often got the worst of both worlds, in terms of human happiness. There are signs, however, of a greater willingness in recent years to employ natives on semi-skilled work in the towns and this problem is being overcome. Training programmes, particularly within government departments, are also helping the natives to acquire the skills necessary to hold down jobs in these departments.

While many natives now congregate in the towns, there still remain large numbers living on the stations and it may be said that they are still largely the backbone of station organization. The males work with the station plant or as drovers or handymen and the females work as domestics. Where numbers are sufficiently large, schools are established by the Education Department and the native children are taught the standard curriculum. Payments are made by the Native Welfare Department to the station for the upkeep of the natives in some cases, and in others the station supports the many relatives of its native workers. The ratio of dependants to workers can be as high as four or five to one. In some cases the natives seem cheerful and happy enough and it is doubtful that they would want to change the system which not only ensures them their minimum food requirements and the basic necessities of life but shelter, often of a crude kind, medical attention and stability. Their lot in life will depend greatly, of course, upon the policy of the station management with regard to native employment and sustenance. Some managers treat their natives with great sympathy and understanding but many on the other hand still adopt a patronising and harsh attitude towards them which creates discontent and unhappiness. It is sometimes difficult for the natives to move from the station which employs them, for various reasons, and this of course tends to weaken their bargaining power and even their willingness to communicate their dissatisfaction to others.

As mentioned above, the basic wage will be payable in 1968 to all native workers in the Northern Territory with certain exceptions, and in the Kimberley the possibility of following this lead is now freely discussed. Many claim that the native stockman, who is currently paid about $6 to $8 per week, and keep, is entitled to the same wage as a white stockman for he is just as competent. Others, while agreeing with this, argue from a different viewpoint that most natives are not capable of handling money wisely and that a great deal of drunkenness and disorderliness will result. Most station managers claim that they will not be able to pay their stockmen the basic wage and continue to maintain the native dependants. If they pay the basic wage the dependants must go. Yet others claim that if they are forced to pay award rates they will replace their natives by fences and other capital improvements designed to save labour and make their operations more efficient. While this latter alternative might ultimately result in better land use and more efficient farming and react to the favour of the remaining natives, such a policy will be costly and will take a long time to implement.

In the meantime a severe problem remains. If the dependants leave the stations where do they go? To the towns, of course. This will obviously create problems for the Native Welfare Department who would no doubt be content to see them remain on the station provided they are happy and are reasonably treated.

One point is certain and that is that if beef prices remain as firm as they have been recently there would be little doubt about the ability of the cattle stations to pay the natives the basic wage. But whether this will be done or not remains to be seen. If they cannot acquire alternative labour or if they cannot introduce more labour-saving machinery or techniques, cattle stations may be forced to capitulate. One cannot be too hopeful about the ability of most stations to do without their natives.

Since the outcome is, however, unknown this seems a rather important social experiment to leave to chance. A great deal of social distress could be caused by the displacement of the station natives if it occurs. It would seem therefore that to introduce the full basic wage for natives by a series of substantial yearly increments leading up rapidly from the current low wage would offer a practical compromise which would enable stations to adjust progressively to the new scales, break the annual flow of displaced natives down to manageable proportions and enable administrators to observe the cumulative effects and adjust their plans accordingly.

As pointed out, in parts of the region where there are few important alternatives to station work, conditions of employment for the aborigines usually differ considerably from those for whites. In the East Kimberley, for example, the pattern of station employment has not changed greatly for some years. Other employment opportunities exist in the area – as at Kununurra where the seasonal labour shortage was so acute at one stage that a group of natives was flown in from the Northern Territory – but they are not great enough to affect the supply of native labour to the pastoral industry. In the West Kimberley the fishing industry has at times provided an alternative employment for natives who were dissatisfied with their lot in station work. But it is further south in the mining areas of the Pilbara that the opportunity for other employment has, in the past, been an important factor affecting the market for native labour. It is there that experiments in a new form of economic and social organization for natives were initiated.[1]

Native leaders, some of them of the older generation who possessed authority derived from tribal status, and others of the younger generation who possessed newer ideas and were able to express them in English had, with the assistance of D. W. McLeod, a white station contractor, arranged several meetings of natives, mainly centred around Port Hedland, in the Pilbara area. These meetings, aimed partially at obtaining better wages and employment conditions for natives but more fundamentally at setting up communally-run pastoral stations and mining activities, culminated eventually in a strike in 1946 which involved native workers from quite a few pastoral properties. The natives were drawn from 13 tribal groups in the area and initially they were known as the Mob or the Group. Later, in 1955, they became known as Pindan, from the name of the company which was then established. Subsequently in 1959-60 a breakaway group from Pindan formed a company known as Nomads Ltd.

As pointed out earlier, alternative employment in mining and fishing was available in this part of the region at the turn of the century. Some small groups of natives were mining independently by 1900. During the early part of this century relations between some aborigines and their white employers on the stations began to deteriorate and, as some of the younger natives found other work, schisms began to develop between them and the older tribal leaders. Thus, when the Group was formed, young leaders were not long in coming forward.

A company known as Nodom (Northern Development and Mining Co. Pty. Ltd.) was formed in 1951 after the Group had enjoyed a successful period of mining activity and a second company (Glen Ern Pastoral Co. Pty.

[1] The discussion of Pindan owes a great deal to the work of J. Wilson whose M.A. thesis 'Authority and Leadership in a "New Style": Australian Aboriginal Community, Pindan, Western Australia', gives a comprehensive account of the formative years of the Group which subsequently went by the name of Pindan. An M.A. thesis by P. Biskup, 'Native Administration and Welfare in Western Australia 1897-1954', gives full documentation of the role played by the Department of Native Affairs in this period.

Ltd.) was established to handle the Group's grazing interests. Although the Group's major activities were mining it was always in the minds of the founders to establish pastoral properties which would be leased and managed and operated entirely by aborigines. The Group, through these two companies, bought several stations – Yandeyarra, which became the head-quarters, Menthina, Ailsa Downs, Glen Ern and Riverdale. These were run by the natives.

Nodom did not last long, however, and after three years, during which it experienced technical mining difficulties and had become involved with a group of Adelaide mining investors which led eventually to litigation, it went into voluntary liquidation in August 1954. The following year a new company was formed with the name Pindan. As well as mining, the Group's activities were widened to include spasmodic activities such as fishing for pearl shell shooting goats and kangaroos for hides and collecting buffel-grass seeds for sale although these activities were very much subsidiary to the main purpose of mining.

The division of interests in the late fifties which ultimately resulted in the splinter faction, Nomads, being formed, crystallised around issues involving leadership and economic policy, in particular what should be the correct proportions between capital and consumer goods in the disposition of the common income.

The significance of the movement is that it represented the first attempt to form a society which combined elements of both Western and Aboriginal culture. At base it was an economic institution but its concept went far beyond the mere idea of collective economic activity into social organization on the broad concept. Early in its existence it aroused the antagonism of pastoralists and of authority as represented by the Native Affairs Department, but it gradually achieved recognition of its aims through strikes and by other means, and it enlisted limited support from other sections of the community and other parts of the state and the commonwealth. It was also responsible for several enquiries into native affairs being set up, and one of the main impacts of the law cases in which it was involved was to modify Western Australia's native welfare legislation. Although it had its internal vicissitudes of all sorts, it provided a means whereby some of the natives could work out their own independent futures. At one stage F. Gare, a Native Welfare Officer (the present Commissioner), reported that in 14 work camps belonging to the Group there were 633 persons.[2]

The present situation in Port Hedland, which has been so stimulated by recent iron ore mining and export as to assume the mantle of a boom town, is that natives find ready employment in a variety of jobs. Members of Pindan and Nomads take advantage of this labour situation from time to time depending upon the state of the mineral market and the other factors,

[2] J. Wilson, 'Authority and Leadership in a "New Style": Australian Aboriginal Community, Pindan, Western Australia', p.89.

but the wider effect of the boom has been to provide another alternative avenue of employment for the unattached native worker. As far as the stations are concerned the mining groups, Pindan and Nomads, and some native miners working independently out from Marble Bar act as a labour pool which can be drawn upon during rush periods. At these times their payments approach award rates.

There is no doubt that the natives in the past have been mistreated and exploited and that in many cases this is continuing. Native administration in the region has, however, recently come a long way in a fairly short time, although not without some prodding of the type provided by the Group. Officers of the Department are, where possible, forcing certain station owners to provide better conditions and are doing what they can within a limited budget to alleviate the native's position. There are social and economic issues of great importance involved in the question of native rights which have yet to be solved to the satisfaction of those who believe in social and economic justice, but their solution will not come overnight. Citizenship and drinking rights have been granted subject to certain limitations, but land rights, perhaps the most fundamental aspect of the native culture, do not exist. There is also the question of mineral rights linked to the land issue.

Leaving the social issues aside, there are good economic reasons why the most should be made of the native workforce available in the region. Even allowing for sub-standard capabilities of some aborigines for the type of work required in the region it is obvious that many more of them could be employed, particularly in mining activities where they have already proved themselves capable of earning a living for themselves within the capital and technical limitations imposed by their modest organization.

This is not the place to examine exhaustively the social implications of the various attempts at assimilation that have been made. One can generalize, however, by saying that there has been some improvement in the economic and social status of the aborigines as indicated both by relative wages earned and by greater employment and educational opportunities. But very much more remains to be done if the aborigines are to play a proper and useful role in the social and economic development of Northwestern Australia. They represent, in fact, the only workers who can be said to be completely adaptable to the climatic conditions of the north. At the same time, in the minds of many employers in the region, native labour is still regarded as inferior in various respects, and this opinion is reflected in the rates they pay and in their general attitudes towards the natives.

The 1958 Special Committee on Native Matters considered that the general objective of official policy towards natives should be their integration in the shortest possible time. They believed, further, that a significant proportion of natives in their state could be integrated within a generation. Following this broad aim they suggested the specific economic aims of : (a) raising the productivity of native workers, (b) advancing scales of wages up to the level of those of the white worker and instituting a policy of equality in employment, including equality of opportunity, (c) inculcating a prudent and beneficial spending of money earned, and (d) developing qualities of leadership and management ability.

These, obviously, are long-term aims though some could no doubt be achieved before others. But to achieve these aims there is needed not only a metamorphosis among the natives but also a re-orientation of thought among many of the whites. It is to be hoped that this can ultimately be achieved, but a realistic appraisal of the possibilities in this direction would suggest that the solution to these economic and social problems is yet a long way off.

Concessions and Other Factors Affecting Labour

The demand for seasonal labour, both skilled and unskilled, is fairly readily met by temporary migration from the south but, because of the disabilities occasioned by the physical and economic characteristics of the region, certain inducements must be offered in order to attract the workers. Some of these have been mentioned briefly above and others are dealt with elsewhere in this book; for example, the subsidization of passenger fares and transport of goods is mentioned in Chapter 9. There are, however, certain other concessions which deserve mention.

Probably the largest single concession to workers north of the twenty-sixth parallel is the taxation zonal allowance. This is available to a person who, in any financial year, is resident for 183 days in the region. The allowance takes the form of a concessional deduction and amounts to a flat $540 for the taxpayer plus 50 per cent more than the standard rates for each concessional deduction allowed for a wife and children and other dependants. Thus the allowance which can be claimed for each member of the family is one and a half times as great as that allowed south of the twenty-sixth parallel.

There is also an education allowance which is paid by the Education Department to parents in respect of children who have to be sent south each year for secondary schooling owing to the lack of teaching facilities in the region. Total fares for these children are met by the state government. In addition to this, subsidized rentals are not uncommon, additional leave conditions are often granted by employers, and other minor concessions in the form of subsidies of one sort and another are available.

There is, for example, provision for payment of fares to the metropolitan area by the state Department of Health in cases where a medical practitioner in the region certifies that the patient needs specialized treatment which is not available in the north. Also, it is now common practice in the region for employers to pay return fares to the south for a worker once yearly and for his family once every two years. It should be pointed out that many of these concessions are not, of course, available to the seasonal worker who is in the region only for three to five months. These special subsidies and other real and financial provisions for workers in the north are designed to make life more attractive in the region, to encourage the expansion of a permanent workforce and the movement of whole families into the area.

There is no doubt that the sum total of these concessions, in money terms, could be considerable but there are still many segments of the community which press for liberalization and extension. There is also no doubt that some of the concessions add considerably to labour costs, in some cases directly and in others indirectly. This, in view of what has already been said in other sections of this work about the distinctive physical and economic features of this area, must be considered inevitable in the region's present stage of development.

3. Living Conditions[3]

The main factors affecting living conditions in the region are: climatic discomfort, which is discussed in Appendix 3, and isolation caused by long distances between population centres.

Northwestern Australia has been characterised since its settlement by extensive-type land use, with the scattered cattle and sheep stations and the isolated mining operations being fed with capital and consumer goods imported from the Perth metropolitan area through the several ports that service the region. One or two small inland centres, like Meekatharra, Wiluna, Marble Bar, Hall's Creek and Fitzroy Crossing, provide communication centres and staging points for the distribution of some goods and services. The ports and the inland centres are all so small that highly competitive retailing, as it is experienced further south, is not possible. When high freight charges are added to this situation the price differential between the regional centres and the metropolitan area becomes very great indeed.

Generally food costs, and most other costs for that matter, tend to increase as one moves north and east. For example, food prices in Carnarvon are about 10 per cent higher than in Perth, in Port Hedland about 30 per cent higher, in Marble Bar about 40 per cent higher, and in Hall's Creek about 70 per cent higher, though variation in some lines is so diverse as to make general comparisons almost impossible. Clothing is much dearer in northern stores and depreciation is much greater on account of the conditions there, so that purchases have to be made more often. There is not, of course, the range of clothing that is available further south but, at the same time, there is not the same need for it in many cases.

Housing erection costs and rentals vary considerably, as one might expect,

[3] Grateful acknowledgement must be made to Mr. H. L. McGuigan, Administrator for the North-West, for general advice and Mr. B. J. Collier, General Secretary of the Civil Service Association, for making available the results of an enquiry conducted by his Association into living costs north of the twenty-sixth parallel.

and again the distance factor is apparent. In the Kimberley, for example, houses cost from two-thirds to three-quarters as much again as in Perth for standard design timber-framed houses, and for a custom-built dwelling one might expect to pay at least twice as much. In Wyndham a typical State Housing Commission rental for a three-bedroom home without subsidy would be about one-third as high again as in Carnarvon. In Hall's Creek the rental would be about one-half as high again.

Most items of household equipment are expensive to buy and then, because of depreciation and high service charges, costly to maintain. Electricity charges in particular make it expensive to attempt to achieve comfort through electrical cooling either by fan or air-conditioner. In Carnarvon and Port Hedland electricity charges for average household use are approximately twice as high as in Perth, in Marble Bar four times as high, and in Hall's Creek six times as high. To operate an air-conditioner for one night to maintain reasonable conditions in one room would cost about two dollars. Gas and water charges are likewise high.

Other everyday items are similarly expensive. For example, newspapers in Derby cost twice as much as in Perth. A bottle of beer in Hall's Creek costs twice as much as in Perth. Vehicle insurance premiums carry a $33\frac{1}{2}$ per cent loading, and running a private car is expensive in the north. Cement is $24 a ton in Perth, $48 a ton in Wyndham and $72 a ton in Hall's Creek.

The standard of tertiary services in the region, the extent of commercial activities and retail trading, the provision of educational facilities and of medical and dental care and the establishment of community associations are discussed in Chapter 8. By and large, while these are adequate for normal needs, there is a need for their extension in some parts of the region.

Thus there are substantial disabilities to be overcome when one compares living costs in the region with those in the larger centres further south. Obviously these disabilities are due in large part to the isolation of the region and its distance from the southern population centres and the southern factories. One has to look very far ahead indeed to see the day when the difference between living costs in these two areas, north and south, are wiped out or even reduced to very small proportions, for this would have to depend upon the growth of population and manufacturing industry in the region on a scale that cannot yet be foreseen. In the meantime wages and earnings need to be adjusted through allowances and other means to take account of these cost differentials, and other forms of monetary adjustment need to be made before the financial strain of living in the region can be brought into equality with that in the metropolitan area of Perth.

Climatic discomfort is the other important factor affecting living conditions. It can be partly overcome by the provision of better living conditions, but this eats up money as already explained and to change existing establishments is also a relatively slow process. However, the construction of new accommodation provides the avenue through which a re-orientation of thought on this matter can be transmitted. Happily there is now abundant evidence that this is occurring.

The township at Kununurra, on the Ord near the site of the diversion dam, is an example of the changed attitude that now exists towards living accommodation in the north. Married quarters are three-bedroom homes set upon concrete stilts and beneath there is room for a car, a laundry and shaded outdoor living. Stoves and refrigerators are electric and there are electric fans in each room. Hot water is provided by a solar heater, and furnishings are a practical blondewood and the laundry is equipped with a washing machine. Septic tank installations are standard with these houses. The township has an airstrip, an open-air theatre, bitumen roads, street lighting and a powerhouse with substantial reserves. It also possesses a modern and comfortable club and hotel, tennis courts, a nine-hole golf course and water skiing facilities at the diversion dam.

A similar situation exists on Koolan Island where B.H.P. commenced mining in 1963. A new township was built which possesses an airstrip, playing field, club, roads, houses of a similar type and cost to those at Kununurra, and power and water supplies. Large blocks of flats have also been built to accommodate single men on the Island. On Cockatoo Island there already existed a well-developed community with good provisions for accommodation. Recreation facilities included a swimming pool, tennis and basketball court, a rugged cricket ground and a recreation club equipped with billiard table, table tennis and library.

The new ports and townships connected with the Pilbara iron ore discoveries and with the United States naval communications centre are more recent still and provide further examples of the new look in northern housing. These are described in Chapter 4. Government and private construction camps in the region are generally of a high standard wherever there are reasonably large concentrations of men. A real effort is being made by those responsible to provide living conditions which are as attractive as possible under the circumstances.

There is no doubt that these measures have assisted in alleviating the lot of the northern residents, particularly in the wet season when the atmosphere is clammy and oppressive, when clothing has to be changed at least twice a day, and sometimes more, and when tempers fray easily and personal relationships become strained under the pressure of humid tropical conditions. Much is needed, however, before all-round conditions can be brought to the point where they will induce whole families to stay in the region and introduce the badly needed element of stability.

Lines along which attempts might be made to improve living conditions are suggested by the facts and opinions already given in the foregoing pages. These may take one of two general forms: by increasing incomes or by decreasing costs, either of which would enable families to afford more of the necessary personal comforts.

To increase incomes in the region by administrative fiat would be a relatively simple matter. District allowances are now so hopelessly out of line with costs that substantial upward adjustments would be needed before they became effective incentives to workers to move into or stay in the area. Their effectiveness would be further increased if they were not subject to taxation as at present. The general question of taxation concessions also needs re-examination since the concessional deductions currently allowed on personal income are not sufficiently generous to create much of an income differential in favour of the north.

To decrease costs in the region would be undoubtedly more difficult in most respects, but some obvious problem areas present themselves for immediate attention. Electricity costs provide a case in point, and substantial reductions in these charges would probably be the single most important element in the improvement of living conditions. Water charges, though not so important, are likewise a further avenue of alleviation. A much more difficult question, and one which is already being partly tackled through the subsidy to the State Shipping Service, is the reduction in transport costs which are all-pervasive in their effects upon costs in general.

Local authorities should be encouraged to extend their capital works programmes and, in conjunction with the state and commonwealth governments, to provide more communal facilities of all sorts for the residents of the region. Financially the shires are not well off, but as well as hoping for some relief or assistance from the state government they should investigate the rating of the properties under their control, in particular the larger pastoral properties, in order to increase their own income.

The crux of the problem is not just to make conditions easier for everyone in the region, for it has been suggested that the transient worker has already sufficient incentives to take him north or he would not now be there, but to make conditions easier for the family unit in order to introduce population stability. The concessions suggested above, coupled with more generous education provisions in the form of boarding allowances and student hostels, should go a long way towards achieving this. It is suggested in Chapter 8 that there is a case for relaxing the student number basis for provision of schools of different grades so that higher education facilities can be introduced into the region earlier than would otherwise be the case.

It has been suggested that business enterprises should be given substantial tax concessions as an inducement to set up in the area and to re-invest a healthy proportion of their profits, but in many cases it can be argued that the concessions of other sorts that existing enterprises have already obtained are generous enough. For instance, in Chapter 3 it is argued that the government has already the power over pastoral properties to ensure that they re-invest to the extent laid down in the leasehold agreements, but that the amount of re-investment required is much too small.

The suggestions made above are all directed towards persons in the region rather than organizations or enterprises, for this should be the prime concern, and the establishment of a stable workforce will in any case make conditions easier for business enterprises. But to be introduced on an effective scale they will cost a great deal of money, and whether or not governments and their electors in the south are prepared to spend this kind of money will depend upon the prior acceptance or rejection of the goal of northern development. This goal is accepted in this study and the reasons for doing so are discussed in Chapter 10 and, incidentally, in Chapter 1 and Chapter 6.

In the past the region has lagged behind the rest of the state in development and has in some cases (for example, road construction allocations) attracted a disproportionately large share of state finance. But the gap is beginning to close and as the north steps up its rate of development it can be expected to be less and less a drain on state finances. But while in many respects the region is regarded as dependant, it must be borne in mind that this in part springs from the role it plays in the state and the national economy. Its contribution to Australia's export earnings should, in this regard, not be forgotten.

4. CONCLUSIONS

Measured in terms of relative population increase, the region is going ahead faster than the state as a whole (at about 7.5 per cent, in fact) but this is not altogether surprising since the initial base was so small. Total population was approximately 20,000 at June 1965. Within the overall regional population movement, the numbers living in the arid gold mining areas of the Central Division have declined while the Kimberley and the Pilbara have expanded rapidly under the stimulus of agricultural and mining development.

Males still predominate and workers outnumber dependants, illustrating the lack of permanent settlement and the relative importance of transient male workers. Socially and economically, employment opportunities for female labour are needed in the towns, but first, female wages would have to be adjusted. At the moment average male earnings are much higher than in the south, but average female earnings are not.

The seasonal pattern of employment in the region will always be one of its characteristics though the moves that are afoot, both for permanent settlement and for gaining a measure of independence from the elements through better transport facilities and the like, should decrease its relative importance slowly. Development in secondary industry should assist this movement, though in the early stages such manufacturing expansion will be largely concerned with processing the region's primary products and thus will itself be somewhat seasonal in character, except for certain mining employment.

There is still a resistance to the widespread use of native labour in skilled and semi-skilled work, and this labour force is still being exploited in some parts of the region. In view of the aborigine's natural adaptability to the harsh environmental conditions and his proven ability to perform semi-skilled work, greater use could be made of this in-built workforce. Conditions of living and employment prospects for natives are, however, improving though there is yet a long way to go and the future change will no doubt be slow. The coming introduction of the basic wage to native workers can be expected to cause hardship and disruption but it may not be as great as some would think.

Costs of living in almost all facets of life are high by comparison with areas further south, and living conditions at some times of the year are unpleasant. Because of isolation and high transport costs and the harshness of the basic environmental conditions, these disabilities, though slowly being overcome, will not be quickly removed or mitigated.

It is clear that at the present stage of development considerable incentives must be offered to attract the right types of labour from the more populous and better developed south. As facilities for comfortable living increase, both for single males and for family units, and as the fringe amenities (such as entertainments, sporting facilities and range of retail goods available) improve, it may be expected that the need for money incentives will decline, but this again seems a very long-term proposition. Even now, however, some private employers have no trouble attracting labour because of the standard of accommodations and other facilities which go with the job. The costs of installing these facilities and of other monetary incentives such as fares, all add to labour costs in the region, and employers feel that while they have virtually no problems in the labour supply side they do have to pay a high price for it. Key personnel as distinct from skilled workers are ordinarily transferred from the south for the duration of a particular job. Where the work of key personnel is of a more permanent nature, special arrangements are normally made to induce them to remain in the area.

In summary, therefore, one may anticipate rapid population growth and no great problem of labour availability provided high labour and material costs do not price the region's industries out of world markets. Except in certain small marginal industries it does not seem that at present labour costs are a critical element of total costs. The really fundamental problem, however, when one considers the long-term development of the region, is that of attracting and holding family units to form the nucleus of a stable population and workforce in the future.

BIBLIOGRAPHY

AUSTRALIAN INSTITUTE OF POLITICAL SCIENCE. *Northern Australia: Task for a Nation,* pt. 4. Sydney, 1954.

AUSTRALIAN NATIONAL ECONOMICS AND COMMERCE STUDENTS ASSOCI-ATION. *Developing the North.* Proceedings of the Fifth Annual Convention. Perth, 1966.

BISKUP, P. 'Native Administration and Welfare in Western Australia 1897-1954.' Unpublished M.A. thesis, 1965. The Library of the University of Western Australia.

BERNDT, R. M. 'The Effect of Area Development on Australian Aborigines.' In *Proceedings of Project Southern Star, Interdisciplinary Projects for Development in the Northern Territory and Western Australia.* Lane, W. Z. (ed.). New York, 1966.

MacDONALD HOLMES, J. *Australia's Open North.* Sydney, 1962.

WEBB, M. J. *Natural Resources 1966-1970.* Proceedings of the Australian Institute of Management National Conference. Perth, 1966.

WILSON, J. 'Authority and Leadership in a "New Style": Australian Aboriginal Community, Pindan, Western Australia.' Unpublished M.A. thesis, 1961. The Library of the University of Western Australia.

TABLE 1

INTERCENSAL POPULATION CHANGE

Statistical Division	Percent Movement 1947-1954	Percent Movement 1954-1961	Percent Movement 1947-1961
CENTRAL			
Meekatharra	+ 3	− 3	—
Wiluna	− 66	− 14	− 70
Divisional total	− 31	− 5	− 35
NORTH WEST			
Ashburton	+ 54	− 7	+ 43
Gascoyne-Minilya	+119	− 10	+ 97
Shark Bay	+ 27	+ 66	+111
Upper Gascoyne	− 8	+ 11	+ 2
Carnarvon[1]	+ 48	+ 25	+ 85
Divisional total	+ 60	+ 8	+ 73
PILBARA			
Marble Bar	− 1	+ 3	+ 2
Nullagine	+ 19	− 28	− 16
Port Hedland	+ 65	+ 25	+107
Roebourne	+ 44	+ 24	+ 79
Tableland	+241	+ 46	+400
Divisional total	+ 60	+ 22	+ 96
KIMBERLEY			
Broome	+ 23	+ 16	+ 43
Halls Creek	+ 32	+ 17	+ 55
West Kimberley	+ 23	+112	+161
Wyndham - East Kimberley	+ 39	+ 79	+150
Divisional total	+ 28	+ 60	+104
Regional total	+ 29	+ 25	+ 62
State total	+ 27	+ 15	+ 47

[1] Municipality.

Source: Commonwealth Bureau of Census and Statistics, *Census of the Commonwealth of Australia,* vol. 5. Australia.

TABLE 2

POPULATION – AGE DISTRIBUTION

as at 30 June 1961

(No. of persons)

Statistical Division	Age Last Birthday				
	0-14	*15-24*	*25-64*	*65 and over*	*Total*
CENTRAL					
Meekatharra	352	163	509	47	1,071
Wiluna	113	39	146	18	316
Divisional total	465	202	655	65	1,387
NORTH-WEST					
Ashburton	136	102	312	19	569
Gascoyne - Minilya	436	243	730	35	1,444
Shark Bay	91	60	213	23	387
Upper Gascoyne	67	77	196	14	354
Carnarvon[1]	661	214	853	81	1,809
Divisional total	1,391	696	2,304	172	4,563
PILBARA					
Marble Bar	85	93	213	13	404
Nullagine	24	25	116	6	171
Port Hedland	370	156	568	26	1,120
Roebourne	157	89	292	30	568
Tableland	258	160	551	11	980
Divisional total	894	523	1,740	86	3,243
KIMBERLEY					
Broome	468	230	707	57	1,462
Halls Creek	141	77	201	17	436
West Kimberley	551	414	1,244	40	1,249
Wyndham-East Kimberley	291	326	887	17	1,521
Divisional total	1,451	1,047	3,309	131	5,668
Regional total	4,201	2,468	7,738	454	14,861
State total ('000 persons)	239.7	105.6	336.2	55.1	736.6
Regional ratio[2]	28.3	16.6	52.1	3.0	100.00
State ratio[3]	32.5	14.3	45.7	7.5	100.00

[1] Municipality.

[2] Ratio of each regional group to total population for region.

[3] Ratio for each state group to total population for state.

Source: Commonwealth Bureau of Census and Statistics, *Census of the Commonwealth of Australia*, vol. 5. Australia.

TABLE 3

POPULATION – MASCULINITY

as at 30 June

(No. of persons)

Statistical Division	1954			1961		
	Males	Females	Masculinity	Males	Females	Masculinity
CENTRAL						
Meekatharra	663	437	1.5	607	464	1.3
Wiluna	215	152	1.4	181	135	1.3
Divisional total	878	589	1.5	788	599	1.3
NORTH WEST						
Ashburton	410	202	2.0	378	191	2.0
Gascoyne-Minilya	1,112	490	2.3	894	550	1.6
Shark Bay	147	86	1.7	254	133	1.9
Upper Gascoyne	244	76	3.2	243	111	2.2
Carnarvon[1]	838	615	1.4	985	824	1.2
Divisional total	2,751	1,469	1.9	2,754	1,809	1.5
PILBARA						
Marble Bar	270	122	2.2	287	117	2.5
Nullagine	190	46	4.1	140	31	4.5
Port Hedland	603	291	2.0	679	441	1.5
Roebourne	315	144	2.2	342	226	1.5
Tableland	415	254	1.6	671	309	2.2
Divisional total	1,795	855	2.1	2,119	1,124	1.9
KIMBERLEY						
Broome	766	495	1.5	882	580	1.5
Halls Creek	249	124	2.0	271	165	1.6
West Kimberley	686	374	1.8	1,539	710	2.2
Wyndham-East Kimberley	602	247	2.4	1,124	397	2.8
Divisional total	2,303	1,240	1.9	3,816	1,852	2.1
Regional total	7,727	4,153	1.9	9,477	5,384	1.8
State total	330,358	309,413	1.1	375,452	361,177	1.0

[1] Municipality.

Source: Commonwealth Bureau of Census and Statistics, *Census of the Commonwealth of Australia,* vol. 5. Australia.

TABLE 4

POPULATION – WORKFORCE RATIO

as at 30 June

Statistical Division	Ratio of Workforce to Total Population(%)		
	1947	1954	1961
CENTRAL			
Meekatharra	54.7	50.6	48.6
Wiluna	44.3	48.5	45.9
Divisional total	49.5	50.1	47.9
NORTH WEST			
Ashburton	63.0	67.0	61.2
Gascoyne-Minilya	67.6	61.8	55.0
Shark Bay	60.1	56.6	57.4
Upper Gascoyne	77.2	75.6	68.9
Carnarvon[1]	45.0	50.0	41.2
Divisional total	59.3	59.2	51.6
PILBARA			
Marble Bar	56.6	65.6	64.1
Nullagine	73.4	71.6	78.4
Port Hedland	63.7	62.0	50.5
Roebourne	65.1	59.0	51.9
Tableland	77.0	52.8	60.5
Divisional total	65.0	60.5	57.0
KIMBERLEY			
Broome	46.9	55.4	49.7
Halls Creek	56.7	55.2	53.4
West Kimberley	66.5	59.4	61.8
Wyndham-East Kimberley	75.9	69.0	70.7
Divisional total	60.3	59.8	60.4
Regional total	58.4	58.6	55.8
State total	41.1	40.4	38.0

[1] Municipality.

Source: Commonwealth Bureau of Census and Statistics, *Census of the Commonwealth of Australia*, vol. 5. Australia.

TABLE 5   ESTIMATED NATIVE POPULATION[1]   30 June 1964   (No. of persons)

District and Division	Aborigines				Part Aborigines				Grand Total
	Adult Males	Adult Females	Children under 16	Total	Adult Males	Adult Females	Children under 16	Total	
NORTHERN									
Wyndham	307	329	320	956	22	20	53	95	1,051
Halls Creek	446	359	319	1,124	40	48	52	140	1,264
Derby	871	872	571	2,314	58	71	159	288	2,602
Broome	280	262	303	845	91	109	294	494	1,339
Divisional total	1,904	1,822	1,513	5,239	211	248	558	1,017	6,256
NORTH-WEST									
Port Hedland	120	99	77	296	147	121	170	438	734
Marble Bar	140	141	180	461	36	31	46	113	574
Roebourne	148	126	147	421	120	82	122	324	745
Carnarvon	160	102	173	435	122	93	221	436	871
Divisional total	568	468	577	1,613	425	327	559	1,311	2,924
NORTH-CENTRAL									
Meekatharra	140	118	196	454	68	70	161	299	753
Regional total (a)	2,612	2,408	2,286	7,306	704	645	1,278	2,627	9,933
State total (b)	3,377	3,025	3,009	9,411	2,728	2,569	6,282	11,579	20,990
(a) as % of (b)	77.3	79.6	76.0	77.6	25.8	25.1	20.3	22.7	47.3

[1] Near approximations only of those persons in the state who possess more than one-quarter aboriginal blood.

Source: Department of Native Welfare, *Annual Report of the Commissioner*. Perth, 1964.

TABLE 6   PRIMARY WORKFORCE BY INDUSTRY as at 30 June 1961   (No. of persons)

Statistical Division	Fishing and Hunting	Agriculture and mixed Farming	Grazing	Dairying	Forestry	Total Rural	Mining and Quarrying	Total Primary
CENTRAL								
Meekatharra	3	1	157	2	—	163	49	212
Wiluna	1	—	70	—	1	72	1	73
Divisional total	4	1	227	2	1	235	50	285
NORTH-WEST								
Ashburton	10	3	182	—	—	195	5	200
Gascoyne-Minilya	—	318	291	5	1	615	12	627
Shark Bay	51	7	51	1	—	110	—	110
Upper Gascoyne	—	1	217	—	—	218	3	221
Carnarvon[1]	57	17	14	—	—	88	1	89
Divisional total	118	346	755	6	1	1,226	21	1,247
PILBARA								
Marble Bar	—	3	102	—	—	105	90	195
Nullagine	1	—	45	2	—	48	48	96
Port Hedland	1	3	92	—	—	96	24	120
Roebourne	3	3	68	1	—	75	7	82
Tableland	—	2	55	—	—	57	407	464
Divisional total	5	11	362	3	—	381	576	957
KIMBERLEY								
Broome	201	5	53	2	—	261	—	261
Halls Creek	1	6	129	—	—	136	8	144
West Kimberley	1	16	154	3	—	174	423	597
Wyndham-East Kimberley	—	10	85	1	—	96	—	96
Divisional total	203	37	421	6	—	667	431	1,098
Regional total (a)	330	395	1,765	17	2	2,509	1,078	3,587
% of total regional workforce	4.0	4.8	21.3	.2	—	30.3	13.0	43.3
State total (b)	1,759	25,190	7,585	5,476	1,156	41,166	7,885	49,051
(a) as % of (b)	.6	9.0	2.7	2.0	.4	14.7	2.8	17.5

[1] Municipality.

Source: Commonwealth Bureau of Census and Statistics. Census of the Commonwealth of Australia, vol. 5. Australia.

TABLE 7   TERTIARY WORKFORCE BY INDUSTRY   as at 30 June 1961   (No. of persons)

Statistical Division	Electricity, gas, water, etc.	Building and construction	Transport and communication	Finance and commerce	Public authority (NEI) and defence services	Community and business services (inc. professional)	Amusement, hotels etc.	Other and indefinite	Total tertiary
CENTRAL									
Meekatharra	8	54	67	29	14	57	57	4	290
Wiluna	1	10	6	16	2	27	7	—	69
Divisional total	9	64	73	45	16	84	64	4	359
NORTH-WEST									
Ashburton	—	53	22	17	11	23	19	1	146
Gascoyne-Minilya	3	23	30	21	16	34	31	5	163
Shark Bay	—	48	12	10	2	7	11	3	93
Upper Gascoyne	—	6	3	—	2	3	4	3	21
Carnarvon[1]	8	141	99	133	46	75	67	18	587
Divisional total	11	271	166	181	77	142	132	30	1,010
PILBARA									
Marble Bar	—	4	13	6	4	5	17	9	58
Nullagine	—	5	2	—	1	7	13	—	28
Port Hedland	1	116	132	52	21	49	48	9	432
Roebourne	2	62	54	26	9	21	25	8	207
Tableland	17	20	11	25	2	19	33	1	128
Divisional total	20	207	216	109	37	101	136	27	853
KIMBERLEY									
Broome	5	79	65	50	46	95	33	13	386
Halls Creek	—	12	3	11	2	24	21	16	89
West Kimberley	8	300	109	50	54	123	38	20	702
Wyndham-East Kimberley	1	384	55	39	36	93	52	37	697
Divisional total	14	775	232	150	138	335	144	86	1,874
Regional total (a)	54	1,317	687	485	268	662	476	147	4,096
% of total Regional Workforce	0.7	15.9	8.3	5.9	3.2	8.0	5.7	1.8	49.4
State total (b)	4,706	25,417	27,092	59,235	11,419	30,990	16,659	4,259	179,777
(a) as % of (b)	1.1	5.2	2.5	0.8	2.3	2.1	2.9	3.5	2.3

[1] Municipality.

Source: Commonwealth Bureau of Census and Statistics, Census of the Commonwealth of Australia, vol. 5. Australia.

TABLE 8

WORKFORCE BY MAIN INDUSTRY GROUP
(Primary, Secondary and Tertiary)

as at 30 June 1961

(No. of persons)

Statistical Division	Total Work-force	Primary Work-force	2 as per cent of 1	Second-ary work-force	4 as per cent of 1	Tertiary work-force	6 as per cent of 1
	1	2	3	4	5	6	7
CENTRAL							
Meekatharra	520	212	40.8	18	3.4	290	55.8
Wiluna	145	73	50.3	3	2.1	69	47.6
Divisional total	665	285	42.9	21	3.1	359	54.0
NORTH-WEST							
Ashburton	348	200	57.5	2	.5	146	42.0
Gascoyne-Minilya	784	627	79.0	4	.5	163	20.5
Shark Bay	222	110	49.5	19	8.6	93	41.9
Upper Gascoyne	244	221	90.6	2	.8	21	8.6
Carnarvon[1]	745	89	11.9	69	9.3	587	78.8
Divisional total	2,353	1,247	53.0	96	4.0	1,010	43.0
PILBARA							
Marble Bar	259	195	75.3	6	2.3	58	22.4
Nullagine	134	96	71.6	10	7.5	28	20.9
Port Hedland	566	120	21.2	14	2.5	432	76.3
Roebourne	295	82	27.8	6	2.0	207	70.2
Tableland	593	464	78.2	1	.2	128	21.6
Divisional total	1,847	957	51.8	37	2.0	853	46.2
KIMBERLEY							
Broome	727	261	35.9	80	11.0	386	53.1
Halls Creek	233	144	61.8	—	—	89	38.2
West Kimberley	1,390	597	43.0	91	6.5	702	50.5
Wyndham-East Kimberley	1,075	96	8.9	282	26.2	697	64.9
Divisional total	3,425	1,098	32.1	453	13.2	1,874	54.7
Regional total	8,290	3,587	43.3	607	7.3	4,096	49.4
State total	279,784	49,051	17.5	50,956	18.2	179,777	64.3

[1] Municipality.

Source: Commonwealth Bureau of Census and Statistics, *Census of the Commonwealth of Australia,* vol. 5. Australia.

TABLE 9

WORKFORCE BY OCCUPATIONAL STATUS
as at 30 June 1961
(No. of persons)

Statistical Division	Employer	Self employed	Employee (on wage, salary)	Helper (not on wage, salary)	Total at work	Not at work[2]	Total in workforce
CENTRAL							
Meekatharra	52	54	395	9	510	10	520
Wiluna	15	17	111	2	145	—	145
Divisional total	67	71	506	11	655	10	665
NORTH-WEST							
Ashburton	28	18	295	2	343	5	348
Gascoyne-Minilya	117	149	504	17	787	7	794
Shark Bay	28	29	163	1	221	1	222
Upper Gascoyne	23	7	207	5	242	2	244
Carnarvon[1]	55	53	608	2	718	27	745
Divisional total	251	256	1,777	27	2,311	42	2,353
PILBARA							
Marble Bar	13	20	220	—	253	6	259
Nullagine	10	12	110	—	132	2	134
Port Hedland	28	23	497	3	551	15	566
Roebourne	25	18	248	—	291	4	295
Tableland	16	16	557	—	589	4	593
Divisional total	92	89	1,632	3	1,816	31	1,847
KIMBERLEY							
Broome	29	29	648	1	707	20	727
Halls Creek	15	7	201	6	229	4	233
West Kimberley	43	23	1,300	1	1,367	23	1,390
Wyndham-East Kimberley	40	22	991	5	1,058	17	1.075
Divisional total	127	81	3,140	13	3,361	64	3,425
Regional total	537	497	7,055	54	8,143	147	8,290
% of Total regional workforce	6.5	6.0	85.1	.6	98.2	1.8	100.0

[1] Municipality.
[2] Includes persons who were:
   (i) unable to secure employment,
   (ii) temporarily laid off from their jobs,
   (iii) not actively seeking work at time of census.

Source: Commonwealth Bureau of Census and Statistics, *Census of the Commonwealth of Australia,* vol. 5. Australia.

TABLE 10   NATIVE EMPLOYMENT as at 30 June 1964   (No. of persons)

Division and District	Males										Females						Grand total
	1	2	3	4	5	6	7	8	9	Total	1	2	3	4	5	Total	
NORTHERN																	
Wyndham	—	—	—	6	82	—	175	—	—	263	—	—	—	—	60	60	323
Halls Creek	—	—	—	11	23	2	240	—	—	276	—	—	—	—	114	114	390
Derby	—	—	5	2	83	—	341	—	1	432	6	2	2	—	305	315	747
Broome	—	—	4	—	37	—	81	28	6	156	6	2	—	10	76	94	250
Divisional total	—	—	9	19	225	2	837	28	7	1,127	12	4	2	10	555	583	1,710
NORTH-WEST																	
Port Hedland	—	4	2	—	32	—	150	1	1	190	1	2	3	6	56	68	258
Marble Bar	—	—	—	—	5	60	40	—	60	165	—	2	35	—	26	63	228
Roebourne	—	—	—	—	14	24	228	—	—	266	—	1	—	—	88	89	355
Carnarvon	—	—	—	12	39	4	125	2	12	194	2	1	—	60	48	111	305
Divisional total	—	4	2	12	90	88	543	3	73	815	3	6	38	66	218	331	1,146
NORTH-CENTRAL																	
Meekatharra	—	—	—	—	—	—	180	—	4	184	—	1	—	19	39	59	243
Regional total (a)	—	4	11	31	315	90	1,560	31	84	2,126	15	11	40	95	812	973	3,099
State total (b)	—	10	28	1,296	674	150	1,860	49	151	4,219	36	29	41	125	1,114	1,345	5,564
(a) at % of (b)	—	40.0	39.3	2.4	46.7	60.0	83.5	63.3	55.6	50.4	41.7	37.9	97.6	76.0	72.9	72.3	55.7

Key to Employment Classification:

MALES:
1. Professional – nursing, teaching.
2. Clerical and commercial.
3. Tradesmen.
4. Rural workers – farm employees, shearers, cleaning and fencing contractors, etc.
5. Industrial workers – factory hands, labourers, fettlers, road workers, truck drivers, etc.
6. Mining industry.
7. Pastoral industry.
8. Pearling and fishing industry.
9. Self employed – artifacts, sandalwood, firewood, goats, grass seeds, etc.

FEMALES:
1. Professional – nursing, teaching, etc.
2. Clerical and commercial – offices, shops, etc.
3. Skilled occupations – dressmaking, photograph tinting, etc.
4. Unskilled occupations (other than domestic) – fruit picking, grass-seeds, etc.
5. Domestics – urban, agricultural and pastoral.

Source: Department of Native Welfare, *Annual Report of the Commissioner.* Perth, 1964.

TABLE 11

FACTORIES, EMPLOYMENT AND EARNINGS[1]
Western Australia and North-West Region

(1959-60 to 1963-64)

Area	1959-60	1960-61	1961-62	1962-63	1963-64
WESTERN AUSTRALIA					
Number of factories	4,279	4,334	4,418	4,492	4,609
Employment	49,651	50,666	51,033	53,435	55,705
Salaries and wages					
Males	£891	£946	£966	£994	£1,037
Females	£502	£535	£544	£554	£566
NORTH-WEST REGION[2]					
Number of factories	86	87	·87	88	104
Employment	516	580	582	641	697
Salaries and wages					
Males	£1,450	£1,430	£1,481	£1,540	£1,604
Females	£586	£515	£517	£654	£582
REGION AS PERCENT OF STATE					
Salaries and wages					
Males	163%	151%	153%	155%	155%
Females	117%	96%	95%	118%	103%

[1] Including working proprietors.

[2] Includes the whole of Central Division as well as the three other divisions.

Source: Commonwealth Bureau of Census and Statistics, *Statistical Register of Western Australia*. Perth.

CHAPTER 3

PASTORAL INDUSTRIES

1. INTRODUCTION

Pastoral activities symbolize the North-West in the minds of most Western Australians. For them it is the land of immense cattle and sheep stations of from half a million to a million acres in extent, sprawled across vast savannah plains; clear blue winter skies, warm balmy days and lazy breezes; hard brown earth broken by rugged, rocky outcrops and gorges which are thrown into refreshing relief by patches of brilliant green and other hues; bracingly cool nights to provide refreshing relief from the heat of the day; acre upon acre of lush savannah type pasture, miles of barren sand, stands of repelling spear grass, and dried up water courses; the shrill cries of white cockatoos breaking the lazy silence as they cluster in their hundreds on the branches of a single tree until it sags under the strain; the swift darting to and fro of the colourful budgerigar and the graceful flight of the brolga and the hasty hopping of the startled kangaroo and the lethargic movement of the python; the cautious and ominous surfacing of the inquisitive crocodile raising its snout out of the muddy waters; the anguished flopping of the captive barramundi; the close-grouped family cluster of bizarre bottle trees watching silently the slow passage of tired cattle being driven from water hole to water hole by sweating white and black stockmen; the coolibah trees and the swaggies and the jumbucks and the frantically busy shearing stands and the flies and the dust; the oppressive heat of summer and the floods and the morasses of mud and broken trees and the bogged trucks and drowned cattle; the yapping dogs at the native camps; the pet donkey at the station homestead and the beads of condensation on the cool pot of beer at the tin-roofed pub; the stock camp under the stars at night where one finds around the campfire all the prototypes of the characters in Mrs. Aeneas Gunn's *We of the Never Never*. These and many others are the visual impressions usually associated with the Kimberley where the main pastoral pursuits of the region are to be found.

Times are changing of course, and these impressions, or many of them, are receding into the mists of the past. The cattle train now roars along the old stock route, the jeep is replacing the horse, the aeroplane has taken possession of the skies, dams are changing the flood pattern, air-conditioners are controlling the oppressiveness, the crocodile and buffalo are harder to find, the roads are tougher and more enduring, more fences are appearing and the pattern of life at the homestead is changing. But the dominance of the pastoral industries in this part of the region is still unquestioned. They are not going; they are merely changing.

The pastoral industry still uses overwhelmingly the largest proportion of the available land and it also still employs the biggest share of the region's workforce.

2. HISTORICAL DEVELOPMENT[1]

The first mention of the Kimberley following the proclamation in 1829 of the Crown Colony of Western Australia appears in 1837-38 following an expedition into the area by Captain Grey. His report on the area as pastoral land was favourable and a further expedition in 1863 returned with similar findings. In 1861 F. T. Gregory led an expedition into the country around the Ashburton, Fortescue, De Grey and Oakover rivers and also commented favourably. These reports aroused interest among southern pastoralists and by 1869 there were nearly 39,000 sheep in the coastal districts of the North-West.[2]

In the Kimberley the first attempt at settlement was made in 1865 by a Victorian pastoral company in the Camden harbour area when 1,200 head of cattle and 6,000 sheep were moved into the new settlement which, unfortunately, was washed out and abandoned in the same year. Another unsuccesful attempt at settlement was made by Western Australians in the Roebuck Bay area, also in 1865.

Eighteen years elapsed before a further assault was made on the Kimberley. During this interim period, surveyor Alexander Forrest explored the Kimberley from 1875 to 1879, following the Ord and Fitzroy Valleys, but he was baulked by the King Leopold Ranges. His reports re-stimulated local and eastern states' interest in the area, and for many years he utilized his knowledge of the area, acting as the Perth agent for many prospective lessees.

Increasing interest in the Kimberley resulted in the framing of pastoral lease conditions by the state government, and by contemporary standards these conditions were quite stringent. Leaseholds were to be of not less

---

[1]Material for this section was drawn heavily from: G. Bolton, 'A Survey of the Kimberley Pastoral Industry from 1885 to the Present'. Historical information on the pastoral industry in the North-West and Pilbara regions is rather scanty. On the other hand, pastoralism in the Kimberley, cause of many clashes of opinion in the state parliament over the years, is prominent in any story of the state's past development.

[2]F. K. Crowley, *A Short History of Western Australia,* was also consulted in the preparation of this section.

than 50,000 acres, at 10/- annual rental per 1,000 acres. Block depth was required to be three times the holding's water frontage, and stock requirements amounted to 20 sheep or 2 cattle per 1,000 acres held. The expiry date of the leases was 1893 and by 1883 more than 51 million acres had been taken up on leasehold.

Settlement of the Kimberley came from two directions: from the south and, at roughly the same time, from the east, and moved from the coast inwards along the Fitzroy valley in the West Kimberley and along the Ord in the East Kimberley. These two lines of settlement effected a division of the Kimberley between east and west which has not yet completely disappeared.

In 1883 the West Kimberley settlement began when John Forrest and other settlers established themselves on the lower reaches of the Fitzroy, Meda and Lennard rivers and the townsites of Broome and Derby were declared. Initial settlement in this area was by sheepmen. By 1884 leases had fallen by 11½ million acres. Stocking requirements were not being met, and gradually the land was returned to the government after the initial onslaught by prospective pastoralists.

In the years 1884-1885 cattlemen from Victoria, Queensland and N.S.W. began to arrive in the East Kimberley, foremost among these being Charles MacDonald, Osmond and Panton, and the Durack family. These men overlanded their stock from the east, whereas settlement in the West Kimberley was effected from the south by ship. By 1884 the first East Kimberley cattle station had been established by Osmond and Panton and named Plymton St. Mary (now known as Ord River), and in 1885 the Duracks established Lissadell, Argyle and Rosewood stations. Gold discoveries in the East Kimberley in 1885 resulted in the port of Wyndham being surveyed and established in 1886, although the original jetty was inadequate as a stock outlet. Nevertheless the discovery of gold in the area was beneficial to the extent that the miners provided a market for the region's beef and the area around Hall's Creek was opened.

By 1885, 14 sheep stations covering 5½ million acres were established in the West Kimberley and a jetty was constructed at Derby at a capital cost of £3,000. This area was subjected to scab infection early in its development but the disease was quickly arrested although some leases had to be abandoned. On the west coast the pearling industry was established at Broome in 1887. The surrounding area was stocked by cattlemen, and expansion continued up the Fitzroy.

The problems confronting the cattlemen at this time were threefold. In the first place they had no dependable market for their beef, second, they were hit by the depression of 1890-95 and forced to turn to the banks and pastoral houses, and finally, stock killing by aborigines reduced their herds. The result was that during these early years many properties were mortgaged.

The decade 1895-1905 witnessed new developments in the industry.

Probably the most significant feature of this period was the tremendous increase in the state's population as a result of the goldrushes. In 1891 the population stood at 50,000; by 1901 it had risen to 184,000. To meet the resultant increased demand for meat, two marketing organizations were established in the Kimberley in 1894. Alexander Forrest and Isadore Emanuel combined forces to form the firm of Forrest, Emanuel and Co. By contracting with the Blue Funnel Line and Adelaide Steamship Company they formed an organized marketing outlet for their own and surrounding West Kimberley stations' products, transporting the cattle to Perth and then on to the goldfields. East Kimberley pastoralists Connor and Doherty established a similar organization and in 1896 the Durack interests merged with them and the firm Connor, Doherty and Durack was established. It is interesting to note that a principal of each firm, Forrest and Connor, represented their respective West and East Kimberley electorates in the Legislative Assembly for a considerable period, prior to the rise of the Labor Party in the state.

The prohibition of entry of Queensland and Northern Territory cattle into Western Australia was announced in 1897. This restricted considerably the East Kimberley turnoff as Wyndham had become the outlet for substantial numbers of Territory cattle. Superimposed on this restriction was a protective tariff on all cattle and sheep entering the state. In addition to these restrictions the East Kimberley was declared an infected area in 1898 and stock movements to other parts of the state were banned. The cattle tick controversy resulted in heated clashes in parliament between the two Kimberley members, who, it has been suggested, were to some extent motivated by their own respective business interests. An attempt by Connor, Doherty and Durack to open a live cattle trade with Singapore was unsuccessful. Later, in 1898, East Kimberley cattle were permitted to enter Fremantle provided infected cattle were slaughtered immediately, and in 1899 the ban on Territory cattle was lifted.

Another feature of this period was the expansion of settlement that took place. A cattle route was formed through the Leopolds and Mt. House station was established, while some of the master pearlers of Broome took up leases and opened up new country for cattle. Prominent in this development was the firm of Streeter and Male. Cattle were overlanded to the goldfields and expansion continued up the Fitzroy. Good wool and cattle prices in the West Kimberley enabled some mortgages to be discharged by 1900 and some capital improvements to be effected. By the turn of the century smaller land holdings were being taken up on the settlement fringes, the flocks and herds in many cases being supplemented, it is said, by 'cleanskins' from the larger properties. As the smaller holdings increased, many of the established pastoralists began to move out. Twenty years of pioneering in rough conditions had resulted in profits adequate to permit them to retire south. By 1905 the absentee-owner class, so frequently criticized subsequently, had come into existence.

The period 1905-19 brought to light new problems in the industry — problems which even now in the 1960's still persist. The drought of 1905 and the late rains of 1910-12 revealed for the first time pasture regeneration difficulties and the need for supplements to the natural water supplies. The vermin problem had also become appreciable by this time and diseases were becoming worse. In 1911 the buffalo fly entered the district from the neighbouring territory and pleuro-pneumonia appeared in the East Kimberley. The West Kimberley was plagued by the Fitzroy floods of 1914 and 1915 and subsequent stock losses caused a substantial decline in sheep numbers (from 300,000 in 1912 to 190,000 in 1917).

In this period the industry was active in its trade links outside the state and tended to neglect the Perth market. In 1910 Connor, Doherty and Durack opened the Manila trade for lightweight cattle and, at the same time, Broome beef was being sent to Java and cattle were being overlanded to Queensland at the rate of about 17,000 annually. Falling wool prices saw the establishment of a fat sheep export trade with Singapore. High transport costs, a decline in Perth prices and the removal of interstate tariffs after federation had reduced the attractiveness of the Perth and goldfields markets. Moves to establish meatworks and freezing works in Wyndham had become a political football in the state parliament.

In 1912 the Labor government, in an attempt to lower meat prices to Perth consumers, established the State Shipping Service with four obsolescent vessels, and subsequently there was a slight fall in consumer prices (2d. per lb.).

Badly needed capital development was retarded between 1910 and 1920 mainly because of insecurity of tenure but in 1917 the expiry date (which had been 1928) was extended to 1948. Attempts were made to prevent large companies from alienating large areas by limiting holdings to one million acres but this provision was successfully bypassed by the large companies. Vesteys placed managers on their properties, each of which was less than the million-acre limit in the East Kimberley, and administered their holdings from the eastern states.

White labour declined in numerical terms partly because of enlistments in the armed services during the Great War and, as a result, more native labour was used by Kimberley pastoralists. A new pattern of absentee-owners, or company ownership represented by managers, appeared on the stations and extension of tenure did not seem to result in any increased capital inflow into the Kimberley despite the increasingly obvious need for herd improvement, the provision of fencing and water, and better living accommodation.

The years 1920 to 1935 have been described as a period of recession in the Kimberley. They encompass the world depression of the 1930's, and yet during these years the seeds for recovery were sown.

In 1919 a state-owned meatworks was opened in Wyndham. Whilst prices paid to the East Kimberley pastoralists were not high, and the meatworks was run at a loss, it helped overcome the marketing problem which had plagued the East Kimberley pastoral industry over the previous years. The year 1920 saw the establishment of the post of Minister for the North-West, first occupied by Mr. (later Sir) Hal Colebatch, and that of Commissioner for the North-West, based at Broome. Whilst the portfolio was short-lived, it revealed an increasing awareness by members of the state parliament of the special problems associated with the district and it was later revived. The airline which is now Mac.Robertson Miller Airlines made its appearance in 1921, providing twice-weekly flights to the region.

The drought of 1924 resulted in heavy stock losses throughout the Kimberley and re-emphasized the need for supplementary water points in the Pindan country. Cattle and wool prices in the West Kimberley were firm, and as a result some bores were sunk and fences erected during the twenties. The East Kimberley pastoralists, operating on a low profit margin, were hit further by the refusal of the State Shipping Service to carry stock from Wyndham for a period of time because the pastoralists were not making sufficient use of the meatworks. Prices in the early 1930's fell with the onslaught of world depression and many properties were sold out or abandoned in the West Kimberley during this period.

The position in the Ord basin was improved in 1932 with the signing of the Ottawa agreement and the introduction of the policy of imperial preference. The creation of preferences by Great Britain, in place of free trade, permitted Australia to compete with Argentina in the British beef market on more favourable terms and in 1934 the first shipment of chilled beef left Wyndham for Great Britain. At the same time increased security of tenure was given the northern pastoralists by the 1932 Land Act which extended leases to 1982. A final feature of this period was the emergence of a new class of management and the emergence of new ideas such as the introduction of stud stock and controlled breeding, experimentation with water conservation, and other changes mentioned below.

From 1935 onwards the Kimberley experienced a period of recovery, a re-orientation of thinking. Wool prices improved after the mid-thirties, and increased capital outlays were made on the Fitzroy sheep runs. Improved transport facilities – road, air and sea – the introduction of the Flying Doctor Service, improved domestic water supplies, the advent of the pedal radio, and improved living quarters on the stations resulted in the gradual disappearance of the bachelor pastoralists and the establishment of family units on the northern pastoral leases, particularly in the West Kimberley. Improved prices and more stable markets had not yet lifted the East Kimberley out of a long period of stagnation.

With the advent of the World War, a labour shortage once again appeared in the industry. In 1940 a second meatworks was established in the region, by the Farrell brothers in Broome. The Canning stock route was reconditioned to compensate for the restricted outlets afforded by wartime shipping (bombing by the Japanese had sunk the *Koolama* at Wyndham) and a market was found for beef in the Northern Territory to feed the large number of troops stationed there. 'The importance of the war years in the Kimberley lies in the fact that they drew the attention of the rest of Australia to the problems and potentialities of the district.'[3]

The post World War years have witnessed many changes, most of which are mentioned elsewhere in this chapter. An all-weather road was re-routed and built from Fitzroy Crossing to Derby financed by an army compensation grant and a regular trade in chilled beef was firmly established between Wyndham and the United Kingdom. William MacDonald, a descendent of one of the original pioneers, established the first registered stud in the north with poll shorthorn cattle at Fossil Downs, and the post-war boom in wool prices led to considerable improvements on the Fitzroy sheep stations. Road transport and air beef had begun to bring a new transport dimension to the region. Heavier government expenditure on roads, schools and hospitals further improved Kimberley living conditions.

The problems now facing the industry are discussed elsewhere. They are remarkably similar to those confronting the pastoralist in 1950 – vermin, disease, transport costs, pasture deterioration, provision of water and fencing, and the absentee-owner who is heavily dependent on the abilities of the paid manager, but there is reason to hope their solution is closer now than it was then.

3. PRESENT CHARACTERISTICS

It will be useful at this point to examine the present characteristics of the pastoral industry insofar as they are revealed by available official statistics, before moving on to consider some of its problems and to examine future prospects. Detailed statistics are given in the tables at the end of the chapter.

Livestock Numbers

In the period from 1954 to 1963 the numbers of beef cattle in the region rose, but only by 42 per cent as against 76 per cent for the state as a whole (unfortunately it is difficult to make comparisons beyond 1963 since the statistical basis for classifying cattle was changed in that year). Thus the region's share of the state total has dropped from 76 per cent to 62 per cent. Within the region itself the Kimberley division – undoubtedly the most important as far as beef cattle numbers are concerned – recorded a 42 per cent increase, while the Central and Pilbara divisions showed increases of 32 per cent and 29 per cent respectively and in the North-West Division the cattle population doubled. These last three divisions have only 9 per cent of the region's cattle.

[3] G. Bolton, 'A Survey of the Kimberley Pastoral Industry from 1885 to the Present', p. 297.

In the period from 1954 to 1964 sheep numbers in the region rose by only 3 per cent compared with a state rise of 54 per cent. As in the case of cattle numbers, the region's proportion of the state total has fallen significantly from 16 per cent to 11 per cent. Within the region itself the Pilbara and Kimberley divisions showed small declines and the Central Division recorded a 39 per cent increase. The most important division from the viewpoint of numbers, the North-West, registered a 2 per cent decline. More recent figures for 1965 indicate a recovery, particularly in the North-West. The region's woolclip increased and the average weight of fleece grew over the decade from 9.0 lbs. to 9.7 lbs. More recent figures show a drop back to 8.2 lbs.

Rural Holdings and Land Utilization.

In the Kimberley in the 1964-65 season some 53 million acres of uncleared land were used for grazing and almost half a million lay idle out of a total for the district of 104 million acres. There were some 119 holdings, an average size of holding of 453,000 acres. This division has some sheep (7 per cent of the total for the region) which would tend to pull down the average property size somewhat, and there are also now some small agricultural holdings on the Ord. On the whole the cattle stations would range in size from half a million to a million acres (the legal limit).

From a grazing viewpoint the North-West Division is the next in importance with 41 million acres used for this purpose in 1964-65. In this division is located the region's oldest-established agricultural area with many small producing units operating under irrigation at Carnarvon. The average size of holding for the division is 204,000 acres but this is misleading since if the Gascoyne-Minilya Shire figures are taken out the average size of the remaining properties, which are mostly sheep stations, is 490,000 acres.

The two Central Division shires and the Pilbara Division have some mining leases, and the Pilbara in particular contains extensive mineral deposits which are now being vigorously exploited. The proportion of land being utilized for grazing and agricultural purposes is by far the lowest in the region (21 per cent). It is greatest in the North-West (88 per cent) and the Kimberley (52 per cent). The modest increase in rural holdings in the region in recent years (from 424 in 1955 to 475 in 1965) has been almost entirely confined to the Kimberley, where irrigated agriculture has developed rapidly on the Ord.

Mechanization

It is difficult to decide to what extent the industries in the region have become mechanized. Generally speaking the rate of introduction of relatively fixed machinery such as shearing machines, shearing stands, electric motors, stationary engines, fell short of that for the state as a whole. As an example, between 1954 and 1964 shearing stands declined in absolute numbers by

3 per cent and as a proportion of the state total by a considerably greater proportion.

When attention is turned to mobile equipment associated with transport and the working of the land, however, the story is different. Motor trucks and utilities are being used in increasing numbers and the increase in tractors is even more marked. Between 1954 and 1964 the number of tractors increased by 57 per cent, and the region's proportion of the state total increased significantly, though from a very small base. As the agricultural industries accelerate their pace of development, tractor use can be expected to rise rapidly. While it seems that mechanization is being introduced in Northwestern Australia it will be noted that most of the increase is associated with agricultural rather than pastoral development. The position with respect to the pastoral industry is still far from adequate.

These generalizations are all based upon official figures published by the Deputy Commonwealth Statistician. Since these figures are based upon returns submitted by individual holdings and not by official census enumerators, there are opportunities for inaccuracies to creep into the figures and at this point it may be wise to warn the reader against accepting the absolute figures as completely correct. More appropriately they should only be used to gain a broad impression of trends. Also, of course, it must be borne in mind that the machinery figures relate only to machines on holdings and not to total machines in the region. It must also be noted that the time periods for which these generalizations have been made differ with different types of machinery. This depends upon the various years in which returns giving machinery details are requested by the Statistician.

Employment

Farm and station employment dropped markedly in the inter-censal period 1947 to 1954 but in the decade from 1954 to 1964 it remained fairly stable at under 2,000 males. Female employment figures are not published.

Over this period – as mentioned elsewhere – there have been forces at work tending to cut down the rural labour force. First of all, increasing mechanization has tended to reduce the need for labour on some of the properties. Second, with the decline of cattle droving and the rapid increase in road transport (which is usually carried out by town firms, the employees of which would not figure in statistics of farm employment), the need for labour of this type has fallen. Third, if the proportion of full-blooded aborigines to white men rises this would show up in the official statistics as a drop in farm labour since full-bloods are excluded from the figures.

The question whether the basic wage should be paid to aborigines is a live issue now in the north, and if this measure is introduced it will undoubtedly have an effect on the employment of natives on some stations. As mentioned in the previous chapter, some owners claim that they would replace native labour by fencing and endeavour in other ways to reduce their labour requirements. To what extent this will take place is impossible to gauge; only the future can provide the answer.

Production Trends

As far as the sheep segment of the pastoral industry is concerned, the relative decline has already been noted. Lambing percentages, as well as sheep numbers and wool clip, have shown little improvement. Actually, year to year fluctuations are quite large and currently the percentage for the region as a whole is about the same as it was in 1947 although in the intervening years it dropped alarmingly at times. The state percentage, on the other hand, has mostly shown steady improvement. As well as variation from year to year, there are marked variations within the region in any one year, as a glance at Table 4 will show.

When one turns from quantity to value figures the story is much the same. The all-time high in gross value of wool production for the region occurred in the boom season of 1951 when more than £10 million worth of wool was produced. Since this spectacular figure the industry has slumped and is currently recording about $8 million to $10 million in gross value of production.

The state of the industry is more sharply reflected in the figures for export of live sheep from the region. In 1950-51 some 22,000 sheep, worth £55,000, were exported whereas the figures had dropped by 1963-64 to 3,000 sheep worth £9,000. Rapidly falling average prices reflected deterioration in quality of the turnoff and easing of demand for sheep from the region. In fact, export cut out altogether from 1955-56 onwards with the exception of two seasons 1958-59 and 1963-64.

The beef segment of the pastoral industry tells a somewhat different story. As an export earner it does not play so large a role as the sheep industry. Nevertheless the value of its overseas exports is substantial and amounts to over $3 million. Export of livestock in the beef industry has taken three forms : some live cattle have been exported overseas through the ports and this trade has grown steadily, others have been shipped interstate, and yet others have been overlanded interstate.

Figures of slaughterings in the Kimberley Statistical Division are available in quantity and value terms. In the first half of the decade 1955-56 to 1964-65, the gross value of slaughterings rose but since then a steady drop has been recorded each year and the 1964-65 figure is equivalent to that of 13 years previously. Some of the cattle slaughtered in the region are overlanded from the Northern Territory to Wyndham and thus they do not truly constitute part of the region's turnoff. Table 12 gives particulars of this movement. It will be seen that the figures have dropped down from a peak of 15,000 in 1958-59 to a figure that is now around 6,000. These in 1964-65 were worth about a quarter of a million pounds.

It should also be noted that numbers of cattle from the East Kimberley are moved eastwards, sometimes to the meatworks at Katherine and, in the case of Vesteys cattle, to Helen Springs Station and thence to the meatworks at Darwin. In 1966, for instance, buyers from Queensland were active in the Kimberley as far west as the Fitzroy Crossing area attempting to buy cattle for movement by road train in stages right through to Townsville.

If an attempt is made to combine the money results of the operations of the various segments of the region's pastoral industry as a whole, some indications can be given of its relative importance to the economy. Subtraction, for instance, of the value of the region's beef and offal exported from the gross value of cattle slaughtered will leave a figure which should represent the beef and offal retained in the state economy. Add to slaughterings value the value of live cattle and sheep exported overseas, interstate and intrastate (less live imports), and then add to this the estimated regional gross value of wool production on the assumption that none of it is retained in the region and the resultant figures would give an approximate picture of the overall course of development of the pastoral industry in the north in money terms.

Table 15 contains some estimates along these lines. The figure of gross value of slaughterings includes the Northern Territory beasts brought in to Wyndham and thus inflates the figure somewhat. But, on the other hand, there is no addition made for live cattle overlanded to the Northern Territory or to the Meekatharra railhead (for example, from southern stations) and sent down to Midland for slaughtering or to agistment in the metropolitan area. Each year there are around 6,000 to 8,000 cattle turned off the region in this way and this will just about counter-balance the Northern Territory imports. From the table it will be seen that, in money terms at least, the beef industry has declined significantly since 1959-60, while the sheep industry has risen slightly but is, on the whole, marking time. The result, seeing the sheep industry is the larger of the two, is that the pastoral industry as a whole has virtually stood still in the past decade. This movement contrasts most markedly with the spectacular increases recorded in the mining industry.

Property Size and Leasehold Provisions

The question of pasture improvement and pastoral management in general, resulting in improved herds and flocks and higher carrying capacity, brings again to light the question of property size. A survey in 1954 of the sheep industry in the pastoral zone of Western Australia by the Bureau of Agricultural Economics reveals that the average size of properties was 468,273 acres over a sample of 33 properties. Almost one half of the properties were between 200,000 acres and 400,000 acres and a similar proportion exceeded 400,000 acres.

It is difficult to generalize on the question of property size as some properties are more favourably situated than others as regards topography, climatic conditions and nearness to markets or transport, but it is certain that with the application of improvements such as fencing and water points, with better animal husbandry and with better vermin control, the carrying capacity of the region could be lifted and the size of many properties reduced to more manageable proportions. With more improvements and smaller holdings, carrying capacity and turnoff could well be doubled in some cases and this will reduce the size of the property that can conveniently be handled. At the other extreme, while properties of up to one million acres might conceivably be the optimum size in a few isolated cases, there seem to exist no convincing arguments for allowing the large pastoral companies to circumvent the intention of the original legislation and hold more than one station.

The early tenure and stocking regulations had undergone some change as knowledge concerning conditions and practice came to hand from stations. The regulations were brought into line in Western Australia in 1933 when all renewals were made on a 50 year basis expiring in 1982. The maximum area to be held by any one person or body corporate was fixed at one million acres, and conditions required improvements to the value of £10 per 1,000 acres and a minimum stocking rate of six beasts per 1,000 acres. The matter recently came under public notice when a motion was introduced into the Legislative Council in 1961 calling for a full enquiry into pastoral leasehold provisions. Following this the Executive Council approved the appointment of a three-man committee consisting of the Surveyor-General, a Wiluna pastoralist and a Perth accountant. This was done in February 1962. The committee became known as the Pastoral Leases Committee and it submitted its report in March 1963.

Leasehold conditions still apply today and many lessees have taken up the recent 1965 offer resulting from the deliberations of the 1962 committee, and have applied for 50 year renewal with voluntary acceptance of revised tenure conditions. The new leases will expire in the year 2015 and they provide for control of stocking rates, complete protection where necessary for eroding areas, and a higher degree of station improvement. Each lessee must, under the amended conditions, submit a plan of development for approval by the Pastoral Appraisement Board and must proceed to finance this work at a minimum rate of expenditure equal to two and a half times the normal rental each year until the approved programme is achieved. Annual rents vary between 60 cents and $2.50 per acre and roughly constitute, in the words of the committee, 'between one per cent and three per cent of the total costs of the operation of a station'.[4] As Treloar, in his recent survey of some aspects of the Kimberley cattle industry puts it, 'with rents so small, the Act will not embarrass many stations'.[5]

[4]Western Australia, *Report of the Pastoral Leases Committee.*
[5]D. W. G. Treloar, 'Investors and Kimberley Cattle'.

As mentioned earlier, absentee-ownership is common in the Kimberley. Of 35 stations in the Ord River area, for example, 23 are owned by four major pastoral companies: Hooker, Vestey, Naughton, and Peel River. One of these companies controls ten stations in the Kimberley and has several more in the adjoining Northern Territory. Treloar's survey mentions 29 absentee-owner stations and 26 owner-managed stations of any significance in the Kimberley. Absentee-owners have come in for a good deal of criticism in the past and the industry as a whole has often been blamed for bad management practices. A recent paper suggests that the fault may not lie entirely with station management and that the government, through its leasehold and other provisions, and the private banks and pastoral finance houses, through their rural credit policies, may be equally to blame at times.[6] Certainly some of the conditions and constraints under which management has to operate in these areas make the management operation complex and hazardous.

Nevertheless, the terms and conditions of the new leases seem very favourable to the lessees and this is borne out by the readiness with which the leases have been taken up again. In particular the annual requirement for capital improvement is far too modest and should be three or four times the present required amount. It is to be hoped also, that the state government will increase its pastoral inspection staff so that it is able, if necessary, to invoke the provisions of the leasehold agreements under which it has power to insist upon adequate development and that, where performances do not measure up to what it regards as reasonable, it will not hesitate to resume properties in the public interest. The eroded land around the Ord catchment area would be a case in point and there are good reasons why this land should be taken back by the government.

4. Pasture Development

One of the main problems facing the majority of pastoralists throughout the region is the degeneration of the natural pastures which has occurred. Various reasons have been advanced for this – overstocking, vermin, and failure to recover from droughts. Each of these factors has contributed to the problem, a problem which now has become acute as revealed by the region's lambing percentages and stock figures. In the case of sheep these have declined relatively and absolutely and in the case of cattle the rate of increase is lagging behind state figures. In an attempt to improve and restore the region's carrying capacity, considerable experimentation has been made in the practical vermin control measures discussed below, and in means of regenerating the highly nutritive natural grasses.

Pasture improvement has been tackled along two lines – the regeneration of natural grasses, and the irrigation of small plots of lucerne and other

[6]K. O. Campbell, 'Problems of Adaptation of Pastoral Business in the Arid Zone'.

fodder crops. The first constitutes an extensive form of agriculture, the second is particularly intensive. Both introduce a new concept to the pastoral industry of Northwestern Australia – the blending of agriculture and pastoralism in the one operation. Prior to the late 1950's agricultural techniques and implements were virtually non-existent in the pastoral area, now the tractor and plough are appearing on an increasing number of stations. Work in many cases has not moved beyond the experimental stage, particularly on the Kimberley river fronts which have been badly eaten out. Both forms of pasture improvement are expensive, and in many areas experiments are still being made to determine the benefits relative to the costs of such plans.

Costs involved are twofold. First, the area selected must be fenced to keep the cattle and sheep off. Fencing in the Kimberley costs up to $400 per mile for materials alone, while in the North-West Division and the Pilbara costs are around $300 per mile. In the Ord River catchment area contract erection costs amount to a further $200 per mile, giving total fencing costs per mile of over $600. The question of fencing in the pastoral industry introduces the general question of selective grazing which is closely connected with programmes of pasture regeneration. The problem is not so severe in the Pilbara where more fencing and waters already exist.

Second, the area must be ploughed and sown. Bearing in mind that properties of up to one million acres in area are involved, it will be realized that if only one per cent of the station is to be treated, this could mean up to 10,000 acres. If the percentage is higher, as it often is, the area requiring remedial treatment may total anything up to 100,000 acres which is equal to 20 average wheat farms in the southern area of the state. Capital and labour costs involved in ploughing, seeding and fencing these areas are considerable and the pastoralist must be sure of a reasonable return from increased carrying capacity before he commences such a programme.

Regeneration of Natural Grasses

Furrows are usually ploughed in a checkerboard design, each furrow varying from one to two chains apart. The furrows are sown with buffel or birdwood grasses. Water accumulates in the opened furrows and the grasses take root. The soil thrown up by the plough tends to form a barrier against which windswept seeds accumulate and gradually the grass cover takes hold and commences to spread out. Intermediate ploughing between the original furrows is often carried out in later seasons and gradually the checkerboard pattern is closed as the natural and introduced grasses provide a cover for the treated area.[7]

The checkerboard system is satisfactory on level land but in areas where

[7]More detailed descriptions of the methods and techniques used can be found in the following articles by W. M. Nunn: 'Pastoral Research in the Kimberleys', 'Solving Pastoral Problems', 'Pasture Regeneration in East Kimberley', and 'Opposed Discs for Furrowing in Pastoral Areas'.

the gradient is appreciable, contour ploughing becomes necessary. Two forms of plough are used – the mouldboard in the lighter, softer soils of the area south of the Kimberley, and the opposed disc plough for the heavier, harder soils of the Kimberley. The opposed disc plough is a local innovation in the Kimberley to satisfy the special needs of the area. In addition to cutting deeper furrows than the mouldboard plough, the opposed discs can be set to a distance apart, varying with the country, to ensure that the maximum soil possible is lifted into the resultant ridge thereby leaving the maximum obstruction possible to ground level winds and to surface water movements. There are advantages too, in having a furrow each side of the central ridge. Wind-borne seeds and debris collect best in the furrow on the windward side of the ridge, so if there is a furrow on both sides then all winds are contributing.

In order to give effectiveness to these pasture regeneration methods it is essential that the practice of deferred grazing be adopted.[8] The carrying capacity of many areas has declined rapidly, mainly by the eating out of the more palatable and more nutritious species and a consequent increase in the less desirable plants in the area. Deferred grazing consists of excluding stock from part of the property after the first rains to permit plants to grow unchecked so that they will mature and produce seed. If the plants are not permitted to mature, but are eaten by stock, they will not only fail to seed, they will also fail to accumulate the necessary root reserves to tide them over dry seasons. Under the pastoral conditions obtaining in the North-West Division, six to eight weeks deferment is considered essential. The stock are brought back into the area at the end of this period to ensure that the seed is trampled into the ground instead of being blown away or taken away by birds and insects. It has been suggested that deferred grazing should be practiced on a third of the run for two successive seasons, so that the whole area is given two treatments every six years.

This extensive method of pasture regeneration is being adopted by an increasing number of northern pastoralists. At present it is largely in the experimental stage. The practicability of the method is proven from the scientific viewpoint, but costs and resulting benefits have yet to be equated by individual pastoralists. A subsidiary but important reason for large-scale pasture regeneration is to halt the substantial top soil losses being experienced in the area, resulting from extensive wind and water erosion.

The most ambitious pasture regeneration project currently being under-taken in the region is in the Ord catchment area where an initial five-year programme involving annual expenditures of £50,000 was completed in 1965. Some 1,200 square miles of badly eroded land are to be found on

[8] A more detailed study of the principles of deferred grazing can be found in the following articles: H. Suijdendorp, 'Changes in Pastoral Vegetation can Provide a Guide to Management', W. M. Nunn and H. Suijdendorp, 'Station Management. The Value of "Deferred Grazing" ', and W. M. Nunn, 'Deferred Grazing'.

the upper reaches of the Ord and the scheme for regenerating these pastures must be seen in its relation to the Ord River scheme, which is described in Chapters 6 and 7. The continued existence of these areas would aggravate the silt problem which is generally common to most northern rivers.

The problem of regenerating these areas has been tackled by contouring and strip cultivation and the species which have been sown are birdwood grass, buffel grass and kapok bush. The land is now mostly stock free and mostly free of vermin (some 25,000 to 30,000 donkeys have so far been destroyed) but regeneration has been slower than hoped for because of drought conditions. It is anticipated that grazing will not be possible for some years to come. Future expenditure on this project is expected to run at about $60,000 per year.

Irrigated Fodder Crops

This form of pasture improvement is of an intensive nature,[9] and it is still in the experimental stages. It differs in principle from the extensive form of fodder cultivation in that the crop is produced as a reserve of feed, or as feed to be used at significant periods.

Lambing percentages in the region have not improved over the past twenty years and are now appreciably below the state figures. Blowfly infestation in southern areas is partly responsible for this. Shearing has been put back to April-May and pastoralists have mated 'off the shears', with a resultant December-January lamb drop. Feed in this period is at its worst, and this is responsible for the low lambing percentags. Irrigated fodder can be used to combat the effects of poor feed both on the ewes and on the lambs as a nutritive supplement to the increasingly poor natural feed available during the latter stages of pregnancy and during the early months of the lamb's life. It may also be baled and used as a reserve against poor seasons. Stock mortality during the poor seasons results, not from a lack of drinking water which is supplied through bores, but from insufficient feed within range of the watering points. Fitzgerald in his 1953 article mentions that the transport cost alone in total fodder costs was then £16 per ton for fodder landed in Fitzroy Crossing – if it was available.

An increasing number of stations in the region are developing irrigated lucerne plots (these are discussed fully in the referenced articles). The average plot would vary from 5 to 20 acres, although some of the more ambitious station managers and owners are thinking in terms of 100 to 200 acres and 2,000 ton crops, which would produce the major portion of the feed ration for 8,000 sheep. Irrigation waters are drawn from artesian bores or from river billabongs. Watering is done by sprinklers, floor, or furrow

[9]Irrigation projects in the region are more fully discussed in : K. Fitzgerald, 'Fodder Conservation in the Kimberleys', J. A. Lawson, 'Producing Lucerne Hay for North-West Pastoral Areas', and W. M. Nunn, 'Irrigation Projects on North-West Stations'.

irrigation. The method selected depends upon the soil types, the variety of crop to be grown, and installation and maintenance costs.

These two forms of agriculture may provide a breakthrough in the region's pastoral industry. The benefits of agriculture are being allied to animal husbandry in an attempt to lift the carrying capacity of the area, and to improve the quality of the animal. In the case of the sheep industry, the application of fodder improvement schemes should lift the low lambing percentages, and provide sufficient replacement numbers to permit pastoralists to cull their herds and remove undesirable strains. At present this is virtually impossible because the replacement rate of many stations is too low even to permit maintenance of flock numbers. Fodder improvements will provide some form of insurance against droughts and resultant stock losses which in turn will assist in maintaining stock numbers and improving stock quality. Pasture improvement programmes will also help to halt the extensive erosion which has become a serious problem in some districts.

The provision of dams on the Kimberley rivers to provide irrigation waters for agriculture is dealt with in Chapter 5. The success of the irrigated lucerne crops provides an interesting line of thought in connection with the large-scale irrigation projects which are under construction or planned for the area. There is the possibility of producing fodder crops on a large scale in these areas for fattening beef cattle before they are transported to the Wyndham or Broome meatworks, or to Derby. Large-scale irrigated fodder crops could raise the quality and quantity of Kimberley cattle, and this would be worth doing if a sufficient increase in returns could thereby be secured.

The possibility of beneficial links between the established agricultural industries and the pastoral holdings in the north has already been suggested. At Camballin, sheep and cattle were pastured on stubble left after rice harvesting. The results proved extremely beneficial and lambing percentages among the ewes were the highest in the region. At Kununurra research has been carried out on the possibilities of saving many breeders on Kimberley cattle stations by the provision of supplementary feed, in particular protein by-products of the cotton industry, at crucial times of the year.

At present the practices of animal husbandry conducted on Kimberley cattle stations are such that bulls run with the herd throughout the year and stock roam at will over hundreds of square miles of unfenced property. Mustering occurs from April to September, when the bullocks are taken from the mob and trucked or driven to the abattoirs. Usually on each station there is a bullock paddock, and steers requiring another year to finish are driven into this paddock so that they will be easily accessible for early delivery the following season. On the station property there are normally two or three branding yards established at different points and the cow and calf herd is usually moved to one of these so that the calves can be branded before the herd is released again to the open range.

Since the bulls are allowed to run with the herd all year, conceptions will occur in any month and calves that are born early in the year have a good chance of surviving and putting on weight while their mothers are on green feed. More often, however, the cow will conceive with the commencement of the green feed period and this will mean that the calf will be dropped during the dry months from September to November and thus mortality amongst breeders and calves is high indeed.

The problem then, in the absence of any attempt to segregate the bulls from the herd, is to find some way of keeping the breeders and calves alive during the crucial dry season. Experiments carried out at the Kimberley Research Station have indicated that the feeding of cotton seed meal as a protein supplement can achieve this. It is clear, however, that unless pastoralists themselves are prepared to improve their properties much more, in particular in respect of fencing, there is little advantage at present in providing this protein supplement. Unless the mothers and calves can be separated from the others in fenced paddocks, the stronger animals – those who least need it – will take the supplementary feed. If, however, through improved animal husbandry practices the pastoralists of the region are able to take advantage of the availability of protein supplements at the right time, the gain to the industry as a whole could be quite significant since it has been estimated that each year some 25,000 to 30,000 breeders, and more than this number of calves, die.

Traditionally shorthorn cattle have been used in the north but since the World War there has been an increasing tendency to introduce into the herds tropical breeds such as the Africander, the Brahman and the Santa Gertrudis. They are more drought resistant and generally mature quicker and are resistant to the ticks which have plagued shorthorns. The tick causes the cattle to lose weight but it may be controlled by dipping, spraying and pasture spelling. Some pastoralists still prefer the shorthorn because it is less temperamental than the newer breeds but it seems certain that in future a greater proportion of the tropical breeds will be found in the north.

In the northern areas very encouraging results have been obtained in the growing of Townsville lucerne, sirato and phasey bean. At Kalumburu Mission, for example, lush pastures have been developed and further south, at Beverley Springs, some fine areas of Townsville lucerne are appearing. This plant has produced startling results in the beef industry on the Queensland coast and in some areas beef production has increased fivefold. At the moment it would appear to be limited to areas receiving more than 30 inches of rainfall annually, which takes in the northern half of the Kimberley, and thus it cannot yet offer hope for better pastures throughout the region. Since this problem is a technical one involving the production of new strains for lower rainfall areas, there seems no reason why research by Queensland scientists already directed to this end will not ultimately be successful. If this comes about it could provide an important technological breakthrough which would have great significance for the future of the northern cattle industry.

5. THE VERMIN PROBLEM

One of the major problems of the pastoral industry is vermin control. Whilst this problem still exists to some extent in the south-west corner of the state, it has so far been more successfully dealt with there than in the north. One of the features of pastoralism in the north is the size of the properties and the very low settlement density and this, to a large extent, makes control of vermin more difficult. The menace of non-domestic animals such as the wild donkey, the wild dog, the red kangaroo, the euro and the wallaby affects the whole area, from the East Kimberley cattle stations to the Shark Bay sheep stations. Different animals predominate in different areas, but the menace is universal.

Research and controlled experiments into the habits of the animals and the most satisfactory and economical way of controlling them have been made both jointly and independently by state Department of Agriculture, Agriculture Protection Board, and C.S.I.R.O. staff, in conjunction with the pastoralists themselves.

The Euro-Biggada or Hill Kangaroo

The shrinking flocks of the North-West and Pilbara divisions have been brought about partly by a deterioration in the pasture vegetation, particularly the disappearance of the more nutritous native grasses on which breeding ewes depended to provide the high protein diet required for the production and rearing of their lambs. Poor seasons are to blame to some extent, but an additional problem in the Pilbara area is that the euro has made pasture regeneration difficult.[10] The euro is a medium sized very powerfully built kangaroo which mainly inhabits rocky places and is rather sedentary in its habits.

In the opinion of the local pastoralists, the main factor in the deterioration of the Pilbara country has been the grazing of euros which had built up to very high numbers as a result of the increased provisions of stock waters. Experiments in the Abydos-Woodstock area refute this claim and have shown that pasture deterioration is due to a stocking policy which has been unsuited to the area's climate and conditions.

The euro has, however, aggravated the problem of pasture degeneration. Extensive studies into the euro's drinking habits were conducted on Abydos-Woodstock Pastoral Research Station. It was found that normally they drink at the same place, although some disturbance could cause them to

[10]Material for this section on the euro has been drawn from: E. H. M. Ealey and H. Suijdendorp, 'Pasture Management and the Euro Problem in the Northwest', and E. H. M. Ealey and R. M. Richardson, 'A Successful Campaign Against the Euro'.

move to water three or four miles away. More important, it was revealed that most euros did not drink very often, even when conditions were dry and temperatures were high. In the worst periods they did not drink daily. To achieve any worthwhile kill by water poisoning, the minimum period for poisoning was found to be six days. It was also found that to be effective, poisoning should be carried out under hot dry conditions, usually not before December, for it is only then that the whole local euro population will be watering with any frequency. Furthermore it was suggested that although a single watering point can be poisoned with good effect, more lasting results could be achieved by poisoning all the watering points over a substantial area of 50,000 to 100,000 acres at once.

Following an effective kill, the chances of the euro migrating from other areas is small. The euro is sedentary in its habits and will usually remain within a one mile radius of its customary drinking point. The reproduction rate in a good season could theoretically approach 30 per cent to 40 per cent per annum, but this theoretical rate would seldom be reached or maintained over a series of seasons since high infant mortality rates are experienced in all but the best seasons. Reinfestation following an efficient poisoning with an 80 per cent kill would require at least a decade. The poisoning policy laid down by the Department of Agriculture will not completely remove the euro population but if applied efficiently should keep them at a level at which their effect on pasture regeneration is negligible. In other words, new eradication measures are becoming increasingly effective.

The Red Kangaroo or Marloo

These are the biggest and most numerous of the kangaroos. As they extend through the Eastern Goldfields, North Eastern Murchison, Gascoyne and Ashburton pastoral areas and even into Nullagine and the lower coastal sections of the Pilbara, they are regarded by pastoralists generally as the most serious kangaroo menace. Although there are resident populations, pastoralists consider that there are large migrations, mainly due to availability of water and feed. Very big concentrations occur, and these large numbers are considered to cause serious pasture loss.

Extensive shooting for skins and meat is conducted by professional hunters but although this causes temporary local reductions, cost considerations usually preclude mounting a programme which will give lasting results. Two kangaroo shooters are stated to have shot 54,000 kangaroos on one station in a year without any noticeable population decline. Water poisoning is advocated as a more precise control measure, but involves absence or exclusion of stock. Baiting has not been successful – as a matter of fact it has only been successful against sand wallabies.

A biologist appointed by the Agriculture Protection Board has now commenced a detailed study of red kangaroos in Western Australia with particular attention to such matters as movements, breeding and feeding.

It is anticipated that these investigations will lead to an understanding of management requirements and methods.

The Wild Dog or 'Dingo'

This animal's destructive power lies in its attacks on stock, whereas the euro competes with stock for available pasture. Because of the rugged terrain in many parts of the region and the sparse nature of settlement, the area is an ideal hunting and breeding ground for wild dogs. Their increase potential is very great – up to 300 per cent per annum.

The Agricultural Protection Board employs up to 60 'doggers' to combat this menace. They are equipped with four wheel drive vehicles and with horses, and they kill by means of strychnine poisoned baits, assisted by trapping and sometimes shooting. Drives are organized in April-May when the breeding season commences and continue into July-August, when the young pups move from their lairs to harry the flocks, with the largest-scale operations in October-November when the dingoes are forced to congregate near water supplies. Drives are sometimes organised in conjunction with pastoralists, who supply the doggers with additional labour and horses. A new development which has been employed in combating this expensive menace is aerial baiting. In 1964 a Cessna aircraft covered over 15,000 miles in 157 hours' flying time, and laid 1,300,000 baits. The introduction of aerial baiting has enabled the programme to be carried into otherwise inaccessible areas.

The Donkey

Originally introduced for transporting wool, hides and sandalwood to the ports, and hauling food, drink, clothing, fencing wire and building materials back to the stations, the donkey became outmoded in the 1930's with the increased use of road transport. Better equipped for living off the country than other introduced animals the donkeys multiplied rapidly roaming the country in large herds which levied heavy toll on the choicest herbage and overran the rich river flats and frontage country.[11]

The most successful method so far used in eliminating this animal has been shooting. Teams of donkey-shooters, equipped with high velocity rifles, usually ex-Army 0.303's, and four wheel drive vehicles, operate around water-holes or range across open country, running down the wild donkey herds. In the East Kimberley two groups of stations employed teams of shooters who destroyed 20,000 donkeys in three years at an average cost of 4/6d. per head. In an attempt to offset costs, the hides were sold at an average of 9/-d. each, but this reduced the killing rate from 200 to 30 a day and defeated the objects of the campaign. The donkey drives have reduced numbers considerably, about 8,000 to 10,000 are shot

[11]P. J. McDonald, 'The Donkeys are Doomed'.

each year, but influxes still occur from other areas. As the campaign intensifies it is expected that donkeys will cease to be a major pest in pastoral areas.

The Camel

Although they have not increased to the same extent as wild donkeys, camels have become a nuisance in some pastoral areas. They can cause considerable damage to fences, and reports have been received of bull camels savaging sheep congregated at watering points. Once again shooting is the method used to control this nuisance.

The Sandy or Kimberley Wallaby

Three classes of the kangaroo family have become menaces to pastoral activity in Northwestern Australia. The euro and the red kangaroo have already been discussed. The third type which infests the Kimberley is the Kimberley or Sandy Wallaby.[12] This small kangaroo has been particularly bad in the Fitzroy area and much damage has been done to river frontage feed, particularly during drought conditions.

Two methods of poisoning have been found to be effective under certain conditions. The first of these methods is water poisoning. Considerable experimentation was necessary to determine the palatability and effectiveness of various soluble poisons, the average weights of male and female wallabies, the quantities of water they consume at their first drink, and the lethal dose required of each poison. To implement this method of water poisoning, all stock must be moved from the paddock, or the poison trough covered during the daytime and the alternative freewater trough shut off at night time. It is imperative that no non-poisoned water be available during the nights when poison is laid. Dams require fencing, and the installation of the poison trough must be carried out at least five days before the programme commences to enable the wallabies to become accustomed to the new source of water. Care must be taken to cover or remove poisoned water during daytime to avoid killing the area's bird life. The poisoning season extends over three months from September to December, i.e., until the wet season breaks. The effectiveness of this method is heavily dependent upon control of non-poison waters and hence is primarily suitable to the country back from the river systems.

The second method of poisoning available is the use of baits, which have given up to a 95 per cent kill in experiments. This form of poisoning the Kimberley wallaby is most effective in the areas near rivers, particularly in times when natural feed is short.

[12]Material for this section on the Kimberley wallaby has been drawn from: A. R. Tomlinson, C. D. Gooding and L. A. Harrison, 'The Wallaby Menace in the Kimberleys', C. D. Gooding and L. A. Harrison, 'Trapping Yards for Kangaroos', and C. D. Gooding and J. L. Long, 'The Kimberley Wallaby, Menace'.

The Blowfly

Blowflies have proved a great menace in the sheep areas and are regarded as one of the major causes of poor lambing percentages in recent years. The fly has forced some pastoralists to change the mating period, with unsatisfactory results.

Generally the fly will attack the youngest sheep for preference and it strikes about May or June. This has, in the past, forced some pastoralists to shear earlier and earlier each year and eventually to change their seasons. Some now shear as early as April in the Gascoyne-Minilya region where the menace is particularly strong. Since the station owners like to mate off shears, mating has been put forward to May and the lambs are dropped in the summertime when feed is at its worst. Lambs are lost because of heat and poor feed and because the ewes are forced to lactate on dry feed.

Once an effective control is developed a return to former mating seasons is possible and in some cases this has already been achieved. Control of the fly through the techniques of spraying and jetting (generally acknowledged as superior to crutching as a blowfly control measure) combined with newer and better insecticides, has enabled some to return to the previous cycle with shearing being carried out in October, mating in November and lambing in May or June. This has resulted in a marked improvement in lambing percentages.

Summary

The destructive nature of vermin is twofold. In the first category are those which compete with the sheep and cattle for the available natural grasses. This group includes the red kangaroo, the euro, the Kimberley wallaby and the wild donkey. Their presence lowers the carrying capacity of the stations, particularly if they are to be found in large numbers. They also make the task of pasture regeneration difficult and to a large extent can nullify a programme of deferred grazing designed to rehabilitate natural resources.

The second category of vermin includes those which attack the stock. The wild dog, camel, blowfly and fox all come within this group. The two basic methods of eradication practised are either by poisoning or by shooting. Poisoning is used in the cases of the kangaroo family, foxes and wild dogs. Wild donkeys, camels and also wild dogs are shot, either by Agricultural Protection Board employees or station staff and private teams employed by the pastoralists or by the Board's employees working in conjunction with pastoral labour. Local vermin authorities (shire councils or elected vermin boards) have displayed an increasing interest in active vermin control in recent years, with some employing doggers and other staff.

Vermin in the region cause considerable damage and loss to the pastoral industry annually and at present there appears to be a lack of co-ordinated effort to remove them from the region. Co-operation has been achieved on the experimental side between commonwealth and state departments and some pastoralists, and as a result combined research is providing the answer to economic and effective killing methods. The application of these techniques, however, appears to lack the integration essential to ensure an effective result. Negligence or indifference towards control and eradication methods on one station can undo the good work of neighbouring stations. To tackle this problem there is need for a comprehensive plan directed by the Agricultural Protection Board and Vermin Control officers, that will be adhered to on moral or legal grounds by the pastoralists operating under the control of local vermin control committees independent of the local governing bodies.

Vermin control in the vast Pilbara area forms the major part of a programme to rehabilitate the Pilbara pastoral industry and was approved by the state cabinet in May 1961. Originally for five years but since extended by another year to 30 June 1967, the plan, which entails an anti-vermin campaign organised by the Agriculture Protection Board in collaboration with a committee of representatives of local vermin boards, was submitted in a report to the Western Australian government by its Consultant on the North-West, Mr. Baron Hay. It was proposed to spend about $100,000 a year – actual expenditure has been about $80,000 – to control wild dogs and kangaroos, mainly euros, the numbers of which would have to be reduced considerably in order to obtain the adequate control over grazing which is considered essential in any overall plan for pasture improvement. The plan has proved an outstanding success, particularly in regard to wild dog control. The special team of doggers has obtained about 1,000 wild dog scalps a year and poisoned many others with the result that sheep losses due to this pest are the lowest in the Pilbara area for many years, if not the lowest on record. Although seasonal conditions and stock movement problems have handicapped control of kangaroos, they have been greatly reduced on many sections of stations requiring pasture regeneration. The scheme has been so successful that the pastoralists in the area, through their committee, have now obtained government agreement for the continuation of a modified plan for a further five years commencing 1 July 1967. Contributions from pastoralists and the government will be on a dollar for dollar basis, estimated to raise $52,000 a year, while in addition, the Agriculture Protection Board will continue to provide its normal staff and services in the region.

6. TRANSPORT

Problems associated with transport both into, within, and out of the region constitute one of the major groups of problems confronting the pastoralists of Northwestern Australia.[13] Remoteness from sources of materials supply

[13]For a more detailed survey of transport in the region see Chapter 9.

and from markets, and the frequent need for double handling add considerably to production and marketing costs in the region. Road haulage is hampered by rough and unsealed roads in parts, and by the washaways which often follow the torrential downpours characteristic of a large part of the area. Vehicle maintenance is expensive, fuel costs are high and the absence of backloading drives up ton-mile freights. Ships have to contend with extreme tidal conditions and in some cases with inadequate jetty facilities either for loading and unloading or for storage. Waterfront labour is expensive. The capital cost of the specially constructed passenger-cargo vessels of the State Shipping Service which service the area is high relative to cargo space. Air transport, whilst fast and reliable, is by its very nature suited only to the carrying of passengers, mails, small freight items and perishables.

Wool

All of the wool produced in the region is freighted out to the Perth woolmarkets and overseas by road, rail or sea transport or a combination of these. The sole railhead in the area to link with the south is at Meekatharra. The wool is hauled by trucks from the stations to the various ports along the coastline, or to the Meekatharra and Geraldton rail terminals and this is usually carried out by the mail contractors who have to operate in most cases over earth-formed roads. The hauls may be anything up to 600 miles in distance and add considerably to the distribution costs of the commodities.

The vehicles used vary considerably in size (usually depending on the capital backing of the operator) and they range up to a 20-ton payload. A feature of the wool haulage business is the absence of multiple vehicle haulage firms; cartage is in the hands of a number of individual owner-drivers. This system must to some extent result in higher transport costs as a result of duplicated maintenance facilities and possibly unused vehicle capacity. At the ports or rail terminals handling of the product once more adds further to costs.

Movement of live sheep within the region, or from the region to Perth markets, does not occur on a large scale. As mentioned elsewhere, the area has difficulty in maintaining its lambing percentages purely for stock replacement, and there is very little scope for commercial disposal of sheep. Experiments have been made with the air-freighting of wool but it has not so far proved a commercial proposition.

Beef

Beef is turned off from the Kimberley either in live form or as frozen meat. Prior to the 1950's beef cattle were walked to the coastal ports of Wyndham, Broome and Derby or to the railhead at Meekatharra. Considerable stock mortality and losses from other factors occurred and the cattle also deteriorated in quality because they lost condition during the long debilitating walks, sometimes over hundreds of miles, in harsh conditions. It was prudent, under this system, to send only beasts of five years or older which were able to withstand the rigours of the drive.

The Wyndham meatworks was established in 1919 and has operated each year since, with the exception of a break due to a strike in 1921, and during the war period 1942-1944, inclusive. The products it now handles are frozen beef and frozen beef offal, edible and inedible tallow, wet and dry salted hides, hair, horns, and blood and bone fertilizer. Heavily subsidized over the years the meatworks has kept alive the beef industry during some of its lean periods. Killing is, of course, seasonal and the killing season for fat cattle lasts for three months. If meat extract could be produced it might be possible to extend this period for another three to four months, thus giving longer employment opportunities in the area. At peak operation it employs about 300 persons.

Air Beef

In 1949, with the formation of Air Beef, a new dimension was added to beef transport in the region. An inland killing works was established at Glenroy lying north of the rugged King Leopold Ranges, and cattle from surrounding stations were slaughtered there and the carcasses air-freighted to Wyndham. Previously, the cattle from this area were forced to undergo a particularly long and arduous walk of 300 miles to Wyndham.

One result of the 1949 operation was an upgrading of the cattle slaughtered. Not only was the condition better on those cattle that otherwise would have been walked to Wyndham, but younger cattle in prime condition could be killed. At its peak, the abattoir slaughtered some 4,000 to 5,000 cattle in a killing season lasting from May to September. This provided three four-ton payloads daily for a DC-3 freighter operated by Mac.Robertson Miller Airlines, in conjunction with Air Beef. In 1959 the enterprise moved one step further and established a processing plant (DEMCO) in Derby, where the boned meat was packaged for export. This diverted the meat from Wyndham to Derby. In the same year Air Beef became an independent entity after having over the decade 1949-1959 received a total subsidy from the government of £101,100.

In 1963 the need for Air Beef vanished with the completion of a beef road through the King Leopold Ranges. The killing works at first continued to operate, with refrigerated trucks taking the place of aircraft in transporting the carcasses to Derby. Very soon, however, a killing works was established at Derby which, in a way, represented a transfer of the works from Glenroy to Derby and at last the Glenroy abattoir became redundant. It was razed by fire in 1966 and now all that remains of this pioneering establishment are a few stockyards and the skeleton framework of the main building surrounded by a few empty huts.

The original conception bore fruit to the point where the obvious need for the inland killing works and the subsequent development was largely responsible for the ultimate opening up of new country and the construction of new communication systems. The enterprise serves to demonstrate how the application of modern transport methods can be used to overcome the physical disabilities of an area which, in many ways, is just moving out of the pioneer stage.

Road Transport

The use of road transport facilities by the pastoralists running sheep is not new. The wool they produce is not affected by rough roads, although of course, the vehicles are. Wool carting by motorized transport has existed since vehicles were available to do the work.

Road transport of beef cattle has also been tried, and proved successful. It has now passed the experimental stage and, within the physical environment, certain operating principles have been established and road transport has become a proven commercial venture although many difficulties still remain.

The receiving depots for the region's cattle are at Wyndham, Derby, Broome, and Meekatharra. Road transport has been found to be most satisfactory over distances ranging from 100-400 miles, and within these limits it has been extensively adopted in the West Kimberley, the focal pickup point being Fitzroy Crossing. The East Kimberley presents a different picture; some of these pastoralists still walk their cattle into Wyndham. The roads in this area still require considerable upgrading, and the fear of bruising the cattle has prevented the widespread adoption of road transport in the area. Transport by road trains is used extensively in the North-West Division to haul cattle to Midland Junction. Ideal truck sizes and loads have been determined from experience and the problem now to be overcome is the provision of all-weather roads along the main northern routes. The present earth-formed roads are dusty during the dry season and prone to washaways and bogging in the wet with a resultant adverse effect on the roads, the vehicles and the cattle. It is encouraging, from this viewpoint, to see an acceleration in the rate at which the bitumen surfacing is reaching out from each major township in the north.

Bitumen road surfaces will not only minimize the continual dust, washaway and bogging hazards, they will also enable the vehicles to speed up their operations, thereby giving them a greater range or enabling them to bring in more cattle per week, with smaller risk of bruising. Road improvement in the East Kimberley should open the way for large-scale use of road trains and if the West Kimberley pattern is repeated, the quality and quantity of turnoff could rise considerably over a period of years. A further advantage of the sealed roads would be to ensure that ships were not forced to leave tidal ports without their full cargo complement, or not forced to fall behind schedule because road transport was held up. The tidal nature of the northern ports places an added strain on shipping servicing the area.

Recognition of the importance of road transport, particularly to the cattle industry, was given by the conclusion in 1962 of an agreement between the commonwealth and state governments to spend £7 million between them on beef roads in the north over a period of five years. This represented a reversal of previous commonwealth policy on beef road finance which had been to avoid long-term commitments in favour of year to year appropriations. Part of the general plan for road construction in the north involves building a road more or less direct from Gibb River to the north, which will open up a great deal of what is now inaccessible country. The existing road through the King Leopold Ranges was also financed under this scheme. This scheme and other aspects of transport in the region are examined in Chapter 9.

The combination of improved roads and improvements to the Wyndham and Derby jetties will permit an increased turnoff from the East and West Kimberley. The completion, in 1966, of a deep-water port at Broome in the West Kimberley, has likewise assisted in the movement of packaged meat in increased quantities from the region. Improved transport facilities throughout Northwestern Australia are essential if the region's output is to be boosted, and if transport costs are to be lowered to a point where they permit the area's produce to compete more than favourably on local and overseas markets.

7. Markets

Some of the main problems facing the pastoral industry have already been discussed and others are dealt with below. The solution of these problems over the passage of time should result in greater possibilities for expansion of the industry, an expansion which will of course, in the last analysis, be limited by the state of demand for the region's product.

The principal market for the region's wool over the last decade was the United Kingdom, followed by France and Japan. Other valuable markets were Italy and the United States of America. Sales to the United Kingdom have, however, been declining year by year and those to Japan have been increasing. Early in the 1960's Japan finally became the most important market for exports of Australian wool.

The possibility of exploiting overseas markets for lamb and mutton should not be overlooked although northern sheep are somewhat different from those in the south – usually they are bigger framed and longer lived – and this may make them less acceptable. However, live sheep are being exported from the south in ever increasing quantities to Singapore and Kuwait, and demand exists in the more northern Asian countries. There is no reason why northern sheep owners should not share in these markets if their product is acceptable and if satisfactory marketing arrangements can be concluded.

The pattern of markets for the region's beef turnoff has, in the past, been reasonably clear. Most export production before the 1950's went to the United Kingdom which was prepared to take first and second quality beef as well as boneless beef. Changes have been occurring in recent years, however, with the exploitation of Asian markets and a vigorous entry into the United States and European markets. United States beef manufacturers entered the Australian market in 1958 and the trade grew rapidly. The 1964 agreement between the United States and Australian governments provides for the export of up to 260,000 tons of Australian meat to the United States in 1966. Since 1950 the proportion of Wyndham meatworks' kill going to the United Kingdom and the Continent has steadily fallen while the remainder, which is mainly 'boned-out' meat for the United States and Asia, and for local Western Australian consumption, has risen. Beef offal (heads, cheeks, tails, udders, tongues, hearts, livers, kidneys and brains) shipped from Wyndham to the United Kingdom has declined in relative terms since 1950, while exports to the United States and Asia from the same source have come into the picture. Broome has been increasing its exports of beef and offal to Singapore and elsewhere in Asia and also to Europe. Live cattle have been exported from Broome and Derby to the Philippines, Hong Kong and Singapore in increasing numbers.

United States' demand for Australian beef has increased considerably in recent years and exports of frozen beef to the United States have increased in value terms from £489,000 in 1958-59 to £3,135,000 in 1964-65. The American buyers are at the moment, however, only buying second and lower quality Australian meat for processing purposes since even the best quality Kimberley beef falls below what is demanded in the American trade for good quality cuts. Kimberley beef is very lean and admirably suited to American processing requirements, and this demand will probably remain firm or increase in the future, subject always to cost conditions and prices. The quality of marketed beef depends not only upon age and configuration, but also upon such other factors as emotional state when killed. In this respect the range cattle of the north, which often have not seen a human being before being taken to the kill, are usually in a highly excited state when killed and this adversely affects the grading.

The possibility of taking advantage of the firm overseas demand for chilled beef should also be given serious consideration. First and second quality beef are at their best when chilled, and third and manufacturing qualities are better frozen. Beef is chilled at about 34° F. and frozen at about 17° F., and there are certain costs at the moment associated with chilled beef that make it less attractive to the exporter than frozen beef. The major drawback of chilled beef in comparison with frozen beef, is that it has to be hung with adequate air circulation assured. Unlike the frozen beef, it cannot be stacked and this increases handling and storage costs. On the other hand, chilled beef is undoubtedly more palatable.

With living standards rising in Asia and other developing areas any slack in other overseas markets may well be taken up, but the character of the demand would probably change from manufacturing beef to a better quality product. Singapore and Hong Kong have been taking first and second quality beef from the Kimberley and this market will probably become firmer and more selective as time goes on. Japan is also now importing larger quantities of beef, though she has not, as yet, taken any Kimberley produce. Her demand is mainly for brisket and other lower quality cuts, and it is expected that the Japanese market will grow.

8. Capital And Labour

Capitalization of Properties

Capitalization of the properties in Northwestern Australia is considerable in some cases but not nearly enough in the eyes of the critics of absentee ownership who claim that the large companies have sunk a minimum of capital into their properties and treated the land as a wasting asset. The generally high costs of materials and labour have undoubtedly proved obstacles to expansion, and the institution of a thoroughgoing stock control programme, particularly on some of the run-down properties, would be beyond the capacity of most stations. Stud stock is itself an expensive item, but the fencing, water supply points and other associated costs are heavy indeed. No station in the Kimberley is boundary fenced and most have no more than one or two large paddocks. Nevertheless, those stations which have recently ploughed profits back into stock control and pasture improvement, even if only in a modest way in the beginning, are already reaping the benefits. These sorts of programmes have a habit of snowballing and those pastoralists who are prepared to sacrifice immediate cash gains for longer term expansion are growing in strength.

A 1958 study throws some light upon the capitalization of sheep stations in the region.[14] The figures were compiled from a sample of 32 properties, averaging 460,000 acres in size and carrying an average of 10,860 sheep each, or about one sheep to every 42 acres.

Approximately 50 per cent of the total capital value of the properties was represented by the value of the sheep they ran. The land had only a nominal value as was indicated by the small proportion (3.2 per cent) of total capital which it represents. The absence of heavy capital cost in respect of land is due to the system of pastoral lease in operation in the region. Net additions to capital from 1952 to 1957 amounted to £2,713 or an increase of five per cent after depreciation allowances. The value of livestock decreased by 2.5 per cent over the period, a decrease which was largely accounted for by dwindling stock numbers. The value of water supply and fencing rose slightly over the period but the most marked movement was undoubtedly the increase in the proportionate importance of plant and building. In both of these cases a 50 per cent increase was

[14]F. Anderberg and J. P. Carney, 'The Sheep Industry of Western Australia'.

recorded in the six-year period. These figures outline the average capitalization of a pastoral lease in the mid-fifties and reveal movements in the components over a six-year period. Figures for cattle stations could be expected to follow a broadly similar pattern with possible increases in the value of fencing and water provisions.

Access to capital does not, on the whole, appear to be a restricting factor within the industry now although some claim that it still is, and that easier rural credit should be made available from banks or from other credit institutions. With programmes of pasture regeneration, irrigated fodder crops and herd improvement, supported by good cattle prices, the capitalization of the pastoral properties may show an increase in the next decade as a result of the purchase of agricultural implements and the need for more fencing. There are signs that the large companies are now putting more money back into their properties as capital improvements.

The Treloar report suggests that one question as yet unsolved, is whether the extra capitalization represented by increased fencing would be justified by a greater increase in the income of the stations. What is needed to answer this question, Treloar suggests, is a research station of commercial size operated by the government. The newly acquired station at Fitzroy Crossing may provide the answer.

Public Capital

The avenues for future government investment in the area, as it directly influences the pastoral industry, have been mentioned throughout this chapter. The most pressing is the need for improved transport facilities. The arterial beef roads, Fitzroy Crossing - Derby - Broome - Flora Valley-Wyndham, the highways, both coastal and inland, of the North-West, Pilbara and Central Divisions, the planned Derby-Wyndham road, and the numerous subsidiary and approach roads, all require continual improvement and maintenance. In this regard it should go without saying that, with the increased public expenditure being made for the benefit of cattle stations, the lessees should justify this public support by being prepared to sink more of their own money into their properties and make them more efficient.

Research facilities to investigate and solve pastoral problems constitute another call upon state funds. The state government has taken over the Abydos and Woodstock pastoral leases in the Pilbara, amounting in all to half a million acres, and has used this area as a base for pastoral research, and recently it has taken over some 90,000 acres near Fitzroy Crossing in order to establish the Fitzroy Pastoral Research Station. Other research stations are located at Carnarvon and at Kununurra. Considerable quantities of agricultural implements, fencing, stock and vehicles are required to carry out research into the problems of the industry, and the maintenance and extension of this service to pastoralists constitutes an important and substantial field of public investment.

Vermin control is another field in which the government is playing an increasing role. It is already spending considerable sums of money in the region, particularly in the Pilbara, and it is hoped that the expenditure of government funds in this way will help to rejuvenate the sheep industry.

There is also the problem of water provision, which is discussed in several places in this book, particularly in Chapter 7. Already the government has spent some millions on dams and irrigation schemes and this form of expenditure can be expected to increase in the future as more of the region's water resources are harnessed and utilized.

Apart from public expenditure directly associated with more efficient production and turnoff in the region there is also, of course, the fact that such expansion, if it does take place, will lead to a strong demand for social capital expenditure in the form of provisions for hospitals, schools and the like as the area is worked more intensively.

Capital for Associated Activities

When considering the capital structure and requirements of the pastoral industry, some mention should be made of the demands of closely allied facilities. One is the meatworks and abattoirs. Three killing units exist in the region, at Wyndham, Derby and Broome. The present turnoff of beef cattle is adequately catered for by these three installations. If, however, transport improvements and advances in pastoral management continue, the result should be substantial increases in the annual turnoff, which will eventually necessitate new or extended meat processing works in the Kimberley unless East Kimberley cattle are sent to the Northern Territory. Allied with an increase in killing and processing facilities, plants can be established, to process what are now treated as waste products from the beef cattle.

A second avenue for increasing associated capital requirements lies in the transport equipment itself. The West Kimberley uses road transport extensively now, and increased turnoff will increase the demand for cattle trains comprising prime movers and two trailers. General acceptance, now emerging, by the East Kimberley pastoralists of road transport would create additional demand for these expensive road trains.

The future capital requirements of the pastoral industry are substantial and diverse. Private capital requirements would appear to be reasonably well catered for, either from the earnings of the pastoralists themselves or to a lesser extent from banks and stock companies. The demand for public investment is enormous and involves the provisions of all-weather roads, high-level crossings, deep-water port facilities, suitable coastal vessels and research facilities. Increased output by the industry will have the effect of increasing demand for allied capital equipment such as killing and processing works and road transport units. At the present stage of development the pastoral industry requires a considerable inflow of public and private capital to overcome its more pressing problems of pasture regeneration, vermin control and for improving transport facilities. If the initial inflow has the desired effect of improving the pastoral output, a secondary demand will arise to cater for the higher level of output in the form of increased transport, processing equipment and social capital.

Labour

Labour, it would appear, does not constitute a basic problem from the point of view of supply and demand within the beef industry. From the point of view of quality there are some complaints. The further north one goes in the region, the more oppressive become the living and working conditions from the climatic point of view, particularly in summer. Wage levels need to be sufficiently high to combat the joint disabilities of isolation and climatic discomfort, and the accepted leave standards have now become two to three months every two years in the Kimberley with each way fares paid to Perth. This has the effect of making unit labour costs high in the region.

In past years considerable use has been made of native labour, particularly for stock work, supervised by white overseers and station managers. Considerable controversy still rages as to the abilities of educated and trained native labour, and the responsibility given to the aboriginal employee is largely dependent on the individual station manager's appraisal of a native's ability. The wages paid in the past was determined on a similar basis.

Developments in transport are releasing station hands from droving duties which previously took them from the stations for substantial periods each year. The labour so released can now be used to carry out essential replacement and improvement work on the stations. This labour supply would appear capable of satisfying demand in the region in the pastoral industry. The quality of this labour is largely determined by wages and working conditions offered by individual stations.

Within the sheep industry the availability of labour of specific types seems to rate fairly high in any list of disabilities from which the industry suffers. Men are available but mostly they do not seem to have the attitude to work or the know-how required by the station managers. It should be realized that this is largely the fault of the managers themselves for they have been unwilling to take the time and trouble to train their station hands and jackeroos. The jackeroos are the managers of the future and, as they progress through the position of overseer to station manager, they must be trained properly if the standard of animal husbandry is not to suffer.

The standard of animal husbandry, in its broadest sense, is a major determinant of the lambing percentage, which, as has been shown, is one of the major keys to the expansion of the industry. Quantity and quality of wool will improve as a result of selective breeding, hard culling, segregation into age groups, all of which can be practised with high lambing percentages and adequate capital resources. Thus the managerial side of station labour, in both its embryonic and final form can be seen to be of crucial importance.

Generally speaking the demand for native labour is easing in the sheep areas, particularly the Pilbara, but is still quite strong in the Kimberley. What effect the payment of the basic wage to all aborigines will have in the future remains to be seen.

9. FUTURE DEVELOPMENT

The most important factors which will determine the industry's future are market prospects, standard of management, vermin control, availability of capital and labour, and transport arrangements.

It cannot be assumed that inadequate demand for the industry's product will prove a limitation to development in the foreseeable future. In fact the prospects for a continued firm demand are bright. World changes in the pattern of demand, and changes in the markets to which Kimberley beef is sent, may eventually force pastoralists to produce a different quality of beef. But as far ahead as one can see the immediate and long-term goal should be to increase turnoff. Unfortunately the bait of high prices has caused some stations to go too far in this regard and to turn off breeders in large numbers. This will have the effect of slowing down and, perhaps in some cases, even reversing the build-up of herds.

Station management must be improved if the industry is to move ahead. Already there are signs of this, and some of the region's pastoralists have demonstrated clearly that they realize the value of better animal husbandry although one could wish that the proportion was greater. They have moved ahead with the agricultural researchers in putting into practice methods which have been proved by experiment to be successful. In the sheep industry attention has to be given to good stock control which, in turn, requires adequate capital resources, scientific management and effective vermin control. In the cattle industry the same is true. In both segments of the pastoral industry the benefits from better animal husbandry usually take some time to appear, but ultimately they are reflected in better quality and larger numbers.

Linked with improvements in animal husbandry is also the question of size of leases. Areas of holdings could in most cases be reduced with a consequent improvement in managerial efficiency. It may well be, too, that the leasehold system might better be replaced by one of conditional purchase, though this has its obvious dangers prominent among which could be landlocking in strategic areas. Reduced property size can lead to greater carrying capacity and to closer settlement than at present, which would bring with it all-round economies of many kinds and would assist in reducing costs.

Vermin has been and still is a major limitation to development. In both of its aspects, the eating of pastures and the savaging of stock, it might be said that the vermin problem has not yet been effectively attacked, though the Agriculture Protection Board has amassed a considerable amount of vital information from experimentation with techniques of control. Tied up with this question is that of who is going to pay for control and what form of organization is to be used. This is a major problem for the industry and its early solution is vital. Meanwhile the programme of vermin control, on the government side, is being stepped up, particularly in the Pilbara, and some enlightened pastoralists are also attacking the problem vigorously.

Transport is again a major limiting factor, though its limitations are much more apparent and serious in the cattle industry than the sheep industry. In its various aspects it affects quality, quantity and cost of beef. The distances are so vast, the terrain so rugged and the water runoff so intense that great amounts of capital would need to be poured into the area before its road system could be considered adequate to meet the full developmental needs of the industry. Looked at in relation to the beef industry alone, the return of social capital invested would seem to be small indeed. But, of course, its benefits in terms of development are not confined to this one industry and the social, if not the economic justification, would seem to exist for the vastly disproportionate sums which are spent by the government upon the region's transport system. Nevertheless, shortage of capital is likely to remain a limiting factor for some years.

The position as regards pastures throughout the region is far from satisfactory. Vermin and exploitative grazing in the past has left the stations with a legacy of denuded or poor quality pasture land. The problem exists in the north of the region but is generally more critical in the southern areas. Here, positive, though as yet minor, progress has been made with the introduction of measures for pasture regeneration spear-headed by experiments conducted by the Department of Agriculture. It is a costly business but the movement is now gaining momentum and the problem is being overcome with increasing effectiveness. As in the solution of the other problems, there is still, however, much to be done.

Labour in the region is really no great problem. Admittedly the quality leaves something to be desired but with some vigorous managers who are prepared to devote some of their time to training their staff, and who are appearing in the region in greater numbers now, the solution may be at hand. Labour costs, like all other costs in the region, are high but, in general, stations seem well able to meet them.

Capital is always a critical factor in development. To meet all of the problems mentioned above in an effective way takes money. Stock control through selective breeding requires expenditures on stud stock, on watering points, on fencing and other capital items. Vermin control eats up time and money. Pasture improvement is very costly. Mechanization means capital expenditure. Given sufficient capital resources to commence these measures and sustain them for a time, they become self-reinforcing and translate themselves into higher profits and thus enable higher appropriations for capital improvements. A snowballing effect commences provided the management is willing to sink a healthy proportion of its profits into

investment of the type designed to improve future profit rates. Although
lack of capital is often advanced as a reason for the degeneration that has
taken place, particularly in the sheep industry, there is little doubt that had
absentee-owners been willing in the past to take less in immediate profits,
the stations would have been more profitable in subsequent years, though
to be fair to the lessees it must be pointed out that this is only one of the
many factors contributing to the decline of the industry. On the whole,
lack of capital even now cannot be regarded as a major limiting factor
except in certain areas. In this respect the solution to the problem lies
mainly in the hands of the owners and the government through their
powers under the leasehold agreements. Lower dividends now may pave
the way for higher dividends later.

There has been a move, recently, towards the taking over of pastoral
properties in Northwestern Australia, both in sheep and cattle, by American
interests with large capital resources behind them and a determination to
spend large sums on capital improvements in an effort to regenerate the
stations. Properties which have been acquired in this way are Anna Plains
and Dunham River, and American capital is entering other properties in
association with Australian capital. It is planned to develop these properties
rapidly, but it is too early yet to assess what effects such takeovers will
have upon managerial and marketing practices and upon the efficiency
of these stations in general. It seems that the development plans will
possibly include a move towards greater diversification, in particular the
introduction of irrigated pastures for legume production.

The climate has not always been kind, in the past, to the sheep and
cattlemen and in particular the sheep industry has taken some almost
crippling blows for lengthy periods, mainly in the form of disastrous droughts.
Little can be done in the future to prevent these conditions but many of
the measures outlined above would, if adopted by pastoralists, help alleviate
them.

All told, therefore, it can be seen that severe problems still confront the
industry. The solutions to some of them seem to be coming more rapidly
than to others. In respect of all of them some positive steps are now
being taken. Barring vagaries of climate like sustained droughts or disastrous
flooding it may be expected that both the cattle and sheep industries are
heading for better days, though too slowly for comfort. The introduction
of an acceptable legume for the drier parts of the region would assist
greatly but the main stimulus for improvement in the industry will have to
come from the pastoralists themselves. They must be willing to plough
much more back into improvements of all kinds than they have done so
far, and must be prepared to lift the standard of their management practices
as well. They can be assisted or persuaded in this by firm action on the
part of the government to ensure that the spirit of the leasehold conditions
is observed and not circumvented. To this end resumption powers should
be used whenever necessary.

10. SUMMARY AND CONCLUSIONS

The pastoral industry is the major form of activity in the region though it will no doubt shortly be surpassed by the mining industry. In terms of employment, the industry absorbs 50 per cent of the primary workforce of Northwestern Australia (1961 census) and 21.3 per cent, or about one-fifth of the total workforce. Returns to the wool grower vary considerably in the region as a result of price movements and poor seasons, but in 1965 the figure amounted to £4.3 million. Official figures of the value of production are not available for the region's beef industry, but estimates would put it at about $4 million.

Sheep numbers in the region have remained fairly stable at around two million over the post-war years, while in the same period the state's sheep population has more than doubled. This lack of increase in the area is due mainly to the low lambing percentage. The region's lambing percentage has varied between 40 per cent and 50 per cent, whilst the figures for the state as a whole have attained almost 70 per cent. The sheep pastoralists on the 40 per cent lambing percentage have difficulty in maintaining their flocks.

Expansion is mainly dependent upon pasture regeneration and improvement, and improved vermin control. Work at Abydos-Woodstock research station and in other areas has shown the value of furrow ploughing of denuded areas, and of deferred grazing. Areas which have been ploughed and rested at vital periods have recovered their grass cover, and the more nutritive of the natural grasses have returned. Deferred grazing over one-third of the property for two years out of every six has proved a practicable method of retaining and improving natural feed.

Pasture improvement and more rigid vermin control, combined with a change back to cool weather lambing (April-May) could help considerably in lifting the area's lambing percentages. The introduction of irrigated and baled pasture crops on an increasing number of stations could provide additional feed at vital times – around lambing and in case of drought. However, despite the research and other rejuvenative activity proceeding in the region, it must be borne in mind that in some areas, particularly in the Pilbara, rainfall will always remain a limiting factor.

The region's annual woolclip has fluctuated fairly closely with movements in sheep numbers, and has averaged around 18 million pounds weight annually over the last decade while the average fleece weight over the same period has been about 9 lbs. Since the boom year of 1950-51 prices have fallen steadily from 137.6 pence per lb. to 55.89 pence per lb. in 1964-65, but returns to the pastoralist, whilst they have declined are still fairly high. As a result of research done in the area, solutions to pasture deterioration have become available. Practical measures are now being adopted to combat the vermin problem on a large scale. As the pastoral industry gradually adopts these new measures the area's carrying capacity in terms of sheep could move towards the old levels of the early thirties though the process would be slow.

The other side of pastoralism — the beef industry — presents a different picture. In 1947 the area contained 486,200 head of cattle. By 1965 this figure stood at 615,900, an increase of some 27 per cent. The vermin and pasture problems are just as acute in the beef producing areas as they are in the sheep country. Large areas of river-front land have been completely denuded, as a result of overgrazing. The same types of solutions apply in the Kimberley as in the North-West and Pilbara, with the techniques and machinery adapted to local conditions which vary considerably. Eventual control of pleuro-pneumonia would also assist by permitting graziers to market their animals, after fattening, in the south of the state.

Transport improvements have opened the way to the marketing of better quality stock in larger quantities. When the use of mechanized transport becomes completely accepted, when pasture regeneration gains momentum, and when the vermin problems are under control, the turnoff of beef cattle from the region should rise considerably. Improved management practices and the ploughing back of profits in the form of capital improvements will also assist in this direction. Alongside these changes and improvements must be considered the potential of large-scale irrigated fodder crops. The water resources of the Kimberley are great and if the capital is available to harness and control them, the scope for irrigated fodder crops is considerable.

It becomes obvious that future expansion in the beef industry is heavily reliant on a substantial capital inflow to implement the agricultural techniques, to develop the transport system, in particular the road network and deep-water port facilities, to provide the associated capital equipment – road trains and killing-processing works — and to provide the dams and irrigation systems. The responsibilities of public investment lie in the provision of deep-water port facilities, an all-weather road network and dams and irrigation schemes. Pasture improvement, including small-scale irrigation areas, vermin control, and the provision of road transport and killing-processing works is more the concern of the private investor.

The financing of public works, under Australia's system of federal government, becomes the joint responsibility of the commonwealth and state governments as the finance involved is usually beyond the means of the state. It is essential that some comprehensive plan of capital development should be constructed, and that the priorities of various capital works be determined, to ensure co-ordinated expansion in the area.

The potential increased carrying capacity of the region introduces another point — the pastoral leases. With improved agriculture techniques and transport facilities it should become possible to turn off an increased number of cattle from smaller acreages in many cases. Smaller holdings, if efficiently managed, could produce increased incomes.

In brief summary, there appears to be considerable scope for expansion in the beef cattle industry of the Kimberley. Future development depends largely on the magnitude of available public and private capital for the area, improved management practices, the continuance of pastoral research, and the formulation of a sensible policy on the conditions of renewal of pastoral leases, and the size of those leases. The sheep industry, on the other hand, requires rejuvenation, rather than development. The two forms of pastoralism together, if they progress along the lines which can reasonably be anticipated, will continue to make a significant contribution alongside the fast developing mining, agricultural and fishing industries, to the region's total primary output.

BIBLIOGRAPHY

ANDERBERG, F. and CARNEY, J. P. 'The Sheep Industry of Western Australia.' *Quarterly Review of Agricultural Economics,* vol. XI, no. 4. 1958.

AUSTRALIAN INSTITUTE OF POLITICAL SCIENCE. *Northern Australia: Task for a Nation,* pt. 2. Sydney, 1964.

BOLTON, G. 'A Survey of the Kimberley Pastoral Industry from 1885 to the Present.' Unpublished M.A. thesis, 1953. Library of the University of Western Australia.

—— *Alexander Forrest: His Life and Times.* Melbourne, 1958.

BUREAU OF AGRICULTURAL ECONOMICS. *The Economics of Road Transport of Beef Cattle, Western Australian Pastoral Areas.* Canberra, 1958.

—— 'Road Transport of Beef Cattle in Queensland.' Beef Research Report, no. 1. Canberra, 1965.

CAMPBELL, K. O. 'Problems of Adaptation of Pastoral Business in the Arid Zone.' *Australian Journal of Agricultural Economics,* vol. 10, no. 1. 1966.

COLEBATCH, H(ed.). *A Story of a Hundred Years: 1829-1929.* Perth, 1929.

CROWLEY, F. K. *A Short History of Western Australia.* Melbourne, 1959.

—— *Australia's Western Third.* London, 1960.

EALEY, E. H. M. and RICHARDSON, R. M. 'A Successful Campaign Against the Euro.' *The Journal of Agriculture,* vol. 1, no. 9. 1960.

EALEY, E. H. M. and SUIJDENDORP, H. 'Pasture Management and the Euro Problem in the North-West.' *The Journal of Agriculture,* vol. 8, no. 3. 1959.

FRASER, R. J. 'Wild Dog Control in the North-West.' *The Journal of Agriculture,* vol. 1, no. 4. 1960.

FITZGERALD, K. 'Fodder Conservation in the Kimberleys.' *The Journal of Agriculture,* vol. 2, no. 5. 1953.

—— 'Soil Conservation in the Kimberley Area.' *The Journal of Agriculture,* vol. 1, no. 11. 1960.

GOODING, C. D. and HARRISON, L. A. 'Trapping Yards for Kangaroos.' *The Journal of Agriculture,* vol. 4, no. 6. 1955.

GOODING, C. D. and LONG, J. L. 'The Kimberley Wallaby, Menace.' *The Journal of Agriculture,* vol. 7, no. 2. 1958.

KELLY, J. H. 'The Captive North.' Paper presented to the Capricornia Society at the Australian National University. 1966.

LAWSON, J. A. 'Producing Lucerne Hay for North-West Pastoral Areas.' *The Journal of Agriculture,* vol. 7, no. 2. 1958.

MALCOLM, C. V. 'Bluebush Seed Supplies.' *The Journal of Agriculture,* vol. 1, no. 3. 1960.

McDONALD, P. J. 'The Donkeys are Doomed.' *The Journal of Agriculture,* vol. 7, no. 2. 1959.

NUNN, W. M. 'Agricultural Extension in the North-West and Kimberley Regions.' *The Journal of Agriculture,* vol. 3, no. 3. 1954.

—— 'Pastoral Research in the Kimberleys.' *The Journal of Agriculture,* vol. 5, no. 5. 1956.

—— 'Pastoral Research.' *The Journal of Agriculture,* vol. 5, no. 3. 1956.

—— 'Irrigation Projects on North-West Stations.' *The Journal of Agriculture,* vol. 5, no. 6. 1956.

—— 'Solving Pastoral Problems.' *The Journal of Agriculture,* vol. 7, no. 6. 1958.

—— 'Pasture Regeneration in East Kimberley.' *The Journal of Agriculture,* vol. 7, no. 1. 1958.

—— 'Mineral Supplements for Kimberley Cattle.' *The Journal of Agriculture,* vol. 8, no. 1. 1959.

—— 'Opposed Discs for Furrowing in Pastoral Areas.' *The Journal of Agriculture,* vol. 8, no. 6. 1959.

—— 'Deferred Grazing.' *The Journal of Agriculture,* vol. 1, no. 4. 1960.

—— 'The Kimberley Pastoral Industry.' Section P, A.N.Z.A.A.S. Congress. 1965.

NUNN, W. M. and SUIJDENDORP, H. 'Station Management. The Value of "Deferred Grazing".' *The Journal of Agriculture,* vol. 3, no. 5. 1954.

SNOOK, L. C. Mineral Supplements for Stock in Pastoral Areas.' *The Journal of Agriculture,* vol. 8, no. 1. 1959.

—— 'Claypans in the North-West Spinifex Areas.' *The Journal of Agriculture,* vol. 3, no. 4. 1954.

SUIJDENDORP, H. 'Changes in Pastoral Vegetation can Provide a Guide to Management.' *The Journal of Agriculture,* vol. 4, no. 6. 1955.

—— 'Observations on the Breeding Habits of Merinos at Abydos Station.' *The Journal of Agriculture,* vol. 8, no. 6. 1959.

SWAN, B. 'Overcoming Stock Watering Problems in the Kimberleys.' *The Journal of Agriculture,* vol. 1, no. 2. 1960.

TOMLINSON, A. R., GOODING, C. D. and HARRISON, L. A. 'The Wallaby Menace in the Kimberleys.' *The Journal of Agriculture,* vol. 3, no. 4. 1954.

TRELOAR, D. W. G. 'Investors and Kimberley Cattle.' *Australian Journal of Agricultural Economics,* vol. 9, no. 1. 1965.

WESTERN AUSTRALIA. *Report of the Pastoral Leases Committee.* Perth, 1963.

WESTERN AUSTRALIA, DEPARTMENT OF AGRICULTURE. *Sheep in the Mulga Zone.* Perth, 1965.

—— *Sheep in the Spinifex Region.* Perth, 1965.

WILCOX, D. G. 'Studies in the Mulga Pastoral Zone – The Grazing of Wandarrie Grass Associations.' *The Journal of Agriculture,* vol. 1, no. 6. 1960.

—— 'Studies in the Mulga Pastoral Zone – Some Aspects of the Value of the Mulga Scrub.' *The Journal of Agriculture,* vol. 1, no. 7. 1960.

TABLE 1

BEEF CATTLE NUMBERS
Year Ended 31 March 1947, 1954, 1961 to 1965
('000)

Statistical Division	1947	1954	1961	1962	1963	1964*	1965
CENTRAL							
Meekatharra	14.2	10.1	13.3	15.2	15.5	16.7	15.6
Wiluna	4.1	7.6	9.6	10.4	7.9	4.7	5.2
Total	18.3	17.7	22.9	25.6	23.4	21.4	20.8
NORTH-WEST							
Ashburton	2.1	3.2	2.8	2.5	4.2	5.6	6.3
Gascoyne-Minilya[1] ..	1.1	.3	.8	1.2	1.3	1.8	2.4
Shark Bay	.2	†	†	.1	†	.1	†
Upper Gascoyne	5.2	4.6	6.3	8.0	10.9	12.3	12.7
Divisional total ..	8.6	8.2	9.9	11.7	16.5	19.9	21.5
PILBARA							
Marble Bar	1.6	1.3	4.5	1.9	2.7	2.3	2.7
Nullagine	14.5	10.0	10.2	10.3	10.3	10.4	11.2
Port Hedland	.9	1.0	.8	1.1	1.5	1.9	2.2
Roebourne	1.7	3.0	2.1	2.0	2.4	2.4	3.1
Tableland	1.0	1.9	4.4	5.0	5.4	5.7	5.3
Divisional total ..	19.7	17.2	22.0	20.4	22.2	22.5	24.6
KIMBERLEY							
Broome	28.5	24.5	24.3	27.7	37.7	41.2	41.4
Halls Creek	172.9	182.8	186.6	196.9	200.2	196.3	157.4
West Kimberley	156.7	128.9	184.6	194.6	208.1	206.8	225.7
Wyndham[2]	81.7	77.4	128.1	131.4	141.6	137.8	124.5
Divisional total ..	439.8	413.6	523.6	550.6	587.7	582.1	549.0
Regional total (a)	486.4	456.7	578.4	608.3	649.8	645.9	615.9
State total (b) ..	588.4	600.2	876.2	982.8	1057.4	n.a.	1038.4
(a) as % of (b)	82.7	76.1	66.0	61.9	61.5	n.a.	59.3

* From 1964 onwards cattle are classified as bred for milk production or for meat production. Figures of meat cattle from 1964 are not strictly comparable with beef cattle figures for years prior to that date.

† Less than 50.

[1] Carnarvon Municipality included in Gascoyne-Minilya Shire.

[2] Renamed Wyndham-East Kimberley as from 1 July 1961.

n.a. Not available.

Source: Commonwealth Bureau of Census and Statistics, *Statistical Register of Western Australia*. Perth.

TABLE 2

SHEEP NUMBERS

Year Ended March 1947, 1954, 1961 to 1965

('000)

Statistical Division	1947	1954	1961	1962	1963	1964[1]	1965
CENTRAL							
Meekatharra	150.7	159.3	220.8	248.0	228.0	243.6	242.3
Wiluna	80.6	99.9	145.0	134.2	106.6	116.7	112.6
Total	131.3	259.2	365.8	382.2	334.6	360.3	354.9
NORTH-WEST							
Ashburton	228.9	293.3	256.6	284.8	289.7	286.7	297.7
Gascoyne-Minilya[1] ..	420.5	478.9	419.6	454.1	482.2	466.7	523.3
Shark Bay	78.9	112.3	111.0	123.8	120.8	126.6	142.0
Upper Gascoyne	237.9	294.3	202.1	236.1	275.2	279.6	284.7
Divisional total ..	966.2	1178.8	989.2	1098.8	1167.8	1159.6	1247.7
PILBARA							
Marble Bar	129.5	115.3	78.5	87.3	78.7	88.8	87.5
Nullagine	65.1	61.7	63.5	68.5	50.1	58.3	59.8
Port Hedland	132.4	128.2	126.6	135.1	133.6	136.6	135.0
Roebourne	158.6	147.8	138.1	142.4	145.8	158.5	178.1
Tableland	53.0	37.7	35.9	36.9	38.6	35.1	37.3
Divisional total ..	538.6	490.7	442.6	470.2	446.8	477.2	497.7
KIMBERLEY							
Broome	49.4	39.3	47.5	54.3	55.0	54.2	54.4
Halls Creek	.8	.4	1.1	1.0	.9	.7	.6
West Kimberley	192.3	142.2	145.3	128.4	132.7	125.7	115.0
Wyndham[2]	†	†	—	—	†	—	—
Divisional total ..	242.5	181.9	193.9	183.7	188.7	180.6	170.0
Regional total (a)	1878.6	2110.6	1991.5	2134.9	2137.9	2177.7	2270.3
State total (b) ..	9787.0	13087.1	17151.4	18313.9	18727.1	20164.9	22391.8
(a) as % of (b)	19.2	16.1	11.6	11.7	11.4	10.8	10.1

† Less than 50.

[1] Carnarvon Municipality included in Gascoyne-Minilya Shire.

[2] Renamed Wyndham-East Kimberley as from 1 July 1961.

Source: Commonwealth Bureau of Census and Statistics, *Statistical Register of Western Australia.* Perth.

TABLE 3

SHEEP AND LAMBS SHORN AND WOOLCLIP

Year ended 31 March 1947, 1951 to 1965

	Sheep and Lambs Shorn ('000's)	Woolclip ('000 lbs.)	Av. weight per fleece (lbs.)
1947	2102.9	17919.7	8.5
1951	2294.1	18749.9	8.2
1952	1989.6	16366.9	8.2
1953	2132.7	19677.4	9.2
1954	2171.8	19588.4	9.0
1955	2103.7	17834.2	8.5
1956	2111.8	19522.0	9.2
1957	2038.1	18341.6	9.0
1958	1992.2	17728.6	8.9
1959	1970.4	18156.9	9.2
1960	2025.6	16336.6	8.1
1961	1913.3	18152.9	9.5
1962	2049.6	18133.8	8.9
1963	2159.8	18641.9	8.6
1964	2076.3	20201.6	9.7
1965	2269.0	18646.0	8.2

Source: Commonwealth Bureau of Census and Statistics, *Statistical Register of Western Australia.* Perth.

TABLE 4

PERCENTAGE OF LAMBS MARKED TO EWES MATED
1947, 1954, 1961 to 1964

Statistical Division	*1947*	*1954*	*1961*	*1962*	*1963*	*1964*
CENTRAL						
Meekatharra	60.9	38.2	58.5	43.1	48.9	56.3
Wiluna	67.4	58.8	43.1	22.0	47.2	46.1
Total	63.1	46.5	53.2	38.3	48.4	52.9
NORTH-WEST						
Ashburton	57.4	44.3	55.6	48.2	41.3	49.7
Gascoyne-Minilya[1]	44.8	49.6	65.9	50.7	42.7	65.2
Shark Bay	55.7	47.7	56.0	47.7	55.3	72.6
Upper Gascoyne	52.5	44.7	51.4	47.0	47.4	49.4
Divisional total	50.8	47.4	58.6	48.0	44.9	58.1
PILBARA						
Marble Bar	48.0	41.1	44.8	27.3	32.5	45.8
Nullagine	48.0	43.4	54.1	17.9	24.7	42.9
Port Hedland	44.6	43.9	33.4	17.8	30.1	21.2
Roebourne	42.9	45.9	47.2	37.3	35.3	51.9
Tableland	43.0	48.2	42.9	17.9	50.8	33.8
Divisional total	47.0	44.4	43.2	25.5	33.0	40.8
KIMBERLEY						
Broome	51.3	53.1	46.7	33.1	44.6	48.3
Halls Creek	46.3	43.7	46.3	16.1	21.7	12.0
West Kimberley	44.5	54.8	29.5	45.9	34.5	31.3
Wyndham[2]	43.7	40.0	—	—	—	—
Divisional total	45.9	54.4	36.9	41.9	37.6	37.1
Regional total	50.7	47.3	52.1	41.3	42.2	52.0
State total	63.1	62.7	69.9	63.3	66.9	67.0

[1] Carnarvon Municipality included in Gascoyne-Minilya Shire.
[2] Renamed Wyndham-East Kimberley as from 1 July 1961.

Source: Commonwealth Bureau of Census and Statistics, *Statistical Register of Western Australia*. Perth.

TABLE 5

LAND UTILIZATION SUMMARY

(Season 1964-65)

Statistical Division	Total area of district	Uncleared land used for grazing	Uncleared land lying idle	Total area of holdings	4 Expressed as a% of (1)
	1	2	3	4	5
	(millions of acres)				
CENTRAL					
Meekatharra	25.18	17.75	0.44	18.19	72.2
Wiluna	81.86	12.09	0.38	12.47	15.2
Total	107.04	29.84	0.82	30.66	28.6
NORTH-WEST					
Ashburton	15.53	12.94	0.16	13.10	84.4
Exmouth Gascoyne-Minilya[1]	13.69	12.06	0.20	12.27	89.6
Shark Bay	5.13	3.90	0.41	4.30	83.8
Upper Gascoyne	14.12	12.41	0.35	12.76	90.4
Divisional total	48.47	41.31	1.12	42.43	87.5
PILBARA					
Marble Bar	29.58	3.72	0.23	3.95	13.4
Nullagine	59.24	7.62	0.39	7.95	13.4
Port Hedland	5.98	3.59	0.18	3.65	61.0
Roebourne	5.41	4.30	0.04	4.35	80.4
Tableland	9.52	3.52	—	3.52	37.0
Divisional total	109.73	22.75	0.83	23.43	21.4
KIMBERLEY					
Broome	13.27	5.70	0.31	6.05	45.6
Halls Creek	35.31	17.80	—	17.79	50.4
West Kimberley	25.38	19.40	—	19.40	76.4
Wyndham-East Kimberley	29.95	10.50	0.13	10.65	35.6
Divisional total	103.91	53.40	0.44	53.89	51.9
Regional total	369.15	147.30	3.21	150.41	40.7

[1] Carnarvon Municipality included in Exmouth and Gascoyne-Minilya Shires.

Source: Commonwealth Bureau of Census and Statistics, *Statistical Register of Western Australia*. Perth.

TABLE 6

RURAL HOLDINGS

1946-47, 1953-54, 1960-61 and 1964-65 Seasons

(No. of Holdings[1])

Statistical Division	1946-47	1953-54	1960-61	1964-65
CENTRAL				
Meekatharra	38	35	37	37
Wiluna	18	18	23	22
Total	56	53	60	59
NORTH-WEST				
Ashburton	27	29	25	28
Exmouth				
Gascoyne-Minilya[2]	90	152	175	167
Shark Bay	11	11	12	13
Upper Gascoyne	30	29	29	30
Divisional total	158	221	241	238
PILBARA				
Marble Bar	16	15	11	10
Nullagine	14	15	14	14
Port Hedland	10	11	12	14
Roebourne	14	11	13	12
Tableland	8	7	8	9
Divisional total	62	59	58	59
KIMBERLEY				
Broome	10	10	12	16
Halls Creek	29	28	29	29
West Kimberley	37	25	33	33
Wyndham[3]	13	11	19	41
Divisional total	89	74	93	119
Regional total	365	407	452	475

[1] No. of holdings from which returns were received.
[2] Carnarvon Municipality included in Exmouth and Gascoyne-Minilya Shires.
[3] Renamed Wyndham-East Kimberley as from 1 July 1961.

Source: Commonwealth Bureau of Census and Statistics, *Statistical Register of Western Australia.* Perth.

TABLE 7 PASTORAL WORKFORCE[1] Census dates 30 June 1947, 1954 and 1961 (No. of persons)

Statistical Division	1947 Census			1954 Census			Percentage change 1947 to 1954 %	1961 Census			Percentage change 1954 to 1961 %
	M	F	Total	M	F	Total		M	F	Total	
CENTRAL											
Meekatharra	184	15	199	154	26	180		141	16	157	
Wiluna	93	5	98	90	6	96		62	8	70	
Total	277	20	297	244	32	276	− 7.1	203	24	227	−17.8
NORTH-WEST											
Ashburton	121	5	126	221	36	257		167	15	182	
Gascoyne-Minilya	336	23	359	292	42	334		272	19	291	
Shark Bay	39	4	43	53	6	59		46	5	51	
Upper Gascoyne	216	13	229	198	16	214		139	28	217	
Carnarvon[2]	18	2	20	29	2	31		14	—	14	
Divisional total	730	47	777	793	102	895	+15.2	688	67	755	−15.6
PILBARA											
Marble Bar	91	4	95	107	15	122		98	4	102	
Nullagine	62	—	62	59	4	63		44	1	45	
Port Hedland	140	6	146	157	12	169		72	20	92	
Roebourne	85	3	88	140	5	145		62	6	68	
Tableland	34	2	36	26	1	27		53	2	55	
Divisional total	412	15	427	489	37	526	+23.2	329	33	362	−31.2
KIMBERLEY											
Broome	42	2	44	35	9	44		48	5	53	
Halls Creek	104	10	114	111	18	129		119	10	129	
West Kimberley	131	8	139	125	16	141		145	9	154	
Wyndham[3]	95	1	96	50	1	51		76	9	85	
Divisional total	372	31	403	321	44	365	− 9.4	388	33	421	+15.3
Regional total	1,791	113	1,904	1,847	215	2,062	+ 8.3	1,608	157	1,765	−14.4

[1] Grazing only.
[2] Municipality.
[3] Renamed Wyndham-East Kimberley as from 1 July 1961.

NOTE: In this and subsequent tables, 'work-force' means persons of all ages who, at the time of the Census, were employers, self-employed, wage and salary earners, unemployed persons and all those who were helping in any industry, business, trade or service, but not in receipt of wage or salary.

Source: Commonwealth Bureau of Census and Statistics, Census of the Commonwealth of Australia, vol. 5. Australia.

TABLE 8

EMPLOYMENT ON FARMS, STATIONS, ETC.

1947, 1954, 1961, 1965[1]

(1) Males Working Permanently. (2) Males Working Temporarily on
Holdings

(No. of persons)

Statistical Division	1947		1954		1961		1965	
	1	*2*	*1*	*2†*	*1*	*2*	*1*	*2*
CENTRAL								
Meekatharra	157	53	117	23	146	20	130	21
Wiluna	75	74	70	9	86	31	64	21
Total	232	127	187	32	232	51	194	42
NORTH-WEST								
Ashburton	103	45	121	14	108	24	113	39
Gascoyne-Minilya	332	113	416	38	440	48	419	51
Shark Bay	45	39	52	10	50	10	58	9
Upper Gascoyne	152	69	160	54	137	19	142	28
Divisional total	632	266	749	116	735	101	732	127
PILBARA								
Marble Bar	102	31	72	14	50	11	34	19
Nullagine	108	6	61	8	36	13	39	14
Port Hedland	56	52	65	17	63	16	65	19
Roebourne	108	4	51	3	76	15	82	13
Tableland	44	—	28	3	31	—	35	7
Divisional total	418	93	277	45	256	55	255	72
KIMBERLEY								
Broome	94	9	25	2	34	5	38	11
Halls Creek	116	2	108	23	120	27	121	4
West Kimberley	171	38	121	18	192	4	164	22
Wyndham[2]	53	4	53	2	94	13	129	28
Divisional total	434	53	307	45	440	49	452	65
Regional total	1,716	539	1,520	238	1,663	256	1,633	306
Regional total	2,255		1,758		1,919		1,939	

† Includes male contractors and their employees working on holdings.
[1] As at 3 March 1965.
[2] Renamed Wyndham-East Kimberley as from 1 July 1961.

Source: Commonwealth Bureau of Census and Statistics, *Statistical Register of
Western Australia.* Perth.

TABLE 9

AVERAGE PRICES OF WOOL (GREASY)
1947-48 to 1964-65
(pence)

Year	Average F.O.B. value per lb.	Average local selling price per lb.
1947-48	41.60	39.24
1950-51	143.43	137.67
1951-52	75.17	66.15
1952-53	80.58	75.99
1953-54	85.02	77.68
1954-55	73.70	66.87
1955-56	61.32	56.73
1956-57	78.74	73.92
1957-58	71.20	60.39
1958-59	50.01	45.70
1959-60	62.79	56.60
1960-61	53.94	48.77
1961-62	59.76	52.40
1962-63	60.63	54.44
1963-64	73.19	66.86
1964-65	65.63	55.89

Source: Commonwealth Bureau of Census and Statistics, *Statistical Register of Western Australia*. Perth.

TABLE 10

GROSS VALUE OF PRODUCTION – WOOL[1]
1947, 1951 to 1965
(£m.)

Year	£m.
1947	1.8
1951	10.8
1952	4.5
1953	6.2
1954	6.3
1955	5.0
1956	4.6
1957	5.6
1958	4.5
1959	3.5
1960	3.9
1961	3.7
1962	4.0
1963	4.2
1964	5.6
1965	4.3

[1] These figures are approximate – they are calculated by multiplying the average local selling price per lb. by the regional total, e.g., 1946-47 average local selling price per lb. 23.97 pence × 1947 regional total 17,919,700 lbs. = 429,295,509 pence = £1,788,708 = £1.8 m.

Source: Table 3 and Table 9.

Table 11

CATTLE SLAUGHTERED IN THE KIMBERLEY DIVISION[1]
1955-56 to 1964-65

Year	Number	Gross Value (£)	Average value (£)
1955-56	46,601	1,133.349	24.3
1956-57	48,857	1,087,323	22.3
1957-58	50,914	1,060,044	20.8
1958-59	56,072	1,437,368	25.6
1959-60	64,877	1,936,241	29.8
1960-61	57,701	1,692,885	29.3
1961-62	62,833	1,614,561	25.7
1962-63	66,766	1,539,181	23.1
1963-64	65,472	1,452,654	22.2
1964-65	41,994	966,730	23.0

[1] Includes cattle shipped to Fremantle and Geraldton from Northern Ports.

Source: Commonwealth Bureau of Census and Statistics, *Statistical Register of Western Australia*. Perth.

Table 12

IMPORTS OF CATTLE INTO WESTERN AUSTRALIA
FROM NORTHERN TERRITORY

1955-56 to 1964-65

Year	Number	Value (£)	Average value (£)
1955-56	8,003	170,390	23.7
1956-57	6,125	116,375	19.0
1957-58	8,789	155,936	17.7
1958-59	14,725	334,326	22.7
1959-60	12,979	350,879	27.0
1960-61	9,920	272,136	27.4
1961-62	10,414	236,272	22.7
1962-63	10,085	226,900	22.5
1963-64	10,305	210,483	20.4
1964-65	5,527	111,550	20.2

Source: Commonwealth Bureau of Census and Statistics, *Statistical Register of Western Australia*. Perth.

TABLE 13

EXPORTS OF BEEF AND OFFAL TO OVERSEAS DESTINATIONS
1955-56 to 1964-65[1]

		Wyndham		Broome		Derby		Regional Total	
		('000 lb.)	(£'000)	('000 lb.)	(£'000)	('000 lb.)	(£'000)	('000 lb.)	(£'000)
1955-56	Beef	13,182	886	—	—	—	—	13,182	886
	Offal	998	86	—	—	—	—	998	86
1956-57	Beef	6,882	412	138	10	6	1	7,026	423
	Offal	313	25	10	1	—	—	323	26
1957-58	Beef	20,780	1,330	557	42	10	2	21,348	1,374
	Offal	1,331	95	15	2	—	—	1,347	97
1958-59	Beef	9,807	731	1,235	101	—	—	11,042	832
	Offal	609	50	64	7	—	—	673	57
1959-60	Beef	7,195	643	1,083	111	7	2	8,286	755
	Offal	496	46	50	5	—	—	545	51
1960-61	Beef	9,658	776	2,121	215	—	—	11,779	992
	Offal	719	70	105	10	—	—	824	80
1961-62	Beef	9,924	871	1,694	179	178	16	11,796	1,066
	Offal	726	57	62	6	21	2	809	65
1962-63	Beef	11,655	1,126	1,798	179	248	23	13,701	1,328
	Offal	776	51	97	9	32	2	905	62
1963-64	Beef	7,459	742	2,268	211	310	32	10,037	985
	Offal	451	31	113	10	65	6	629	47
1964-65	Beef	11,909	1,542	—	—	150	19	12,059	1,561
	Offal	1,053	100	—	—	10	1	1,063	101

[1] Relates to period of record which is not necessarily period of export.

Source: Commonwealth Bureau of Census and Statistics, *Statistical Register of Western Australia*. Perth.

TABLE 14

EXPORTS OF LIVE CATTLE – QUANTITY AND VALUE
1955-56 to 1964-65

	Derby		Overland		Total	
	No.	£'000	No.	£'000	No.	£'000
1955-56	710	44.4	2,485	17.3	3,195	61.7
1956-57	2,296	79.0	—	—	2,296	79.0
1957-58	2,125	55.9	—	—	2,506*	63.6*
1958-59	2,342	75.9	2,150†	51.4	4,492	127.3
1959-60	2,464	68.5	2,618†	60.8	5.082	129.3
1960-61	5,280	147.9	—	—	5,280	147.9
1961-62	—	—	—	—	—	—
1962-63	—	—	—	—	—	—
1963-64	2,042	54.3	4,037	36.8	6,079	91.1
1964-65	4,884	66.5	2,657	25.7	7,541	92.2

† By sea from Derby.
* In 1957-58, 381 live cattle were exported from Broome, to the value of £7,600.

Source: Commonwealth Bureau of Census and Statistics, *Statistical Register of Western Australia*. Perth.

TABLE 15

VALUE OF PASTORAL OUTPUT

1955-56 to 1964-65

(£m.)

	Livestock Exported[1]	Gross Value of Wool	Gross Value of Slaughterings	Total
1955-56	.06	4.6	1.1	5.8
1956-57	.08	5.6	1.1	6.8
1957-58	.06	4.5	1.1	5.7
1958-59	.14	3.5	1.4	5.0
1959-60	.13	3.9	1.9	5.9
1960-61	.15	3.7	1.7	5.6
1961-62	—	4.0	1.6	5.6
1962-63	—	4.2	1.5	5.7
1963-64	.10	5.6	1.5	7.2
1964-65	.10	4.3	1.0	5.4

[1] Both cattle and sheep.

Source: Tables 10 to 14.

CHAPTER 4

MINING

1. INTRODUCTION

Northwestern Australia possesses varied and extensive mineral deposits but, generally speaking, these were not really tapped in any thorough-going way until the decade of the 1950's. In Appendix 2 a description is given of the extent and location of the region's mineral wealth and in this chapter the emphasis is upon what man has done and is currently doing to exploit these resources.

Mineral exploitation played an early part in the region's development but in the 1950's production of minerals in both quantity and value terms, took a big step forward. This expansion has been based mainly upon the extraction of iron ore and asbestos, though minerals such as manganese, tin and cupreous ore and concentrates have also played their part.

Broadly speaking, the surge in mining development in the region has taken place because of a change in methods of mining, and because prospecting by individuals and small groups has been to a considerable extent replaced by exploitation by highly capitalized companies operating with modern techniques. Also of importance has been the growing industrialization of Australia and the growing domestic demand for minerals, improvements in transport and in methods of working deposits with highly mechanized processes, growing overseas demand for certain minerals, and changes in government policy regarding exports of certain minerals.

2. HISTORICAL DEVELOPMENT

Mining activity in the region assumed an increasing importance in the 1950's, and in the decade of the 1960's it will dominate northern development. The region's contribution to the state's mineral production rose from £400,000 in 1950 (3.5 per cent of the state total) to approximately £3.5 million in 1960 (15.6 per cent of the total). The story of the years preceding this phenomenal rate of increase is somewhat sketchy. This is probably due partly to the nature of the pre-war industry which was characterized by individual prospectors rather than large companies.

probably due partly to the nature of the pre-war industry which was in 1848 with the location of lead and copper deposits near Northampton, on the southern fringe of the region. Twenty-four years later rich copper ore deposits were found at Whim Creek in the Pilbara, and the output from these mines was shipped to England.

In 1883 the Surveyor-General, John Forrest and the Government Geologist, E. T. Hardman, visited the Kimberley and reported that the district might contain gold. As a result of this report some prospecting was carried out in the area lying between the headwaters of the Margaret and the Ord Rivers. Charles Hall and Jack Slattery discovered gold in August 1885, and precipitated in the then infant colony the first of the gold rushes which were to have such a profound influence on the state's later development.

The state's first goldfield, the Kimberley, was proclaimed in 1886. It was located in remote and inhospitable country 300 miles from Derby and 250 miles from Wyndham, and there the small shanty townships of Hall's Creek, Ruby Creek and Brockman sprang up. Food and water were scarce. Horses died from a local disease and many of the 2,000 men on the goldfield by 1886 died of scurvy and dysentry. The surface workings did not reach expectations and it became obvious that companies with capital equipment would be needed to mine the reef gold. The miner's licence fee of £1 for a Miner's Right and the export duty on gold were unpopular and avoided when possible. By 1890 only one mining company on the goldfield was paying expenses. Mining population had dwindled to 300 as men moved to the southern fields, and the collapse of the goldfield accentuated an already serious unemployment problem being experienced in Perth.

The Kimberley goldfield has been described as the most inaccessible and least valuable field in the state.[1] It was, however, valuable to the extent that it provided a beef market for the struggling East Kimberley pioneer pastoralists at a vital time,[2] and it provided a prospector class which subsequently moved through other parts of the state and was responsible for the larger and more important discoveries of the 1890's.

In 1888 the Pilbara goldfield was proclaimed following the gold discoveries by H. Wells, N. W. Cooke, W. G. Lorden and the Withnell brothers east of Roebourne. A rush began and Marble Bar became the centre of a newly found rich alluvial field. The following year the Ashburton goldfield was proclaimed and the discovery of the various goldfields was

[1]F. K. Crowley, *Australia's Western Third*, was used extensively for this section.
[2]See Chapter 3.

followed by a spate of company formation in Perth, Melbourne and London, followed by the eventual failure of a large proportion of these syndicates.

Gold brought an influx of temporary population into the region. It provided the area with an itinerant prospecting group who, when the supply of alluvial gold was exhausted, focussed their attention on other minerals, and the mining population provided a ready market for the beef and mutton of the region's pastoralists. In the 1890's gold constituted an important source of income for the north, particularly in the Pilbara and Ashburton fields. During this early period 20,000 fine ounces were won from the region's fields.

Gold in particular and mining in general, alongside pastoralism, were largely responsible for the improvement in communications. By 1894 Marble Bar was connected to Perth by telegraph. In 1912 the Port Hedland-Marble Bar railway was opened, and earlier, in 1889, a submarine cable had been laid between Java and Broome. Since 1900 gold has assumed a role of decreasing relative importance in Northwestern Australia, but it was the gold discoveries of the 1880's which gave a fillip to the initial impetus given by the pastoralists in the development of the resources of the area north of the twenty-sixth parallel.

Following the gold discoveries, mining lapsed into the doldrums for the next forty years. The industry was largely based on the labour of individual prospectors and the annual value of regional mineral production had only reached £400,000 by 1950. The output of the small units which character-ized the industry from 1900 to 1940 was largely determined by world prices. Large companies were not willing to incur the substantial capital expenditures which were necessary to develop access to the region's minerals and to work them. Useful exploratory work was carried out by individual prospectors, and some of the companies engaged in limited exploration and operation.

In 1905 operations commenced on tantalite alluvial deposits in the Pilbara when Tantalite Ltd., an Adelaide company, commenced mining operations at Wodgina 60 miles south of Port Hedland. During the 1920's, Freney drilled unsuccessfully for oil in the Kimberley. A report by E. S. Simpson in 1929 stimulated interest in asbestos in the Pilbara, and specimens from Mt. Margaret and Weeli Wolli Spring brought favourable comment on commercial possibilities.

During the 1930's the Pilbara witnessed increased activity in asbestos mining. The main problems involved were the 200 mile road haul by truck to Roebourne and the fluctuating export prices. Production depended upon individual prospectors and upon the Asbestos, Molybdenum and Tungsten Co. which commenced operations at Lionel but moved to Yampire Gorge in the Hamersley Ranges in 1939. Operations in this region com-menced in 1937-38 although occurrences of asbestos had been reported as far back as 1917. The first mine was located at Yampire Gorge and the mute skeletal remains of mining machinery and other evidences of the earlier activity are still to be seen on the way to beautiful Dale's Gorge where asbestos has also been reported. Another company, Australian Blue Asbestos Pty. Ltd., a subsidiary of Colonial Sugar, commenced operations at Wittenoom Gorge in 1943. By 1950 Australian Blue Asbestos had established the township at Wittenoom and had become the area's sole producer of crocidolite (blue asbestos). Large-scale capital was at last entering the region's mining industry.

During the early years of the World War mining for gold, silver and other minerals was virtually at a standstill although gold prices stood at an all time high of £10.14.0 an ounce in 1940 and rose to £10.15.3 in 1945. In 1937 some interest was shown in the iron ore on Koolan Island, but with the placing of an export embargo on iron ore to Japan in 1938, development plans were permitted to lapse for several years. As the war progressed, a steady world demand for tin, silver, wolfram, manganese, tantalum, molybdenum and tungsten stimulated mining in the Pilbara. The oil search was temporarily revived in 1940 at Exmouth Gulf until Learmonth became a base for the armed services.

Beryl production in the pre-war years was negligible but, as a result of war-stimulated demand, hundreds of tons were mined in 1943 and 1944 at Wodgina and Yinnietharra. From 1947 to 1958 export was restricted and beryl was shipped to the United Kingdom under license, and in 1958 and 1959 the Australian Atomic Energy Commission became the sole buyer of the mineral. In January 1960 the export ban was lifted to approved destinations.

In the meantime Australian Iron and Steel Pty. Ltd., (a subsidiary of B.H.P.) commenced a plan to equip Cockatoo Island for iron ore production. A township was established and in 1951 the first shipment of iron ore was sent from Yampi to Port Kembla for processing. Prospecting for tantalite, manganese, tin, wolfram and scheelite continued.

The inception of ore shipments from Cockatoo Island was the successful conclusion to a long period of search followed by development expenditures on a large scale.[3] As early as 1927 interest was displayed in this island as a possible source of iron ore when Hoskins Iron and Steel Co. Ltd., acquired mineral leases on the island. When Hoskins and others merged to form Australian Iron and Steel Ltd., in the following year, the leases passed to the new company. In 1930 the island was surveyed, and stores and living quarters were erected. The depression of the early thirties put an end to this activity. It was not until 1935 that interest was once more revived, and by the outbreak of the World War developmental work was under way.

A vigorous renewal of the oil search began in 1951. American capital, equipment and technical skill were brought into the area by the Ampol-Caltex teams who carried out surveys in Exmouth Gulf. On 4 December

[3]Broken Hill Proprietary Co. Ltd., *Quarterly Review*.

1953 oil was found, but not in payable quantities. The occurrence of oil fired the public's imagination and 5/- shares rocketed to £5 within a few days. The turnover of shares during these few weeks was enormous, but gradually prices and turnover slipped back to 'normal' as the optimism of late 1953 died, and no further strikes were made. In 1956 West Australian Petroleum Pty. Ltd. (Wapet) commenced drilling operation in the West Kimberley for the Commonwealth Bureau of Mineral Resources. Shell joined the Ampol-Caltex oil search merger in 1958 and their combined capital continued to finance Wapet's exploratory activities.

In 1954 larger-scale mining of manganese began in the Pilbara. The mineral, previously exploited by individual prospectors, now became the object of company exploration despite an embargo which hampered export markets. Westralian Ores Pty. Ltd., Northern Mineral Syndicate and D. F. D. Rhodes Pty. Ltd., all entered the manganese production market, hauling the ore 240 miles into Port Hedland.

From this brief historical sketch of the region's mining industry three stages in its development can be distinguished. First, the period 1885-1900 when the area was the centre of the state's first gold rushes. Substantial quantities of the valuable mineral were won, and although the finds were insignificant compared to those of the Eastern Goldfields, they nevertheless had an appreciable influence on the development of Northwestern Australia. Population flowed into the region and provided meat markets for struggling pastoralists. Increased population brought with it a demand for improved transport and communications which, after the gold rushes, were of benefit to the pastoralists. Exploitation of the mineral lay in the hands of individual prospectors and companies and several companies remained in the Pilbara after the surface gold was won. The prospectors provided a type of person so necessary in the mining industry to ensure further discoveries.

In the second stage, from 1900 to 1940, mining played a minor role in the region's economy. The industry, such as it was, was based on the efforts of individual prospectors. The principal contribution of this era lay in the discovery of minerals which were later to become the object of company attentions. Output was largely influenced by export prices and transport costs. The World War drew attention to the strategic importance of some of the region's mineral wealth.

The third stage was the post-war period when the era of the large company dawned. Australian Blue Asbestos became the sole producer of crocidolite at Wittenoom Gorge in the Hamersleys. A new township was sited and built around the industry. On Cockatoo Island, Australia Iron and Steel commenced large-scale mining of iron ore. Once again a company township sprang up. With the introduction of large earth-moving equipment the alluvial tin fields were opened up by large companies. Manganese likewise became the object of company activity and mining camps mushroomed throughout the area. The capital resources behind those interested in oil was enormous. The era of company exploitation and large-scale production had arrived. The exploitation of Pilbara iron ore resources, described in detail elsewhere in this chapter, was an extension of this new type of development though on such a scale as to overshadow completely the other developments mentioned.

3. PRESENT CHARACTERISTICS

Workforce

Mining and quarrying in the North-West at the 1961 census date occupied 1,078 persons and this constituted about one-eighth of the total workforce of the region. The regional figures for the mining and quarrying workforce hardly changed between the census dates of 1947 and 1954, but changed considerably between 1954 and 1961. Some important shifts in the workforce occurred within the region itself between these two dates.

The North-West Division recorded a large relative decrease (81 per cent) after the early oil exploration activity died down and the two Central Division shires likewise registered a substantial fall (47 per cent) between the two census dates. Within this division a marked shift occurred in favour of the Wiluna area.

The mining workforce of the Kimberley Division declined between the census dates 1947 and 1954, mainly because construction activity was brisk on Cockatoo Island in the earlier year, and by 1954 the workforce had settled down to a normal figure. By 1961, however, activity had stepped up again with the development work on Koolan Island, and the division recorded a substantial increase (over 200 per cent) between 1954 and 1961.

The Pilbara Division experienced a surge of mining activity between 1947 and 1954, due mainly to growth in the production of asbestos and manganese. The growth in the mining workforce in this period was close to 100 per cent but in the following inter-censal period, 1954-1961, the increase was much more modest at about 20 per cent. Since then, however, with the spectacular mining developments described below there has been a concomitant increase in the mining workforce. Unfortunately detailed results of the 1966 census will not be available for some time and so no accurate figures of the workforce increase can be given. Some indication of the probable rate of increase may be gained, however, from the fact that the population of the Pilbara Division grew by almost 50 per cent in the one year from June 1964 to June 1965.

Value of Production by Gazetted Goldfields

When one examines figures of the value of mineral production for the region over the past decade a picture of steady progress emerges. Value of production is four times as great as it was ten years ago. The reason, of course, is not that mining in all its aspects has expanded, but that several new industries have emerged in the last decade to boost the figures. Iron, manganese, asbestos and tin have been the main contributors to this movement. They will be dealt with in more detail below.

Within the gazetted goldfields in the region some disparate movements have taken place between 1955 and 1965. West Kimberley, for instance, has increased its production considerably from £.5 million in 1955, and is currently producing minerals worth $4.6 million annually. This has occasioned by the exploitation by Australian Iron and Steel of the iron deposits in Yampi Sound. The Pilbara is also expanding rapidly, from £.3 million in 1955 to £1.5 million in 1965. It is now safe to assume that the Pilbara, in 1966, will take over as the leading producer in the region. Iron ore, manganese, asbestos and tin are responsible for this.

As might be expected from the spectacular increases recorded in the region, its relative rating with the rest of the state's mining activities has improved markedly. In 1950 it contributed 3.5 per cent of the state's total value of mineral production, in 1955 the figure had risen to 8.1 per cent, in 1960 it was 15.6 per cent, and by 1965 it had risen to 18.9 per cent. By 1970 it will dwarf all other mineral production.

Value of Principal Minerals

Of the principal minerals in the region, the most important is iron ore. In quantity terms it has increased from .5 million tons in 1955 to 2.3 million tons in 1965. In value terms the figures are the same, since the price at which B.H.P. sells the ore to itself is a notional £1 per ton. If this production were valued at the world price the value of ore won from Yampi Sound would be much greater. As the recently developed mines in the Pilbara come into production (exports have already flowed from Mt. Goldsworthy) the value of iron ore produced in the region will increase immensely, and with every passing year this mineral will draw away from the others as the principal mineral produced.

Second in importance in 1965 was manganese which recorded a value approaching that of the early 1960's after two or three lean years. Currently, this mineral is once more being exploited vigorously and with the developments that are occurring at Port Hedland, if new loading facilities can be made available to the manganese operating companies, the possibilities for further production and value increases are fairly bright providing the world market holds firm.

The third important mineral is asbestos, produced at Wittenoom Gorge. Only three years ago this was the major mineral produced in the region but it has now slipped back to third place. Tin is the fourth principal mineral and is gaining in importance yearly. From 1955 to 1965 it increased more than 20 times in value and in the last five years the increase has been almost 50 per cent. Its current value is almost three-quarters of a million pounds.

These four minerals between them account for 97 per cent of the value of mineral production in the region.

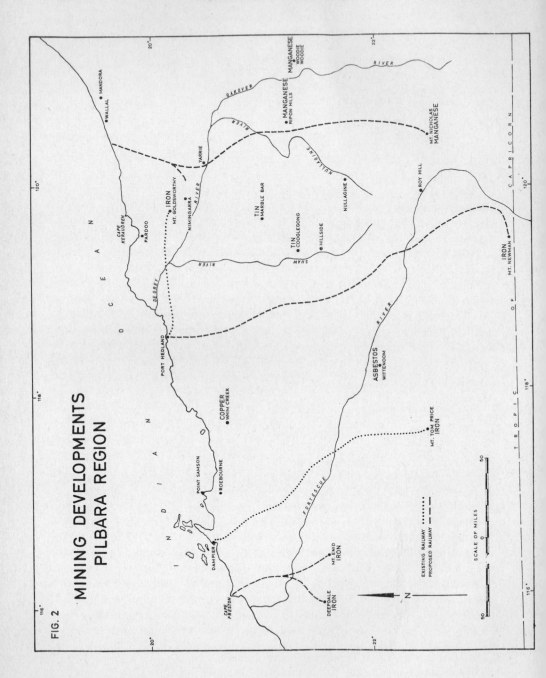

FIG. 2

MINING DEVELOPMENTS
PILBARA REGION

4. ASBESTOS MINING

The early history of the asbestos industry has already been mentioned above. The industry, centred at Wittenoom, really got under way in the post-war era. In 1943 Colonial Sugar acquired large holdings in Wittenoom and Dale's gorges and commenced mining operations, and in 1945 a treatment plant was established.[4]

Technology

The Hamersley Ranges, where the crocidolite is mined, lie south of Port Hedland and Roebourne. The western end of the ranges is roughly 75 miles south of Roebourne, and the eastern end is about 175 miles south of Port Hedland. Although the mineral is distributed throughout the Hamersleys, the heaviest deposits are in the gorges mentioned, and the company's centre of operations is at Wittenoom Gorge. Reserves in this deposit are estimated to amount to three million tons of recoverable fibre.

Generally, two series of fibre exist spaced some 20 feet apart and parallel to each other, and they are mined as the upper and lower seams. At present 60 per cent of the mine's production comes from the upper seam, which is being worked in advance of the lower seam for safety reasons. The Colonial mine and treatment plant, latest producer for the company, lies deep in the gorge in a setting of great beauty. It runs down in a series of steps from the mine entrance about half way up the side of the gorge to the loading point for the finished product in the bottom of the gorge. The unusual colours of the rock formations in the Hamersleys have already made these gorges a successful tourist attraction.

Mining operations are carried out under very difficult conditions due to the vertical dimensions of the stopes. The seams, which are up to three inches in thickness, are worked in stopes approximately 300 feet square and 43 inches high, with 10 per cent being allowed to remain as rock pillaring for support. This means that the miner cannot at any stage stand to full height; he has to operate much of his time in a crouching or sitting position. At this point in the operations, and also in the loading sheds, particles of asbestos dust are a danger to the worker's respiratory system. The company is currently experimenting with long-wall stoping methods using a stope height of seven feet in which the top 60 inches is blasted back in the form of waste fill, the remaining 24 inches being fired independently and transported to the mill as mill feed. If this method proves successful it will obviously improve working conditions for the miners. Into the bargain, the company will recover a higher grade of ore.

After the ore is won from the stopes it is tipped on to a conveyor belt running the length of the main shaft (or adit) and taken up to the

[4]Australian Blue Asbestos Ltd., 'Report of Operations at Wittenoom Gorge'.

surface. The 2,250 feet conveyor belt, made up of two flights, is capable of handling 200 tons an hour to a storage ore pocket, and from there it is taken to the treatment plant when wanted. Here it begins its trip down the gorge, each step being marked by another building and another phase of treatment. The use of gravity in this way when nature assists with the contouring of the land eliminates the excessive use of inclined conveyors and reduces handling costs.

When the ore has been crushed, screened and cleaned the fibre is put into jute bags and machine-sewn, and the final process is to load the great semi-trailer trucks and prepare them for the 230 mile journey overland to Point Samson. The trucks can carry loads of up to 33 tons of bagged asbestos and are equipped with 175 h.p. prime movers, but generally speaking the carriers prefer to take about 27 tons per trip.

Labour

A complete township has been built at the entrance to Wittenoom Gorge to accommodate the company's 400 workers and their families. Executives live in the delightful setting of the gorge itself where the rocks reflect the most brilliant and unusual colours. Here they are close to the centre of operations. The facilities in the township, which houses 1,000, include a cinema, library, hotel, churches, cafe, and general store, and apart from housing, school, postal and police services, and hospital accommodation which are state government responsibilities, it is virtually a company town.

Living and working conditions are not easy, particularly in the heat of summer and in view of this and the isolation of the area, it is not surprising that labour turnover is high. Mainly there is a shortage of skilled labour but the problem also extends to the ranks of the unskilled and also into the administrative ranks. The management feels that the iron ore developments, by drawing away men through higher wages, have recently heightened what has always been a problem. Labour turnover is currently about 150 per cent per year, including staff, and in an effort to obtain more stability in the labour force the company has sponsored migrants from Great Britain and the Lebanon.

Some 200 men are employed underground and they can earn very high wages, with overtime – sometimes as much as $150-$200 per week. Minimum rates are $80 per week for a 45-hour week. The total annual wages and salaries bill for the establishment currently amounts to over $1.5 million. Accidents have, in the past, taken their toll in terms of injuries to workers and lost production time but these have now been cut to a minimum and the accident rate is very low.

Markets

The principal use for the fibre in Australia and overseas is as a reinforcing material in the manufacturing of asbestos cement sheet for covering the exteriors of houses, and as a reinforcing agent in asbestos cement pressure pipe for water supply purposes. It is also used in the spinning and weaving of certain cloths and in the manufacture of plastics. There is a widely distributed demand for the Wittenoom product and, apart from the substantial domestic demand, the main export markets are in Asia, in particular India, Singapore, Malaya, Japan and the Philippines. The United States, which previously was a large buyer now takes less than 1,000 tons annually. In 1964, exports to Asia accounted for 33 per cent of total production and the domestic Australian market absorbed 57 per cent. The company's main competitor is South Africa which produces asbestos of approximately the same quality, though the Australian fibre is somewhat longer.

Asbestos prices have remained fairly stable and demand on world markets is likely to remain firm in the future. The export market is seen by the company as the outlet for production over and above what is required by Australian manufacturers, and the main aim is to increase production towards capacity output so that the benefits of economies of scale can be derived.

Future Prospects

Once production got under way in the post-war period substantial increases were recorded. In the decade 1955-1965 asbestos production more than doubled in quantity terms but, because of fluctuations in the average price per ton, caused by demand variations and variations in the quality of fibre produced (the longer fibre being higher priced), the increase in value of production in the same period was roughly 80 per cent. In 1963 and 1964, demand was weak and production was controlled because of this but in 1965 when demand firmed, the company was prevented by labour shortages from taking full advantage of the situation.

The development of the company has not been without its problems. A drop in overseas demand in the 1950's, for example, became a cause of considerable concern until a subsequent large United States order made possible a profitable level of operations. Labour troubles, too, have dogged the firm and have been responsible for production below capacity, which is about 20,000 tons. In 1960 a cyclone struck the area causing severe flooding which interfered with production for several weeks and resulted in a final production figure well below that which was expected. Another cyclone recently damaged the port facilities.

Because of these problems it may be said that asbestos mining, at the present moment one of the most important mineral extraction processes in the region, is not likely to remain a major income earner and employer of labour in the north for long, unless demand remains strong enough to enable the continued operation of the industry at economical cost levels.

5. Iron Ore Extraction

Location of the Ore

On 21 July 1951 the *S.S. Iron Yampi,* belonging to the Broken Hill Proprietary Co. Ltd., began to load the first cargo of ironstone from the jetty at Cockatoo Island. This opened up a new ore supply for Australia's largest steel producing enterprise to feed its New South Wales furnaces.

Cockatoo Island lies some 85 miles north of Derby in the maze of islands and rocky outcrops at the entrance to Yampi Sound, and active interest in its possibilities as a source of iron ore dates back to 1927 when Hoskins Iron and Steel Co. Ltd., acquired its mineral leases on the island. They passed to Australian Iron and Steel Ltd. in 1928. Recently the iron ore quarrying operations of B.H.P. in W.A. passed to a subsidiary, the Dampier Mining Co. Pty. Ltd., which is responsible for operating not only the Yampi deposits but all others held in Western Australia.

Cockatoo Island itself is just under four miles long and has an area of two square miles. It is estimated that the ore reserves are about 20 million tons. The township lies at the north-western tip of the island, and mining operations are conducted on the southwestern coast which is fringed by steep cliffs. It was the second principal source area of Australian ore, the other being Iron Knob and the adjacent Middleback Ranges in South Australia. Rising steeply from the sea, it contains high grade ore, much of it in a soft, powdery form.

There are at present 51 homes in the township. They are provided with sewerage, electricity and basic items of furniture. The population of the island is about 350, including 75 children, about 10 of whom are away from the island for secondary education. A two-teacher school, staffed by the Education Department gives primary teaching to about 40 children. Recreation facilities include a swimming pool, tennis and basketball courts, open-air cinema, a rugged cricket ground and a recreation club equipped with billiard table, table-tennis table and library. The township is a well integrated and contented community. In the cyclone season the conditions for a pleasant life are less obvious, since high winds and heavy seas batter the island.

The open-cut quarrying is done by mechanical means, and electric shovels load up to eight tons of ore at a bite into 28-30 ton capacity diesel trucks. These trucks take it to a crushing plant where primary and secondary crushers, capable of treating a four feet cube weighing 8-10 tons, reduce the ore to an average size of four inches, suitable for blast furnaces. A belt conveyor 42 inches wide then delivers the ore to a storage bin capable of holding 20,000 tons. From here another belt conveyor, with a shuttle and hinged boom at the off-shore end, loads direct into the ship's hatches.

Cockatoo Island in 1960 produced more than three quarters of a million tons of high grade ore valued at more than three quarters of a million pounds. By the end of 1961 production had reached a rate of 1.5 million tons of ore per annum and, since the adjacent Koolan Island has come into production, it has now steadied down to about one million. Since the extraction of the raw material is carried out by the same company that uses it, the average price per ton is a notional one. At 19/6, a figure which has remained constant since the inception of production, the ore is valued at a price far lower than would result from open sale.

Construction on Koolan Island, lying close to Cockatoo, was commenced in 1960 and completed at the end of 1964 at a cost of £7.5 million. The plant itself, similar to that at Cockatoo Island but larger in scale, is capable of producing 2 million tons per year and production commenced early in 1965. A labour force of about 200 is employed.

When the commonwealth lifted its export embargo in 1960, the islands of Yampi Sound remained a restricted area but in 1965 opposition to B.H.P. exporting from Cockatoo and Koolan finally dissipated, and negotiations are currently being carried on for the export of more than a million tons of ore a year to Japan from Yampi.

With the lifting of the state embargo on exports of Yampi ore and the almost certain granting of commonwealth export licenses and the early possibility of substantial Japanese ore contracts, Yampi Sound will undoubtedly play an increasingly important part in the mining activities of the region. B.H.P. is in the fortunate position of having completed the capital expenditure necessary to exploit these deposits, and with proven reserves of 70 million tons of high-grade hematite and substantial reserves of lower-grade ores, there would appear to be no major problems limiting further expansion in the area. Under previous agreements B.H.P. has been paying 1/6d. per ton in royalties to the state government and will continue to do so on all locally used ore, including iron ore concentrates produced from locally used ore by secondary processing (pelletisation). However, under the new arrangements recently negotiated, royalties on future exports of ore will range from: (a) on direct shipping ore, 7.5 per cent of f.o.b. revenue with minimum of 6/- (60 cents) per ton, to (b) on fine ore, 3.75 per cent of f.o.b. revenue with minimum of 3/ (30 cents) per ton, to (c) on fines, 1/6d (15 cents) per ton.

Prior to the 1960's the best known deposits of iron ore in Northwestern Australia were those at Cockatoo Island. The existence of other deposits had been known about in general but not much was known of the quality of the ore. On the broader Australian scene, Broken Hill Propriety, Australia's largest industrial enterprise, had been exporting annually some 200,000 tons of ore in the decade prior to 1938. This ore went mainly to the U.S.A., the Netherlands and Japan. Just prior to the World War an embargo was placed on the export of ore and this remained in force in the 1940's and 1950's. Discoveries in the mid-1950's in Northern Australia (Northern Territory and Queensland) altered the estimate of Australia's known resources sufficiently to permit pressure to mount for the removal of the embargo and, finally, in December 1960 it was lifted except for a few prohibited areas, among which were Cockatoo, Koolan and Irvine islands in Yampi Sound. This prohibition on these areas has now been removed.

Almost immediately after the lifting of the embargo, staggeringly large deposits were announced in the Pilbara. By 1962 the overall estimate had mounted to 8,000 million tons of high-grade ore and the estimate now stands at 15,000 million tons. The major part of these finds (two-thirds) is hematite, graded between 55 per cent and 68 per cent, while the remainder is limonite, at between 50 per cent and 60 per cent. Details are to be found in Appendix 2. These reserves are exceeded only by those of the U.S.S.R., Bolivia, India (including Goa) and Brazil, and are roughly equal to Canada's.

It goes without saying that the announcement of these discoveries transformed the potential of the region's mining industry. Almost as startling as the magnitude of the discoveries themselves has been the rate at which they are being exploited. Several large international companies moved into the scene in combines to develop the resources in different parts of the Pilbara area. They are listed and their operations discussed briefly below (the main statistical details are given in Table 4):

Mt. Goldsworthy Mining Associates

This is the first company to export its ore from the Pilbara. The first shipment left Port Hedland in May 1966. The company is owned by Consolidated Goldfields (Aust.) Pty. Ltd. (33⅓ per cent), Cyprus Mines Corporation of California (33⅓ per cent) and the Utah Construction and Mining Co. of California (33⅓ per cent). They hold reserves in the Pilbara region and the Hamersley iron province and are developing Mt. Goldsworthy first. A new mining town has sprung up at Mt. Goldsworthy and a recently completed 70 mile standard gauge (4 ft. 8½ in.) railway links this with a new port on Finucane Island, opposite Port Hedland. This has an initial capacity for 40,000 d.w.t. ore carriers and will subsequently be able to handle vessels of up to 70,000 d.w.t.

The agreement the Company has with the state government involves a three-stage programme and the first is completed. The second stage calls for secondary processing, and the third stage involves additional upgrading of beneficiated ore at an estimated cost of $40 million.

Hamersley Iron Pty. Ltd.

The operating company is owned by Conzinc Riotinto of Australia (60 per cent) and Kaiser Steel Corporation of California (40 per cent), representing a combination of a mining group and a steel company. They hold large reserves and at the moment are developing Mt. Tom Price, in the Hamersley Ranges. A new mining town has sprung up at Mt. Tom Price and a recently completed 179 mile standard gauge railway links the town with a new port which has been built at Dampier. The port in its initial stages can handle vessels of 65,000 d.w.t. and after subsequent dredging will be able to take ships of up to 100,000 d.w.t.

The agreement which the company has with the state government calls for a three-stage programme, the first of which is now completed. The second stage will involve the construction of a plant for pelletising the ore, and the third stage involves the expenditure of some $80 million on an integrated iron and steel industry.

Mt. Newman Iron Ore Company Ltd.

This company is owned by American Metal Climax (50 per cent) and The Colonial Sugar Refining Company Limited (50 per cent). They have several reserves, including Mt. Whaleback, near the Mt. Newman homestead. A mining town will be established at Mt. Newman and will be linked by a 260 mile standard gauge railway to a port at Port Hedland.

The agreement which the company has with the state government calls for a three-stage programme. The initial development will be the export of ore, and the second stage involves processing into pellets. The third stage, costing an estimated $80 million, calls for an integrated iron and steel industry. These developments are proceeding at a slower rate than the two already mentioned and the first shipments are due to commence in 1969.

Cliffs Western Australian Mining Company Pty. Ltd.

This company is owned by Cleveland-Cliffs Iron Company of Ohio (51 per cent), Mitsui and Company Ltd. of Tokyo (35 per cent), Garrick Agnew Pty. Ltd. of Western Australia (7½ per cent) and other interests (6½ per cent). It has large limonitic deposits in the Robe River area and plans to construct a large pelletising plant. A mining town is to be constructed at Mt. Enid and linked by a 70 mile standard gauge railway to a new deep-water port at Cape Preston capable of handling large ore carriers.

The agreement which the company has with the state government calls for a minimum outlay of $70 million on the first stage of the capital works. It is interesting to note, in view of the large amounts of fuel usually required by the pelletising, the recent announcement of Western Australia's first commercial oil and gas field at nearby Barrow Island.

The Broken Hill Pty. Co. Ltd.

Australia's first iron ore and steel producer, this company has also reserves in the area as well as its holdings in Yampi Sound and elsewhere in the state. It has formed the Dampier Mining Co. Ltd. in which it will hold equal shares with its largest subsidiary, Australian Iron and Steel Pty. Ltd., which is already working Yampi. This company has reserves of limenitic ore at Deepdale near the Robe River similar to those of the nearby Cliffs area.

Since the negotiations of the original contracts and agreements with the state government which are described above, certain difficulties have been experienced by some of the companies concerned in carrying their plans forward. In particular some of the cost estimates are now thought to be too low and there is talk of some companies withdrawing. The exploitation of the Mt. Enid and Deepdale deposits may be postponed and a consortium of all the companies concerned may concentrate their combined resources on the development of the Mt. Newman deposits in the first instance. What is certain at the moment is that Mt. Goldsworthy and Hamersley are operating and the pattern which the exploitation of the remaining resources will eventually take may become clearer by the end of 1966. The original plans of Mt. Newman, B.H.P. and Cliffs are presented here to illustrate the extent and type of development ultimately envisaged at the time the agreements were first drawn up.

The state government is currently negotiating with the D. K. Ludwig organization for the establishment of an up graded iron and ferro-manganese export industry in the Pilbara.[5] The plan provides for the development of iron ore deposits at Nimingarra 100 miles east of Port Hedland, with an export outlet on the Eighty Mile Beach east of Cape Keraudren, to be linked by a 45 mile railroad with Nimingarra. Estimated reserves of high-grade ore at Nimingarra are 30 million tons. The proposed upgrading process would reduce the oxygen content of the ore and improve pig-iron production. The Sentinel Mining Company would spend a minimum of $30 million on the development of the deposits.

Longer-term plans envisage the development of the extensive holdings of low-grade manganese to be found throughout the Pilbara from Mt. Nicholas near Mt. Newman in the south, to Nimingarra in the north. A further 135 miles of railroad would be needed to link Mt. Nicholas with the Nimingarra line. The upgrading plants for both the iron and manganese would be established at the port site.

The company is expected to seek markets for its ore in Europe and North America as well as in Japan, but Commonwealth approval will be needed for export and for the prices and terms of the contracts negotiated.

The Impact of Iron Ore Development

In all, some $686 million has been contracted for in the way of initial development expenditure, and contracts worth a total of $2,600 million have already been negotiated by the companies mentioned above. This will involve the extraction of some 270 million tons of ore and will bring in royalties of approximately $120 million. The construction phase of all the large projects will employ an estimated 7,200 persons, and when the plants settle down to regular production a workforce of 3,000 will be required. At least four new towns and three new ports will have been

[5] *West Australian,* 7 July 1966.

constructed, and also a network of standard-gauge railway covering some 600 miles, four pelletising plants by the mid 1970's and two new steel industries by the 1990's providing the agreements are carried through.

The impact of all this development on the previously underdeveloped northern region of Western Australia will be remarkable to say the least, and it raises many issues of major importance. Some are more obvious than others, some can be examined more easily by statistical evidence than others, all have been raised in public debate throughout Australia, and indeed overseas, and some of them have become contentious.

Several characteristics of the present situation are immediately apparent, and beyond argument. Australia has suddenly become a major supplier of bulk iron ore in the world. Australia's major market for the ore to be exported under existing contracts is Japan. Australia in this regard is competing against the other major world suppliers, in particular, India, Malaya, Chile, Brazil and Peru. Australia is exploiting her resources at a rate which involves capital expenditures on a scale far beyond anything she, herself, can provide. Even so, she has so far committed for export less than two per cent of her estimated reserves. A great deal of the capital involved – probably about two-thirds – is foreign. Many of the price agreements arrived at with the Japanese buyers have been below those previously concluded with other countries. Most of the contracts are for longer terms than ever previously written into ore contracts. Australia will gain in export income and company income tax. Western Australia will gain in rents and royalties and the development of community centres.

The repercussions of this development for the regional, the state and the national economies are many and varied and will be felt to different degrees in the different economies.

To take the regional economy first. The immediate result of this development is the creation of townships, railways and ports. But none of these can function without people. Population in the Pilbara has almost doubled since 1960, with the prospect of many more to come. In the year June 1964 to June 1965, the population increased by 49 per cent. Some of these are, of course, construction workers and can be expected to leave the area once the major developmental works are completed. Many more, however, will stay. In the meantime resources of every sort in the region are strained to breaking point. Port Hedland, still the focal point of activity in the area, and the main port, is bulging at the seams as anyone wanting accommodation at short notice will soon discover.

The atmosphere is charged with bustle and rush. Hotel rooms are cluttered with extra furniture and one has to pick one's way among beds lining all available verandah space. Hotels have spent some $300,000 recently on extensions but are still inadequate to cope with the demand. Material of all sorts – sleepers, drilling equipment, pipes and rails, sheets of asbestos and iron – is piled in the cluttered and untidy lots fronting the main streets of the township. The bars are crowded with workers and visitors of all nationalities, and even the price of beer, at 50 cents a bottle, does not arrest their constant thirst. Engineers, geologists, surveyors, graziers, tradesmen of all sorts, and unskilled labourers rub shoulders with the inquisitive tourist, and at night their chatter is drowned by the constant roar of diesel and petrol engines as heavily laden trucks roar out of the township into the inland darkness. Jeeps, land rovers, Toyotas, some of them equipped to the hilt with every conceivable type of accoutrement, jostle for parking space in the busy streets and taxis ply their endless trade with an air of urgency.

Out in the hinterland the countryside plays host to drilling rigs, land cruisers of all colours, great trucks and all kinds of earth moving equipment, and the skies are busy to the drone of aircraft of all sizes and shapes. M.M.A., with its Fokker Friendships and DC-3's is struggling to cope with the overwhelming demand for its services for passengers and freight. Where formerly it had five flights per week scheduled through Port Hedland it now has 18 and there are still problems.

Sited on a restrictive delta-like piece of land, Port Hedland is already experiencing severe growth pains. A plan for the townsite development is badly needed if it is not to get completely out of hand. The contrast is provided by the new mining towns and ports with their well-planned streets and well-equipped homes and community facilities.

The population surge alone, apart from the industrial construction projects, will bring with it demands upon the state budget for social capital expenditure of many sorts, though not as great as might have been thought, since the agreements place the onus for most of the development upon the mining companies. Some idea of what will be involved on both sides is gained from the agreements signed between the state government and the operating companies.

Each company is required to lay out and develop complete townsites at the mine and the port and provide adequate and suitable housing, recreational and other facilities and services, roads, schools, water and power supplies, air strips, police stations, quarters and hospitals. The company may levy charges, where reasonable, on facilities such as water, power, and housing, and they are not responsible for meeting the operating expenses in respect of education, hospitals and police. If public facilities already exist – e.g. in Port Hedland – and the company wishes to make use of them, it must meet its share of the capital charges involved in any addition to the public facilities such as schools, hospitals, police-stations, water, power, roads, necessitated by the extra demand.

The main obligation of the state in respect of the agreements is to allow each company to enter and survey crown lands, allow capital site leases to be taken up (at normal rentals or freehold in the case of townsite blocks) and grant 21 year mineral leases (with rights of renewal) for approved areas at prescribed rentals per acre per annum. At the companies' request and expense the state will, where reasonable, upgrade existing roads and survey the area. It will also, where reasonable, assist with labour requirements by encouraging state, national and international migration to the area. The only continuing and permanent charges to the state in respect of iron ore in the north will be the operating costs of police, education and hospital services.

The harbour sites must be available for full use of third parties, including the state. They are to have access to all facilities, harbour installations, wharf machinery and equipment at a cost agreed to by the state. Rival companies and third parties exporting more than 500,000 tons annually may be charged for a share of capital costs and maintenance of harbours, channels, navigation aids, beacons, markers, etc. Non-rival parties shipping less than 500,000 tons annually will pay levies, if any, to the state.

As far as railways and roads are concerned, companies are obliged to transport passengers and carry freights for the state and for third parties at reasonable terms and charges providing company operations are not prejudiced. Third parties may use company roads free of charge, providing such use does not prejudice the companies' operations in any way, except for certain minor exceptions where terms and conditions are laid down.

Third parties carrying on legitimate business at port townsites are to be allowed full use of water, electricity, recreational, health and other services and facilities provided or controlled by a company. A company may charge for such facilities, for which purpose it is given the power of a Water Board, under the Water Boards Act 1904, and of a Supply Authority, under the Electricity Act of 1943. Each company may charge rent for houses which it lets to third parties and each company has municipal powers in respect of its townsites unless they are declared townsites by Order-in-Council.

The state economy will also benefit in a number of ways. Royalties – perhaps the most obvious and direct benefit – will rise from $180,000 in 1966 to $6.7 million in 1980, amounting in all to some $124 million. In the absence of precise contract price details these royalty estimates have been made on the basis of minimum royalties per ton payable for different grades of ore set out in the Agreement Acts. Already capital expenditure of probably some $20 million has rubbed off on the Perth metropolitan area in the form of orders for sleepers, housing materials, engineering supplies etc. and a great deal of current or operating expenditure is flowing to Perth. Mineral lease rentals could amount to $300,000 per year in addition, if each company takes out a 21 year mineral lease on the maximum area permitted under the agreements. Other rentals will increase by 25c per ton after 15 years in the case of some companies and 30 years in other cases. The additional rental will be payable on all ore, pellets and concentrates produced, whether used locally or not. The construction of the deep-water ports and the standard-gauge rail links, with access allowed to other users than merely the companies themselves, represent an important gain, and the capital assets represented by the whole townships constructed by the companies, with their accompanying facilities, are vast. The development of the region could mean back-loading for ships and trucks and could thus help to reduce transport costs in Northwestern Australia. Finally, the savings on state debt charges which would have been incurred in the construction of the normal social infrastructure such as schools and hospitals, needs to be taken into account.

All in all, the state stands to gain a good deal – certainly far more than sufficient to outweigh the stresses and strains it has to undergo.

The nation as a whole will also benefit to a considerable extent. Most obvious will be the effect upon the balance of payments of increased export earnings. These are estimated to rise to an annual figure in excess of $180 million. Further to this is, of course, the company income tax payable to the commonwealth government, which should rise to a substantial amount by the mid-1970's. Since the commonwealth's avowed policy is one of population growth and decentralisation the development in the Pilbara should be welcomed. But discontented rumblings in Canberra have been heard ever since the first contract was signed and attention must now be paid to some of the issues that have been raised in public debate in the last year or two.

The recent developments in the exploitation of Pilbara reserves have first to be viewed in a world setting. Altogether some 260,000 million tons are currently estimated as world reserves, and this figure will no doubt increase over time as existing assets are reassessed and new deposits discovered. The major sources of these reserves have already been mentioned.

There are certain characteristics of the world trade worth mentioning. First, the ore is a bulky cargo of low economic density which is normally produced in large quantities so that considerable economies of scale are in fact attained in the big plants which require vast capital outlays. This has necessitated long-term contracts. Second, since freight constitutes an unusually large proportion of the raw material price, the pattern of the world's markets has assumed a regional character. While the main suppliers of ore on international markets are South and North America, Europe, and India, to be joined soon by Australia, the main international markets for ore are in the United States, Europe, and Japan. Japan, lying relatively close to Australia, is a logical market though orders from European mills have already been placed with Australian exporters. Third, immense ore carriers have now made their appearance, and this, together with a significant improvement in mechanization and ore handling facilities, has brought down the proportion of sea-freight cost in the raw material price. A fourth characteristic is the recent growth of pellet production which enables the use of fines, and is a means of upgrading poor quality ore, and which has distinct freight advantages.

Thus Australia, closer to Japan than any other major competitor, with large-scale production, with ports capable of taking large carriers, with modern handling facilities, and with plans for the early establishment of several pelletising plants, should be in the van of potential suppliers to Japan for some years to come. The amount actually supplied will depend, of course, upon prices and other factors negotiated in the agreements.

Demands from Japanese steel makers for raw material seem likely to remain firm. Actually Japanese steel production has grown at a staggering rate. In the last decade it has more than quadrupled, and the industry is continuing to expand its capacity. While a repetition of the growth of the last ten years is unlikely in the next ten, it would be reasonable to expect that within another five years the annual demand for iron ore in Japan will be over 50 million tons, about one-third of which will be supplied from Australian mines.

One of the factors which will bear upon the question of price is the existence of alternative sources of supply. Japan now gets its ore mainly from India, Malaya, Chile, Peru and Brazil. India, the closest large rival is some 35 per cent further away from Japan than the Pilbara ports (3,500 miles as against 4,800), and thus has a freight disadvantage. Despite its freight advantage, however, Australia has to reckon on the existence of several large and aggressive rivals, including the South American countries. Attempts to drive too hard a bargain may have the effect of driving Japanese buyers to competing sellers.

This question of price has already caused considerable controversy on the Australian scene. During the latter months of 1965, commonwealth ministers had been warning against contracting for low prices. Positive commonwealth action came early in 1966 when the federal government refused an export permit to Hamersley Iron on the grounds that the price was too low. Subsequently the contract was re-negotiated on the basis of a revised price and a shorter term with larger annual quantities, but the refusal of the export permit threw into relief a schism between the federal and state governments on the matter of pricing policy.

It is extremely difficult to compare world prices since many elements enter into their determination, including grade of ore, shipping costs (prices may be compared f.o.b. at port of export or c.i.f at port of destination, and the comparison in the case of Japan is complicated by the fact that she carries the ore in her own ships), length of contract time, and quantity involved. Larger quantities over longer periods mean that lower prices can be offered by sellers while still maintaining a reasonable profit margin. Some of the contracts already written have several different prices, appropriate to the timing phase of export, and all of them contain price revision clauses.

There is little doubt, however, that the prices agreed to were below those obtained by India in 1961 but higher than those obtained by Brazil in 1962. There is also no doubt that the Japanese buyers acted in concert while the Australian sellers acted individually. Whether higher prices could have been obtained would be known only to the Japanese buyers. But

with world iron ore supplies on the increase, one may expect price reductions in the future and it may well be that in five years' time the prices
negotiated in recent contracts will appear favourable.

In the final analysis, and in fundamental economic terms, the price level
of iron ore will obviously hinge on elasticities of supply and demand.
Because of the vast initial capital investment necessary to get the industry
off the ground and because the decisions to commit such investment are
virtually irreversible, the supply of ore may be regarded within fairly
broad limits as relatively price-inelastic. Similarly, because there is now
available to steel producers a relative abundance of iron ore from various
sources, demand for iron ore will tend to be relatively price-elastic. The
major advantage that Australian-based companies have over other nations
such as India and Brazil in relation to the Japanese contracts is the lower
freight costs.

Whether the Western Australian government acted too hastily in permitting
the massive exploitation to get under way is another contentious point.
There is little doubt that the development occurring in the Pilbara has
thrown severe strains on several segments of the state economy. Metropolitan resources have been strained in several directions, and labour has been
drawn away from Perth. It has also been drawn from the eastern states.
The consumer price index for Western Australia has moved up more
rapidly than that for Australia (4.8 per cent increase, against 4.5 per cent)
and the ratio of vacancies to persons on benefits has almost doubled in
Western Australia whereas it has halved in Australia as a whole. The
excess labour demand has already resulted in a considerable upward
pressure on wages and earnings.[6]

A slower rate of exploitation would undoubtedly have meant that a
greater proportion of the benefits would have accrued to the state economy
provided it could have been guaranteed that all the contracts now signed
would eventually have been agreed to. Orders have gone to the eastern
states and overseas because local industrial capacity could not expand rapidly
enough to fulfil them. But it is doubtful whether the same contracts could
have been concluded in the distant future, and the state government's policy
of taking what was offering in the short run rather than opting for slower
and more controlled development was the right one even from a national
point of view. Also, there was no possibility of alternative uses for the
capital which was offering; it was a case of Pilbara development or nothing.

As to the charge that valuable resources are being virtually given away,
it should be borne in mind that less than 2 per cent of the reserves are
committed for export and the capital drain in developing them has been
slight as far as domestic capital is concerned. In return for the ore the
state has acquired new transport links, new communications, new towns
and ports and continuing income from rents and royalties, and the common-

[6]*Economic Activity in Western Australia,* vol. 9, no. 3.

wealth has gained not only from extra income tax but also from the fact that as royalties and rents flow to the state its requirements in the way of financial assistance from the commonwealth are progressively reduced.

When one considers the balance of payments effect upon the Australian economy of all this development, allowance should be made for that part of the gross export income which will be subsequently repatriated to the foreign companies involved. That is to say the net effect upon the balance of payments is the important issue, particularly in the long term. While the initial impact of the Pilbara development on Australia's balance of payments will be beneficial, there will come a time when repatriation of dividends could strain current resources and cause some concern. The outward drain could be as much as one-third of the total, but it is unlikely to be as high as this. Even so, out of an estimated total of $180 million this would leave some $120 million a year as a welcome addition to Australia's overseas funds.

The final issue is perhaps the most important of all. From the thinly veiled clash of interests between the state and commonwealth governments it is obvious that an explicit export pricing policy and an overall development policy for the exploitation of iron ore resources should be formulated. The commonwealth may have good reasons for its rejection of the Hamersley contract, for example, but it has never stated them in detail. Until it does so the state government and the companies do not know where they stand, and future contracts will be negotiated in the dark. This may damage the prospects for their successful conclusion.

6. Manganese and Tin

Manganese has increased considerably in importance in the last 10 years as a glance at Table 2 will show, though the rise has been anything but steady. After passing the £1 million mark in 1959, the value of manganese production fell for two years, then rose to a new peak in 1962 and subsequently declined even further than previously. In 1965 it once more exceeded £1 million and is expected to be considerably higher in 1966. The location and nature of manganese and tin deposits are dealt with in Appendix 2. Their commercial exploitation is the subject of this section.

The ore is currently mined at Woodie Woodie on the edge of the Great Sandy Desert in the Pilbara, and at Ripon Hills, some 50 miles further west, by Mt. Sydney Manganese and Westralian Ores. Mt. Sydney is owned two-thirds by Western Australian interests and one-third by British Metal Corporation, a large British mining company with extensive international interests which is the selling agent in Japan for all Western Australian ore. Westralian Ores, also extracting manganese in the region, is owned by Bell Bros., a Western Australian cartage and earth-moving company. Sentinel Mining (a subsidiary of the large international Ludwig Group) have taken over leases in some areas from Rhodes Ltd., another Western Australian cartage and earth-moving company, but so far they are not working them. Their interest may eventuate in a combination with iron ore interests and the creation of additional port facilities, should the economics of such an exercise be proven.

Technology

The ore is extracted from open cuts by mechanical shovels with a three-yard bite and transported to on-site crushing plants by heavy rear-dump trucks. Apart from crushing, screening and some hand picking, no further beneficiation is carried out. No economic processes for upgrading the manganese by chemical or other ore dressing methods are carried out, but the practice of crushing and discarding fine ores does raise the grade slightly to meet the buyers' specifications on grade and sizing with a minimum of permissible fines.

After crushing and screening, the ore is transported the 240 miles to Port Hedland by 90-95 ton trucks. The trucks currently used are being replaced by 345 h.p. Scamel 95 ton trucks. The eight-wheel prime mover, of 35 tons, has two tandem-wheel trailers, each of 30 tons. The ore is stockpiled at Port Hedland to await shipping space and then, when needed, it is transported to the ship's side by semi-trailer trucks carrying the ore in 2 ton kibbles (steel buckets). The ship's gear tips the contents of each kibble into the hold and returns the empty kibble to the attendant truck. A daily loading rate of between 1,500 and 2,000 tons is achieved on a two eight-hour shift basis.

Over the 13 year period that manganese has been exported, the resultant trade has added to the activity of Port Hedland. In the immensity of the iron ore developments in this area one tends to forget this and to overlook the economic significance of manganese development in the past. There is no doubt that it contributed in a substantial way to the township's port activity and its general prosperity.

A severe limitation to the development of this mining activity has always been imposed in the past, however, by the nature of the port and its facilities. Because of the inability of large-draught vessels to enter the port, ore carriers were limited to a maximum of 19 feet 6 inches, which limited shipment to 4,000 tons. This did not really constitute an economic load size and imposed a severe cost limitation upon the mining companies in the international market for manganese. More recently, because of the dredging that has been carried out for iron export, loads of 6,500 tons have been sent off and, in the future, it is hoped to export manganese in loads of 10,000 tons and greater. The manganese producers have thus benefited from the iron ore developments in a practical way and this is one of the factors contributing to the bright prospects which now exist for greatly expanded manganese production from the region. This is but one tangible example of the creation of external economies, of benefit to others, which arise when regional development of this kind takes place.

Markets

Manganese is used mainly in steel making and thus the demand for manganese is closely tied to steel production. The bulk of manganese from the region is at present exported to Japan where it is converted into ferro-manganese, which is directly used in the manufacturing of steel. Low-grade, high-iron manganese ores are used by direct smelting with iron ores in steel production. Limited amounts have been exported to Europe, mainly to France and Germany, and recently some keen inquiries have been made by buyers from the United States. Australia's steel producer, B.H.P., has also used small quantities of Western Australian manganese. Apart from exporting the ore, local producers also supply manganese oxide, which is used in brickmaking and as a pigment in paint manufacture. The current Australian consumption of manganese oxide is about 6,000 tons, of which Western Australia supplies some 1,500 tons. Grinding and market preparation of Western Australian ore is caried out in Perth by the Universal Milling Company but they are unable to satisfy the entire domestic Australian requirements and the balance is imported.

In view of the prospects for increasing Japanese steel production, already mentioned above in the section dealing with iron ore, one may expect Japanese demand for manganese in the future to remain firm and, because of the improvements in facilities which have made possible more economical load sizes, the Northwestern producers should be able to maintain their hold on the market by virtue of the grade which is equal to the best available in the world for lump ore. One result of the bigger loads being sent out of Port Hedland will be that the Western Australian producers will be restricted to shipping into Japan through three major ports capable of taking the larger ore carriers, instead of half a dozen as at present. However the initial problems created by this situation are expected soon to be overcome with beneficial results to both parties. It is possible also that prospects for more vigorous entry into the European markets will improve as larger loads become possible. For these markets, loads would have to be within the range of 10,000 tons to 20,000 tons.

The main competitors of the Western Australian producers at the moment are Ghana, the New Hebrides, and India, but the Western Australian ore is of a higher grade than the ore produced in these countries and the local producers are not apprehensive about the ability of their international competitors to cut into the demand for their ore, which is firmly established in Japan in the ferro-manganese market.

There is, however, another potential source of competition, the development of which will be watched with interest by Western Australian producers. Important and extensive deposits of manganese ore of medium to high grade, suitable for the production of ferro-manganese, are currently being developed by B.H.P. at Groote Island, off Arnhem Land in the Gulf of Carpentaria. The B.H.P. company has plans to achieve a production rate of some 200,000 tons by 1967. A beneficiation pilot plan was operating in 1965 and the company plans in the first phase of development to bene- ficiate the ore to the sintered stage. The second development phase allows for a large ferro-manganese plant. Initially, the grade of Groote Island ore should not worry Western Australian producers, but by the end of the first phase the production of beneficiated ore at the rate of 200,000 tons could present a serious threat to their present markets, though to what extent is hard to assess. With the production of ferro-manganese in the second phase, repercussions may be felt in Japan since a plant of the size pro- posed by B.H.P. will be much more economical to operate than the several smaller plants, at present producing in Japan, and could provide Japanese producers with strong competition, if allowed to. This could indirectly affect the market for Western Australian ore if some of these plants are driven out of production.

Apart from this there is the Ludwig ferro-manganese proposal, mentioned above, in connection with the development of the Nimingarra iron ore deposits. A sophisticated plant is proposed and if the project ultimately comes to fruition the operation could represent a severe challenge to the producers currently operating, particularly since the newer exporters will be aiming at the same market. The resistance of the Japanese steel-makers and the Japanese government to imported ferro-manganese may, however, protect the interests of the companies already exporting ore which is not upgraded.

Future Prospects

In the past, reserves of manganese in the region have been regarded as small, but in recent years it has become apparent that some millions of tons, at least 7 to 10 million, remain to be mined. Production has been held back partly because of the Australian government's desire to husband what were thought to be meagre resources. The position was similar to that with iron ore before the 1960's. Only one-third of proven reserves (in some special cases, one-half) could be exported and this was an inhibiting factor in the development plans of the producers. Still only a small proportion of the estimated reserves are proven, but producers hope that the export restriction will be removed or modified in the near future. In the meantime the companies are intensifying their exploration and proving activities. Mt. Sydney, for example, are carrying out extensive geophysical survey and drilling operations. Detailed investigation is also being carried out by some overseas mining companies and as a result of these operations, it is anticipated that known reserves will increase sub- stantially in the future.

The first export shipments were made in 1953. Quantity production passed the 100,000 ton mark in 1965 and in the light of recent developments it could even reach 150,000 tons by 1967. By 1970 it is possible that some 200,000 tons of manganese will be produced annually in the region not allowing for the Ludwig development. Thus, in the assessment of future prospects for the companies involved, reserves cannot be regarded as an inhibiting factor. At an export rate of 200,000 tons per year there is an estimated 50 years' supply in the area at the moment.

A further factor which has worried the producers has been the problem of transport. Because of the distance from the port and the nature of the terrain and the roads, costs of transport have been high enough to impose severe limitations upon the expansion of the enterprise. A further aspect of the present handling arrangements, not previously mentioned, is the double-handling which takes place at the port site. Because of the need to stockpile from the large ore trucks to await ships, the ore has subsequently to be loaded into kibbles and taken to the ships. The process of ship-loading is slow and costly and may be regarded as a further element in the overall transport and handling operation which has added greatly to costs.

The producers are actively investigating the possibility of reorganizing their transport arrangements to coincide with modern loading facilities at the port, and this should increase considerably the efficiency of the operation by enabling greater tonnages to be moved at lower costs per ton handled. These companies have always been limited in their capital expansion programme by the factors mentioned above and the current plans would, if carried to fruition, assist in removing these obstacles.

These developments, taken together and related to the expected future firm demand for manganese ore, suggest that prospects for the future expansion of manganese mining in Northwestern Australia are reasonably bright, particularly if competition from B.H.P. beneficiated ore from Groote Island and possibly upgraded ore from Mt. Nicholas can be met by greater economies and highly competitive prices or by Japanese protection. The ability to meet future competition is undoubtedly going to be a crucial factor in determining the future prospects for the companies currently operating. It seems that manganese should hold its ranking as the region's second most important mineral for some time until overtaken by oil.

Tin deposits are usually of high grade, some of the producing areas carrying as much as six lbs. per yard. The deposits are usually confined to small, shallow creeks and are, on the whole, relatively small with an average pay dirt width of two or three chains. In the case of tin, as with other minerals in the region, large companies with substantial capital resources behind them have moved in, and tin mining seems to be enjoying a revival based partly upon rising international prices. Production has increased tenfold in the last decade, from 60 tons to 645 tons, and indications are that this year the rapid rate of increase will continue.

The biggest operator in the area around Marble Bar, where most of the region's tin is mined, is Pilbara Tin Pty. Ltd., which is at present installing a gravity treatment plant worth about $2 million at the Moolyella field about 10 miles from Marble Bar. This company is a subsidiary of

Kathleen Investments which bought out Mineral Concentrates Pty. Ltd. and moved into the area in 1964. British Metal Corporation also has an interest in tin as well as manganese and its main mine is at Cooglegong, 40 miles south west of Marble Bar. The mine is capitalized at $850,000. The Hillside mine, owned by the Johnston family and B.M.C., is the third biggest producer. There are five or six small mines also operating in the district.

The mineral is first extracted by earth-moving equipment working in dry shallow water courses on alluvial ground. The concentrate is then obtained by the usual gravity processes of sluicing and jigging and one of the main problems, therefore, is to obtain an adequate supply of water. In this arid area water has always been considered a problem, or rather it has been the lack of capital to explore for water by boring which has provided the main limitation. Water supplies are obtained from catchment dams and from bores and are now generally regarded as satisfactory. But in any event, to reduce dependence upon rainfall, local mining concerns have developed a treatment method which makes use of a shallow dish, known as a concentrating cone, rotating about an inclined axis. Its operation requires very little water.

The concentrate, packed in drums, is transported in some cases from the mine direct to Fremantle in order to take advantage of cheap backloading charges. In other cases it is taken from the mine to Port Hedland. Used mainly in tin-plating processes, the concentrate finds its chief market in Sydney. With the revival in world tin prices problems of marketing have diminished, and with the amount of capital, in the order of $3 million, now being put into the mines by the large companies controlling them, one would expect the general operations to become much more efficient. Despite foreseeable production increases it seems that reserves are substantial enough to cause producers no immediate worry. In any case, and again no doubt in response to the price stimulus, the companies operating at the moment are also undertaking a substantial programme of investigation.

7. OIL EXPLORATION

The first traces of oil in Northwestern Australia were reported from West Kimberley in 1921 when indications of mineral oil were found while boring operations for water were being carried out at Price's Creek. The Freney Company drilled several wells in the Canning Basin between 1922 and 1941 until the war intervened.

Recent Developments

In 1952 the first large-scale oil exploration in Western Australia using modern geophysical and drilling techniques was started by Wapet in the Carnarvon basin. The company achieved spectacular but short-lived success with its first well, Rough Range No. 1, which in December 1953 produced oil at the rate of 500 barrels a day. The discovery attracted investment, allowing Wapet to make long-range plans, and stimulated the formation of several new companies. But further drilling at Rough Range proved that the quantity of oil was not sufficient for commercial production and search activity slowed down somewhat over the next few years. The discovery of oil in Queensland in 1961 and the widening of the base of the commonwealth oil subsidy to include all types of physical methods used in the search for petroleum were among a number of factors encouraging exploratory activity, and the tempo has increased each year since then. As well as the subsidy, the commonwealth offers taxation concessions.

In 1964 the first oil flow in the region since that at Rough Range was produced at Barrow Island. To June 1966, 26 wells had been drilled on the island, of which 24 had produced oil or gas, and a commercial oil field was proclaimed.

Between 1955 and 1965 the area held under Permits to Explore, which cover surface survey, nearly doubled. The Permit is issued for an area of at least 1,000 square miles and for a term of two years with the right of annual renewal. The License to Prospect, which is for drilling, is issued for an area between 8 and 100 square miles and for a term of two years with the right of three annual renewals. The Lease, which is for commercial production, may be granted for an area between 4 and 100 square miles and carries an annual rental of $20 per square mile and royalties ranging from 5 to 15 per cent of gross value of production. Holders of all types of tenements are required to carry out a satisfactory amount of work in their areas.

The Commonwealth Bureau of Mineral Resources has undertaken geological and geophysical surveys and stratigraphic drilling in the Canning and Carnarvon basins, aerial magnetometer and geological surveys in the Bonaparte Gulf basin, and regional geological and seismic surveys in the South Canning and Amadeus basins. These surveys have made a significant contribution to the geological knowledge essential to the search for petroleum. The Geological Survey of Western Australia has taken part in geological surveys and assisted exploration by providing information to companies.

By far the greater part of the search for oil has been conducted by Wapet which was formed as an operating company in 1951 by Caltex Oil Co. and Ampol Petroleum Pty. Ltd., and joined in 1958 by Shell Development (Aust.) Pty. Ltd. The company is now owned by California Asiatic Petroleum, Texaco Overseas Petroleum, and Shell Development (Australia), each with two-sevenths and Ampol Petroleum with one-seventh. Its extensive exploratory activities have been concentrated on the Canning and Carnarvon basins. Survey operations in the former have been mainly in the Fitzroy basin where drilling began in 1954, and by 1962 some 14 oil-test and 3 stratigraphic wells had been completed. Some indications of oil and gas were recorded but no oil flows and in 1963 the company began geological and geophysical surveys in the south-east portion of the Canning Basin. Drilling began there in 1965.

Wapet continued its surveying and drilling in the Exmouth Gulf area and substantial showings of gas were recorded at Cape Range and showings of oil or gas at some other locations. Elsewhere in the basin, extensive geological and geophysical surveys have been conducted and holes drilled at many locations in the northern half but only at Warroora have signs of oil been found. Seismic survey work extended to the off-shore area in 1961 and the company had its first success in this area in 1964 when Barrow No. 1 well produced up to 11 million cubic feet a day of gas and up to 985 barrels a day of oil. The drilling programme was directed largely to an assessment of the Windalia sand formation until the existence of sufficient oil to make production economically feasible was proved, and since then the company's operations on Barrow Island have centred on the development of production and shipping facilities. The search for oil goes on, concentrated in the islands near Barrow, the adjacent mainland, and the offshore areas. Recently Wapet has made farm-out agreements with Continental Oil Co. of Australia, French Petroleum (Aust.) and Australian Aquitaine Petroleum, Australian Superior Oil, Phillips Australian Oil, Sunray DX Oil, Gewerkschaft Elwerath, Anacapa Corp. and Canadian Superior Oil.

Associated Freney Oil Fields N.L. took over the Freney interests in 1954 and drilled three wells in the Fitzroy basin without success but since 1961 activity by other companies has increased. Hunt Oil Co., in association with Placid Oil Co., carried out a vigorous exploration programme in the Officer basin but this ended abruptly in July 1966 when the only hole drilled struck bottom at a shallow depth. Beach Petroleum N.L. and its associates carried out surveys and began drilling in the Amadeus basin in 1965. Burmah Oil Co. of Australia, as the operating company for a group, has been conducting marine seismic surveys in Woodside (Lakes Entrance) Oil Co.'s offshore area.

The Impact of Oil Discoveries

The direct impact of oil exploration on the regional economy has not so far been very significant although about $80 million has been invested in the search for oil in Western Australia, most of it in the North-West region. Investment in the Barrow Island operation totalled $6 million to May 1966, and the construction of production and shipping facilities will raise this to $26.5 million. However, much of the work has been carried out by contractors from overseas or elsewhere in Australia so that relatively little of the amount invested has directly flowed into the region's economy. The labour force employed by Wapet in the state is about 560, but no estimate is available of how much of this workforce is employed in the region except for Barrow Island.

As many as 200 men may be employed there during the construction phase of this operation, but the permanent workforce will be about 50.

The commercial development of the Barrow Island field is unlikely to bring important direct benefits to the region beyond its effect in encouraging further exploration. Its importance lies more in the region's contribution to the state and Australian economy. The field, conservatively estimated to contain 85 million barrels of high quality oil, is the largest in Australia. Installations and operating facilities are expected to be completed by May 1967 when production of oil at the rate of 9,000 barrels a day will begin. This will rise in two years to about 20,000 barrels a day providing future wells produce at the same rate as those so far tested. Such a rate of production which is more than double the current output of the Moonie and Alton fields in Queensland, would almost meet Western Australia's current needs and will raise Australian oil production to about 10 per cent of its requirements.

The location of the deposits on Barrow Island poses some problems. The production rate is not expected to be high because of the very low permeability of the Windalia sands which contain the main reservoir of oil. However, the company hopes that the introduction of new techniques now under study will improve the recovery rate. Shipping problems arise because there is no suitable deep-water access to the Island. The oil will be stored at a tank farm on the east coast and conveyed by a submarine pipeline to a mooring buoy installation which will provide anchorage for tankers six miles offshore. This installation will be vulnerable to cyclones.

Estimates of the value of the field are hazardous. The oil is owned by the partners in Wapet, who are free to dispose of their shares within Australia independently, and it is expected that it will be refined at Kwinana, the nearest refinery. Ampol Exploration Ltd., which owns one-seventh of the oil, estimates the price at Kwinana at $3.24 a barrel, set by the Tariff Board formula which will remain operative until 1970. The current freight charge from Barrow Island to Kwinana is about 38c. a barrel, so that the net well-head sale price would be about $2.86 a barrel. Ampol estimates the costs of producing its share (12 million barrels) to be $9 million so that its estimated net income from the total operation would be $25 million, of which $2.5 million would have been earned by 30 September 1968 and the remainder would accrue at the rate of $2 million a year on the anticipated annual rate of production. The other partners can be expected to benefit in proportion to their shareholdings.

The state will benefit from royalties. If the oil lease is granted on the basis of the minimum royalty of 5 per cent of an estimated annual gross production of $21 million the royalties will eventually amount to about $1 million annually. Royalties payable on any offshore production will be 10 per cent.

8. Salt Farming

In recent years salt production has emerged as one of the promising newer industries of the north and five companies have now shown interest in the possibilities of solar salt farming. Shark Bay Salt. Pty. Ltd. was the first in the field with its decision in 1963 to construct a £750,000 salt works. In 1966 an agreement between the state government and Leslie Salt Co. of San Francisco was concluded. Other companies currently investigating possibilities in the north are The Commonwealth Aluminium Corporation at Dampier, The Exmouth Salt Co. Pty. Ltd., near Onslow, and the Continental Oil Co. of Australia Ltd., at Shark Bay.

Shark Bay Salt is a $3 million joint venture by Garrick Agnew Pty. Ltd., and the Adelaide Steamship Co. Ltd., and it is supplying to Japan. Leslie Salt is investigating reserves covering 150 square miles at Port Hedland. Hamersley Iron has been granted reserves covering 224 square miles at King Bay where the Comalco group will establish salt fields covering 25,000 acres. It is associated in this venture with two Japanese companies, Maubeni-Iida and Nissho Trading Co. It plans to produce 350,000 tons of salt annually by 1970 and one and a half million tons annually by 1975.

The Leslie Salt proposal, which is the largest of the current development plans, allows for the eventual establishment of a $7 million industry, with evaporating ponds covering some 48,000 acres of tidal flats. The company hopes to begin exports in about three years at a rate of 475,000 tons a year and to export a minimum of one million tons a year when the plant is fully operational. Initially, 45,000 ton carriers will be used. By 1975 annual production may be raised to 2 million tons. Royalties on this operation will be 5c. a ton on the first 500,000 tons in any one year, 6.25c. on the second 500,000 tons, and 7.25c. on any amounts over one million tons. The agreement will allow for the construction of a 600 ft. general purpose jetty south of the existing wharf in Port Hedland.

Conditions required for salt production are ideally a combination of low rainfall, high evaporation and impervious soil, and on these criteria the area between Port Gregory and Broome is ideal, particularly at Roebourne and Onslow. The usual method of salt farming is to block off low-lying areas of land from the sea by earth embankments and pump into the bays sea water which is then allowed to evaporate. When the water becomes brine it is pumped into specially levelled, impervious bays where further evaporation ultimately deposits salt which can then be harvested by scraping.

World salt consumption is increasing steadily for industrial as well as household use. Its main chemical derivatives – chlorine, sodium carbonate and caustic soda – are used in the manufacture of many products including petroleum, aluminium, paper, plastics, rayon, glass, insecticides, weed killers, soap and detergents. Industrial use of salt is increasing in

Australia but it is probable that the principal market for salt produced in the north will be Japan whose rapidly growing chemical industry is demanding larger and larger quantities each year. The Japanese market absorbs $3\frac{1}{2}$ million tons of salt annually. In 1965 Japan placed an order for the construction of a 138,000-ton bulk carrier to transport salt from Mexico to Japan.[7]

9. OTHER PRINCIPAL MINERALS

Gold, as already noted, was responsible for much of the early mineral discoveries in the region and also for supporting the pastoral industry in part. The State Batteries at Marble Bar, Bamboo Creek and Nullagine treat prospector's ore, which is fairly high in grade, and as a generalization it may be said that the gold deposits are spectacular but not extensive. Various attempts to market antimony concentrates have been made but the present practice is to treat the ore for its gold content only. In recent years 1952 represented the year of peak production in value terms, since then the value of gold produced in the region has declined markedly.

Copper deposits, if large enough, can be worked economically even when the grade is below one per cent, but the treatment of such deposits usually requires some method of upgrading on-site, either by concentrating or by smelting. Since, however, none of the known deposits in the region is big enough to support a smelter, the sulphide ore has to be shipped away and thus only a high-grade ore of, say, 10 per cent or better, is profitable.

There is a keen demand for carbonate copper ore for use as an additive to fertilizer. This is found at the surface above primary ore bodies, and it is usually above 10 per cent in grade which makes it an economic proposition. But when this is exhausted it is usually found that the underlying primary ore is not suitable for use with fertilisers and is usually not rich enough to export unless above 10 per cent. The result, therefore, is that the exploration of copper ore bodies at depth is very much neglected, although deep mining is gradually being introduced.

The production of cupreous ore and concentrates in the region reached an all-time high in 1959 when over 11,000 tons, worth £175,000 (see Table 2) were won, but production fluctuates considerably from year to year. As a result of recent moves it is probable that the Whim Creek mine will soon be operating once more and there are signs of increased exploration activity by several companies and increased interest in the possibilities of further copper production in the region. For instance Pickands Mather and Co. International have reported indications of economic deposits of copper in the Bow River area, north of Hall's Creek, and promising indications of lead, zinc and nickel. Pickands Mather have been joined in a prospecting programme in the Kimberley by two

[7]*West Australian,* 21 July 1965.

Australian companies, North Broken Hill and Ampol Mining, and four overseas companies, Dominion Foundries and Steel, of Canada, and Cerro Corporation, Interlake Iron, and Pocantico Oil and Gas, of the United States. Western Mining Corporation are also actively prospecting over a big area around the Warburton Range.

Among other recent mineral discoveries in the north are promising signs of Bauxite in the Admiralty Gulf area. The U.S. Metals Refining Co. believes that bauxite deposits of an economic size may exist in four temporary reserves totalling 2,560 square miles that it holds in the area south of Admiralty Gulf. The company, which is a wholly owned subsidiary of American Metal Climax Inc. (AMAX), has been exploring by helicopter in the region between Couchman Range and Admiralty Gulf, and if extensive deposits are proved in the area this could have implications for the tidal power possibilities discussed in Chapter 7.

Coal is another mineral for which temporary reserves have been granted in the West Kimberley. Thiess Bros. Pty. Ltd. and Premier Properties Pty. Ltd. have been granted reserves totalling 2,900 square miles in the northern part of the Fitzroy basin and in a 100 mile radius east and south-east of Derby. So far, the few discoveries of thin seams of coal in the Kimberley which have been intersected at shallow depth during water boring and oil drilling operations have had no economic value though geological conditions in the area are favourable for coal formations.

10. FUTURE PROSPECTS

It may be said that future prospects for the mineral industry in Northwestern Australia are exceedingly good. The actual degree to which they will play their part and contribute to the region's rapid economic growth will depend, however, upon five main factors.

First, the minerals must be there in adequate quantites. With respect to asbestos reserves, the position is not clear. Manganese is scattered throughout the region but no really large deposits have yet been found. The same may be said of gold, tin and copper. Known oil reserves at the present time and at the anticipated extraction rate, are sufficient for 12 years' production. However, it cannot be stressed too much that so little is yet known of the varied mineral resources of this vast region. Exploration is proceeding apace and even in five years' time the story may be quite different with respect to some of the minerals mentioned above or some of the many other minerals mentioned in Appendix 2.

Iron ore, at this point, deserves particular mention. It has been pointed out that good reserves exist in Cockatoo and Koolan islands. Taking into account the reserves of some distance below sea-level they could amount to more than 200 million tons, representing maybe 75 years' supply at the estimated 3 million tons annual production when fully developed. But the reserves so far estimated for the Pilbara dwarf the Yampi reserves and erase completely any question of their depletion for many hundreds of years, even with a greatly accelerated rate of extraction.

A second condition essential to the successful exploitation of the region's minerals is that the reserves are accessible and capable of being worked. It has already been pointed out that in the case of asbestos, tin, manganese and copper the deposits are accessible and capable of being worked and treated within fairly narrow limits set variously by the nature of the deposits, by the climate, and by transport costs.

In the case of iron ore the position varies with the location of the deposits. At Yampi, where operations are well under way, the company has successfully overcome its extraction and handling problems with the expenditure of large capital sums and is well placed to load directly on to the ships. In the Pilbara area rail links were necessary to open up the deposits which were several hundred miles inland in some cases. This has been a very costly business but much of it is now completed.

The third problem is that of getting the ore to its markets. This involves the use of the road and rail access links and, in addition, the provision of adequate deep-water port facilities somewhere on the coastline. Some of the problems in this connection and some of the attempts that have been made to achieve a solution to them are described in Chapter 9. New ports have been developed, existing ones dredged and upgraded, and all of them equipped with modern loading facilities.

The fourth problem is that of obtaining the necessary development capital. Private capital had to be provided for the working of the deposits on a scale that could not have been supported or sustained by Australian financiers. This necessitated the entry of foreign capital and thus raised problems of profit remittances, taxation provisions, royalty and lease agreements and the like. At the same time it required public funds to develop ancilliary services and facilities and here, of course, the state government comes up against strong demands for development capital from other industries in the region. These points are all dealt with above.

The final problem is certainly not the least. It is the problem of markets. If all the other conditions are met over time, as may reasonably be anticipated, the successful promotion of these proposed ventures will turn upon the demand for the region's mineral products in relation to the price at which they can be supplied. In this case prediction for the future is rather hazardous. Gauging the strength of future demand for minerals in a changing technology is at best an uncertain business. With respect to the well known and widely used minerals, however, some broad generalizations are possible.

Most of the region's known mineral wealth is concentrated currently in three main types of deposit, iron ore, manganese and asbestos, with oil and salt rapidly entering the picture. Taking asbestos first, it would seem that at the moment there is not too great a deviation between costs of production and the world price. For the future, the position seems uncertain since there exists a need for cost reductions in the form of a reduction in hours lost through better employer-employee relations, a reduction in transport charges through improved handling and carting facilities, and a reduction in production costs through working more easily accessible seams if the company is to be able to achieve an economical scale of production.

With respect to iron ore, the position is more definite. Contracts involving 275 million tons of lump ore and pellets, stretching over the next 25 years, have been negotiated with Japan and there seems little doubt that these will be followed with further contracts over the next decade. A contract has already been concluded to supply Great Britain. Western Germany, Italy, and Taiwan are other possibilities being freely discussed. But the advantage of shorter freight hauls between Australia and Japan disappears in the European case and added to this is the fact that the Australian industry is being developed to handle the largest types of ore carriers. It has been reported that there is not one port in the whole of Western Europe capable of handling ore carriers greater than 40,000 deadweight tonnage.

Under the Agreements the region should have two fully integrated iron and steel industries by the 1990's but only time will tell whether these will eventuate. The steel products will probably be directed to export since the local domestic market will already be adequately catered for by the future integrated Kwinana iron and steel industry, which itself should be able to export a proportion of its production.

Oil production is now commencing and if the anticipated eventual production rate of 7 million barrels a year is achieved the field will last 12 years on current estimates of the reserves available. It is reasonable to assume that before then further oil discoveries will have been made in the region, particularly if the intensity of exploration steps up, since there is a positive relationship between the footage of wells drilled and the oil reserves discovered.[8]

In the case of manganese, export markets will be firm enough and the real problem will be to keep operating costs at a level which will allow the local producers to compete with other international and Australian suppliers, in particular B.H.P. and the Ludwig Group. Proposals for this involve larger-scale production, more efficient port handling and the export of much greater quantities at a time.

With most of the other minerals the relationship between prices and costs is crucial and a change one way or the other can affect production considerably. There is little doubt that the general improvement in communications and transport and other facilities in the region, and particularly in the Pilbara area, will result in fringe benefits which may boost

[8]M. J. Webb, *Natural Resources 1966-1970.*

the production of these other minerals via a reduction in the costs of producing and exporting them. Also, as more people trained to recognize rock formations move into the area more minerals will be discovered.

On the whole, therefore, the long-term prospect for the region's minerals are good. Mineral extraction will shortly become not only the most important form of economic activity in the north, but in the state as a whole, and may well provide the basis for long-term industrialization which will transform the economy of Western Australia.

BIBLIOGRAPHY

AUSTRALIAN BLUE ASBESTOS LIMITED, *Report of Operations at Wittenoom Gorge*. Perth, undated.

BROKEN HILL PROPRIETARY COMPANY LIMITED. *B.H.P. Review*. This publication is published from 4 to 6 times a year.

CROWLEY, F. K. *Australia's Western Third*. London, 1960.

Economic Activity in Western Australia, vol. 9, no. 3. 1966.

IAN POTTER AND COMPANY. *The Search for Petroleum*. Melbourne, 1964.

—— *Iron Ore in Australia*. Melbourne, 1965.

PETROLEUM INFORMATION BUREAU. *Petroleum Search in Australia*. Perth, 1965.

WEBB, M. J. *Natural Resources 1966-1970*. Proceedings of the Australian Institute of Management National Conference. Perth, 1966.

West Australian. 1965-66.

WEST AUSTRALIAN PETROLEUM PTY. LTD. *West Australian Petroleum Pty. Ltd. Report 1964-65*. Perth, 1965.

WESTERN AUSTRALIAN GOVERNMENT. *Iron Ore – Western Australia*. Perth, 1966.

WESTERN AUSTRALIAN MINES DEPARTMENT. *Annual Report* and *Quarterly Press Release*. Perth.

TABLE 1

VALUE OF MINERAL PRODUCTION[1]

(by goldfield)

(£'000)

Year	Pilbara	West Pilbara	Kimberley	West Kimberley	Ashburton	Peak Hill	Gascoyne	Regional total	State total	Regional total as a % of state total
1950	119.9	160.7	19.2	.2	23.2	76.5	—	399.7	11,489.2	3.5
1951	206.2	237.1	2.0	13.0	62.6	38.6	—	559.5	12,706.2	4.4
1952	381.1	604.3	6.4	218.5	97.3	140.7	—	1,448.3	16,920.4	8.6
1953	236.5	708.2	4.0	690.7	41.6	321.5	1.4	2,003.9	19,124.4	10.5
1954	357.3	570.5	1.3	631.9	21.9	683.5	2.4	2,000.1	19,764.6	10.1
1955	289.5	527.0	3.0	493.3	1.4	360.5	1.9	1,676.6	20,599.4	8.1
1956	532.4	838.9	2.8	323.9	11.8	690.9	10.3	2,411.0	21,367.6	11.3
1957	535.5	1,245.0	1.1	386.4	15.7	755.2	4.4	2,943.3	22,924.5	12.8
1958	549.8	1,345.1	.8	532.4	7.2	634.5	5.3	3,075.1	21,797.5	14.1
1959	974.7	1,623.1	.6	666.6	3.3	439.3	9.1	3,726.9	23,224.3	16.0
1960	918.0	1,420.9	.3	830.3	2.0	195.8	20.1	3,387.4	21,826.5	15.6
1961	1,145.0	1,554.7	.2	1,274.2	3.3	187.1	21.0	4,185.5	22,376.8	18.7
1962	1,276.4	1,705.7	.8	1,309.9	2.6	324.4	8.8	4,628.7	23,096.8	20.0
1963	860.6	1,256.4	1.7	1,267.0	7.4	132.5	5.8	3,531.4	21,076.6	16.8
1964	1,089.0	1,116.4	.2	1,369.7	.7	58.7	3.1	3,637.9	24,741.8	14.7
1965	1,525.5	883.1	.3	2,314.0	.2	368.1	2.0	5,093.2	26,912.7	18.9

[1] Total value of minerals of all types produced in each gazetted Goldfield.

Source: Western Australian Mines Department, *Report*.

TABLE 2

VALUE OF PRINCIPAL MINERALS PRODUCED[1]

(1950–1965 inclusive)

(£'000)

Year	Asbestos	Iron ore	Manganese	Tin	Silver, lead ore and concentrates	Cupreous ore and concentrates	Tanto columbite	Beryl	Gold
1950	143.5	—	55.5	8.5	45.5	8.5	.7	.4	114.4
1951	225.6	10.3	33.3	21.6	92.1	11.7	—	8.0	148.3
1952	595.1	205.2	35.6	44.8	154.4	14.7	1.6	11.5	293.8
1953	707.4	682.2	151.0	39.7	76.5	8.1	9.6	19.0	269.7
1954	555.7	629.3	603.2	40.1	30.8	32.3	69.0	20.7	232.8
1955	502.0	492.7	423.8	33.3	25.9	78.1	21.2	31.7	68.0
1956	826.1	322.9	644.9	137.0	90.9	99.2	88.1	53.4	45.4
1957	1,237.7	386.4	925.2	125.3	58.4	67.6	4.7	56.5	22.7
1958	1,343.4	532.4	953.3	70.9	8.5	94.8	6.9	27.7	32.0
1959	1,628.5	666.6	1,015.6	141.9	19.4	175.1	4.3	45.1	33.4
1960	1,420.4	830.1	742.8	157.4	—	125.7	12.8	31.6	74.3
1961	1,535.2	1,274.1	884.3	224.3	—	142.5	17.5	37.8	69.6
1962	1,693.0	1,305.6	1,155.9	320.2	—	71.5	32.6	15.5	30.4
1963	1,202.8	1,267.0	513.0	379.5	—	119.6	10.4	3.4	35.7
1964	1,105.8	1,270.2	457.3	565.0	99.4	117.0	1.2	1.9	20.0
1965	901.9	2,222.3	1,075.9	744.2	91.7	47.0	.3	—	9.9

[1] Other minerals, produced in varying quantities in the region, include: antimony ore and concentrates, copper ore and concentrates, emerald, fergusonite, scheelite, zinc ore, ochre, corundum, emery, wolfram, opal, bismuth, chromite, petroleum and salt.

Source: Western Australian Mines Department, *Report.*

TABLE 3

QUANTITY OF PRINCIPAL MINERALS PRODUCED

(1950–65 inclusive)

(long tons)

Year				Asbestos[1]	Iron Ore	Manganese	Tin	Cupreous ore and concentrates	Gold (fine oz.)
1950	....	....	....	1,019	—	11,962	21	915	7,383
1951	....	....	....	2,119	10,384	5,257	39	960	9,572
1952	....	....	....	3,592	204,945	5,045	62	1,233	18,965
1953	....	....	....	4,401	687,895	16,329	49	845	17,313
1954	....	....	....	4,097	634,514	40,581	78	3,720	11,687
1955	....	....	....	4,762	496,882	37,491	60	5,996	4,226
1956	....	....	....	8,047	327,815	57,323	227	6,627	2,271
1957	....	....	....	12,494	389,686	63,937	221	3,954	1,172
1958	....	....	....	13,265	536,713	61,440	124	6,565	1,707
1959	....	....	....	15,312	672,239	69,973	227	11,353	1,599
1960	....	....	....	12,983	837,147	53,788	261	6,888	3,611
1961	....	....	....	14,243	1,284,768	67,652	321	6,494	4,451
1962	....	....	....	15,669	1,320,355	89,603	443	4,239	1,944
1963	....	....	....	11,105	1,277,631	39,357	529	2,782	2,284
1964	....	....	....	11,150	1,280,864	38,824	579	1,907	1,283
1965	....	....	....	9,682	2,240,939	100,208	645	939	635

[1] Asbestos includes chrysotile and crocidolite.

Source: Western Australian Mines Department, *Report*.

TABLE 4

PILBARA IRON ORE AGREEMENTS

(as at January 1966)

Company and value of agreement with state government	Export contract period	Capital investment[1] ($million)	Miles of railway	Workforce		Export tons (millions)	Amount of contract ($million)	Royalties ($million)
				Construction[2]	Permanent			
Goldsworthy Mining Pty. Ltd. $96 million.	1965-73 7 years	48 (ore) 56 (pellets)	70	920	300	16.5	144	10.8
Hamersley Iron Pty. Ltd. $156 million	1966-84 18 years	90 (ore) 36 (pellets) 80 (steel)	179	2,500	1,010	95.1	812	43*
Mt. Newman Iron Ore Company $156 million	1969-91 22 years	150 (ore) 96 (pellets & steel)	260	1,800	680	100	820	57.6*
Cliffs Western Australian Mining Pty. Ltd. $70 million	1969-39 21 years	Combined 130 (pellets)	70	2,000	1,030	71.4	782	7.4
Dampier Mining Co. Ltd. (Deepdale) $50 million	1972-79 7 years					5.5(a)	54(a)	n.a.
Total $528 million	1965-91	686	579	7,220	3,020	290.5	2,612	118.8

* Approximate figure.
1 Companies' Capital Investment in many instances has already exceeded Government Agreements.
2 Peak construction workforce.
n.a. not available.
Source: Western Australian Mines Department, Report.

CHAPTER 5

FISHING

1. INTRODUCTION

Established before the turn of the century, the fishing industry of North-western Australia has changed its character considerably in recent years. At its present stage of development it is located primarily in the Shark Bay-Carnarvon-Onslow area but commercial quantites of fish are reported to exist in the more northern waters (Broome-Derby-Wyndham) and these are now being surveyed for early exploitation. However, the pearling industry, which is centred almost exclusively on Broome, and pearl culture at Kuri Bay, north of Derby, are the only forms of fishing currently practised on a commercial scale in the northern sector of the region.

The industry can be conveniently divided into three categories : pearling, shellfishing (crustaceans) and scale fish caught for human consumption. Each is a separate entity within the fishing industry, and each may be distinguished from the others according to differences in stages of development, transport, marketing and capital requirements, and future possibilities.

Employment in the industry rose substantially between the 1947 and 1954 censuses, from 121 persons to 583, but between 1954 and 1961 it dropped to 330. The low 1947 figures reflect the influence of the World War on the industry; boats were commandeered by the armed services and had not, at the time of the 1947 census, been completely replaced. By 1954 pearling had been re-established in Broome with the re-introduction of Japanese divers, and whaling stations had been established at Point Cloates in 1947 and Babbage Island in 1951. By 1961 the numbers employed in the whaling industry had dropped considerably as had the numbers engaged in pearling at Broome. The whaling industry has since ceased to exist and a further large decline in pearling is evident. Thus the 1966 census figures when they come to hand will show a further drop in fishing employment in the region. However, with the current prospects for expansion within the industry of large-scale commercial fishing this figure may be expected to rise once more in the near future.

2. Early History[1]

Fishing was one of the early activities in Northwestern Australia, as indeed it was on the southern and south-western coast, but its extent was very limited and the ventures sporadic. After the settlement on the Swan River was officially established, venturesome individuals began to fan out on journeys of exploration. In the early period their activities were mainly confined to the south-west of the state between the Swan River settlement and the settlement which had been made earlier at Albany. In 1839, however, the Gregory brothers passed through the Shark Bay area, which had been previously rejected as a possible site for settlement prior to the first settlement at King George Sound in 1826. Grey had also crossed the mouths of the Murchison and Gascoyne rivers in 1838.

Probably the earliest productive activity in the region associated with the sea was the shipping of several loads of guano from the Shark Bay area, under licence, in the early 1850's. Whalers were also operating up and down the coast though mainly they confined their activities to southern waters. By the late 1860's pearling and *beche-de-mer* gathering was being carried on in the Nichol Bay area, with about ten boats operating. Aborigines were frequently used for the diving operations and the industry was quite well established and flourishing. In the 1870's and 1880's this industry continued to expand and the search for pearl shell and pearls was widened to take in the coastline between Shark Bay in the south and the Eighty Mile Beach in the north. As the ease with which these products could be gathered diminished, so the organization, equipment and methods of the pearlers changed. Sea-going schooners were acquired, deeper waters were worked for longer periods and the diving suit with air line replaced the bare skin and the human lung. The character of employment also changed and this period saw the introduction of Asian labour into the pearling industry. By the early 1870's there were 80 boats operating and between them they won pearl shell in 1874 worth £62,000, and pearls worth £12,000. At this stage even some pastoralists turned to pearling.

The industry atttracted labour of many nationalities, and assumed the cosmopolitan air that was to become characteristic of this part of the north and which was to provide the industry with a source of colourful history in subsequent years. By 1874, for example, over 500 Malays were employed in pearling and reports of their ill-treatment led to the appointment of an inspector in 1879. In 1876, as the result of a

[1] F. K. Crowley, *Australia's Western Third,* has been heavily drawn upon for the information contained in this section.

cyclone, 69 men were drowned in the Exmouth Gulf area and 12 luggers were wrecked and their crews lost in 1881 from the same cause. In 1887 another cyclone struck on the Eighty Mile Beach, sinking 18 luggers and drowning nearly 200 men, most of whom were Malays.

By the turn of the century the pearling industry, which had suffered setbacks in the 1890's, had recovered and was producing at the rate of more than £120,000 a year. The industry was now centred at Broome, whence it had moved from Cossack, and employed more than 2,000 men of whom about 1,700 were Malays and Japanese. There was also a smattering of Chinese, Filipinos and Aborigines, and life there was raw. By 1912 the industry had more than 400 luggers and employed about 3,000 men. It was then the fifth largest exporting industry in the state.

The collapse of the market for pearl shell during the Great War dealt a severe blow to the industry and never again did it achieve the heights of the early period of the twentieth century. Speaking of this period, Crowley writes: 'During the lay-up season, when the luggers and tenders were being refitted, Broome was the most polyglot community in Australia. In the shacks and sheds along the foreshore, in the whitewashed iron shanties of Chinatown and scattered in the many huts within walking distance of the hotels and stores of the town were hundreds of Japanese, Koepanger and Malay divers and deckhands. Chinese pearl buyers were doing extremely well, and there was such a varied collection of unscrupulous "white adventurers" as to prompt one resident to remark that "the coloured were a trifle the whiter". The mixture of nationalities and races, the illicit buying and selling of "snide" pearls and occasional crimes of violence were all part of life in this outpost of Asia. The industry was allowed to flourish in this far-distant pearling port as the exception which gave justification to the otherwise rigidly enforced White Australia Policy. The occupation was considered too perilous, too strenuous and too uncongenial for white labour'.[2]

There was some recovery after the Great War and once again Broome and the industry assumed a prosperous air. About the only incident which marred the colourful but reasonably controlled life of Broome was a civil riot in 1920 which followed a fight between Japanese and Koepangers and which lasted for three days. By the 1930's a decline in the industry set in and has persisted to this day except for the temporary resurgence of pearling after the World War.

Several factors were responsible for the decline in the 1930's, chief among which was the world depression. Foreign vessels operating outside Australian territorial waters with cheap labour and low operating costs also contributed to the decline in prices by flooding the world market with pearl shell. There was also a rise of pearl culture in Japan

2F. K. Crowley, *Australia's Western Third*, p. 178.

which hit the natural pearl segment of the Australian industry. Also, in 1935 another cyclone struck, destroying 20 luggers and drowning 140 men of the Lacepede Islands. By the end of the 1930's there were only about 50 luggers remaining in the industry. The figures of employment, equipment and production presented in Table 3 give some idea of the course the industry has taken since 1950.

Whaling as an industry in the north did not really have its beginnings until the operations of the Norwegian Whaling Company in the 1912-16 seasons although, as mentioned earlier, whalers had operated in the region in spasmodic fashion through most of the second half of the nineteenth century. The Norwegian Whaling Company operated from the Point Cloates area and used modern equipment. By 1921 a local company had commenced operations but after two seasons its activities in the area ceased. From 1925 to 1928 a Norwegian company again operated from Point Cloates and treated nearly 3,500 whales in the four successive seasons. During the 1930's most of the whaling in the region was carried out by foreign owned boats manned by foreigners, and the industry then lapsed during the World War to be revived in 1949.

The early gathering of guano has already been mentioned. This activity continued and there is a report of a cyclone in 1877 causing havoc among the boats loading guano in the Lacepede Islands in the West Kimberley. Guano was exported in the years 1878-79 and deposits of this fertilizer were to be found also in the Abrolhos Islands. Leases were taken up here at the turn of the century.

By the 1930's commercial fishing for scale fish for human consumption had become established in the region, though still in a small way, employing a handful of men. The most favoured areas were in the vicinity of Carnarvon and Shark Bay, and snapper, kingfish and sharks were the main species caught. This industry has expanded considerably since the World War and the story of its recent growth is given below.

Other more recent developments in the fisheries of the north are described below but one segment which has now passed into history is the whaling industry. Formerly a million pound industry based upon Point Cloates and Babbage Island in the Carnarvon area, employing many seasonal workers, it is now defunct as a result of the decision of the International Whaling Commission to protect humpback whales completely. The last catch of whales was taken in 1963 and the whaling factory and other facilities at Babbage Island are now used partly for processing prawns.

The growth of shellfishing and pearl culture and the possibilities of exploiting the free swimming fish which abound in northern waters is described below.

3. Scale Fish For Human Consumption.

This form of fishing is based almost entirely on the Shark Bay-Carnarvon area. Table 1 highlights the concentration of men and boats in this area.

Of the other centres of the region, Carnarvon and Broome are largest. Fish production by species for the Shark Bay-Carnarvon area is given in Table 2. Between 1950 and 1960 the catch trebled but since then the industry has declined, particularly in 1964-65.

Whilst a large variety of fish are caught in the area, fishermen rely heavily on three species, snapper, whiting and mullet. The fish are caught either by net or hand line and a few traps are used for the catching of snapper. The majority of the boats are motor powered and are equipped with snap freezers and cold storage space ranging from 10 to 80 ton capacity. Mostly they come from Fremantle and stay on the snapper grounds for two or three weeks before taking their catch to Geraldton or to Fremantle. Fishing in this vicinity requires an intimate knowledge of local conditions built up over a considerable period of time, to ensure large catches. The most successful fishermen in the area gross figures in excess of $10,000 annually.

Fishing has been described as an industry which does not require much government capital expenditure and this is to a large extent correct. With the completion of the bitumen road to Carnarvon, however, improved marketing of the district's fish became possible. Fast heavy transport was able to reach the metropolitan area with the minimum of delay from the flooding and from the mechanical breakdowns usually experienced with non-sealed roads, and the operating and maintenance costs of the vehicles were also reduced. Thus the marketing side of the operation became much more efficient.

Apart from road transport, the State Shipping Service is being used more extensively now as an alternative means of transport to get the catch to the metropolitan area. The mother ships operating with the fleets in the Exmouth Gulf area rendezvous at sea with southbound vessels of the State Shipping Service and tranship their cargoes for carriage to Perth. Since this is welcome backloading the freight charges are low and it can be said that transport costs, either by sea or by road, are certainly not a limiting factor to the expansion of the industry.

A processing works was established in Denham and this takes a large proportion of the catch from the Shark Bay fishermen. Most of the catch is packaged into 35 lb. packs for the use of shipping companies, hotels and restaurants and some is exported to the eastern states in 5 lb. filleted whiting packs. The attraction of these packages has been the freshness of the fish which are processed immediately upon entering the plant and distributed to the Perth retailers within four days or less of being caught. The private investment of $200,000 in processing plant and refrigerated transport has helped to stabilize what would otherwise have been a somewhat precarious industry, while government investment on the improved road enabled the product to be transported quickly to consumers.

The future of this segment of the region's fishing industry seems to be sound enough. Improved packaging to cater for a wider class of consumer should ensure increased demand for the area's products, particularly with an expanding population in the south-western corner of the state, providing costs can be kept within reasonable limits. The expansion of factories to process other fishing products in the area, which is mentioned below, is also adding to general development and contributing to overall economies of operation. For instance, the construction of a new freezer factory for prawns by Planet Fisheries at Shark Bay is expected to provide adequate electricity for other enterprises as well.

4. PEARLING

The history of pearling in Northwestern Australia has already been described. In its early days the industry extended along most of the coastline from Shark Bay to Derby. In studying its development over time, three distinct phases are apparent. The industry was first established to fish for pearls; pearl shell was secondary. In many cases the beds were fished out and eventually the industry receded along the coastline until now Broome is the only centre of any importance. With the depletion of many of the beds, pearls became secondary to pearl shell which grew considerably in importance until the late 1920's and then declined also, though for different reasons. The third and more recent development is pearl culture, which is mentioned in more detail below. Some pearling and pearl shell gathering still remains. Table 3 outlines the post-war course of pearling and its decline is quite evident. In the last five years the number of men employed has dropped to almost one-third, the number of boats to less than one-half and the production of pearl shell to one-fifth.

Returns from natural pearls vary enormously. As with pearl shell, the price of pearls is heavily dependent on world prices which are controlled by international cartels in Europe. The peak post-war year was 1958 when pearls realized £20,869. 1960 returns amounted to £11,710, but the average return per annum over the post-war period, would not exceed £6,000.

The pearl shell found in Australian waters is of a high grade and can compete more than favourably on world markets, given a controlled supply. With the entry into Australian territorial waters of pearling fleets from other nations, particularly Japan, there was an overproduction of pearl shell with a consequent depressing effect on the world prices.

Pearling technique and equipment have improved beyond recognition over the past 70 years. Modern luggers are motor powered and equipped with powered air pumps for the divers. Likewise living conditions aboard the luggers have improved immeasurably. One thing, however, has not changed. Asiatic labour is still used for the actual task of diving. Generally speaking there is no white labour offering for diving and the pearler has the choice between indentured Asiatic divers and aborigines. They generally prefer the Asiatics because they are skilled in the art from long training, and they are capable of greater individual production figures. This demand for Asiatic divers has led to the introduction of a system of indenture under which necessary Asian labour is permitted to enter Australia for a period of two years. The divers are indentured to master pearlers who are responsible for their maintenance, conduct and transport to and from their homeland over the two-year period. Payment of the divers is usually by means of a basic wage plus bonuses on pearl shell recovered.

The mother-of-pearl is much sought after for inlay work, jewellery and ornaments because of its distinctive lustre, and it is particularly favoured for button-making because of its strength and resistance to boiling. Since the mid 1950's, however, the demand for shell for most purposes has fallen off, particularly under the pressure of competition from plastic substitutes which are steadily improving in quality. Pearl shell prices have fluctuated and stocks have built up, compelling local pearlers to limit their takes severely at times. An international sales promotion campaign has not sufficed to revive the industry and pearl shell gathering is now at a low ebb in Broome.

In past years the United States was the major buyer of Australian shell, but since 1958-59 Germany has taken more than half of the quantity exported and has paid higher prices than American interests. Other purchasers include Italy and the United Kingdom. The shell is finally processed by the button industries and jewellery manufacturers of the United States and Europe, the cutlers of Sheffield, and by craftsmen throughout the world, who ornament their products with inlay work.

To take its place another segment of the pearling industry has grown up in the region. Pearl culture, established in 1956 by Brown and Dureau in conjunction with the American firm of Gerdan and a Japanese pearl farmer, Hiro Awaki, is now flourishing. There are now three companies growing cultured pearls in northern waters : Alf Morgan and Son at Exmouth Gulf, Dean Brown and Son at Cape Leveque, and W.A. Pearls Pty. Ltd. at Kuri Bay. In all there are 15 farms operating in Western Australia, the Northern Territory and Queensland, mostly joint Australian-Japanese ventures. The Western Australian farms are managed and controlled by local interests. The Kuri Bay enterprise markets its pearls through the Japanese company of Nippo Pearls of Tokyo which contributed half the cost of the equipment at Kuri Bay.

Natural pearls are produced when the oyster secretes nacre, the substance with which it lines its shell, around some irritant which has become lodged in its flesh. A cultured pearl results when a living oyster covers with nacre a shell bead deliberately inserted into its body, wrapped in a piece of oyster mantle tissue. The live oysters for Kuri Bay are gathered at Broome and sent north and the gathering of the shells has proved profitable for Broome's remaining eight pearlers. For the shell, which is of good quality, they receive approximately $2,000 a ton, which is equal to the price of best quality shell on the world market. It is estimated that the Kuri Bay industry is currently contributing annually about $110,000 to the Broome luggers.

Although the culture principle is simple, great skill is needed to insert the bead in a part where it will form a perfect pearl without killing the oyster. Continuous attention is then necessary for a number of years to keep the oyster under conditions which will allow it to grow satisfactorily to produce a marketable pearl. The farm requires a precise combination of water conditions, temperature, food content, freedom from parasites, suitable current movements, and shelter from storms.

At Kuri Bay the pearls are grown in baskets hanging from acres of rafts anchored in the shallow water of the bay. Each raft carries 1,000 pairs of shells in 100 baskets. Two sorts of pearl are grown : the round pearl which is known by everyone, and the half pearl which is not so well-known in Australia. The half pearl grows as a dome on the inside of the shell where the mother-of-pearl is laid down. Production of pearls is now about one ton per year, compared with a total Japanese production of about 50 tons. The pearls grown in northern waters come to maturity in about two years, one-half of the time taken in Japanese farms.

The Western Australian cultured pearls have proved to be of exceptional size and beauty and some have been valued at over $2,000 each. The demand for these pearls is assured and the industry has a bright future. Current Australian production is now worth over $3 million annually.

5. CRUSTACEANS AND SHELLFISH

This form of fishing has been introduced relatively recently to the region and should be thought of in terms of future development rather than past production. Four basic species have been fished commercially in the region in the last decade : crayfish, crabs, prawns and oysters.

First caught in 1952, crayfish in the region yielded 19,380 lbs. in 1956. 1961 witnessed a peak production of 294,000 lbs. and following this large catch, a rapid decline set in until now there is no recorded take of crayfish in the area at all. Crabs and oysters have both been caught in the area on occasions, but it has apparently not been worth anyone's while to fish for them on a large-scale commercial basis, despite reports that they exist in substantial quantities.

Prawns are prolific in the Carnarvon area. The varieties caught, the king, and tiger prawns, are large and palatable. The first company to attempt commercial prawn fishing was based on Carnarvon. Operations were commenced in May 1960 by the Australian Pearling Co. Ltd., using three trawlers, two of which were converted luggers. The company was backed by eastern states and overseas capital but the venture was not financially successful for a number of reasons. As was too often the case in this region in the past, company management was based in Perth and operations lacked on-the-spot direction and financial control by company executives. Weather conditions in the particular season were adverse and the trawlers did not get out often enough. The company invested about £100,000 in the venture, including a six-ton refrigerated International truck to transport the prawns to Perth.

Several large companies are currently fishing for prawns in the Exmouth Gulf-Shark Bay area which is rapidly increasing in importance. Ross Fisheries (Aust.) Pty. Ltd., the largest company currently operating on the Western Australian coast, has plans to extend its activities considerably. Already the 272 ton *Ross Endeavour* is acting as base ship for five trawlers. The Ross Group of Britain became established in the region in 1960 when it took over the local firm of International Fisheries. The company hopes to replace the crayboats currently used with a fleet of locally designed 45 foot prawning trawlers capable of trawling to 90 fathoms as against the 45 fathoms limit of most local boats. It has already explored the northern coast as far as Wyndham where it carried out two surveys in Cambridge Gulf for new prawning grounds and it plans to establish a fisheries training school to teach local fishermen new techniques. The three-year development plan of the company involves the expenditure of approximately one million dollars on equipment and evaluation of the fisheries.

M. G. Kailis (Gulf Fisheries) Pty. Ltd., operates a shore based prawn processing works at Exmouth Gulf and Ross Fisheries operates a floating factory ship at Exmouth Gulf. Wm. Anglis, Australia, have taken over North-West Whaling and Planet Fisheries, two other local fishing ventures which were active in northern waters. Planet Fisheries Ltd., a wholly owned subsidiary of Engineer and Marine Services Pty. Ltd., intends to expand its prawning activities considerably in the near future.

The prawn fishery is proving to be a sound enterprise and results in recent years have been encouraging. High prices are being offered for prawns caught in the Shark Bay and Exmouth Gulf areas and the demand for them is keen. For the last two seasons more than one and a half million lb. of prawns have been caught of the king, tiger and banana variety measuring up to eight and nine inches in length. Frozen prawns bring 95c. per lb. on the Japanese market but processing and shipping costs in the remote northern areas are high. Nevertheless the industry is currently earning about $2 million annually in export income.

6. Off-shore Fishery Development

Any development of fisheries in northern waters must be based upon some form of on-the-spot processing followed by export to other areas, since the isolation and lack of population have meant that there is no local market to absorb the catch. This is the reason why commercial development of the region's fish resources has, except in one or two instances, been slow. Although a great deal of research and investigation is needed in order to establish the location, types, quantities and habits of fish in northern waters, it is known that paucity of resources has not been a limiting factor.

The species which are most common and abundant around the Broome area northwards, where small vessels find ideal anchorages, are yellowfin tuna, northern bluefin tuna, spanish mackerel (both narrow and broad barred), and north-west salmon. Oysters also abound but they are quite small with hard shells and do not offer commercial prospects. There are also great numbers of edible green turtle. Small surface fishes suitable for conversion to fish meal also abound in the area.

Japanese tuna fleets have visited the area each year and this has demonstrated to local fishermen that these fish have commercial prospects. The Japanese are taking big quantities of tuna (40,000 to 50,000 tons) each year between 100 and 200 miles off the west coast and have fished tuna along the Continental Shelf about 200 miles west of Carnarvon and Broome. Apart from the Japanese, Russian ships have been fishing off the north-west coast and West German companies are interested. Because of the long haul involved, these fleets would have to operate with large vessels, some of which are freezer-trawlers displacing 10,000 tons and capable of remaining at sea for three months at a time. Russian plans are to build vessels of 40,000 tons capable of trawling at great depths. These trends may set the pattern for the future development of the region's fisheries. There is not much place now for the single operator who is giving way to the large companies with fleets of all-weather ships, expensive gear and highly trained personnel.

Ross Fisheries has plans to exploit the tuna fishery in northern waters by 1967 with a $300,000 tuna boat of about 300 tons. Freezing and processing works will be established at one of the northern ports. Preliminary research has been undertaken and already quantities of tuna have been caught using the poling method. Next season the company plans to experiment with purse-seining in the tuna fishery. Other large international companies are interested in the fisheries of the north and inquiries have been received by the Fisheries Department from Britain, the Netherlands, Scandinavia, the United States of America, Peru and Japan. These companies have discussed tuna fishing, the processing of 'trash' fish into meal and fertilizers, and the extension of the present prawn fisheries.

The development of the tuna fishery with land-based fishing enterprises, which will allow smaller vessels to make many more trips than their larger rivals, should give these companies an advantage over those from other countries, provided they can be assured of a stable local cannery and cold stores, and provided they have adequate port facilities for direct overseas shipment. The main tuna market would be the United States for frozen or canned exports. Tuna prices have trebled in the international market in the past five years and future demand is expected to remain firm at up to $500 a ton.

Much oceanographic study needs to be done in this area; research is one aspect of the northern fishing industry which has lagged. The state government is, however, soon to begin a long range research programme which will cost $90,000 per year. It will be partly financed by contribution from the industry itself and will study fishing grounds up to 100 miles off-shore in waters around Carnarvon and further north. The 5 to 10 year programme will be mainly aimed at proving the extent of the tuna grounds which the Japanese fleets have been successfully exploiting off-shore.

7. Conclusions

The growth of the fishing industry in Northwestern Australia in the last half decade has been marked by diversity and change. Five years ago the most important segment of the industry was whaling; now it no longer exists. Five years ago the value of pearl shell gathered far exceeded that of pearls, either natural or cultured; now pearl shell sales are very low and cultured pearls are bringing in millions of dollars annually. Five years ago a quarter of a million lb. of crayfish was taken in the region; last year the figure was zero. Five years ago a total of 100 lb. of prawns was taken in the north; now the figure is about two million lb.

Table 5 gives an approximation of the results of these quantity variations converted into money terms. For the scale fish and shell fish figures average prices for each species were applied to the quantity figures. The consumer price index was used to adjust prices for years either side of the 1962 and 1963 base period. For whaling £800 per whale was used as an average in 1961. It will be appreciated that this is not a sophisticated calculation but it is, nevertheless, sufficient to provide a guide to the relative importance, in value terms, of the principal segments of the industry. The figures suggest that the industry is declining but the total is misleading. The cessation of whaling affected it considerably and the exclusion of the value of cultured pearls leaves an important segment of the industry out of account. The period of the last two or three years, and possibly the next year or two, should perhaps best be thought of as a transition stage while the industry as a whole is changing gear. Large-scale commercial operations can be expected to inject new vigour into northern fishing which will be reflected in much higher production values in the near future.

The change that has characterized the industry has not only been one of types of fishing but one, also, of techniques of fishing and methods of organization, particularly with the entry of large international enterprises into the field. Although the experience of the last decade is sufficient to indicate the danger of trying to predict developments, the current indications and the plans of the companies concerned suggest that this industry will grow considerably in the future.

One of the major problems of which the Fisheries Department is well aware, is to ensure that when new fisheries are found and developed, as in the case of prawns, for example, they are not exploited so rapidly as to exhaust them. Limitations upon the number of boats allowed to operate in specific areas for specific types of fishing, under closely controlled regulations, is one way of ensuring this. This has also been used as a means of guaranteeing the larger companies an adequate return upon the large capital investment they are prepared to make, though this, too, has to be administered carefully for obvious reasons in order to protect the smaller fishermen who have operated in the area in the past.

The new developments and the interest of other countries with much deep-sea fishing experience, in the potential of the state's northern waters, have brought with them an awareness of the need to rationalize fishing techniques and to increase the efficiency in the industry in all of its phases of operation. The proposed developments involve the establishment of processing factories in addition to those which have already been constructed in the last year or two, and the contribution this will make to manufacturing activity and general development in the north and to the generation of additional export income, though modest in relation to the size of the region, must not be underestimated.

Of fundamental importance in all of this is the urgent need for a greatly stepped-up programme of research, some of which will be undertaken by the private firms concerned, for their own interest and profit and for the general good, and some of which will be carried out by the state and commonwealth governments. Fortunately there are signs that this is now occurring and it is to be hoped that the government and private efforts in terms of money and equipment will be on a scale large enough to guarantee adequate results upon which to base future operations which, within the necessary limitation of prudent husbanding of fishery resources, will enable the full exploitation of the industry's potential.

BIBLIOGRAPHY

BANK OF NEW SOUTH WALES. *Bank of New South Wales Review*, no. 47. Sydney, 1961.

BARON HAY, G. K. 'Development of Northwestern Australia.' *Rural and Industries Bank 15th Annual Report*. Perth, 1961.

BOWEN, B. K. *The Shark Bay Fishery on Snapper Chrysophrys Unicolor*. Western Australian Fisheries Department report no. 1. Perth, 1961.

BROWNFIELD, E. J. 'The Pearlshell Industry in Western Australia.' *Western Australia Fisheries Department Monthly Service Bulletin*, vol. 11, no. 4. 1953.

CROWLEY, F. K. *Australia's Western Third*. London, 1960.

TABLE 1

FISHING LICENSES ISSUED

(i) Professional Fishermen, (ii) Fishing Boats, (iii) Value of Boats and Gear

		1960	1961	1962	1963	1964	1965
Shark Bay							
Fishermen	No.	45	49	57	46	56	51
Boats	No.	44	52	56	51	71	53
Value	£	41,100	36,295	44,160	64,486	59,565	73,890
Carnarvon							
Fishermen	No.	6	—	4	1	45	6
Boats	No.	3	—	—	1	2	3
Value	£	2,540	—	—	2,000	1,550	1,840
Broome							
Fishermen	No.	12	11	7	11	21	30
Boats	No.	1	2	3	4	6	3
Value	£	3,000	6,300	9,750	17,750	14,180	1,300
Port Hedland							
Fishermen	No.	7	8	4	14	10	9
Boats	No.	4	3	4	5	6	5
Value	£	2,700	910	1,804	4,780	1,960	2,330
Onslow							
Fishermen	No.	2	2	1	5	3	1
Boats	No.	2	1	1	5	3	3
Value	£	810	260	750	2,990	2,840	3,950
Regional total							
Fishermen	No.	72	70	73	77	135	97
Boats	No.	54	58	64	66	88	67

Source: Western Australia, Department of Fisheries and Fauna.

TABLE 2

SHARK BAY[1]

Fish Production by Species

('000)

Species	1950	1960	1961	1962	1963	1964	1965
River Kingfish	4.6	—	5.7	—	5.5	†	†
Sea Kingfish	—	1.6	3.0	11.0	4.9	†	†
Shark	6.6	18.2	.2	3.8	6.5	1.1	15.9
Mullett	184.6	284.7	332.7	356.7	418.2	433.3	313.3
Schnapper	241.8	1,539.3	1,616.0	1,287.0	1,319.7	348.7	249.2
Skipjack	10.2	7.4	12.4	8.7	9.0	†	†
Tailer	77.5	74.7	85.9	108.3	96.7	118.7	93.7
Whiting	220.9	382.4	450.3	417.1	430.5	389.6	333.0
Garfish	2.8	.8	.6	2.3	29.3	†	†
Groper	.2	1.0	---	—	.1	†	†
Yellow Fin Bream	45.9	55.2	56.1	52.1	38.5	43.5	43.5
Jewfish	4.9	1.1	1.0	.9	.8	2.0	—
Cod	2.0	6.8	15.2	10.6	18.0	†	†
Whitefish	—	1.4	4.4	1.9	—	†	†
Ruffs	—	—	.7	—	—	—	2.0
Spanish Mackerel	—	58.4	102.1	92.6	191.0	19.1	19.4
Tuna	—	.9	.2	.4	7.2	15.0	8.2
Turtle	—	38.7	54.2	48.5	214.5	—	88.6
Other fish	.1		15.8	10.1	23.3	49.4	53.3
Total	802	2,473	2,756	2,412	2,813	1,420	1,220

[1] Includes Carnarvon.

† Production not available separately, included in Other fish.

Source: Western Australia, Department of Fisheries and Fauna.

TABLE 3

PEARLING

Employment, Equipment and Production

Year	No. of men	No. of boats	Value of boats and equipment (£'000)	Shell production tons	Value of pearls and pearl shell[1] (£'000)
1950	216	25	69	352	166
1960	297	27	210	646	281
1961	225	24	113	358	160
1962	217	23	114	349	160
1963	174	21	116	242	113
1964	103	10	174	138	92
1965	107	11	182	160	130

[1] Does not include value of cultured pearls.

Source: Western Australia, Department of Fisheries and Fauna.

TABLE 4

SHELLFISH PRODUCTION

Year	Oysters	Crayfish	Prawns	Crabs
1960	759	57,037	4,208	—
1961	1,389	294,154	100	—
1962	279	220,592	383,182	6,614
1963	6,861	15,733	1,196,357	381
1964	235	8,556	1,951,014	1,803
1965	870	—	1,650,557	310

Source: Western Australia, Department of Fisheries and Fauna.

TABLE 5

GROSS VALUE OF FISHING PRODUCTION

(£'000)

Year	Scale fish for human Consumption[1]	Shellfish[1]	Pearls and pearl shell[2]	Whaling	Regional total
1950	10	—	166	310	486
1959	154	8	293	438	894
1960	132	8	282	352	774
1961	204	57	160	380	801
1962	181	85	160	428	854
1963	209	141	113	103	566
1964	105	217	92	—	414
1965	92	188	130	—	410

[1] Calculated at average prices for 1962 and 1963 and adjusted by Consumer Price Index, Perth, Food Group, supplied by Deputy Commonwealth Statistician, Western Australia.

[2] Excluding cultured pearls.

Source: See text and previous tables.

CHAPTER 6

AGRICULTURE

1. Past Development

The character of agricultural production in Northwestern Australia has, until recently, been determined mainly by the size of the local market and the distance from the main metropolitan centres. Within this general limitation, individual crops have largely followed the pattern known to be appropriate to local soils, climate and topography. One of the basic problems has been to overcome the seasonality and unreliability of the region's rainfall. Part of the solution has been found in irrigation, and the areas where agriculture has so far gained a foothold are those where the topography, soils and water resources are such that irrigation is feasible.

An examination of the climatic characteristics of the region and its soil types has so far suggested two broad areas suitable to agriculture : the Kimberley and the Carnarvon district. The former is now being developed and little can be said about the past since the industry is barely under way. The latter area, while also a relatively recent entry into the agricultural field, does at least provide statistics and experience going back for roughly three decades and the industry has now been established long enough for some observations to be made on the course of its past development.

The first consignment of bananas from the Carnarvon district was carried off in 1930 and since then the industry has grown markedly. It has had its ups and downs but since the World War the story has largely been one of steady and sometimes even rapid expansion, interrupted by cyclones and floods, and hampered by problems connected with the water supply.

Generally speaking, production in all fields has expanded and in the decade of the 1950's the total acreage producing beans, tomatoes, pumpkins and bananas increased by more than 60 per cent. The oldest established

industry, banana growing, declined somewhat in area under crop, although
recent higher yields per acre have resulted in an increase in both the
quantity and the gross value of production. The decline in area devoted
to bananas was more than made up by the increases recorded in the area
devoted to tomatoes, beans and pumpkins, and in respect of these products
significant increases were recorded in actual production. This is an indication
of the diversification which has been a characteristic of the more recent
development of the industry. The area also produces rock melons, cucumbers
and some citrus fruit. Production figures for recent years are given in
Table 1, but too much reliance must not be placed upon the acreage
figures since there is reason to believe that the reporting of acreages by
producers is not as accurate as it could be.

Carnarvon is 100 miles south of the Tropic of Capricorn and more
than 600 road miles from Perth and, because of the previous infrequent
and comparatively slow shipping service, one of the main problems in
the industry was that of disposing quickly and effectively of its produce,
all of which is perishable in varying degrees. Throughout the industry's
development this problem has gradually been overcome with steady
improvement in roads, with better vehicles and a more efficient transport
service, and with the use of refrigeration and of air services.

Another problem affecting the development of the industry in the past
has been the effective control of the waters of the Gascoyne River for
irrigation purposes. With an annual average rainfall in the district of only
9 inches, and with extreme unreliability – some yearly rains have been as
low as 2 inches – the problem of water conservation has always been acute.
Wells and bores are sometimes expensive to install and to run, and the
river has not been found suitable for the construction of a major dam
near Carnarvon. Experiments have been made with a clay barrier but
these cannot yet be said to have been successful. The water problem did
not loom large in the early stages of the industry's development but since
the large expansion of the 1950's the problem of ensuring adequate water
supplies has assumed major importance.

As it has developed, the industry has absorbed greater numbers into
its workforce. In the Carnarvon Municipality and the Gascoyne-Minilya
Shire, employment in agriculture and mixed farming increased from 155
to 335 persons between the censuses of 1947 and 1961, and the expansion
of the industry is having an impact upon the pattern of production and
employment in the area. The increase in share-farming practices is noted
below. Of the total workforce engaged in primary industry alone, more
than one half were engaged in agriculture in 1961 and this proportion is
still rising.

2. CARNARVON AGRICULTURE – PRESENT CHARACTERISTICS

Climate, Soils and Water Resources

Because of the climatic factors mentioned earlier, the big problem in this district is to cope with the unreliability of the rainfall. This area is far enough south to come under the influence of the westerlies which bring mainly winter rains and dominate the weather in the south-west region of the state. The Carnarvon area is, however, just on the northern fringe of the area affected by the westerlies and the result is that the rainfall pattern is rather irregular. Because of this unreliability, irrigation is necessary to achieve independence of the rainfall for the growers, who must have an evenly distributed and dependable supply of water. The rain, itself, can be both a help and a hindrance. It can supplement irrigation supplies and thus help to reduce costs of irrigating but, on the other hand, it can, if coinciding with cold weather, adversely affect the crops and reduce financial returns. The average relative humidity of the area is high and during most summer afternoons high winds, known as 'southerly busters' sweep through the township and plantations. When the wind is not blowing, very high temperatures can be recorded.

Cyclones occasionally visit the area, sometimes causing great damage, and the district also experiences occasional droughts, floods and isolated frosts. Cyclones cannot be said to be a regular feature of the climate each year and in some years no cyclones have been experienced at all. They can, however, affect the Carnarvon area through precipitation in the upper reaches of the Gascoyne which ultimately brings floods to Carnarvon. The incidence of droughts and floods in Carnarvon is basically determined by what happens to water supplies from 100 to 300 miles inland and not by the incidence of precipitation in the Carnarvon area itself. Nevertheless the climate in Carnarvon is clearly one that is well suited to the growing of fruit and vegetables as an examination of the production figures and yields will show.

The soils on the south bank of the river are deep fertile loams and it is here that the majority of bananas are grown. On the north bank there is a variation from sandy loams to loamy sands, while in the gullies clay loams are usually found. The soils in the district are moderately supplied with phosphates and well supplied with potash, but the nitrogen content is only poor to medium.

In the past, settlers drew their entire water supply from the river sands which are approximately 12 to 20 feet deep. This is known as 'top water' and is of good quality. But because supplies of this water are dependent upon the flow of the river (they are replenished completely whenever the river flows) the position of the growers becomes precarious during drought periods. Further water supplies of good quality are found in the deeper sands lying below the clay layer which underlies the surface sands. This static 'second water', which has been found around 40 feet, differs from the top water in that it is not replenished completely each time the river flows and in fact its quantity seems to be decreasing steadily over time. This gives rise to a problem of water conservation which can be expected to become more and more acute as time goes on. Salinity is also a serious problem associated with the water supply. These problems are examined in Chapter 7.

Size and Type of Holding

There were roughly 1,500 acres cultivated for agricultural activities in 1964-65 in the Carnarvon area yielding a variety of products. The plantations themselves, varying from 10 to 300 acres in area,[1] mostly front on to the Gascoyne River and extend for a distance of approximately 12 miles from its mouth. Since the early 1950's when land sales boomed and land values rose, large areas have been opened for selection by the government and taken up. Also some of the larger freehold blocks have been sub-divided. It is virtually impossible to determine what would be the size of a representative holding and what types of crop would be grown thereon, since the variation in a relatively small total number of holdings is very great. Some planters concentrate solely on the production of bananas, others combine banana-growing with vegetables and other fruits, and yet others concentrate solely on vegetables.

Properties are freehold and land values would probably average around £150 per acre in 1965, although quoted prices of properties include all improvements and as these vary so much, it is very difficult to arrive at a valuation for land alone. Soils vary so much from property to property and are constantly changing due to the influence of floods in shifting large masses of sand and topsoil, that the position is further complicated. In addition, water endowments can vary radically between a property and the one adjoining, and this affects the purchase price.

Type of Crop and Technology

Bananas and beans are the main crops in the area. Cyclones in 1953, 1956 and 1961 have encouraged bean production as a form of insurance against the effects of the weather upon the banana crop, and the development of eastern states markets has reinforced this trend. The result is that the area under beans is now considerably larger than that under bananas. Generally speaking, beans and other crops are grown in conjunction with bananas during the winter season. The most important of the other crops are tomatoes and pumpkins, as shown in Table 1, although opinions seem to vary about what will be the important 'out of season' crops of the future.

[1]For an economic appraisal of the Carnarvon area – a report based upon a sample survey of irrigation properties in 1962-63, see: J. S. Nalson and M. L. Parker, *Irrigation on the Gascoyne River – An Economic Appraisal.*

Some idea of the variety of such production is given by the statistics in Table 2. Apart from the many types of fruit and vegetables mentioned in this table, the area produces or has produced lettuce, marrow, beetroot, cape gooseberries, cabbage, oranges, passion fruit, sweetcorn, bean seed, mandarins, peanuts, garlic, carrots, potatoes, olives, ochra, avocadoes, strawberries and grapes. Most of these latter mentioned items have, however, been produced only in small quantities so far and cannot be said to have reached a commercial scale of production.

From Tables 1 and 2 it will be seen that the character of production on the Carnarvon plantations is steadily changing in the direction of diversification. Where bananas were without doubt the dominant crop a decade ago, beans have surpassed them in acreage in recent years, and the area devoted to pumpkins and tomatoes has likewise grown. Production of cucumbers, capsicums and melons has also expanded considerably. On the other hand banana acreages are low compared with 10 years ago.

Bananas are grown under irrigation and this is normally done by flooding. The area is levelled and the bays from 8 to 18 feet in width and 2 chains in length are formed. Water is brought from a cement irrigation channel into each bay by means of cement spoon drains, though on some properties wasteful earth channels still exist. Generally, on the heavier soils of the south bank, watering to a depth of four inches is carried out at least once a week in summer and twice every three weeks in winter, depending upon rainfall. On the lighter northern soils watering is twice weekly in summer and once weekly in winter.

Water economy is important since the misuse of water resources reflects itself in increased costs to the grower through higher pumping costs per acre. Water shortage can also raise acute problems in this respect. When the water level is low the pumping unit operates below maximum efficiency and this means higher operating costs. It also takes much more of the grower's time in attending to his pumping equipment and tends to increase the salinity of the water, the safe maximum of which, for bananas and beans, is considered to be 60 grains of sodium chloride per gallon. Water is generally obtained from wells or bores and pumped out by diesel-driven centrifugal pumps of 2 inches to 4 inches outlet diameter, whence it is taken by pipeline to a spill pool from which run the cement drains. On some properties large irrigation tanks of up to 150,000 gallons capacity have been erected to build up a large head of pressure at times when only a small flow can be pumped.

The seven month period from August to March is the main planting season and planting material is usually obtained from old patches which are being abandoned. It seems to matter little, in terms of the final result, what type of planting material is used (e.g. butts, bits or small suckers) provided it comes from good stock. Early planting yields the best production results but they come at a time when fruit is plentiful and prices keen. Planting in the hotter months is more of a gamble but the stakes are higher.

Because of the high winds, mentioned earlier, wind-breaks are a common feature of banana growing in the Carnarvon district, but these have their disadvantages and experiments are still continuing at the Research Station to determine the best variety of tree to use and the best method of siting the breaks.

Capital and Labour

Generally speaking, the industry is not one demanding high capital outlay. Equipment needed by the grower will include a pumping unit, fixed cement channels or fibrolite piping, water storage reservoirs (ideally), a tractor (perhaps), and a rotary hoe. A runabout or utility is desirable and, of course, a packing shed and a home to live in. Capital equipment of this sort may cost anything from $7,000 for working a small property to $80,000 or $100,000 for a larger plantation.

The industry is not very amenable to mechanical production processes and is, in fact, labour intensive. For this reason the plantations are generally small and capable of being handled by one man assisted by the members of his family in times of pressure, such as at picking and planting time. On the larger plantations the share-farming technique is employed and some growers have several share-farmers working parts of their property usually on vegetables rather than bananas. Arrangements vary but usually the returns are split on a 50-50 basis between the share-farmer who provides the labour and skill, and the owner who provides the land and the capital equipment. The share-farmers are mostly Southern Europeans, some of them newly arrived in the country, and the larger planters are mostly Southern Europeans too or descended from that stock. In all, probably more than half of the cropped area in Carnarvon is share-cropped. Because most plantations are family affairs and because of the share-farming practices, the number of wage-earners in the industry is quite small and no problem of labour availability really exists.

Costs and Returns

Current production costs consist of wage payments, fuel costs (for tractor, runabout, pumping and lighting units), weed, pest and disease control (fungicides and fumigants), fertilizers, packing cases, rates and taxes, transport costs, crop insurance, and the occasional charges for capital installations damaged by cyclones. These production costs are considerably higher than those in New South Wales which is the main competing production area in Australia. (The Carnarvon district produces more than one-half of the requirements of bananas for the Perth metropolitan area, the remainder coming mainly from New South Wales, and occasionally from Queensland.) The need to irrigate is the main factor responsible for the discrepancy in production costs but the cost differential in respect of transport is usually sufficient to wipe out this disadvantage.

An attempt has been made, in the Nalson and Parker report, to calculate the net return to banana production on two properties from which details of production and marketing costs were obtained. Assuming production of 502 cases per acre it was estimated that the net returns on the two properties, after allowing for family or hired labour, all other cash costs, and depreciation and operator's labour, was $1,126 in one instance and a loss of $1,048 in the other. The report stresses the decline in farm incomes generally that has occurred in recent years.

But the difficulties of trying to describe the operation in these terms become immediately apparent when one realizes that gross returns have, at times, been as high as $27.10 per case, that yields as high as 1,000 cases per acre have been obtained on good properties, that net returns as high as $4,000 per acre have been realized, and that land acquisition can vary from $150 to $700 per acre, depending upon the numerous factors mentioned above. The position is further complicated by the fact that banana growers also plant other crops. One such case is that of a grower who netted $4,600 from two-thirds of an acre of tomatoes which just hit the Perth market at the right moment.

What one can say is that providing growing conditions are ideal, providing cyclones, floods or other natural calamities are not experienced, and providing there are few enough acres planted to avoid over-production in any line, a great deal of money can be made in a very short time in this area. With such luck capital costs could be recouped in four or five years and from then on the planter is ahead. But bad luck in the initial stage can cripple a planter financially for a long time. Basically, the operation is a gamble but the prize is tempting. Evidence of this is the fact that 80 per cent of the growers interviewed by Nalson and Parker in 1962 indicated that if they had more water they would grow bananas or increase their present area of bananas. Overproduction of vegetables and the extension of the growing season, which renders the growers liable to competition from other areas, has tended to bring banana growing back into favour in recent years.

Production and Yields Per Acre

Banana production has varied considerably over the last 10 years from a peak of 108,000 bushels in 1959-60 to a low of 7,600 bushels in 1960-61, when the crops were devastated by a cyclone, and then rapidly to a new peak of 145,000 bushels in 1964-65. The gross value of production has likewise varied, from a peak of £345,000 in 1954-55 to a low of £18,000 in 1960-61, to a new high of £475,000 in 1964-65, and is determined as much by the outside forces affecting Perth prices as by the Carnarvon production figures.

Average yields per acre from the Carnarvon crops are higher than in New South Wales or Queensland and, indeed, are much higher than in most of the truly tropical areas where most of the world's bananas are grown. In Central America and West Africa 10 tons is regarded as a good yield. In the Canaries 19 tons has been obtained. In Carnarvon a yield of over 35 tons was obtained in nine months from one patch. Average yields for the whole district, which are at present below 15 tons, have increased considerably in the last 10 years.

Weeds can run riot and completely ruin a patch if the grower lets them get away to a good start. The soft and flabby-rooted bananas are no match for the vigorous competition of the weeds. Probably the most important pest is the eel-worm, which attacks the root and sometimes penetrates into the underground stem, but an effective water miscible fumigant has been developed. The absence of pests and diseases is no doubt an important factor contributing to the high yields obtainable in this district. Diseases such as banana blight or wilt, sigatoka disease, blood sickness and anthracnose are widespread among the major banana producing areas of the world, and some of them are found in Queensland and New South Wales, but so far Carnarvon has remained free. As far as these diseases are concerned the district is in the fortunate position of being far removed from any other centre of banana production and of having a strict policing of quarantine measures designed to prevent infestation. The result is that there is no serious disease problem on the Carnarvon plantations.

Transport and Marketing

The road from Perth to Carnarvon has been sealed since 1961. This has enabled the build-up of a fast efficient road transport service from grower to market and is undoubtedly an important factor making it possible to market Carnarvon bananas in Perth at prices which can generally compete with those offered for eastern states' produce. In the early stages of the industry's growth its produce was sent by a road-rail combination and this had the disadvantage of being slow and hard on the bananas and costly to the grower because of the extra handling required. Now, however, fast diesel trucks specially designed for the trade can carry the produce straight to the Perth metropolitan market in little more than 20 hours.

The service is operated by a subsidiary of one of the several large stock firms in the state. The trucks have fluted metal sides for maximum ventilation, and are capable of carrying 18 to 20 tons of produce. Prime movers are of 150 b.h.p. and the structure is of the semi-trailer type. Despite the fact that some growers would argue for the establishment of a second competing transport company, there is a lot to be said for the whole resources of the area being directed at present towards one company which is then in a position to establish maintenance installations which will guarantee a reliable service. If the industry shows further rapid growth the establishment of a competing transport company would no doubt remove any monopoly elements which may exist in the present arrangement.

Markets, as mentioned previously, lie mainly in Perth, but partly in the eastern states. All of the banana crop is disposed of in Perth – in fact local banana production cannot yet hope to satiate the local demand – and there is no reason to expect a substantial export trade in this fruit to grow up in the near future. On the other hand some of the supporting crops find a ready market in the eastern states. Substantial quantities of beans are sold in Adelaide – where they can be marketed in the off-season – and in 1960 Geraldton absorbed nearly 500 bags. Also, 1960 saw the export of cucumbers to Adelaide for the first time. An expanding market in Melbourne, mainly for beans, was explored recently but results were not encouraging. It may be assumed, also, that an increasing market for Carnarvon produce will open up in the north as the Pilbara mining developments take shape and as the roads improve.

Bad packaging is still one of the worries on the freighting side of the industry and improvements will be needed if produce is to be adequately protected and efficiently transported. It is alleged that the absence of any grading provisions for the local market is also a factor which can influence considerably the reception of Carnarvon produce on interstate markets, since poorer grade vegetables can be purchased in Perth and then sent on to the eastern states buyers as Carnarvon produce. Over-production in some lines and lack of unity among growers are other factors affecting stability in the industry and this, in turn, places limitations upon the forward planning of transport and marketing facilities.

3. CARNARVON AGRICULTURE – FUTURE PROSPECTS

Undoubtedly under ideal conditions banana growing in Carnarvon, and its associated off-season vegetable growing, can offer the opportunity for a quick return on capital (maybe within four or five years). It is really the climate and the associated physical features of the Carnarvon hinterland that provide the main obstacles to rapid physical development. Unreliability of rainfall and the topography of the area give rise to a water problem in that there is often not enough water, and even when there is the country is not suitable for dam construction to conserve it. On the occasions when nature jumps the other way to provide torrential downpours or cyclonic conditions inland there is no way of preventing floods or severe wind damage.

Productivity in bananas has increased encouragingly in the past year or two and this may be put down to several factors, chief among which would be the control of the eel-worm and better use of scarce water resources and fertilizers. Apart from gains in physical productivity, there is the possibility of lowered costs for the grower (for example, due to better use of more efficient capital equipment) and of higher prices to the grower resulting from better packaging and waxing and better and speedier transport.

There is no general shortage of capital except on some of the smaller, poorer properties since this is not a capital-intensive industry, and no shortage of labour due to the share-farming technique presently employed. A labour force may be required in the long term to cope with the seasonal activities such as picking and packaging, and extra capital or insurance may be required to cope with emergencies. Undoubtedly the opportunity to insure the crop will take some of the risk element out of agricultural activity in the area and make the operations more attractive to prospective growers.

A consideration of these latter factors together might lead one to conclude that the potential of the area is great and that a considerable degree of expansion can be expected. There are, however, certain other factors which constitute severe limitations to the future possibilities of the area.

Water is undoubtedly the greatest physical problem confronting the industry, as has already been explained, and under present circumstances the only solution seems to be to adopt some system of water conservation. Future proposals, as mentioned, provide for tapping the sands further upstream. Further in the future lies the possibility of damming the Gascoyne some distance – perhaps 100 miles – from the mouth of the river. This would be costly, but provided the industry could find the markets to support expansion it may well be the only feasible long-term solution to the problem of water shortage.

Some recent proposals are contained in a report prepared for the government of Western Australia by a firm of consultants in 1961.[2] Briefly, the report recommended that as well as instituting a system of water rationing, supported by charges for water supplied, the government should construct a series of bores or wells along the river banks, equipped with suitable pumping machinery and should study the possibility of using movable barrages to trap the water at periods of low or zero flow. The possibility of a major storage at Kennedy Range was seen as a development which could occur considerably later.

The productivity of the area is so great under ideal conditions, and markets within the state are so limited within the season in which Carnarvon possesses an advantage over metropolitan market gardeners, that there is the ever-present danger of overproduction in any one particular line. Often remunerative prices will depend upon getting the Carnarvon produce to market at a time when metropolitan produce is not available. A slight change in the season can affect this timing and remove the expected profit margin.

[2]R. M. Scott and H. G. Furphy, *Report for the Government of Western Australia – Gascoyne River.*

So far the demand for Carnarvon produce has come mainly from the Perth metropolitan area, and if this pattern continues the economic limit to Carnarvon production will be set by population growth in this area. Extension of the growing season by Carnarvon growers has already brought them into severe competition with growers in areas around the city and has removed the 'out-of-season' advantage they had, thus depressing prices. Nalson and Parker estimate that on the most favourable assumptions of Western Australian population increase and consumption per head and banana yields per acre, some 1,200 to 1,500 acres of bananas could be needed by 1975. This would represent an increase in area of roughly 200 per cent over 10 years, which is quite substantial. The area under vegetables might be expected to expand by around 100 per cent in the same period. Altogether, this would amount to a total increase, in 10 years, of about 150 per cent. In the 10 year period, 1953 to 1963, the increase was 140 per cent. For expansion of this magnitude to take place the position with respect to water supplies would have to be improved considerably.

What market prospects are there for expansion beyond this point? First, further markets in the eastern states and overseas could be exploited for products which will stand long-distance transport, but present transport and marketing arrangements would have to be improved for this to become possible. Second, it may be feasible at a later stage to set up processing plants for canning fruit and fruit juices and for canning or snap-freezing certain vegetables, possibly even in conjunction with the fishing industry. This would modify the seasonality aspect of the industry's production, give it a measure of stability and create a product of greater economic density. Thus larger markets may be opened up for the growers in the Carnarvon area.

In both cases, however, prospects do not seem bright. While the Adelaide market is still a favourable one and can be expected to grow as population grows, attempts to enter the Melbourne market have not yet met with success. Carnarvon growers may also have to face increasing competition in eastern states markets from other 'out-of-season' areas such as Alice Springs, for example. Possibilities of finding new export markets in South-East Asia are also remote since these areas already produce tropical fruits and vegetables and the export market is usually a demanding one in which consistent quality is of prime importance.

The question of fruit and vegetable processing also raises severe problems. Quality control is of paramount importance and only certain varieties are suitable for canning. Growers, providing they were able to meet these conditions, would have to be prepared to commit themselves on contract to supply certain quantities at pre-arranged prices and this would preclude them from taking advantage of more favourable prices for the fresh produce as the opportunity arose. Costs of local materials would be high, and with a limited Western Australian market producers would have to export interstate and possibly overseas. Since production of this nature has to be large-scale to operate economically, any new establishment would be under intense competition from already established producers in the eastern states now selling throughout Australia.

At times in the past the planters and growers of Carnarvon have been divided broadly into two groups – the small planters and the big ones. At other times they have been united in one single association. At present they are separated and the split was occasioned by proposals for conserving water, although the divergence of economic interests and practices and of social attitudes would seem to be more fundamental than just this. Marketing arrangements for the export of produce to other states and elsewhere are unsatisfactory while two different associations exist. Until this is ironed out it seems that effective exploitation of these markets will be severely hindered. Inspection of produce and proper grading for local markets is also virtually impossible while two separate factions exist. Finally, until the industry stabilizes from within, the growers cannot really expect wholehearted government support in plans for its long term development.

The Nalson and Parker report, which examines the problems of the Carnarvon irrigation area, concludes with certain policy recommendations based upon an assessment of the potentiality of the industry in relation to possible markets. After reviewing the major problems associated with irrigated agriculture in the area – water availability, overproduction, high production and marketing costs, grower disunity, climatic factors – the authors recommend an immediate policy of stabilization of the existing industry rather than one of further development.

To support this recommendation they propose that about 10 per cent of existing properties should be withdrawn from production by the government as they become available for purchase. At the same time more research should be undertaken on the hydrology of the area, for any future expansion must be based upon a better knowledge of the underground water potential and the potential for storing water further up the river. There is little doubt at the moment that this provides a major limitation to safe expansion. To remove another major obstacle to quality and marketing control, and even water control, they also recommend that a Carnarvon produce authority be established. This is an attempt to remove or modify grower disunity, which has been a major limiting factor. They recommend also that research into the growing of medium and long staple cotton at Carnarvon be commenced, and they see this as a long term project. Some very good yields have, in fact, been obtained at the Research Station. In view of the plans for cotton production on the Ord, which are discussed below, and the intense opposition these have already aroused in some quarters, this would not seem a feasible proposition at the moment, particularly since the state government has repeatedly suggested that Carnarvon irrigation development involving dam construction should, as in the case of the Ord dam, be a charge on commonwealth funds for northern development rather than solely on state funds. Finally, they recommend that if increase in population is a prime aim of development in the north, alternative sites for settlement on the Carnarvon pattern should be sought further north since it may be possible to establish these at a lower cost than would be incurred by providing extra water at Carnarvon and thus concentrating population in one centre.

In summary, the physical and climatic limitations in the Carnarvon area have only become so apparent since the opposing physical and climatic attractions have induced rapid development. The bigger Carnarvon grows the worse the problem becomes, and a workable solution to the problem of water shortage must be found if the industry is to progress much further. As regards the economic aspects of the industry, considerable future growth presupposes the solution of problems of costs, markets, and possible processing activities.

4. RICE AND FODDER CROPS AT CAMBALLIN

For some years now rice has been grown under irrigation at Camballin some 80 miles from Derby on the Fitzroy. Cultivation was first commenced in 1949 by Northern Developments Pty. Ltd. under the management of Mr Kim Durack.

The project is situated on the Liveringa plains and draws upon the resources of the Fitzroy River which delivers an immense volume of water in season and which is regarded as having a great potential for supplying water to irrigation projects of the Ord River type. Undoubtedly the water resources of this river system will eventually be harnessed to bring closer settlement to this tract of country, but this may lie well into the future. In the meantime irrigated agriculture is being carried on there on a modest scale.

Water was originally pumped from the Fitzroy into Uralla Creek, an anabranch of the Fitzroy, which is seven feet higher than the river and which runs past the Camballin area, and it was carried 17 miles downstream to a diversion dam situated adjacent to the rice growing area. In December 1961 a barrage dam across the Fitzroy at the point where it meets Uralla Creek was completed to allow the water to flow by gravity feed and thus eliminate the present necessity for pumping. Some 35 million gallons daily were formerly pumped into the creek.

Production Characteristics

The aim of the project has been to prove the suitability of the area for rice growing and so far the company can be said to have met with only limited success. Its dry season crops have given more consistent yields than its wet season crops, although experimentation with different varieties is continuing in an effort to improve the so far disappointing yields obtained from the wet season crops. Average yields from dry season crops have exceeded one ton and, in some cases, yields of one and a half tons to the acre have been obtained, though from limited areas.

The area itself has certain advantages over the Murrumbidgee Valley, Australia's major rice producing area, chief of which is the fact that it is capable of producing a good semi-long grain rice whereas only the soft short grain varieties come from the Murrumbidgee area. In this respect, however, it is worth noting that experiments are proceeding vigorously to develop a semi-long grain rice on the Murrumbidgee and initial results have been encouraging. Thus the older established industry is moving to meet the challenge. Its proximity to South-East Asia gives the region a certain geographical advantage, though to what extent will be determined ultimately by more intensive market research and also by the development of better transport and handling facilities.

Field crops which have been sown to date at Camballin include long and short grain rice, safflower, linseed, sudan grass and sorghum alum, but at present the operating company is concentrating on the production of long grained rice and sorghum alum, the latter to be used as a hay and a grazing crop. At the same time the Department of Agriculture is conducting research into correct fertiliser practice, time of planting for rice, depth of water for rice, possible rotation with rice, new variety testing, and pasture species establishments.

The type of sorghum grown at Camballin has proved suitable to the area as it will withstand flooding as well as long spells without water at the end of the dry season. If watering intervals are carefully regulated, hay quality is excellent and cuts of up to 8 tons per acre of green matter are possible. Intervals between cutting vary from 6 to 10 weeks depending on seasonal conditions and fertiliser applications.

Up to 59 sheep per acre were carried for short periods during the 1963 dry season. Liveringa flock was shorn in October and approximately 27,000 sheep were held on the irrigated sorghum areas until December when they were moved out onto the Pindan areas (scrub and spinifex with some grass) before the wet season started. The advantages of carrying stock on irrigation during the dry season are obvious. Sorghum is also sold to local stations for stock feed as well as for the feeding of live cattle during shipment to Robb's Jetty, near Fremantle.

Milling of the rice is carried out only in a limited way and the produce is exported mainly as brown rice to London and Asia. The brown rice is produced at the field mill at Camballin; as yet equipment is inadequate to produce white rice on a commercial basis. The export market does not, at this limited stage of development, present any great problems to the company and there exists a strong demand in London, Europe and the Far East.

One aspect of the Camballin development is significant from the viewpoint of land tenure in the Kimberley. Under the agreement with the state government, Northern Developments was eventually to take up four parcels of land, each of 5,000 acres. Rice was to be grown for a minimum period after which freehold of the land would be granted to the company. One such parcel has already passed to the company. A similar provision applied to the land on which the company grew rice at Kununurra. This has introduced the concept of freehold for irrigation development in the Kimberley, the extension of which is seen in the provision for freehold on the Ord farms after a minimum period of leasehold tenure.

Problems of the Industry

Certain basic problems which have emerged in the early phases of development of rice growing at Camballin may be mentioned briefly.

First, there is an urgent need to control the floodwaters on the plain of the Fitzroy. The area is subject to large-scale flooding and considerable damage can be done by inundation in this region. In this respect it is not an ideal area for the establishment of large-scale experimentation of this sort. Control of flooding by the construction of levees is possible but the levees would have to be very long (up to 25 miles in length) and there is always the problem of their maintenance. Flood control at this site will thus be a costly undertaking, but if the area was to develop rapidly such expenditure could become economically justified.

Second, there is a need for more effective methods of vermin control. The main nuisance is from birds which cause considerable damage to the ripe crop, not from eating it but from alighting on the heads and breaking the delicate stalks. Experimentation is proceeding with methods of controlling this menace.

There is also the need to find a suitable type of rice from the viewpoint both of production and of marketing, for this question is by no means settled. The problem has two aspects: what can be grown and what can be sold. The second issue has logically to be tackled first, at least to the extent of finding out what restrictions on choice are imposed by the market. As mentioned earlier considerable disappointment has been experienced with wet season crops so far, although experimentation is continuing. The main varieties so far grown have been Zenith, Magnolia, Caloro and some Calrose, with the more recent introduction of HD19.

Future Prospects

Some of these problems will no doubt be solved in the future; others may prove more intractable. On the whole the future prospects do not seem encouraging if one considers this merely as a rice growing area in terms of the original conception. But if one looks forward to the use by the surrounding pastoralists of milling by-products and the association of stock running and stock feeding with this type of agriculture, the possibilities seem more favourable.

In this respect some notable successes have already been achieved. Cattle boats and the surrounding local stations demand fodder crops at certain times of the year and some fine crops of Sudan grass, oats and sorghum alum have already been sold from Camballin. Stock have also been run on the Camballin property. Sheep from adjoining Liveringa station have been pastured on the irrigation area and the results were most promising. In the dry conditions, when other stock were losing weight the Liveringa sheep were putting on condition and according to local sources they recorded the best lambing percentage in the district. As mentioned in Chapter 3 the contribution that irrigated agriculture can make, may have a rejuvenating effect upon the region's pastoral industries and may help to provide a breakthrough to a new phase of development in both the sheep and the cattle industries.

5. The Kimberley Research Station

Interest had long been centered upon the possibilities for agricultural production in the Ord River area when the Kimberley Research Station was established in 1945. Individuals had seen the possibilities of using this land in the north for intensive agriculture,[3] and one or two farmers had actually attempted to grow crops in the area. It was realized that an essential part of any long-term plan to test the agricultural potential of the area was a programme of controlled experiment as well as an intensive soil survey programme. Both were set in motion in the early forties.

The Kimberley Research Station (K.R.S.) was established following upon preliminary proposals to dam the Ord River. Land reconnaissance and soil surveys indicated that there was an area of between 100,000 and 200,000 acres that had irrigation potential, and K.R.S. was set up as the joint responsibility of the State Department of Agriculture and the Commonwealth Scientific and Industrial Research Organization. The station itself is 2,000 acres in area and is situated on the Ord near Ivanhoe station some 60 road miles from Wyndham.

The immediate objectives of the research programme were to determine the suitability of the soils for irrigation and to experiment with crop cultivation and pest control in order to determine the physical potential of the area for agricultural development. In the early stages experience was gained with a wide range of crops on the heavy-textured Kununurra clay soils of the K.R.S. and subsequently in 1952 the K.R.S. Policy Committee decided that efforts should be concentrated on those cash crops, particularly sugar-cane and rice, which showed the most promise of forming a basis for agricultural settlement in the area.

Sugar-cane is an easy crop to grow in the area and is particularly free from trouble with pests. Yields of at least 35 tons to the acre, based on

[3]See for example, L. J. H. Teakle, 'The Kimberley Project'.

expected yields of 100 to 120 tons of cane for a three year crop, have
been forecast and results from experiments have produced returns better
than those from the best areas in Queensland. The existence of international agreements on sugar exports, however, and the large capitalization
required makes the production of sugar in the Kimberley doubtful.

Rice had already been established at Camballin and many considered
that the prospects for its development in the East Kimberley were bright.
Under experimental conditions at K.R.S., yields of over two tons to the
acre have been obtained, and under commercial conditions at Camballin
one and a half tons to the acres have been harvested, though the average
is considerably lower than this. The area, like that at Camballin, has the
advantage over the Murrumbidgee valley that it can produce a high-grade
semi-long grain rice which is more acceptable in Asiatic markets than the
soft short grain varieties of the Murrumbidgee area. So far, however, the
results of rice growing have been disappointing, to say the least.

Safflower has been grown successfully at K.R.S. and finds a ready
market as a replacement for linseed oil. It is a member of the thistle
family and has been grown in the East from ancient times, where it was
raised both for oilseed production and for a yellow dye obtained from the
flower. This is used in paint and chemical manufacture and a valuable
by-product is the protein-cake which can be used for stock feed providing
the grain is milled in the area.

Cotton is another crop which seemed to have potentialities. However
the native hibiscus species in the area harbour many pests which readily
attack the cotton plant and this originally proved a major problem.
Nevertheless, because of the high yields and high money return, this was
thought to be the most lucrative of all the crops grown. It also produces
a valuable protein by-product. By the time the first five farmers at the
Ord were ready to commence production it had been decided that cotton
offered the best prospects of all the crops grown under experimental
conditions and since then cotton has been the main crop. The search still
continues for a second crop and those which are favoured most at present
are grain sorghum and wheat.

With an expected commercial yield of three tons per acre, based upon
experimental yields of 8,000 lbs. per acre, grain sorghum is considered
a likely cash crop for the area. It could be grown either as a supplementary
crop to cotton, and in rotation with it, or on the cotton farms in flat areas
unsuitable for cotton production or as a monoculture on farms with no
land suitable for cotton.

Wheat is another crop which is considered to have a potential roughly
equal to that of grain sorghum and to have the same possibilities for
cultivation. Irrigation varieties have given encouraging results at the
Research Station.

Experimentation is still proceeding in many forms at K.R.S. and the
activities of the research staff are by no means confined merely to growing

those crops mentioned above. However it may be said that the station has now filled its original prime functions, which were to establish the suitability of the soils for irrigation and to develop suitable crops for cultivation in the area. The next stage, and one that is currently being undertaken on the farms, is to establish commercial production of these crops. At this point it should be noted that the scientists at K.R.S. have not always been concerned with examining the economic feasibility of these crops. Success in growing them under control conditions at the Research Station and even success in growing them under commercial conditions does not guarantee success in marketing them at competitive prices. This aspect of the industry is examined below.

6. THE ORD RIVER PROJECT

The main aim of the Ord River Project is to promote closer settlement in the East Kimberley by developing intensive agriculture in the area.

The engineering features of the scheme are more fully described in Chapter 7. Briefly, they involved constructing a main dam on the Ord, with a diversion dam some 30 miles downstream to feed an irrigation area. The diversion dam was to be constructed first to service an area of some 30,000 acres. In a way this would serve as a pilot scheme and should it be successful the construction of the main dam would follow and a total of 175,000 acres would eventually be irrigated. The diversion dam was completed in 1963, and officially opened by the Prime Minister.

By 1962 sufficient progress had been made on the provision of irrigation channels and preparation of the land for applications to be called from farmers wishing to take up properties for cotton farming. Five farms were allotted and by 1963 the first farmers, who had come from different parts of Australia, were busily preparing their properties for planting. In 1964 they harvested their first crops. Twenty farms were in operation by 1965 and in 1966 the number had grown to 31. In three short years technology improved rapidly and so did yields and returns until at present the future of the area as a major cotton producer seems bright.

Climate and Soils[4]

The area has a warm, dry winter and a hot, wet summer season. Temperatures generally exceed 70°F during winter and remain around 90°F during summer and the area is completely frost free. The mean annual rainfall is 30 inches, most of it falling between early December and mid-March, but the duration of the wet season and the quantity of rainfall and its distribution within the season are very variable. The high intensity of some falls of rain and the rainfall distribution give rise to cultivation and drainage problems which are accentuated by the nature of the soil.

[4]J. J. Basinski, *Cotton Growing in Australia*.

The land suitable for irrigation consists of nearly flat alluvial plains with a uniform cover of heavy cracking black soil described as Kununurra clay, the permeability of which is low. The plains are not prone to river inundation though they are subject to sporadic flooding from heavy rains and, to a lesser degree, from run-on from adjacent higher land. When dry the Kununurra clay becomes hard and difficult to work and when wet it is plastic and sticky. Fertiliser application is essential for crop growth since this soil in its virgin state is low in nitrogen and phosphate.

Technology and Yields

Since 1958, when intensive cotton variety testing began at the Kimberley Research Station, over 100 varieties have been introduced from Africa, Argentine, India, Pakistan, Queensland, U.S.A. and U.S.S.R. The American bred varieties, Rex and Deltapine, have been used exclusively by commercial farmers, with Rex by far the most popular because of its resistance to disease and its potentiality for high average yields. While the fibre quality of Rex is satisfactory for spinning it is inferior in certain respects to some other varieties. It should be noted that the prospects for introducing improved varieties are very good. In a cotton introduction trial at Kimberley Research Station in 1965, five different American varieties yielded over 4,000 lbs. of seed cotton. Important features of this experiment were the high lint conversion percentages obtained and the excellent yields from varieties which produce cotton with a high Presley strength.[5]

The main cotton crop is planted in late November and early December. This timing allows farmers to complete the operation before the summer rains. On occasions when land preparation has been late or re-seeding has been necessary, planting has been as late as February. The satisfactory results obtained from these crops have shown that summer rains are not as serious a problem for cotton production as was originally thought.

Land preparation begins immediately the cotton crop is picked, the main months for the various operations being October and November. The old crop is first slashed and generally this is followed by ploughing and by several cultivations before the seeding process begins. Phosphatic fertilizer and nitrogen are applied at seeding time and nitrogen is again applied during crop growth. After plants have emerged there are several inter-row cultivations and sometimes hand-weeding is required.

The nature of the soil calls for fairly high tractor power and heavy cultivation equipment but, in future, savings on cultivation costs should be possible. In 1965-66 one farmer, on part of his crop, dispensed with the normal pre-seeding cultivations and carried out the minimum row work to form a seed bed. The average yield of this crop was among the best obtained in the area and the excellent results were attributed to the fuller use of the nitrogen remaining in the soil from the previous crop.

[5]Kimberley Research Station, *Kimberley Research Station Annual Report.*

Another interesting development which should also have important cost-saving effects is the growing of stub cotton. After harvest, the cotton stalks are slashed close to the ground and left unattended until the new season opens, at which time they are watered and fertilised. Obviously considerable savings in many cost elements can be made in this way. It is estimated that this technique gives a saving of up to $30 per acre and that it can be carried out on half the total area planted. In 1965-66 such a stub crop grown by a commercial farmer gave an average yield of 1,200 lbs. of lint per acre (approximately 3,700 lbs. of seed cotton).

Weeds[6] and Pests[7]

Pre-irrigation, followed by tillage and inter-row cultivation are standard techniques for weed control. The main weeds on older land are pigweed (*Trianthema portulucastrum* and *Portulaca oleracea*) and chloris grass (*Chloris barbata*), while on virgin land *Serbania, Chionachne, Corchorus* and hibiscus species can be troublesome weeds. Chemicals are required in the wet season to control weeds in irrigation channels and drains, and in the dry season they can be controlled by delving and burning. Diuron has proved the most effective herbicide for the cotton weeds.

Cotton is subject to attack from a large number of insect pests and there are six major pests in the Ord Irrigation Area, namely, the tobacco cluster grub (*Prodenia litura*), the rough bollworm (*Earis huegeli rog*), the pink bollworm (*Pectin ophora gossypiella*), the climbing cutworm (*Heliothis punctigera wallengr*), the cotton looper (*Anomis planalis*) and the cotton semi-looper (*Cosmophila flava*). The tobacco cluster grub (*Prodenia litura*) has caused considerable havoc and remains a serious pest because during the winter it is able to maintain relatively large numbers on vegetation growing on the farms and throughout the area. It can be effectively controlled in cotton crops, however, with methyl parathion, a chemical which was first used to good effect during the 1964-65 season.

Capital and Labour

In 1965 the average total capital per farm was estimated at $69,000.[8] Since there had not been any land sales, the cost of development, which had averaged about $43 per cleared acre, provided the valuation basis. By August, 1965, more than three-quarters of cultivable land on farms had been cleared. The various components of the total capital were: land and improvements $21,700; structures $2,600; vehicles $4,700; tractors $10,200; pickers $19,400; plant and machinery $10,100; giving a total of $68,700.

[6]P. J. Van Rijn, 'Weeds and Weed Control'.
[7]K. T. Richards, 'Insect Pests of Cotton in the Ord River Irrigation Area'.
[8]G. D. Oliver and A. W. Hogstrom, 'The 1965 Ord River Cotton Crop'.

The source of farm labour is usually the farmers themselves, members of their families, and employees who went with them to Kununurra. Togther they form an efficient labour force and rely very little on casual workers. Permanent men are paid the equivalent of about $3,000 per year. Some casual workers, usually natives, have been employed for weeding during the summer months, on a daily basis.

Costs and Returns

The average net position of farmers in the Ord scheme for the years 1964 and 1965, and costs of production for the same years are given in Tables 3 and 4. From these tables it will be seen that while cash costs increased by 38 per cent and total costs by 23 per cent, the gross value of cotton increased by 48 per cent and the gross farm return by 58 per cent. The widening of the gap between costs and returns was sufficient to increase the average profits per farm, after allowing for operators' return and depreciation and interest, from a nominal £65 in 1964 to £5,324 in 1965.

Although more fertilizers have been used in 1966, and this has been partly responsible for the increased yields, other cost elements have not increased at the previous rate and in some cases cost reductions have been achieved. It is probable that in absolute terms costs will not be much greater than in 1965. The introduction of stub cotton crops, as mentioned above, could further reduce costs considerably. Thus, with the much greater yields per acre being obtained in 1966, the gap between costs and gross returns will be further widened and the farmer's net return will be considerably higher than in 1965. In fact it appears that about one-third of the growers on the Ord could, in this current season, have operated profitably at a non-subsidized price.

Processing and Marketing

The first gin on the Ord was provided by the state government at a capital cost of £250,000 and was rented to Wesfarmers, who organized a co-operative among the farmers. The rental charge is approximately one cent per lb. of lint. A second gin is being constructed at the same site and will be ready for operations in the 1967 season.

The growers in the co-operative are charging themselves one cent per lb. as a capital charge to defray the capital costs of the second gin and this is included in total ginning costs, including marketing costs, of 9.5c. payable in the 1966 season. Of this total, marketing costs amounted to 4.5c. per lb. and actual ginning costs were 4.0c. It is expected that with larger quantity throughput in future considerable economies in ginning costs can be achieved.

In 1966 the throughput should be close to 7 million lbs. of lint, or 22 million lbs. of seed cotton. Lint is sold to spinners in Brisbane, Sydney, Melbourne and Adelaide, and transported by sea. Cotton seed (two-thirds approximately of seed cotton) will all be sold to Japan for approximately $60 per ton f.o.b. Wyndham. Eventually there will be an oil mill at the Ord River. It is estimated that this will double the growers' net returns from cotton seed which is expected in 1966 to be $28 per ton.

Economic and Social Aspects

The Ord scheme was financed in the first place mainly by the commonwealth government, and early in 1965, with the completion of the first stage approaching, the state government submitted a case to the commonwealth for further funds to proceed with the next stage. The 1965 request was refused and a further approach one year later was also refused. The original submission on the Ord project in 1963 was based partly on a benefit-cost analysis prepared by the Commonwealth Bureau of Agricultural Economics[9] and an analysis of secondary benefits prepared by Dr. C. A. Cannegieter of the University of Western Australia.

During the years 1964 and 1965 a controversy developed over the wisdom of proceeding with the whole scheme and many opinions were expressed in public by politicians, administrators, economists, agricultural economists and others.[10] A great deal of public interest was aroused in the course of the debate and the controversy on the Ord was indissolubly linked with the much larger issue of northern development as a whole. The commonwealth government, which had been accused of adopting a negative attitude to northern development,[11] established a Northern Development Division in its Department of National Development in 1964. By 1965, however, critics were claiming that the work of the division was being rendered ineffectual by continued commonwealth government apathy.[12] Towards the end of that year the inaugural Director of the Northern Development Divison resigned. At the time of writing the debate on general northern development continues.

One way of examining a project of this nature is to determine the expected yield and by relating costs and prices to this, to decide whether the scheme is profitable or not. This was the procedure adopted by Dr. B. R. Davidson in 1965 in a report on cotton growing on the Ord which

[9]Bureau of Agricultural Economics, *The Ord River Irrigation Project: A Benefit-Cost Analysis.*

[10]See for example, I. Bowen, 'A Comment on the Ord Controversy', K. O. Campbell, 'An Assessment of the Case for Irrigation Development in Australia', C. A. Cannegieter, 'The Secondary Benefits of the Ord River Scheme', B. R. Davidson, *The Northern Myth,* D. R. Gallagher and W. F. Musgrave, *Location and the Australian Cotton Industry,* A. G. Lloyd, 'The Controversy on Northern Development', W. F. Musgrave and J. N. Lewis, 'The Ord Controversy: A Rejoinder', R. A. Patterson, 'The Economic Justification of the Ord River Project', People of the North Committee, 'North Australia Development', and H. Raggatt, 'The Development of Northern Australia'.

[11]See for example, J. H. Kelly, 'The Captive North'.

[12]See for example, K. O. Campbell, 'Discussion to Sir Harold Raggatt's Paper'.

was included in his book dealing with the question of northern development in general.[13]

Davidson suggests in his preface that northern development is largely a myth perpetuated by politicians and the press, and claims that whatever can be grown north of the Tropic of Capricorn can be grown far more cheaply south of it. With respect to the Ord – only one of the areas he comments on – this leads to the conclusion that the irrigation proposals represent a misuse of national resources.

Davidson's detailed budgeting approach, in relation to expected yields, involves assumptions regarding the technology employed, variety of crop grown, method of processing and marketing, and so on. On the assumptions made he concluded that at an assumed long-term yield of 1,450 lbs. of seed cotton per acre (two-thirds of the average experimental yield) the net return per farm, without the government subsidy, would be minus £30,000 on a 1,000-acre farm and minus £10,700 on a 300-acre farm. His method is acceptable but his figures and assumptions with respect to cotton were based upon inadequate preliminary data and his conclusions now need severe modification. His estimated yield of 1,450 lbs. was exceeded by 40 per cent in 1965 and seems likely to be exceeded by 65 per cent in 1966. The yield in 1964 was 1,330 lbs. While three seasons may not, under normal circumstances, be taken as adequate upon which to base assumptions about future yields they are, in this case, the first three seasons of commercial production available, and it would be too pessimistic not to assume that the farmers are still learning rapidly and yields will increase still further though occasional future years will no doubt be disappointing. Technology has improved and costs, while increasing, have not grown commensurately with yields, so that in 1965 the average return to the farm was quite substantial and will be even greater in 1966, as shown above.

An alternative approach to determining the feasibility of such a scheme is to examine costs in relation to yields, given the technology, and to determine what would constitute a break-even yield. Various break-even yields have been calculated at different times, ranging from Dr. Patterson's 1,088 lbs. of seed cotton per acre at the current domestic prices and 1,764 lbs. of seed cotton per acre, at import parity prices,[14] to the Department of Agriculture's 2,700 lbs. of seed cotton per acre at the non-subsidized price, not allowing for the sale of seed and other products.

The 1965 average yield of 2,016 lbs. of seed cotton per acre was 51 per cent higher than the 1964 yield and the yield in 1966 is likely to be 25 per cent higher than in 1965. Experimental yields of over 4,000 lbs. and commercial yields of well over 3,000 lbs. have been obtained, and yields from stub cotton grown under commercial conditions have been

[13]B. R. Davidson, *The Northern Myth*.
[14]R. A. Patterson, 'The Economic Justification of the Ord River Project'.

over 3,600 lbs. Current yields have therefore already well exceeded Patterson's estimated break-even point. Valuable experience relating to farming techniques appropriate to the soil and the climate, size of farm, control of weeds and pests, has already been gained and it can be anticipated that yields will increase further in the next few years.

Equally important, of course, are the costs incurred in obtaining these yields. Costs from commercial farming are now available for three years and this provides a sounder basis for projecting them ahead over a limited time than was available when Davidson was writing. Subtracting actual costs from actual returns, the farmers in 1965 averaged over £5,000 net profit from their operations, as pointed out above, after allowing £2,000 operator's allowance as a cost item together with interest and depreciation. While gross farm returns increased by 60 per cent, over 1964, total costs increased by only 20 per cent and it seems likely that the net return will be even greater in 1966. As long as the gap between total costs and gross returns continues to widen, as it has in the past, net returns will improve year by year.

The money returns mentioned above were obtained at a subsidized price and it has been argued by those who oppose the scheme that it would collapse if the subsidy were removed. On reasonable – perhaps even slightly pessimistic – assumptions about future trends, this seems most improbable. Assumptions for instance, that on a 450-acre crop average, yields will settle at 900 lbs. of lint and that the future non-subsidized price will be slightly lower than the present price, and that total farm costs per acre will remain at approximately their present level, may be considered rather conservative. A target of 1,000 lb. of lint is probably more realistic if one looks ahead some years. International cotton prices, after dropping in the 1950's, have levelled out in the 1960's, though year-to-year and month-to-month fluctuations are apparent. Cotton consumption and the consequent demand for raw cotton will continue to rise but competition from synthetics will remain vigorous. Future prospects for Australia will depend also upon efficiency within the Australian cotton spinning industry. On the whole, and particularly with the gradual decrease in stocks in the American industry, which is subsidized, there are no clear indications that cotton prices will fall in the future. Finally, with increases from the current farm size to acreages of 450, one may expect total costs per acre to decline relatively, or at least not to rise significantly in absolute terms.

On these assumptions a net return of $13.5 per acre or approximately $6,000 per farm may be expected. To this may be added returns from the sale of seed cotton which are currently running at 2.5c. per lb. of lint. Since the demand for cotton seed oil and oil cake is strong and is in some respects independent of the demand for lint, there is no reason to expect returns from this source to fall in the future. At the current price this extra income would amount to $22.5 per acre or approximately $10,000 in total. If stub cotton is grown on half the area, the anticipated cost saving per acre based on this year's experience could increase the farmer's net return by a further $6,500, making $22,500 in all. It would take a substantial fall in prices or rise in costs or fall in yields to wipe out an unsubsidized profit of this size.

Thus with yields increasing rapidly and with costs decreasing in relation to them, it can be expected that over the next few years most of the farmers will approach the point of profitable production at a non-subsidized price. In the 1965 season, 3 of the 18 growers went close to a non-subsidized net profit and, as pointed out above, it is likely that in 1966 one-third of the growers at the Ord will have reached this position.

Considering costs in relation to the world price for cotton, the commonwealth government has suggested that the Ord scheme which, in its entirety, will absorb some $82 million of public capital should remain in its first phase, costs for which are $12 million, until more data on the economics of cropping are available, but in this respect it should be pointed out that certain economies on the cost side will not apply until the scheme is operating on a larger scale. The installation of an oil seed crushing plant is a case in point; when throughput is large enough to justify such a plant, ginning costs will be lowered significantly. The sale of oil, seed cake and other by-products could reduce the break-even yield by as much as 200-300 lbs. of seed cotton to the acre which could bring the non-subsidized break-even figure of the Department of Agriculture down to say, 2,400 lbs. This may well prove to be the 1966 average yield.

The other possibilities which have been mentioned as currently being investigated are stub cotton and the introduction of a second crop, probably grain sorghum or wheat. Either of these alternatives could increase the chances of reaching the break-even point at an earlier date. As Patterson points out, the alternative crop, if grown in rotation with cotton, will utilize the productive irrigable land that is lying idle as well as taking advantage of the fixed capital involved on the farm, and as long as the extra income gained is greater than the extra costs incurred, the enterprise is financially sound. Grain sorghum has a firm export market and would provide a useful backstop in the event of a fall in cotton prices. Results so far are encouraging and suggest that a substantial extra return could result from growing 300 acres of grain sorghum in association with a cotton crop. Patterson puts the profit from this crop at $16,000, over and above the profit from cotton.

Mention has been made of a hidden subsidy at the Ord, in the sense that the nation is expected to pay for the headworks, and in this respect it is worth pointing out that this is normally expected of all large irrigation projects, a charge being made to users for the water consumed. The charge at the Ord is similar to that paid elsewhere and since the cost to the government of $5.2 per acre-foot of water supplied is much lower on the Ord than in many other irrigation schemes (e.g., $65.6 for the Keepit), the Ord farmers are paying relatively more and the hidden subsidy is that much less.[15]

It has also been suggested that as yields increase on the Ord, with better technology, they will also increase elsewhere and thus the prospect of increasing yields cannot be used as an argument for investing money there rather than in other ventures where yields are currently better. But it should be borne in mind that in a newly developing area such as this, where lessons about climate, soils, pests, etc., are still being learned, the chances for a much higher proportionate increase in yields are considerably greater than in the longer-established industries situated elsewhere which have settled down to a pattern of production. Experience on the Ord in the first three years has already demonstrated this.

One of the dangers of pursuing too closely the 'least cost' argument – that national resources should be invested where they will bring in the greatest returns on the basis of current costs – is that it is a short-term view. It is hazardous to predict how prices will look in ten or twenty years from now and thus to assume that the present position regarding relative prices will persist. A policy of diversification, and this involves not just cotton growing, would seem justified at this stage rather than one which tends to keep the same eggs in one basket.

But more importantly, the pursuit of such a least-cost policy can have the effect of inhibiting development in regions that are lagging behind others. It can result in a widening of the gap between the developed regions and the underdeveloped regions in a national economy. One's view of whether this matters or not depends upon the assessment of many factors, economic, social and political, but if governments do not wish to abrogate responsibility for the welfare of citizens living in one particular area, gaps between various regions must not be allowed to grow too large. It has yet to be demonstrated, for example, that alternative, south-located investment of the funds required for completion of the Ord scheme will, in the long-run, contribute more to the overall national economy in the broadest sense than if the scheme were immediately proceeded with. On this point it may be assumed, in any case, that the commonwealth government is just as favourably disposed to a general policy of decentralization as are the state governments.

There is little doubt that if short-term economic considerations alone are the criteria upon which the decisions of government and private planners, administrators and operators are based, then much development of a path-breaking nature would not take place. There would mostly be extensions at the margins of existing industries, where the return to capital invested is safe and sure even if unspectacular. The fact is, however, that new large-scale developments have often ultimately justified themselves on their own grounds and through the attraction of other activties and the

[15]H. Raggatt, 'The Development of Northern Australia'.

creation of economies which could be shared by others. Often this type of investment involving long-term risk capital is made because the developers have been looking beyond the short-term. If the commonwealth government is serious about its intentions to develop the north of Australia it has to be prepared to encourage structural changes and new activities as well as merely extending at the margin of existing industries.

Certain non-economic arguments have also been discussed in the general context of the Ord controversy. Estimates have been made in money terms of political and other benefits which will accrue from the development of the Ord[16] and these should be considered as additional to the primary benefits associated with the scheme itself.

It has been argued, for example, that the scheme will indirectly assist in Australia's defence against aggression by developing the country and attracting population, though one can also argue that the more developed the country is the easier it might be for an aggressor to overrun it. It has been suggested further that populating a hitherto relatively under-developed portion of the Australian continent will provide an earnest of Australia's intentions to develop its natural resources in a land-hungry world. There is some strength in this view and Davidson's counter-arguments are not altogether convincing. Obviously some weight must be given to arguments of this nature in any overall assessment of northern development projects, but it is difficult to put any generally acceptable quantitative values upon them and the question becomes largely one of subjective assessment which supplements economic considerations.

Apart from these somewhat intangible but nonetheless real benefits, there are the secondary or associated economic benefits that will also be felt. General commercial and small scale industrial development in the area, long-term benefits to the beet industry which could be quite significant and far-reaching provided the industry itself responds to the stimulus, the growth of population and the provision of services of one kind and another, these all add significantly to the long-term net worth of the scheme. But these are extra benefits and although they may be quite substantial the scheme is able to stand on its own merits if attention is confined solely to the economics of cropping in the area.

At this stage no serious arguments have been officially advanced by the commonwealth government to suggest that it considers the Ord scheme unsound. The commonwealth government has, in effect, indicated in 1965 and 1966 that it is adopting a wait-and-see policy based mainly upon the implication that insufficient evidence is yet available to indicate clearly that cotton production on the Ord will be profitable at a non-subsidized price or that a satisfactory alternative or supplementary crop can be grown. In some ways such a policy expressed early in 1965 would appear reasonable on the grounds that no great harm would be done by waiting,

[16]C. A. Cannegieter, 'Some Socio-Economic Aspects of the Ord River Scheme'.

but, on the other hand, in the light of the subsequent 1965 and 1966 results, one may wonder what is required to demonstrate the potential of the scheme. Also, as pointed out earlier, it is incorrect to judge a scheme by its pilot phase when certain economies of scale appropriate to the larger scheme are lacking.

Much acrimonious discussion and comment would, of course, have been avoided if the commonwealth government had clearly stated at the beginning of the negotiations for the first phase of the scheme that it would be prepared to consider financing the second phase after it had been able to examine the results of, say, four or five seasons of experimental growing and two or three seasons of commercial growing. In this event, all parties to the agreement would have known where they stood.

One argument that could be considered as relevant to the debate on the main Ord scheme has not been used officially but has been advanced in other quarters,[17] though there is no doubt that it is a major consideration affecting the decisions of the commonwealth government. Gallagher and Musgrave suggest that on certain yield assumptions applied to possible irrigation acreages in 1977-78, total Australian production of seed cotton would be 316.8 million lb. in that season. Using a lint extraction rate of 33 per cent they conclude that 105.6 million lb. of raw cotton would be produced and they measure this against an expected demand from Australian manufacturers, in 1977-78, of 76 million lb. of raw cotton or 218 million lb. of seed cotton, a prediction which seems reasonable in the light of current trends.

The authors state that the predicted domestic demand would only be satisfied from domestic sources if the Ord scheme were carried to completion but if this happens 'it seems likely that Australia would have an exportable surplus of cotton'. Irrespective of whether this is considered a desirable state of affairs or not, and the authors themselves do not consider it desirable, it should be pointed out that the calculations are based on an assumed increase in irrigated cotton acreage of something like 300 per cent throughout Australia. On the authors' own figures, it can be shown that if the Ord scheme were completed but the predicted increases in other schemes were not realized Australia would not, as they suggest, have an exportable surplus. In point of fact, should the present bounty be removed it is unlikely that total acreages will increase by this amount.

The danger of floods in the Namoi valley is mentioned, and this is the area which the authors believe currently offers the greatest possibility for the development of cotton production in New South Wales. Also, although the effect of drought conditions on the Namoi growers is not mentioned by Gallagher and Musgrave, note should be taken of the serious setback to production which has occurred in the current season. Thus,

[17]D. R. Gallagher and W. F. Musgrave, *Location and the Australian Cotton Industry*.

it is by no means certain that an exportable surplus would emerge as soon as might be expected in the report and it is not certain that to proceed with the Ord scheme would, of its own, guarantee its emergence, although it seems probable. In any case, as pointed out above, this would not affect the Ord growers since they would be able to compete internationally.

The question of export rests not only upon local costs and prices but upon freight and other handling charges to possible overseas markets. On this point Davidson and Patterson differ. Davidson rightly claimed that the Australian and New Zealand Shipping Conference quote the freight rate to Japan from Wyndham at 4.5 pence per lb. of lint,[18] while Patterson pointed that, be that as it may, Japanese lines had quoted the Western Australian government 3d. per lb.[19] Since then a quote of 2.5 pence has been officially received. Opinions also differ on the payment of a quality premium on Ord cotton. Davidson dismisses the possibility of a quality premium while Patterson assumes a premium of 1.74 pence per lb. and is supported by Basinski of C.S.I.R.O.[20] Thus the export position is by no means clear, but if the Japanese shipping lines charge their quoted freight rate and the quality premium is obtained, as seems likely in view of the quality of the 1966 crop, export prospects in Japan for Ord cotton seem encouraging, given the ability of the farmers to produce at export parity. In fact, Patterson claims that 'if the cotton bounty were removed, it would be more profitable for Ord farmers to market their cotton in Japan than send it to the eastern states of Australia'.[21]

The volume of comment that has so far been offered against proceeding with the Ord scheme may be reduced to four main propositions : that the scheme is uneconomic in the sense that it would need continued subsidy, that it would result in a surplus that would have to be exported and Australia does not want an export industry for cotton, that there is no other feasible alternative crop to cotton, and that there are no good reasons for developing the north.

It has been suggested here that the first issue has been virtually resolved in favour of the scheme by the results so far obtained, that an exportable surplus probably will emerge, and the issue here depends upon one's assessment of the future trend in world cotton prices and in Ord yields and production costs, that there are alternative crops to which the growers can turn should cotton prices fall significantly, and that there are good reasons for developing the north.

[18]B. R. Davidson, 'The Economics of Pastoral and Agriculture Development in Northern Australia'.

[19]R. A. Patterson, discussion of Davidson's paper referred to in footnote 18 in People of the North Committee, *North Australia Development*.

[20]J. J. Baninski, discussion of Davidson's paper referred to in footnote 18 in People of the North Committee, *North Australia Development*.

[21]R. A. Patterson, 'The Economic Justification of the Ord River Project'.

There is not the space in this general survey of the various development problems of such a large region to enter into detailed argument of the pros and cons of the Ord scheme. The aim in this section has been to present the main considerations that have been debated. Sufficient references have been given for the interested reader to pursue the case in detail if desired, exploring both sides of the controversy in the process. What is suggested, however, is that results to date have justified the optimism of those who instituted the scheme as it now stands and of those who much earlier set about commencing the necessary preliminary research. Claim and counter-claim have been made until the lay reader finds himself bogged in a morass of figures and guesses which he has no way of checking. The facts that stand above the detailed arguments are that the Ord farmers are obtaining surprisingly good yields and are making a handsome profit on their operations.

Long-term effects

The basic aim of the scheme has been officially stated as essentially to promote closer settlement in the north of Australia by utilizing water to provide agricultural development based on irrigation; although the other arguments mentioned above have from time to time been brought forward in its support. The population of Kununurra at present, with 31 farms operating, is approximately 1,000, and when the scheme is complete it is expected that some 10,000 people will be living in the area. Thus its population induction effect in the East Kimberley will be considerable, in relative terms. The development has, of course, rubbed off on to the port of Wyndham, too, and population there has more than doubled since 1961. Further substantial increases can be expected in the future.

Another effect of the scheme will be to expand the region's primary industry export trade and thus there would be no immediate alleviation of the one-way transport problem. On the other hand, as the region grows it may be expected that smaller manufacturing activities will spring up as they did in the South-West region in the wake of the group settlers in the 1930's. The growth process feeds upon itself with a snowballing effect and once the movement has been started the availability of cheaper electric power as anticipated should hasten the trend.

A by-product of the scheme, which could do much to induce other developments in the area would be the partial alleviation of the flood danger in the district because of the ability to control the water flow at least partially. This can be a very substantial benefit, for apart from the reduction in flood damage itself, almost continuous communications may be maintained throughout the region, thus facilitating commerce and inducing greater all-round activity.

The pastoral industry could eventually benefit from the protein byproducts of the agricultural produce as mentioned in Chapter 3, and, of course, in the future the scientists may be able to produce a satisfactory pasture so that the cattle industry can benefit from the irrigated lands. Patterson has dealt at some length on the benefits which might be expected to accrue in this way to the pastoral industry.

There is also the possibility that fairly cheap electric power would attract heavier industries into the area though this may be looking well ahead. It has been estimated by the Public Works Department that with electricity sold at one cent per unit, a return of over $2 million per year could be obtained from the scheme and it is felt that if power were available at that rate the possibilities of refining ores, such as bauxite, are rather encouraging. Again, of course, the one-way transport problem exists.

Although the scheme, by itself, is relatively small it is a start on the general problem of inducing closer settlement in those areas of the north which lend themselves to this type of development. More schemes can be expected to follow but this does not mean that the extensive grazing technology to which so much of the Kimberley is suited will suffer. In fact, it should benefit from the associated development.

7. Summary and Conclusions

Agriculture in the region is not yet developed to any great degree but its extension may ultimately prove to be a turning point in the history of the region's growth. Although the temperature conditions allow the growing season to extend throughout the year, the amount of precipitation is a limiting factor. A combination of warm temperatures with an assured water supply guaranteed through irrigation, and good irrigable soils would give great production possibilities. There are several areas in the region where this combination may be achieved.

At Carnarvon, planters have been growing bananas since the 1930's but the industry has recently grown rapidly and production has diversified. The area now produces a great amount of out-of-season vegetables and some fruit as well as the banana crop. Generally speaking the area has a great production potential but at the moment it is limited by several factors. Among the main obstacles to immediate expansion are shortage of suitable water, lack of unity and cohesion in the industry, lack of an assured demand to support large-scale development, and lack of processing industries. Climatic and weather conditions, which give the area its great growing potential also, from time to time, can be destructive and, in the form of cyclones and floods, wreak havoc in the plantations. One cannot foresee development occurring in the next decade at the rate of the last decade unless solutions can be obtained to some of these problems.

The next area to be developed for agriculture was the rice-growing area at Camballin in the West Kimberley. Here commercial production has now been undertaken for some years but has met with only limited success. Crops have varied in yield, dry season proving better than wet season, and the search for the most suitable variety is still proceeding. A new and more important phase in the development of the industry has come with the running of stock in conjunction with irrigated agriculture. At Camballin fodder crops are also grown and the milling of by-products from the various grain crops will undoubtedly assume greater importance as the industry develops. The main problems in this area are those associated with obtaining adequate water supply and effective flood control, and with vermin control.

The third area, and the largest of the three, is the Ord irrigation area. The development of this area for tropical agriculture involves the expenditure, ultimately, of at least $82 million for capital works, and associated development costs. Construction work on the diversion dam followed several years of experimentation at the Kimberley Research Station which was charged with determining the suitability of the area for irrigation and for the production of tropical cash crops. In its final stages the scheme envisages the irrigation of up to 175,000 acres and the provision of hydro-electric power to the area and involves the construction of a large dam on the Ord River with three and a half million acre-feet capacity, some 30 miles upstream from the diversion dam.

The scheme itself, which has so far achieved encouraging results in cotton growing, is an example of bold planning in an underdeveloped area and, if it is ultimately successful, its effect will be to change the pattern of land use and production in the area. As well, it should have salutary effects upon the pastoral industry which has been the backbone of the regional economy and it could lead to the development of other small industries in the area.

The success of the scheme would be the starting signal for proceeding with other major irrigation projects in the Kimberley designed to promote closer settlement and to make use of the immense and, at present, largely uncontrolled water resources in the region. On the broader horizon its success could also point the way to the more intensive exploitation of the whole of tropical northern Australia and it could well provide the example needed to lift these areas into a new phase of economic growth.

BIBLIOGRAPHY

AUSTRALIAN INSTITUTE OF POLITICAL SCIENCE. *Northern Australia: Task for a Nation.* Sydney, 1954.

BARNETT, G. B. 'Banana Culture in Western Australia.' *Journal of Agriculture,* vol. 24, no. 1. 1947.

BASINSKI, J. J. *Cotton Growing in Australia.* Melbourne, 1963.

BEECH, D. F. 'Safflower – An Oil Crop for the Kimberleys.' *Journal of Agriculture,* vol. 1, no. 3. 1960.

BOWEN, I. 'A Comment on the Ord Controversy.' *The Economic Record,* vol. 41, no. 94. 1965.

BUREAU OF AGRICULTURAL ECONOMICS. *The Ord River Irrigation Project: A Benefit-Cost Analysis.* Canberra, 1964.

CAMPBELL, K. O. 'An Assessment of the Case for Irrigation Development in Australia.' *Australian Academy of Science: Water Resources, Use and Management.* Melbourne, 1964.

—— 'Discussion to Sir Harold Raggatt's Paper.' The Economic Society of Australia and New Zealand; New South Wales and Victorian Branches. *Economic Papers,* no. 21. 1966.

CANNEGIETER, C. A. 'Some Socio-Economic Aspects of the Ord River Scheme.' *The Economic Record,* vol. 40, no. 91. 1964.

—— 'The Secondary Benefits of the Ord River Scheme.' *Economic Growth in Western Australia: Economic Studies,* no. 1. 1964.

—— 'Comparison of the Ord with some Dutch River Basin Projects.' *Economic Activity in Western Australia,* vol. 8, no. 2. 1965.

DAVIDSON, B. R. *The Northern Myth.* Melbourne, 1965.

—— 'The Economics of Pastoral and Agriculture Development in Northern Australia.' *North Australia Development.* Proceedings of a symposium held at the University of New South Wales by the People of the North Committee. Sydney, 1966.

GALLAGHER, D. R. and MUSGRAVE, W. F. *Location and the Australian Cotton Industry.* Armidale, 1966.

KELLY, J. H. 'The Captive North.' Paper presented to the Capricornia Society at the Australian National University. 1966.

KIMBERLEY RESEARCH STATION. 'Kimberley Research Station Progress Report 1957.' *Journal of Agriculture,* vol. 7, no. 2. 1958.

—— 'Kimberley Research Station. A Progress Report.' *Journal of Agriculture,* vol. 1, no. 12. 1960.

—— *Kimberley Research Station Annual Report.* Perth, 1965.

KOCH, L. E. 'Rice Stem Borers at the Kimberley Research Station.' *Journal of Agriculture,* vol. 1, no. 12. 1960.

LAWSON, J. A. 'Peanut Growing on the Levee Soils of the Gascoyne River.' *Journal of Agriculture,* vol. 3, no. 2. 1954.

—— 'Banana Cultivation at Carnarvon.' *Journal of Agriculture,* vol. 2, no. 4. 1961.

LAWSON, J. A. and REES, R. A. 'Vegetable Growing at Carnarvon.' *Journal of Agriculture,* vol. 7, no. 6. 1958.

LLOYD, A. G. 'The Controversy on Northern Development.' *Review of Marketing and Agricultural Economics,* vol. 33, no. 3. 1965.

McDONALD HOLMES, J. *Australia's Open North.* Sydney, 1963.

MUSGRAVE, W. F. and LEWIS, J. N. 'The Ord Controversy: A Rejoinder.' *The Economic Record,* vol. 41, no. 96. 1965.

NALSON, J. S. and PARKER, M. L. *Irrigation on the Gascoyne River – An Economic Appraisal.* Perth, 1963.

OLIVER, G. D. and HOGSTROM, A. W. 'The 1965 Ord River Cotton Crop.' *Journal of Agriculture,* vol. 7, no. 1. 1966.

PATTERSON, R. A. 'The Economic Justification of the Ord River Project.' 38th Congress, Australia and New Zealand Association for the Advancement of Science. Hobart, 1965.

PEOPLE OF THE NORTH COMMITTEE. *North Australia Development.* Proceedings of a symposium held at the University of New South Wales by the People of the North Committee. Sydney, 1966.

RAGGATT, H. 'The Development of Northern Australia.' The Economic Society of
    Australia and New Zealand; New South Wales and Victorian Branches. *Economic
    Papers,* no. 21. 1966.

RICHARDS, K. T. 'Insect Pests of Cotton in the Ord River Irrigation Area.' *Journal
    of Agriculture,* vol. 5, no. 2. 1964.

SCOTT, R. M. and FURPHY, H. G. *Report for the Government of Western Australia –
    Gascoyne River.* Perth, 1961.

TEAKLE, L. J. H. 'Terraced Soils of the Gascoyne River at Carnarvon.' *Journal of
    Agriculture,* vol. 12, no. 3. 1935.

—— 'The Kimberley Project.' *Journal of Agriculture,* vol. 27, no. 4. 1944.

VAN RIJN, P. J. 'Weeds and Weed Control.' *Journal of Agriculture,* vol. 6, no. 5. 1965.

VON LOESECKE, H. *Bananas – Chemistry, Physiology, Technology.* New York, 1950.

TABLE 1

CARNARVON AREA

Agricultural Production – Major Items

Season – 1947-48, 1950-51 to 1964-65

Year	Tomatoes		Beans		Pumpkins		Bananas		
	Acres	Half bushel cases ('000)	Acres	cwt. ('000)	Acres	cwt. ('000)	Acres	bushels ('000)	Value[1] (£'000)
1947-48	1	.1	19	1.2	4	.2	320	57.7	—
1950-51	—	—	29	1.3	—	—	540	91.3	269.3
1951-52	1	.3	35	2.3	17	.9	540	73.3	274.8
1952-53	1	.8	47	2.7	9	.5	517	69.0	344.5
1953-54	2	.9	75	6.6	4	.1	556	41.8	187.9
1954-55	—	.1	109	9.2	3	.3	563	76.7	345.0
1955-56	1	.8	154	12.0	10	1.1	490	68.5	248.5
1956 57	6	4.6	317	23.8	10	1.2	331	34.1	136.5
1957-58	25	23.3	301	24.9	24	3.5	357	43.8	173.6
1958-59	53	54.2	343	36.2	26	4.2	408	70.8	198.3
1959-60	34	41.4	431	42.4	46	11.1	398	107.9	302.1
1960 61	38	52.9	520	47.5	63	10.8	253	7.6	17.7
1961-62	59	74.0	650	51.7	134	19.9	259	48.1	112.3
1962-63	82	81.6	534	59.0	136	16.8	305	76.6	218.7
1963-64	62	78.9	665	53.5	105	18.4	397	140.6	336.2
1964-65	76	112.4	647	57.8	122	22.5	469	145.1	475.0

[1] Value of bananas only.

Source: Commonwealth Bureau of Census and Statistics, Perth.

TABLE 2

CARNARVON AREA

Fruit and Vegetable Production

1955-56 and 1960-61 to 1964-65

Vegetable	Unit	Season					
		1955-56	1960-61	1961-62	1962-63	1963-64	1964-65
Cucumbers	doz.	13,741	49,620	59,182	67,488	75,340	111,848
Capsicums	cwt.	58	1,670	2,760	2,498	2,333	3,705
Grapefruit	bush.	204	147	132	112	150	478
Pawpaws	bush.	—	—	140	325	1,887	911
Eggfruit	doz.	1,056	662	2,500	5,684	2,624	4,196
Onions	cwt.	60	220	236	221	10	202
Chillies	lbs.	—	5,950	2,350	29,580	13,088	18,432
Peas	cwt.	—	—	—	—	13	—
Rock Melons ..	doz.	—	20,060	20,020	46,740	29,844	24,162
Mangoes	bush.	30	—	215	179	711	228
Watermelons	doz.	10	60	329	1,250	1,784	4,063

Source: Commonwealth Bureau of Census and Statistics, Perth.

TABLE 3

ORD IRRIGATION SCHEME

The Average Net Position of Farmers

1964 and 1965

Details	1964	1965
No. of farms	5	18
Average area planted (acres)	272	283
Total lint (lb.)	121,870	180,076
Average price per lb. (d)	49.6	49.5
	£	£
Gross value of cotton	25,180	37,165
Less gining and marketing[1]	7,108	8,629
Farm gross return	18,072	28,536
Less cash costs[2]	12,480	17,165
Depreciation	2,882	2,447
Interest (balance to 6 per cent of total capital)	645	600
Operator's allowance	2,000	2,000
Net return	65	6,324

[1] 14d. per lb. of lint in 1964 and 11.5d. per lb. in 1965.

[2] Including all hired and family labour (expect operator) and interest paid.

Source: G. D. Oliver and A. W. Hogstrom, 'The Ord River Cotton Crop', in *The Journal of Agriculture,* vol 7, no. 1. 1966.

TABLE 4

ORD IRRIGATION SCHEME
Average Costs of Production

1964 and 1965

(£)

Cost items	1964		1965	
	Per farm	*Per acre*	*Per farm*	*Per acre*
Spraying	4,415	16.2	7,167	25.3
Defoliation	—	—	468	1.6
Fertilizer	2,806	10.6	3,305	11.7
Seed	—	—	95	0.3
Water	909	3.3	1,417	5.0
Fuel and Oil	496	1.8	836	3.0
Labour	2,700	9.9	2,221	7.8
Repairs	186	0.7	401	1.4
Licences	226	0.8	46	0.2
Insurance	—	—	113	0.4
Interest paid	650	2.4	771	2.7
Other	92	0.3	325	1.2
Total cash costs	12,480	46.0	17,165	60.6
Depreciation	2,882	10.6	2,447	8.7
Interest – Balance to 6 per cent on capital	645	2.4	600	2.1
Operator's allowance	2,000	7.4	2,000	7.1
Total costs	18,007	66.4	22,212	78.5

Source: G. D. Oliver and A. W. Hogstrom, 'The Ord River Cotton Crop'.

CHAPTER 7

WATER CONSERVATION

1. INTRODUCTION

Agricultural and pastoral development in parts of Australia is limited by poor water resources. The driest of the continents, Australia has an average annual rainfall of 16.5 inches and the percentage of run-off is lower than the world average, amounting to 10 per cent or 1.6 inches. Total average annual discharge of Australian rivers, or the surface run-off, has been estimated at 280 million acre-feet per annum,[1] 60 per cent of which occurs on the eastern seaboard, on the ocean side slopes of the Great Dividing Range and around the Gulf of Carpentaria.

Water Resources[2]

The position in Northwestern Australia is more promising than in other parts of the state. For instance, the Ord has an average annual flow of 4.3 million acre-feet per annum drawn from a 21,000 square mile catchment area which averages an annual rainfall of 21 inches.[3] Estimates by the Australian Water Resources Council have revealed the total catchment area of the Kimberley to be in the vicinity of 107,600 square miles and the calculated run-off of the Kimberley rivers is an average of 31.6 million acre-feet per annum. In comparison, the catchment area of the Murray-Murrumbidgee-Darling rivers system is 408,000 square miles and the run-off amounts to 19 million acre-feet.

The resources of the remainder of Northwestern Australia are not great. The Pilbara and North-West divisions are served by the De Grey, Fortescue, Ashburton and Gascoyne river systems and so far there are no comprehensive

[1] Australian Water Resources Council, *Australia's Water Resources (Stream Flow and Underground Resources) 1963.*
[2] Material for this Chapter has been drawn heavily from Public Works Department files.
[3] The median flow is, however, only 3.0 million acre-feet. Thus it will be seen that arithmetic average figures can be misleading and have to be treated with caution.

records of the flows of these rivers, which are spasmodic. The catchments are large and relatively bare and large floods are experienced at times. In general, salinity is not a problem except in some parts of the upper Gascoyne. The total water resources of this part of the region could be several million acre-feet per annum, but high evaporation and uncertainty of flow makes storage a rather difficult proposition. The hydrology of some of the Pilbara rivers is currently being investigated as a result of the mineral developments now occurring in the area. Some investigation and survey work has also been undertaken along the Gascoyne as a result of water shortages experienced by irrigation farmers around Carnarvon, and this river would appear to be the first one in the area where a hydraulic structure of any size might be built in the future.

It is worth noting the dearth of accurate knowledge as regards river flooding and flows, erosion and silt factors, and possible damsites in the region. The Ord has been examined and surveyed, likewise with parts of the Fitzroy and Gascoyne, and reconnaissance work has been conducted on some potential Kimberley damsites. A comprehensive plan has been drawn up by the Public Works Department for the installation of recording equipment on the region's rivers and acquisition of further knowledge is now in progress.

As previously pointed out, Northwestern Australia is predominantly a pastoral economy although mining and agriculture are assuming increasing importance in the region in terms of employment and value of production. The harnessing of the region's water resources is of vital importance in any plan to increase production and employment because the existing utilization of land, dominated as it is by the pastoral industry, tends to inhibit the intensive development and exploitation of natural resources. The soil is not generally cultivated and rivers flow virtually untouched to the ocean. To the extent that more intensive exploitation is desired, efficient ways of using the region's water resources need exploring.

Since the World War, public interest has increased in the potential of Northern Australia and attention has been focussed upon the fact that the Kimberley is well endowed with water and potentially irrigable land. Investigations by the State Public Works and Agriculture departments, and C.S.I.R.O. have revealed agricultural possibilities in certain areas within the region and these have already been examined in Chapter 6. These areas or sub-regions have become fairly clearly defined. They are based on river systems or drainage patterns. Foremost amongst these is the Ord-Victoria-Baines system, extending across into the Northern Territory. Next are the Fitzroy-Margaret valleys. Other 'river regions' include the Lennard which is adjacent to the Fitzroy, the King Edward-Carson-Drysdale system of the North Kimberley, and the Gascoyne-Lyons system in the North-West Division. In addition to these areas are the Pilbara rivers and the Kimberley north-west coastal rivers.

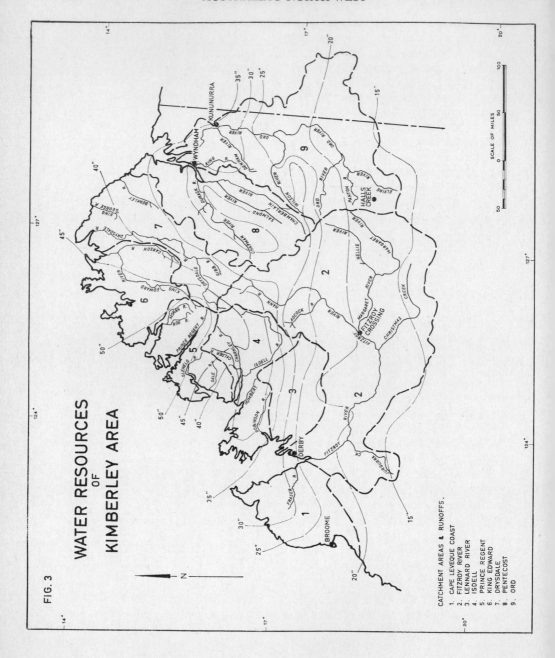

FIG. 3

WATER RESOURCES
OF
KIMBERLEY AREA

CATCHMENT AREAS & RUNOFFS.

1. CAPE LEVEQUE COAST
2. FITZROY RIVER
3. LENNARD RIVER
4. ISDELL
5. PRINCE REGENT
6. KING EDWARD
7. DRYSDALE
8. PENTECOST
9. ORD

Survey Work

Investigations and surveys of these river systems have been carried out in varying detail. In the case of the Ord, construction is complete on the diversion dam, first stage of the development plan, and sufficient survey work has been done to enable engineers to proceed with the next stages when funds are made available. A weir has been erected on the Fitzroy to divert water to a small irrigation area. The upper reaches of the Fitzroy and Margaret rivers have been surveyed and possible damsites located. Hydrological investigations are now proceeding in this river, the irrigable potential of which is expected to exceed that of the Ord in terms of total area served. Development based on the use of the water from the Lennard river is also considered possible in the future.

The rivers of the Northern Kimberley have not been examined in the same detail from the point of view of water resources and irrigable land, although surveyor J. F. Morgan traversed the Drysdale-Carson-King Edward rivers in 1954.[4] His mission was to examine the area with the view to assessing pastoral potential and to plot possible access roads and his report did make possible some estimate as to the extent of irrigable land in the northern river valleys. No detailed investigation has yet been carried out on the other Kimberley rivers.

Of the North-West and Pilbara rivers, the Gascoyne is the only one to have aroused any interest until recently, for reasons previously mentioned. South of the Fitzroy, rivers have an unreliable flow and whilst this also applies to the Gascoyne, special factors have focussed interest on this river. In the 1930's irrigation agriculture was commenced near the mouth of the Gascoyne, and industry developed in the first instance through its ability to compete favourably on the Perth banana market. Later the industry expanded and diversified by supplying off season vegetables.

The post-war years have witnessed considerable growth in Carnarvon agriculture and the water resources of the river are now over-taxed. Water is pumped from the sand lenses, a form of natural storage, after the Gascoyne has ceased to run and whilst these natural reserves are adequate to supply the plantations with water for a limited period after a river flow, they are incapable of meeting requirements following a prolonged dry spell. For these reasons pressure is being placed on the state government to rectify the inadequate water reserves. Among other measures taken a clay barrier has been placed in the Gascoyne in an attempt to store greater quantities of water, but the growers see a dam as the only feasible long-term solution.

Since the recent mining development in the Pilbara, rivers in this area have been subjected to closer examination in order to establish their potential for industrial and domestic water supplies. Desalination is in

[4] J. F. Morgan, *Report on Central North Kimberley Region.*

operation at Dampier, and this provides an alternative to surface or underground water, but in other areas it will be necessary to utilize what surface water there may be. The Fortescue, Shaw, Coongan and Harding are currently being gauged and suitable damsites on them have been located, while investigation is being planned for others.

The water resources of the region are thus considerable, and although at present the region's economy is mostly oriented towards pastoralism, more intensive land occupation must rely on agricultural development and, in turn, agricultural development must rely on the conservation and diversion of the region's water resources. Mineral development, which will intensify in the future, will also make heavy demands upon the water resources of the Pilbara. Further discussion in this chapter will be concerned with specific details of various projects or proposed projects in the region, and with some mention of the town water supplies and private irrigation schemes.

2. WATER CONSERVATION – KIMBERLEY

Ord River Project

HISTORICAL BACKGROUND

The World War was largely responsible for awakening public interest in the Kimberley, which previously had been virtually the exclusive domain of the pastoralists. In 1941, as a result of interest shown in the possibilities of irrigation agriculture in the Ord basin by the then Director of Works, Mr. R. J. Dumas and by Mr. K. M. Durack, an agricultural experimental station was established at Carlton Reach, 60 miles from Wyndham, and not far from the site of the recently completed diversion dam.

By 1944 soil and land investigations in the potentially irrigable area had been carried out. Of the 86,000 acres examined adjacent to the Ord, 50,000 acres were found to be potentially irrigable and a further 125,000 acres which were not examined in detail, appeared to be satisfactory. In 1945 the commonwealth and state governments jointly established the Kimberley Research Station on a cost-sharing basis. A supervisory committee was set up consisting of representatives from C.S.I.R.O., the Department of National Development and the state Agriculture and Public Works departments. In 1957 the Research Station published its first annual report and findings with reference to irrigation agriculture in the area, and has continued to publish annually.

The state government in 1949 made submissions to the commonwealth requesting financial aid to develop the region and their proposals included a dam for the Ord. Inadequately supported, statistically, the broad plan failed to attract finance from the federal authorities and in 1955 and 1956, new reports based on revised and more detailed information were submitted.

The period 1957-60 witnessed increased activity in state departments in the collection of data. The Public Works Department extended their gauging and sampling activities, the Lands Department air-photographed the entire storage basin and produced a contoured map at 10 feet vertical intervals, hydraulic model studies of the proposed dam were carried out by the University, and tropical agriculture recommendations became available in the Research Station's annual reports. In 1959 further proposals were prepared for the commonwealth, backed by a wealth of detail, and on this occasion finance was made available for the first stage of the proposed four-stage development plan – the construction of the diversion dam and allied works.

DEVELOPMENT PLAN

The main engineering features of the scheme are : (i) a main rockfill dam situated some 90 river miles from Wyndham, to provide a reservoir of 3.5 million acre-feet capacity, (ii) a diversion dam, 30 miles downstream from the storage dam, to raise and divert the water released from the storage dam into the irrigation system, (iii) an irrigation area of approximately 170,000 acres of black-soil plains, (iv) the generation of hydro-electric power by water released from the storage dam and the reticulation of power as required throughout the irrigation area, (v) the establishment of a township at Kununurra and the necessary ancillary development such as roads and water supply.

This proposal may be considered as part of a regional plan for the development of the whole Ord-Victoria region. The scheme is essentially one to promote closer settlement in the north of Australia by utilizing water to provide agricultural development based on irrigation.

The scheme has been planned to be developed in three stages. Stage 1, which is now completed, is the construction of the diversion dam and the development of 30,000 acres of irrigable land. Stage 2 embraces the construction of the main storage dam and the development of the balance of the irrigation area. Stage 3 is the construction of the hydro-electric power station and the reticulation of power. Complementary to this development is the provision of the essential towns, roads, water supplies and the establishment of small industries.

HYDROLOGY

The area covers some 32,830 square miles and lies between the lines of latitude 14° south and 18° south. It is drained by three main river systems: the Ord, which flows into Cambridge Gulf, the Keep and the Baines. It is characterised by two distinct seasons, a 'wet' and 'dry' season. During the wet season, which occurs between November and March, cyclonic storms occur bringing intense rainfall. Falls of six inches per day with a recurrence interval of five years have been recorded at the Kimberley Research Station. The rainfall over the area is not high, varying from 18 inches in the south to about 30 inches at Wyndham in the north, but it

[5]K. C. Webster, 'Water Resources and Engineering Aspects of the Ord Irrigation Project'.

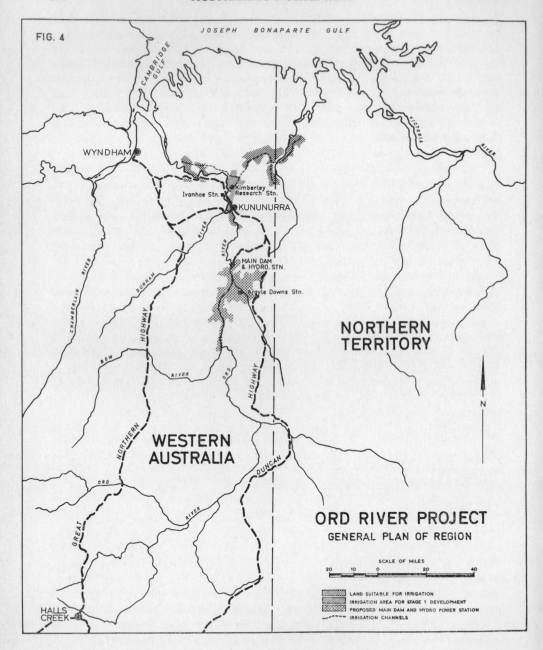

FIG. 4

JOSEPH BONAPARTE GULF

CAMBRIDGE GULF

VICTORIA RIVER

WYNDHAM

Ivanhoe Stn.
Kimberley
Research Stn.
KUNUNURRA

RIVER

DUNHAM RIVER

HIGHWAY

MAIN DAM
& HYDRO. STN.

Argyle Downs Stn.

BOW RIVER

ORD

HIGHWAY

CHAMBERLAIN RIVER

NORTHERN TERRITORY

N

NORTHERN HIGHWAY

WESTERN
AUSTRALIA

DUNCAN

ORD

GREAT

RIVER

HALLS
CREEK

ORD RIVER PROJECT
GENERAL PLAN OF REGION

SCALE OF MILES

20   10   0   20   40

LAND SUITABLE FOR IRRIGATION
IRRIGATION AREA FOR STAGE 1 DEVELOPMENT
PROPOSED MAIN DAM AND HYDRO POWER STATION
IRRIGATION CHANNELS

is reliable and severe droughts are infrequent. This intense rainfall leads to very considerable floods on the major river systems with consequent soil erosion and moderately high silt content in the flood flows.

The total catchment area drained by the Ord River is 21,050 square miles and the estimated median flow is 3 million acre-feet. Upstream from the proposed main damsite are 17,800 square miles of the catchment, and the calculated median flow at ths point is 2.45 million acre-feet. The catchment areas of the Keep and Baines rivers are much smaller, being only 4,740 square miles and 7,040 square miles respectively, with estimated median flows of 600,000 acre-feet and 900,000 acre-feet.

The cyclonic rainfall leads to large flood flows during the wet season, and two storms which occurred in 1956 and 1959 precipitated floods exceeding one million cusecs on the Ord River. River flows have been measured only from 1945 at gauging stations upstream of the damsite, but rainfall records for the past 60 years have been examined and all major storms studied. This study has resulted in the determination of a design flood for the Ord River main dam of 1.8 million cusecs.

The silt problem is a major one in the Ord River scheme and in any development in the north of Australia. Silt contents during floods have been measured since 1945 by throwing in a bottle from the bank and more recently by depth integration sampler from a cableway. The average silt content is between 0.5 per cent and 1 per cent by volume, but can rise as high as 1.5 per cent by volume depending on the state of the catchment and the intensity of the rain. It has been estimated that the Ord River brings down 12,500 acre-feet of suspended sediment and bedload in an average year, and allowance has been made for this in the determination of the safe yield from the reservoir. It is also to be expected that catchment reclamation measures will have had a measurable effect within the next 10 years.

Catchment reclamation is vital, but no improvement is allowed for in consideration of silt storage. A reconnaissance survey was made by the Department of Lands and Surveys of the soil erosion situation in the catchment area as long ago as 1944 and an estimate then prepared showed an area of 1,130 square miles, adjacent to the Ord River in Western Australia and the Negri in the Northern Territory, to be subject to erosion of varying degrees of severity. Some of the more severely eroded areas are being regenerated on the upper reaches of the Ord. This is described in Chapter 3. In recent years officers in the Department of Agriculture have been actively engaged in demonstrating methods of regenerating pasture cover on the more mildly eroded areas and formulating plans for attention to the more severely affected sections. Legislation exists under the State Soil Conservation Act to enable compulsive action if necessary in the Western Australian section.

THE MAIN STORAGE DAM

Since 1955 the whole of the storage basin has been flown and photo-
graphed at a scale of 14 chains to an inch. Horizontal and vertical ground
control was established by the Lands Department in conjuction with the
Public Works Department and the whole area was contoured at 10 feet
intervals by stereoplotting machine. This has resulted in a detailed picture
of the storage basin which would have taken many years to obtain by
normal methods. The capacities at various levels have now been determined and it is known that 3.5 million acre-feet is stored at 290 feet above
Wyndham mean springs. The water surface area is approximately 250
square miles. The reservoir will inundate the Argyle Downs homestead
and airstrip in addition to several miles of the Wyndham-Nicholson Road
and will back up close to the Lissadell homestead.

The main dam will have a thin sloping core rockfill dam some 200 feet
high above streambed which will have a total volume of some 1.7 million
cubic yards of rock and earth. A rock-excavated concrete-lined spillway
will be located in a natural saddle immediately downstream from the dam.
The excavation for the spillway will be over 200 feet deep and 300 feet
wide, and it involves a total excavation of approximately 1.4 million cubic
yards of rock, a large percentage of which may be used in the rockfill
dam. The design flood is 1.8 cusecs but by the provision of 50 feet of flood
storage in the reservoir, the maximum designed spillway discharge has
been reduced to 400,000 cusecs and, apart from reducing the cost of the
spillway structure, this in turn will reduce the risk of flooding downstream
from the main dam.

A concrete-lined tunnel some 14 feet 6 inches in diameter and 800 feet
long will be located in the right bank and will release up to 5,000 cusecs of
irrigation water through downstream control valves located in an irrigation
structure immediately adjacent to the dam. In the ultimate development
this tunnel will also be used to supply water to two of the hydro-electric
turbines. With a total storage of 3.5 million acre-feet, and making allowance
for both evaporation and siltation, the safe annual irrigation draw has been
calculated to be 1.25 million acre-feet.

The construction of the embankment will be completed in two years but
because of the large floods experienced during the wet seasons, normal
diversion is not possible. The embankment has therefore been designed to
pass flood-flows over the top during the one wet season. This has been
made possible by limiting the height of construction during the first year
and by protecting the clay core, the top surface and the downstream face
with large rock of approximately three feet in diameter.

THE DIVERSION DAM

The diversion dam is built across Bandicoot Bar some 30 miles downstream from the proposed major damsite, and is an integral part of the
total project. It comprises a concrete spillway 1,000 feet in length

with earth and rockfill embankments on each side, and four miles of
low levee bank to protect the irrigation area in times of flood. The
spillway consists of a broad concrete sill, keyed into the natural rock bar
and having thin vertical piers, 6 feet wide and 50 feet high, at 55 feet
centres. Between each pair of piers is a steel radial gate 37 feet high by
50 feet wide. There are 20 such gates, each weighing 95 tons. The gates
are operated automatically to pass the flood flows of up to 1.5 million cusecs
and so prevent flooding of the irrigation area. Flood flows in excess of
this amount will pass over the top of the western levee bank which is
remote from the irrigation area. Spanning the top of the dam is a two-lane
prestressed highway bridge providing an all-weather road link from the East
Kimberley to Wyndham. A 20 ton gantry crane straddles the roadway
and will be used to place stoplogs in slots in the piers so that the routine
maintenance may be carried out on the gates.

The storage behind the diversion dam is 80,000 acre-feet, of which
approximately 60,000 acre-feet is available for irrigation. At present only
the top 5 feet of the diversion dam storage provides gravity command
to the irrigation area. When the water drops below this level it is necessary
to pump into the irrigation channel through three 150 cusec vertical spindle
pumps. When the main dam is built, however, water will be released
downstream to maintain the level at the diversion dam and pumping will no
longer be necessary.

THE HYDRO-ELECTRIC POWER STATION

In the ultimate it is envisaged that the water released for irrigation will
be used for the generation of hydro-electric power and, in planning the
project, provision has been made for the location of a power station
immediately downstream from the dam in the right bank. Because of the
high tail-water levels, it was initially thought that the station would be
better underground; however, after thorough investigation and the decision
to provide 50 feet of flood storage, a surface power station, which is an
extension to the existing irrigation outlet, was found to be the most
economical solution. The installed capacity of the station will be 30
megawatts, comprising four 7.5 megawatt generators driven by Kaplan
turbines, installed progressively as power demand increases.

THE IRRIGATION AREA

The irrigation area covers some 170,000 acres and stretches from the
banks of the Ord River across to the Keep River valley. The area consists
of extensive black soil plains. Stage 1 involves the development of approximately 30,000 acres of these plains. Water for the irrigation area is
diverted from the diversion dam into the main irrigation channel which
has a capacity of 800 cusecs. At intervals along the main channel, subsidiary
channels branch off to supply the farms. Drainage of surplus water from
the farms is collected in main drains and led back into the Ord River at
convenient points. The development of this area involves the construction

of many structures ranging from highway bridges and pumping stations to small checks and farm turnouts. Each farm is a nominal 600 acres and consists of three 200 acre units, each unit having a supply of water through a 5 cusec Dethridge meter.

The reticulation and drainage design presents no difficulties, as the general slope of the country is of the order of 3 feet per mile. It is evident from experience so far that the permeability of the black soil, once wetted, is extremely low and channel losses from seepage are fairly small. Experience so far has shown that not only is drainage no problem but, also that the black soil stands up well under moisture conditions.

ECONOMIC AND SOCIAL ASPECTS

Such a development scheme as outlined above must, of course, have significant effects upon the character of the region's economy and upon its social structure, but it is not intended to describe them in this chapter. In Chapter 6 certain of the economic and social changes which will follow the implementation of these schemes are discussed, with particular reference to the position of agriculture as a junior partner in the region's primary and extractive industries. In Chapter 3 the effect of these schemes upon the senior partners, the pastoral industries, is considered. Throughout this survey, in fact, may be noticed the implicit assumption that the region's primary industries could be moving into another spurt of development. In Chapter 2 some of the changes in living conditions which can be expected to accompany more intensive development are discussed.

If the wider technical and economic problems mentioned in these previous chapters are solved, there can be little doubt that the successful completion of the harnessing and controlling of the waters of the Ord will have profound economic and social effects upon the Kimberley and upon the state as a whole.

Fitzroy-Margaret River System

Second in size and importance of the Kimberley rivers is the Fitzroy-Margaret system with a catchment area of 33,400 square miles and an estimated average annual run-off of 5.0 million acre-feet. While the Ord system provides the drainage pattern for a large sector of the East Kimberley, and its produce outlet is the recently extended port of Wyndham, the Fitzroy and Margaret rivers flow through the West Kimberley and the produce outlets are Broome and Derby.

The land settlement pattern created some form of division between the East and West Kimberley in their early stages of development. The first settlers in the Ord basin were predominantly eastern states cattlemen; those of the Fitzroy were sheepmen from the southern parts of Western Australia. Considerable rivalry, and on some occasions political antagonism, manifested itself between the two sectors of the Kimberley which developed as individual units based on their particular characteristics and economic situations. In subsequent years, with transport improvements and joint parliamentary representation, the separate identities of the East and West Kimberley tended to merge into one – that of the Kimberley. But the intensive development of the area's water resources may eventually introduce a new, perhaps milder, division between East and West, based, not upon earlier interests, but upon the two major river regions, the Ord valley and the Fitzroy valley. The Ord scheme has already been discussed. A section of the Fitzroy near Liveringa has, however, been under irrigation for some time.

Interest in the potential of the Fitzroy river's alluvial flats was awakened in 1950 following a visit to the area by Mr. Peter Farley of Associated Rural Industries Ltd. and the then federal Minister for the Interior, the Hon. H. V. Johnson, M.H.R. Favourable reports of the Fitzroy as a rice growing area were received from the New South Wales Department of Agriculture. Mr. Kim Durack, a descendent of one of the East Kimberley pioneering families, carried out initial experiments on an area of land adjoining Uralla Creek, approximately 8 miles from Liveringa homestead. Up to 80 acres of rice and safflower were irrigated from a pool in Uralla Creek.

In 1957, by Act of Parliament, an agreement to develop the area which has now become known as Camballin was reached between the state government and Northern Developments Pty. Ltd., a firm financed by Associated Rural Industries Ltd. Under the terms of the agreement the state government resumed 20,000 acres of Liveringa's pastoral lease and made it available to Northern Developments Pty. Ltd. on a rental basis with the right of eventual purchase. In addition, the state government provided the necessary engineering works to control and supply irrigation water, access roads, creek crossings and housing and water supply for the township of Camballin. The company in turn agreed to proceed with rice production and other rotational crops.

This scheme, whilst it was initiated before that of the Ord, has no pretensions to developing and exploiting the full water and land resources of the Fitzroy Margaret river system. The weir which has been built has not been designed for flood control and this is one of the weaknesses of the scheme; its prime function is to divert water into Uralla Creek and to provide limited storage. In terms of total development of the Fitzroy-Margaret river system it comprises a relatively small segment.

DAMSITES

Three possible damsites have been located and examined on the Fitzroy, the Margaret and the Leopold rivers. At present the hydrology of the system is largely unknown.

The main damsite on the Fitzroy is located at Dimond Gorge, 40 miles from Fitzroy Crossing, and access to the damsite is from Fossil Downs up Connor's Valley and over some ranges through boulder-strewn country. The rock is sound at the damsite and the geology simple. It has been estimated that a 200 foot dam wall would provide a storage comparable to the Ord. The proposed Margaret River damsite is located in a gorge 50 miles east of Fitzroy Crossing where the river leaves the King Leopold Ranges at the junction of Fossil Downs, Gogo and Louisa Downs stations' boundaries. It is estimated that a 100 foot dam wall would pond water back along the river just beyond the confluence of the Margaret and O'Donnel rivers. The dam wall would probably be 1,000 feet long at the top, 400 to 500 feet across at the base. The estimated catchment area behind the proposed damsite is in the vicinity of 5,200 square miles and estimated storage behind a 100 foot wall is 400,000 acre feet or 110,000 million gallons. Up to the present, work on these damsites has not progressed beyond the location and survey stages. The future of large-scale irrigation agriculture on the Fitzroy may be heavily dependent on the success of the Ord, in which the commonwealth government has a stake, for the capital financing of such large scale engineering projects is beyond the resources of the state government.

CAMBALLIN PROJECT

As previously mentioned, a small scheme has been initiated in the lower Fitzroy at Camballin. The Fitzroy Weir is a diversion structure on the Fitzroy River forming the headworks of the Camballin rice project, located 120 miles from Derby.

The rice area itself is being farmed by Northern Developments Pty. Ltd. who were the first to initiate commercial irrigation in the north of Western Australia. The state government undertook to supply water to the boundary of the company's property. For this purpose the Fitzroy Weir serves to divert water down Uralla Creek, which is a long anabranch of the Fitzroy, and this natural water course has been deepened and widened where necessary. About 17 miles down Uralla Creek there is a structure known as the 17 mile dam which raises the water in Uralla Creek to provide gravity command to the irrigation area. There are two supply channels, one to the western area with a concrete box siphon under Uralla Creek and one to the eastern area.

The general area might best be described as an alluvial flood plain, and in a major flood the whole area becomes a sheet of flowing water which causes severe damage to crops, check-banks and irrigation structures alike. The gradient of the plain is only about one foot per mile, so that the velocity of flow is not very fast, but nevertheless the area has been denuded, due to overstocking and kangaroos, to the point where sheet erosion is a serious problem. The soils in the area are typically a black sticky cotton soil on the plain, with silty red levee soils along the river and water courses. The higher land surrounding the flood plain is a sandy 'pindan', almost useless for agriculture.

HYDROLOGY OF THE FITZROY RIVER

The catchment of the Fitzroy River up to the weir is approximately 24,000 square miles. The lower half of this catchment is in a geologically old alluvial valley without any relief of importance, and the upper half is in extremely rugged country comprising massive quartzite and sandstone ranges together with some limestone, mudstone, phyllite, schists and other metamorphic rocks. The vegetation cover is very sparse; the trees are small and widely scattered except along the water courses. There is quite good natural grass cover in the lower half of the catchment, but in the upper half this is mostly confined to spinifex.

The average rainfall on the upper catchment is 22 inches per year and on the lower catchment 20 inches per year, and this comes in a fairly short wet season from December to the end of March. The rainfall is derived from three main sources: local thunderstorms, monsoonal depressions and cyclones. In each case the intensity is quite high and severe local or general flooding occurs quite often. While no accurate gauging has yet been possible it may be said that the magnitude of the peak floods on the Fitzroy approaches that of the Ord.

In the dry season the Fitzroy usually stops running in June and does not flow again until the first rain of the next wet season, about December, and consequently the weir can only divert run-of-river flows for wet season crops such as rice and cotton. There is a small storage of some 3,500 acre-feet in the weir, which can be utilized, and 4,500 acre-feet in the 17 mile dam, but otherwise water cannot be supplied all the year round until a major storage dam is built in the upper catchment.

Sediment in the form of both bedload and suspended load is a serious problem on the Fitzroy. Any diversion structure will affect the sediment regime of the river and of course it is desirable to keep as much sediment as possible out of the intake channel. In addition to sediment, the Fitzroy in flood brings down considerable quantities of debris in the form of leaves, twigs, branches and whole trees up to 30 feet long. While the amount carried is not as much as in the Ord, nor the flow so fast, the debris problem is troublesome in relation to gate operation, sluicing and offtake works.

THE WEIR

The large river-flows, the flat flood plains always prone to erosion, siltation of the river, and difficulties of access during the wet season were problems to be overcome in the design of a suitable structure to be built across the Fitzroy River. Full investigations and considerations were made of existing structures both overseas and in Australia. Finally, following a visit to India and Pakistan by Departmental engineers, a design was adopted which was based on the type of structure successfully developed in those countries.

Briefly, the weir consists of a broad concrete sill built on the compacted sand of the river bed with a steel sheet piling cut off driven through the sand into the impervious clay sub-soil. The spillway section which is 458 feet long, is surmounted by 47 steel shutters each 6 feet high and 8 feet long. The shutters are hinged in such a manner that they automatically collapse and lie flat on the crest of the sill when the river reaches a pre-determined level. The structure will therefore offer a minimum of interference to the large flood flows of the river. The shutters may be raised again in an upright position by a gantry which travels on rails along the concrete sill. A series of 8 sluice gates have been installed at the northern end of the structure to facilitate removal of silt from the vicinity of the Uralla Creek intake.

Other Kimberley Resources

The review of Australia's water resources prepared for the Australian Water Resources Council delineates 197 river basins, of which 9 are in the Kimberley. Two of these, the Ord and the Fitzroy, have been described in some detail above; the remainder may now be mentioned briefly. They are: The Cape Leveque Coast (basin No. 1), the Lennard River (No. 3), the Isdell River (No. 4), the Prince Regent River (No. 5), the King Edward River (No. 6), the Drysdale River (No. 7), and the Pentecost River (No. 8). These are shown on the map on page 188. They have been reported on briefly in Sadler.[6] The report, which contains tabulated statistical details, is based upon aerial reconnaissance and air-photo interpretation but does not cover the Cape Leveque basin which is thought to have limited surface water potential.

The principal rivers of the Lennard basin are the Lennard River and its tributary the Barker. Of lesser importance are the Hawkestone and Alexander creeks. The Lennard and Barker in their lower areas course through flood plains parts of which are very suitable for irrigation. Further upstream the Lennard and Barker both flow through the limestone Napier Range in the Winjina and Barker gorges respectively. Immediately behind both gorges the country is extremely flat, perhaps too flat to provide efficient storage reservoirs although they would provide excellent flood regulation. There is a possibility that water backed up by dams in these two gorges would flow around the Napier Range. Above Napier Range, from the vicinity of Kongorow Pool to well back near the Leopolds, the Barker River flows through hilly granitic country. The hills are low 'domes' of massive granite. A storage site, though perhaps not a good one, could probably be found in this area. In higher reaches of the Lennard between Mt. Joseph and the Leopolds the river runs through hilly country which may offer storage sites. A site has been noted on the Richenda in this area.

The principal rivers of the Isdell basin are the Isdell, Charnley and Calder. Lesser rivers are the Robinson, Humbert and Swift. There are also

[6]B. S. Sadler, 'Notes on Water Resources of the Kimberleys'.

numerous minor streams draining into Collier Bay and the Buccaneer Archipelago. The catchments of the Isdell, Charnley and Calder rivers are dominated by the sandstone plateau of the King Leopold, Artesian, Isdell, Phillips, Edkins and Harding ranges and through these sandstones the rivers have incised many gorges. Areas of volcanics having more open valleys also occur and contrast with the sandstones. The Humbert and Swift flow through rocky country where possible storage sites are formed by hills, but the Robinson-Tarraji is flat, braided and poorly contained. Storage prospects may be summarized as follows: good sites have been noted low down on the Isdell and Charnley but the Calder is more difficult and a good site may not exist, the Humbert and Swift appear to have reasonable sites low down but the Robinson-Tarraji is rather hopeless except in their extreme headwaters.

The principal rivers of the Prince Regent basin are the Prince Regent, Moran, Roe, Sale and Glenelg. The Prince Regent basin is an uplifted plateau, almost entirely sandstone, through which the rivers have incised some spectacular gorges on their path to the sea. Subsequent to the uplifting there has been a lesser subsidence which has partly drowned the lower ends of the valleys, forming impressive fiords. The basin, particularly around the Prince Regent River, includes some of the most rugged and inaccessible country in Western Australia. Some of the rivers offer good storage sites but unless it be to utilize a limited power potential any development of them seems a very remote prospect.

The principal rivers of the King Edward basin are the King Edward, its major tributary the Carson, and the Mitchell River. The King Edward is known to be perennial and perhaps other rivers in the area are perennial also. The main limb of the King Edward, the Mitchell River, and the Morgan River, a tributary of the Carson, all drain from a rocky plateau of relatively gentle relief, which is a mixture of sandstones and volcanics. The Carson drains an area of degraded volcanics bounded to the east by the more resistant sandstones which form the spectacular Carson escarpment. The storage prospects on the major rivers of this basin are disappointing.

The principal river of the Drysdale basin is the Drysdale but the basin also includes the King George and Berkeley rivers. The Drysdale River catchment is physiographically complex, embracing many land types of the North Kimberley. In its upper reaches the Drysdale, including the Gibb, drains a gently undulating plateau with good soil cover, the river being in a wide flat valley. Downstream of the Gibb confluence are to be found occasional hills and scarps which increase in number until in the vicinity of Wallis peak the country is quite hilly. Below here the country begins to open and the river descends through the plateau by small falls and rapids in a long sandstone gorge which has sufficient storage volume to be a damsite. Downstream of this the grade flattens again and the river is in long pools on a low coastal plateau, a mixture of volcanics and sandstones. Possible storage sites have been located on the Drysdale but they are not outstanding. The King George River drains a predominantly rough sandstone plateau of low relief which extends to the coast where the river drops into the sea over a spectacular waterfall. There may be a poor storage site between low hills a little above the fall. Upstream, the river grade is flat except near Seppelt Range where there is a short section of rapids. A possible storage site exists above these rapids. Apart from possible hydro-power development there would seem little use for the King George River. The Berkeley River in its lower reaches has incised itself through the plateau, and the river runs on a low grade through the tidal gorge to the sea. Above Seppelt Range is a section of rapids but the invert apparently does not rise greatly until above the Collision Range. There is a good storage at the Campbell Range.

The principal rivers of the Pentecost basin are the Durack, Pentecost and Forrest rivers and all appear to have good prospects for major storages should there be a demand for such. The Durack catchment is a tableland comprised mainly of sandstones and, for the most part, relief is moderate and there is apparently reasonable soil cover. However, towards the lower end, the river cuts down through the tableland in a continuous sandstone gorge which appears to have an evenly graded bed. Storage should be available in this gorge section. The Pentecost River has three main branchs, namely, the Salmond, the Chamberlain and the relatively minor Pentecost. Only the lower part of the Salmond was covered by survey, and here the river twists through a long, deep, generally wide sandstone gorge having an apparently evenly graded bed. A good storage was noted at the lower end of this gorge. The Chamberlain is a peculiar and spectacular river which drains a deep valley between Durack Ranges and Elgee Cliffs. The catchment is extremely narrow and long with hundreds of short tributaries which run directly and orthogonally into the river from the Durack Range on the east. There is a wonderful gorge at the lower end which appears to form a fine damsite. The Pentecost was not covered by survey but a study of contour maps suggests a good storage is available not far from its confluence with the Chamberlain. The Forrest River has cut its course on an even grade down through the sandstone plateau. The sandstones contain the river in what appears to be a good site at the river mouth. This storage would drown the Forrest River Mission but other sites would exist, at least on the tributaries, above the mission.

Conclusions

The water resources of the Kimberley average a total of 31.6 million acre-feet (arithmetic mean) annually from a catchment of 107,600 square miles. These resources comprise about 11 per cent of Australia's total resources. The rainfall for the area averages 21 inches per annum.

When it is completed, the first major attempt to harness one of the northern rivers, the Ord, will provide the East Kimberley with an irrigation area of up to 170,000 acres, depending on the crops grown, and an installed capacity of 30,000 k.w. of hydro-electric power. The dams will provide a considerable degree of flood control of the Ord, storage of up to 3.5 million acre-feet of water and facilities for diverting water into the irrigation area. From this it will be seen that upon completion of the scheme a more intensive form of land use will exist side by side in the Kimberley with the now dominant extensive pastoral industry. Some guesses at the likely population increase resulting from such a development are given in Chapter 6. The East Kimberley should expand considerably with these agricultural developments, and eventual population increase could also create the demand for a number of light secondary industries in the Ord River region.

Future development in the West Kimberley will probably depend heavily on the degree of success attending the Ord scheme. Should the scheme provide close settlement and a sound agricultural economy, the Fitzroy-Margaret system with its 5 million acre-feet of annual run-off will probably be the next area to be developed and the Camballin project will provide essential data to assist in planning such development. Damsites have been located on the upper Fitzroy and Margaret rivers in the preliminary surveys already undertaken, but before any concrete plan for development can be formulated for the West Kimberley, a more comprehensive hydrological survey of the rivers is essential.

Thus, development of the Kimberley's substantial water resources in the immediate future is likely to be confined to the two major river systems, the Ord of the East Kimberley and the Fitzroy-Margaret of the West Kimberley. Should these developments prove successful from an economic and social viewpoint, then it is quite likely that increased attention will be focussed on the other virtually untapped and extensive resources of the Northern Kimberley.

3. WATER CONSERVATION – PILBARA AND NORTH-WEST

In direct contrast to the water resources of the Kimberley, those of the remainder of the region are scant and irregular. South of the Fitzroy the region's climate changes from one of tropical savannah to one of steppe and desertland characterised by a low rainfall which tends also to be irregular – in some inland areas drought conditions have been known to extend over several years. As with the Kimberley, rain, when it comes, is characterized by heavy downpours and temporary flooding of large areas.

The major rivers of this part of the region are the De Grey, Fortescue, Ashburton and Gascoyne but, as yet, they have no flow records. Due to extremely variable rainfall and a high rate of evaporation, flow is spasmodic but when it does occur large floods are experienced because of the existence of large and relatively bare catchment areas. The rivers are not saline, except in the case of the upper reaches of the Gascoyne. Preliminary work has commenced on the Fortescue, Shaw, Harding and Coongan rivers by way of aerial photography and preliminary survey. A large programme of river gauging has also commenced.

It has been estimated that the total water resources of this area could be in the order of several million acre-feet per annum, but the uncertainty of flow makes storage rather unattractive. Despite these unfavourable climatic characteristics, considerable interest is being shown in the Gascoyne as a result of past development of irrigation agriculture at the mouth of the river. The Gascoyne is the only river of the Pilbara and North-West rivers on which detailed investigations are being carried out at present. The commonwealth government has agreed to assist the state government with these investigations.

The Gascoyne River

In the 1930's irrigation agriculture was commenced at the mouth of the Gascoyne as described in Chapter 6. The sub-tropical nature of the climate permitted the production of bananas which could compete favourably on the Perth market with Queensland and New South Wales produce. Later the growing of off-season vegetables was commenced. In the post-war period the industry expanded considerably, new growers being attracted to the area by the promise of high returns.

Irrigation water, when the river is not flowing, is drawn from sand lenses, a form of natural storage beneath the river, but with the increased number of producers on the river the natural storage capacity has become overburdened and the growers have become reliant on regular river flows to provide them with their required quantities of water. The importance of the industry has resulted in the state government taking some notice of demands for improved water supplies. Three lines of action have been taken: an extensive survey of the Gascoyne for possible damsites by the Public Works Department and a firm of private consultants, the erection of a clay barrier in the river, and the introduction of a pilot pumping scheme.

A survey of the Gascoyne was carried out by the Public Works Department in May-June 1960 in order to discover possible damsites.[7] Two were found : one at Kennedy Range 103 miles upstream from the mouth, and the other at 'Chalby Chalby' 190 miles upstream. Outside consultants were called in to examine the position and they made some specific recommendations in connection with the Kennedy Range site.[8] Engineering investigations for a dam at Kennedy Range are now in progress and the extent of the potential irrigation area in the Gascoyne is being assessed.

[7]Public Works Department, *Gascoyne River Water Resources*.
[8]R. M. Scott and H. G. Furphy, *Report for the Government of Western Australia — Gascoyne River*.

The possibility of establishing a major flood control and storage dam in the area is, however, subject to certain qualifications. First, such a proposal would be expensive; it could well cost somewhere in the region of $15 million for the complete scheme. Second, the industry is at present plagued by overproduction in some sectors (this aspect is covered more fully in Chapter 6). Before any further major expansion in output can be contemplated, a food processing and preserving industry would probably need to be established in order to handle the large-scale production increase which would probably result from the construction of the dam and which, in any case should be regarded as necessary to justify the expenditure on the dam in the first place. At the moment the ratio between total capital costs and the area to be serviced seems to be excessive by comparison with alternative projects in the region.

In an attempt to increase the river's underground storage capacity, a clay barrier was completed early in 1957. Since the barrier was erected the river has flowed on many occasions and the flow has been very irregular. In 1959, for instance, the river failed to reach the plantations at all. In August of that year it stopped half a mile upstream from the Gascoyne bridge, the upstream boundary of the plantations. Since 1957, weekly readings of water levels in a number of selected bores and wells have been taken and plotted so that variations in water levels can be watched and the effect of the barrier established.

The construction of this bar envisaged the holding up of river waters in the top sands to provide better conditions for replenishing the lower aquifer waters. There is no evidence to conclude that this action is taking place. In fact the growers immediately downstream of the bar have experienced further deterioration rather than improvements in their supplies. It would appear that the immediate effect of the bar has been to bulk up supplies of top water immediately upstream of the bar for possibly 60 to 80 chains and to deplete the supplies for a similar distance downstream. The overall effect of the bar appears to be purely local and, at this stage, it can be concluded that no overall improvement in supply has been effected. The whole area is therefore directly dependent on regular flows of the river.

Ten farmers have been re-located upstream of the bridge as a result of their properties having sustained severe damage in recent floods. There is also a tendency for properties near the mouth of the river to become more saline than others at certain times of the year and this was a further reason for the re-location. The new plantations seem to be doing well.

Conclusions

The question of stabilizing water resources on the Gascoyne produces an interesting problem. Solutions which have been offered to date are of three types : the small-scale clay barrier, the pilot pumping system which brings temporary alleviation to a few planters but no overall remedial result and which costs in excess of $200,000 per scheme, and the large-scale project with flood control and storage dam and allied works, the cost of which runs into millions.

The future development of irrigation agriculture in the area should be carefully considered before further expenditure is made to stabilize the water supply, and foremost in such considerations should be an appreciation of the industry's future markets. Should food processing industries commanding an interstate or international market be attracted to the area, justification for a major dam may be made but at present the market possibilities do not call for a greatly increased output and stop-gap expenditure may thus be of doubtful value economically, though justifiable from a social or moral viewpoint. A comprehensive assessment of the industry's future is essential before any large-scale financial commitments are entered into. This problem is examined in more detail in Chapter 6.

Interest is quickening in the possibilities of utilizing the waters of the other rivers, the Ashburton, the Fortescue and the De Grey. Large quantities of water are now required for domestic and industrial use because of the mineral development now occurring in the Pilbara and elsewhere. This has resulted in a closer look being taken at the economics of surface storages in the area which is one of the three main water sources. The other two are desalination which is already being carried out at Dampier, and underground water (examined in Section 5 below).

4. Town Water Supplies

The town water supplies of the region are drawn either from artesian bores or from wells on the banks of rivers, or, in the case of Wyndham, from permanent pools in the King River. As can be seen from the following assessment compiled by the Public Works Department, the quality and availability of domestic water supplies in the region vary considerably. In average terms consumption varies from 1,270 gallons per day at Point Samson to 280,000 at Carnarvon. Peak consumption ranges from 1,600 gallons per day at Point Samson, which is reliant on restricted supplies from the state ships, to 402,000 at Broome. The towns of Derby, Broome, Port Hedland, Wyndham and Carnarvon have facilities for supplying shipping with water. Gallons consumed per head per day are lowest at Point Samson (18) and highest at Camballin (270). Broome also has the highest annual consumption, 94 million gallons.

Table 2 outlines the number of water services in northern towns from 1957 to 1966. The largest aggregate in 1966 was at Carnarvon and the least number of services, 10, was at Gascoyne Junction. The highest percentage increase over the period 1951-1966 is to be found at Hall's Creek, 137 per cent, and the lowest at Roebourne, 6 per cent, Onslow recorded a 12 per cent decrease. Water supplies in individual townships are commented on below.

Shark Bay (Denham)

The township supply supports an estimated population of 387 and has an average daily consumption of 21,300 gallons. Total salinity of the town's water supply amounts to 4,400 parts per million, while chloride content is 3,200 p.p.m. The water supply is drawn from an artesian bore 1,584 feet deep, located on Lot 8 in the centre of the town and there is sufficient pressure in the bore to deliver water to the storage tanks on high ground. All water is aerated, settled and filtered through sand beds before entering the storage tanks and the supply is not visibly affected by seasonal conditions. It has been operating since early 1957 and a new bore was completed in March, 1966.

Carnarvon

The township supply supports an estimated population of 2,400 and has an average daily consumption of 280,000 gallons. Total salinity of the town's water supply amounts to 615 p.p.m. minimum to 1,100 p.p.m. maximum, while chloride content is 286 p.p.m. minimum to 733 p.p.m. maximum. The supply for Carnarvon is pumped from two 12 inch bores and two wells adjacent to the Gascoyne River approximately three miles from the town. The wells are each 55 feet deep and the bores on a nearby island are 54 feet and 60 feet deep respectively. The salinity of the water varies with seasonal conditions and is at its freshest immediately after the river has flowed. Irrigation water for plantations is also drawn from the Gascoyne River sands and a heavy draw can affect the town supply if there is an extended period of low rainfall.

Gascoyne Junction

The township supply, which is in the course of construction, will support an estimated population of 50. Total salinity of the town's water supply amounts to 390 p.p.m. while chloride content is 206 p.p.m. The water is pumped from one well in a shallow in the river bed half a mile from town.

Exmouth

The township supply supports an estimated population of 1,000, some of whom are living in caravans, though development of the town is still proceeding rapidly and the population will continue to increase. This is the only township in the region that is sewered. Exmouth has an average daily consumption of 52,700 gallons. Total salinity of the town's water supply amounts to 1,170 p.p.m. while chloride content is 757 p.p.m. The water is pumped from 12 six-inch bores, ½ mile-1½ miles west of the town, varying in depth from 107 feet to 255 feet. Additional bores are being drilled in 1966. There is also a reservoir with one tank of half a million gallons capacity and one under construction.

Onslow

The township supply supports an estimated population of 300 and has an average daily consumption of 38,700 gallons. Total salinity of the town's water supply amounts to 243 p.p.m. while chloride content is 29 p.p.m. The water is pumped through four-inch fibrolite pipe from bores adjacent to the Cane River, approximately 18 miles from Onslow. There are four bores each cased with six-inch bore casing varying in depth from 85 feet to 150 feet. One bore is equipped with a windmill and three have diesel operated jack pumps. Since the scheme was installed in 1957 the supply has not deteriorated during dry spells.

Roebourne

The township supply supports an estimated population of 550 and has an average daily consumption of 53,800 gallons. Total salinity of the town's water supply amounts to 860 p.p.m. while chloride content is 497 p.p.m. The water for Roebourne is pumped from a well or from two bores on the east bank of the Harding River approximately half a mile from the town. The quality of the water varies slightly throughout the year but the supply has been known to deteriorate seriously only during extended drought conditions.

Point Samson

The township supply supports an estimated population of 80 and has an average daily consumption of 1,270 gallons. Investigations have shown that ground water supplies near Point Samson have a very high saline content and are unsuitable even for a small town supply. All water is delivered by State Shipping Service vessels from other ports between Fremantle and Darwin. Water is pumped ashore into storage tanks by ships' pumps and is reticulated throughout the town, each of the 22 houses being allowed an absolute maximum of 25,000 gallons each per annum. Houses were first connected to the scheme in September 1960 and septic systems are being installed, there is expected to be an increase in the present daily consumption.

Wittenoom Gorge

The township supply supports an estimated population of 950 and has an average daily consumption of 79,300 gallons. Total salinity of the town's water supply amounts to 360 p.p.m. while chloride content is 60 p.p.m. The water for Wittenoom was originally drawn from a spring approximately five miles up the gorge. The flow from this spring, which was gauged at 67,000 gallons per day, reduced eventually to 31,000 g.p.d. which was inadequate for the town's needs. Consequently four eight-inch bores approximately four miles from the town in the opposite direction on the Roebourne Road have been equipped and are now operating. These bores are between 123 and 158 feet deep.

Nullagine

The township supply supports an estimated population of 30 and has an average daily consumption of 2,300 gallons per day. Total salinity of the water supply amounts to 240 p.p.m. while chloride content is 51 p.p.m. The water is drawn from one well and one bore.

Marble Bar

The township supply supports an estimated population of 350 and has an average daily consumption of 11,500 gallons. Total salinity of the town's water supply amounts to 420 p.p.m. while chloride content is 47 p.p.m. The water for Marble Bar is pumped from a well 40 feet deep in Sandy Creek which runs through the centre of the town and a six-inch bore 84 feet deep at Sandy's Camp half a mile from town. Another six-inch bore drilled nearby is shortly to be equipped to supply the township.

Port Hedland

The township supply supports an estimated population of 2,970, approximately 900 construction workers included, and has an average daily consumption of 192,000 gallons. Total salinity of the town's water supply amounts to 320 p.p.m. while chloride content is 100 p.p.m. Since 1954, water for Port Hedland has been pumped from a series of bores at the Turner River approximately 20 miles from the town. Six eight-inch bores at present in use vary in depth from 85 feet to 148 feet. The source of supply varies considerably depending upon seasonal conditions and upon whether or not the river has flowed. Immediately following a run of the river, water is pumped from a shallow sump in the river bed. The population of Port Hedland is expanding rapidly and greater demands will be made from these water resources in the near future.

Broome

The township supply supports an estimated population of 1,500 and has an average daily consumption of 268,000 gallons. Total salinity of the town's water supply amounts to 303 p.p.m. while chloride content is 153 p.p.m. The Broome town water supply came from an artesian bore 1,543 feet deep in the centre of the town near the school. Water was reticulated under natural pressure and there was sufficient pressure in the bore to supply water to all mains in the town at most times. This was abandoned in 1962 and a new source of potable water has deen developed eight miles from the town along the road to Derby, the salinity being 303 grains per gallon total, of which 153 are chlorides. Five eight-inch diameter bores of depth 217 feet to 326 feet have been equipped to supply the township.

Derby

The township supply supports an estimated population of 2,000 and has an average daily consumption of 225,000 gallons. Total salinity of the town's water supply amounts to 413 p.p.m. while chloride content is 283 p.p.m. The water for Derby is pumped from seven bores in the town and the supply from this source is not materially affected by seasonal conditions. The depth of the bores varies from 80 feet to 100 feet. Five miles out of Derby is Mayalls Bore which was drilled in 1911. This is an artesian bore 1,056 feet deep, which is used for watering stock being brought into Derby from outlying stations. Its salinity is 400 p.p.m. The flow from this bore, which was 69,400 gallons per day in 1911, has now diminished to 15,000 gallons per day.

Camballin

The township supply supports an estimated population of 39 and has an average daily consumption of 10,500 gallons. Total salinity of the town's water supply amounts to 258 p.p.m. while chloride content is 100 p.p.m. The water comes from two bores in the township.

Halls Creek

The township supply supports an estimated population of 440 and has an average daily consumption of 35,000 gallons. Total salinity of the town's water supply amounts to 120 p.p.m. while chloride content is 14 p.p.m. The water is pumped from a well and four bores near the town. It is small, approximately 1,200 gallons per hour, and is not materially affected by seasonal conditions. The well is 46 feet deep and the six bores vary in depth from 145 feet to 172 feet.

Wyndham

The township supply supports an estimated population of 960 and has an average daily consumption of 148,500 gallons of which the Wyndham Meatworks is the major consumer. Total salinity of the town's water supply amounts to 78 p.p.m. while chloride content is 13 p.p.m. Water for Wyndham is drawn from two pools in the King River approximately 20 miles from the town. These pools can be affected by seasonal conditions. The population and water consumption is greatest during the killing season at the meatworks from May to September when the average daily consumption is as much as 270,000 gallons. A storage tank of one million gallons capacity is sited near the township plus a one million gallon tank at the Meatworks.

Kununurra

The township supply supports an estimated population of 921 and has an average daily consumption of 176,000 gallons. Total salinity of the town's water supply amounts to 380 p.p.m. while chloride content is 61 p.p.m. The water is pumped from four bores plus a pump in the reservoir.

5. Underground Water Supplies

So far this chapter has been concerned mainly with surface water and its conservation and control. The resources below the surface are, however, still of great importance, as they have been in the past, and a short description of them is essential to any appraisal of the complete water resources of the region.[9]

Two main types of underground water may be distinguished: ground or non-pressure water, and confined or pressure water. Pressure water may further be sub-divided into artesian and sub-artesian, depending on whether or not the pressure is great enough to force the water to the surface through the bore hole. All of these types are found in Northwestern Australia.

On the basis of the type of underground water generally found in the area the region can be separated into clearly defined zones, namely, sedimentary artesian basins in which artesian and sub-artesian supplies can be expected, and crystalline, igneous and metamorphic rock areas in which utilization of ground water predominates.

The sedimentary artesian basins of the region are : the Bonaparte Gulf basin, the Ord basin, the Canning basin and the Carnarvon basin. The crystalline rock complex occupies the remainder of the region and throughout it variable ground water conditions exist. Generally speaking, it should be noted that whereas no chance of pressure water exists within the crystalline rocks, non-pressure ground water can be encountered within all the artesian basins, given favourable conditions.

Underground Pressure or Artesian Water.

All of the artesian areas mentioned above are composed of varying thicknesses of sedimentary and, more rarely, volcanic rocks which, depending on favourable structures within these sedimentary sequences, carry supplies of water. These supplies are used mainly by the pastoral industry, as seen in Chapter 3. The utilization of any of these aquifers is largely governed by depth below the surface, by known reliability as a producer, by salinity, by rainfall on the intake beds and, most important, by the proper siting of the bore.

The Bonaparte Gulf basin is situated in the north-eastern corner of Western Australia and straddles the Northern Territory-Western Australian border. It covers an area of some 7,500 square miles (about 2,500 square miles in Western Australia) of low lying coastal country of which only about one-third is suitable for pastoral use. Records of only one artesian bore are available; this was drilled in the course of oil exploration during 1959-60. Water was encountered in the vicinity of 1,000 feet and flowed at the rate of some 2,000 gallons per hour. The water is warm and contains sulphuretted hydrogen but it is suitable for human consumption.

[9]This section is based upon information supplied by the Geological Survey of Western Australia.

The Ord basin, covering an area of some 50,000 square miles of pastoral country, yields good sub-artesian water at depths of up to 300 feet. Yields are in the vinicity of 1,200 gallons per hour from pervious beds inter-bedded with limestones and shales of the sedimentary sequence. Associated with the sedimentary beds of the basin are basal volcanic flows which cover an area of some 10,000 square miles of excellent grassland. Bores put down to an average of 75 feet give supplies of water in the vicinity of 1,200 gallons per hour.

The Canning basin is the largest of the artesian basins in Western Australia; it covers an area of some 143,500 square miles. Approximately two-thirds of this area is desert country of no pastoral value. It is split geologically into two parts, the Fitzroy trough, which occupies an area of some 13,500 square miles along the northern margin, and the Canning basin proper. Whilst they share the same aquifers, their water conditions vary considerably and it is convenient, therefore, to examine them separately.

In the Fitzroy trough underground artesian water supplies within the sedimentary sequence are, generally speaking, restricted to two sources. There is, first, a series of deep aquifers which require holes up to 5,000 feet in depth at the centre of the basin. Second, there is a shallower sequence of younger sediments which is usually a reliable source of water but is known to contain saline beds. Derby obtains its water from these shallower source beds.

The tapping of underground water in the Canning basin is rather more restricted than in the Fitzroy trough, due to the fact that the most prolific aquifer is so situated that, in order to obtain sufficient hydrostatic head, holes must be drilled topographically below the 80 foot contour. This restricts optimum bore siting to a narrow coastal strip some 10-20 miles wide. Shallower source beds do exist and these are drawn from, but their reliability regarding salinity is questionable. As well as this, deeper aquifers which are encountered in the Fitzroy trough may be tapped further inland but little information is available as to their reliability and depth.

The Carnarvon basin is a coastal basin covering an area of some 35,000 square miles, and from the small amount of information available, indi-cations are that the water is too saline for human consumption and in many cases unsuitable for stock. Information obtained from boreholes drilled for oil in the northern portion of the basin shows highly saline water at depths ranging from 1,000-5,000 feet. In the southern part of the basin bores average 200-300 feet in depth and produce water with a salinity of approximately 4000 parts per million.

Ground or Non-Pressure Water

Favourable structures for the retention of underground water of the non-pressure variety are of two main types. There are, first of all, the weathered zones of the earth's crust which vary in depth from a few inches to several hundred feet, and also fractures, joints and cavities. Then, second, there are the surface deposits of a porous nature such as alluvial or transported deposits, both recent and fossil.

Ground water yields are generally much smaller than artesian, due to lack of storage structures, and the depths at which water is encountered is usually much less, probably not greater than 150 feet. In certain circumstances, however, large quantities of water are recorded from non-pressure sources at shallow depths. For example, a tested pump yield in excess of 400,000 gallons per day has been recorded from a shallow bore which penetrated a fossil drainage channel in the Wiluna area.

In contrast to artesian sources, ground water replenishment is directly related to seasonal fluctuations of rainfall in the locality where the water is needed. Whereas drought conditions do not usually affect artesian sources, ground water supplies can be easily exhausted through over-development. Thus ground water conditions vary considerably throughout Northwestern Australia, each locality having individual characteristics dependent on soil type, topography, rainfall, vegetation and depth of weathering.

In recent years, use of aerial photographs and geophysical methods within the region have greatly increased the chances of siting successful bores, and it is due to these methods that in the more arid portions of the state the importance of fossil drainage channels is now being recognised as a source of ground water. As these drainage channels are found to occur in many parts of Northwestern Australia, it is likely that the next decade will see important developments in the utilization of these supplies.

6. TIDAL POWER RESOURCES

The possibility of utilizing tidal ebb and flow for the generation of electric power in the region has been given some attention of late, and a recent report summarizes the interesting results of research in this field which was carried out by Mr. J. G. Lewis while an officer of the State Public Works Department.[10]

Basically, the proposal is prompted by the fact that the region has no source of cheap power – one of the essentials for economic development. The report claims that of the three basic fuels used throughout the world in power generation, coal has generally been found to be the most satisfactory; the economics of using fuel oil for this specific purpose usually makes any comparison with coal unfavourable though fuel oil is admirably suited to traction. Nuclear power stations are still relatively inefficient and uneconomic by comparison. The region has none of these fuels as yet and would have to import them. But it does possess an enormous power potential in the great tidal movements on the north-western coast of Australia and Lewis's purpose is to draw attention to this.

[10]J. G. Lewis, 'The Water Resources of the Kimberley'.

Tidal energy varies with the square of the tidal range and the area of the water basin. Thus large basins with large tidal variations offer the best prospects for this type of power generation. Large tidal variations of up to 40 feet, resulting from the combination of natural forces and topography, occur only in a few areas in the world and one of these is the Kimberley coast of Western Australia. An additional characteristic of this coastline is that it has some very large basins with suitable sites for dam construction.

The Lewis report summarizes the tidal power resources of the whole north-west coast from La Grange Bay to Darwin Harbour. Altogether 45 schemes are examined and from these some 25 have been selected as possibilities which could prove economically attractive after further detailed analysis. Within these 25 schemes Lewis makes a ranking based upon power output per mile of dam, without taking account of the overall economics of the schemes, although elsewhere in the report he does assume that 'the economics and practical possibility of tidal power in the Kimberley can be reduced to costs of the tidal installation itself.' On this assumption and the assumption that costs of the dam construction do not vary greatly this is, no doubt, as good a general way of ranking as any. In most of the schemes examined the power output per mile of dam is very high, by world standards. Table 3 gives some statistical details of the 25 schemes mentioned above.

Three methods of utilizing tidal power are examined. The first is simply the emptying of the basin, under uni-directional turbines. In this method, which is the least costly from the viewpoint of capital installation, considerable power potential is lost. The second method is double flow which utilizes both the ebb and flow tides, using the universal turbines. The advantage of this method is that the plant is operative for a greater proportion of the time and thus more power is extracted from the scheme. The third method is the double basin system which makes use of two interconnected basins. Costs are highest in this method and suitable sites are not so plentiful but it has the advantage of being able to generate power continuously. When power extraction is considered in relation to cost, the double flow system is favoured and Lewis examines the alternative schemes in the Kimberley from this point of view, though provision is made for extending six of them to double basin systems if required in the future.

The report is largely technical and exploratory and the economic aspects of the schemes, though mentioned, are not examined in great detail. For that matter Lewis emphasizes that the technical features themselves need further analysis in much greater detail, and for this purpose a great deal of additional information would have to be gathered in the area concerned. The technical possibilities of linking up to the Australian national grid with a D.C. transmission line present no insuperable problem in Lewis's view, and the main economic problem is the vast capital expenditure needed on the tidal installation itself.

One of these sites has already been investigated in some detail. The state governments in conjunction with Sogreah, a firm of French consulting engineers, have examined the feasiblity of a tidal power scheme at Collier Bay just north of Derby. The proposal consisted of closing off the main entrance to Secure Bay with rockfill dams and surrounding the rockfill dams with sluice gates for the adjustment of basin levels. Further sluice gates and turbines would be located in rock cuts on either side of the rock embankments. The proposal envisages the installation of thirty 19 M.W. bulb units giving a totalled installed capacity of 570 M.W.'s. To provide power during the inoperative periods and during neap tide a pumped storage scheme using an adjacent high level basin is required. Two rockfill dams each 230 feet high would close the openings from the basin and form a high level storage of 145,000 acre-feet and a 36 feet diameter tunnel 4,000 feet long would connect the reservoir to the pumping/power station. The station would include six pumps with a total capacity of 400 M.W., three of which would be coupled to generators of 170 M.W. It is estimated that the continuous power output would be 150-200 M.W. at unit load factor. After careful study to obtain the optimum scheme it is estimated that such a proposal would cost between $240 million and $280 million depending on interest rates demanded for the capital needed to complete the scheme.

Although the possibilities for generating electric power from the tides in the Kimberley are obviously great, it seems at the moment that a technological breakthrough would be needed in at least two and possibly three aspects of the proposed schemes before these could be considered to be an economically feasible proposition. First, the capital costs need to be reduced. In this respect the possibility of using nuclear devices for moving the rock has distinct advantages. At least it would be possible to do this in some of these remote locations where the treated area could be left for two or three years to clean up, without undue disruption to economic or social life. This would represent an advantage peculiar to the Kimberley area. Second, operating costs would need to be reduced substantially in order to drive the cost of producing electricity down from one cent per unit to something like 0.5c or 0.6c. Any technical breakthrough of this nature would also, of course, be capable of application elsewhere in competing areas although its application might not be immediate because existing capital installations might not be able to be scrapped or modified without considerable expense. Finally, reticulation costs would have to be reduced considerably except in the unlikely event of vast quantities of power being needed on the spot. The promising bauxite deposits in Admiralty Gulf spring to mind as one possibility for this type of development.

All in all, one may say that the realization of the electricity generating potential of the tidal power resources of the Kimberley would seem to lie well in the future.

7. Conclusions

With more than 100,000 square miles of catchment area and an annual run-off in the order of 30 million acre-feet of water the Kimberley area is well endowed with water resources. For the remainder of Northwestern Australia, the figures are not reassuring and prospects for large-scale conservation and irrigation are less bright.

The region possess supplies of underground water in the form of both artesian and sub-artesian basins and of non-pressure or ground water. Four main artesian basins can be distinguished and there is considerable variation in depth, rate of flow, salinity and other properties. The total extent of these basins, lying within the region, is 231,000 square miles, or nearly one half of the region's total area. In the remainder of the region non-pressure water is found under varying conditions.

Of the main Kimberley surface water systems, the Ord and the Fitzroy-Margaret, the first is currently being developed on a fairly large scale and the second is being developed on a lesser scale. The other area in the region where conservation and irrigation is being practised is Carnarvon and here the development is still confined to a relatively small area of the Gascoyne delta.

Techniques of water conservation and irrigation have two broad aspects – the solution of engineering problems and the solution of economic and social problems. It is probably true to say that given the necessary economic resources, and experience and initiative on the part of the engineers, the solution of the technical engineering problems is merely a matter of time. Ideally, a great deal of analytical work should be done, before the inception of any scheme, in order to determine both the basic aim of the scheme and the economic organization and measures necessary to ensure its successful completion. Indeed, upon some of these answers will depend the engineering techniques and solutions adopted.

One thing does seem sure and that is that if the Ord scheme proves successful, it will be followed by the other projects of a similar nature designed to capitalize upon the natural water endowments of the region. The development of the Fitzroy valley will probably be the next stage in the long term exploitation of the Kimberley resources.

In the Pilbara, a rapid population influx in response to the vigorous mineral development occurring there has necessitated a re-orientation of thinking on the time-path of water resource development. Added to this is the industrial demand for water which will accompany the exploitation of the deposits and the subsequent processing operations. The net effect has been to accelerate the investigation of all types of water resources, including the possibility of inducing rain through convection from bitumenized areas.

A different aspect of the utilization of the region's water resources is emphasized in proposals for the development of hydro-electric power based upon the great tidal variation in conjunction with the topography of the north-western coastline. Sufficient detailed information is not yet available but it does appear probable that at some time in the future these unutilized resources will be turned to good purpose and the region, and indeed the nation, may profit from the provision of greatly increased power supplies. Installation, operation and reticulation costs are the limiting factors at the present time, for the proposed projects are technically feasible. This sort of development, except on a very small, localized scale, may still lie many years in the future.

BIBLIOGRAPHY

AUSTRALIAN WATER RESOURCES COUNCIL. *Australia's Water Resources (Stream Flow and Underground Resources) 1963.* Canberra, 1963.

KELSALL, K. J. 'Water Resources.' Paper presented to Kimberley Consultative Council. 1965.

LEWIS, J. G. 'The Water Resources of the Kimberley.' *Industrial Review and Mining Yearbook.* Perth, 1959.
—— *The Tidal Power Resources of the Kimberley.* Perth, 1962.

MORGAN, J. F. *Report on Central North Kimberley Region.* Perth, 1954.

PARKER, J. E. 'Developing the Kimberleys.' *Australian Civil Engineering and Construction.* 1965.

PUBLIC WORKS DEPARTMENT. *Margaret River Damsite Survey.* Perth, 1953.
—— *Gascoyne River Water Resources.* Perth, 1960.
—— *Fitzroy River – Dimond Gorge Damsite.* Perth, 1961.
—— *Camballin Irrigation Area.* Perth, 1961.
—— *Lennard River Project.* Perth, undated.
—— *Gascoyne River – Irrigation, Investigation and Design.* Perth, undated.
—— *Gascoyne River – Supply to Banana Plantations.* Perth, undated.
—— *North-West Town Water Supplies.* Perth, undated.

SADLER, D. S. 'Notes on Water Resources of the Kimberleys.' Prepared by engineers of the Water Resources Section, Public Works Department, Perth. 1966.

SCOTT, R. M. and FURPHY, H. G. *Report for the Government of Western Australia – Gascoyne River.* Perth, 1961.

WEBSTER, K. C. 'Water Resources and Engineering Aspects of the Ord Irrigation Project.' Paper presented to the Australian and New Zealand Association for the Advancement of Science, Hobart. 1965.

TABLE 1

KIMBERLEY WATER RESOURCES

River basin	No.	Total area (square miles)	Average annual rainfall (inches)[1]	Annual run-off (mill. acre-ft.)
Fitzroy	2	33,400	14-39	5.0
Lennard	3	5,430	19-37	1.5
Isdell	4	7,480	26-50	4.0
Prince Regent	5	5,450	34-52	4.5
King Edward	6	6,550	33-51	4.5
Drysdale	7	9,870	28-50	4.5
Pentecost	8	11,140	26-33	3.0
Ord	9	21,700	15-31	4.3

[1] Spatial range.

Source: Australian Water Resources Council, *Australia's Water Resources (Stream Flow and Underground Resources) 1963.*

TABLE 2

TOWN WATER SUPPLIES – NUMBER OF SERVICES[1]

	1957	1961	1966	Percentage increase 1961-1966
Shark Bay	41	62	76	23
Carnarvon	378	465	635	37
Gascoyne Junction	—	—	10	n.a.
Exmouth	—	—	321	n.a.
Onslow	87	101	89	— 12
Roebourne	68	85	90	6
Point Samson	—	24	24	0
Wittenoom	174	192	222	10
Nullagine	—	—	11	n.a.
Marble Bar	26	33	37	12
Port Hedland	174	250	368	47
Broome	—	310	344	11
Derby	186	266	417	57
Camballin	—	7	14	100
Halls Creek	11	27	64	137
Wyndham	—	127	259	104
Kununurra	—	—	172	n.a.

[1] A service is a single connection to the main.

Source: Western Australia, Public Works Department.

TABLE 3

KIMBERLEY AREA

Tidal Power Resources

Basin	Area (square miles)	Maximum tide (feet)	Length of dam (miles)	Possible economic priority
Port Usborne	22	33	0.4	7
The Graveyard	16	33	0.3	8
King Sound	1,650	30	15.3	5
Dugong Bay	12	36	0.3	11
Talbot Bay*	92	36	3.7	15
Secure Bay I	11	36	0.25	9
Secure Bay II	25	36	0.5	6
Walcott Inlet	110	36	0.35	1
George Water	70	36	0.6	3
Doubtful Bay	175	36	4.5	12
Collier Bay I	267	36	14.3	18
Collier Bay II	1,000	33	32.0	14
Brecknock I	54	30	3.1	23
Brecknock II*	109	30	6.2	24
St. George Bay I	102	33	0.6	2
St. George Bay II*	150	32	1.3	4
Prince Fred. I	140	30	5.3	19
Prince Fred. II*	190	30	5.8	17
Brunswick Bay	542	30	27.3	21
York Sound	502	27	19.5	20
Admiralty Gulf	850	21	25.0	25
Cambridge Gulf I	30	24	0.3	10
Cambridge Gulf II	88	23	1.0	13
Cambridge Gulf III*	152	22	2.9	16
Cambridge Gulf IV	518	18	10.0	22

* Denotes possible double basin.

Source: J. G. Lewis, 'The Water Resources of the Kimberley'.

CHAPTER 8

SECONDARY AND TERTIARY INDUSTRY

1. Introduction

It is possible to describe the development of a region partly in terms of shifts in the workforce between the broad industry groupings, primary, secondary and tertiary. This three-fold classification originated in the empirical studies of Colin Clark and A. G. B. Fisher, who produced some general arguments, backed by statistical indicators, to show that countries with the higher per capita incomes in the 1930's tended to have the lower percentages of employment in the 'lower' sectors. Similarly, over time, some economies had shifted towards the 'upper' sectors as per capita income increased.[1] There were important exceptions for which special reasons had to be found, and the universal applicability of this scheme has been critically scrutinized and questioned since it was first propounded.

Many regions certainly pass through a series of stages, as they develop, as Perloff has shown, starting from an early subsistence economy to one that specialises in the export of tertiary activities.[2] Whichever stages of development a region passes through, the movement is likely to reflect shifts both in demand and in labour productivities. A shift up the sector ladder implies rising labour productivities in primary industry and a surplus of resources made available for specialized tertiary services. Perloff's framework emphasizes the shift out of a subsistence pattern to a market economy. However, neither of these simple patterns fits the north pattern, even in outline.

Northwestern Australia has not been a subsistence economy since a market economy was forcibly imposed directly upon the hunting economy of the

[1] See for instance, C. Clark, *The Conditions of Economic Progress,* or A. G. B. Fisher, *The Clash of Progress and Security.* For criticism see P. T. Bauer and B. S. Yamey, 'Economic Progress and Occupational Distribution', pp. 741-55.

[2] H. S. Perloff, E. S. Dunn, E. E. Lampard and R. F. Muth, *Regions, Resources, and Economic Growth.*

primitive tribal aborigines, nor have tertiary activities been lacking from
the outset. The region being so sparsely settled, government activities
have always been important.

The pattern of change in the distribution of the workforce is all the
more interesting for not fitting into many pre-conceived ideas of development, and it deserves to be studied carefully. Comments on the relationship
between primary, secondary and tertiary industry are given in Chapter 2.
The relative increase in primary employment compared with secondary
employment is undoubtedly in this instance an indication of development,
not of retrogression, for reasons that the preceding chapters have given.
For a region such as this, the first stages of development may well result
in a rising proportion of primary employment, due to the opening up of
new land, and to the exploitation of mineral resources. Tertiary employment
rather than secondary, is likely to increase in a marked degree initially.
In addition, Northwestern Australia is peculiarly sensitive to the demand
for its exports, and much of that demand comes from overseas. Periods
of rapid growth can result from exogenous changes in demand rather
than from surpluses developed in the region itself — a good reason why
any 'normal' growth pattern will be departed from. For example, the
demand for pearl shell, for asbestos and for meat has shifted substantially
from one decade to the next, and the relevant export industries have in
turn transmitted high demand or low to the local wholesale and retail
enterprises that serve them.

Any explanation of growth that has relevance to Northwestern Australia
must be one that takes account both of export markets and of the activities
of government. Government expenditure is a distinct item since budgets
are not drawn up out of any direct relationship to current export earnings.
With optimistic assumptions as to the future of export markets and of
government and private investment programmes, the surpluses earned by
primary industry can become very significant. Some of them spill over in
the form of demand for secondary or tertiary activities in the region. How
far this has already occurred can only be guessed at; the following sections
on secondary and tertiary industry give the principal known facts about
the development of these sectors.

2. SECONDARY INDUSTRY

Present Characteristics

A factory is defined by the Commonwealth Statistician as 'any establishment which is engaged in the process of manufacturing, assembling, treating
or repairing and in which four or more persons are employed during any
period of the year or power other than manual is used'. In the three major
statistical divisions in the region some 86 factories were operating in
1963-64. Of these most were establishments for motor repairs, and next

in numerical importance were factories satisfying the demand for consumer non-durable goods such as bread, ice, drinks, etc., and then factories engaged in the provision of heat, light and power. The remainder, only 10 factories, were linked to the need of the region's primary industries. Details of these, by industrial classification, are given in Table 1. Statistical details are not yet available for years later than 1963-64 but the recent trend has undoubtedly been to consolidate the previous pattern with more light engineering establishments being set up, particularly in Port Hedland. Subsequent development, with pelletising plants being erected in the Pilbara and plans for eventually establishing a fully integrated iron and steel industry in the area, will of course change the entire manufacturing complexion of the region and will undoubtedly induce great population influx and the establishment of associated light and heavy engineering works and other factories catering for consumer demand. The implications of this are discussed in Chapter 4 and mentioned below.

Figures of employment by industry are presented in Chapter 2. In that chapter the general question of employment, earnings and incentives is also discussed. In terms of numbers employed, the principal factories in the region are the meatworks at Wyndham, Derby and Broome. Considerable numbers are employed in mining but these establishments are not included by the Commonwealth Statistician in factory statistics and thus do not appear in Table 1.

Figures of the book values of land and buildings, plant and machinery, value of output and net production are available by statistical divisions. The value of output is the selling value 'at the factory' (i.e. the value at the point of sale less all selling and distribution costs) of all goods made or processed during the year. It includes the amount received for other work done such as repair work, assembling and making up for Net production is the value added in the course of manufacture. It is customers. Any bounty or subsidy received on finished products is included. derived from the value of output by deducting the value of goods consumed in the process of production. The values deducted are those of materials used, fuel, power, and light, lubricating oil and water, repairs to plant and buildings, tools replaced, and containers and packings. Net production thus represents the sum available for payment of wages, rents, depreciation, other sundry expenses, interest and profit.

The latest year for which these figures are available is 1963-64, when the values of land and buildings stood at £1.3 milion, or about 2.1 per cent of the state total, while plant and machinery was almost twice as high at £2.3 million, or about 3.0 per cent of the state total. Value of factory output was £4.5 million, or 1.6 per cent of the state total, and net production was £1.9 million, or 1.6 per cent of the state total. The reader will have noted from these figures that the ratio of output to capital in the region is lower than for the state as a whole.

Future Prospects

The establishment of manufacturing industry in the area depends upon a number of factors among which is the provision of adequate quantities of cheaply available power and water. These the region does not possess at present. Coal is not readily available, hydro-electric power sources have not yet been developed, and power generation at the moment must rely upon the use of heavy-cost liquid fuels brought in from outside. Electricity costs are extremely high. Poor water has also been a hindrance both as regards quantity and quality, though the distribution of this varies from one area to another and some areas are quite well endowed.

Obviously the small population of the area and its scattered nature have constituted a limiting factor as regards the establishment of manufacturing enterprises oriented towards the local economy. Carnarvon is the largest population concentration in the region and even here there are less than 2,500 people. Most of the few townships have between 1,000 and 2,000, though rapid growth is now occurring.

When manufacturing for export is thought of, there is ready availability of raw materials but the question of transport facilities and costs both into and out of the region assumes vital importance. This is acknowledged to be one of the most important problems in this vast area, and is dealt with in detail in Chapter 9. While improvements are on the way and significant changes are beginning to occur, the position is still unsatisfactory and transport is a major limiting obstacle in the development of export-oriented manufacturing.

From what has been said of labour in Chapter 2 it will be seen that although availability of labour of the right type presents no insuperable problems, there exists the problem of high costs since extra incentives have to be provided to attract workers and to reduce labour turnover. Other factors which would determine whether manufacturing enterprises could be established would include the location of markets in relation to the region, the extent of the markets in relation to expected production potential, and the climatic and physical characteristics of the region. These have all been examined in the preceding chapters and in the appendices and have been seen to constitute, in some cases, limitations to secondary industry development.

Thus, if one examines the factors determining the location of manufacturing industry – fuel and power, water, raw materials, labour, transport facilities, climatic and physical characteristics and local and external markets – one can see no reasons why the growth of manufacturing in Northwestern Australia in the past should have been anything but slow and halting. There is, at the same time, no doubt that as the region experiences economic growth, which will be reflected in an expanding population and greater local incomes and expenditure, the possibilities for expansion of localized manufacturing activity will increase, although

responses to this type of stimulus will take place over the long-term and
would not lead to any rapid build up of industrialization. But certain other
changes will result from the large-scale development schemes now proceeding
in the region. On-the-spot processing of agricultural products from the Ord
is already occurring and establishment in the area of plants to press oil
seeds and cotton textile plants can be seen as possibilities in the future.
Likewise the rather remote possibility of establishing plants to process
the products of the agricultural and fishing industries at Carnarvon is
discussed in Chapter 6, and the possibilities of fish canning and other
fish processing works in Chapter 5. The projected manufacturing developments consequent upon the exploitation of the region's iron ore resources
are outlined in Chapter 4 and, as these come to fruition, they will undoubtedly lead to population growth and the establishment of associated
manufacturing activities.

All of these changes, though leading to increased industrialization, will
be linked to the region's primary and extractive industries and it seems
that this pattern may be expected to extend well into the future. The
region may thus now be set to follow the development pattern which was
experienced in the earlier days of the South-West, namely, increased
employment in manufacturing activity tied to the region's export industries.
Any deviation from this pattern in the next decade or two could be caused,
it seems, only by deliberate government inducements, through concessions
of various kinds, to industries which would not otherwise see any peculiar
locational advantage in establishing in the region.

3. TERTIARY INDUSTRY

Although tertiary industry has been restricted in the region due to the
very small aggregate population, relatively many more people have found
employment in tertiary industry than in secondary industry. Normally
in a developed area the public authorities (commonwealth, state, local and
semi-governmental) supply the basic communal needs of the population for
essential services. In an underdeveloped area, such as Northwestern
Australia, some of these basic needs may be met by private industry.
Thus the provision of electricity or the water supply may be functions
assigned in the early stages of development to specific enterprises which
happen to exist at the focal points of population concentrations.

The tertiary industries include wholesale and retail distribution, building
and construction, the provision of electricity, gas and water, transport
and storage, communications, finance and property, public authority and
professional activities, entertainments, accommodation and personal services.
Of these, the most important in the region in terms of numbers employed
in 1961 were: building and construction (1,317 persons), transport and
communication (687), business and professional (662), finance and commerce (485), entertainment, accommodation and personal services (476),

public authority and defence (268) and the provision of electricity, gas and water (54). Some of these main tertiary activities will now be examined briefly.

Government Administrative Agencies

State government offices and agencies are established throughout the region. The following are the main departments represented.

The Police Department, with stations at Broome, Derby, Fitzroy Crossing, Hall's Creek, Marble Bar, Nullagine, Port Hedland, Roebourne, Wittenoom, Dampier, Mt. Tom Price, Koolan Island and Kununurra – all under the Broome headquarters of the Roebourne and Kimberley District – and at Shark Bay, Carnarvon, Onslow, Meekatharra and Wiluna – all under the Geraldton headquarters of the Western District.

The Department of Agriculture, with research stations at Carnarvon, Kununurra, Abydos-Woodstock, and Wiluna, agricultural and cattle advisors at Kununurra, Derby, Broome, Port Hedland, Wiluna and Carnarvon, who range far and wide across the country, and vermin control officers at Wyndham, Derby, Meekatharra, Port Hedland and Nullagine.

The Crown Law Department, with travelling magistrates based at Broome and Carnarvon, clerks of courts at Broome, Carnarvon, Derby and Port Hedland, and police officers and mining registrars to act as clerks of courts in other areas in the region.

The Mines Department, with inspectors in Port Hedland, a warden at Meekatharra, mining registrars at Marble Bar and Meekatharra, and police officers to act as mining registrars in other areas in the region.

The Fisheries Department, with inspectors at Broome and Shark Bay and the research vessel *Peron* which is concerned with carrying out exploratory fishing in northern waters.

The Harbour and Lights Department, with officers at all northern ports and an agent at Shark Bay, concerned with handling cargoes, stevedoring and operating all harbour facilities within the region.

The Main Roads Department has administrative headquarters for the Kimberley area centred at Derby and for the North-West area centred at Carnarvon. These maintain servicing and repair depots at the centres mentioned and, in addition, there are depots at Port Hedland and Wyndham. Also there are construction organizations and maintenance patrols operating throughout the region. Road plans are described in detail in Chapter 9.

The Public Works Department has officers in each port and in the main townships.

The Department of Native Welfare has expanded its activities in the region considerably in recent years. The staff it maintains in the north are situated at Derby (Superintendent, Assistant Superintendent, District Officer, Welfare Officer), Wyndham (Assistant Superintendent, District Officer, Welfare Officer), Hall's Creek (District Officer), Broome (District Officer, Welfare Officer), Port Hedland (Superintendent, Assistant

Superintendent, Welfare Officer), Marble Bar (District Officer, Welfare Officer). In addition it has two mobile welfare units in the Northern and Northwestern divisions consisting of a married couple who travel by truck and caravan, the husband doing maintenance on the reserves' facilities and the wife assisting the Welfare Officer. It also maintains a Project Officer in Port Hedland who assists natives in their mining claims, buffel seed gathering, etc. It has, in addition, native hostels at Hall's Creek, Marble Bar, Onslow and Roebourne and operates native camping reserves in all northern townships.

The Medical Department operates district hospitals and medical and nursing services throughout the region, as well as a leprosarium at Derby. Health services are dealt with in more detail below.

The Education Department has teachers at 32 schools in the region. Educational services are discussed in more detail below.

Other state government departments operating in the region include: the Public Health Department, mostly represented by local governing bodies, the Geological Survey which carries out intensive survey work in the region, the Department of Labour which is concerned with administering the provisions of the Act, the Lands Department which is mainly concerned with survey work, the Department of Local Government which is in direct line of contact with the governing bodies of the shires, the State Housing Commission – its building programme is discussed in more detail below – and the State Shipping Service which provides passenger and cargo carriage to the north, and is considered in detail in Chapter 9. The Wyndham Meatworks is also a government concern.

In addition to the state government agencies, numerous commonwealth agencies operate in the region, either with permanent personnel and establishments or with itinerant teams or through appointed agents. Among commonwealth agencies are the following: the departments of the Army, Navy and Air, the Commonwealth Bank, the Commonwealth Electoral Department, the Commonwealth Bureau of Census and Statistics, the Commonwealth Employment Service, the Department of Primary Industry, the Department of Customs and Excise, the Postmaster General's Department, the Health Department, the Bureau of Meteorology, the Department of Civil Aviation, the C.S.I.R.O., the Overseas Telecommunications Commission, the War Service Land Settlement Division, and the Department of Works.

Power and Water Supplies

All towns in the region are equipped with 240 volt A.C. power, and in some cases electricity charges are extremely high, as pointed out in Chapter 2. Lack of volume-demand is one of the main factors responsible for this and the economics of the future of power supply in the area will depend largely upon the flow of population and industry. The possibility of cheap power supplies at Kununurra has already been mentioned and it has been pointed out that this could have a salutary effect upon surrounding industry and could assist in further development and in the encouragement of light industry.

Details of town water supplies are given in Chapter 7. Generally speaking supplies are adequate at the moment but in some cases it will not be long before new works will be needed to keep pace with development. The same may be said of sewerage facilities in the region.

Postal, Telegraph and Telephone Facilities

The Overseas Telecommunications Commission operates coastal radio stations directly at Broome and indirectly at Wyndham through the Department of Civil Aviation. The Postmaster General's Department provides for the transmission of radio messages, and facilities for radio-telephone conversation with Perth are established at Derby, Broome, Kununurra, Marble Bar, Port Hedland, Onslow and Wittenoom. There are also some private radio-telephone facilities where contractors for large development projects operate the service. Normal postal facilities exist at all townships in the region where post offices are established.

Rapid development in the north, particularly in the Pilbara area, has highlighted some unsatisfactory aspects of the region's communications system and it is now proposed to establish a broad-band telephone system which will link the north with the Perth metropolitan area. The first stage of this will be to link Geraldton with Perth. Carnarvon will follow, and then Port Hedland. The communications link thus established will provide many telephone and telegraph circuits for rapid communication and would be able to carry sound broadcasts and television if required. This project, which was announced by the Director-General of Posts and Telegraphs in February 1966[3] will probably be completed by 1970 at a cost of $12 million and will give Port Hedland the same telecommunications facilities that exist between Melbourne and Sydney.

In addition to these facilities there is, of course, the Flying Doctor Radio network. The first flying doctor base in Western Australia was established at Port Hedland in 1935, and since then bases have been established at Carnarvon, Derby, Meekatharra, Kalgoorlie and Wyndham with some 392 fixed and 420 mobile stations using pedal wireless. A great volume of traffic passes through the system and apart from emergency messages 75,000 telegrams are handled annually by the service.

Housing

At 30 June 1961 there were 2,837 occupied houses in the region, and 79 unoccupied. Carnarvon had the greatest housing concentration, followed by the shires of West Kimberley, Broome and Gascoyne-Minilya, in that order. Detailed figures are given in Table 3.

[3]*West Australian,* 22 February 1966.

Since 1945 the State Housing Commission has erected some 1,250 housing units north of the twenty-sixth parallel at a cost of approximately $10.6 million. Half of this cost has been financed through the Commission and half by other departments for which the Commission has erected homes. It has also designed and erected various facilities such as native hostels, toilets and ablution blocks, offices and stores and living quarters for workers and for nurses, on behalf of several different government departments. In all there are 22 centres in the north in which the Commission has been active.

During 1947 to 1952 the township of Wittenoom was built, and with Commission finance 152 houses were erected for persons employed in asbestos mining. Over the past few years 31 reinforced-gypsum-wall houses, clad and roofed with fibro-cement sheeting, have been erected. Steel framing was used for all door, window and roofing structures. This class of construction was adopted, after considerable research, in order to overcome the high incidence of termite damage and to reduce maintenance costs in such a remote area.

Houses for farmers at Kununurra were designed and erected by the State Housing Commission, together with houses for employees of government departments. Altogether some 93 homes have been built there. As well, several native hostels costing $100,000 each have been built for the Native Welfare Department in the region. Since 1963, duplex houses, each unit of two or three bedrooms, have been erected at a lower capital cost which has enabled a consequent reduction in rentals. This type of accommodation has achieved popularity among smaller families, and is still being provided.

Special finance arrangements have been made to provide houses at Exmouth for Australian personnel to be employed at the United States Navy Communications Centre, mentioned below, and in the essential supporting services. Some 44 houses have been completed and another 88 are under construction. At Carnarvon, the Commission has built 54 houses for the Shire Council, as part of the N.A.S.A. tracking station project.

The housing projects associated with the iron ore developments in the Pilbara at Mt. Tom Price, Mt. Goldsworthy, and Dampier are not part of the Commission's activities. Generally speaking the average costs of the houses being erected in these centres are higher than those of other houses in the region. Plans for housing development in these centres and the rights and obligations of the companies concerned are described in Chapter 4.

Attention in recent years has been given by the Commission to house-planning for specific areas. Cross-ventilation has been considerably improved and insulation has been incorporated in roof and walls. Each rental house is now fitted with a ceiling fan and heat absorbing glass, and many houses are equipped with liquid petroleum gas stoves. The houses themselves are better oriented, through greater attention to land subdivision, for experience has shown that it is necessary in the north to site houses facing north or south with no windows in the east or west walls. To match the climatic and cyclonic conditions special design and construction methods are essential and these, together with higher transport, insurance, and labour charges, make the total cost much higher than in the south of the state.

Increasing attention is now being given to architectural problems in northern areas, in particular design, materials and siting,[4] and it is recognized that because of the physical and social characteristics of isolated areas it is important to plan housing facilities which will reduce to a minimum the physical and mental stresses often found in these areas. Of particular importance is the need to study physical layout and planning of dwellings, cooling methods, the relationship of dwellings to surrounding open spaces, types of local or imported materials most suited to each area, and the way in which dwellings are linked to community facilities and services.

For example, should the planner attempt to introduce the idea of compact group housing with attached dwellings providing less surface exposed to the sun, and how acceptable will this be to families who are accustomed to at least a quarter-acre block separating them from neighbours? How does one reconcile the fact that lightweight materials, which are so much cheaper to import into isolated areas, lack the insulating qualities of bulk protection normally associated with massive construction? What greater use can be made of prefabrication, possibly using plastics for complete units such as plumbing systems? Since structural insulation is virtually pointless in humid areas with low diurnal temperature variation, how best can cooling be achieved, and what are the costs involved? How can the land waste, which is seen so clearly today in some northern townships with widespread settlement and many vacant townsite blocks separating groups of houses, be eliminated?

Local interest in some of these problems, apart from the efforts of the State Housing Commission, was aroused in 1965 by a Perth architect and eventually crystallized in the establishment of a Scholarship for North-West Architectural Research which was awarded to Simon Holthouse. Supported by local architectural and business firms, it enabled Mr. Holthouse to spend some months in the north in 1966, studying the sorts of problems mentioned above. In particular he was charged with investigating housing throughout the north especially in regard to both single and multiple units and as to: (a) problems of living and conditions for comfortable living, (b) use of traditional building methods, materials and techniques, (c) the possibility of using new or untried building methods, materials and techniques, (d) comparisons between (b) and (c), (e) costing of housing

[4] See for instance, R. M. Campbell, 'Designing for Comfort in a Tropical Climate', and B. S. Saini, *Human Habitations in the Arid Zone – Problems of Remote Settlements in Central Australia.*

considering (a), (b), (c) and (d) above, (f) planning for resolution of problems. His report should be available by the end of this year. The Faculty of Architecture in the University of Western Australia is also planning a group project to study dwelling and office design and township planning in a northern port.

Education

The provision of a completely developed primary to high school educational system depends mainly upon population size, and, in country areas, the concentration of children to make such a system worthwhile has to be achieved by artificial means. Where small communities exist relatively close to one another, such concentration may be achieved on a day-to-day basis by the provision of bus or train or other transport services taking the children to school and home again each day. This position obtains in most parts of the more populated southern parts of the state. But where large distances separate small population groups, as in Northwestern Australia, the only way to achieve the concentration of children is to take them on a continuous basis, as for example in a hostel or in private homes away from their own family. Provision for a solution of this nature is, as yet, far from adequate and so far sufficient finance has not been available to enable the education authorities to establish in the north a complete educational system to take the child from primary to high school graduation. Attempts have been made, however, by the Education Department and by private organizations to bring the advantages of at least primary education into as many parts of the north as possible. It should be noted that a three-year high school now exists at Carnarvon and junior high schools are established at Derby and Port Hedland.

There are some 32 government schools and 10 private schools in the region. Details of the location and type of government schools are given in Table 2, but it should be pointed out that some of these are schools situated in native missions but staffed and run by the Education Department. This is so in the case of the Church of England mission at Forrest River, the Roman Catholic missions at Balgo Hills, Kalumburu and La Grange, the United Aborigines Mission at Fitzroy Crossing, the Apostolic Mission at Jigalong and the Seventh Day Adventist Mission at Karalundi. There are also the native schools at Go Go, Argyle Downs, Cherrabun, Christmas Creek, Kimberley Downs and Nullagine. It should also be mentioned that there is a technical training section at the Derby junior high school which takes a high proportion of the students who are enrolled there for secondary schooling. More than half of the students enrolled at Derby are aborigines.

As well as the government schools, there are private schools established in the north as follows : convents at Broome, Wyndham, Carnarvon, Meekatharra, Port Hedland, Derby, Wittenoom; native missions at Lomba-dina and Beagle Bay; and a Seventh Day Adventist school at Wiluna. In addition to these services there is also the government 'school of the air' with two teachers at Meekatharra and one each at Derby and Port Hedland. These schools have 55, 29 and 22 students enrolled, respectively, and the teachers carry out marking and all correspondence operations connected with their teaching.

Although the Department is providing good schooling facilities in relation to numbers of students and is coping admirably with the distance and other problems involved in northern education, there is a case, if northern development is desired, for relaxing to a greater degree the student number requirement for classification of schools. This problem, in relation to the need to attract a stable family population into the region and to hold it, is discussed in Chapter 2. The only high school at the moment is at Carnarvon and this does not assist parents in the Kimberley. There is an urgent need to rectify this position and Derby would seem to be the logical town for the early establishment of a high school for the extreme northern areas.

Health

The Medical Department is well established in the north and although medical facilities are not as extensive as in the more populous areas, various schemes, such as the Flying Doctor Service and the institution of fare payments and the subsidizing of specialist visits to the region, have been adopted to overcome some of the more obvious disabilities.

District hospitals exist at most of the townships in the region, and at Wyndham and Port Hedland native hospitals are also operated. At Derby the native hospital, which formerly was separate, has now been integrated into the district hospital, with the construction of a new wing for natives. In Broome the same policy is being followed. In Wyndham similar plans have been made, as also in Port Hedland where the rapid development has necessitated further thoughts on the development of medical services. The Department aims ultimately to integrate native and European treatment in the one hospital. There are no private hospitals in the north, the nearest one being situated at Geraldton, where also a regional hospital gives a much greater range of facilities. There is a leprosarium at Derby, and there is also at Derby a salaried medical officer of the Department who is making a nutritional and diseases survey of the native population in the north. At Derby, too, there is a laboratory and a qualified laboratory technician located at the hospital.

General practitioners are salaried medical officers of the Department and, in addition to those resident at Meekatharra, Roebourne, Port Hedland, Broome, Derby, Exmouth and Wyndham, there are private doctors operating at Yampi and Wittenoom. There are also three salaried dental officers in the region, at Derby, Port Hedland and Wyndham. These are primarily located in the north to attend to school children, but they are also allowed to treat adults and additional remuneration is given for this by the Department. Statistical details of hospital and other health facilities are given in Table 4.

The Flying Doctor Service has already been mentioned in several connections. It is impossible to overestimate the valuable part that this pioneering service has played in the development of medical services in the northern outback. It has undoubtedly saved many lives and much distress, and the operators have been dedicated, courageous men, like those commemorated in the memorial at Derby.

There are other ways in which the government has endeavoured to compensate for the disabilities under which residents of the north suffer when expert medical advice is needed. For instance, as mentioned in Chapter 2, return air fares to the metropolitan area are paid by the Department in approved cases where urgent consultation with specialists is deemed necessary. This service costs approximately $60,000 per year. Also specialists are induced to visit the region and their visits are subsidized for this service. Infant health sisters are stationed at Broome and Derby, and the Department sends infant health sisters to visit the north frequently. Among other duties, they frequently give talks on health matters over the Flying Doctor radio service. Infant health centres exist at all the main townships in the region. Two nurses, based in the East Kimberley and the West Kimberley travel to all points of settlement in their areas in conjunction with the Australian Inland Mission. They give treatment for trachoma, examine matters of native hygiene and give advice on infant health matters. As well as this, the Department has established a well-patronized correspondence service on infant health matters whereby advice by letter is sent into the more remote areas. A further development has been the establishment of health inspectors at Derby and Port Hedland.

Local Government Organization and Finances

Local government in the region is administered by the shire councils, each with members elected by ratepayers, a president elected by the members, and a shire clerk, the chief executive officer, who is appointed only with the consent of the Minister for Local Government. There are 16 such shires in the region, some of which have been renamed in recent years. The major changes that have taken place in this regard have been the incorporation of Carnarvon, which was formerly a municipality, into the Gascoyne-Minilya Shire in March 1965 and the creation of a new shire, Exmouth, in January 1964.

In addition to exercising the usual powers and functions of local authorities they are concerned with enforcing local health regulations for which purpose they are proclaimed local Boards of Health, with the construction and maintenance of roads other than main roads which fall under the care of the state government, with the control of vermin in cases where they are empowered to administer the Vermin Act, with controlling water supplies where they are constituted Water Boards, with the control of traffic under the Traffic Act, and with the issuing of building permits. Revenue is derived from rates, licensing fees, government grants and reimbursements, fines, interest and receipts from the hire of halls and other property. Expenditure is incurred on construction works, maintenance and development of properties, interest, debt redemption, and grants and donations to hospitals, fire brigades and the like. Receipts and expenditures for 1963-64 are given in Table 5.

United States Government Activities

Apart from the Australian commonwealth, state, local and semi-governmental authorities with interests in the region, the United States government has personnel stationed there, in particular at the N.A.S.A. tracking station in Carnarvon and at North-West Cape, where a Very Low Frequency communications system has been established for submarine communications. Both of these projects have brought money and general development into the area and of the two the North-West Cape project is the larger.

An agreement between the United States and Australian governments was signed in 1963 and construction began on the $80 million project. The townsite of Exmouth, now with a population exceeding 1,000, was established and in 1964 the Shire of Exmouth was gazetted. The post and the townsite have gone ahead rapidly and this has been a contributing factor to the marked upsurge of activity that has characterised this part of the north.

Other Tertiary Activity

There are not many bank branches in the region, as a glance at Table 6 will show. However, agencies exist in some settlements where there is no branch established and, of course, there are the widespread Commonwealth Savings Bank facilities normally provided at the post offices situated throughout the region. Other commercial services are rather sparse and scattered. Credit and other facilities akin to those of a bank are given by the large stock firms operating in the north but the absence of widespread banking facilities is undoubtedly a handicap to orderly local development.

Retail and wholesale trading activities in 1961 accounted for less than 15 per cent of the persons employed in tertiary industry. At the 1956-57 retail census there were 159 establishments in the region and the value of retail sales amounted to £3.5 million, representing 1.8 per cent of the total value of retail sales for the state. By 1961-62 the number of establishments had increased by a mere 10 and the value of sales had increased by £1.5 million, bringing the total to 2 per cent of the state total. The greatest activity in the retail trade in 1961-62, in terms of number of establishments and value of sales, was at Carnarvon followed by Derby, Port Hedland and Broome in that order. Undoubtedly more recent figures would show large gains made by Port Hedland, in particular, and by Wyndham and Kununurra. Unfortunately the number of establishments in some towns and in some branches of retail trade is so small that detailed figures cannot be released by the Commonwealth Statistician and no analysis of the results can be made.

Information regarding the provision of entertainment and sporting and other community activities and the numbers and types of social and citizen organizations existing in each town or village in the north was obtained from the respective local government authorities. From this it would seem that social activities are reasonably well developed in most areas where there are centres of population. Some of the new company towns such as those described in Chapter 2 and Chapter 4 have been designed with a view to providing a wide range of sporting and social facilities in order to attract and hold a stable labour force. Almost every township has its hall which is used for all types of entertainment from association meetings to dances. There are approximately 30 such halls in the region and they are used for entertainment on an average of about twice weekly, apart from association and other business meetings.

Many social and citizen organizations can be found in the townships in the north ranging from sporting clubs to lodges and children's organizations. Some of the organizations represented are: churches of all denominations, the Country Women's Association, the Returned Soldiers League, Masonic and R.A.O.B. lodges, Rostrum, Rotary, Lions and Apex clubs, chambers of commerce, golf, basketball, badminton, sailing, rifle, race and tennis clubs, Girl Guides, Brownies, Boy Scouts and Cubs groups, parents' and citizens' associations, other youth organizations, and social and trade or professional bodies. There are some 30 churches in the north and about the same number of sports grounds which cater for a range of events from basketball, football and cricket matches to race meetings.

Tourist Facilities and Attractions

Tourism in the region is developing rapidly and tours are now being arranged by bus, air and sea, with roads improving, with more frequent air flights in faster and more comfortable aircraft and with growth in the number and quality of tourist facilities. Many more people are now moving into the area in the dry winter season and are learning what the north has to offer for the person who wants to escape the cold, wet winter of the south and visit country that is as different in so many other ways as it is climatically.

As well as hotel accommodation, there are guest houses and camping areas and caravan parks at most centres. Although they vary considerably the average standard of these facilities is rising rapidly under the stimulus of competition from other areas of the state and, also, because of the growing local realization that the north has certain natural advantages which will induce tourist inflow provided accommodations of a reasonable standard can be guaranteed. Table 7 gives certain information regarding accommodations in the region and it is quite apparent that the tourist cannot exercise much choice in the matter of where he shall sleep and eat.

Generally speaking, hotel facilities have been most unsatisfactory in the past and it is probably true to say that the poor standard of accommodation has dissuaded some from visiting the area and others from returning to it.

This position, happily, is now changing. Hotels throughout the north are being rebuilt or renovated and the standards of service and accommodation offered are steadily improving, particularly, but not only, in those centres where competition exists. This is a prerequisite in any development of tourism and there is still much more improvement needed. Although the region has much in the way of unusual flora and fauna, climatic attractions, unusual sporting facilities, magnificent scenery, historical places and other attractions to draw people into the area, the upgrading of tourist accommodation is essential.

The natural beauty of Northwestern Australia makes an immediate impact on the visitor. From the rich colours of Cockatoo Island in its Archipelago setting to the east across the savannah grassland to the rugged bluffs of the Kimberley, then south across the desolate waste of parched, caked, red desert soil, and west to the variegated mountains hiding the spectacular beauty of deep gorges like Wittenoom, and finally north to the green, white and brown coastline, the land abounds with perfect settings for the artist or the camera enthusiast. This beauty, sometimes soft in form, as in the myriad wild-flowers to be found in season bordering the roads, sometimes hard, as in the fiery glare of ironstone hills thrown into relief by the afternoon sun or the full red-brown of a giant anthill, is one of the great natural assets of the region and its potential is now being realized and exploited by tourist agencies.

Hunting, fishing, and other active pastimes offer something quite different in the north. There is a wide variety of fish to be taken, both along the coast and in the rivers, with crocodiles, both estuarine man-eaters and Johnson fish-eaters, to add spice to the hunt. The estuarine crocodile often grows to 20 feet or longer. He is sluggish when on the river sand banks but extremely fast in the water. He is cunning and extremely powerful, sometimes seizing cattle on the river banks and drowning them within a matter of seconds. His favourite habitat is the deeper water of the estauries, which abound along the coast and are bordered by mangrove swamps, but he has been found up the rivers at distances of 50 to 100 miles from the coast. The Johnson, a smaller species growing up to about 10 feet in length, is usually found further up the rivers and in the past a favourite and lucrative pastime has been to catch these crocodiles and mount them as trophies for sale. It is said that the Johnson will not attack a human being except under extreme circumstances, and natives and whites swim in rivers which abound with Johnsons.

Ocean fishing offers the possibility of catching many different types, but in the rivers the main species to be found are barramundi, mullet, catfish, perch, bream, golden salmon, kingfish, groper and sawfish. Some shark and stingray also swim up rivers on occasions. The barramundi is the pride of the north, as far as fish are concerned, and rivals the southern jewfish for pride of place on the table. It grows up to 50lbs. and 60lbs. in weight, a good average probably being about 15lbs. Game fish abound in the ocean, and other species, some of them quite large, can be caught from jetties.

Bird life in the north also offers great attractions for the nature lover. Most of the larger birds have attractive colouring and are not classed as pests. Many are protected by law. Of the large birds perhaps the brolga, or native companion, is the most plentiful and the best known. It is found north of Broome and in the plains of the Kimberley. Essentially community birds, they get together in large groups for the mating ceremonies, where they will be seen circling and weaving in and out of the other dancers and bowing to their partners. Another large bird is the jaberoo. This, unlike the brolga, is a water bird and it is not given to moving in communities. After jaberoo have mated, they remain together in pairs for the whole of the mating season. They are found north of Broome and in the Northern Territory, and being shy and quiet they are often hard to find. When one does find a pair of them, however, the sight of these large black and white birds flying in the marshes is sufficient reward for any trouble that may have been taken in the search.

The wild turkey is protected and it is surprising how many of them are 'knocked down' by motor cars or 'shot in self-defence'. They are reputed to be highly palatable. They are not community birds but they sometimes team up into groups of up to three pairs. The pelican and the wedgetail eagle and the magpie goose are three other large birds found in the Kimberley. The pelicans stand together in small groups to muster their fish prey into one small area, whereupon they proceed to devour them with mightly gulps. The wedgetail is reputed to be the highest flying bird in the world. The goose, a swamp bird, can become quite a pest where crops such as rice are grown in well watered bays. Most of the large birds are edible.

Many varieties of small birds exist in the Kimberley. Finches and budgerigars predominate and other well-known types to be seen are the magpie lark, the honey bird, the cockatiel parrot, known by the native name of weiro, and the kingfisher. There are over one hundred species of small birds, half a dozen species of wild duck and half a dozen species of brilliantly coloured parrot.

Apart from the natural attractions of the region in terms of scenic beauty, climate, bird, fish and animal life, the area has much to offer of historical interest. There are, for instance, native rock paintings throughout the region and some of them, particularly those on Depuch Island, are extensive and well preserved. There are the remains of the Lilmalura Police Station near Winjina Gorge in the Napier Ranges where Pidgen, the outlaw of the Leopolds, killed Constable Richardson. There is the famous prison baobab tree, out of Derby, scene of many incidents in the early days.

There is the Japanese cemetery at Broome, the Cossack and Roebourne cemeteries, all in a state of disrepair and all telling their mute story of the past. There are the tumbledown, neglected buildings of the old settlement at Cossack, the Mount Anderson cave paintings, 80 miles from Derby, the old townsite at Hall's Creek, scene of the state's first gold rush, and the roadside grave of the head stockman in Mrs. Aeneas Gunn's *We of the Never Never*.

These, and many other points of historical interest too numerous to mention, paint the picture of the early history of the north and much work needs to be done to preserve them and to make some of them more easily accessible to the interested tourist. There is no doubt at all that many of them could be so developed as to become focal points of interest to visitors and thus to increase the attractions of the region.

In many countries the national heritage is carefully cultivated and nurtured at all levels. To help achieve this in the north, the Western Australian Historical Society in conjunction with other interested bodies at the state and local government level should, before it is too late and records and memories recede into the dim past, establish the exact place at which important events took place and mark them well with large explanatory signs. This technique is used effectively throughout the U.S.A. where warning signs strategically placed for the speeding traveller indicate the position of historic markers which are usually set well back from the road with adequate parking space so that the interested traveller can pull off the highway. This makes the visitor's journey more interesting and fosters local pride and knowledge of local history.

Picnic and rest areas are desirable, at least on main routes, but toilet facilities are generally not required so long as clean rest rooms are provided at service stations en route. The encouragement of road travel is essential since of all the tourist modes, it brings the greatest income into the region. A good tourist map showing historical and other points of interest, camping areas and other accommodation, as well as the normal geographical information is also required for the region as a whole.

Camping facilities in the U.S.A. have been developed greatly in the last decade and now more than 80 million Americans camp out each year. This astounding figure has been achieved in a country of which the major part is suitable for camping only for a few months each year. How much more of an advantage, in this regard, has Northwestern Australia! An amalgam of the best points of various camping areas in the U.S.A., which may be regarded as a long-term ideal towards which local government authorities in the north should move, would produce a camping area in which : (a) there is a camp ranger in attendance to police the area and to advise campers on interest points and to give lectures, (b) each campsite is individually marked out to avoid overcrowding and to ensure the adequacy of the established facilities, (c) each campsite has a permanent steel barbecue grill set in a concrete base, (d) each campsite has a large wooden table with attached seats, anchored in some way, (e) there are ample stocks of fuel placed at various points around the camping area, (f) there is a general store conveniently situated on or close to the campsite, (g) there are water points with upright fountains for drinking and conventional taps for filling containers, with suitable drainage for spillover, (h) there are adequate toilet facilities with modern porcelain fittings, septic tanks or sewerage, tiled shower recesses, hot and cold water, power points for shavers and other appliances, and good lighting, and (i) there are adequately sized laundry facilities with automatic washing machines and drying machines (coin in the slot). Facilities of this standard may be a long time coming in the north but there is no doubt that they would induce a far greater tourist movement in the region, particularly if the visitor can rely upon a reasonably uniform standard of facilities throughout.

There is no doubt whatever that the income generating potential of the tourist industry in the north has not yet been fully capitalized. In the adjoining Northern Territory, it is estimated by the Tourist Board that in 1966 more than $14 million will be spent there by tourists. The advantages of tourist development are that it offers opportunities for the big investor and the small man alike since there is room and, indeed, the necessity for both in the provision of tourist facilities. It also offers much-needed employment opportunities for women, in contrast to mining, agricultural and pastoral development, and can thus introduce greater population stability into the area. There is no doubt that the vigorous development of this income-elastic industry would greatly assist the region's rapid growth.

4. Summary and Conclusions

Primary industry is by far the dominant activity in Northwestern Australia and various segments of the agricultural, pastoral, fishing and extractive industries are dealt with in previous chapters. Tertiary industry, because of the very nature of the region, with long distances and many government services to be maintained and because of the current and continuing surge of building and construction activity, also figures large. Manufacturing industry exists, but on a very small scale indeed. Because the region does not have a large population and therefore lacks a strong all-round demand, those manufacturing activities which do exist are concerned with very localized consumer production, for example, the baking of bread, or with processing the region's primary products.

No great change can be foreseen in this pattern for some time to come unless some of the basic limitations to development such as problems connected with transport, water and power, are removed by the expenditure of considerable capital sums. All the foreseeable developments in this direction, if realized, will apply in any case initially to the primary field. At the moment it would seem that any large scale diversification in manufacturing activity in the region would have to come as a result of deliberate government policy directed to changing the pattern of production, and this would involve large expenditure and financial concessions.

In the tertiary field the most important activities, in terms of numbers employed, are building and construction and the provision of government services. With the large development schemes now under way it seems that the hand of government will continue to figure large in the region for some time. Many government administrative agencies are represented in the north either directly, with staff located permanently at various points, or indirectly, through agents. Indirect representation has in some cases been a bone of contention and northern residents sometimes complain of the remoteness of government control. This point is taken up in the concluding chapter. As the region grows in importance, direct government representation will likewise grow in absolute terms but may be expected to decline in relative importance.

Other tertiary activities are limited to the bare minimum necessary to maintain the localized flow of goods and services and to cater for the personal comforts of the population. Some of these services, particularly the provision of hotel accommodation, are very poor and although changes in this regard are taking place, there is very much more that can be done. This has particular relevance to the tourist trade which is now beginning to quicken its pace of development and for which a bright future can be foreseen.

Thus one might, for the next decade, see a continuing emphasis upon the primary and tertiary fields with manufacturing continuing to lag until the natural development of existing and new centres of population eventually induces a movement into the region of types of manufacturing, probably on a small scale initially, other than those which exist at present to cater for a very small localized demand or for the primary industries.

BIBLIOGRAPHY

BAUER, P. T. and YAMEY, B.S. 'Economic Progress and Occupational Distribution. *Economic Journal,* vol. LXI. 1951.

CAMPBELL, R. M. 'Designing for Comfort in a Tropical Climate.' *Tropical Building Studies,* vol. 2, no. 2. 1965.

CLARK, C. *The Conditions of Economic Progress.* London, 1940.

FISHER, A. G. B. *The Clash of Progress and Security.* London, 1935.

PERLOFF, H. S., DUNN, E. S., LAMPARD, E. E. and MUTH, R. F. *Regions, Resources, and Economic Growth.* Baltimore, 1960.

SAINI, B. S. *Human Habitations in the Arid Zone – Problems of Remote Settlements in Central Australia.* Mimeographed paper. Melbourne, 1966.

STATE HOUSING COMMISSION. *Annual Reports.*
West Australian. 1966.

WESTERN AUSTRALIAN GOVERNMENT TOURIST AND PUBLICITY BUREAU. *The North West of Western Australia.* Perth, 1965.

TABLE 1

FACTORIES CLASSIFIED BY NATURE OF INDUSTRY
1963-64

| | Statistical Division | | | Total |
	North-West	Pilbara	Kimberley	
CLASS IV:				
INDUSTRIAL METALS, MACHINES, ETC.				
Plant, Equipment and Machinery (incl. tools)	2	1	3	6
Other engineering	—	—	1	1
Motor repairs	8	7	12	27
Motor bodies	—	1	—	1
Aircraft	—	—	1	1
CLASS IX:				
FOOD, DRINK AND TOBACCO.				
Cereal foods and starch	—	—	2	2
Bakeries	2	2	5	9
Meat and fish preserving	3	—	5	8
Aerated waters, cordials, etc.	1	—	4	5
CLASS XVI:				
HEAT, LIGHT AND POWER.				
Electric Light and Power—				
Government	—	1	3	4
Local authority	2	1	2	5
Other	—	3	4	7
OTHER	4	—	6	10
Total	22	16	48	86

NOTE: Meekatharra and Wiluna Shires are not included in this table.

Source: Commonwealth Bureau of Census and Statistics, *Statistical Register of Western Australia*. Perth.

TABLE 2

LOCATION AND TYPES OF GOVERNMENT SCHOOLS
1965

Type of School	Where located
Junior High Schools	Carnarvon (Class I), Derby (Class II) Port Hedland (Class II).
Class I Schools	—
Class II Schools	Roebourne, Wyndham.
Class III Schools	Balgo Hills*, Broome, Cockatoo Island, Exmouth, Fitzroy Crossing*, Forrest River*, Jigalong*, Karalundi*, Kununurra, Koolan Island, Marble Bar, Onslow, Shark Bay, Wittenoom Gorge, Meekatharra.
Class IV Schools	Argyle Downs†, Camballin, Cherrabun†, Christmas Creek†, Gascoyne Junction, Go Go†, Kalbarri, Kalumburu*, Kimberley Downs†, La Grange*, Nullagine†, Wiluna.

NOTE: A Class IV school has up to 30 pupils and one teacher, a Class III school from 30 to 120 pupils, a Class II school from 120 to 300 pupils, and a Class I school from 300 to 600.

* Mission schools.
† Native schools.

Source: Western Australia, Education Department.

TABLE 3

DWELLINGS IN LOCAL GOVERNMENT AREAS
1961

L.G.A.	Occupied Dwellings	Unoccupied Dwellings	All Dwellings
Carnarvon	417	17	434
Ashburton	104	1	105
Broome	277	8	285
Gascoyne-Minilya	275	1	276
Halls Creek	62	—	62
Marble Bar	94	3	97
Meekatharra	251	19	270
Nullagine	34	—	34
Port Hedland	224	12	236
Roebourne	106	—	106
Shark Bay	74	3	77
Tableland	185	6	191
Upper Gascoyne	52	—	52
West Kimberley	370	8	378
Wiluna	85	1	86
Wyndham-East Kimberley	227	—	227
Total	2,837	79	2,916

Source: Commonwealth Bureau of Census and Statistics, *Census of the Commonwealth of Australia*. Australia.

TABLE 4

HOSPITAL AND OTHER HEALTH FACILITIES

Town	Hospitals	Beds	Resident Doctors	Other facilities
Broome	2 (D and N)	26 and 31	2	Dentist
Carnarvon	1	47	2	Dentist
Derby	2 (D and N)	40 and 31	4	Dentist
Exmouth	1	6	1	Visiting Dentist
Fitzroy Crossing ..	1	17	—	Visiting Doctor and Dentist
Halls Creek	1	9	—	Visiting Doctor and Dentist
Kununurra	1	5	—	Visiting Doctor and Dentist
Marble Bar	1	7	—	Visiting Doctor and Dentist
Meekatharra	1	25	1	Visiting Dentist
Port Hedland	1 (D and N)	24 and 35	2 and 1 Part time	Dentist
Onslow	1	14	—	Visiting Doctor and Dentist
Roebourne	1	29	1	Visiting Dentist
Shark Bay	1 (N.P.)	1	—	
Wiluna	1	35	—	Visiting Dentist
Wittenoom	1	13	1	Visiting Dentist
Wyndham	2 (D and N)	43 and 30	2	Dentist

D = district hospital; N = native hospital; N.P. = nursing post.

Source: Western Australia, Medical Department.

TABLE 5

LOCAL GOVERNING AUTHORITIES
Revenue, Expenditure, Assets and Liabilities

1963-64

	Licensing of Vehicles	Govt. Grants	Total Revenue	Total Expend.	Assets†	Liabilities
	(£'000)	(£'000)	(£'000)	(£'000)	(£'000)	(£'000)
Meekatharra	7.5	16.8	43.1	44.0	99.2	48.5
Wiluna	1.6	8.7	14.1	18.5	48.1	13.1
Ashburton	2.4	3.4	15.1	15.7	23.9	7.4
Exmouth	.9	—	1.6	.9	1.5	.8
Gascoyne-Minilya	10.2	20.0	46.2	51.2	29.3	1.1
Shark Bay	1.4	—	3.1	2.3	12.8	.5
Upper Gascoyne	1.5	10.4	18.2	20.7	18.5	3.0
Carnarvon	16.2	3.3	58.1	74.5	356.1	252.6
Marble Bar	3.8	.6	10.8	10.6	15.8	3.5
Nullagine	.9	2.0	6.8	5.5	10.1	3.8
Port Hedland	9.5	11.8	32.6	30.8	133.1	63.8
Roebourne	4.0	4.1	13.3	13.2	17.7	9.5
Tableland	3.2	6.0	15.9	15.4	34.7	27.5
Broome	4.0	6.7	23.9	26.4	109.6	95.2
Halls Creek	2.3	4.3	12.7	16.5	45.9	32.2
West Kimberley	8.6	6.3	34.3	36.3	113.7	87.1
Wyndham-East Kimberley	8.4	1.5	21.7	32.4	84.2	54.2
Regional total	86.4	105.9	371.5	414.9	1,154.2	703.8

† Including Electricity Undertakings.

Source: Commonwealth Bureau of Census and Statistics, Perth.

TABLE 6

FINANCE AND AUXILIARY SERVICES
1965

Township	Banks and Agencies	Public Accountants	Other[1]
Broome	Commonwealth A.N.Z. Savings N.S.W. Savings	2	nil
Carnarvon	Commonwealth A.N.Z. R. & I.	1	2
Derby	A.N.Z. National Commonwealth	nil	2
Exmouth	Commonwealth N.S.W.	nil	nil
Gascoyne Junction	Commonwealth	nil	nil
Halls Creek	N.S.W. A.N.Z. Cwlth Savings	nil	nil
Kununurra	National R. & I. Commonwealth	nil	nil
Marble Bar	Commonwealth	nil	nil
Meekatharra	N.S.W.	nil	nil
Nullagine	Commonwealth	nil	nil
Onslow	N.S.W. Savings Cwlth Savings	nil	nil
Roebourne	N.S.W. Cwlth Savings	nil	nil
Wiluna	Cwlth Savings	nil	nil
Wittenoom	National Cwlth Savings	nil	nil
Wyndham	National R. & I. N.S.W.	nil	1

NOTE: Bank agencies are established in those townships where regular branches do not exist. Post offices normally serve as agencies for the Commonwealth Savings Bank.

[1] Estate agents, valuers or auctioneers.

Source: Answers to questionnaires. Some questionnaires were not returned.

TABLE 7

ACCOMMODATION

1965

Township	Hotels	Beds	Other accommodation
Broome	2	46	Motel with 14 beds, guest house with 40 beds, **C.P.**
Carnarvon	4	156	1 guest house with 120 beds, C.G.'s, 4 C.P.'s, motel.
Derby	1	54	C.G., C.P.
Exmouth	1	26	1 guest house with 6 beds.
Gascoyne Junction	1	10	
Halls Creek	1	30	C.G.
Kununurra	1	30	
Marble Bar	1	20	
Meekatharra	4	66	
Nullagine	1	12	C.P.
Onslow	1		C.G., C.P., 1 guest house.
Port Hedland			
Roebourne	1	55	C.G., C.P.
Shark Bay			
Wiluna	1	30	
Wittenoom	1	24	C.G.
Wyndham	2	48	C.G., C.P.

C.G. Camping ground.
C.P. Caravan park.

Source: Answers to questionnaires.

materials and climate. Gravel is not readily available in all parts of the region, particularly along the coast, and consequently new soil stabilization techniques have been developed. In some cases roads have had to be re-routed to areas where the soils are suitable for road stabilization.

A feature of the climate is the torrential downpours which lead to severe flooding in many areas and consequent washing away of roads and bridges. The road from Derby to Fitzroy Crossing, for instance, was re-located in 1949-51 and it now runs along higher ground where previously it had followed the Fitzroy valley. Also a section of the North-West Coastal Highway is now being deviated further inland through Nanutarra. The severe flooding to which many parts of the region are subjected has necessitated the construction of reinforced concrete bridges and crossings which are expensive items in the Main Roads Department outlay. Some miles east of Carnarvon, where the main road crosses the Gascoyne, one of the largest bridges in the state has been constructed. Built of reinforced concrete piles with a steel and timber superstructure, it has a total length of 720 feet. Bridges of similar pattern have been erected along the coastal highway where it is intersected by major rivers. In periods of full flood these bridges and the surrounding roads are often submerged.

In the Kimberley, timber and concrete crossings have been constructed over the major rivers and streams and have provided a part solution to the bridging problem. The major structures of this type in the region are Fitzroy Crossing, which crosses the river some 165 road miles east of Derby, and the Ord River crossing, located at Ivanhoe south of Wyndham. There is a necessity for high-level bridges if the road from Derby to Wyndham is to become an all-weather road. High-level bridges have been built above the Ord River diversion dam at Bandicoot Bar and over the Dunham River nearby. These, together with other subsidiary crossings, have cost well over one million dollars. Five smaller concrete bridges have also been constructed recently in the East Kimberley on the route of the Great Northern Highway. It is proposed to build two high-level bridges over the Fitzroy River, 30 miles south of Derby, in a joint $900,000 state and commonwealth project. One of these, 1,280 feet long, will be the longest bridge ever built in Western Australia. These bridges will replace Langi Crossing which is impassible for two to three months during the wet season when the Fitzroy River is in flood.

Thus it may be seen that to provide all-weather roads involves not only bituminous or concrete surfaces but also the construction of expensive bridges and high-level concrete crossings over the numerous creeks and rivers which traverse the region and which, at present, periodically disrupt transport and communication through flooding. The aim is to provide bituminous surfacing of the more heavily trafficked roads and high-level bridges over the major rivers so that the principal road routes will be serviceable in all but exceptional flood conditions.

The region is dependent upon pastoral, mineral and agricultural production for its economic survival at this stage of its development. Produce moving to and from the ports along the road system is bulky by nature – mineral ore, live cattle, baled cotton, and wool and construction materials – and unusually heavy haulage equipment has been introduced in order to minimise transport costs. When operating on unsealed roads in the north, most hauliers obtain special permits which enable them to exceed statutory axle loading limitations, particularly with the transport of minerals.

Where bitumen roads are provided, it is necessary for the axle loadings to be reduced to conform with the statutory requirements designed to protect the heavy public investment in this type of high-class road. While excess axle loadings can be permitted on earth or gravel roads as compared with bitumen roads because road maintenance costs of earth roads are relatively low, vehicle operating expenses and operating costs per ton mile are lower on bitumen roads. Hauliers in the region are therefore being encouraged to develop transport units with a large number of axles. In this way axle loadings can be confined to the 16 ton tandem axle load limit and the total payload remains the same. Also, for some classes of haulage such as live cattle, smooth dustless roads have clear advantages. Sealed roads are also necessary for developing the tourist industry.

It must also be mentioned that the earth-formed roads have three major drawbacks, which can affect the heavy transport vehicles considerably. First, wear on tyres is considerable and this is a costly item in these areas. Second, the dust hazard can become considerable, increasing accident risks and also vehicle maintenance costs. The final drawback is the time and, sometimes, the cargo lost as a result of the bogging of vehicles through flooding. On rare occasions transport drivers have even had to release their cattle into open country when bogged down for long periods. Delayed road transport can result in the upsetting of shipping schedules, or can force ships to leave ports without their full cargo load. Thus the provision of sealed roads will assist considerably because, although it will not solve the flood problem, it will enable transport to move more quickly after floods.

The road conditions in Northwestern Australia are to some extent reflected in the freight rates charged by hauliers operating in the region. Haulage rates for northern runs are announced periodically by the W.A. Road Transport Association. At the end of 1965, the first year of operation of the standard rates, the charges per ton for loads of 10 tons and over, from Perth, were: Mt. Newman £21.5, Learmonth £22.75, Dampier £28.5, Roebourne £29, Port Hedland £30.5, Mt. Tom Price £31, Mt. Goldsworthy £32, Broome £42, Derby £45, Kununurra £61. It is extremely difficult, however, to establish a representative figure, for evidence indicates that the hauliers deviate from the charges laid down. Shipping rates are one-third to one-quarter of the road charges, though the service is not, of course, door-to-door.

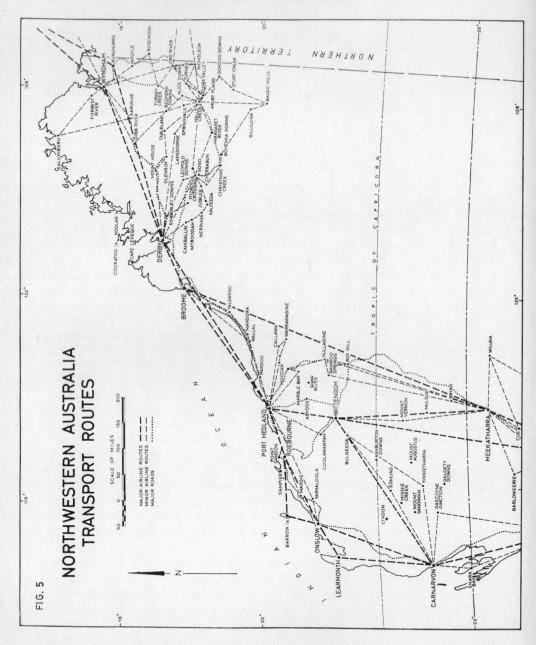

FIG. 5

NORTHWESTERN AUSTRALIA
TRANSPORT ROUTES

Construction and Maintenance

The responsibility for road construction and maintenance in Northwestern Australia lies with the Main Roads Department and to a much lesser extent the 16 shires which comprise the region. Figures showing road construction as at 30 June 1965 are to be found in Table 1. At this date there were 2,216 miles of surfaced road and 10,040 miles of formed but not otherwise prepared roads located in the region. This represents an increase in surfaced road of 27 per cent over the 1960 figure and in formed but not otherwise prepared road, of 20 per cent. The number of vehicles using these roads has increased substantially in the same period. There were, in June 1965, some 2,608 motor cars on register in the region, an increase of 180 per cent from the 1960 figure, while commercial vehicles increased by 54 per cent to 3,563 (see Table 3).

The Main Roads Department has statutory responsibility for the main roads leading to Carnarvon and Meekatharra; north of these two centres all roads are the legal responsibility of the various local authorities. However, because of their limited finances, the local authorities are unable to improve or maintain the main routes in a serviceable condition and the Main Roads Department has therefore assumed responsibility for the construction and maintenance of the principal routes in the northern part of the state. The major commitments of the Department are four-fold. First, there is the Great Northern Highway running from Meekatharra through Nullagine, Marble Bar, Anna Plains, Broome, Derby, Fitzroy Crossing, Hall's Creek to Wyndham via Turkey Creek. Second, there is the North-West Coastal Highway running north from Geraldton to Carnarvon, Onslow and Port Hedland. Third, there is the Duncan Highway, from Hall's Creek via Nicholson to Wyndham, which traverses country to the east of the Great Northern Highway. Fourth, there is the new road being developed from Derby through the King Leopold Ranges to Mt. House and on to Gibb River to serve the undeveloped area between Derby and Wyndham. Two subsidiary roads under the Department's control are the feeder road from the North-West Coastal Highway to Denham on Shark Bay, and the connecting road running through the pastoral country from Meekatharra to Carnarvon via Gascoyne Junction. There is also the much used Wittenoom Gorge-Port Hedland road. The principal roads in the region are shown in Fig. 5.

The road network in the region is responsible principally for providing access to the ports and to the Meekatharra railhead. To a lesser but increasing extent, the road system is now also catering for tourist traffic. Gradually the bituminous sealing is being extended from the northern townships, but costs are high. Nevertheless, progress has been made in recent years and there are now 350 miles of bitumen sealing in the region. Because of the nature of the traffic and the climatic conditions, roads may require resealing at more frequent intervals than those in the south-west part of the state. While maintenance costs on earth-formed roads are relatively low, these costs increase when the roads are improved and strengthened with gravel. When this occurs it becomes feasible to consider sealing as an alternative when costs over the long-term are taken into account.

Awareness of the need to provide essential road communications in the region has led the Main Roads Commissioner to budget for larger and larger allocations for Northwestern Australia. The budget for 1966-67 now amounts to over $7 million, a figure which is high when measured against the region's population. With about three per cent of the state's population the region will receive 27.8 per cent of the Main Roads Department's annual commonwealth grant for road construction of more than $25 million for 1966-67. Financial assistance provided by the commonwealth government has made it possible for the state government to push ahead with a major beef roads scheme in the Kimberley area. The commonwealth has provided $7 million for Kimberley beef roads during the last five years and has agreed to provide a further $1.5 million in 1966-67. Since the state is at least matching the commonwealth contributions, an amount of over $17 million will have been allocated for the development of Kimberley beef roads in the six-year period 1961-62 to 1966-67, inclusive.

This programme provides the basis for developing a transport system in the Kimberley area and includes improvements to the Great Northern Highway between Broome, Derby and Wyndham, involving 160 miles of sealing to June 1966, and the construction of bridges at Mistake Creek and Bow River, and a number of smaller structures between the Duncan Highway junction and Wyndham. Also included are improvements to the Duncan Highway and the construction of high-level bridges over the Ord and Dunham rivers, thus providing an all-weather access road from Wyndham to the Kununurra irrigation project. A further development is a new road route from Derby through the King Leopold Ranges to Mt. House and Gibb River. This route will be eventually pushed through the vast pastoral areas towards the north coast at Kalumburu. Two bridges are to be built over the Fitzroy River to replace Langi Crossing. Since the Kimberley beef road scheme is now in its sixth year, work on most of the projects is well advanced.

An appreciation of the extent of the up-grading of Kimberley roads planned for the year 1966-67 can be obtained from the allocations in the Main Roads Department's programme for that year. On the three principal beef roads in the Kimberley, the allocations will amount to $1.8 million for the section of the Great Northern Highway, $520,000 for Duncan Highway and $280,000 for the Derby-Mt. House-Gibb River road. These allocations will provide for extending the black top on Kimberley roads by as much as 108 miles in 1966-67, representing an increase of one-third on the total mileage of bituminized sealing in Northwestern Australia. As pointed out in Chapter 3 the pastoral industry will have to improve methods and increase turnoff if the full benefits from these expenditures on northern roads are to be realized.

Further south, the Department is also active. Recently a plan was approved by the government for the sealing of the North-West Coastal Highway as far as Port Hedland. This highway, which on the present alignment is approximately 580 miles in length between Carnarvon and Port Hedland, acts as the principal supply line for the development of the extensive Mt. Tom Price and Mt. Goldsworthy iron ore deposits. It is also an important route for serving the pastoral industry and the new oil field being developed at Barrow Island situated off the coast in this area. Being the main north-south artery, the route also serves an increasing number of tourists and hauliers.

The huge mineral developments have generated a large build-up of heavy haulage road traffic transporting construction materials and heavy equipment, and have also increased other traffic associated with these projects. Counts taken on the section of the North-West Coastal Highway approximately 100 miles north of Carnarvon have shown that traffic has built up from 36 vehicles a day to a peak of 125 within the last 12 months. As other projects get under way, this traffic volume is likely to increase even further and already it is causing considerable strain on the existing lightly constructed roads in the area.

In its present condition the highway requires continual and costly maintenance and is subject to frequent closure during flooding. The government has, therefore, approved a nine-year sealing programme which will involve the sealing of approximately 550 miles of road and will commence with the extension of black top surface by 44 miles during 1966 67. In subsequent years, distances of 50-70 miles will be sealed annually. The total cost of this project, which will be the longest sealing operation on a single road yet undertaken in the state, is estimated to be $17 million. As it will be necessary to re-construct and strengthen the road formation prior to sealing, it is proposed to relocate troublesome sections of the highway to eliminate low-lying areas which cause lengthy delays to traffic following upon rains. Some of these deviations will be extensive and will shorten the existing route by approximately 30 miles. It is proposed to deviate the highway from Barradale through Nanutarra, where a high-level bridge is being constructed over the Ashburton River, and then on to Peedamulla. Investigation is currently in progress to relocate the section, approximately 100 miles in length, between Minilya and Barradale. Other proposed deviations are from Peedamulla to near Cape Preston, and in the vicinity of Dampier, and near Port Hedland. Investigations will be carried out to plan a satisfactory access road between the already constructed Barradale-Peedamulla deviation and Onslow.

Traffic usage must be sufficiently high before a sealed road is justified on economic grounds. For the southern region of the state a traffic density of

75-100 vehicles a day is generally required before a sealed road can be economically justified. For Northwestern Australia fewer vehicles per day constitute a criterion for sealing, given sufficient funds, for the nature of the traffic and the economic or social significance of a road must be taken into account; by and large there is a much greater economic return per vehicle in the north than in the southern regions.

It should, finally, be noted that the heavy haulage vehicle is not the only type of vehicle using the road system. As the region grows, increasing emphasis will be placed upon the small, fast commercial vehicle to supply the every-day needs of an expanding population, and it can be expected that the private car will also be more extensively used. Figures of motor vehicles on register are given in Table 3. In an era when people are becoming increasingly travel-conscious and a vehicle is becoming an integral part of most families, the north has joined the tourist circuit and holiday-makers are flowing there in increasing numbers. The natural attractions, combined with major developmental works such as the Ord and Fitzroy dams and the iron ore and asbestos mines, are bound to increase the flow of tourists. Already the road and air transport services in the region have combined forces in an attempt to exploit the potential of the area. Travelling by air and by motor coach, it is possible for the tourist to take a 15-day 'Spinifex Walkabout', a 13-day 'Sunshine Safari' or a 14-day 'Tropicana Tour' or a selection of other northern trips. The eventual linking of all northern towns by bitumenized road will undoubtedly prove a great stimulus in this respect.

Freighting of Specific Commodities

The cattle industry holds a prominent position in the economy of the region, particularly in the Kimberley area which contains more than 50 per cent of the cattle in the state, and to a much lesser extent in the North-West and Pilbara statistical divisions which carry about five per cent of the total. In recent years, some 65,000 cattle per year have been turned off properties in the Kimberley and moved to the various trans-shipping or processing points.

Cattle in the region are either transported by road or walked in to the ports and the coastal or the inland abattoirs. In the West Kimberley the number of stock carried by road has risen from less than 2,000 in 1952 to 23,000 in 1960 and 37,000 in 1965. In the North-West Division some 7,000 head of cattle are transported by road to the railhead at Meekatharra, and in the East Kimberley road transport is now becoming more accepted by the pastoralists. As the potential turnoff in the Kimberley area is much greater than the present figures and some 90 per cent of this would be able to be carried by road, there is still much room for the expansion of road haulage in the beef industry.

The cattle are hauled by road trains over four principal routes: from the pickup point at Fitzroy Crossing to either Broome or Derby, from Gibb

River and Mt. House to Derby, from the North-West and Pilbara cattle
stations to the railhead at Meekatharra, and in the East Kimberley, from
as far as Hall's Creek along the Great Northern Highway and the Duncan
Highway to Wyndham. The operation is seasonal, occupying the months
between April and September. Road trains in the Kimberley region average
26,000 miles annually, whilst those in the North-West average 35,000 miles.

Costs per unit are, of course, greatly affected by the capacity of the road
trains. Droving costs are about $1.00 per head, per 100 miles, for mobs
of up to 400, and the mobs make about 10 miles a day, whilst average road
transport costs are $3.50 per bullock, per 100 miles, and they can make
up to 300 miles a day. The capital cost of a road train is in excess of
$24,000 for the 150 b.h.p. prime mover and $5,000 each for the two trailers.
Although there have been experiments with larger units, hauliers still consider
a 150 b.h.p. vehicle pulling two trailers, with an overall capacity of about
50 large bullocks, to be the most efficient unit under present conditions. The
size of the road trains are limited by several factors among which are initial
capital outlay, road conditions, and the need to avoid jolting and sway.

There are certain advantages in road transport which offset the cost
disparity. Road transport permits the release of station droving plants to
carry out essential improvements and works on the station which could lead
to increased capacity. It also enables the turning off of younger stock which
would not be able to stand up to droving conditions. This, in addition to
supplying better beef, enables a much greater annual turnoff to be achieved.
The movement of cattle through tick and pleurisy areas can be carried out
without the risk of infection. There are no losses due to poor feed and water
on stock routes, and stock from drought-affected areas can be moved
speedily. Road transport also eliminates stock losses usually associated with
droving through eaten-out country, and losses from strays.

The cattle turnoff from these areas by road transport is undoubtedly considerable but certain minimum requirements have to be observed in the
roads themselves. They need to be straight enough to prevent jolting and
bruising, broad enough to prevent ruts developing through vehicles having
to follow the same tracks all the time, provided with adequate bridges and
crossings to make the carriers independent of floods, and free of steep
grades which jolt the cattle. The principal disadvantage of road transport
is the bruising of cattle, sometimes as a result of poor road surfaces,
sometimes due to inexperienced drivers.

As pointed out above, the main routes in the region are being improved
to provide more efficient transport of beef cattle. The access roads, on the
other hand, are poor generally but are being steadily improved. In parts
of the region trucking points may be anything up to 60 miles from the main
road and the state of the access roads has undoubtedly, in some cases,
dissuaded pastoralists from attempting to truck their cattle.

The sheep industry mostly covers that part of the region which lies south
of the Fitzroy. It is predominant in the North-West, Pilbara and Central

statistical divisions, whereas in the Kimberley it plays a secondary role to the cattle and mining industries. The Fitzroy may be roughly described as a demarcation line between the two forms of pastoralism. Over two million sheep and lambs were shorn in the region during 1965. Table 9 reveals the movement of wool and sheep skins through the ports of the region for the last three years by the State Shipping Service. It must be remembered that a large quantity of the region's wool is moved by road transport to the Meekatharra railhead and then railed direct to Perth. It should also be noted that a small amount of wool is airfreighted but the quantity is not economically significant.

Movement of wool and sheep to the ports is carried out by road transport using the principal roads and the numerous feeders and cross roads which link the transport system to the main roads in the region and to the ports. Generally, it may be said that the transport of sheep and wool, because of the smaller size of the vehicles and their lower capital and operating costs, does not require the concentrated mobilization of financial resources and equipment that is apparent in beef transport. There are thus more and smaller operators in this field.

Many of the roads used for the transport of sheep and wool are earth-formed, with the danger and wear and tear factors which have already been mentioned. The climatic conditions of the North-West and Pilbara statistical divisions, which are the basic sheep areas, tend to accentuate the hazards associated with earth-formed roads. Long dry spells increase the dust hazard and torrential downpours lead to flooding and the risk of bogging. However, as pointed out above, the roads are being steadily improved and more high-level bridges are being provided.

Agriculture in the region, because of the rainfall pattern, is mainly reliant upon irrigation. Three irrigation centres exist on the major rivers, the Ord, the Fitzroy and the Gascoyne. Of the three areas the Gascoyne is the most diversified and developed and the industry there produces for a particular type of market – that for domestic fresh fruit and vegetables. The growers in this area produce bananas, beans, tomatoes, cabbages and other vegetables and channel the produce into the Perth metropolitan or eastern states market in the off-season for the local producers. The nature of the produce from this area gives rise to transport problems different from those of the remainder of the region since the type of commodity produced requires fast, well ventilated transport to ensure that it reaches the markets in the best possible condition.

Gascoyne Traders, a subsidiary of Wesfarmers, freights the perishable agricultural produce from Carnarvon over the 600 miles of bitumenised road to Perth. It also carries Carnarvon prawns to Perth. The ideal type of vehicle for haulage of perishables over this distance has been found to be a prime mover of 125-150 b.h.p. with a semi-trailer capable of carrying 20 tons. The company has refrigerated trucks in which the refrigeration unit and a chiller compartment and freezer compartment are located in the trailer. These vehicles cost $40,000 and there are nine units operating at present. General purpose trucks of the same carrying capacity, costing $30,000 also ply to Carnarvon and to other northern centres such as Exmouth, Roebourne, Onslow, Marble Bar and Port Hedland. The company has about 20 such trucks. Average haulage rates for the 600 mile journey from Carnarvon are $24 per ton. Since the company has suitable trucks and can find considerable freight for back-loading from Perth to Carnarvon, freight rates can be kept down, and, in fact, they have not increased since 1961. Each vehicle is manned by two drivers to enable the 600 mile journey to be made non-stop, excepting for meals. The trip, including loading and unloading, is made within 24 hours. Sleeping quarters of reasonably comfortable proportions have been constructed in the rear of each cab to ensure adequate rest for the crew throughout the journey.

The perishable nature of the cargo and the distance it has to be hauled are the principal factors which influence the company's decisions, as the journey must be covered in the minimum safe time to ensure that the fruit and vegetables reach their markets in good condition. This places heavy emphasis on the importance of good maintenance and repair facilities. Repair depots have been established in Geraldton, Perth and Carnarvon, and mobile repair units and spare vehicles are maintained to guarantee the punctual arrival of the product in the event of breakdown or accident.

Output from the Ord and Fitzroy projects is different in character. It is essentially bulky and of a less perishable nature and is moved by road to the ports for carriage by overseas or state vessels. Transport costs from the Kimberley irrigation areas to Derby, Broome and Wyndham are still high. Somewhat similar problems to those of beef transport are encountered by vehicles operating on earth-surfaced roads, although the bruising factor does not apply.

Mineral deposits for the region are both varied and widely scattered. Mining organization ranges from highly capitalized companies employing substantial quantities of labour to one-man prospector rights. The principal minerals found in the area include iron ore at Koolan and Cockatoo Island, in Yampi Sound and in many parts of the Pilbara, blue asbestos in the Hamersley Ranges at Wittenoom Gorge, manganese and tin in the Pilbara, and beryl, copper and gold widely distributed throughout the area.

Road transport is closely tied in with the production of three of these minerals : asbestos, manganese and tin. The iron ore is shipped direct from Yampi Sound to the eastern states processing plants and is railed from the Pilbara areas to coastal ports for export overseas. Asbestos from Wittenoom Gorge is hauled 200 miles to Point Sampson from where it is shipped to overseas markets. An alternative road has been constructed by the company to Port Hedland, a distance of approximately 200 miles, to provide a second line of communication if Point Sampson should become unserviceable through weather conditions or cyclone damage. Asbestos tonnages moving through Point Samson totalled 10,000 in 1965. Manganese is mined in the Pilbara district, about 180 miles south-east of Port Hedland, and the ore is hauled to Port Hedland from whence it is shipped to the eastern states or overseas. In 1965 manganese transported by road to Port Hedland totalled 100,000 tons. Some 645 tons of tin were roaded partly to Perth and partly to Port Hedland in 1965.

It has been suggested that the provision of bitumen roads will lower transport costs in this area and while this applies generally, the road-freighting of some minerals may provide exceptions to this generalization. The average load of the manganese vehicles is 50-60 tons, which is in excess of that which would be permitted on sealed roads because of the heavy tyre loadings on the vehicles currently in use. If the roads used for hauling manganese were sealed, either the loads carried by the vehicles would need to be reduced or the vehicles would have to be modified with a sufficient number of axles and wheels to keep tyre-loading within reasonable limits. The vehicles used to haul asbestos and manganese to the ports are primarily flat-top semi-trailers, and the trucks at present are loaded to their maximum capacity in an attempt to minimize transport costs for cargoes which have to compete on world markets. Sealing of roads for this particular type of traffic may not therefore provide the complete answer and a suggested combination of road systems for manganese, involving the construction of a private earth road and the use of road trains with much greater capacity which would enable maximum loads to be carried, would provide an interesting example of an attempt to achieve the necessary goal of lower transport costs.

3. AIR TRANSPORT

The carriage of cargoes and passengers by air has, like sea transport, been of vital importance to the development of the north in many ways though its contribution came later than that of shipping. The present company now serves an area of more than half a million square miles and a population of over 20,000 and has progressed a long way from the time of the first uncertain flights into the area.

Past Development

The first regular air service in Australia was commenced in Northwestern Australia in 1921 when Major Brearley, as Managing Director of West Australian Airways, flew the 1,121-mile route from Geraldton to Derby. The present company, Mac.Robertson Miller Aviation Co. Pty. Ltd., began its operations in the north of the state in 1934 when it tendered successfully for the mail contract between Perth and Daly Waters. Three DH-84 Dragon aircraft were used to operate this weekly service and four days were required to complete the northbound journey which was originally planned to follow the overland telegraph. In 1936 a twice-weekly service was introduced, and in 1938 the Perth-Wyndham-Darwin service was inaugurated. After the World War the company introduced DC-3's and re-routed the Derby to Wyndham flight across the King Leopold Ranges instead of along the Fitzroy River as before. At the same time the Kimberley Stations and the Northern Territory Stations services were introduced and on these runs Avro Ansons and DC-3's were used extensively. Mac.Robertson Miller Aviation amalgamated with Airlines (W.A.) Limited in 1955 to form Mac.Robertson Miller Airlines Limited, and in 1959 the company purchased its first turbo-prop aircraft, the Fokker Friendship. This plane carried 9,400 lbs. of freight, 36 passengers, and cruised at 270 m.p.h. which enabled a considerable speeding-up of operations to be achieved. The company now operates four of these aircraft and the next major development is expected to be the operation of pure jet aircraft carrying 60 passengers at 500 m.p.h. before 1970.

Present Operations

The company has an unduplicated route mileage of 26,390 miles which are built around 92 regular ports of call and 10 other landing points where aircraft will call by arrangement. The M.M.A. network principally services the area north of the twenty-sixth parallel although other flights are made including those to Albany, Esperance, Kalgoorlie, Rottnest and the Northern Territory. To service the extensive network, M.M.A. maintains a fleet comprising four Fokker Friendships, one Piaggio, one Dove and eight DC-3's which can be used for passengers or as freighters. A summary of the fleet's operations is given in Tables 4 to 6, where the impact of recent mining developments upon both cargo and passengers carried can be clearly seen in the case of Learmonth, Port Hedland and Roebourne, and where the effect of agricultural development at Kununurra is also clearly evident. A great amount of cargo and many passengers have, of course, been carried to the other mining centres in the Pilbara, but since these have been charter flights the figures have not been included in the tables.

As far as freight is concerned the cargoes carried are usually either light and small, or urgent. The airline provides a speedy adjunct to the road and shipping services – which mainly handle the bulky, non-perishable cargoes – and enables the carriage into the region of fresh vegetables, medical supplies and other urgently required equipment. When the company completed its first year of operations in 1935, some 28,000 lbs. of freight had been carried; now the figure is in excess of five million lbs. Passenger figures have likewise increased significantly. In 1935 approximately 830 passengers were carried; in 1965 the figure was 79,000 and in 1966 more than 157,000. A study of the joint cargo and passenger figures for M.M.A.'s operations in recent years brings home very forcefully the change and growth occurring in the region and suggests the problems which the company itself must be facing in trying to cater for yearly increases in demand of this magnitude.

The need for air transport services is quite apparent in a remote area such as this to cope adequately with the movement of mails, perishable foods, and urgently needed equipment as well as passengers. Another post-war use to which air transport was temporarily diverted was the freighting of slaughtered cattle to the meatworks at Wyndham and Derby from the more inaccessible stations around the Glenroy area. Aircraft are also used by the Flying Doctor Service for the removal of patients from the stations and mining towns to the better equipped hospitals of the coastal ports or Perth. In both of these cases the introduction of air transport has been a pioneering move, requiring the qualities of courage and vision, and has resulted in further economic development of the region as well as in the provision of amenities designed to make life in the more remote areas more attractive. Air travel has also been extensively used in mineral ex-ploration and development in recent years, and many different types of aircraft, including helicopters, are now to be found in the north.

Light aircraft are being used more and more in the cattle industry of northern Australia, though they seem at present to be favoured more in the eastern than the western areas. Aircraft of the Beechcraft, Cessna, Auster, Piper and Autocar type are being used for fence patrols, for urgent errands, for distributing wages to widely scattered or isolated camps and even for rounding up stock. This is, indeed, an age of mechanization and of revolution in transport methods; even motor bikes are used to muster sheep! As well as the conventional light aircraft, helicopters are being used in increasing numbers in the north, and in the rugged Kimberley and Hamersley areas they have proved particularly useful. They can be used for such operations as oil surveying, mineral prospecting, crop spraying and cartographic surveys.

Problems and Prospects

With newer faster aircraft, airports require longer sealed runways to provide year-round operation whereas most landing strips in the region are now mainly earth-formed. Of necessity, the new turbo-prop aircraft are, as future jet aircraft may be, compelled to use the landing strips constructed to serve old piston-engined DC-3's, with the risk of wet season unserviceability. The provision of sealed airstrips in the region introduces similar cost considerations to those involved in road construction, and although the need for all-weather landing strips is readily apparent, particularly as the air service provides the region with its emergency transport, it may be some time before completely satisfactory landing and take-off facilities are available throughout Northwestern Australia.

Another problem encountered in the north is the lack of sufficient back-loading on most trips. This problem, which has already been mentioned in respect of road transport, also figures largely in sea transport. Large quan-tities of cargo are air-freighted into most of the northern centres — far in excess of the quantities carried out — and this is due, of course, to the fact that the products of the area are usually either bulky and/or alive, and hence unsuited to air transport. This is one of the reasons why the airline and the shipping service have both been obliged to operate with the assistance of a government subsidy. The air subsidy in 1964-65 amounted to $92,000 for foodstuffs and perishables and $31,000 for student fares.

A development which may well revolutionize travel in the North-West is the recent invention of the hovercraft. It has already been pointed out that one of the main problems in respect of ground communications is that even a good road system will be disrupted at certain times of the year by climatic factors. Over the flat ground which is most prone to flooding, the hovercraft may well come into its own in years to come, but without thorough testing in the area it is difficult to say just what its future role may be.

The importance of air transport for the development of the region can hardly be over-stressed. The north, in fact, provides a classic example of the type of country – forbidding, impassable at times, and brutal on occasions – which needs air services to open it up. There is no doubt that the airline with the assistance of the government has accepted the challenge and has contributed in a very real way to improving many economic and social aspects of life in the region. Its contribution in the future can be just as great.

4. SEA TRANSPORT

Until the World War the pastoral industry dominated the north, a prosperous pearling industry operated in the waters between Onslow and Broome, limited mining ventures produced tin and copper in the Pilbara district, a meatworks operated at Wyndham and a banana industry flourished at Carnarvon. These industries provided the main southbound cargoes for the State Shipping Service.

Today, as pointed out elsewhere in this survey, most of those industries still exist, but additional meatworks have been established at Derby and Broome, many thousands of tons of asbestos processed at Wittenoom Gorge in the Pilbara district are shipped out through Point Samson, vast quantities of iron ore are shipped from Cockatoo Island, bulk shipments of manganese ore are exported from Port Hedland, and iron ore and cotton are being shipped in increasing quantities from Pilbara ports and from Wyndham, respectively. The successful operation of these industries depends upon the maintenance of adequate shipping facilities.

Past Development

The State Shipping Service began before the Great War and over the years the maintenance of a northern coastal shipping service has become a government function, as have the railway systems in other parts of the commonwealth. The extreme isolation and comparative backwardness already mentioned have retarded the growth of industrial development and population and have been the main influence in the establishment of a heavily subsidized sea transport service. The commonwealth government assists through the Grants Commission to meet this subsidy but the state must find the capital to purchase or build the necessary fleet of ships to carry on the service.

In the past a considerable number of small auxiliary sailing craft found profitable work running to station landings with stores and periodically bringing out wool either directly to Fremantle or to a coastal port for on-carriage by a larger ship, but these traders have now all disappeared with the development of motor transport between stations and ports. For many years coastal class Blue Funnel vessels running between Fremantle and Singapore carried northward and southward cargoes between Fremantle and northern ports, but since the World War their northward service has been confined to the greatly increased Singapore trade. They call at northern ports to lift sheep, wool, asbestos and other minerals destined for overseas ports, and they bring predominantly livestock from northern ports to Fremantle on their southward voyages.

Another feature of coastal shipping services that existed prior to the establishment of the meatworks at Wyndham was the seasonal chartering of four or five interstate cargo vessels to bring cattle down to Fremantle from Wyndham or Derby during the winter months. These charterings ceased for almost 40 years and it is only within the last year or two that additional ships have been brought in to transport Kimberley cattle from Derby to Fremantle or Queensland ports, with other shipments going to Manila and Hong Kong.

The use of road transport to the metropolitan area by an expanding agricultural industry at Carnarvon resulted in considerable inroads being made into sea-borne traffic to and from that port, and a changeover to the use of the road vehicles to and from the greater part of the Gascoyne district has now occurred. Carnarvon is no longer a port of call, servicing of the port having been discontinued since January 1966.

Nature of the Trade

Ship design becomes an important factor in the operations of the coastal service to ensure that the fleet can best meet the conditions prevailing in the trade in respect of both the nature of the traffic to be carried and the ports of call. As will be seen from Table 7, some ships are purely cargo vessels, while others carry passengers as well, and they vary in size from 2,400 tons to 4,100 tons. Restricted dry-docking facilities at Fremantle, together with the limitations of depth of water and berthing space at northern ports as well as frequency requirements, necessitate the use of comparatively small ships of 2,000-2,500 tons deadweight capacity - including fuel, water and stores, etc. The present coastal fleet consists of eight such ships of which four carry passengers as well as cargo, and three are solely freighters.

These ships must have ample refrigerated space for perishable foodstuffs on northward voyages and for frozen meat southward from Wyndham, Derby and Broome. They must have facilities for lifting heavy packages – the present limit is 20 tons – and stowage capacity for extremely bulky items such as fabricated steel sections, deck and hold space for heavy road-making machinery and long jetty piles, and specially equipped space for the carriage of large quantities of aviation and motor spirit in drums. Not all ships carry livestock, but the whole fleet must provide sufficient space for northward shipments of stud stock – rams, ewes, bulls – and southward shipments of fat cattle for the metropolitan market from the Kimberley and Pilbara districts, and for sheep as required. A summary of types of cargoes carried north and south is given in Tables 10 and 11.

The provision of space for such diverse traffic requirements in ships of limited dimensions involves skilful arrangement on the part of naval architects and places the ships in a special class category. When to this is added the complications of air-conditioned passenger accommodation with essential dining and lounge-room amenities, the result is a fleet of ships with a much higher capital value in relation to earning capacity than is customary in other normally profitable trades.

The one-way nature of the trade, evident also in road, air and rail transport, has serious effects on shipping operations. In 1960 northbound freight earnings to the five major ports listed in Table 10 amounted to £486,000, while the southbound freight brought in £201,000. By 1965 the northbound feight had almost doubled to £901,000 while southbound freight earnings had remained virtually static, at £210,000. Thus the already marked imbalance between the two increased even further from £285,000 to £691,000. Northbound shipping cargoes are mainly general cargo, fuel, timber and vehicles, while southbound cargoes are mainly wool and skins, empties and minerals.

In 1964, to enable products of the north to be shipped direct to eastern states ports the Service inaugurated its round-Australia voyages traversing the continent from Fremantle north-about via Darwin. This has ensured the shipment direct to Brisbane, Sydney and Melbourne of cotton from the Ord, as well as asbestos from the Wittenoom mines. The State Shipping Service uses its cargo-passenger vessels on these voyages thus offering accommodation for tourists as well.

Cost of Sea Transport

The heavily subsidized character of the Coastal Shipping Service is indicated by the amount of subsidy which is currently $2.4 million per annum. This situation results from a number of causes of which the immediate one is the comparatively low scale of freight and passage rates in relation to capital and operating costs fixed by state government policy to afford all possible assistance to northern areas in the matter of transport costs.

It is calculated that, including overhead charges, it costs approximately $2.1 to handle one ton of cargo on an overall-average basis, from wharf to ship's hold and out again in the state's cargo ships. The overheads include capital cost of ships, and cost of administration of the State Shipping Service. To this must be added the cost of conveying the goods from port of shipment to port of discharge, which varies of course with the type of ship and the length of run, but is estimated to be approximately $7 per ton overall, on the cargo ships. Vessels are usually filled to roughly 90 per cent of capacity leaving Fremantle, but over the complete northward voyage, with nine discharge ports and with a lack of any substantial interport cargo, a vessel would not average more than 50-60 per cent capacity. The picture is considerably worse on southward voyages. Other cost factors which inflate the amount of subsidy required are the restricted size of coastal ships – ships of twice the capacity could be built and operated for much less than twice the cost of the small ship – the jetty-type ports, which necessitate slower handling rates per gang-hour and the employment of a lesser number of gangs to avoid jetty congestion, and the tidal nature of the trade, which necessitates working a great deal of overtime to avoid excessive delay and demurrage costs. Improvements currently being made in port facilities in this area are described below. The recent Wayne Report[1] which makes certain recommendations relevant to northern transport generally is also discussed below.

Passenger Traffic

Programmes are arranged to give each port a regular frequency of calls which vary between 6 and 12 days apart. Variations are caused by the different speeds of ships and lengths of voyages, and the utmost care is necessary at all times from the cost viewpoint to avoid the need for week-end overtime stevedoring work at the terminal ports, Fremantle, Derby, Wyndham and Darwin, and of course at all other ports where possible.[2] Early programme planning is essential for two reasons : first, to make sailing dates available for the purpose of passenger reservations, and second, to enable the southward fat-cattle loading programme ex Derby to be arranged. Cattlemen need the information some months ahead to enable them to plan the delivery of the requisite number of cattle at Derby to coincide with the arrival of the ship.

It has been suggested in the Wayne Report that in the interests of overall efficiency the state ships should concentrate more on the carriage of cargo than on passenger services. The acquisition by M.M.A. of its Fokker

[1] C. G. C. Wayne, *Overall Review of Transport in Western Australia.*
[2] The Wayne report recommends that stevedoring and wharf handling at northern ports should pass to the State Shipping Service wherever it has branch offices or local representation.

Friendship aircraft has somewhat reinforced this argument since travel in these aircraft is undoubtedly much more pleasant than in the DC-3, and much quicker than by ship. Apart from travel by northern residents an important segment of passenger traffic is now the winter tourist flow which has already been mentioned, and in this respect the shipping service is subjected to increasing competition from road and air transport as bitumen roads spread through the north and as M.M.A. acquires more and speedier aircraft. By the elimination of passenger traffic the opportunity is available to avoid the difficulties associated with maintaining an itinerary which will avoid the ship being neaped at some northern ports.

Navigational Problems and Port Facilities

Coastal waters are not well charted, many of the last surveys having been carried out before the turn of the century. A survey programme is now being carried out in selected areas, but local knowledge in close waters has been, and still is, essential. Wyndham, Broome and Port Hedland are the only gazetted pilotage ports north of Geraldton. Overseas ships engage pilots at Fremantle for the other more hazardous ports. Calls at other ports by overseas vessels for manganese ore, iron ore, asbestos or live cattle are increasing each year.

All northern ports are tidal, with a rise and fall at top springs varying between 5 feet at Carnarvon and 34 feet at Derby. During neap tide periods, 2 to 5 days at Derby, vessels take the ground at low water, with the sea receding some two or three miles from the jetty. To meet this condition vessels must be suitably strengthened in their hull structure. Wyndham and Derby are situated in Cambridge Gulf and King Sound respectively and these waters as well as the inner passage between Yampi Sound and Cambridge Gulf must be navigated in daylight. For all its beauty the area is a hazardous one for shipping and the Wayne report recommends that the State Shipping Service should restrict its calls at Derby to an absolute minimum, and that early action should be taken to provide navigational aids to bring Wyndham into line with other 24 hour deep-water ports.

At all northern ports the silting problem is ever-present with new banks forming in different places. Added to these hazards is the cyclone season which can make navigation in these waters dangerous and time-consuming. When one considers these disabilities it is small wonder that skippers and owners of overseas ships were reluctant to take contracts to pick up along the northern coast. Quite apart from this there was the impossibility of berthing ships with large displacement. This meant that ore and other cargo had to be trans-shipped at Fremantle. In a competitive international market such diseconomies could not be tolerated for very long and the Western Australian government pressed ahead with the provision of adequate deep-water port facilities. Derby is the one remaining northern port where port facilities are still unsatisfactory, and in Wyndham the problem of night navigation still remains.

In particular, the newly constructed ports at Dampier and Exmouth leave very little to be desired and the changes that have taken place in the last two years at Port Hedland have transformed it as a port. The port at Dampier, developed to take iron ore from Mt. Tom Price, gives unrestricted access to vessels of 60,000 tons and admits vessels of 100,000 tons at high tide. Port Hedland, which previously had badly limited access, has so far been dredged to take ships of 50,000 tons on high tide and dredging is continuing. This port currently handles iron ore from Mt. Goldsworthy and later will handle large quantities of salt for Leslie Salt (see Chapter 4). If it is also called upon to handle iron ore from Mt. Newman, its annual throughput will eventually amount to some 25 to 30 million tons a year involving a turn round of 500 to 600 ships of 50,000 tons.

Shipping Finance

Since its inception the State Shipping Service has generally been unable to achieve yearly earnings to match its yearly expenditure. With some exceptions in the inter-war period it has incurred continuing deficits due mainly to the deliberate government policy of subsidizing the north and encouraging its development. To this end, both passenger rates and freight charges have been kept low which, with the other disabilities of operating the ships along the northern coast, have ensured that a deficit will be incurred, though operations have been maintained as efficiently as possible within the constraints imposed. Charges have naturally risen over the years and fares, which constitute roughly 10 per cent of total earnings, have more than doubled since 1952; currently they are $77 to Port Hedland and $113 to Wyndham. Freight rates, constituting 90 per cent of earnings, have also more than doubled since 1952; currently the rates for general cargo, Class A (clothing, groceries, foodstuffs, furniture and household commodities) are $18.75 per ton to Port Hedland and $21.25 to Wyndham.

The extent of the deficit in recent years is indicated in Table 13. In 1961 it exceeded one million pounds for the first time and has remained above that figure since then. Since 1960 it has averaged approximately 47 per cent of total expenditure and in the preceding five years the proportion averaged 48 per cent. Since 1960 total expenditure has increased by 53 per cent and revenue by 62 per cent and the deficit has increased by 43 per cent.

The deficit incurred by the State Shipping Service has been explicitly recognized by the Commonwealth Grants Commission as one of the contributing factors to the large special grant made yearly to Western Australia by the commonwealth government. Coupled with this is the more general need to maintain services to the northern area of the state in the face of heavy costs. The Commission has, at times, commented on the scales of charges and the performance of the State Shipping Service in carrying out its tasks, and queried whether the whole of the annual deficit should be reimbursed in the special grant. On the whole the Commission has tended in the past to take a sympathetic view of the problems faced by the service and thus has tended to oppose the views of the commonwealth treasury that high priorities on State Shipping expenditure should be offset by lower priorities on other expenditures. In 1965, however, it finally imposed, for the first time, an adverse adjustment of £26,000.[3]

In attempting to determine the main factors responsible for the continued deficit the Commission concluded, on the basis of a comprehensive report by Captain Williams,[4] that efficiency in administration and operation was not one of them. The physical, climatic and economic factors already mentioned were partly responsible and certain self-imposed economic factors, in particular persistently low fares and freights, also contributed substantially to the loss.

The Commission felt that if the entire loss of the State Shipping Service were to be treated as a subsidy for northern development, this should be done so explicitly by the commonwealth government rather than concealed in the special grant procedure. However, this has not been done. Nevertheless, the commonwealth government, in answer to a request from the Commission to clarify its attitude in the matter, considered that some limit should be imposed upon the extent of the losses it would be prepared to support and the Commission settled upon £1.2 million, though without any precise detailed evidence to support this. The payment for this was to remain within the special grants procedure. Since the deficit in 1965 was £1,226,000 an adverse adjustment of £26,000 was made, as mentioned above. The Commission contends that the new arrangement will act as a strong incentive for the Service to achieve some economy in operation and states that it will require strong evidence in the future that increased losses could not be covered by economies in operation and increased charges on those using the service.

The drawback of such a limit upon losses is that it may well help to impair efficiency in the Service in the immediate future. The Commission itself has seen the rise in interest payments and depreciation, resulting from repeated re-equipment and modernization of the fleet, as the dominant factor affecting the size of losses, and has noted that on this account the losses can be expected to continue for some years. Any cheeseparing in this respect may have direct effects upon the efficiency of the Service's operations and will, at the same time, force an upward revision of fares and freight charges.

Future Development

Both the Williams and the Wayne reports have drawn attention to the adverse conditions under which the Service operates and have suggested

[3]Commonwealth Grants Commission. *Commonwealth Grants Commission 32nd Report.*
[4]J. P. Williams, *An Inquiry into the Affairs of the State Shipping Service.*

remedial measures designed to increase the general efficiency of the transport facilities offered, taking into account the limitations imposed by the nature of the trade and the social and economic needs of the region. The Williams report is the more comprehensive of the two, since it was specifically an enquiry into the affairs of the State Shipping Service, while the Wayne report covered all aspects of transport in Western Australia.

The Williams report recommends changes in the control of cargo operations, sailing schedules, freights and fares with the object of reducing the present deficiency by one-third. This would involve capital expenditure leading to long-term improvements designed to speed up the traffic as a means of utilizing individual ships more intensively. On the operating cost side, stevedoring and wharf handling by the Service and the provision of a permanent berth for state ships at Fremantle also offer considerable scope for economies, possibly to the extent of $200,000 a year, whilst savings in port time and crew overtime from simultaneous loading and discharging at outports will also be made. In areas where road or rail transport or both can cater satisfactorily for the business offering, Captain Williams recommends progressive withdrawal by the Service as a further means of reducing the loss.

The report forsees some disturbance of present schedules and existing practices which will bring opposition from some quarters and recommends therefore the establishment of a Commission or some independent body which will act as a shield for management.

Rationalization of the State Shipping Service is rightly seen as a major problem in the Wayne report, and various suggestions made as to how this may be achieved or, at least, how the present cost-revenue position can be improved and the deficit reduced. The report recommends, for instance, that the Service should concentrate on the deep-water ports of Dampier, Port Hedland, Broome and Wyndham. Onslow and Point Samson should be closed, with asbestos delivery re-routed to either Dampier or Port Hedland, and state ships should no longer call at Geraldton. Calls to Derby should be reduced to a minimum. This is part of a plan for 'speeding up' the Service which Mr. Wayne considers essential, and in which Captain Williams concurs. Fare and freight rises, as in the Williams report, are also recommended and likewise a further development of sea-container traffic is seen as an integral part of the emphasis upon cargo rather than passengers. Both reports agree, also, on the provision of a permanent berth at Fremantle.

The Williams report was presented in 1962 and many of its recommendations have been put into effect. Among other moves, the Western Australian Coastal Shipping Commission, a corporate agency of the crown, was established by the state government in November 1965 and in its planning of replacement tonnage is currently investigating various new types of vessels.

Under consideration is a vessel of revolutionary design, termed a barge carrier or 'lash' vessel – the initials stand for Lighter Aboard Ship. Each barge would be an oversize container with a gross weight of 200 tons and carrying capacity of 160 tons and a ship could carry up to 25 such barges. Loading and unloading of barges would take about 15 minutes by ship's gear. This type of cargo handling would speed up the whole coastal operation since ships would not need to wait for wharf or jetty space as the barges could be unloaded midstream. Also, discharge of cargo from barges could be carried out in normal working hours at a special terminal. They could be loaded and made ready for a later southbound trip. If this proposal is adopted the Fremantle-Darwin-Fremantle trip, now taking about 30 days, could be cut to little more than a third, servicing five or six ports and providing 4,000 tons of cargo capacity each way.

With the progressive implementation of the proposals contained in both reports as a move towards greater rationalization of the shipping service, one may see the various transport modes in the north moving closer to some loose kind of co-ordination or partnership. The ultimate aim would be to have them operating in a complementary rather than competitive fashion. In the meantime the problems of northern sea transport remain closely tied to the general character of development in the region and this will continue to impose cost disadvantages for many years. Despite this the sea link with the south must be maintained even at the cost of a substantial government subsidy in the short-term.

5. Railway Transport

Of the four major transport modes – road, rail, sea and air – rail transport is the least developed in the north. Small lines have existed in the past at the ports but the region could not be said to have had a railroad system unless it be the line from Marble Bar to Port Hedland. This in any case was finally torn up and the rails used for building structures in the period of acute steel shortage after the war. From then on the only railroad in the north was the Meekatharra railhead which played an important role in servicing the southernmost areas of the region and continues to do so.

In recent years, however, standard gauge railways constructed at high cost have branched out from Port Hedland to link with Mt. Goldsworthy, 70 miles to the east, and from Dampier to link with Mt. Tom Price, 179 miles to the south-east. Further proposals are for a line from Port Hedland to link with Mt. Newman, 225 miles to the south, and a line from Cape Preston to link with Deepdale and Mt. Enid, 70 miles to the south. Another proposal is for the construction of a line to link a new coastal port near Cape Keraudren with Mt. Nicholas 180 miles to the south. These proposals are outlined in Chapter 4 and if they all come to fruition will result in a total standard gauge rail mileage of 724 miles. The Hamersley railroad, which was constructed in 15 months, is one of the world's heaviest duty railroads and is capable of accommodating a train carrying 18,200 tons of ore at 45 miles per hour.

This represents a significant investment in heavy transport facilities in a surprisingly short time, all of which has been carried out to move one mineral – iron ore. The agreements concluded between the state government and the companies concerned allow for the carriage of passengers and freight for the state government and for third parties at reasonable rates and it is conceivable that the rail system so developed will assist in the exploitation of other minerals and in the carriage of other goods into and out of the region.

6. Summary and Conclusions

Because of the climatic characteristics, the terrain, the great distances between towns, and the economic characteristics of the region's production, the question of transport looms large in any discussion of the economic growth of Northwestern Australia. The physical and economic characteristics of the region affect all four modes of transport – sea, air, rail and road, to varying degrees.

Road transport is vitally affected by the physical factors as they become translated into vehicle depreciation and maintenance costs and operating hazards and into the costs associated with the construction and maintenance of roads. In conjunction with these, one must consider such economic factors, as population and motor vehicle densities and the character of the region's production which is mainly primary, with vast quantities of produce exported and much smaller quantities imported, leading to a one-way goods traffic flow and to the need for specialized vehicles. Possibilities for back-loading and the economic density of cargoes carried must also be taken into account.

Commonwealth road grants are based upon a formula of one-third for area, one-third for population and one-third for vehicle registration, and the seemingly disproportionate allocation of funds to the north has to be considered in this light. For instance, while northern-based vehicles rarely move out of the region, vehicles such as heavy-duty trucks, passenger buses and cars which are registered elsewhere make relatively high use of northern roads. The remote areas, by the nature of their trade, also contribute substantially to petrol tax and other taxes on fuels, which form an important source of commonwealth revenue from road useage. Nevertheless, without the slightest doubt, northern road transport will have to be assisted in the future as it has in the past and the question is just how far this assistance is to go. A great deal of money, for example, can be spent in sealing northern roads; a million dollars would achieve little and in fact a $17 million scheme is currently operating in the far north. In the pastoral areas expenditures on this scale can only be justified by greater turnoff of cattle and wool and the state must demand that pastoralists play their role by developing their properties and improving their efficiency. There is no justification for a subsidy which is not matched by much greater efforts on the part of those who will most benefit.

The first major long-term aim should be to develop one great arterial sealed highway connecting all the major centres of activity in the region. This could be serviced by feeder roads, the further development of which could come at a later stage. Such a system would allow the operation of a fast efficient transport fleet and could also facilitate the quicker turnoff of the region's produce in many ways. In addition it will undoubtedly have a marked effect upon tourism, an industry which could be a great money earner in the north but which is, even now, virtually untapped. Transport costs generally would also be lowered with consequent all-round economic and social benefits. Annual capital and maintenance costs on this alone would amount to more than is being spent currently on all roads in the region. Such a development, the second stage of which is now under way with the sealing of the road from Carnarvon to Port Hedland and the extension of the bitumen from other northern ports, could also change the whole character of the region's trade flow, just as the sealing of the highway through to Carnarvon radically changed the traffic flow. This should work to the advantage of the State Shipping Service in the rationalization of its schedules as road transport of heavy bulky goods to the smaller ports takes over from sea transport.

Difficulties encountered in the development of air transport in the region are not quite so much physical as economic. There are physical characteristics of the area which give rise to difficulties of construction and maintenance of airfields and aircraft, but the major problems are the familiar ones of backloading and economic density of the cargoes carried. In spite of these problems M.M.A. has a remarkable record of aircraft utilization.

The air transport system does provide a much-needed means of getting perishables and high-value, urgently needed goods to the region quickly. In its own right, and in many of its variants such as Air Beef and the Royal Flying Doctor Service, air transport has undoubtedly assisted greatly in the development of the region. But again, it is heavily subsidized to the extent of over $100,000 per annum and the subsidy will need to be extended well into the future if it is to continue to play its role in the region's growth. The future expansion of air services will involve the building of new aerodromes, the extension of existing ones and the acquisition of more, larger and faster aircraft. In very broad terms the transport subsidy for these could well take up more than a million dollars a year because of material and labour costs associated with capital projects and the high operating costs associated with trying to maintain a wide network of frequent calls to isolated areas with a very low traffic density.

Sea transport, like the other modes, can exist in its present form only with a heavy subsidy of over $2 million. To the cost of subsidizing the State Shipping Service must also be added the cost of constructing and maintaining deep-water ports, although in several cases this cost is currently being met by the large ore companies. Climatic and physical conditions affect sea transport through the tidal rise and fall and the tricky navigation in northern waters, as well as through silting up of harbours and the presence of cyclonic conditions at certain times of the year. Economic factors also exercise a significant influence; they make it impossible for the coastal shipping line to operate anywhere near an economic level.

The development of rail transport can be expected, at least in its initial stages, to follow the dictates of economy and profitability in relation to the transport of iron ore. The railroads already privately constructed can be expected to be added to and utilized to a greater extent in the future and it is important that as with previous agreements, provision be made for the carriage of passengers and of freights for the state and for third parties on reasonable terms.

It can be seen, therefore, that the region has a very severe transport problem – one which is not likely to be removed in the foreseeable future, even by rapid economic development. Subsidies will have to remain for a long time. One could probably say that transport services as a whole in the region are subsidized to the extent of perhaps $10 million annually at present. There is, of course, a responsibility upon the government to ensure that this money is being spent in the best way, taking the overall view, and a case can be made out for urging the formation of a northern transport co-ordinating committee responsible for formulating a transport development plan for the region as a whole into which would be fitted the different developmental requirements of the four different transport modes.

Research into all aspects of transport in the region would be the principal task of such a committee which should comprise economists, engineers and administrators. Knowledge is needed of the capital and operating costs of the various transport modes under differing conditions, as well as of the capacities available from the different carriers. Estimates are needed of the quantities of various classes of goods expected to be moved in different directions. Given such information it would be possible, with the aid of mathematical programming and other econometric techniques, to develop transport models and case studies supplemented by input-output analyses, benefit-cost analyses and regional studies. From this could be developed a long-term plan which would provide a rational basis for transport development in the north. In this respect it is worth noting that acceptable information on capital and maintenance charges and operating costs for sea, rail and air transport is now available, but in respect of road transport there is virtually nothing on which the planner could work. It is, of course, a much more atomistic industry than the other transport modes and it is certain that the required information would not even be recorded at present by any but the big operators. Until the required information is recorded by the operators and made available to the committee, a co-ordinated transport system cannot be evolved. There is thus an urgent necessity to remove this statistical bottleneck.

That successive state governments, at least in recent years, recognize the necessity for gathering planning information, is indicated by the number of different consultants called in to undertake specific surveys directly in the field of transport or indirectly linked to it. There is, however, no indication that at any time these consultants have worked together on the possibilities of co-ordinating their efforts according to one overall transport plan for the region. The setting-up of a transport authority for the state as a whole is one of the recommendations in the Wayne report. Should this eventuate it would be possible for a northern transport co-ordinating committee to work within the general framework so established. Because of the isolation and the peculiar characteristics of the region, however, it is sufficiently different from the remainder of the state to warrant separate study, and for this reason one would hope that the problems of northern transport would not receive less emphasis or attention than should be the case if they were handled by the central authority. In fact there is a good case for linking the northern committee in some direct way with the office of the Administrator of the North-West.

Development is now taking place rapidly in the north and the necessity for long-term planning and budgeting in the transport field is evident. For instance, if some of the transport development work in the north is to be carried out by private contracting firms they will often need to be assured that work will continue for a long enough period to justify moving expensive capital equipment into the area. Again, the state government departments most directly concerned, particularly Public Works, must also know as soon as possible just what role they are expected to play over a reasonably long period. This basic information is needed in order that the various departments will be able to plan for future requirements in the form of technical staff, equipment, designs and so on. Such a long-term plan must weigh the relative merits of the different transport modes in the region, and must establish priorities designed to suit the money currently available as well as lesser priorities in the time scale which could be realized earlier than planned if other monies became available unexpectedly. The formulation of such a plan should be the task of a body of men representative of the three main transport modes. The overall aim should be the most efficient utilization of the financial resources available having regard to both short and long-term factors.

Bibliography

AUSTRALIAN INSTITUTE OF POLITICAL SCIENCE. *Northern Australia: Task for a Nation.* Sydney, 1954.

BUREAU OF AGRICULTURAL ECONOMICS. *The Economics of Road Transport of Beef Cattle – Western Australian Pastoral Areas, 1958.* Canberra, 1958.

COMMONWEALTH GRANTS COMMISSION. *Commonwealth Grants Commission 32nd Report.* Canberra, 1965.
—— *Annual Reports.*

MAC.ROBERTSON MILLER AIRLINES LIMITED. *Annual Reports.*

MAIN ROADS DEPARTMENT. *Annual Reports.*
—— 'Road Transport's Vital Role in North-West Cattle Development.' *Australian Journal of the Institute of Transport.* 1962.

PYKE, L. H. 'Economics of Transport: North Western Australia.' Unpublished M.Ec. thesis, 1965. Library of the University of Western Australia.

STATE SHIPPING SERVICE. *Annual Reports.*

WAYNE, C. G. C. *Overall Review of Transport in Western Australia.* Perth, 1966.

WESTERN AUSTRALIAN GOVERNMENT TOURIST AND PUBLICITY BUREAU. *The North-West of Western Australia.* Perth, 1965.

WILLIAMS, J. P. *An Inquiry into the Affairs of the State Shipping Service.* Perth, 1962.

TABLE 1

ROAD MILEAGES

(as at 30 June 1965)

(No. of miles)

Statistical Division	Surfaced	Formed but not otherwise prepared	Unprepared but used for general purposes
CENTRAL			
Meektharra	611	1,198	2,281
Wiluna	28	1,097	14
Divisional total	639	2,295	2,295
NORTH-WEST			
Ashburton	19	1,147	162
Exmouth	66	—	—
Gascoyne-Minilya	142	255	1,308
Shark Bay	76	327	n.a.
Upper Gascoyne	—	1,511	55
Divisional total	303	3,240	n.a.
PILBARA			
Marble Bar	11	800	n.a.
Nullagine	172	432	30
Port Hedland	265	271	148
Roebourne	118	103	338
Tableland	16	450	124
Divisional total	582	2,056	n.a.
KIMBERLEY			
Broome	60	437	109
Halls Creek	67	1,136	344
West Kimberley	371	648	672
Wyndham-East Kimberley	194	228	783
Divisional total	692	2,449	1,908
Regional total	2,216	10,040	n.a.

Source: Deputy Commonwealth Statistician, Western Australia.

TABLE 2

ALLOCATION FOR ROADS FROM COMMONWEALTH FUNDS

(£'000)

	1955-56	1960-61	1966-67	1965-66
Northern Roads (1)	612	1,630	3,121	3.558
State total (2)	5,450	8,250	12,307	12,783
(1) at % of (2)	11.2%	19.8%	25.4%	27.8%

Source: Western Australia, Main Roads Department, *Annual Reports.*

TABLE 3

MOTOR VEHICLES ON REGISTER
(as at 31 December 1965)
(No. of vehicles)

Statistical Division	Motor Cars	Commercial Vehicles[1]	Motor Cycles	Total
CENTRAL				
Meekatharra	147	268	9	424
Wiluna	50	76	16	142
Divisional total	197	344	25	566
NORTH-WEST				
Ashburton	80	149	1	230
Exmouth	87	152	3	242
Gascoyne-Minilya	889	723	42	1,654
Shark Bay	56	60	2	118
Upper Gascoyne	48	103	2	153
Divisional total	1,160	1,187	50	2,397
PILBARA				
Marble Bar	63	118	2	183
Nullagine	31	60	14	105
Port Hedland	274	419	22	715
Roebourne	104	354	4	462
Tableland	129	129	13	271
Divisional total	601	1,080	55	1,736
KIMBERLEY				
Broome	164	164	13	341
Halls Creek	27	135	2	164
West Kimberley	221	318	26	565
Wyndham-East Kimberley	238	335	22	595
Divisional total	650	952	63	1,665
Regional total	2,608	3,563	193	6,364

[1] Utilities, vans, trucks and buses.

Source: Deputy Commonwealth Statistician, Western Australia.

TABLE 4

AIR TRAFFIC CARRIED TO ALL NORTHERN PORTS
1960-1965

Year ended 31st December	Passengers carried (No.)	Cargo carried ('000 lb.)
1960	38,942	5,806
1961	41,025	6,276
1962	44,370	6,362
1963	52,109	3,725
1964	60,515	4,072
1965	72,689	7,910

Note: Cargo from 1960 to 1962 includes air beef.

Source: Mac.Robertson Miller Airlines Limited, *Annual Reports.*

TABLE 5

AIR CARGO TRAFFIC TO AND FROM MAJOR NORTHERN PORTS

(1960-61 to 1965-66)

('000 lbs.)

	1960-61		1961-62		1962-63		1963-64				1965-66*	
	Off	On	Off	On	Off	On	Off	On	Off	On	Off	On
Carnarvon	169	57	183	64	184	60	227	64	220	73	263	111
Broome	155	50	190	64	164	40	233	40	287	58	351	70
Derby	2,769	1,015	3,030	1,155	1,150	819	819	342	836	327	1,151	532
Fitzroy Crossing	27	2	42	5	41	4	33	3	45	3	42	4
Halls Creek	100	14	161	21	177	16	205	21	196	19	170	18
Learmonth	24	4	26	4	27	4	87	12	143	28	292	49
Marble Bar	62	3	76	5	45	5	18	7	54	6	62	9
Meekatharra	97	46	114	63	119	66	112	45	84	31	91	29
Onslow	86	13	62	24	76	19	68	20	82	80	101	46
Port Hedland	357	165	407	214	422	249	435	274	508	283	953	425
Roebourne	89	16	85	20	86	14	101	13	194	19	315	30
Shark Bay	30	12	22	6	26	3	29	3	26	4	18	3
Wittenoom Gorge	201	25	124	39	133	25	114	33	118	32	171	59
Wyndham	315	120	417	258	406	132	420	101	449	79	459	95
Kununurra	38	1	143	10	211	18	275	32	376	32	501	37

* For information regarding the newer iron ore townships see text.

Source: Mac.Robertson Miller Airlines Limited, *Annual Reports.*

TABLE 6

AIR PASSENGER TRAFFIC TO AND FROM MAJOR NORTHERN PORTS

(1960-61 to 1965-66)

(Number of Persons)

	1960-51		1961-62		1962-63		1963-64		1964-65		1965-66*	
	Off	On	On	Off	On	Off	On	Off	On	Off	On	Off
Carnarvon	2,187	2,202	2,264	2,153	2,410	2,389	3,000	4,120	3,622	3,827	4,772	4,882
Broome	1,477	1,603	1,739	1,720	1,860	2,055	2,255	2,309	2,713	2,842	2,952	3,020
Derby	3,985	3,798	4,714	4,565	4,981	5,143	5,324	5,354	5,550	5,682	6,321	6,578
Fitzroy Crossing	136	101	109	175	238	213	159	152	170	113	168	170
Halls Creek	267	257	317	396	292	285	295	305	434	420	426	470
Learmonth	176	148	145	173	443	419	1,674	1,431	2,844	2,463	6,438	5,856
Marble Bar	183	180	180	19_	178	189	143	156	218	243	342	299
Meekatharra	865	1,024	952	807	682	829	807	919	709	838	922	975
Onslow	603	523	574	550	738	848	703	733	968	998	1,069	1,125
Port Hedland	2,177	2,317	2,451	2,403	2,757	3,034	3,082	3,246	4,306	4,331	8,084	8,242
Roebourne	506	498	514	536	609	573	635	677	1,517	1,135	2,155	2,208
Shark Bay	176	163	128	148	180	144	304	243	359	313	186	158
Wittenoom Gorge	1,327	1,238	1,454	1,577	1,371	1,392	1,595	1,613	1,599	1,485	2,103	1,956
Wyndham	2,7_2	2,587	3,485	3,305	2,376	2,585	2,144	2,016	2,247	2,422	2,377	2,590
Kununurra	237	184	566	867	1,224	1,145	1,737	1,722	1,925	2,106	2,198	2,423

* For information regarding the newer iron ore townships see text.

NOTE: These are the main ports serviced. Many more that these are visited by aircraft from M.M.A. Ltd.

Source: Mac.Robertson Miller Airlines Limited, *Annual Reports.*

TABLE 7

STATE SHIPPING SERVICE

Fleet Information

	Koolama	Koojarra	Kabbarli	Dorrigo	Dulverton	Delamere	Kangaroo	Wangara
When built　…　…　…　…　…　…	1958	1956	1957	1946	1948	1946	1962	1954
Where built　…　…　…　…　…	Glasgow	Newcastle	Newcastle	Newcastle	Brisbane	Whyalla	Brisbane	Newcastle
Gross tonnage　…　…　…　…	3,777	2,959	2,983	2,898	2,411	2,835	4,129	2,459
Net tonnage　…　…　…　…　…	1,942	1,656	1,561	1,388	1,134	1,424	2,551	1,274
Length (ft.)　…　…　…　…	285	282	279	279	279	279	323	270
Propulsion (type)　…　…　…	Motor	Motor	Motor	Steam	Steam	Steam	Motor	Motor
Speed (knots)　…　…　…　…	13	12	12	10	10	10	13	10
Passengers (nos.)　…　…　…	60	61	55	nil	nil	nil	94	nil
Crew (nos.)　…　…　…　…	60	55	53	37	34	38	66	30
Refrigeration (cu. ft.)　…　…	14,160	17,920	11,240	12,420	nil	7,880	17,107	7,050
Heaviest lift (tons)　…　…　…	5	10	17	20	20	20	20	20
Live cattle (head)　…　…　…	320	nil	nil	295	nil	405	310	nil

Source: State Shipping Service, Western Australia.

TABLE 8

PORT ACTIVITY

Port	Vessels Entered	Cargo			
		Discharged		Shipped	
		Tons Weight	Tons Measurement	Tons Weight	Tons Measurement
Broome					
1960	90	3,470	9,153	1,898	3,142
1965	96	17,272	2,929	6,484	550
Carnarvon					
1960	76	7,269	3	8,653	1,212
1965	81	18,049	26	2,017	51
Derby					
1960	97	6,660	10,895	5,748	4,660
1965	111	9,202	13,002	18,031	5,622
Onslow					
1960	80	6,180	470	2,724	102
1965	79	2,357	97	1,367	—
Port Samson					
1960	106	4,166	5,495	16,470	795
1965	110	22,651	6,146	8,420	740
Port Hedland					
1960	97	5,000	12,764	60,848	3,008
1965	131	31,603	—	72,881	—
Wyndham					
1960	64	6,847	11,707	8,149	4,702
1965	98	16,820	19,287	6,718	5,559
Yampi					
1960	100	4,105	117	774,049	—
1965	192	9,529	—	1,510,652	—

Source: Deputy Commonwealth Statistician, Western Australia.

NOTE: Part of the cargo is recorded in tons weight and part in tons measurement. As the total cannot be described accurately as either 'tons weight' or 'tons measurement', each is recorded and published separately. One ton measurement equals 40 cubic feet.

TABLE 9

NORTHERN PORTS

Wool and Sheep Skins Carried South

1960 to 1965

(Number of Bales)

Ports	1960	1961	1962	1963	1964	1965
Derby	1,603	1,362	1,616	2,061	2,121	1,968
Broome	306	137	137	417	366	402
Port Hedland	4,006	4,893	4,613	2,659	3,412	3,044
Point Samson	3,267	2,876	2,205	2,514	2,803	3,090
Onslow	4,798	1,922	4,728	3,880	4,272	4,045
Carnarvon	250	81	47	5	—	—
Total	14,253	11,271	13,346	11,536	12,974	12,549

Source: State Shipping Service, Western Australia.

TABLE 10

SUMMARY OF SHIPPING CARGOES CARRIED NORTH

1960 and 1965

Major Ports[1]	General	Timber	Cement	Petrol	Aviation Gas	Kerosene and Oils	Vehicles	Bulk Oil	Freezer	Wines and Tobaccos	Dangerous	Others	Inter-port	Total	Horses and Cattle	Rams and Sheep	Freight Value
	Tons	Tons	Tons	Tons	Tons	Tons	Tons	Tons	Tons	Tons	Tons	Tons	Tons	Tons	No.	No.	£'000
Point Samson																	
1960	3,271	305	219	936	85	683	59	—	200	56	84	154	46	6,098	3	468	38.3
1965	7,807	464	929	255	161	708	44	—	147	31	144	203	159	11,052	3	557	97.1
Port Hedland																	
1960	5,183	347	600	1,991	441	2,491	156	1,432	662	135	176	166	271	14,051	14	4,061	88.3
1965	13,145	855	2,353	1,086	306	1,326	393	496	989	119	320	1,021	80	22,489	20	1,038	211.6
Broome																	
1960	4,480	476	372	1,053	195	1,467	264	307	607	92	182	129	260	9,884	12	1,038	68.6
1965	9,742	950	1,237	725	86	1,031	251	801	832	79	353	1,397	131	17,615	10	61	161.1
Derby																	
1960	7,725	794	795	2,301	820	1,862	777	786	676	93	171	135	336	17,251	13	3,864	121.4
1965	10,271	545	1,079	1,251	248	1,227	571	320	970	90	407	73	287	17,349	34	591	163.1
Wyndham																	
1960	11,636	2,081	1,289	1,656	535	1,230	1,262	181	519	82	161	145	1,017	21,604	24	—	169.5
1965	17,095	1,107	1,212	897	338	1,885	1,181	—	731	130	479	54	972	27,081	4	25	267.9

[1] Ports with tonnages exceeding 5,000 in 1965.

Source: State Shipping Service, Western Australia.

TABLE 11

SUMMARY OF SHIPPING CARGOES CARRIED SOUTH

1960 and 1965

Major Port¹	General	Empties	Fertiliser	Asbestos	Pearl Shell	Ores	Vehicles	Tallow	Meat and Fish	Hides and Skins	Others	Wool and Sheep Skins		Inter-port	Total	Cattle	Sheep	Freight Value
	Tons	Tons	Tons	Tons	Tons	Tons	Tons	Tons	Tons	Tons	Tons	Bales	Tons	Tons	Tons	No.	No.	£'000
Port Samson																		
1960	74	751	—	5,992	—	108	4	2	6	1	—	3,267	652	33	7,623	—	—	32.5
1965	199	621	—	3,819	—	288	—	—	13	—	—	3,090	618	3	5,561	—	—	29.8
Port Hedland																		
1960	227	2,477	—	50	—	2,114	206	—	—	1	—	4,006	803	706	6,584	432	—	32.2
1965	185	924	—	464	—	538	50	—	1	—	—	3,044	610	72	2,844	273	3,304	25.2
Broome																		
1960	306	2,228	156	—	110	—	108	123	439	162	—	306	61	317	4,010	—	—	19.7
1965	209	794	994	—	155	1	87	569	2,063	465	—	402	79	2	5,418	—	—	48.3
Derby																		
1960	623	2,634	—	—	4	—	457	—	585	87	—	1,603	321	231	4,942	6,365	—	73.6
1965	359	1,495	—	—	—	1	300	—	497	—	—	1,968	394	235	3,281	6,546	—	64.5
Wyndham																		
1960	242	2,064	381	—	—	—	188	650	1,485	599	—	23	5	372	5,986	—	—	43.3
1965	458	3,192	211	—	—	12	585	16	366	47	483†	17	3	688	6,061	—	—	42.4

¹ Ports with tonnages exceeding 5,000 in 1965.

† All cotton – 2,165 bales, 483 tons.

Source: State Shipping Service, Western Australia.

TABLE 12

NORTHERN PORTS

Summary of Passengers Carried

1960 to 1965

Port	North		South	
	Direct	Inter-port	Direct	Inter-port
Carnarvon				
1960	97	—	95	2
1961	40	4	33	—
1962	15	—	18	—
1963	27	—	9	—
1964	16	—	6	—
1965	2	—	1	—
Onslow				
1960	34	4	30	2
1961	21	1	25	2
1962	19	—	19	—
1963	12	—	6	—
1964	9	—	13	—
1965	4	1	27	—
Point Samson				
1960	35	5	35	1
1961	43	12	61	3
1962	27	11	46	6
1963	37	2	48	—
1964	22	—	19	—
1965	26	3	33	—
Port Hedland				
1960	139	22	124	13
1961	108	11	161	5
1962	96	8	101	—
1963	147	10	127	9
1964	115	6	145	—
1965	115	3	139	9
Broome				
1960	124	21	157	3
1961	142	7	131	2
1962	63	16	100	—
1963	90	15	132	5
1964	106	11	138	7
1965	85	4	103	1
Derby				
1960	152	28	193	17
1961	193	9	199	6
1962	197	16	305	8
1963	285	14	230	4
1964	206	11	214	2
1965	176	6	220	13
Cockatoo Island				
1960	36	9	25	—
1961	85	44	15	1
1962	61	9	65	4
1963	65	12	17	1
1964	54	13	40	4
1965	26	2	29	—
Wyndham				
1960	162	77	156	8
1961	185	26	216	14
1962	224	34	183	11
1963	197	37	166	9
1964	205	18	184	9
1965	173	22	164	23

Source: State Shipping Service, Western Australia.

TABLE 13

SHIPPING FINANCES

(£'000)

Year	Expenditure (1)	Revenue (2)	Deficit (1) - (2)	Deficit as per cent of Expenditure
1960	2,005	1,071	933	46.5
1961	2,333	1,191	1,142	48.9
1962	2,248	1,118	1,130	50.3
1963	2,552	1,334	1,218	47.7
1964	3,062	1,730	1,330	43.4
1965	3,441	2,073	1,365	39.7

Source: State Shipping Service, Western Australia.

CHAPTER 10

FUTURE DEVELOPMENT OF THE REGION

1. CONTINUITY AND STRUCTURAL CHANGE IN REGIONAL GROWTH

Any attempt to look even ten years ahead in the economic growth pattern
of Northwestern Australia must be something akin to crystal ball gazing. For
if anything can be said about the region with certainty it is that radical
changes in techniques of production have begun and will continue. True,
many of the changes which are now occurring have their roots well in the
past; particularly is this so in respect of the region's old established industry,
pastoralism. On the other hand, it is equally true that there can be no
accurate element of predictability in mineral exploitation such as that which
has occurred recently in the Pilbara. Likewise, who would have predicted
ten years earlier, that the first farms in the Ord irrigation scheme would be
operating in 1963?

Nevertheless a study of past development is useful for several reasons.
Prime among these is the fact that while discontinuities and break-throughs
are more prone to occur in relatively underdeveloped areas such as Northwestern Australia than in more settled areas, one may still agree generally
with the dictum *natura non facit saltum*; economic development is a continuous process in the sense that certain pre-requisites generally have to be
achieved as a necessary preliminary to further growth of whatever form. Thus
a study of the character of the foundations upon which the regional economy
has been built is essential to an understanding of the range of possibilities
for future development. The brief study of Northwestern Australia's past
development contained, *inter alia,* in these pages has shown that economic
growth has taken place despite the restrictive effect of certain physical and
economic limitations. These limitations have been progressively modified but
they will continue in part to determine the growth pattern.

The past has been discussed in the preceding pages not merely to point out
some of the early difficulties experienced in the north, but also in order to
assess which of them might persist. Among the early difficulties were :
transport and the distance barrier, scanty population and limited local demand,

changing world markets for mineral and agricultural products, high labour and material costs, lack of cheap fuel, harsh terrain and climate, inadequate coastal handling facilities and a very large tidal rise and fall, a serious vermin menace, and lack of capital, both private and public. Offsetting these were many natural advantages in the region, including vast land resources of mixed quality, widespread and varied mineral wealth, a long growing season and a good growing climate, good water resources and great natural beauty. These taken together are still the characteristics which will determine the region's potential for growth in the future. To the extent that the problems can be overcome and the advantages turned to good purpose, in whole or in part, the growth pattern will change and the balance between various industries and activities will alter.

2. The Pattern of Development to 1950

In the field of primary industry, including mining, the pattern of past development is fairly clear. The country was first opened up by the pastoral pioneers making their way into the rich range country of the north with their cattle, and into the open country of the south with their sheep. In both cases the land was worked extensively and, because land was so plentiful, little capital was ploughed back into the holdings in the form of improvements. By the end of the nineteenth century, the absentee landlord had appeared and the pattern of pastoral activity began to assume a degree of stability. Some important changes occurred in the first half of the twentieth century among which were the restrictive quarantine provisions imposed upon northern cattle, the establishment of the State Shipping Service, the establishment of a coastal abattoir, the emergence of pasture regeneration problems and the growth of the vermin menace.

In the years immediately following the World War, primary industry was in a parlous condition. A boosted wartime demand was insufficient to stave off the cumulative effects of problems that had been growing in importance over the years, most of which had their roots in the past. Stock quality had fallen off due partly to lack of capital improvements such as fencing and water points which are among the pre-requisites for good animal husbandry, and partly to other important factors. Large tracts of good country had been eaten out by stock and vermin alike and were now reduced to claypans. Vermin, through ineffective control, had increased to the extent that they constituted a serious menace to the industry. On top of all this, the industry had been subjected to a series of disastrous droughts, particularly in the 1930's, which had reduced livestock numbers very considerably. Thus by 1950 the pastoral industry, still the dominant activity in the north, had run down and was badly in need of major re-orientation on several crucial points if satisfactory development were to be achieved.

Mining also figured early in the region's history, and in fact the early mineral discoveries of the 1880's resulted in the state's first goldfield being proclaimed in the north. Here, as elsewhere in Australia and indeed throughout the world, the lure of minerals provided the stimulus to open up the country. But its effect was relatively short-lived and the early enthusiasm soon waned so that by 1900 mineral exploration was desultory and small-scale. This pattern – individual prospectors or small groups working their way across the country – characterized the first half of the twentieth century, and with one or two exceptions very little of value in the way of minerals was extracted from the region.

Fishing, mainly for pearls and pearl shell, was also an early activity in the north and led to the growth of some ports on the north-western coast. Throughout the nineteenth century this industry had its ups and downs but always remained a useful income generator. It attracted a fairly substantial population of mixed nationalities, traces of which still remain in the coastal communities. Until 1950 the only major change in the pattern of the industry, apart from technical improvements in equipment, was the introduction of whaling which became an important employment and income generator and boosted the industry's gross output considerably.

Agriculture began much later in the region, and it was not until the decade prior to the World War that the first attempts were made to establish an irrigated agriculture industry on the Gascoyne delta. This remained the only pocket of agriculture in the north until the 1950's.

Development was slow in the field of secondary industry. No distinctive industrialization pattern emerged and manufacturing activity was limited almost solely to processing the primary products of the region or providing small-scale local services. In the period prior to 1950 this consisted of killing beef cattle and providing processed foodstuffs for purely local demand. The small size of the local market restricted any general growth of secondary industry.

Tertiary industry developed as the north grew, with the hand of government always prominent in the process. Retail and wholesale distribution outlets were limited in number and in range of goods provided, and never really moved ahead of demand.

What do we learn from the region's past growth? Basically, it is a story of early and wasteful exploitation, no different from the way in which countless other countries have been opened up. Minerals were taken only when they were easy to obtain and prices were good; high labour costs, directly affected by the distance factor, ensured this. Pastoral properties were worked for short-term profits and the long term was rarely taken into consideration. While there was plenty of good land it was wasted in this way, but eventually the lack of forward planning manifested itself in the form of denuded land, poor stock and inefficient operations. Of the four main primary industries, only fishing and agriculture seemed to be in a reasonably healthy position by 1950, and then only in some respects. The physical and economic factors mentioned previously and the human management factor, government and private, had influenced the pattern of northern development until 1950. They

FIG. 6

PASTORAL INDUSTRIES PRODUCTION
QUANTITY AND VALUE

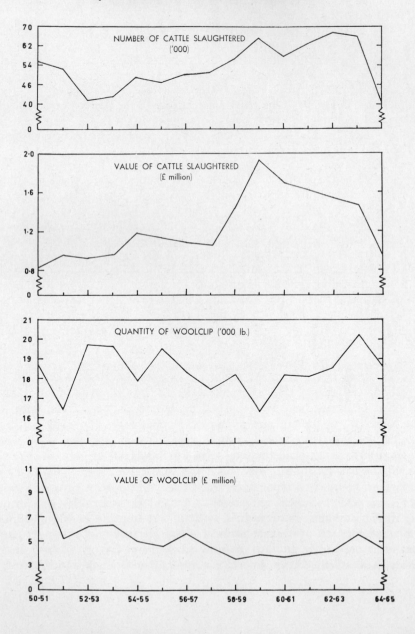

are still the underlying determinants of the region's growth pattern but there are new technologies and skills now available to control and modify the restraints, and the story of development since 1950 is largely one of the successful application of these measures.

3. THE PATTERN OF RECENT DEVELOPMENT (1950-1965)

In all four fields of primary industry, which includes mining, the period since 1950 has seen changes in techniques and changes in emphasis which have led to changes in the basic pattern of the industries themselves. The picture of the course of the main northern industries in this period, in quantity and value terms, is given in Figures 6 to 9.

The sheep industry had fallen on hard times for a number of reasons, all of which had a cumulative effect upon the fortunes of the industry as a whole. Most of the problems have been analysed and attacked with varying degrees of effectiveness in recent years and changes are becoming apparent. The introduction of irrigated pastures and pasture regeneration have made it possible to run greater numbers of stock on some properties. Vermin control methods, greatly improved in recent years and to be extended in the future, are producing the same result. These various improvements, all of which attack the problem of stock feed, have been introduced on a very limited scale and are certainly not yet representative of the whole area. Partial control of the blowfly has enabled a change in the mating season, leading to a better lambing percentage, and capital improvements to provide more watering and feeding points to combat drought conditions have reduced stock losses. Better lambing, more fences and better feed through pasture regeneration have given some pastoralists the opportunity to practice stock control and to cull more heavily. These changes in stock feed, numbers and quality give a more solid foundation to the industry and have provided a rejuvenating influence which gives promise of better times to come. They have been brought about by co-operation between the Department of Agri- culture, which has initiated fundamental research both on its own research stations and on private properties, and those pastoralists who have been astute enough to grasp the benefits of scientific research and assist in the experiments or to apply the findings to the solution of their own particular problems, with beneficial results for themselves and for the industry as a whole. Unfortun- ately these pastoralists still represent a minority, but in time the benefits of improved practices should be transmitted to others.

The cattle industry has also been undergoing a period of change. Among the main changes that have taken place since 1950 are : changes in methods of transporting livestock, with motor transport rapidly taking over from the old droving system; increasing, though still limited, use of irrigated pasture; the establishment of further seaport abattoirs at Broome and Derby; the establishment of the pioneering Air Beef Scheme with an abattoir inland at Glenroy, now defunct; changes in methods of animal husbandry, particularly

FIG. 7

VALUE OF MINERAL PRODUCTION

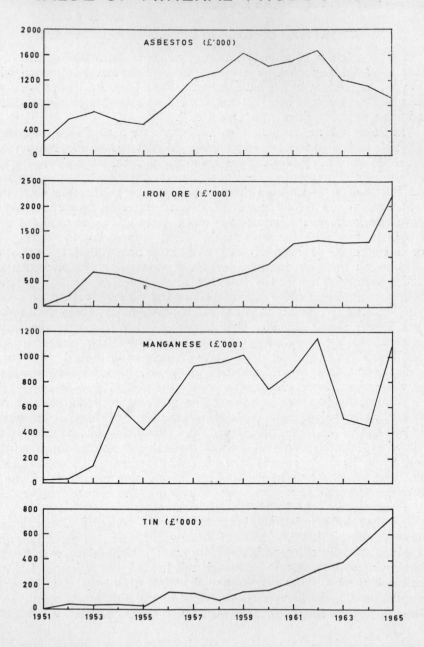

stock breeding which was formerly confined to but a few of the more progressive pastoralists; increasing mechanization; and orientation towards new markets. In the short space of 15 years some of the former practices have all but disappeared and the new practices have given an air of rejuvenation to the industry which for too long had operated in an unchanging pattern.

The change which has occurred in the region's mining industry since 1950 has been more spectacular than in the other industries partly because it has boosted production values twelve-fold in 15 years, and partly because it is much more fundamental and obvious. The era of the individual prospector now belongs to the past, and though there is still a place for him in the north, he is disappearing rapidly. This is the age of the large prospecting and development company, with its massed capital resources and technical know-how. In the 1950's two new large-scale mining ventures transformed the industry: iron mining at Yampi backed by the resources of B.H.P. and asbestos mining at Wittenoom financed indirectly by C.S.R. Since then further iron ore exploitation on an immense scale in the Pilbara, the gazettal of a commercial oil and gas field at Barrow Island, a rapid build-up in the export of manganese and tin, and the development of a large solar salt industry have further transformed the northern mining industry. Once again in the state's history, mineral exploration and development is initiating economic growth and opening up the country on a scale hitherto unprecedented and in a way which has changed completely the character of the industry.

The fishing industry, too, has undergone a fundamental change since 1950. Its pearling segment has acquired a new constituent, pearl culture, which in a few short years has outstripped the older pearl shell industry in value terms. Its whaling segment, after rapid growth in the 1950's, has now completely disappeared. Its scale fish segment, also after rapid growth in the same period, has now ceased to expand. A new segment, prawn fishing, has grown rapidly to a position of prime importance. These changes have been accompanied by, and in some cases have been the result of, the concentration and application of large-scale financial resources to research and fishing techniques and equipment. With shore and sea based factories appearing in the region and with radio controlled fishing fleets operating well offshore, using expensive equipment, the fishing industry has experienced a change as fundamental in some respects as that in the mining industry.

Finally, agriculture has undergone changes which will eventually turn out to be as significant as those which have occurred in any other branch of the region's primary industry over the last 15 years. Irrigated agriculture at Carnarvon has developed far beyond its post-war level of activity. The main changes which are apparent in this section of the industry are: the diversification of crops to include out-of-season vegetables, a move which has been very successful; a greater diversification in size of properties, which has resulted in the introduction of larger plantations and of share farming on a

FIG. 8

VALUE OF FISH PRODUCTION

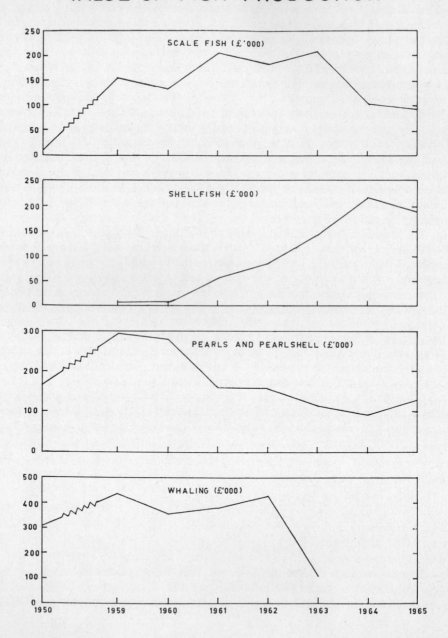

large scale; vastly improved irrigation methods; the recent growth of a fast, efficient transport service to Perth; a more acute water problem, as increasing acreages are making greater demands on the meagre and unreliable supply; and a degree of instability in the industry due to the inability of the heterogeneous group of growers to agree upon a common policy with regard to production, prices and selling methods. To this well-established agricultural industry have been added two new segments. The first, chronologically, is the rice growing venture at Camballin on the Fitzroy. The second is the much more ambitious Ord River Irrigation Scheme, also in the Kimberley. These schemes represent a significant departure from the previous pattern of land use in the north since they allow for the land passing freehold to the occupier after certain conditions are met, and if successful they will transform the northern economy and raise the agricultural component of the region's primary industry to a position of considerable importance.

Thus in all phases of primary industry the region can be seen to be changing. The present pattern of development when contrasted with the period stretching well back before the World War is marked by significant changes in basic methods and techniques. What then can be learnt from the immediate past?

The basic physical and economic limitations mentioned previously still exist in the north but they have been modified very considerably in some respects. The physical factors may be considered first. Distances cannot be shortened but improvements in transport and communications have shortened time schedules, reduced costs and opened up new production possibilities – as witness the Air Beef venture. Improvements to roads and ports have had a significant effect in this regard. Mineral exploration has also revealed further rich natural resources. Climate is still impossible to control, but man is making himself less vulnerable to its vagaries. Architectural design is now more suited to the area, cooling devices are being widely used and water, previously wasted, is now being utilized instead.

What of the economic factors? These, in a way, have proved harder to control or turn to advantage. Population is still small though now growing quite rapidly. Costs are still high. World markets continue to change, and the region's industries are changing with them. But in the field of management and production techniques, real progress can be reported. The scientific approach to management in all parts of industry is accepted, and the new methods which have already been described are being adopted. New transport techniques, better management practices, increasing mechanization, and continual experimentation are aspects of this change.

4. FUTURE DEVELOPMENT (1965-1975)

In most underdeveloped regions, the first industries to be developed are the primary and extractive industries. Based upon natural resources and dependent upon world markets, they are subject to rapid growth or decay

FIG. 9

CARNARVON AGRICULTURAL PRODUCTION

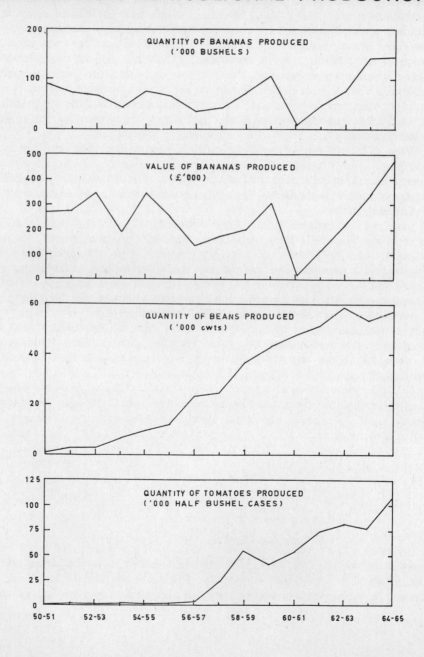

to a greater extent than most manufacturing industry, and Northwestern Australia has been no exception in this. Particularly in mineral extraction but also in fishing and to some extent in the pastoral industry, fortunes have waxed and waned, sometimes in a most dramatic way.

It is apparent that the economy of Northwestern Australia has undergone some fundamental changes since 1950, the more recent of which have hardly got under way. Even so, there are already some broad indications as to how these changes will affect the regional economy in the next decade. For example, the phasing and the magnitude of operations of the iron ore companies are known in general terms from the details of the agreements concluded with the state government. The pattern of fishery development, as large companies move into the field with long-term plans, is now beginning to take shape enough to give some indications of its growing importance in the near future.

Were it certain that these significant changes of direction and emphasis would not soon be matched by others equally significant, one could guess in broad terms about the course of the region's development in the immediate future. But the period 1950-1965 has demonstrated quite clearly how the exploitation of the region's resource endowment can suddenly take a series of new and unexpected turns. And it is not only in the field of mineral development that these dramatic changes have taken place. In two branches of the fishing industry and in agriculture, as well as in iron, manganese, and tin, structural changes of a far-reaching nature have become manifest. One cannot guess about developments of this nature, but it is possible, nevertheless, to make certain broad generalizations about the region's future growth, based upon what is known now about the regional economy.

The future course of the pastoral industry may be examined first. The quantity of wool produced in the region has not risen in the last 15 years and its value has fallen slightly if the abnormally lucrative 1950-51 season is ignored. The previous long-term downward trend in wool production is apparently halted and the industry has stabilized to a certain extent, though at a level which is regarded as unsatisfactory. The reasons for this have already been discussed in Chapter 3, as also have the attempts to re-build the industry. It is obvious from the figures that these attempts have not yet borne fruit on a scale large enough to affect the total though there are encouraging signs that a gradual rejuvenation is taking place. This is however essentially a long-term prospect, the effects of which will be slow to materialize, and between 1965 and 1975 there is no doubt that the industry will continue to lose ground to other industries in the north as a major income earner, even allowing for a modest rise in the wool clip.

In many ways prospects for beef cattle are more encouraging and have been so for some years, but even here the increase in cattle turnoff in the last 15 years is somewhat disappointing. Discounting the 1964-65 figures, which are unusually low because of a bad season, the numbers of cattle slaughtered in the Kimberley have risen since the early 1950's from about 50,000 to about 65,000 at a simple average annual rate of 2 per cent. The values of these slaughterings have risen from about £950,000 to about £1,500,000 at an annual rate of about four per cent. Average prices in recent years have fallen, from about £30 in 1959-60 to about £22 in 1963-64, due to the turnoff of increasing numbers of young cattle, but this trend will probably now be halted and returns to pastoralists should once more rise as turnoff increases. Projecting these trends it is possible to anticipate a 20 per cent increase in turnoff between 1965 and 1975, so that killings in the region could, by then, total about 80,000 providing that there is not a drain to the northern territory and that breeders are not reduced by unwise killing practices.

In view of the amount of public capital now being allocated to infrastructure development designed primarily to assist the beef industry, it is essential that the rate of growth in the region's turnoff should be much higher than this. There is no doubt as to the capacity of the region to carry much more stock,[1] but to realize this potential would, as pointed out in Chapter 3, demand greater effort on the part of the pastoralists to ensure widespread use of better techniques. This would involve heavy private capital expenditure, the economics of which need further investigation. It would also demand new or enlarged abattoir facilities either in the region or in the Northern Territory, but initially, at least, this may be catered for by an extension of the killing season made possible by transport improvements. As in the case of sheep, building up efficiency and turnoff in the beef cattle industry is a long-term proposition and startling short-term results cannot be expected.

In the mining industry, the position is clearer in some respects. Known plans for iron ore extraction already guarantee that the industry will dominate all others in the region by 1975. By then, three major producers will be operating in the Pilbara, at Mt. Goldsworthy, Mt. Tom Price and Mt. Newman, with the possibility of being joined by the Ludwig Group at Nimingarra and the Cliffs Group at Mt. Enid. Added to this will be the continuance of iron ore extraction at Yampi Sound. The Barrow Island oilfield will be at full production in 1975, with annual throughput of seven million barrels. At least two major salt companies will be exporting at combined annual rates of three and a half million tons. The prospects for greatly increased tin and manganese production are on the whole bright and of the region's major mining ventures, asbestos is the only one for

[1]For an estimate of the region's carrying capacity see J. H. Kelly, *Struggle for the North* which came to hand too late to be referred to in previous chapters of this book. Like Davidson's *The Northern Myth* it is controversial but should be added to any list of essential reading for those interested in problems of developing northern Australia as a whole.

which the future does not look too bright.[2] Costs in relations to price will, however, mainly determine the course of development of these three latter minerals, as explained in Chapter 4, and one cannot be so certain of their future course as with iron, oil and salt.

The fishing industry seems to be headed for better days after some serious setbacks since 1950. Prawning and pearl culture have risen to take the place of whaling and pearl shell production, and in both of these new activities future prospects are bright, as explained in Chapter 5. The future market for cultured pearls is assured, and in northern waters the potential for prawning is hardly tapped despite very large catches in the Exmouth Gulf-Shark Bay area in recent years. The newest development in this industry is the exploitation of tuna and other free-swimming fish in northern waters and of trash fish for canning. Although, on current indications, prospects seem bright for the rapid growth of this activity much more basic research is essential before the full potential of the area can be assessed. The interest already displayed by large international fishing companies ensures that if a good potential is established it could be exploited immediately.

With respect to agriculture the future is less certain. In the Carnarvon area, for example, development cannot proceed at the same rate as previously unless one or two basic problems, in particular the problems of water supply and markets, are overcome. There are good grounds for arguing that until a satisfactory solution can be found to the water problem, probably involving the construction of a dam, any considerable extension in the number of properties taken up in Carnarvon would be unwise. On the other hand, gains resulting from improvements in physical productivity, lowered costs and higher prices may be expected, as pointed out in Chapter 6, and these could lead to production increases and general improvement in the existing industry.

The Camballin rice growing experiment has not proved highly successful for the reasons already mentioned. Looking ahead ten years one cannot see this as a rice growing area of any consequence, but one can foresee a change in its role. Already the combination of irrigated pastures and stock raising has emerged as a successful departure from the original concept. Unless a suitable rice variety is found or an alternative crop developed and unless the flooding and other problems can be controlled much more effectively than at present, it may be expected that by 1975 Camballin will be a flourishing centre for livestock breeding and the production of fodder crops for sheep and cattle. As an agistment area, for example, it could carry one and a half cattle to the acre.

[2]At the time this book went to press, the surprise announcement was made by C.S.R. general manager, Sir James Vernon, early in December 1966, that the asbestos mine at Wittenoom would be closed down at the end of that month. The reasons given were labour problems and uncertain and low-grade reserves leading to inefficient operation and recurring losses. Thus a previously important segment of the region's mining industry may shortly pass out of existence.

Irrigated agriculture at Kununurra which was still in the experimental stages in the decade of the 1950's, has now proved to be an economic proposition. With 31 farms covering approximately 15,000 acres of irrigated land, fed by a dam constructed on the Ord, it is the largest agricultural undertaking in the region. The first stage of the project is completed but ultimately it is anticipated that a larger dam will be constructed to irrigate 170,000 acres of land in Western Australia and in the Northern Territory. Already there is a flourishing community of 1,000 persons at Kununurra and on completion of the total scheme there will be several more such communities in existence, with a total population of between 10,000 and 15,000. The project has been financed mainly from commonwealth funds and there is yet no clear indication when finance will be forthcoming to proceed with the larger dam and the development of the remaining land. If this is commenced in 1968, it may be expected that by 1975 some 115,000 acres will be under irrigation and 175 farms will be operating. Agriculture will then have established its place as a major industry in North-western Australia.

Thus we have in prospect a picture of radical change in the region in terms of the balance between those primary industries which are of greatest importance at the present time. Pastoralism will give way to mining as the region's dominant activity in terms of employment, value of production, and overall income generation. Agriculture will rise at least to equality with pastoralism in value terms, but will surpass it in terms of employment and income generation. Fishing will substantially improve its position relative to pastoralism, but will still be the minor partner in the region's primary industries.

In 1975 the basic problems in the north will still exist. Its physical characteristics will still impose their stamp upon the pattern of regional production though much less effectively than at present. The economic problems will also still be there, but their influence will be on the wane. The growth of secondary industry associated with some of the foreseeable developments mentioned above will be significant and far-reaching in its effects, particularly upon population inflow and upon income and demand generation within the region. As centres of activity expand, shire boundaries will alter and new shires will be gazetted; as population increases other possibilities for limited local manufacturing will emerge; as transport facilities and communications improve costs will decline relatively; as townships grow permanent labour will be attracted in larger numbers, and as attitudes change greater use will be made of the indigenous native labour force. All of these characteristics will be in greater evidence at the conclusion of the next decade of the region's growth.

The accelerated pace of northern development in the last ten years has brought its problems, but they have not been insuperable and have not been sufficient to dissuade would-be developers from moving in. Just how fast the region *will* grow in the next ten years is a matter of judgment but just how fast it *should* grow is a matter of opinion; what the pattern of growth *will* be is a matter of judgment but what the pattern of growth *should* be is a matter of opinion.

5. Government and Private Development

The economic development of a relatively underdeveloped and fairly isolated region like Northwestern Australia may be undertaken by government or it may be left to private enterprise. Generally speaking, however, these are really not feasible alternatives except at the project level, and even here one finds government and private enterprise being jointly involved. This being so, the problem is one of evolving ways and means of ensuring a correct balance and a workable operating arrangement between the two.

Private companies, acting in response to purely economic stimuli, will develop an area if the possibilities for reasonably quick and profitable returns on capital seem to exist. Governments, since they do not always follow rigorously the dictates of the profit motive and are also concerned with welfare considerations, can take a longer view. In some cases the economic prospects of a region do not reveal themselves as attractive until a large amount of public capital has raised its infrastructure development (transport and communication links, power generation, public utilities) to the point where expected returns from production, manufacture and distribution compare favourably with costs. External economies which may result from specific development projects are also significant in attracting further industry. It is in the sphere of infrastructure development, therefore, that government probably has its biggest contribution to make to regional development.

In Northwestern Australia development has proceeded as an amalgam of private and public enterprise and the region provides some interesting examples of the different ways in which they have worked together on recent schemes.[3] The Ord irrigation project provides an example of a government-financed development scheme. The prior research and investigation and the ultimate development of the headworks and irrigation channels and the establishment of the township and amenities was carried out by the government, with the private farmers being asked to contribute to the operating expenses of the services. The Mt. Goldsworthy project, on the other hand, provides an example of a privately-financed development scheme. The research and investigation and capital works costs, including most of the infrastructure, have been met by the private company developing the reserves. Other schemes, such as the Wittenoom development,

[3]For a description of some of the arrangements recently made by the Western Australian government see C. W. M. Court, *Interdependence of Government and Private Enterprise in the Modern Society.*

have embodied capital works financed by the company and infrastructure financed by the government.

On the whole, mineral extraction, where grades and extents of deposits are known with a reasonable degree of certainty, lends itself to private development. Particularly is this so in the case of the recent Pilbara iron ore projects where the development expenditures are on such a scale as to rule out completely the possibility of government exploitation at a comparable rate. On the other hand, the past history of land exploitation by private companies in some instances is such as to suggest that the financing and organizing of agricultural schemes is better left to government if funds of sufficient magnitude are available. As far as one can judge, northern development in the next decade, 1965-1975, will continue along these lines, with the government making its major contribution in the form of services and utilities.

6. Administrative Aspects

The relative isolation of the region has been stressed throughout this book, and the government of Western Australia has always been aware of the problems which stem from this. Among most northern residents there is a feeling of being remote from the centre of government, and no doubt the distance barrier has been responsible for many misunderstandings and frustrations in the past. Because of improvements in transport and communications and the recent rapid development of the region, visits by government ministers and officials are more frequent than previously but still not frequent enough to satisfy the demands by some residents that their voice be heard.

A move in the direction of meeting these obligations was made by the government in 1962 when Mr. H. L. McGuigan was appointed to the newly created position of Administrator for the North-West, with responsibilities in administration and planning. He is directly responsible to the Minister for the North-West for the effective co-ordination of government departmental activities, and is charged also with maintaining continuing contact with all sectors of the community in order to investigate proposals and problems affecting the region. He acts as Chairman of the Divisional Consultative Councils and of their various sub-committees, and participates in current and future planning for the region by virtue of his membership of the North-West Planning Authority.

The Administrator and his small staff are based at Derby and from there they travel constantly to all points in the region. The Administrator is partly a 'trouble-shooter', since one of his functions is to search out problems and try to find solutions to them or channel them to those who can. He is partly a planner, since another function is to suggest lines of development, and to this end he is a member of the North-West Planning Authority which comprises : the Director of Engineering, as Chairman, the Commissioner for Main Roads, the Director of Agriculture, the Surveyor-General, the Deputy Under-Treasurer, and the Administrator for the North-West. This authority reports direct to the Minister for the North-West. He is partly an administrator since his office provides a co-ordinating mechanism for various northern-oriented government activities. It is not intended that he should intrude on or supersede the function of statutory authorities, but one of his main interests is to maintain close contact with and to assist local authorities. To help him appraise and act upon regional problems he is assisted by three consultative councils comprising 34 specially appointed northern residents who are experienced in local affairs. There is a council for the Kimberley, one for the North-West, covering the Carnarvon and Gascoyne districts, and one for the Central North, covering Port Hedland to Meekatharra.

The setting up and operation of this office represents an important contribution to the possibility of coming to grips with some of the administrative and planning problems of the north, and in a relatively short time the Administrator has succeeded in making his office a focal point for regional interests. It stands to reason that properly representative citizen advisory bodies can present a balanced cross-section of opinion, both expert and lay, upon specific problems and proposals. As well as this they can assist in gathering technical detail which is important for planning purposes, and they can provide focal points for fostering a regional consciousness. In order to do this effectively it is essential that they be truly representative of all sections of the community and that they be comprised of citizens who are willing to take a regional rather than a narrowly sectional viewpoint on major issues. They must be prepared to accept the fact that most development proposals will affect some parts of the region more than others in the first round, but that subsequently the region as a whole will gain when the development rubs off on to other activities. Better transport and communications facilities, for instance, are the immediate and obvious benefits of Pilbara mining development and the Kununurra project. If repercussions of this sort are appreciated by the advisory committees, this could go a long way towards ensuring a greater regional cohesiveness than ever before. Specific proposals can then more readily be accepted on their economic worth for the region as a whole rather than on their appeal to sectional or parochial interests.

There is the broader question of where the ultimate responsibility for regional development in the north will rest. Many suggestions have been made over a long period as to how northern development should proceed,[4] and most of these embody the idea of a northern development authority embracing the Northern Territory and the northern parts of Queensland

[4]Examples of four recent suggestions would be: Australian Institute of Political Science, *Northern Australia: Task for a Nation;* C. W. M. Court, *Development of Northern Australia;* J. H. Kelly, *Struggle for the North;* and People of the North Committee, *A Plan for the North.*

and Western Australia. This authority would ideally represent a partnership of interests between the states and the commonwealth, and would be quite different in concept from the existing Northern Development Division in the Commonwealth Department of National Development, mentioned in Chapter 6.

The arguments in favour of such a move are substantial. Northern Australia, conceived in these terms, has much to commend it as a separate economic region. Climatically the segments are similar, the basic industries are similar, and similar administrative problems exist. A partnership between the states and the commonwealth should also guarantee a national viewpoint being taken of all development proposals for the north.

7. RESEARCH AND PLANNING

For a region to have economic cohesion and good prospects for rapid growth certain conditions must be fulfilled. Except for densely populated, well-developed regions which are virtually self-sufficient – and these, naturally enough, are even more difficult to find than self-sufficient nations – the region's growth possibilities will be largely dependent upon its export industries. Its exports may flow either to other parts of the national economy or to overseas, but in either case there will be an export multiplier effect in the region. The character of the regional economy of Northwestern Australia which gives it a distinctive exporting role in the overall state economy has already been stressed. What happens to the income that is earned by the region's exports will depend upon the economic, social and institutional characteristics of the regional economy which will determine how much of the export income is retained in the regional economy, and thus how fast it will grow.

Different types of multiplier effect will be experienced with different industries. For example, the extraction of heavy minerals like iron ore demands, among other things, the establishment and maintenance of adequate transportation facilities and services within the region. Labour-intensive industries result in large wage bills being paid in the region. Intensive agricultural development of the 'family unit' or 'share farming' type generally leads to most of the income generated remaining in the region, providing services such as education are sufficient to induce the whole family to live there. Absentee-ownership means that a proportion of the income generated flows out of the region. The greater the amount of such income retained in the region, the greater will be the multiplier effect tending to expand the markets within the region for goods and services produced internally or externally. As the region's internal economic structure grows and diversifies, it will retain an increasing proportion of its own export income and the change will be self-reinforcing. As the region develops in this way the dominance of the export industries tends to diminish. At the same time the dependence on imports into the region, which may be regarded in one sense as a negative multiplier or as a leakage tending to depress the value of the export multiplier, is lessened.

Ideally, if a region is to grow rapidly it should concentrate upon products which have extensive forward and backward local linkages, which have a high local multiplier in the sense that the income generated results in demands for locally produced goods and services, and which have a high income elasticity of demand. The first condition will increase demand for the products of other local industries taking outputs from or supplying inputs to the export industry, the second condition will result in an increase in the demand for local goods and services in general, and the third condition will ensure that as economic development takes place and incomes rise in the external markets for the export product, the amount demanded will progressively increase. Apart from these basic considerations one must also consider the extent to which external economies are created – the extent to which installations intended for one particular operation provide a means of reducing costs in another possibly unrelated operation. The construction of railroads or power lines or port facilities which can be used by producers other than those for whom they were originally intended would be cases in point.

The brief mention above of the cumulative effects of the export multiplier, of forward and backward local linkages, of the generation of external economies, and of the development of industries for which the income elasticities of demand are high, would suggest that there is a strong case for encouraging more rapid development of this kind in Northwestern Australia, providing that the exploitation of the region's resources offers the possibility of reasonable returns initially. It has already been pointed out that its industries, particularly minerals, meat and fish and, to a lesser extent, its agricultural products can expect buoyant future demand, but for the region to retain the full effect of this it must develop its internal structure. Steps must be taken at the same time to try to ensure that only the minimum amount of export income is taken out of the region so that the multiplier effect is sufficient to generate further growth.

Increasing industrialization is one means of assisting the region's rapid growth, and attention could well be given to the possibilities of attracting 'footloose' industries into the north. There are industries which are not tied in a direct way with any particular resource endowment or locational market and will settle wherever the fringe benefits are greatest. In Northwestern Australia in its present stage of development these fringe benefits are few, and a policy of practical governmental encouragement in the form of concessions of one sort or another may, in fact, be needed before any such industrial growth could become feasible.

It is in these ways that decentralization can become a positive policy for lessening regional differences in economic growth and welfare, and efforts should be made to encourage increased activity in the north which will ultimately reduce the wide gap between northern and southern areas in respect of transport, labour and material, and other social and economic costs. 'In a less developed area – where social overhead facilities, such as public utilities, have to be built up and new services have to be brought into being – a given amount of manufacturing growth will generate more economic expansion than it will in a "mature" region which is already well equipped with facilities and services.'[5] The all-round activity generated will thus be greater as derived demands for these facilities are expressed.

As well as assisting the region towards a self-sustaining growth point, which may still lie well in the future, such a policy will eventually reduce its present dependence upon subsidies and its heavy demands on the state budget. On the other hand, a policy of holding back northern development because there are better short-term returns to investment of public funds in the southern areas of the state or nation, will only perpetuate, and indeed increase, cost differentials and widen the gap between the developed and the underdeveloped regions.

Planning for regional development may take one or all of several different forms. Perhaps the least rigorous and most common is what may be called 'trouble-shooting'.[6] This consists of locating trouble spots or bottlenecks in the economy and taking action to remove them. It is in this category that one would place the present planning responsibility of the Administrator for the North-West. This type of planning assumes largely private development, and presupposes that it is the government's function to ensure that things proceed as smoothly as possible.

A more specific type of planning is project planning which involves the appraisal of specific development projects, such as the Ord River scheme. Benefit-cost analyses and other analytical devices are used to establish economic feasibility in these cases. It seems evident, from a recent Commonwealth Treasury white paper that state governments will be expected to make increasing use of these techniques when requesting special assistance from the commonwealth for development purposes.[7]

Two other types are sectoral planning, and region planning or target setting on an overall basis. Both of these are much wider in scope than either project planning or trouble-shooting. They involve a much greater government intervention in the planning process and entail the setting of targets for capital formation, production and employment in specific sectors of the regional economy or for the region as a whole. Neither of these methods has been used in Northwestern Australia or indeed in Australia, though they are now widely used throughout the world.

The basis of any type of plan, if it is to have a chance to succeed, is comprehensive and reliable statistical information. Although much is already

[5]H. S. Perloff, E. S. Dunn, Jnr., E. E. Lampard and R. F. Muth, *Regions, Resources, and Economic Growth*, p. 94.
[6]Benjamin Higgins, *Economic Development*.
[7]Commonwealth Department of Treasury, *Investment Analysis*.

known of the north much more information is needed. Apart from intensive analytical research on the structure and problems of individual industries, there is the need for inter-industry research which will draw upon the industry studies for its basic material. Movements in the broad economic aggregates of the region must be studied and estimates made of income flows, of regional multipliers, and of regional interdependence of various activities. Such information can come from routine government enquiry, from research by consulting firms and other bodies, from private firms engaged in exploration and development operations, and from independent research by universites and other professional institutions. For example, the Department of Economics in the University of Western Australia is currently studying the local multiplier effects of the recent Pilbara iron ore exploitation. The estimation of regional multipliers is a new and relatively undeveloped field of economic enquiry and a great deal of work is needed to advance it to the point where it can provide a quick and useful means of assessing the economic worth of alternative projects according to criteria (employment or income generation, for example) which have been set down. M. L. Parker, working in the John Thomson Agricultural Economics Centre in the University of Western Australia, has produced a highly useful pioneering study of input-output relationships in the Western Australian economy,[8] and ideally this work should be extended to cover regional economic relationships. As this is done and the flow of research information increases, government planning decisions will come to rely more and more on the results of scientific enquiry which will provide a reliable basis for sound judgment.

8. Proposals For Policy

This study suggests that although Northwestern Australia is now developing rapidly and its future looks bright, it is still very much underdeveloped by comparison with many other parts of Australia. In the interests of decentralization and balanced regional development, growth of Northwestern Australia should continue to be stimulated and encouraged by the injection of public capital in conjunction with private investment. The prospects for some northern industries, as indicated above, are sufficiently sound to justify their development on short-term economic grounds alone, and private enterprise is already seeing to this in many instances. In other cases the government's policy of decentralization involves more embracing concepts, such as the encouragement of closer settlement, which must be viewed in a longer term context.

The main aims of the government programme should be: to improve general working and living conditions for the people in the area, including the native inhabitants, to provide a framework of social capital which will attract further private investment in secondary and tertiary activities

[8]M. L. Parker, *An Inter-Industry Study of the Western Australian Economy*.

as well as in primary industry, and to ensure that the private development which does take place is not inimical to the best long-term interests of the state and of the nation as a whole.

To this end, and in the absence of an overall plan for the development of the region as a whole or indeed for any sub-region within it, certain broad policy recommendations may be made. The basic physical, economic and social problems of the region have been discussed in this study and it is towards the removal or mitigation of these problems that policy measures should be directed, bearing in mind that until a comprehensive programme of research and planning is set in motion, such measures can only be discussed in broad terms. In the ultimate, since the underlying reason for economic development is the improvement of living standards and the enrichment of human life, such measures should be considered in terms of their effects upon the individual, even though they may be translated in specific cases into technological or economic regulations affecting a particular industry.

General working and living conditions in some areas are still far from satisfactory in their effects upon population and employment. The major problem is to improve them to the stage where they will induce families to settle permanently, thus establishing a population stability which is lacking at present. Although progress in this regard will come slowly and will be costly, some obvious problem areas suggest immediate attention. The measures discussed below for instance, would go a long way towards mitigating some of the main working and living disabilities in the north.

In order to increase disposable money income for the family man there should be :

1. A substantial increase in the concessional deductions for personal income taxation purposes allowed to persons working in the region permanently.

In order to increase available real income for the family man there should be :

2. A substantial reduction in electricity and water charges.
3. The encouragement and subsidization of youth clubs, in particular, and other community activities that are not sectionally oriented.
4. A more rapid expansion of higher educational facilities through relaxing the student-number basis for grading schools.
5. Construction of student hostels in high-school townships. This would be partly compensated for by a reduction in the amount of money now paid by the government for students proceeding south.

In order to improve native conditions and increase native employment there should be :

6. A firm insistence on improvement of native living conditions on stations which fall below standard.

7. An accelerated programme for training native labour, and a much wider use of the native labour workforce in occupations other than those associated with the pastoral industry.
8. A progressive rise in an established legal minimum native wage until it reaches equality with the basic wage.
9. The construction of more native hostels.
10. A very substantial increase in the annual vote for the Department of Native Welfare to enable it to expand its representation and its activities in the region and to continue the good work it is currently performing on a severely limited budget.

Liberalization of personal income tax concessions would not cost the commonwealth government very much at all in terms of foregone income, for the population is so small, but the marginal effect on individual incomes could be instrumental in inducing greater population stability. On the other hand the cost to the state government of implementing the proposals suggested here would be quite substantial in some cases. When coupled with the additional proposals made below they would impose a severe burden upon a state budget which is always strained to capacity.

It has already been suggested that the shire councils may help to defray some of their own costs by revising certain of their rates upward and also by streamlining the townsite areas they have to administer. More attention to town planning alone could produce closer-knit development with consequent savings in the provision of community services such as water mains and electricity. Land in some townsites is cheap but the cost of servicing it is not, and the region's townships cannot afford to sprawl over large areas. Some local government authorities and state government departments are making a positive contribution to the problem of native employment by employing and training increasing numbers of aborigines.

The commonwealth government, through the normal federal financial structure, assisted by the operation of the Commonwealth Grants Commission and the Loan Council, contributes to the cost of state administration and development in many ways.[9] General-purpose revenue grants, originally to cover tax reimbursement, but now much wider in scope, are made annually on a per capita basis. Special grants to enable the attainment of a certain overall standard of services throughout the states of Australia are made annually to Western Australia and Tasmania through the Commonwealth Grants Commission. Road grants are made annually to all states. Capital outlays are financed annually through the Loan Council. Finally, money is made available from the commonwealth to the states to an increasing extent nowadays by way of special-purpose grants which include grants for additional assistance to ease budgetary problems, grants for education, grants for railway projects and grants for development projects. These special-purpose grants are usually conditional in the sense that they

[9] K. M. McKenna, *Commonwealth State Financial Relations.*

require a matching contribution by the state, and they mostly seem to be given for projects of importance to the national economy which are beyond the immediate resources of the state.

It has, from time to time, been suggested that the revenues from northern mining activities now flowing in to the state treasury in the form of licences, rents and royalties should be earmarked for reinvestment in the region, particularly in the form of infrastructure development. However this income cannot be so used since it passes into general revenue in the state's Consolidated Revenue Fund. The immediate effect is to reduce the extent to which the state is dependent upon extra assistance from the commonwealth government and this should be welcomed since it represents a move towards greater self-sufficiency. It does not, however, offer any immediate relief in the way of extra finance for northern expenditure.

The federal government may well take the view that it has contributed substantially in the past to northern development and that the swelling of state C.R.F. revenue on account of the mining developments is a long overdue offset against this. But this viewpoint would deny an underdeveloped region much of the fruits of its own subsequent development and it does not seem unreasonable to suggest that for the reasons already mentioned above (pursuit of decentralization and levelling of standards of economic and social welfare) the commonwealth should allow at least some of these gains to be withheld from the state Consolidated Revenue Fund and earmarked for northern infrastructure development. To the previous programme we may therefore add :

11. Exemption by the commonwealth government of a certain proportion (say 20 per cent) of mining rents and royalties from inclusion in state C.R.F. revenue.

When the mining developments are in full swing this would release $1 million each year for use in the north. These funds should be used for development throughout the region and not just in the areas where mining development has taken place. This will add support to the fostering of a regional outlook, help to break down localized and sectional interests, and strengthen the hand of the Administrator in trying to achieve all-round regional development.

When attention is turned from general working and living conditions to conditions within each industry in the north, certain other policy guidelines suggest themselves, as pointed out in previous chapters. Social capital has already been spent on providing beef roads and upon research into pasture regeneration, erosion control and vermin control. In order to ensure the best response of the industry to these expenditures the following minimum requirements would be necessary :

12. Revision of leasehold provisions on pastoral properties to require a larger minimum proportion of annual rents to be devoted to station improvement.

13. The enforcement of higher minimum standards of management on pastoral stations, by an enlarged team of pastoral inspectors.
14. Greater use of resumption powers where the requirements of the pastoral leases are not being satisfactorily met.
15. More rigid insistence on adequate vermin control and erosion control measures by individual pastoralists.

Such policies would not impose a financial burden upon the government, nor upon pastoralists who are managing their properties adequately. It would, however, establish minimum management standards and lift the efficiency of the whole industry with consequent benefits in terms of turnoff and income generated. The problem of absentee-ownership, while a contentious issue, is second in importance to the prime problem of lifting efficiency in the industry in order to justify the public capital that has been expended.

Recent mining developments in the Pilbara have raised contentious issues, including questions of overseas ownership and questions of pricing policy. As pointed out above it is essential to ensure that as many as possible of the benefits of such development are retained in the domestic economy and to this end it is important that government policy should include :

16. Insistence upon the right of the state and of third parties to make reasonable use of the infrastructure facilities set up by the developing companies.
17. The greatest possible development of local processing facilities for the ore which is mined.
18. Wherever possible the placing of contracts for materials and construction for mining developments with local rather than overseas firms.

The government of Western Australia is aware of the need for these measures in respect of mining development in the region and has written these provisions into the agreements it has made with the companies, as explained in Chapter 4. It is anxious to see the greatest possible benefits accruing to the domestic economy and it is essential that the government insists upon adherence to these provisions.

The fishing industry, which is currently undergoing a transformation to large-scale operation will, for its adequate development, require :

19. A greatly accelerated programme of research, and development based upon private exploitation controlled by the state and the commonwealth to ensure adequate husbanding of the fisheries in northern waters.
20. Within the proviso above, concessions to large companies which are prepared to sink substantial capital into fishery development.

21. Encouragement, in the way of infrastructure development, for companies which are prepared to establish processing factories on the mainland.

The fishing industry appears to be entering a new phase of development which, if carefully controlled, can lift its regional importance considerably. Close control, which would involve substantial expansion of the research and inspection activities of the Fisheries Department, is essential to ensure that subsequent development is in the best interests of the region and the nation.

Irrigated agriculture is now developing rapidly in Northwestern Australia, based upon a prior research programme which has been undertaken for many years. From the discussion in Chapter 6 the following policy proposals suggest themselves :

22. In the East Kimberley, the completion of the Ord River scheme, and the continuance of research into crop diversification.
23. In Carnarvon, continued research in pursuit of increased productivity and crop diversification supported by greater attention to marketing and packaging in order to improve the produce exported from the area.
24. In Carnarvon, research into the longer-term prospects for processing vegetable produce, possibly in conjunction with fish processing.
25. In the West Kimberley, continued research at Camballin into possible cash crops and encouragement of the development of irrigated fodder crops in conjunction with pastoralism.

The state government is anxious to complete the Ord scheme but at the moment no finance is available for its continuation. By the end of 1966, the position should be clearer, but if commonwealth assistance is not forthcoming, finance from elsewhere could be employed. As suggested earlier, if this happens, very close attention will have to be paid by the government to the terms and conditions under which such assistance is obtained since ultimate freehold tenure is one of the basic features of the scheme and this could easily be abused.

Since irrigated agriculture depends upon water control, and little is yet known of the water resources of the region, a basic condition for further agricultural development planning is :

26. A stepping up in the current programme of water resource surveys and hydrological investigations.

This work is detailed and slow, and its benefits lie well in the future since it can be expected that any further large-scale development of irrigated agriculture will probably have to await the eventual outcome of the Ord scheme. In the meantime, the basic information must be collected.

In the field of secondary industry, some developments, particularly in connection with the mining industry, are already in progress. In addition it should be, and is, the aim of the government to achieve :

27. Expansion of local service factories, such as light engineering works, maintenance depots and building materials manufacture.
28. Attraction of footloose industries, by means of limited concessions if necessary.
29. Development of secondary processing in industries other than mining, particularly in agriculture and fishing.

The successful pursuit of these aims will require :

30. Research into regional linkages and multiplier effects, and the development of regional input-output studies.
31. Investigation into the possible fringe benefits available in the north to footloose industries and small scale growth industries.

The prime aim should be to encourage the establishment of those activities which have the greatest local income and employment effects. This is a policy which has been stressed and encouraged for some years by the state Department of Industrial Development as one of the means of achieving its aim of greater decentralization of industry in the state.

The field of tertiary activity is wide and there are many ways in which tertiary services could be improved in order to induce greater northern development. In the field of public services, education, water and power have already been mentioned above. Transport is mentioned separately below.

Town planning is another field in which the present position is unsatisfactory. There is a great deal to be said for appointing experienced planning consultants to advise the shire councils of the more rapidly developing areas. Port Hedland is a case in point where a townsite plan is urgently needed. In this case, however, the completion of such a plan awaits a final decision on the Mt. Newman development, which could have vast repercussions on the town and port area. Even better than the ad hoc appointment of consultants would be:

32. The establishment of a section in the government's existing regional planning authority to plan town development in country areas.

This would regularize town planning throughout the North and ensure a consistent regional approach. The activities of this section in respect of the northern region would need to be integrated with the activities of the government's North-West Planning Authority.

One tertiary activity which is largely in the hands of private enterprise and which offers great prospects for future development is the tourist industry. The state government is well aware of this and pursues a vigorous promotional campaign designed to interest tourists both within Australia and overseas in the attractions of the north. Its Tourist Development Authority also offers substantial assistance to local authorities who are prepared to develop caravan parks and other facilities. This is really a case where it is now up to the local authorities and private individuals and companies to take the initiative and capitalize on the assistance offered bv the government. As pointed out in Chapter 8, an immediate move could be made to establish :

33. Clearly defined historic markers and road signs indicating other points of interest to the tourist.
34. Adequately equipped picnic spots and rest areas.
35. Improved camping facilities conforming at least to uniform minimum standards laid down by local authorities.
36. Joint local authority consultation to ensure common standards throughout the region upon which the tourist may rely.
37. Co-operation between local authorities, the Administrator, chambers of commerce, oil companies, other interested bodies, and private individuals in the production of tourist promotion literature which deals with the region as a whole rather than with specific areas.

These measures could go a long way in a short time towards inducing much greater tourist flow into the region.

Perhaps the greatest single problem in the north, or at least the principal all-pervasive one, is the problem of transport, as discussed in Chapter 9. High transport costs affect all sectors of the northern economy and it is unlikely that this position will change greatly in the foreseeable future. But without doubt economies can be effected and the first move in this direction should be to establish :

38. A regional transport co-ordinating committee.

The immediate task of this committee should be to gather all available relevant information on northern transport services, including capital, operating and maintenance charges. There are grave gaps in available information and the committee should have power to ensure that it gets the information which is necessary. Once the information is available, the way would be clear to evolving a plan which would co-ordinate the development of the region's four transport modes with the prime aim of reducing costs and improving the service. Such a rationalization of northern transport is long overdue.

These are some of the ways in which the development of Northwestern Australia can be assisted and guided. Many of them require no financial commitment on the part of any government, some involve expenditure and effort by local authorities, some entail outlays by the state government and yet others require financial assistance, in the form of concessions, by the commonwealth government. The foregoing policy proposals are suggestions for government action, but the pages of this book demonstrate clearly that Northwestern Australia is a mixed economy in the development of which private enterprise has played and will continue to play a significant role. Thus there is also a challenge to those who operate within the private sector in the north, be they sole traders or executives of large companies, to make a commensurate effort to work within a policy framework which will ensure optimum development of the region from a national point of view.

BIBLIOGRAPHY

AUSTRALIAN INSTITUTE OF POLITICAL SCIENCE. *Northern Australia: Task for a Nation*. Sydney, 1954.

COMMONWEALTH DEPARTMENT OF TREASURY. *Investment Analysis*. Canberra, 1966.

COURT, C. W. M. *Development of Northern Australia*. Melbourne, 1965.
—— *Interdependence of Government and Private Enterprise in the Modern Society*. Rotterdam, 1966.

HIGGINS, BENJAMIN. *Economic Development*. London, 1959.

KELLY, J. H. *Struggle for the North*. Sydney, 1966.

McKENNA, K. M. 'Commonwealth State Financial Relations.' *Economic Activity in Western Australia*, vol. 9, no. 1. 1966.

PARKER, M. L. *An Inter-Industry Study of the Western Australian Economy*. Mimeographed paper, 1965. The Library of the University of Western Australia.

PEOPLE OF THE NORTH COMMITTEE. *A Plan for the North*. Townsville, 1966.

PERLOFF, H. S., DUNN, E. S. Jnr., LAMPARD, E. E. and MUTH, R. F. *Regions, Resources, and Economic Growth*. Baltimore, 1960.

APPENDIX 1

PHYSIOGRAPHY AND GEOLOGY[1]

1. INTRODUCTION

Northwestern Australia encompasses approximately half a million square miles of country in Western Australia north of the twenty-sixth parallel of latitude. Because of its vast extent this region exhibits a great diversity in geological structure and consequent physical relief. Although meteorological and biological factors have a great influence upon build, it is the immediate dependence of physical features upon rock structure and composition which will be discussed in this appendix.

The region contains some of the oldest rocks of the globe. They are a complex of igneous and folded sedimentary rocks and are Precambrian in age and are often referred to, as a whole, as the Precambrian shield.

The Precambrian shield has probably been covered in part, intermittently, throughout geological times by younger sediments of Palaeozoic, Mesozoic and Kainozoic age and all of these rocks have, throughout time, been subject to minor folding, faulting and tilting, coupled with erosion and weathering. From the late Tertiary onward, laterization,[2] associated with bevelling of all these rocks resulted in a surface of peneplanation. Since then this land has been somewhat uplifted, faulted and warped, and dissection has progressed below the level of the laterite surface, leaving ironstone-capped hills.

The Precambrian shield outcrops in areas which, as unities, are known as the Kimberley block, the Nullagine platform and the Yilgarn block;[3] the younger sediments are preserved in the Gulf (Bonaparte), Canning and Carnarvon basins. Along the coastal margins the basins are generally of

---

[1] I am indebted to the Director of the Geological survey of Western Australia and his officers for their assistance in the preparation of this appendix.

[2] See Appendix 4.

[3] Unless otherwise stated, nomenclature of physiographic units (e.g. Kimberley block) is taken from J. Gentilli and R. W. Fairbridge, *Physiographic Diagram of Australia*. A close relationship can be seen between the units adopted by I. W. Whitehouse, 'The Surface of Northern Australia', and those above.

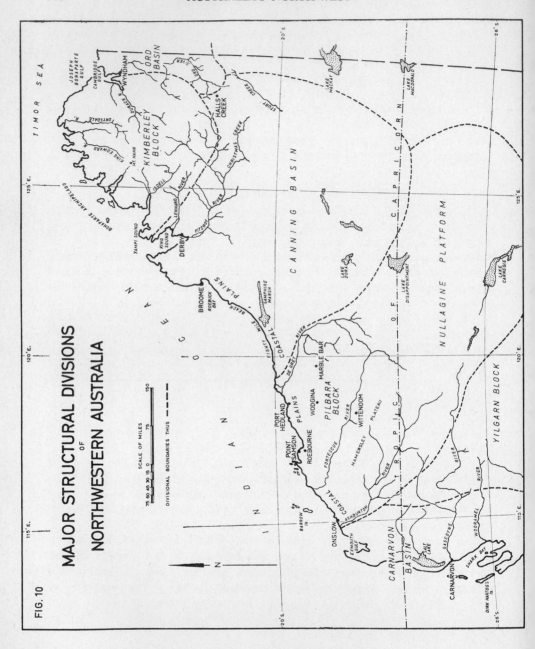

FIG. 10

MAJOR STRUCTURAL DIVISIONS
of
NORTHWESTERN AUSTRALIA

low elevation and are fringed by sediments of more recent age (Kainozoic to Recent). Here they form the physiographic unit known as the 'coastal plain'. Coastal plain lands stretch in an almost continuous arc around the coast of Northwestern Australia.

Northwestern Australia may thus be divided into two areas of physical difference determined principally by their underlying geology, namely : the old Precambrian shield and the younger sedimentary basins and their coastal plains. The latter are discussed under separate headings. Figure 1 shows the major structural divisions below, and Figure 2 shows the topographical features of Northwestern Australia.

2. Precambrian Shield or Plateau[4]

The oldest rocks of the plateau, comprising mainly granites, gneisses, greenstones, and metamorphosed sediments, are of Archaean age and cover wide areas of the state. They represent a very early geological era when the oldest known sediments were extremely contorted and subject to periods of granitization and subsequent intrusions of both acid and basic magmas. Where these expanses of Archaean rocks have been eroded, they have given rise to a predominantly uniform plateau level between 1,000 and 1,500 feet, as over most of the south-west and central parts of Western Australia.

In places the Archaean complex has been overlain by two series of sediments and volcanic rocks of probable Proterozoic age. These rocks rest unconformably upon the former indicating a long time lapse until their disposition. The Proterozoic sediments lying unconformably on the Archaean, are the least disturbed Nullagine series, now known to be composed of more than one sequence of rocks separated by unconformities; they are represented by a succession of conglomerates, sandstones and shales interbedded with basic igneous rocks. They are often less folded than the Archaean rocks and readily dissected by the agents of erosion. These Proterozoic systems are developed in Northwestern Australia on the Nullagine platform and in the Kimberley block, and account for the extremely broken topography of these areas.

The central region of the plateau is obscured by extensive tracts of desert sand dunes, dry claypans and salt lakes. The underlying rocks are believed to be of a comparable composition and age to the Archaean. The salt lake and sand ridge regions of the plateau constitute the most desolate and uninhabitable areas of the state. The former maintains only a sparse mining population, while the latter remains largely unexplored and as yet is of no economic importance.

[4]Geological sequence and terminology taken from: R. T. Prider, *Geology of Western Australia.*

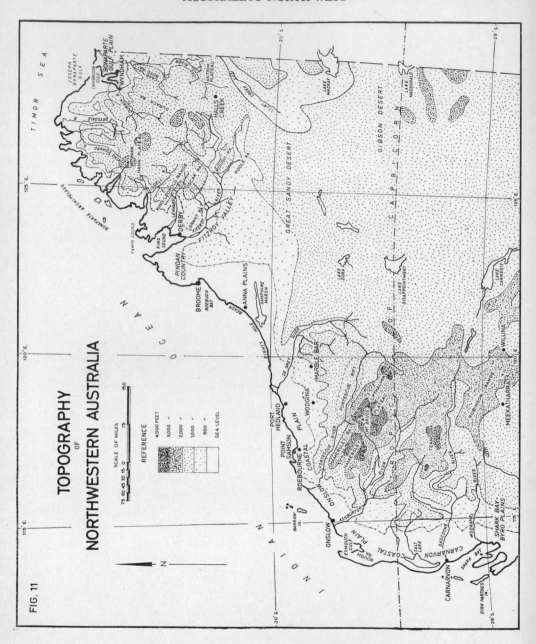

FIG. 11

TOPOGRAPHY
OF
NORTHWESTERN AUSTRALIA

The Kimberley Block

The Kimberley block occupies some 70,000 square miles of land in the extreme north of Western Australia and represents the northernmost extension of the great plateau of Western Australia. It is composed of Archaean and Proterozoic rocks; the nucleus of the Kimberley is the Hann plateau, composed mostly of sandstone and interbedded basic lavas (basalts) of Proterozoic age. To the west of the plateau these sediments are domed about a north-south regional anticlinal axis, rising from the general level of 1,000 feet to the highest point, Mt. Hann (2,800 feet). The basement rocks of the region are Archaean metamorphic rocks and Proterozoic granites and gneisses which outcrop in the marginal areas to the south and west of the Kimberley proper.

According to Jutson, the Hann plateau is an uplifted and dissected pene-plain.[5] River action and weathering have produced deeply incised gorges separated by flat-topped divides of almost horizontal sandstone. A more gentle relief is found in areas underlain by basalts and as this rock weathers to give a rich soil and good pasture such localities offer most to the pastoralist. They are however limited in extent and isolated within the confines of the rugged plateau region. Drainage of the plateau is structurally determined and, generally speaking, rivers flow in a radial pattern outwards from Mt. Hann. The major rivers are the Durack flowing north-east to Cambridge Gulf, the Drysdale and King Edward flowing north to the Timor Sea, and the the Prince Regent and Charnley draining westward to the Indian Ocean. Drainage to the south is controlled by the Isdell and Fitzroy rivers and their tributaries.

A ria coastline has been produced by the downwarping of the north-west margin of the Kimberley block. Drowning of the immaturely eroded river valleys in the sandstone has produced precipitous cliffs (200 to 800 feet) along the coast. The coastline is deeply indented and dotted by many steep-sided islands. Although the water is deep and many inlets would provide good anchorage, a high tidal range (20 to 40 feet) and the rugged nature of the coast and its hinterland make the development of port facilities in this area difficult and costly. Likewise the rough and inaccessible terrain, despite some pockets of good grazing land, has been a deterrent to pastoralists.[6]

The King Leopold Ranges mark the south-western limit of the Kimley block. A residual band of strongly folded Archaean rocks, broken into many sections by the water gaps of the Lennard and Fitzroy rivers and their tributaries, constitutes these ranges. Their average height is approximately 2,000 feet, but some isolated peaks are over 3,000 feet.

[5] J. T. Jutson, 'The Physiography of Western Australia', p. 40.
[6] For a more detailed discussion on the topography and economic potential of this Kimberley region see, Commonwealth Scientific and Industrial Research Organisation, 'Lands and Pastoral Resources of the North Kimberley Area, Western Australia'.

The Durack and Carr Boyd ranges bound the Kimberley block to the south-east and east respectively. Little is known about these ranges. They mark the line of division between the country dominated by Nullagine sediments and that underlain by the granitic basement. This latter eastern belt of crystalline rock passes southward from the southern end of the Carr Boyd Ranges to the vicinity of Hall's Creek and forms a transition zone of high plain land (e.g. Nicholson Plains) between the Kimberley block and the Antrim region.

The Nullagine Platform

The Nullagine platform extends over an area of more than 200,000 square miles, stretching from central Western Australia to the north-west coast where it is fringed by the Onslow coastal plain. It is a large and geologically complex region of Archaean and Proterozoic rocks, the weathering of which has produced a more varied topography than that of the plateau to the south. An extensive outlier of Proterozoic sediment mantles the Archaean basement to the west, while to the east the surface is obscured by the gibber plains and sand of the Gibson and Great Sandy deserts. Mining and pastoral pursuits are the main economic activities of this region.

One may distinguish three main topographical areas in the Nullagine platform, namely : the Pilbara block, the Hamersley plateau, and the Fortescue valley.

The northern section of the platform, known as the Pilbara block, is composed of granites and highly altered sedimentary and volcanic rocks which are relatively resistant to erosion and give the plateau here a flat or gently undulating surface. Laterization is widespread and mesas and buttes are characteristic. The area reaches its maximum height of approximately 1,200 feet in the south-east in consequence of which the De Grey and its tributaries drain towards the sea. The Pilbara block is bounded by the Fortescue River to the south.

The Hamersley and Ophthalmia ranges have been etched out of the Proterozoic sediments which overlie the Archaean basement in this area. Dissection of the Hamersley plateau has resulted in the deep scarring of the slightly metamorphosed sediments and interbedded lavas and doleritic sills of Proterozoic age. The topography is immature and rugged by comparison with the remainder of the Nullagine platform and the Precambrian shield here reaches its greatest height in the residual Mt. Bruce (4,024 feet). The deep gorges and ravines of this area, which provide a great tourist attraction, are the result of the erosion, by the Fortescue and Ashburton rivers and their tributaries, of an undulating tertiary peneplain.

As a result of Archaean igneous activity in this area, widespread mineralization has occurred, enriching the Pilbara with deposits of gold, for which Marble Bar and Nullagine were at one time famed. Iron occurs in great quantities and is now being exploited vigorously (see Chaper 4). Today, non-auriferous minerals are produced on the Pilbara goldfield for which Port Hedland and Point Samson provide the outlets. Wodgina is the centre of an area noted for tin and tantalum.

The Hamersley plateau comes within the limits of the West Pilbara goldfield. Post-war development of mining here has mainly been confined to the production of crocidolite, or blue asbestos, taken from seams in the banded ironstone formation within the Nullagine sediments. Deposits have been exposed along the cliff faces of the deep gorges, of which Wittenoom is the best known. Ports of access to the plateau are Port Hedland, Onslow and Point Samson.

Separating the Pilbara block and the Hamersley plateau is the Fortescue valley which is flanked to the north by steep-sloped Proterozoic sediments. This depression is occupied by Tertiary alluvial soils, and has a good natural grass cover.

The Yilgarn Block[7]

Due to the characteristic levelling of the plateau where it is underlain by granites and gneisses, the northern part of the Yilgarn block reaches an average height of approximately 1,000 feet. A triangular projection of the greater mass of the southern plateau, this section is wedged between the south-western edge of the Nullagine platform and the eastern rim of the Carnarvon basin.

The level of the plateau is broken by table-topped hills, some of which are capped with laterite. These have been undercut below the capping and are bounded by low cliffs (breakaways) and rocky talus slopes. They have been produced under semi-arid conditions. Monadnocks of resistant meta-sediments and igneous dykes occur above the laterite level and are usually ridged or elongated along their strikes.

The Gascoyne and Murchison rivers drain the north-western section of the Yilgarn block while to the east is an area of interior drainage. Here precipitation collects in shallow basins which, after heavy rains, merge into more or less connected streams. Aridity causes these lakes to become dry and salt-encrusted. This region is the northern section of Jutson's 'salina-land.'[8]

This area, like the Pilbara, is underlain by highly mineralized igneous rocks and constitutes part of the Ashburton, Gascoyne, Peak Hill and Murchison goldfields. Although the latter mineral region is mostly outside the area of this survey, it has been in the past one of the richest goldfields in Western Australia and is worthy of note. Carnarvon provides port facilities for the northern area of the Yilgarn block.

[7]These comments refer only to that area of the Yilgarn block north of the twenty-sixth parallel.

[8]J. T. Jutson, 'The Physiography of Western Australia', p. 94.

3. SEDIMENTARY BASINS

Composed, as they are, of uplifted and only slightly disturbed sediments, these basins contain the prerequisites for the occurrence of artesian water and, with the exception of the Gulf basin, they are all large in area. All mark the past location of ancient seas. Their constituent sediments, sandstones, siltstones, conglomerates and limestones, range from Lower Palaeozoic to Pleistocene in age. Topographically they vary in height with a general development from sea level, on the coast, to between 1,000 and 2,000 feet onwards towards the interior plateau.

The Gulf Basin (Ord Basin)[9]

The sediments of the Gulf basin outcrop in the region of the Antrim plateau and the Ord River basin to the east of the Kimberley block. At the base of this Palaeozoic sedimentary sequence are Cambrian basalts. These are overlain by sandstone, limestones, shales, and conglomerates ranging in age from Lower Cambrian to a Tertiary sequence of terrestrial siltstones and marls, and are considered by Jutson to be an extension of the interior plateau. The area provides a strong contrast to the rough landscape of the Kimberley for the rocks tend to wear away into great rolling expanses. Essentially, therefore, the topography is one of open downs above which rise the mesas and buttes marking the plateau level of approximately 1,500 feet. Where basalts provide the source rock for soils, a rich grassland prevails and beef cattle raising is the dominant economic activity, though irrigated agriculture has recently been established in the area (see Chapters 6 and 7).

The plateau has been dissected by the Ord River and its tributaries, and is traversed by the Ord River basin (300-400 feet above sea level) which merges seawards with the coastal plain. The youngest section of the basin flanking the north coast contains Permian sediments which appear to be the source beds of artesian water.

The Canning Basin (Desert Basin)

The Canning basin covers an area of probably over 150,000 square miles, not including its seaward extension on the continental shelf. The basin extends from the coast at the Eighty Mile Beach in a general south-easterly direction towards the Western Australian border. The exact location of its eastern boundary is unknown. To the north it is flanked by the sediments of the Fitzroy valley and its southern limit is marked by the De Grey River. The area is the northern region of Jutson's 'sandland'.

The rocks of the basin are best observed on its northern border where

[9]This term is here inclusive of both the Antrim plateau and the Ord River basin and is, generally speaking, synonymous with 'Ordland' of J. T. Jutson, 'The Physiography of Western Australia', and the 'Antrim Region' of E. de C. Clarke, 'Natural Regions in Western Australia', and J. Gentilli and R. W. Fairbridge, *Physiographic Diagram of Australia*.

sediments, ranging in age from Ordovician to Triassic, outcrop in the Fitzroy Valley. In the larger Canning Desert portion, sediments range from Permian to Lower Cretaceous, with Jurassic sediments most abundant. However, much of this region remains unexplored. With the regression of the Mesozoic sea, Cretaceous sediments were laid down on what is now Dampier Peninsula. Overall, the strata dip gently towards the centre of the basin, but are interrupted by local folding. Igneous activity occurred in post Triassic times, as evidenced by intrusive dykes and volcanic necks cutting through the sedimentary sequence in the Fitzroy valley.

One may distinguish three main topographical areas in the Canning basin, namely, the Fitzroy valley, the Pindan[10] country, and the Canning basin proper.

The Fitzroy River forms part of the radial network of channels draining the Kimberley block from whence it passes southwards through a gap it has carved in the King Leopold Ranges. Through the activity of the Fitzroy and its tributaries the area has been reduced to an extensive plain-land of elevation between 500 and 1,000 feet, commonly called the Fitzroy valley. Though in places obscured by alluvial deposits, the valley is underlain by Permian sediments of the basin proper. Sandstones in the Permian sequence are the artesian water-bearing beds of this basin. The general level of the valley is broken by a series of sub-parallel sedimentary residuals forming the Grant, St. George's, Poole and Rough ranges, and by igneous intrusions in the form of volcanic necks, e.g. Machell's Pyramid.

The rocks underlying this region are thought to be Cretaceous in age, but are masked at the surface by large tracts of unconsolidated red sands and gravels. The area is typified by a low sclerophyllous woodland with which the name, Pindan, is commonly associated. Due to its good soils and accessibility the valley has been extensively occupied by pastoralists running either beef cattle or sheep. Production of irrigated crops, mainly rice, is carried on on the alluvial soils at Liveringa on the Fitzroy. The port of Derby services this region.

The fertile river flats of the Fitzroy valley stand in strong contrast to the Pindan country of Dampier Land. The port of Broome is situated in the south of the Pindan area on the northern shore of Roebuck Bay and provides an alternative to the outlet at Derby.

The Canning basin is a vast plainland underlain by the artesian water-bearing sediments of Palaeozoic age. Mesozoic rocks outcrop in the large central desert portion of the basin. Here the terrain passes from a few rocky outcrops (laterite-capped mesas and buttes) into the region of un-consolidated sands and dunes which feature prominently in the journals of the early explorers. These dunes exhibit a parallel development under

[10]Pindan is the native name referring to the land away from the rivers and permanent water. L. J. H. Teakle, 'A Regional Classification of the Soils of Western Australia', p. 117.

the influence of the prevailing winds tending in a west-north-west to east-south-east direction and may be either moving or fixed with a sparse cover of spinifex and stunted eucalypts. They vary in height, width, and interval between the ridges.[11]

The region has no surface drainage, and sporadic rainfall collects in claypans in depressions between the dunes. The basin is arid and, despite its artesian water potential, it offers little encouragement to settlement. The line of bores marking the Canning Stock Route has fallen into disuse since the establishment of northern outlets for beef cattle. All told, it is one of the most inhospitable and inaccessible areas in Australia.

The Carnarvon Basin (North-West Basin)

This basin lies westward of the plateau between the Ashburton and Murchison rivers, and constitutes an area of approximately 50,000 square miles. It is entirely composed of sediments which outcrop in wide bands parallel to the coast. The eastern margin of the basin is occupied by a very thick sequence of marine limestones, sandstones, glacial beds, and shales which range from Devonian to Permian in age. They exhibit a regional dip towards the west and, in places, outcrop in a series of cuesta escarpments. The central band of exposed sediments is mostly Cretaceous sandstones, shales, marls and limestones which lie uncomfortably on the former sedimentary sequence. Although slightly folded, these rocks give rise to a wide plainland area east of North-West Cape, passing south-wards into the Shark Bay-Byro Plains area. The younger sediments along the coast have been gently folded. In the North-West Cape-Exmouth Gulf region, both Cape Range and Rough Range mark the position of anti-clinal structures (domes) and this area has been the site of intensive oil exploration in the last decade. The most recent sediments are those laid down along the coastal margin comprising an overlay of Tertiary strata, mainly limestone.

The port outlet for the basin is at Carnarvon where irrigated agriculture is established in addition to the sheep raising of the hinterland.

4. COASTAL PLAINS[12]

The north-western coastal plains are a continuation of the low-lying Kainozoic, Quaternary and Tertiary sediments of the south-west. These encompass the coastal belt, from the shoreline inland to the 500-foot contour, and form a continuous strip from Shark Bay to King Sound. They are almost totally absent from the steep and rugged shoreline of the

---

[11]Height – 50 to 100 feet; width – 150 to 1,500 feet; interval between ridges – from a few chains to a mile. See J. T. Jutson, 'The Physiography of Western Australia', p. 121.

[12]Much of the detail contained in this section was observed by W. H. Woolnough, *Report on Aerial Survey Operations in Australia during 1932*, in aerial recon-naissance.

Kimberley, but are manifest again in a small area on the coast of **Bonaparte Gulf.**

The Plains vary in width, being more extensive in the vicinity of Port Hedland and Carnarvon. With the exception of the Onslow area most of these plains contain artesian water, as they form the coastward extension of the great sedimentary basins. Likewise, where they fringe such basins they form an intermediate zone between a wide continental shelf and the interior.

In view of the great tidal range along the north-western shores, tidal flats and salt marshes are common from Carnarvon northward, including Bonaparte Gulf plains. Beaches are generally low, shelving and sandy, and coastal ports make use of long jetties and causeways to link the point of anchorage with the dry high ground of the port township. From Onslow northward, mangroves are common and mangrove tidal flats are found between here and Bonaparte Gulf in those situations where inlets and bays are lined with muddy shores. The low topography of the coastal plains of the north-west gives access by road (not an all-weather road) to the northern towns and ports, the North-West and Great Northern highways traversing the plains from Carnarvon to Derby.

The Bonaparte Gulf Plain

This northern plain is a low-lying area of coastland extending across the Western Australian border into the Northern Territory. It is underlain by Devonian and Permian sediments which have been masked along the northern coastal fringe by Tertiary deposits. It is drained by the Ord and Victoria rivers which bring down vast volumes of water and silt to the shallow waters of Cambridge and Bonaparte gulfs. Despite the drowned nature of the Ord River mouth, sedimentation has reduced depth to make navigation southward as far as Wyndham difficult. However, the same sedimentation has provided the alluvial soils of the plain, a product of the weathering of the limestones, sandstones and basalts of the interior. It is on these soils that the irrigated agriculture of the Ord scheme is established. As elsewhere in the north of the state, mangrove tidal flats are common along the coast.

The Eighty Mile Beach

This western edge of the Canning basin is in an area of shelving beaches on a wide continental shelf. Along the beach, salt marshes merge into red pindan sands and in the vicinity of Wollal they culminate in an extensive samphire marsh. The shoreline at the north-eastern end of the beach, near Anna Plains, features the development of parallel coastal sand dunes of Kainozoic age. These dunes continue southwards, merging with the bays of salt marsh on their windward side and the Pindan sands to their leeward.

The Eighty Mile Beach marks the seaward margin of a dry tract of land with no exterior drainage. However, situated as it is on the edge of the Canning basin it has a good supply of artesian water. The De Grey River may be regarded as the southern limit of this strip of coastal plain.

The Onslow Coastal Plain

Unlike its northern counterpart the Onslow coastal plain is bordered by rocky headlands and coral islets. The plain is the coastal extension by the Nullagine Platform and is drained by the De Grey, Fortescue and Ashburton rivers. Mangrove tidal flats and salt marshes are common from Port Hedland southward to Onslow. From the Fortesque River southwards vast redsoil plains pass into salt marsh towards the coast. Claypans are common and extend to the eastern shores of Exmouth Gulf. A belt of red sand ridge country from the mouth of the Ashburton passes down the coast to Salt Lake on the Carnarvon coastal plain.

The Carnarvon Coastal Plain

From Exmouth Gulf to Shark Bay the coastal plain widens and resumes its dune-lined shore. The low-lying Shark Bay-Byro plain is generally sandy except on Dirk Hartog Island where high sandstone cliffs face seawards. In the region south of Exmouth Gulf, the Minilya River and other small creeks drain into Salt Lake, a depression lying parallel to the coast. The Gascoyne River cuts the plain at Carnarvon giving rise to fertile agricultural soils where alluvium has been deposited. Tropical agriculture is carried out here under irrigation. White sand dunes and Tertiary coastal limestone are common coastal features in the southern part of the plain and it has artesian water resources.

5. SUMMARY

Based upon geological criteria, it has been convenient to divide the physiography of Northwestern Australia into two main structural areas – the plateau and the sedimentary basins and their associated coastal plains.

Two types of topography are manifest on the plateau. The first is that of the gently undulating tableland and relief produced as a result of the denudation of large expanses of Precambrian igneous and metamorphic rock as evidenced by the northern section of the Yilgarn block. The second is that of the rugged and greatly dissected tableland where an overlay of less resistant slightly metamorphosed Precambrian sediments has been scored with deep narrow gorges and clefts. Such topography is found in the Kimberley block and on the Nullagine platform where large areas of old sandstones and limestones have thus suffered destruction by running water. Perhaps in past ages such sediments were widespread over the plateau but have by now been removed, leaving only certain areas standing somewhat above the level of the igneous basement. These are the highest points in Western Australia and are source areas of the major northern rivers.

Of lesser elevation than the plateau, is the surface of the Palaeozoic and Mesozoic sedimentary basins. Erosion of these basins has been consequent upon their structure and exhibits a wide variation due to local folding and faulting. Generally speaking, where the sediments are horizontal they have been denuded to give large expanses of open country marked by the mesa and butte type of residual with their characteristic breakaway escarpments. Such topography is best exemplified in the Gulf basin. Where sediments have been tilted, cuestas have been formed. These may be seen in the Carnarvon basin. Where water has given way to wind as the major erosive force, sand-dune development has obliterated surface structure. Thus the arid interior of the Canning basin has been reduced to a vast desert of ridged sand dunes.

The coastal fringe of this country may be viewed as the seaward extension of the sedimentary basins, but the coastal plain is the characteristic feature along the entire coastline, the only exception being the cliff-lined Kimberley shores. The coastal plains, named for their location - Bonaparte Gulf, Eighty Mile Beach, Onslow and Carnarvon – are low-lying sedimentary areas in which sands predominate, so that they are almost invariably lined with coastal dunes, often marshy and, in the north, prone to mangrove growth.

Northwestern Australia demonstrates a great variation in geology and physiography. This huge area of country is nowhere broken by chains of high mountains. From coastal plain to the Western Australian border, over a distance of hundreds of miles, there is a rise of only a few thousand feet in height. Thus, although in many places the terrain is rugged, the over-riding physical factor which will greatly influence the development of this area is the immensity of the land surface and its isolation rather than its configuration.

Bibliography

CLARKE, E. de C. 'Natural Regions in Western Australia.' *Journal of the Royal Society of Western Australia,* vol. XII, no. 14. 1926. Clarke's natural regions of Western Australia are based upon geological and climatic criteria. Factual detail contained in his article has been used in compiling the physiographic and geological detail for this appendix.

COMMONWEALTH SCIENTIFIC AND INDUSTRIAL RESEARCH ORGANISATION. 'Lands and Pastoral Resources of the North Kimberley area, Western Australia.' *Land Research Series,* no. 4. 1960. This survey contains a very detailed appraisal of the physical resources of the North Kimberley. It assesses the economic potential of the area with special reference to the pastoral industry.

GENTILLI, J. and FAIRBRIDGE, R. W. *Physiographic Diagram of Australia.* New York, 1951. This work contains an up-to-date and comprehensive survey of the physiography of Australia. It divides the continent into physiographic regions which are discussed in detail with reference to geology and physical structure, climate and vegetation.

JUTSON, J. T. 'The Physiography of Western Australia.' *Geological Survey of Western Australia Bulletin,* no. 95. 1934. There is a great wealth of physical data contained in this volume – geology, physiography, climate, vegetation and so on. It is a standard reference, outdated only in regard to some geological interpretations of structure and to statistics given.

PRIDER, R. T. 'Geology of Western Australia.' *Official Yearbook of Western Australia.* Perth, 1958. A concise survey of the geology of Western Australia and resultant physical features, including a *precis* of the geological history of the state.

TEAKLE, L. J. H. 'A Regional Classification of the Soils of Western Australia.' *Journal of the Royal Society of Western Australia,* vol. XXIV. 1937-38. A comprehensive survey of the soils and geology, physiography, climate and vegetation.

WHITEHOUSE, I. W. 'The Surface of Northern Australia' in Australian Institute of Political Science, *Northern Australia: Task for a Nation.* Sydney, 1954. Dealing as it does with the immediate problems of the north, this book contains a regional survey of all physical and economic aspects.

WOOLNOUGH, W. H. *Report on Aerial Survey Operations in Australia during 1932.* Canberra, 1932. This work contains many personal observations of physiographic features seen from the air by the author. This survey was conducted by the Commonwealth in order to locate possible oil structures in Australia. It has been especially useful for detail of sedimentary areas in North-West Australia.

APPENDIX 2

MINERAL RESOURCES[1]

1. INTRODUCTION

Mineral discoveries have been, throughout the world and at all times, among the main factors responsible for surges of economic development. Even in Northwestern Australia, commonly regarded as the land of cattle and sheep stations, the influence of early mineral discoveries may be seen in the development of various towns and setlements. Nevertheless, until recently income from mining in the region has been relatively small when measured against that from pastoral pursuits, though it is now increasing rapidly. The story of recent development is contained in Chapter 6.

This is not to suggest that the region's mineral resources are limited. Quite the reverse, in fact. As will be seen in the following pages, a great variety of mineral wealth exists to be tapped when markets and prices are buoyant enough to overcome the transportation problems created by vast distances and the nature of the terrain, the labour problems created by isolation and climatic discomfort, and the capital problems connected with the establishment of large-scale operations. In many cases these problems have already been partly or wholly overcome, and the region is now experiencing a surge of mineral development on a hitherto unprecedented scale.

The chemical elements comprising commercially valuable mineral resources are dependent upon geological structure for their distribution. Due to differences in mode of occurrence there are major differences in the mineral resources of the sedimentary basins of the Precambrian shield. Coal, oil, water and deposits of mineral salts are usually associated with the sedimentary basins, while most metalliferous deposits are found on the plateau where they were formed in Precambrian times as an aftermath of igneous activity.

The major exploitation of mineral resources in the region (with the

[1]Grateful acknowledgement is made to the Director of the Geological Survey of Western Australia, and his officers, for their assistance in the preparation of this appendix.

exception of artesian water) has so far been confined to the plateau, though oil search activities are now directing more attention to the sedimentary basins. The distribution of the minerals of the plateau has not been haphazard; certain 'laws' have governed their location and association with other mineral types. Metalliferous minerals, and associated non-metalliferous minerals, are concentrated in small areas rather than spread throughout the mass of crystalline rocks. Ore enrichments have been due to the invasion of these areas by igneous intrusions which have solidified in the form of dykes, veins and pegmatites. These constitute lodes or ore bodies and their overall composition predetermines the minerals found therein. For instance, the two main types of intrusions, acid (granitic), and basic (doleritic), contain different associations of minerals. The former contains the lighter metals and associated minerals, while the latter is often rich in base metals.

Thus, over the northern plateau where granitic intrusions are common, tin, tantalum, niobium, beryllium, lithium, tungsten, antimony, radio-active minerals, mica and felspar are found. They are mined from acid intrusions associated with the younger granites of Archaeozoic age and their occurrence is particularly important on the Pilbara block; the Pilbara goldfield has the largest output of these minerals. Where basic intrusions are common, copper, silver-lead ore and vanadium are found. Such intrusions occur in limited areas throughout the northern goldfields. As a rule the minerals associated with acid intrusions will not be found in association with those of the basic type, and *vice versa*. Gold may, however, be found in association with both types of intrusion and thus has a wider distribution.

The two important minerals, iron and asbestos, which are also found in the rocks of the shield, do not always depend for their origin upon igneous intrusions. Iron ores originate as a result of the alteration and enrichment of banded iron formations. This enrichment results either from supergene processes associated with movements of groundwaters, as in the case of the Hamersley ores, or from the influence of magmatic fluids derived from granite intrusions, as in the case of ores of the Mt. Goldsworthy type. The Yampi ores are original sedimentary accumulations and, as such, are freakish and practically unique.

There are two types of asbestos in the North-West. The most important in terms of present production is the amphibole asbestos, crocidolite, which occurs as a constituent of banded iron formations in the Hamersley Ranges. The second type is chrysotile asbestos which is related to metamorphosed ultrabasic rocks and is itself a product of the metamorphism. Iron ores occur over a wide area of the Pilbara, in banded iron formations and associated sedimentary deposits in the Hamersley and Opthalmia ranges, in the Port Hedland district, notably at Mt. Goldsworthy, and at Yampi Sound in the West Kimberley. Asbestos is confined to the Nullagine sediments of the Hamersley Ranges in the West Pilbara goldfield.

The discovery of minerals in Northwestern Australia is attributable to the early explorers, private prospectors and geologists of the Government Geological Survey. Apart from gold, the existence of iron, copper, tin, tantalum, asbestos and other minerals, in the north, had been acknowledged for many years even as early as 1900.[2] Their commercial extraction has been dependent upon suitable market prices in relation to extraction and transport costs, and these have changed sufficiently in more recent years to warrant production. The growth of industry and the advance in technical knowledge and mineral processing have widened the demand for many minerals and have made payable some of the known deposits of the north.

Over much of Northwestern Australia prospecting has been simplified by the nearness of mineral deposits to the surface. Lack of rainfall, particularly in the North-West Division, has prevented the growth of a heavy vegetation cover. Soils are often skeletal and only form a thin mantle over the country rock. Thus residual minerals have been found more or less *in situ,* on the surface, very close to the source ore body. However, easily located mineral deposits have not necessarily been developed with ease. The inadequacy of water supplies has always been a problem in the mining areas of the north. Distance from ports has limited exploitation in view of freight costs, and it has been difficult to attract suitable labour to isolated mining towns. Since the decline of the alluvial miner, large-scale production, involving expensive machinery and treatment plants, has usually been dependent upon capital investment by the larger mining companies, and the whole character of the mining process has changed (see Chapter 4).

Based as it is upon the exploitation of a wasting asset, the mineral industry of Northwestern Australia has been subject to considerable changes. Mining localities change as ores are exhausted or as the demand for new minerals arises. Likewise the emphasis upon the development of certain types of mineral production alters. Whereas gold was the predominant mineral mined in the late nineteenth century and early twentieth century, today the most important minerals are iron, manganese and oil, and the area's potential for rare metals and radio-active minerals may be called upon at some future date.

In the following pages an attempt has been made to point to the geological mode of occurrence of the minerals of importance in Northwestern Australia, giving some details about their past development and some notes concerning their present exploitation. A fuller description of the economic aspects of the mineral production of the region is given in Chapter 4.

2. ASBESTOS

Of the two varieties of asbestos found in Western Australia, crocidolite or blue asbestos, accounts for more than ninety per cent of the total production of asbestos fibre. It occurs in seams of closely packed parallel

[2]See A. Gibb-Maitland and A. Montgomery, *The Geology and Mineral Industry of Western Australia.*

fibres running transverse to the borders of the seam in the flat-dipping
banded ironstones and quartzites of Nullagine age in the Hamersley Ranges.
Because the asbestos seams are exposed on the cliff faces of the deep
gorges within these ranges, they can be cheaply mined by open cutting and
stripping before underground mining is necessary. The best known deposits
are found at Yampire Gorge and Wittenoom Gorge, the latter location
marking the present site of development. At Wittenoom crocidolite is taken
from two seams lying between 150 and 200 feet up the cliff face of the
gorge. The lower seam contains crocidolite fibres up to two inches in
length while in the top seam fibres vary from one-eighth inch to one inch
in length.

Chrysotile is found in rocks in the Warrawoona System and is at present
mined at several places in the Pilbara, including Lionel and Nunyerri.
In this area serpentine rocks associated with jasper and conglomerates
are transversed by shear zones which constitute the asbestos lode. In view
of this fact, it is necessary to work ore bodies by underground mining
methods.

Little credence was attached to reports of the occurrence of asbestos
in the Hamersley Ranges until 1929 when E. S. Simpson, the Government
Analyst and Mineralogist, reported favourably on specimens found at Mt.
Margaret and Weeli Wolli Spring.[3] Later geological studies proved the
area's potential and when market prices permitted, small parcels of asbestos
were exported by individual prospectors. The inaccessibility of the mineral
field in the West Pilbara rendered exploitation uneconomical when prices
were low, for the asbestos had to be transported for 200 miles over bad
roads to Point Samson.

In 1937 and 1938 when asbestos ore was bringing £75 sterling per
ton, the output was such that the market was flooded, and many miners
left the district. Prior to the war, production of chrysotile was carried
out by the Asbestos, Molybdenum and Tungsten Co. Ltd. operating a plant
at Lionel. In 1939 this concern moved its plant to Yampire Gorge and
concentrated on the production of crocidolite. Until the war the asbestos
resources of the Pilbara had been subject to sporadic exploitation but
in 1943, with the establishment of a plant at Wittenoom Gorge by the
Australian Blue Asbestos Co. N.L. (an associate of the Colonial Sugar
Refining Co. Ltd.), the mining of crocidolite was put on a more permanent
basis. By 1950 the Australian Blue Asbestos Co. had become sole producer
of blue asbestos fibre.

The state Government has been responsible for building a completely
new township at Wittenoom Gorge which houses the dependants of men
employed on the mines. Its future now seems much less secure than it
appeared in the early 1960's. It is connected by road to Port Hedland and

[3]K. R. Miles, *The Blue Asbestos-bearing Banded Iron Formations of the Hamersley Ranges*, p. 37.

Roebourne and Point Samson, and is serviced by Mac.Robertson Miller Airlines. Because of the scenic attraction of the gorge it is now a well visited tourist centre.

3. BERYL

The mineral beryl is the commonest source of berryllium, a rare metal used in the production of copper alloys and in atomic reactors. It is found over a wide area of the Precambrian shield of the North-West of the state. Beryl is one of several minerals associated with the end-phase of the younger granitic intrusions, a product of Archaeozoic igneous activity in Western Australia. Deposits of beryl are found together with tin, tungsten, molybdenum, tantalum and niobium, lithium, radio-active minerals, mica and felspar, all of which are largely found within pegmatites produced as offshoots of the younger granitic magma.

Production of beryl was negligible until stimulated by wartime demand. In 1943 and 1944 hundreds of tons of beryl ore were mined mainly from the Pilbara, particularly at Wodgina, and the Gascoyne goldfields, at Yinnietharra. Between 1947 and 1948 the export of beryl ores and concentrates was restricted and the output was shipped to the United Kingdom under licence. During the following two years export was prohibited when the Australian Atomic Energy Commission purchased all good-grade material. The buying programme of the Commission was suspended in January 1960, when producers were allowed to export ore to approved destinations. Production rose to 261 tons in 1961, but with poor demand and lower prices, it fell to 80 tons in 1964.

Northwestern Australia has produced most of the total Western Australian output of beryl, mainly from the Pilbara. Ore has come from Marble Bar, Cooglegong, Abydos, Moolyella, Mt. Francisco, Strelley, Tabba Tabba, Wodgina and the Nullagine area. A new field was reported at Roebourne in 1960 and has produced about 70 tons of ore. In 1965, when the total state output was only 13 tons, Mt. Francisco was the only Pilbara producer. Yinnietharra on the Gascoyne goldfield is the main producing centre outside the Pilbara.

4. COPPER AND CUPREOUS ORE

Practically the whole of the copper production in Northwestern Australia consists of cupreous ore and concentrates of fertiliser grade. Despite the discovery of copper ore – particularly that at Whim Creek near Roebourne in 1875 – there has been little development of such deposits in recent years.

Copper and cupreous ore occur over a wide area of the Precambrian shield in the North-West Division, and also in the Kimberley. It mostly occurs in quartz reefs associated with igneous intrusions, but some deposits are probably original sedimentary concentrations enriched by ground water movements. The main copper period of formation in Western Australia was probably in the Proterozoic era when extensive base metal-enriched doleritic intrusions forced their way into the rocks of the Nullagine sytem. Such intrusions now remain as small copper-bearing lodes which usually contain rich secondary ore near the surface. Many lodes have been picked over at the surface and abandoned once the more easily won richer ores were exhausted. The present demand for copper to remedy trace element deficiencies in the soil has made exploitation of the ore more worthwhile. Production for chemical fertilizers commenced in 1947 for this purpose.

Copper and cupreous ores commonly occur in the Peak Hill, Pilbara, West Pilbara and Ashburton goldfields, the first two areas usually having the largest output. In the Peak Hill district mining has been carried on at Thaduna, Ilgararrie, Peak Hill and Kumerina, primarily by open cut methods, but developing into deep mines. In fact, only Thaduna now remains as an open cut. This is also the only mine producing concentrates. In 1959-63 the Copper Hills Mine, south of Marble Bar in the Pilbara, was processing cupreous ore to obtain copper sulphate. In 1964 most of the ore produced in the Pilbara goldfield came from the Glen Ellen Pool deposits. Uaroo and Red Hill, on the Ashburton goldfield have been copper producers in the past but transport costs have prevented all but highest-grade ores being transported to Onslow for shipment. The West Pilbara goldfield was renowned for its copper mining activity when the Whim Creek mine was in production. Mining operations were resumed in July 1963 and ceased in 1964. Some ore was mined from an open cut but most of the ore treated was from old dumps. Whim Creek was the leading copper producer in the region in 1964, and considerable reserves of ore remain. Several localities in the area are noted for copper – Mons Cupri, Croydon and Roebourne. However, rich surface ores have been picked out at these sites, and normally the West Pilbara contributes but a small percentage of the state's cupreous ore.

There are copper deposits in the East Kimberley in the area between Wyndham and Hall's Creek. At present, however, there is no production recorded from this region. In the past, copper ores have been smelted from Mt. Neville in the West Kimberley. Some ore has been mined at Yampi Sound and several other deposits are known. Exploratory surveys by the Western Mining Company failed to find indications of commercial deposits.

5. GOLD

It was in 1882 in the Kimberley, between the headwaters of the Ord and Margaret rivers that gold was discovered in Western Australia by E. T. Hardman.[4] Later discoveries followed, including that by Hall and Slattery in 1885. Although the find was a modest one and the field, the Kimberley goldfield (proclaimed in 1886), was very quickly worked out,

[4] See F. K. Crowley, *Australia's Western Third,* pp. 83-87 for history of discoveries.

it marked the beginning of an industry which greatly stimulated the colony's economic development. The government had long believed that the discovery of gold might confer great benefits on the colony and the ensuing strikes were to prove such optimism well founded. A rush to the Pilbara occurred in 1888 and the Pilbara goldfield was proclaimed, and Marble Bar and Nullagine became the centres of a rich alluvial goldfield. Further prospecting resulted in the proclamation of the Ashburton and Murchison fields in 1889 and 1891 respectively. The finds of the north were eclipsed in 1892 by the gold discoveries of Bayley and Ford at Coolgardie which led to the most spectacular rush in Australian history. Finally the strikes culminated in that of 1893 when Hannan, Flannagan and O'Shea made the discoveries that were to establish Kalgoorlie and the 'Golden Mile' as the foremost Australian gold producer.

The gold discoveries which began in such a small way in the Kimberley had marked repercussions on the social, economic and political history of the colony. They also had the effect of intensifying prospecting activity and many non-auriferous minerals were found in the process of looking for gold.

Gold has been the chief metallic mineral produced in the state and occurs in the rocks of the Precambrian shield, having been deposited as an aftermath of igneous activity. The principal gold formation epoch in geological times is believed to have been that associated with the intrusion of basic and granitic rocks from early Precambrian times.[5]

There are two main types of gold deposits, namely those associated with sulphide lodes in greenstones, and those of the quartz reef-type. The principal gold-bearing lodes in Western Australia are those of the former type and are common from Meekatharra southwards on the Yilgarn block. The gold-bearing rocks of the north are usually of the latter type, where lodes of the 'fissure vein' variety are more common. Here gold is believed to be a product of the end phase of granitic intrusions which have cut into the pre-existing granites, gneisses and meta-sediments of Archaeozoic age. The invading granitic magma has intruded into rocks of the Warrawoona and Mosquito Creek Systems enriching them with many quartz and porphyry veins and pegmatites which remain as ore bodies. These lodes often contain many non-auriferous minerals such as cassiterite (tin), tantalite, beryl, felspar and mica.

In the early days of gold prospecting in the north, alluvial mining was common and fields were soon exhausted. The Kimberley field for instance had about a ten-year life, and only one shaft mine of any significance, the Ruby Queen at Hall's Creek, was sunk. Much gold, claimed as alluvial, was in fact eluvial gold found on or near the original lode. Mining of surface alluvial gold was usually followed by shaft mining, but none of

[5]Western Australian Government Mineral and Chemical Laboratories, *The Mineral Resources of Western Australia*, p. 3.

the northern goldfields has developed on any scale the extensive deep mining as on the eastern goldfields. The Comet at Marble Bar and the Blue Spec at Middle Creek were perhaps prominent exceptions.

Today the goldfields of Northwestern Australia produce less than one per cent of Western Australia's output; the entire area, having been principally subject to alluvial or eluvial mining, has enjoyed only a passing importance as a producer. Of the northern goldfields, the Pilbara makes the largest contribution, producing mines being the Prince Charlie at Bamboo Creek about 40 miles north-east of Marble Bar, and the Barton at Middle Creek near Nullagine. The only other producers of any note are the Horseshoe Lights mines on the Peak Hill field. In other northern fields output is low and sporadic.

6. IRON[6]

Iron ore bodies are found within the confines of the Precambrian shield. They are mostly associated with the banded ironstone formations or jaspilites which are considered to result from the chemical precipitation of colloidal silica and iron compounds in rocks of sedimentary origin.[7] Generally speaking jaspilites are composed of alternating layers of silica or chert, and iron oxides interbedded with highly metamorphosed sedimentary and volcanic rocks of Archaean age. At the surface of the iron-bearing outcrops iron oxides are usually in the form of hematite and, to a lesser extent, magnetite and limonite. Hematite in both high and low-grade ore bodies is the predominant iron ore mineral and, when pure, yields seventy per cent iron.

Iron ore occurs in four parts of the Precambrian shield: The Hamersley plateau, and the Pilbara, Kimberley and Yilgarn blocks.

The Hamersley iron field contains more than 95 per cent of the known iron ore reserves of the state, and its resources rival those of India, Brazil and the U.S.S.R. Inferred reserves were estimated in 1964 to be about 14,000 million tons of ore of grade higher than 50 per cent iron, and about 8,000 million tons of this is ore of direct shipping grade. The iron ores are associated with three banded iron formations, of a total thickness of nearly 4,000 feet, which form part of a series of Proterozoic sediments and lavas. These sediments extend over about 25,000 square miles. The thick, resistant banded iron formations form the Hamersley and Ophthalmia ranges.

The formation of most economic importance is the Brockman iron formation, which contains most of the iron deposits as well as the Wittenoom Gorge asbestos deposits. The Brockman iron formation is more than 2,000 feet thick and, like the other formations in the series, is remarkably uniform in thickness and lithology. It consists of jaspilite alternating

[6]Much of the information in this section is taken directly from, J. McAndrew (ed.), *Geology of Australian Ore Deposits.*
[7]R. R. Connolly, *Iron Ores in Western Australia,* p. 16.

with bands of shale, chert and carbonate. In the unaltered formation iron is present as magnetite, forming from 20 to 35 per cent of the jaspilite, which contains about 50 per cent silica. The iron ore occurs in the jaspilite and in detrital deposits as a result of selective leaching of silica and supergene enrichment of the jaspilite through the action of meteoric and ground waters. Within the jaspilite the product has been a hematite-goethite ore containing more than 60 per cent iron, and less than 4 per cent silica.

Enrichment of the jaspilite has occurred in synclinal troughs near the base of the Brockman iron formation. The largest and richest deposits of hematite ore are in the areas of regional folding, in the south-west and centre of the Hamersley Ranges near Mt. Brockman and Mt. Turner, and in the east in the Weeli Wolli Spring area, and along the south flank of the Ophthalmia Range. The Mt. Brockman area has the highest concentration of ore bodies found so far in the limbs of the Mt. Brockman Syncline. Inferred reserves in this area amount to about 2,000 million tons of ore grading from 58 to 63 per cent iron. The largest high-grade ore deposit in the region is at Mt. Tom Price near Mt. Turner, where the ore body is about four miles long, up to 4,000 feet wide, and up to 400 feet thick. Proved reserves amount to more than 200 million tons of hematite grading about 64 per cent iron with phosphorous averaging 0.05 per cent, and inferred reserves amount to about 300 million tons.

The Weeli Wolli Spring area has large deposits of hematite, with inferred reserves amounting to more than 2,000 million tons. The deposits along the south flank of the Ophthalmia Range are large and of grade between 60 and 63 per cent iron. The nearby Mt. Whaleback deposit is among the largest high-grade hematite deposits in the state, some of the ore grading as high as 68 per cent iron. Many hematite deposits occur in the area between Weeli Wolli Spring and Mt. Whaleback.

Outside these areas the main occurrences of hematite ore are in the northern part of the Hamersley Ranges, where there has been less folding and the deposits tend to be smaller than in the south and east. A group of small high-grade deposits has been found near Hamersley Station, and other deposits occur at Mt. Pyrton, Mt. Lockyer and Mt. Farquhar. At Roy Hill and in the Chichester Range west of Roy Hill some rich deposits occur in the Marra Mamba iron formation, one of the sedimentary units underlying the Brockman iron formation. In all, more than 100 hematite ore zones are known in the Hamersley iron field, most of them with ore of grade exceeding 60 per cent iron. Features of the Hamersley hematite deposits favouring development of the region as a major source of iron ore are the consistent type and grade of ore over the whole field, and the relative ease with which the deposits can be quarried.

In addition to the ore which occurs within the jaspilite, there are considerable reserves occurring in detrital deposits derived from the banded iron formations. Hematite conglomerate ore occurs as scree on the lower slopes of jaspilite hills, associated with high-grade hematite ore bodies.

At Mt. Tom Price the thickness of these deposits reaches 80 feet. The ore consists of angular fragments of hematite in a matrix which is generally limonitic. The average grade of the hematitic conglomerate is about 60 per cent iron, and most of it would be mined in the course of mining the hematite ore bodies.

Another ore type which occurs in vast deposits all along the valleys of the ancient streams which drain the Hamersley and Ophthalmia ranges is a pisolitic limonite. This is an unusual type of sedimentary ore which appears to have been derived from the jaspilite formations. The ore is mainly limonite and goethite, with minor amounts of hematite. It contains between 50 and 60 per cent iron, with a low content of phosphorous, sulphur and aluminium, and makes excellent pellets with an iron content of about 64 per cent. The largest deposits occur along the Robe River, Duck Creek, the Beasley River, and the headwaters of the eastern Fortescue River.

The deposits along the lower course of the Robe River, between Deepdale and Warramboo, are of the greatest economic significance. These are the largest deposits, and contain the higher-grade ore. The western-most deposits are only about 25 miles from the coast. Proven reserves amount to more than 100 million tons, and the ore of the richest deposits contains between 52 and 60 per cent iron. Deposits occur all along the Robe River covering about 30 square miles in area, and averaging 80 feet in depth. The larger individual deposits are up to six miles long and two or three miles wide.

The deposits in the valley of Duck Creek and its tributary Boolgeeda Creek contain estimated reserves of grade exceeding 50 per cent iron amounting to about 800 million tons. The ore occurs in thinner layers and is of lower grade than that of the Robe deposits. The Beasley River has extensive pisolite deposits for about 15 miles along its valley. The ore is usually between 30 and 50 feet thick and contains between 53 and 57 per cent iron. Inferred reserves amount to 250 million tons. Some quite extensive deposits occur along Yandicoogina and Weeli Wolli creeks, but the remoteness of this area makes these deposits of little economic significance.

In the Pilbara area, iron ore is associated with Archaean jaspilites which generally occur as steeply dipping lenses in strongly folded, faulted and metamorphosed volcanics and sediments and are less thick and laterally extensive than the Proterozoic jaspilites of the Hamersley region. The jaspilite crops out in an arc of hills around the best known deposit at Mt. Goldsworthy. This deposit consists of five ore bodies in a thick banded iron formation of jaspilite, chert, meta-sediments and mudstones. The main ore body at Mt. Goldsworthy is a lenticular, steeply dipping lode of dense massive hematite with an average iron content of more than 65 per cent. It is 2,200 feet long and up to 400 feet thick. Proven reserves are about 30 million tons. The associated ore bodies contain about the same amount of lower-grade hematite-goethite ore which has resulted from supergene enrichment of the iron formation close to an old land surface. Other deposits of hematite and goethite ore occur at Ord Range, Strelley Gorge, and Yarrie. Total reserves of hematite are estimated to be about 200 million tons of ore with more than 55 per cent iron content. Detrital deposits occur in association with the jaspilites. Limonite ore of similar type and origin to that of the Hamersley field occurs as fillings in former stream systems which drained the jaspilites.

In the third area, the iron ores of the Kimberley block occur in Proterozoic banded iron formations which are of clastic origin and are quite different from the jaspilites of chemical origin of the Hamersley region. The Yampi Sound deposits are the most important in the Kimberley area, but there are other deposits, the largest being at Pompey's Pillar and Bandicoot Range. The Yampi sedimentary beds consist of quartzites, sandstones, conglomerates and schists, nearly all of which contain hematite in varying quantities.

The ore deposit at Cockatoo Island has produced all the ore mined in the region to 1964, amounting to 10 million tons. The high-grade zone of the deposit consists of nearly pure hematite, and the lower-grade zone of hematitic sandstone and schists mingled with hematite. The ore is friable below the surface and needs sintering before reduction. Reserves amount to 21 million tons up to 40 feet below sea level, and the average grade is 64 per cent iron. The ore outcrops in a sea cliff for a distance of 7,000 feet, and is well placed for mining and shipping.

The Koolan Island ore bodies occur in a formation which consists of hematite sandstone, hematite conglomerate and hematite, and much of the ore is porous and friable. The largest of the five ore bodies is 7,000 feet long and 100 feet thick, and has an average iron content of 66 per cent. Reserves up to 40 feet below sea level amount to 45 million tons of hematite, with five million tons of hematite conglomerate containing about 58 per cent iron. A deep water channel on the south side of the island allows easy access for large vessels. Minor deposits in the Yampi area have been found on Irvine and two other islands.

The Pompey's Pillar deposit consists of hematite and hematitic sandstone interbedded with other sandstone and shale, forming the capping on a high range for about eight miles. The sandstone bed is about 30 feet thick and the grade averages between 40 and 50 per cent iron, with about 10 million tons of hematite of higher grade.

The fourth area, the Yilgarn block, is an Archaean shield area consisting mainly of granite and gneiss with extensive remnant belts of meta-sediments including banded iron formations. At Mt. Gould, about 100 miles north-west of Meekatharra, are reserves of iron ore of high quality, estimated to amount to approximately 15 million tons. Here the ore bodies occur as well defined lenses of almost pure micaceous hematite in banded ferruginous jaspilites.

7. Manganese[8]

Manganese occurs mainly in two distinct regions of Northwestern Australia : in the Peak Hill goldfield and in the Pilbara. The Pilbara is the main source of high-grade metallurgical ore in Australia, with an average annual production of about 30,000 tons in the five years to 1964, though this is now rising rapidly.

The Pilbara deposits are spread over a large area along the eastern edge of the Pilbara block. All the deposits are on, or in, sediments of the Proterozoic Nullagine Series, or on Tertiary rocks in areas of outcrop of Nullagine sediments.

The ore bodies, which all crop out, occur in three forms : sheets, mounds and cavity fillings. Sheets are the most common form. These deposits have a large surface area, sometimes covering several acres, and a depth which may be less than 10 feet, and is rarely more than 50 feet. Mound-shaped deposits are sometimes remnants of sheets, and are sometimes formed by surface enrichments at the outcrop of steeply dipping manganiferous sediments. Some small deposits have formed by direct deposition from surface water at changes of slope of the land surface. Cavity filling deposits have a small surface, but are high-grade and over 50 feet deep. These occur where manganese has been deposited from solution in cavities formed in Carawine dolomite.

Most of the Pilbara deposits have not been sampled in sufficient detail for an accurate grade to be determined. The grade varies with the type of manganese minerals as well as their proportion. The deposits range in size from 50 tons to many thousands of tons, but most of the high-grade deposits are in the 500 to 5,000 tons range.

The principal deposits are Ripon Hills, Mt. Sydney, Woodie Woodie, Skull Springs, Bee Hill, Mt. Cooke-Davis River, Ant Hill-Mt. Cooke, Balfour Downs and Mt. Nicholas. The deposits at Woodie Woodie and Mt. Sydney are high-grade ore bodies forming cavity fillings in dolomite, extending to more than 100 feet depth. Woodie Woodie has been mined continuously since 1954, produces most of the region's output of ore, and still has reserves of more than 100,000 tons. Mt. Sydney has been mined intermittently, and several thousand tons of high-grade ore remain.

The Ripon Hills and Balfour Downs deposits are large sheet deposits associated with manganiferous shales with a high iron content. It is possible to upgrade these ores by magnetic separation after reduction roasting, but the recovery of manganese and the grade of concentrate achieved in tests have not been entirely satisfactory.

At Skull Springs, Bee Hill and Mt. Cooke-Davis River the ore occurs as sheets or mounds on chert breccia. Skull Springs has produced more than 30,000 tons of moderately high-grade ore, and several thousand tons remain.

[8]For further detail, see L. E. de la Hunty, 'Manganese Deposits of Western Australia'.

The Bee Hill deposits often contain hematite impurities. One deposit has an estimated 10,000 tons of ore. Ten miles north of Mt. Cooke there is a group of deposits in which the ore is on the surface and edges of a dissected plateau and in stream beds. The Ant Hill deposit, formed by supergene enrichment of manganiferous shale, has been mined, and contains several thousand tons of moderately high grade ore.

In the Peak Hill goldfield, the other large area of manganese production, the deposits occur in the south near the headwaters of the Gascoyne and Murchison rivers. The northern part of the manganese area consists of the flat-lying Proterozoic Nullagine Series, containing manganiferous sediments. Archaean granite and gneiss and steeply dipping Archaean meta-sediments form the southern and central part. Sub-horizontal manganese deposits occur along former drainage channels on a sloping tertiary land surface.

Of the total of 324,630 tons of manganese ore produced in the Peak Hill field up to the end of 1964, more than 300,000 tons have come from Horseshoe. Only two deposits at Horseshoe have been worked. The southern deposit is 2,700 feet long, up to 1,400 feet wide but averaging probably less than 400 feet, and in places more than 50 feet deep. The ore is usually massive and heavy, and occurs in association with pisolitic ore, limonite and clay. Some of the ore is more than 50 per cent manganese, but about 40 per cent is probably about 40 per cent manganese, a further 40 per cent low grade ore, and the rest gangue. This deposit has produced most of the ore from Horseshoe and reserves have been depleted. The northern deposit, a mile from the southern deposit, is similar to it in disposition, but smaller in extent. At the eastern end of the deposit the ore has a high iron content, but probably most of the ore contains more than 40 per cent manganese.

Other deposits of ore in this area occur at Mt. Fraser and Peak Hill. The Mt. Fraser deposit, which forms the cap on a mesa, contains about 20,000 tons of medium to high-grade ore. Peak Hill has produced battery-grade ore and chemical ore from a small deposit. At Murphy's Well a deposit in the form of a ferruginous, manganiferous capping on weathered schistose Archaean rocks is estimated to contain about 2,800 tons of ore above 40 per cent manganese.

Deposits which lie outside the Peak Hill and Pilbara manganese provinces are those at Nimingarra, Yarrie, Roy Hill, Warrie, Marillana and Mulga Downs stations in the Pilbara and West Pilbara goldfields; Mt. Florrie in the Ashburton goldfield; and Ilgararrie Station and Nabberu in the Peak Hill goldfield.

8. Mineral Oil

Traces of oil and gas have been found in most of the sedimentary basins of Northwestern Australia, indicating that conditions for the formation of petroleum have existed in the past and structures favouring the accumulation of oil and gas are known to occur in all the basins. As yet none of them has been thoroughly explored for petroleum, although the Carnarvon basin, because of its high oil potential and its relative accessibility, has attracted more exploratory activity than any other.

Oil has been produced at Rough Range, oil and gas at Barrow Island, and gas at Cape Range. At Rough Range, which is an anticlinal structure, oil flowed from a depth of 3,605 feet from the Birdrong Sandstone Formation. Barrow Island is on the crest of a large surface anticlinal structure developed in tertiary limestones and its geological structure is complex. Oil and gas have flowed from two levels, Jurassic sediments at more than 6,000 feet and the Windalia sands at little more than 2,000 feet. The latter formation is 90-100 feet thick, laterally extensive and has good porosity but its permeability is poor.

The Fitzroy Basin has about 30,000 feet of sediments. Permian rocks folded into long anticlines form vast potential oil reservoirs and lower Carboniferous dolomitic sandstones are potential sources and reservoir rocks. All the Ordovician rocks which occur are potential sources, and Devonian sandy limestones are potential reservoirs. The extent and variety of the sediments in the Fitzroy basin have attracted most of the oil search activity outside the Carnarvon basin. Indications of oil and gas have been found in wells drilled in the west of the basin at Meda near Derby and in the Goldwyer No. 1 well near Broome, at Nerrima Dome and Frome Rocks, and at Poole Range and Price's Creek in the east.

The Bonaparte basin underlies the northern part of the Gulf basin physiographic division and extends offshore. The basin contains about 15,000 feet of Paleozoic sediments, in which there has been little folding but much faulting which could have produced structures forming traps for oil. The area and geology of the offshore extension is unknown. By 1964 two wells had been drilled near Wyndham. One produced from Lower Carboniferous beds the first flow of hydrocarbons in this area, a gas flow of 1.15 million cubic feet per day.

The Ord basin, south of the Bonaparte Gulf basin, covers about 3,000 square miles and contains about 7,000 feet of Cambrian volcanics and marine sediments. Bitumen was found in two areas in the basin in 1920, and one dry hole was drilled in 1924. A geological survey in the 1950's was not encouraging and there has been no further serious prospecting.

The geology of the Canning basin south of the Fitzroy basin is little known because of its vast extent and desert surface. It contains Paleozoic and Mesozoic sediments generally about 6,000 feet thick, although in its south-east part deeper sediments occur. Drilling began in 1965 at the Kidson site in the south, and at the Sahara location in the south-east.

South-east of the Canning basin lies the Amadeus basin extending eastwards into the Northern Territory where it contains the Mereenie gas field. Late in 1965, drilling in the Western Australian portion was commenced at Point Moody. South of the Canning basin is the Officer basin covering about 75,000 square miles, of which about half lies in Northwestern Australia.

It generally contains about 6,500 feet of sediments, and stratigraphic drilling began at Browne Range in 1965.

9. SILVER-LEAD ORE

Silver is usually produced as a by-product in the mining of gold, copper or lead. Because of the large production of gold in Western Australia, most silver has in the past been obtained from gold recovery processes, the native gold of the state averaging about 10 per cent silver. As gold mining no longer plays an important role in the north, silver produced from this source is now negligible. Low market prices for lead experienced by Western Australian producers after 1957 caused a severe decline in production. In 1963 no lead ore was mined in the state.

In 1964 the lead-zinc ore bodies at Narlarla in the Napier Range in the West Kimberley were mined after a lapse of 12 years, and 8,000 tons of ore were produced. High lead-zinc prices and the imperial smelting process for lead-zinc ores made the exploitation of these deposits economic.

The Narlarla deposit is a massive, finely crystalline lead-zinc sulphide deposit overlain by an irregular mass of secondary ore. The latter is low in lead content, containing up to 32 per cent lead, with up to 32 per cent zinc and about 4 fine ounces of silver per ton. The sulphide ore contains between 27 per cent and 68 per cent lead, and zinc.

Indicated reserves remaining at the end of 1964 were about 3,500 tons, but the deposit has not been fully explored. The ore bodies occur in Upper Devonian limestone, which overlies Precambrian gneiss, schist and granite. This is the only known lode of its kind in the state, and the youngest dated ore body.

Lead ores are known in the East Kimberley, but have not been mined.

The most important lead-producing centre on the Pilbara field was Braeside in the Gregory Ranges where galena (lead sulphide) occurs in rocks of Proterozoic age. These deposits, in the form of long solid lenses of galena up to 5 feet in width, carry only 1 to 4 ozs. of silver per ton. Samples from Cooglegong and Tambourah have shown 60 and 75 ozs. of silver respectively. Similar occurrences at Whim Creek and Andover on the West Pilbara goldfield have yielded a small tonnage of lead, that from the former locality being rich in silver.

Outcrops of lead are common on the Ashburton goldfield where the Uaroo Mine had, until the war, produced concentrates averaging 20 ozs. silver and 50 per cent of lead. The Kooline field was in production until 1959. Working of other localities (Mt. de Courcey, Mt. Edith, Mt. Stuart, Mt. Alexander) has been prevented by high operating and transportation costs. Bangemall is the main centre for lead on the Gascoyne goldfield.

10. TANTALITE

Tantalite and other genetically related minerals, principally columbite,

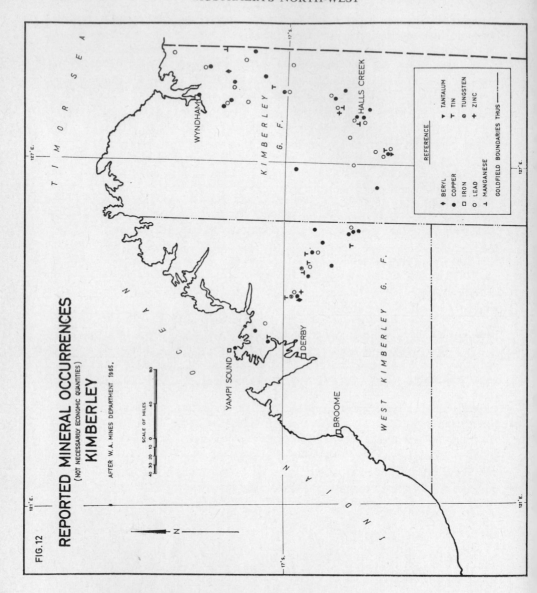

FIG. 12

REPORTED MINERAL OCCURRENCES
(NOT NECESSARILY ECONOMIC QUANTITIES)
KIMBERLEY

AFTER W.A. MINES DEPARTMENT 1965.

provide the source of the metal tantalum. These minerals occur in association with cassiterite, beryl and others within pegmatites of Archaeozoic age. As previously mentioned, such pegmatites are found intruding into rocks of the Warrawoona and Mosquito Creek systems and are common over a wide area of the Pilbara block. In the past the main tantalum ore-producing centres have been Wodgina, Strelley, Tabba Tabba and Pilgangoora, all of which are located on the western edge of the Pilbara goldfield. Wodgina, the most important of these, is located some 60 miles south of Port Hedland, the port of export.

Mining at Wodgina is carried out in the highly folded and steeply dipping rocks of the Warrawoona System. Pegmatite dykes cutting these rocks contain manganotantalite which is intergrown with the mineral albite. Occurrences of the former may range in size from small specimens to pieces weighing 50 or more pounds. The main source of supply has been alluvial deposits, but since working of these began as early as 1905, they have now been worked out. Lode-mining yields about three pounds of tantalite ores per ton and grades are, on the whole, high (67-68 per cent tantalum oxide).

Prior to the World War, the tantalite deposits of the Pilbara goldfield (and those of Greenbushes in the South-West) supplied approximately 90 per cent of the world's demand for high-grade ore. Because tantalum-bearing minerals were placed on the list of strategic minerals during the war, the deposits of the Pilbara assumed increasing importance as a source of supply of this rare metal. During this time the production and handling of tantalum concentrates was taken over by the Commonwealth Department of Supply and Shipping, when concentrates were shipped to America. Before the government took charge of wartime production, Tantalite Ltd., an Adelaide company, was responsible for the working of leases at Wodgina, Strelley and Tabba Tabba, while those at Pilgangoora were held for speculative purposes and worked intermittently by private owners. However, the industry is now very quiet, and production of tantalite in the region is at present virtually negligible.

11. Tin

Tin is obtained from the mineral cassiterite. It is found in three types of deposit: in albite pegmatite veins frequently in association with tantalum (lode tin), in detrital or residual deposits close to the outcrop of the above (eluvial tin), and in true alluvial deposits (stream tin) or deep leads.

The occurrence of cassiterite is restricted to the Precambrian rocks of Archaeozoic age and in all cases is found in close association with granites. In view of the association between tin and tantalum, the tantalum producing district of the Pilbara goldfield has also become the main tin producing area of Northwestern Australia. At Moolyella near Marble Bar, cassiterite is found in a series of pegmatite veins, but production in the past has mainly been from 'picked over' eluvial ore or stream tin from the small creeks in the area. Cassiterite is found at Wodgina in a number of pegmatite

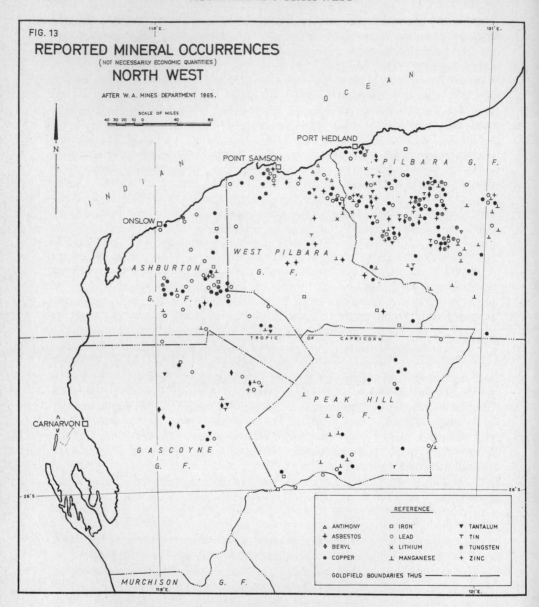

FIG. 13

REPORTED MINERAL OCCURRENCES
(NOT NECESSARILY ECONOMIC QUANTITIES)
NORTH WEST

AFTER W. A. MINES DEPARTMENT 1965.

SCALE OF MILES

REFERENCE

△ ANTIMONY □ IRON ▼ TANTALUM
✦ ASBESTOS ○ LEAD ⊤ TIN
◆ BERYL ✕ LITHIUM ⊛ TUNGSTEN
● COPPER ⊥ MANGANESE ✚ ZINC

GOLDFIELD BOUNDARIES THUS ———·——

veins closely asociated with tantalite, tourmaline and albite. These veins are offshoots from the main mass of granite which covers a large area of the district. At times they have been sufficiently rich in cassiterite to constitute lodes. There is more lode tin than stream tin in the area.

Present development is confined to the Pilbara where Hillside, Cooglegong and Moolyella are the main centres. The high price of tin in the past two years has given a great stimulus to production. Water has always been a problem in the Pilbara, and activities are seriously interrupted by drought conditions. The Pilbara produces approximately 90 per cent of Western Australia's tin, while Greenbushes, in the South-West Division of the state produces the remainder. The mining of cassiterite in the Pilbara is handled mainly by Kathleen Investments Ltd.

12. Miscellaneous Minerals

Although the minerals mentioned above represent those of economic importance to Western Australia in terms of value of production, this is by no means an exhaustive survey of all the minerals that have been produced in the north or of those which await possible future development. A brief summary of this latter group of minerals will be given below to complete the discussion on the mineral resources of Northwestern Australia.

ABRASIVES

On the 1952 mineral deposits map of the Department of National Development, the Richenda River area of the West Kimberley is cited as a centre for the mining of emery.[9] An extremely dark-grey rock yielding abrasive material of highest quality was quarried from this locality near the Napier Range during the World War. Thirteen tons of this emery rock were obtained to 1944 to replace supplies normally obtained from Greece, but which were then unavailable. Despite the high grade of the abrasive material obtained from the Richenda River, the area is rather inaccessible, and the high cost of transport at present militates against the development of these deposits.

ANTIMONY

Antimony production has, in the past, been confined to the Pilbara and West Pilbara goldfields. It was first discovered in the North-West at Mallina in the West Pilbara goldfield. In an area north-east of Roebourne, antimony was obtained from stibnite and stibiconite found associated in bunches with gold, in quartz veins. Mallina, Peewah, Sherlock Crossing and Mt. Negri were the only exporters for the few years prior to the war. In the Pilbara area this metal was obtained from auriferous stibnite from the Blue Spec Mine at Middle Creek.

[9]Commonwealth Department of National Development. *Mineral Industry*.

RED OCHRE

Deposits of red ochre, which occurs as an alteration product of banded ironstone formation in the Opthalmia Range, were worked during the World War. The material is of excellent quality as a substitute for spanish red pigment.

BAUXITE

In 1965 extensive deposits of bauxite were discovered in the North Kimberley region south of Admiralty Gulf. These deposits occur as remnant cappings on Precambrian basalts. Reserves have not been estimated but preliminary investigations suggest that the total could be substantial.

BISMUTH

Bismuth carbonates are found at Yinnietharra on the Gascoyne goldfield. Here they occur as small thin irregular veins in the quartz of a large pegmatite dyke. The Gascoyne is the only area which has produced bismuth in Western Australia.

CHROMITE

The largest deposit of chromite in Australia occurs at Coobina near the eastern end of the Opthalmia Range. The chromite occurs as thick veins in a serpentine rock of the Warrawoona System.

Rare metals, associated with granite intrusives, are of frequent occurrence between the North-West coast, and Albany and Ravensthorpe in the south. Commercial quantities of lithium, beryllium, yttrium, cerium, thorium, vanadium and tantalum are known to occur in the north, while deposits of uranium and radium are available in small quantities.

LITHIUM

There are a number of lithium-bearing minerals, the commonest of which is lepidolite (lithia mica). Lepidolite is characteristic of granite pegmatite veins and occurs throughout the metalliferous area of the Pilbara block. In recent years this mineral has not been listed amongst those produced on the Pilbara goldfield, but it is known to occur in varying quantities at Wodgina, Melville, Mt. Francisco, Tabba Tabba and Tambourah. Larger deposits of lepidolite occur at Londonderry on the Coolgardie goldfield. Lepidolite is used as a source of lithium compounds.

BERYLLIUM

See under Beryl.

VANADIUM

Minerals containing vanadium have been found in varying quantities at Braeside in the Pilbara goldfield. They are contained in the lodes of lead and copper found in this area.

YTTRIUM METALS

Deposits of minerals containing yttrium are known in Western Australia although, with the exception of a ton of gadolinite which was exported in 1920, they have not been worked solely for this metal. A few hundredweight of yttrotantalite, tanteuxenite and tantopolycrase (sources of the metal yttrium) have been collected for experimental purposes, and all have contained a small quantity of uranium. If needed, further supplies are obtainable from the Pilbara district, especially from Cooglegong, Abydos, Eley, Mt. Francisco and Tambourah.

CERIUM METALS AND THORIUM (also see under Uranium and Radium)

As with yttrium metals, the collection of ores containing cerium metals and thorium – the main source being the mineral monazite – has been for experimental purposes. Monazite has been recorded from the Pilbara area at Cooglegong, Eley's, Moolyella and Mt. Francisco.

TANTALUM

See Tantalite.

TUNGSTEN

The principal ore of tungsten, scheelite (calcium tungstate) is not common on the northern goldfields. Prior to the war it had been marketed from Friendly Creek in the Pilbara, but not in any quantity. The occurrence of wolfram (tungstate of iron and manganese) is known at Wodgina although this is at present a non-productive locality. Before 1924 two tons of concentrates containing ferberite (tungstate of iron) were mined from small quartz veins at Clara Hill in the Kimberley.

NIOBIUM

The metal niobium is obtained in varying quantities from those minerals mined for their tantalum content. As both columbite and tantalite are niobates of iron and manganese (they grade almost insensibly from normal columbite, the nearly pure niobate, to normal tantalite, the nearly pure tantalite) they provide the source of niobium. As mentioned previously, these minerals have been obtained from the Pilbara where Wodgina is the main producing centre.

URANIUM AND RADIUM

The main source minerals of uranium and radium, pitchblende and carnotite, are unknown in Western Australia. However, the pegmatites at Wodgina contain four minerals rich in uranium, radium and thorium. These are maitlandite, nicolayite, pilbarite and hydrothorite.

Apart from the minerals mentioned above, yttrotantalite, tanteuxenite and tantopolycrase from Cooglegong, carry respectively two, three and seven per cent of uranium oxide with corresponding amounts of radium.

MICA

Mica (muscovite) is found in 'books' associated with felspars and quartz in the pegmatites of the plateau. Such 'books' are only of sporadic occurrence, a feature which makes mining specifically for this mineral, difficult. Quantities of muscovite mica occur at several localities in the north of the state, but Yinnietharra is the only centre at which considerable production has occurred. Shortages of high-class strategic mica during the war caused the Yinnietharra deposits to be worked. As mica then constituted a strategic mineral, production was handled by the Commonwealth Department of Supply and Shipping.

SALT

Salt is the raw material for chlorine, sodium carbonate and caustic soda, which are being used in increasing amounts in the chemical industry.

The coast of Northwestern Australia is favourably placed to produce solar salt and export it to Japan. The coast between Port Gregory and Broome has a low average annual rainfall and a high average annual rate of evaporation, which are ideal climatic conditions for the production of solar salt. At Useless Loop near Shark Bay, the Shark Bay Salt Company is bringing a solar salt plant into production for export to Japan, and other companies are investigating prospects for salt extraction at Port Hedland, King Bay, Lake McLeod, Carnarvon and Broome.

13. Summary and Conclusions

The mineral resources of Northwestern Australia are exceedingly varied. Minerals of igneous and metamorphic origin are found over wide areas of the plateau where the Precambrian shield is the source of many valuable metallic and non-metallic minerals. Due to the mode of occurrence peculiar to certain mineral types, there is a close association between groups of minerals and particular rock formations.

Of the seven goldfield divisions which have been arbitrarily super-imposed upon the shield north of the twenty-sixth parallel (West and East Kimberley, Pilbara, West Pilbara, Ashburton, Gascoyne and Peak Hill) each have rock formations representative of the above but in one or two cases the outcrops of certain minerals are particularly noticeable within a restricted area. For instance, blue asbestos is confined to the Nullagine sediments of the West Pilbara goldfield, while those minerals associated with the younger granites are found in abundance on the Pilbara goldfield. This latter is perhaps the most highly metalliferous area in the north. Although the area of the shield encompassed by these seven goldfields has been well explored and its mineral resources annotated, prospecting has mainly been confined to that region along the western edge of the shield drained by the major northern rivers. To the east, much of the shield is as yet unexplored and its potential unknown. Likewise, knowledge of the mineral resources of the sedimentary basins in Northwestern Australia is limited. They supply valuable artesian water and may yet prove to be reservoirs of mineral oil. To date, despite an active oil prospecting programme over the last 14 years, oil in commercial quantities has not been located in either the Canning-Fitzroy or the Carnarvon basins, except at Barrow Island (see Chapter 4).

The following is a summary of the more important minerals of the plateau in Northwestern Australia and the rock formations in which they are found:

ROCK TYPES	MINERALS
Proterozoic	
Basic rocks (basic lava flows,etc.)	Lead, vanadium, some silver-lead ore.
Nullagine sediments	Blue asbestos, iron
Archaeozoic	
Granites (pegmatite dykes and quartz veins)	Gold, tin, tantalum, niobium, beryllium, lithium, mica, felspar, radio-active minerals, copper.
Mosquito Creek System (meta-sediments)	Copper.
Warrawoona Series (meta-sediments and meta-basic rocks)	Gold and sulphide lodes, copper, iron (Mt. Goldsworthy), chrysotile asbestos, chromite.

Thus, with the exception of water, exploitation of the mineral resources of the north has virtually been confined to the Precambrian shield. The northern mineral fields were at first exploited for their gold, but with the exhaustion of this metal, emphasis has been placed on the mining and quarrying of the utility minerals, such as iron, asbestos, and manganese.

BIBLIOGRAPHY

BROKEN HILL PROPRIETARY COMPANY LIMITED. *Broken Hill Proprietary Company Limited Review*, vol. XXVIII, no. 4. 1951.

CARROLL, DOROTHY. *Census of Western Australian Minerals.* Western Australia Department of Mines Bulletin, no. 1. Perth, 1945.

COMMONWEALTH DEPARTMENT OF NATIONAL DEVELOPMENT. Atlas of Australian Resources, 1st series, with commentaries. *Mineral Industry,* 1959. Canberra.

CONNOLLY, R. R. *Iron Ores in Western Australia.* Western Australia Geological Survey. Mineral Resources of Western Australia Bulletin no. 7. 1959.

CROWLEY, F. K. *Australia's Western Third.* London, 1960.

DE LA HUNTY, L. E. 'Manganese Deposits of Western Australia', in McAndrew, J. (ed.). *Geology of Australian Ore Deposits,* 2nd edition.

ELLIS, H. A. *Some Economic Aspects of the Principal Tantalum-bearing Deposits of the Pilbara Goldfield, North-West Division.* Western Australia Geological Survey. Mineral Resources of Western Australia Bulletin no. 104. 1950.

FOXALL, J. S. *The Blue Asbestos Deposits of the Hamersley Ranges and their Economic Importance.* Western Australia Geological Survey. Mineral Resources of Western Australia Bulletin no. 104. 1950.

GIBB-MAITLAND, A. and MONTGOMERY, A. *The Geology and Mineral Industry of Western Australia.* Western Australia Geological Survey. Mineral Resources of Western Australia Bulletin no. 89. 1924.

GUPPY, D. J., LINDNER, A. W., RATTIGAN, J. H. and CASEY, J. N. *The Geology of the Fitzroy Basin, Western Australia.* Bureau of Mineral Resources Bulletin no. 36. 1958.

HARMS, J. E. and MORGAN, B. D. 'Pisolitic Limonite Deposits in North Western Australia.' Proceedings of the Australian Institute of Mining and Metallurgy.

HENDERSON, S. D., CONDON, M.A. and BASTIAN, L. V. *Stratigraphic Drilling, Canning Basin, Western Australia.* Bureau of Mineral Resources Bulletin no. 60. 1963.

LOW, G. H. *Copper Deposits of Western Australia.* Western Australia Geological Survey. Mineral Resources of Western Australia Bulletin no. 8. 1963.

MILES, K. R. *The Blue Asbestos-bearing Banded Iron Formations of the Hamersley Ranges.* Western Australia Geological Survey. Mineral Resources of Western Australia Bulletin no. 100, part 1. 1942.

McANDREW, J. (ed.). *Geology of Australian Ore Deposits,* 2nd edition. Eighth Commonwealth Mining and Metallurgical Congress. Melbourne, 1965.

WcWHAE, J. R. H., PLAYFORD, P. E., LINDNER, A. W., GLENISTER, B. F. and BALME, B. E. 'The Stratigraphy of Western Australia.' *Journal of the Geological Society of Australia.* 1956.

PETROLEUM INFORMATION BUREAU. *Petroleum Search in Australia.* Melbourne, 1965.

PRIDER, R. T. 'Igneous Activity, Metamorphism and Ore Formation in Western Australia.' *Journal of the Royal Society of Western Australia,* vol. 31. 1944.

REID, I. W. 'The Geology of Cockatoo Island, Yampi Sound, Western Australia.' *The Australasian Institute of Mining and Metallurgy Proceedings.* Stillwell Anniversary vol. 188. 1958.

TRAVES, D. M. *The Geology of the Ord Victoria Region, Northern Australia.* Bureau of Mineral Resources Bulletin no. 27. 1955.

VEEVERS, J. J. and WELLS, A. T. *The Geology of the Canning Basin, Western Australia.* Bureau of Mineral Resources Bulletin no. 60. 1961.

WESTERN AUSTRALIA MINES DEPARTMENT. *Western Australia Mines Department Report.* 1959 to 1964 inclusive. Perth.

WESTERN AUSTRALIAN GOVERNMENT. *Official Year Book of Western Australia,* no. 4. Perth, 1964.

WESTERN AUSTRALIA GOVERNMENT MINERAL AND CHEMICAL LABORATORIES. *The Mineral Resources of Western Australia.* Perth, 1945.

APPENDIX 3

CLIMATE[1]

1. INTRODUCTION

Northwestern Australia lies within the tropical and sub-tropical zones of the Southern Hemisphere. In relation to the world wind belts and sources of preciptation, the region, with such a vast interior, suffers the fate of other western margin lands in similar latitudes. Much of its land surface experiences the rigours of an arid or semi-arid climate. This is, of course, to be expected in continental areas as far removed from the sea as the northern interior of Western Australia.

Its coastal lands have been spared the desiccation that has occurred in Africa and South America and, unlike the plantless sand deserts of those continents, it provides many hundreds of square miles of useful pastoral land. That this should be so is attributable to the occurrence of tropical cyclones, which, with some winter rains, enable the growth of a steppe vegetation.

In the extreme north of the state, the Kimberley region benefits from monsoonal rains which favour the growth of woodland and savannah grassland. However, the weak nature of the North-West Monsoon has so far precluded the widespread development of tropical agriculture in this area, and where agricultural rather than pastoral activities are contemplated, irrigation is a necessary supplement to natural precipitation.

Thus the most conspicuous aspects of the climatic pattern of Northwestern Australia are three in number : the monsoonal regime in the Kimberley, the tropical cyclone in the North-West Division, and the prevailing dryness over large tracts of the northern interior. For ease of exposition the following discussion of climatic data will be related to the following areas : the Kimberley – comprising the physiographic regions of the Kimberley block, Ord basin, Fitzroy valley and associated coastal plains; the North-West – comprising the western sections of both the Nullagine platform and the

[1]Grateful acknowledgements are made for advice and assistance given by the Regional Director of the Bureau of Meteorology, Perth, and his officers.

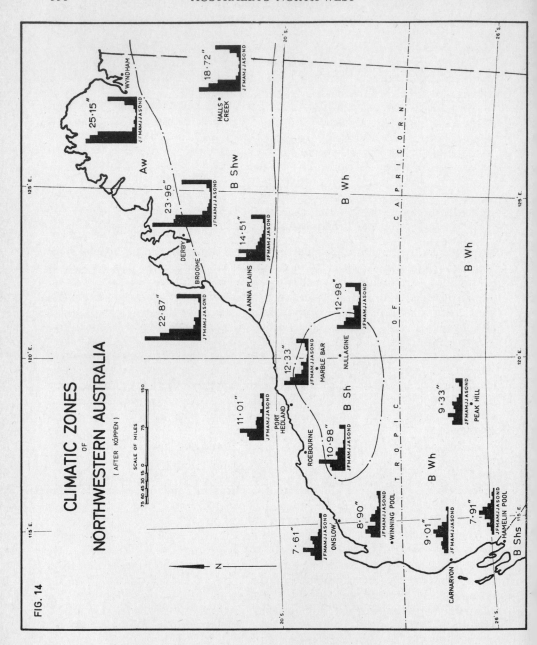

FIG. 14

CLIMATIC ZONES
OF
NORTHWESTERN AUSTRALIA
(AFTER KÖPPEN)

SCALE OF MILES
75 60 45 30 15 0   75   150

Yilgarn block, the Carnarvon basin and associated coastal plains, including the Eighty Mile Beach; the dry interior – comprising most of the Canning basin, the eastern Nullagine platform and north-eastern Yilgarn block.

Before proceeding to a detailed discussion of the climatic characteristics of these three regions, perhaps something more should be said generally about climate in Northwestern Australia as a whole.

Broadly, the overall warm to hot temperatures constitute a unifying rather than a distinguishing climatic element. The classification into climatic zones is thus determined principally by precipitation and the nature of its seasonal distribution. The region has no high mountain ranges inland which would affect the climatic classification. In the tropical cyclone area there is no feature to make it any different from other similar areas, and even in the Kimberley the monsoon climate has not the individual differences that one finds in similar climatic zones in Asia. Thus there is only the very simple division between a wet climate with a hot summer and a dry climate with a hot summer. Broadly speaking, the north of the region falls into the first category. In the winter although day temperatures may be in the eighties, the nights are quite cool and in the interior heavy frosts are not uncommon.

A further refinement of the simple division above is necessary to place Northwestern Australia into a world-wide climatic perspective. Köppen, using temperature, precipitation and vegetation as criteria, has distinguished between the megathermal – tropical rainy – climate of the north-western Kimberley, and the xerophilous – dry – climates of the remainder of the region (see figure 14 opposite). His climatic divisions give the following regions:

Aw   Tropical Savannah Climate with dry winter. This climatic region lies to the north and west of a line running between Broome, Derby and Wyndham – inclusive of these towns.

BShw   Tropical and Sub-tropical Steppe characterized by high temperatures and winter drought. This zone lies to the south of the Aw region and extends approximately to the 20th parallel.

BSh   Tropical and Sub-tropical Steppe. A pocket of this steppe occurs in Region BWh and corresponds to the Pilbara and Hamersley highlands.

Bwh   Tropical and Sub-tropical Desert. This climatic division extends southwards from the 20th parallel, around the highland steppe region and to the coast near Hamelin Pool – including the dry interior.

BShs   Sub-tropical Steppe having a summer dry period. This climatic type is found in the vicinity of Shark Bay.

Relating this classification to the three areas delineated above gives the following result :

Kimberley:
    a.   North and West Kimberley – tropical savannah.
    b.   South Kimberley – tropical steppe.

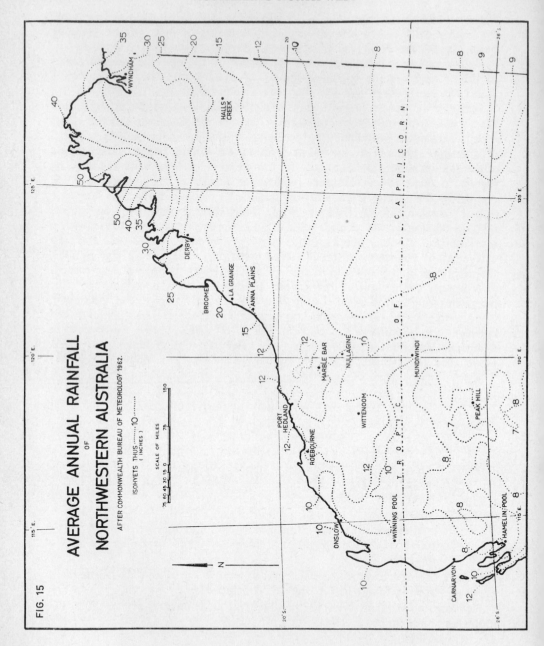

FIG. 15

AVERAGE ANNUAL RAINFALL
OF
NORTHWESTERN AUSTRALIA

AFTER COMMONWEALTH BUREAU OF METEOROLOGY 1962.

ISOHYETS THUS ......10......
(INCHES)

SCALE OF MILES

North-West:
 a. Pilbara and the Hamersley Ranges – tropical and sub-tropical steppe.
 b. Coastal (Port Hedland to Hamelin Pool) – tropical and sub-tropical desert and steppe.
 c. Shark Bay and Dirk Hartog Island – sub-tropical steppe.
Dry interior:
 a. North – tropical desert.
 b. South – sub-tropical desert.

It must be realised that a climatic survey on a global basis such as that of Köppen, is subject to inaccuracies on a detailed level, and thus allowances must be made for local anomalies within the region.

2. The Climate of The Kimberley

Rainfall

A study of both the rainfall statistics (Table 1) and the average annual rainfall map of the region (Figure 15) indicates an annual average rainfall of between 14 and 40 plus inches in the Kimberley area. There is a rapid decline from the north and west coastal areas in the vicinity of the Bonaparte Archipelago where rainfall may reach 50 inches,[2] and where more than 80 inches has been measured in a wet year, to the south and east where the annual average of Anna Plains is 14.51 inches and that of Hall's Creek, 18.72 inches. Average figures for Wyndham, Derby and Broome are 25.15, 23.96 and 22.87 inches respectively. Most recording stations have a rainfall lower than that of Perth (35.05). Discounting the plateau region which has a rainfall between 30 and 40 inches plus, those areas occupied by pastoral holdings have an average rainfall between 14 and 30 inches only.

The Kimberley has a marked seasonal distribution of rainfall, the maximum precipitation occurring in the 'high sun' months of December to March. In contrast to the south of the state the long dry season is experienced during the winter months. Opening rains may fall at any time during the months of October to December, and the close of the season may be just as variable.[3] The rainy summer period, or wet, is not of a continuous nature; rainfall comes in a series of short bursts, and may be interspersed with spells of fine sunny weather which quickly evaporates surplus moisture. However, when rain does fall, as much as 17 inches may be recorded in one day and the effect of such downpours is to cause the sudden flooding of water courses. The average monthly distribution of rainfall, as shown in Table 1, adequately illustrates the nature of the summer rainfall regime and winter drought.

Owing to the nature of the dynamic processes controlling rainfall, monthly and yearly totals are subject to a variability ranging between 20 and 30 per

[2]J. Gentilli, *Weather and Climate in Western Australia*, p. 16.
[3]L. H. J. Teakle, *The Kimberley Project*, p. 7.

cent. Because most rainfall is received from cyclonic depressions and thunderstorms which are themselves erratic within the season, there is a marked variation between monthly recordings from year to year. The variation occurs both in the frequency and the intensity of rainy periods. The frequency of tropical cyclones bringing rainfall is about 0.3 in December, 0.9 in January, and about 0.8 in February and March. Thus if one disturbance too few, or one too many, is experienced during such a month, the rainfall may vary by as much as 100 per cent above or below the average.

Yearly rainfall figures are usually somewhat more reliable than monthly averages which may often be misleading. Actual falls recorded show that even in the summer certain months may be dry in one year and receive between 10 and 20 inches in others.[4] Likewise, winter months with recorded averages of approximately an inch may in fact represent years of drought interspersed with years in which falls of from four to six inches occur. By way of illustration, Table 2 gives actual monthly figures of years chosen at random for Wyndham and Derby.

Monthly figures show a greater variability in the summer than in the winter. For example, Wyndham in 1896 received 19.29 inches in January whereas four years later drought conditions prevailed in that month with only .51 inches recorded. Likewise Derby received 31.65 inches in January 1917 and for the same month in 1924 received only 2.55 inches. Rainfall during winter months is at a constant low for both centres with only occasional high recordings as at Derby where 6.39 inches fell during May 1895.

It is thus clear, if rainfall figures for particular months in given years are compared with the averages in Table 1, that there are major differences. Because variability is such a feature of the rainfall in the Kimberley, the climate is not as suited to non-irrigated tropical agriculture as it is to pastoralism, for natural grasses have developed efficient root systems to cope with periods of drought and with fluctuations in the summer rainfall.

Rainfall intensity (measured by dividing the average rainfall by the average number of wet days, i.e. days on which at least one point is recorded) for the Kimberley is approximately between 60 and 80 points per wet day. The significance of this high incidence of rainfall per wet day can be realised when it is remembered that the wet days themselves are mostly limited to a four month season and occur after a long period of drought when the ground is dry. Seepage into the soil cannot take place so thoroughly and much precipitation is lost as run-off. Plant growth is therefore not as great as total rainfall figures would suggest; flooding is a constant danger and soil erosion is aggravated. Rainfall intensity must therefore be taken into account when determining the effective rainfall of pastures and crops and when dealing with hydrological problems.

The frequency of thunderstorms increases from 15 to 20 days over the arid interior of Western Australia to over 80 days a year on the Kimberley

[4] J. Gentilli, *Weather and Climate in Western Australia*, p. 16.

coast.[5] Most thunderstorms result from the development of cumuliform clouds when moist tropical maritime air is heated over the land. These clouds usually yield heavy showers. Approximately 10-15 per cent of the rainfall of the Kimberley plateau owes its occurrence to this phenomenon when heating and orographic factors initiate thunderstorm activity during the summer months.[6] Precipitation due to thunderstorms influences both rainfall intensity and rainfall variability in this area.

As mentioned above, floods are common in tropical areas where rainfall is seasonal and variable within the season. Flooding is thus a feature of the wet in the Kimberley and has been the cause of stock losses, damage to property, dislocation of communications and even the loss of life. Many exceptional floods have been experienced in the Kimberley in the past, and perhaps typical of the reports of these reaching Perth, was that of the Inspector of Police in Broome when on 26 January 1914 he reported 'Record floods in West Kimberley . . . losses in stock exceptionally heavy, cattle in hundreds, sheep, pigs and kangaroos being swept down by the floods. The Post Office at Fitzroy Crossing was surrounded by water for miles, and men camped on the Fitzroy River had to take refuge in the trees.'[7]

At such times those river beds which have been in the dry a series of water holes, become quickly filled and often flow across wide flood plains towards the sea. Unless rainfall continues, their waters ebb almost as quickly as they bank up. However, although conditions have not changed over the years, past experience and more accurate weather forecasting now allow a certain amount of preparation to be made to meet an impending flood. Effective reconnaissance of flooded areas enables warnings of the impassability of roads and crossings to be given, thus minimizing tragedies.

It must always be borne in mind that the Kimberley is an area of normal seasonal drought wherein for as many as five months of the year in winter no rain may be received whatsoever. Added to this there is a degree of variability in the summer rainfall which, if taken on the average, is fairly reliable but in any one year may be far below average. In Table 2, for example, it is obvious that 1924 was a drought year for Derby with a rainfall only one-fifth of normal.

Various droughts have taken toll of stock in the Kimberley. Such a one was that of 1952-53 when it was estimated that losses of cattle in the East and West Kimberley were about 50 per cent. In this year spinifex and native trees died and parts of the Kimberley was as 'bare as bitumen'.[8] Fortunately good rains fell in January and April 1954. Because of the nature of the climate, drought is an ever present possibility which the

[5]Commonwealth Department of National Development, *Rainfall*.

[6]J. Gentilli, *Die Klimate Australiens, Die Erde*.

[7]Commonwealth Bureau of Meteorology, *Results of Rainfall Observations made in Western Australia*, p. 103.

[8]Commonwealth Bureau of Meteorology, *Fifty Years of Weather in Western Australia, 1908-1957*, p. 14.

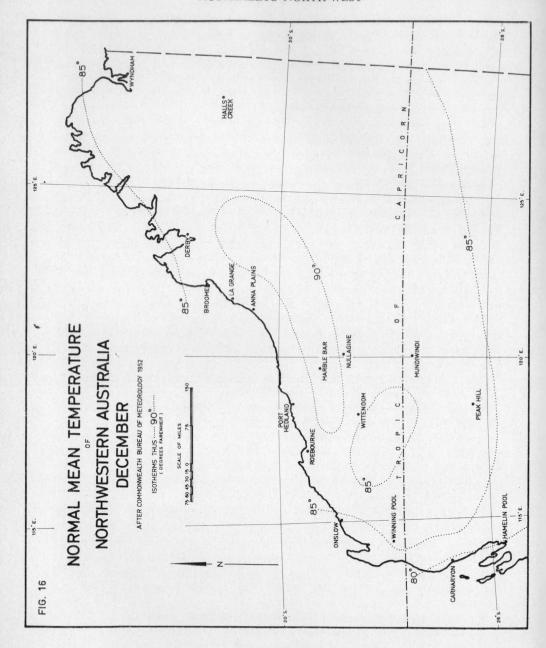

FIG. 16

NORMAL MEAN TEMPERATURE
OF
NORTHWESTERN AUSTRALIA
DECEMBER

AFTER COMMONWEALTH BUREAU OF METEOROLOGY 1952

ISOTHERMS THUS ...... 90° ....
(DEGREES FARENHEIT)

SCALE OF MILES

75 60 45 30 15 0   75   150

pastoralist has to risk. There is, however, far less risk of drought in the Kimberley than in the pastoral areas of the North-West.

Temperature

Located north of the Tropic of Capricorn, the Kimberley is subject to higher temperatures throughout the year than is the south of the state. Likewise the seasonal variation is not as great as in the south and, as the period of heaviest rainfall coincides with the summer, there is not the usual lag of maximum temperature following 'high sun'. The increasing humidity and cloudiness of the summer months have a cooling effect, so that the higher temperatures are experienced at or about the time of the onset of the wet after the build up of heat during the latter months of the dry season. Thus, as can be seen from Table 3, Wyndham experiences its highest average daily mean temperature in November, while Anna Plains, Broome, Derby and Hall's Creek experience their highest mean in December. On the other hand the lowest average daily mean temperatures for Anna Plains, Broome, Derby, Hall's Creek and Wyndham are recorded in July.

Based upon the averages in Table 3, the annual ranges of temperature for these stations are as follows : Wyndham, 14.4 degrees, Broome, 16.9 degrees, Derby, 17.0 degrees, Anna Plains, 19.6 degrees, Hall's Creek, 23.7 degrees. Actual figures vary greatly above and below these averages for any given day. The high range of temperature recorded at Hall's Creek is attributable to its inland location, while the modifying influence of the sea can be seen in the smaller seasonal variation of other centres mentioned above. Altitude does not have any affect on the four coastal stations, which range between 10 and 53 feet above sea level, and the influence upon the reduction of temperature at Hall's Creek (1,225 feet) would be masked by the over-riding influence of the surrounding land mass.

Temperature is a much less variable climatic factor than rainfall, and although there is a seasonal difference, continuous warmth is a feature of the north. The seasons are thus determined more by the presence or absence of precipitation. They are characterized by a wet humid period from December to March, when the combination of high temperatures and heavier rainfall cause a rise in humidity and consequent discomfort and a dry period of mild temperatures from May to August when, with a fall in temperature and humidity, the climate is more comfortable. There is a larger diurnal range of temperatures with afternoons seldom above 90 degrees.[9] Night temperatures are bracing and permit more refreshing sleep. In June and July frosts may occur on the plateau and surrounding highlands, and early morning mists are not uncommon in the valleys.

The months of September-October, March-April mark the transition period from hot days to hot and wet days and the reverse. As they herald either the beginning of the uncomfortable living and working temperatures,

[9]L. H. J. Teakle, *The Kimberley Project.*

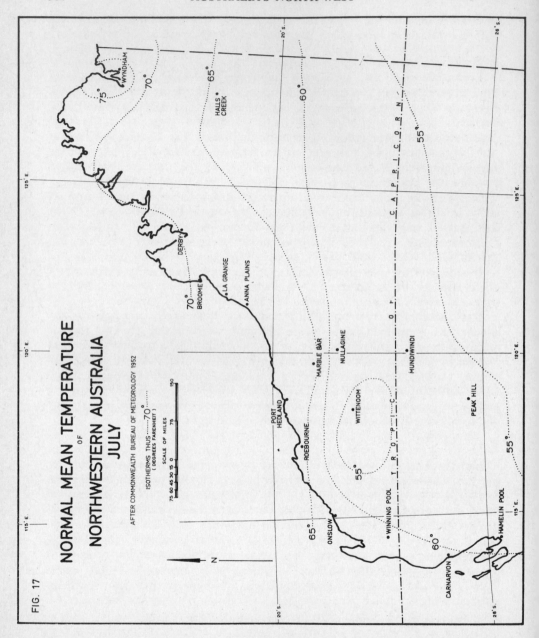

FIG. 17

NORMAL MEAN TEMPERATURE
OF
NORTHWESTERN AUSTRALIA
JULY

AFTER COMMONWEALTH BUREAU OF METEOROLOGY 1952

ISOTHERMS THUS········70°········
(DEGREES FARENHEIT)

SCALE OF MILES
75 60 45 30 15 0   75   150

N

or the end of the long and tiring wet, the most trying times of the year are said to occur in these months. In some ways these intermediate periods may be regarded more as a time of transition than as separate seasons. Consistent with the seasonal temperature range, the diurnal range of temperature is greater inland, so that, although its day temperatures are high, Hall's Creek, for instance, has the lowest night temperature and hence a greater diurnal range (average 28.1 degrees) than a coastal station such as Broome (19.1 degrees).

During the wet, the inflow of moist air and cloudiness lowers the temperatures so that in the north the highest temperatures are recorded in November when the average may be between 85 and 90 degrees. Afternoons register temperatures which are sometimes above the century, but which decrease during the season due to the cooling effects of the rain and the evaporation which follows. Interior temperatures are, of course, more extreme. Night temperatures vary less and are between 74 and 80 degrees with some cooler nights dropping to 65 degrees. Cool winds from the interior influence the temperatures of the mild season bringing particularly low temperatures at night and some valley frosts. Temperatures vary from an average of 63 degrees in July in the interior, to 76 degrees along the northern coast where they are modified by the influence of the ocean.

The period of greatest moisture loss due to evaporation occurs during the wet season when abundant moisture and high temperatures combine to give an evaporation figure between 10 and 15 inches during October and November.[10] However, during the actual tropical rainy period itself evaporation is at a minimum due to the moist, saturated condition of the atmosphere.

In June evaporation occurs at the rate of six or eight inches a month. It will be realized that such figures combined with the wastage of precipitation due to run-off, greatly reduces the effective rainfall.

Humidity

The characteristic feature of humidity in the Kimberley is its increase in the wet season. As Table 4 shows, the port of Broome records the highest humidity, namely 76 per cent in February. Broome also records the highest mean average of 63 per cent for the year. Even the easterlies can be moist in Broome for they come in across the mud flats. On the other hand, as one might expect, Hall's Creek registers the lowest summer mean humidity (54 per cent, in February) and its yearly average mean humidity is only 45 per cent. In explanation of this fact, it should be pointed out that Hall's Creek is subject to the drying easterly winds blowing outward from the semi-stationary high-pressure area over central Australia. There is a considerable decrease in relative humidity in the dry season, with figures ranging from a low mean of 52 per cent for Broome in July, to a figure of 35 per cent for Hall's Creek in September. Such periods bring relief from the humid summer

[10]J. Gentilli, *Weather and Climate in Western Australia*, p. 16.

months and help explain why Hall's Creek is less hampered by the climatic discomfort suffered in coastal towns.

Pressure and Winds

SUMMER

The climate of Western Australia is dominated by the weather systems. These bring Southern Ocean depressions and anti-cyclones, which move from the western seaboard across the continent to the east. They give rise, respectively, to zonal winds which have a dominant westerly or south-easterly component and are thus known as the westerlies and the south-east trades. In winter these systems control the weather of the whole continent – the westerlies bring rain to the south, and the trade winds bring generally fine and dry weather to the north except on the north-eastern seaboard where they do bring rain. However, as northern Australia lies within the tropics it is subject to greater insolation and in summer is occupied by a semi-stationary low-pressure area. Towards this area there moves an inflow of moist tropical air from the northern oceans which intrudes upon the normal winter zonal pattern which retreats southwards.

Such an inflow of tropical air is usually associated with the southward movement of the inter-tropical convergence zone over the northern extension of the hot continent. With this movement of the front, come winds from the north-west, the monsoons, and from the north and the north-east. It is in years when this tropical moist tongue of air moves over a wide area of Australia that record precipitation occurs.[11] Such incursions are relatively infrequent and, although the Kimberley is said to have a monsoonal climate, the rainfall received from the true monsoon is but a fraction of the annual total. The winds that are usually associated with the Asian winter monsoon, those to the north, do push southwards and reach the Australian coast, but the air in these monsoon 'air streams' reaches greater heights (20,000 feet) than the commonly experienced local onshore winds (about 3,000 feet). When the former air streams do reach the Kimberley in January and February, rain is widespread and falls are heavy. Likewise, rain may be experienced over wide areas of inland Australia.

As the prevailing winds of the dry season are the regular south-easterlies, the reversal of seasonal winds indicated by the term monsoon would imply winds from the north-west during the wet. Surface observations show that many heavy falls of rain in fact occur with the north-east and south-east winds, but it is still to some extent true to speak of the north-west summer monsoon.

When considering daily rainfall in relation to winds systems or the influence of topography, it is apparent that the dynamic processes in the atmosphere are of the greatest importance in causing the large-scale rising of air necessary for widespread precipitation. Of the factors contributing to rainfall, the

[11]Commonwealth Department of National Development, *Climatic Regions,* p. 8.

tropical low-pressure system and the instability in moist air masses, giving rise to strong convection and thunderstorms, are the most prevalent in the Kimberley.

Tropical lows or troughs of weak to moderate intensity cause the mass rising of air and consequent precipitation. These troughs are often located on the southern extension of the inter-tropical convergence zone and may be more effective if they either intensify, forming a tropical cyclone or willy-willy, or are continued upwards at height combining with an upper-air low. The tropical low of moderate intensity contributes the least rainfall, while the fully developed tropical cyclone and the surface low associated with an upper-air low produce heavy and widespread falls. Such low-pressure patterns occur early in the summer and, as they cause air to be drawn inwards towards their centres from a north and north-westerly direction, they are difficult to dissociate from the monsoon.

WINTER

During the winter with the retreat of the moist tropical maritime air associated with the inter-tropical front, winds blowing outwards from the interior prevail. These are zonal winds originating from the equatorial side of the southern anti-cyclonic belt and are south-easterly in direction. These south-easterly winds which are analogous to those in the Pacific Ocean, are felt in tropical areas throughout the year, but blow with greater steadiness from May to September.[12] During the summer they tend to be drawn into the clockwise air circulation of the heat low and in consequence lose their easterly character. They are primarily responsible for the period of winter drought in this northern region. The occasional good winter rains occur when the cold southerly air lifts warm moist air (a cold front).

Weather associated with the south-east trades is dry and clear (little cloudiness), so that day temperatures are high and night temperatures often very low.

3. The Climate of the North-West Zone

Rainfall

The North-West zone has an annual average rainfall of between 8 and 14 inches. Generally speaking the rainfall is highest on the Pilbara block — 10 to 14 inches — with two small areas receiving over 14 inches east of Marble Bar and just inland from Roebourne. From the Hamersley Ranges southwards to the vicinity of the Gascoyne River the rainfall varies between 8 and 10 inches. Stretching in a band eastwards from Wooramel and Hamelin Pool through Meekatharra and Wiluna there is an exceedingly dry tract of country with a rainfall of less than 8 inches per annum. In the area of the Peron Peninsula and Dirk Hartog Island, there is an increase of rainfall, from 8 to 14 inches, which marks the influence of the rain-bringing systems

[12]Royal Australian Air Force, *Weather on the Australian Station*, p. 15.

controlled from the south. Otherwise the gradation of rainfall decreasing southwards illustrates a northerly or tropical influence on the precipitation received. Following this pattern the best pastoral prospects are in the north while the least occur about the twentieth parallel. The North-West is a sheep grazing area.

Annual rainfall averages for the centre within this region appear in Table 5. The trend of figures marks a decline in rainfall from the north of Marble Bar (12.33 inches) and Nullagine in the Pilbara, through from Port Hedland, Roebourne, Winning Pool and Carnarvon to the southern-most station at Hamelin Pool (7.91 inches).

When considering the seasonal distribution of rainfall there are several features which are notable. A study of the maximum and minimum rainfall shows that there is a division between the north and the south of the region with reference to coastal stations. In the north the maximum is a summer one, while at Carnarvon and Hamelin Pool the rainfall regime is akin to that of the south of the state with a maximum in June and minimum in November and December respectively. The summer rainfall of southern coastal towns reaches its peak in March and clearly reflects the influence of the tropical cyclone systems which are responsible for much of the precipitation of the North-West. On the north-western highlands, however, maximum rainfall is received in January at Marble Bar and Nullagine after the pattern of the Kimberley. This is because this area receives rain from both the tropical cyclones and thunderstorms associated with the monsoonal regime of the north, during the same period. The rainfall regime of this area differs from that of the Kimberley in that winter rains form a larger proportion of the annual total.

The reliability of rainfall in the North-West zone is exceedingly low due to the complete unpredictability of tropical cyclones. Admittedly they do come within the summer and autumn period, but in any one such period there may be only one as in December 1950, or as many as five, as in February 1951.[13] In some years no cyclones have been experienced, and thus rainfall has been severely limited.

Part of the North-West zone experiences the highest rainfall variability of any place in Australia. At Onslow, for instance, it is 60 per cent.[14] This feature is directly attributable to the erratic visitation of the north-western coast by the tropical cyclones. A series of rainfall recordings for four years chosen at random (Table 6) illustrate the great variability in this area and shows of how little value is the concept of rainfall average within such a climatic region. Annual totals for Onslow range from a half an inch to 28 inches. At Whim Creek more than 29 inches have been recorded in the

[13]J. Gentilli, 'Tropical Cyclones as Bioclimatic Activators'.
[14]Commonwealth Department of National Development, *Rainfall*, p. 40.

one day,[15] while in 1924 the whole year's total was only 17 points.[16] Thus rainfall averages in drier areas can give a very distorted impression of the climate if no account is taken of the variation in both monthly and annual totals.

When it is realised that a relatively unreliable rainfall of high variability is coupled with a high rainfall intensity per wet day within the season, it is easier to account for the high proportion of droughts and floods suffered in the North-West. The year's rainfall may be received within a few months when floods are common, leaving the remainder of the year virtually waterless. These three factors, combined with a total yearly rainfall which is low to barely moderate, have had marked repercussions in the plant life of the North-West zone. Only those native shrubs and grasses which have become adjusted to the climate can withstand the stresses of such an erratic rainfall. Fortunately many such plants are palatable as stock fodder and thus enable the pasturing of sheep in this area.

Because of the rainfall characteristics, flooding of river beds and surrounding lowlands is an ever present danger in the North-West zone as it is in the Kimberley. Communications are disrupted due to flooding, and stock losses are common on river valley properties. The Gascoyne River in recent years, as in 1961, has been responsible for the spoilation of banana and vegetable plantations on the Gascoyne flood plain at Carnarvon. Likewise, damage to homesteads and roads has cost the township thousands of dollars.

Droughts are a common feature of the North-West and as with floods sometimes involve financial losses. They are more prevalent there than in the Kimberley, and have a greater adverse affect on pastoralism because plant life, which is so difficult to regenerate in this semi-arid area, can be readily eaten out. Even under normal conditions the area experiences a lengthy dry season, and the failure of seasonal rains combined with high temperatures can lead to prolonged droughts.

Temperature

Unlike the Kimberley the North-West zone has a great variation in range of temperatures, showing marked seasonal differences. Also, as the North-West stretches some distance both north and south of the Tropic of Capricorn, there is a difference between the temperatures of the north and the south of this area. Generally speaking, temperatures are less severe in the south and are also modified along the coast by proximity to the ocean. The greatest build-up of temperature occurs on the plateau, particularly in the Pilbara region where the town of Marble Bar has the highest mean maximum temperature in Australia. Although this area has not recorded the highest individual temperature in Australia (Cloncurry, 127.5 degrees F)

[15]Royal Australian Air Force, *Weather on the Australian Station*, p. 38.
[16]Commonwealth Bureau of Meteorology, *Fifty Years of Weather in Western Australia, 1908-1957*, p. 7.

nor the highest in Western Australia (Eucla, 123.2 degrees F.), its average readings make this the summer heat-centre of the continent.

Maximum temperatures, both monthly and annual, are recorded in January and February (see Table 7). During both these months the 90 degree isotherm envelopes an area from Exmouth Gulf, along the north-west coast across the plateau and into the Canning basin region. At the heart of this area the 100 degree isotherm encloses that section of the Pilbara around Marble Bar. This town has the Australian record of 160 consecutive days when the temperatures recorded exceeded 100 degrees. Minimum temperatures for all stations are recorded in July varying from the average daily minimum of 41.4 degrees at Mundiwindi to 55.6 degrees at Port Hedland.

The daily temperatures of the zone are at times quite erratic due to the rapid heating and cooling of the continental interior. The lowest average daily range of temperature is 17.5 degrees recorded at Carnarvon where insolation is not as great as further north and where temperatures are moderated by the influence of the sea. North of the Tropic the range at coastal towns is between 20.4 degrees (Port Hedland) and 24.8 degrees (Onslow). Extremes of temperature inland cause an increase in range, the lowest being at Peak Hill in the south (23.8 degrees F) and the highest at Nullagine (29.6 degrees F).

During the coolest month, July, day temperatures average between 60 and 70 degrees. Night temperatures range from 40 to 50 degrees and frosts, which occur on occasions north of the Tropic, are not uncommon during this month. Mundiwindi, almost on the Tropic, has recorded 22.4 degrees – temperatures lower than 20 degrees have not been recorded in Western Australia. In July, day temperatures rise to 80 degrees, even to over 90 degrees at interior stations. Summer temperatures on the other hand may be on average 70 degrees, with interior centres sometimes lower in the night time, rising to a morning average of 80 to 85 degrees. Afternoons average 95 to 107 degrees in January, but the mercury may often reach 110 degrees, particularly on the plateau.

During the months of June and July evaporation is at a minimum with an average of three to six inches a month. However, with an increase in temperature the rate rises and during November and December water loss occurs at the rate of 11 to 14 inches a month. Under the circumstances indigenous plant life which is adapted to the semi-arid conditions survives, but agriculture is out of the question except perhaps in river valleys where irrigation may be used, as at Carnarvon.

Humidity

Table 8 indicates an overall low relative humidity for the North-West zone. As might be expected, coastal towns are more humid, with a maximum of 64 per cent relative humidity at Carnarvon and a minimum of 37 per cent at Peak Hill. The higher humidity of Carnarvon may be attributable to the regular breeze and to the increase in overcast days associated with the weather systems brought by the westerlies. The lower relative humidity inland makes working conditions a little less oppressive than on the coast.

Pressure and Winds

SUMMER

The characteristic feature of the North-West is the occurrence of the tropical cyclone, an intense low-pressure system which originates sometimes over land and intensifies as it passes over the sea. Cyclones often turn inland, striking the North-West coast between Onslow and Broome. They are distinguished by their low pressure, and the high wind and precipitation that accompanies them.

The North-West tropical cyclones often originate over the Timor Sea between latitude 10 and 15 degrees south. From this area they travel in a south-westerly direction. Between the latitudes 20 and 25 degrees south they recurve and cross the North-West coast. From here they pass along a south-easterly track over the continent, gradually modifying and dying out over the Great Australian Bight. Unusual paths of the cyclone are not infrequent and even cyclones originating in the east of Australia have travelled westward across the north of the continent and thence down the North-West coast. Likewise, recurving of the western origin cyclone does not always take place and the cyclone may continue southward along the west coast into temperate latitudes, or continue westward into the Indian Ocean.

A most unusual tropical cyclone during February and March 1956 passed along the normal course turning inland over La Grange.[17] Its path took it directly to the north-east of Alice Springs where it described a loop 800 miles long, by 200 miles across, and passed westward to the Indian Ocean again. Continuing southward, the 1956 cyclone crossed the coast between Mandurah and Bunbury and passed out to sea again west of Albany. This was recorded as one of the very few cyclones which have described loops in their paths and it was noteworthy for its sustained intensity and the almost state-wide rains it brought in its wake.

The cyclones make their appearance in summer and autumn. Of the recorded cyclone days in Western Australia, 96 per cent occur between 7 December and 7 April. However, the months most prone to cyclone development are February and March.

It should not be thought that cyclones are a completely regular feature of the climate of this zone. Their frequency varies, and not all cyclones pass inland in this area. Between three and five cyclones may be recorded in any given year, but years may pass when they are completely absent. At the Perth Weather Bureau, 78 were recorded between 1870 and 1955, giving an average of two per annum. More undoubtedly did occur, but were not recorded due to the small number of reporting stations in the early days.

[17]J. Gentilli, 'Tropical Cyclones as Bioclimatic Activators'.

The centre, or 'eye', of the tropical cyclone is windless and subject to extremely low pressures of 950 to 960 millibars. Some reports even take pressures down to as low as 914 millibars. This low pressure area, with its associated clockwise-moving wind circulation, travels at a rate of 10 to 20 miles per hour, a rate which increases if the cyclone intensifies. Within the depression, however, winds may blow at 60 to 80 miles per hour and in an intense cyclone at more than 120 miles per hour. In 1963 the wind recording instrument installed at Onslow registered cyclonic winds which reached 144 miles per hour, probably an Australian record at ground level.[18] As evidence of the force of such winds is a line of steel telephone posts at Exmouth Gulf which at a height of four or five feet from the ground, are bent over at right angles, the upper half of the posts being almost parallel to the ground.

Because the storm is limited to a diameter of perhaps 50 to 100 miles, damage is confined to a limited path. The rains which accompany these cyclones are widespread. Thus the area which is benefited is usually far larger than that which suffers the ill-effects of a cyclone. Many pass inland between towns and thus do little harm; many, on the other hand, wreak great havoc.

Composed of moist maritime air, cyclones bring in their wake beneficial rains. Although tropical cyclones cross the coast most often between Onslow and Broome, in January cyclones are more prone to visit the coast between Roebourne and Wyndham while in February the favoured section is from Hamelin Pool northwards to Roebourne. Hence at some time during the cyclone season any area north of Hamelin Pool may benefit from cyclonic rains. Precipitation is thus brought to an area that would otherwise be dry for months on end.

Heavy downpours may bring up to 14 inches of rain in one day. Flooding is manifest under such circumstances, but these rains sustain plant growth for many months. During the cyclone season average falls for the four months January through to April vary from a high of 7.6 inches at Wyndham in January, to a low of 0.4 inches at Carnarvon in January. The heaviest rainfall from this source occurs north of the Hamersley Ranges. Unfortunately the highlands have an adverse affect on the areas to the west, south and east, for to a certain extent they shelter these lands from the cyclonic rains. March is a month of heavy rainfall for most centres influenced by the cyclones. However, the northern highlands, under the influence of both tropical cyclone and monsoonal convection, receive their highest recordings in January.

The area has a history of destruction of property and loss of life due to cyclonic storms. Damage to buildings and shore installations is sometimes severe, and it is not unusual in this area to see roofs tied down with wire

[18]Commonwealth Bureau of Meteorology, 'Proceedings of the Tropical Cyclone Symposium', p. 15.

cable, and houses specially constructed to withstand stormy winds. However, the greatest damage is usually that suffered by shipping along the coast.

During the year 1908 two cyclones in April and December struck the pearling fleet off the Eighty Mile Beach with the consequent loss of 140 lives and damage estimated at £60,000. The following year at Broome another cyclone caused the loss of 24 men and 4 vessels. The force of the storm was such that a pearling lugger and a laden collier were carried a half and a quarter of a mile inland, respectively. Another bad cyclone followed in 1910 when houses were blown down in Broome, 26 pearling luggers were sunk or dismasted and the lives of 40 divers were lost. As well as the loss of craft and seamen, there is the great battering that wharf installations take at such times. In recent years damage to the Onslow jetty has recurred so often that in 1961 it was decided to abandon its rebuilding and to use lighters for the port trade.

One of the worst disasters recorded in this area was the loss of the coastal vessel S.S. *Koombana* in March 1912 along with other vessels. The *Koombana* put to sea from Port Hedland in an attempt to ride out the storm, 'as the *Koombana* left the port she was so light her propeller was out of the water and in the small swell at the entrance, was racing. Once outside Captain Allen had no other course open to him but that which led the ship right into the vortex of the tremendous elemental strife which prevailed at sea.'[19] The ship was never found nor was there any trace of its crew members and 76 passengers.

The outstanding cyclone of 1956 can be cited in evidence of the beneficial effects of tropical cyclones. The estimated total amount of rainfall brought to Australia during its passage in February and March was some 87,410,250 acre/feet of water, or on average, 2.47 inches over the whole 666,800 square miles of country affected. This estimate is exclusive of the 12,000,000 acre/feet of water deposited over the Northern Territory.[20] Although remarkable, this was perhaps less than would otherwise have resulted had not so much of the path of the cyclone been over the sea. It should be obvious that against the physical damage caused by tropical cyclones, should be weighed the immensely beneficial effects on plant life and consequent good effects on the pastoral industry, for they determine the habitat of the grassland and steppe of the arid region.[21]

As in the Kimberley, thunderstorms in the North-West zone are an additional source of precipitation in the summer. They are influenced by the low-pressure systems of the tropics and thus are more frequent in the north. Their occurrence is increased over the plateau region where a rise in altitude sets in motion the lifting of air which is taken to great heights by convection. Cumulo-nimbus clouds are the harbingers of stormy conditions

[19]Commonwealth Bureau of Meteorology, *Results of Rainfall Observations made in Western Australia*, p. 181.
[20]J. Gentilli, 'Tropical Cyclones as Bioclimatic Activators'.
[21]C. A. Gardner, 'The Vegetation of Western Australia'.

and the source of rainfall, which may vary from several points to many inches in one thunderstorm. The frequency of these storms in the early summer gives the Pilbara and Hamersley Ranges a maximum rainfall in January and links the area with the monsoonal type rainfall regime of the north.

WINTER

Whereas summer winds are more variable under the influence of tropical cyclones, in winter the North-West is under the influence of the high-pressure area located over central and northern Australia. Winds are mainly out-blowing, easterly and south-easterly, and are therefore not rain-bringers in this season. Winter is thus a time of drought in most of the North-West region but more particularly in the northern coastal and highland section, though occasionally very good winter rains are experienced.

The southern coastal towns benefit from the marginal effects of the westerly winds which bring to the south the alternation of high and low pressure systems. Depressions of southern ocean origin have effect as far north as Carnarvon and Hamelin Pool, which have decided winter rainfall maxima. The amount received in the four winter months, May to August, is small being 5.59 inches at Carnarvon and 4.16 inches at Hamelin Pool, but it is still more than half of the annual total received. The effects of the westerlies quickly diminish inland for such winds as do penetrate, very soon become desiccating.

This southern area is thus on the fringe of rains of temperate latitude origin completely removed from monsoonal influences, and it benefits only occasionally from the tropical cyclones. It forms an intermediate region the climate of which is basically controlled by the dry continental air of the interior.

4. THE CLIMATE OF THE 'DRY INTERIOR' ......

Within this dry interior area the climate, generally, and other physical features are such that agricultural or pastoral activities are virtually im-possible. However there are several pockets of fertile grazing land in the area where some attractive pastoral stations exist. Because of the lack of extensive and accurate weather recordings for this area, the discussion which follows is necessarily of a general character.

Rainfall

The over-riding feature of inland Northwestern Australia is its prevailing dryness. This great land surface, principally occupied by the Great Sandy and Gibson deserts, is the least fortunate of the climatic regions. Located in the western interior of a large continent, it suffers from its isolation from the sea and its proximity to the source of the dry offshore south-east trades emanating from central Australia. Because of its low elevation and practic-ally uniform topography, the build of the interior does not give rise to the development of those dynamic processes in the atmosphere that lead to precipitation. Many thousands of miles of country are cut off from the rain-bringing systems in the north, north-west and south. Thus rainfall is completely inadequate and it is only through aeons of adaptation that the native flora has been able to withstand the country's aridity and give a sparse cover to the soil in more favoured localities.

Occasional rains are brought inland by the unusual penetration of the moisture-bringing weather systems previously discussed, namely, the monsoon of the north, the tropical cyclone in the north-west and the southern ocean depression in the south. Such cases are more the exception than the rule, and rainfall is very unreliable.

The northern districts receive rainfall in summer and autumn while the southern districts have a precipitation maximum in winter. Again the rainfall averages can be misleading. A great proportion of the dry interior falls within the 8 inch rainfall isohyet but rainfall may vary from 3 to 4 inches in dry years, to 10 to 12 inches in wet years. Rainfall for a wet month is over one inch, rarely 2 inches.

Temperature

The continental nature of this area causes a very rapid heating and cooling of the land surface. The outstanding feature of the temperatures of the interior is their large extreme annual range; winter nights are cool to cold, while summer day temperatures soar. The diurnal range is less spectacular, but can still be 25 to 30 degrees in winter. Generally speaking the range is less in the north and more in the south.

A major factor contributing to the great range of temperature inland is the absence of cloud cover, and low humidity. Clear skies, and lack of moisture in the air readily allow both a rapid heating up of the land surface in the day time, leading to extreme maximum temperature readings, and appreciable nocturnal radiation and extreme minimum temperatures. Although the interior of Western Australia does not experience the extreme minimum temperatures recorded in the eastern highlands which are under the influence of increased elevation, this region receives what is presumed to be the maximum amount of sunshine in Australia, approximately 80 per cent of the possible hours.

July is usually the coldest month, when below-freezing temperatures are responsible for frosts. 39 to 40 degrees at night are usual for July, when temperatures average 60 to 65 degrees. The highest temperatures are recorded in January in the north (85 degrees average) and February in the south (75 degrees average). Night temperatures are still cold in the south sometimes falling to 50 degrees, whereas in the north, while they average over 70 degrees, they can still fall many degrees below this on occasions. Day temperatures reach 90 degrees in the south in the afternoon, and are about 10 degrees higher in the north, centuries are not uncommon.

Pressure and Winds

The controlling feature of the weather in this area is the dominance at all times by the south-east trades which in the interior are desiccating winds – moisture-collecting rather than moisture-precipitating.

During winter the interior of the continent is controlled by the southern high-pressure belt with resultant cool, descending air. As it flows outward from the centre following the anti-clockwise movement of winds in such pressure systems, it becomes warmed by pressure, by contact with the heated land surface, and by friction. Such winds blowing from an easterly and south-easterly direction are pleasantly dry during the daytime. They do not bring rainfall, but may recede under the influence of a mass of moist southerly air which may at times push inland during this season, bringing limited rains to the south.

Likewise in summer, the easterlies are predominant but they are of less importance when a tropical low-pressure system moves over the north and north-west of Australia sometimes bringing rain to the northern interior. Cyclones, because of their intense nature, and the inland path they tend to follow, are a factor contributing to rainfall. If such a cyclone should move into a trough connecting with a southern depression, and pass eastwards over the continent, widespread rains occur inland. Such conditions unfortunately are the exception rather than the rule, and at most times dry, easterly-flowing air brings dry weather.

5. CLIMATIC DISCOMFORT

One of the major difficulties in the settlement of tropical lands is the enervating effect of the climate on bodily comfort. Continuous heat and high humidity lower working efficiency and reduce output. The cooling of the body is essential to the maintenance of physical efficiency in work; when the cooling power of the air in contact with the body is lessened physical capacity is reduced. Thus in humid climates the efficiency of the workforce is limited and costs of production are increased. Where there is little daily variation in the climate, psychological factors such as boredom, and depression add to the physical lassitude and increase the climatic discomfort.

In the north of the state, coastal towns with their more uniformly hot and humid climates are subject to a higher degree of climatic discomfort than inland towns where greater diurnal and seasonal ranges of temperatures, and lower humidity have recuperative influences on the health and state of mind.

An awareness of the factors contributing to climatic discomfort has had an important bearing on living conditions, where home-building, eating and dressing habits, times of rest and other activities have been adapted to the climate, and on working conditions, where amenities and compensations are continually appearing in the region.

The criteria of climatic discomfort of towns in Northwestern Australia has been the subject of study by Gentilli[22] and Gaffney.[23] The concept of effective temperature has been used by both writers to determine discomfort zones. Effective temperature takes into account dry and wet bulb temperatures and wind speed which are plotted on a nomograph.

The Sub-Committee on District Allowances appointed by the Joint Council of the Commonwealth Public Service has adopted in the years following the world war, the concept of effective temperature as the only available satisfactory measure of climatic discomfort. For its purpose this Committee chose the limit of 65 degrees effective temperature as that below which the normal sedentary worker does not feel any discomfort. Gentilli, on the other hand, using figures based on the working day exclusive of the rest hours, chose 69 degrees effective temperature as the criterion of climatic discomfort. In any case a basis of comparison between areas can be derived by computing the number of day degrees above the starting point for each month and for each year.

A nomograph was used to derive mean monthly effective temperatures which were used as a basis to determine discomfort zones.[24] The total number of day degrees in excess of 69 was computed by taking the effective temperature in excess of 69 degrees for each month and multiplying by the number of days in the given month. Such computations appear in Table 9. Gentilli, working from the annual number of day degrees over 69 degrees effective temperature, mapped heat discomfort zones for every 600 annual day degrees above the effective temperature minimum

From the figures given in Table 9 and from the map, it can be seen that Northwestern Australian may be divided into six zones, the least comfortable of which is centred on Wyndham, and the most comfortable of which includes Carnarvon. The zones with 3,000 and 3,600 plus annual day degrees above the comfortable effective temperature provide the greatest problems as regards living and working conditions.

Part of the difficulty of attracting labour to the north may be due to climatic discomfort and thus there is a need to offer greater inducement in providing higher wages, longer leave periods, and comfortable living amenities such as refrigeration and air conditioning, which in turn lift production costs and reduce profits. It is partly due to climatic discomfort that many pastoralists return to the south in summer or often do not appear in the north to manage properties at all. Such absentee-ownership may result in inefficient management in some cases and this, of course, has a detrimental effect on the pastoral industry as a whole. Climate also affects stock, for the condition of cattle deteriorates if they are forced to walk many miles in the heat to killing centres. Standards of health are more difficult to

[22]J. Gentilli, *Climatic Discomfort in Western Australia.*
[23]D. O. Gaffney, 'The Economic Development of the Kimberleys with Particular Reference to Climate'.
[24]J. Gentilli, *op. cit.*

maintain and the breeding of stock is a particular problem because fertility is reduced, particularly in the case of sheep.

These and the associated human problems which are directly attributable to climatic discomfort must be taken into account when considering future proposals for the closer settlement of the north. It is heartening to note that more attention has been given recently by private and governmental agencies to this aspect of life in the North-West, and there has been a general improvement in the standards of amenities and working conditions in the region.

6. SUMMARY AND CONCLUSIONS

Because of its size, Northwestern Australia comes under the influence of several wind and pressure systems and has several different and distinctive rainfall and temperature characteristics in different parts of its vast area. For this reason it becomes necessary, at least for expository purposes, to sub-divide the region into three smaller zones which come under a broad climatic classification. There is the Kimberley area, a monsoonal type, the North-West, a tropical cyclone type, and the dry interior, a vast arid zone.

In the Kimberley the rainfall varies from an annual average of 14 inches to over 50 inches. The heaviest rainfall is recorded on the north and west coast and decreases as one proceeds towards the south and east. There is a marked seasonal distribution, with usually fairly heavy summer rain, brought by the monsoons and tropical cyclones, and virtually a winter drought. The rainfall in the Kimberley is extremely variable and unreliable, both as to the frequency and to intensity of rainy periods. Over 30 inches have been recorded in one summer month and as low as half an inch in the same month of another year. There is, at times, considerable thunderstorm activity, though this is most marked on the Kimberley coast (100 days a year) and decreases as one moves towards the interior (15-20 days a year). Floods are a common occurrence in the wet and have caused immense damage of all kinds. There is a normal seasonal drought in this area and when this is combined with an abnormally low summer rainfall serious hardship can be caused.

Temperatures are generally high, with a fairly small seasonal variation. The average daily range is only around 15 degrees to 30 degrees although daily ranges can be considerably higher. The hottest days occur in the summer months, with temperatures in the 80's and 90's, and the coldest in the winter months, with temperatures in the 50's and 60's. The build up of heat during the dry season runs into the onset of the wet and makes conditions very uncomfortable in the period from November to February. On the whole, however, temperature is a much less variable climatic factor than rainfall in the Kimberley and thus the character of the season is more determined by the presence or absence of precipitation.

The most prevalent of the common types of atmospheric pressure patterns contributing to rainfall in the Kimberley are the tropical low-pressure systems and the instability in moist air masses resulting in thunderstorms. In the winter the south-east trades dominate the Kimberley, bringing generally fine and dry weather, but in the summer a large low-pressure area draws in moist tropical air from the north, and gives rise to monsoonal rains.

In the North-West zone the rainfall varies from 8 inches, annual average, to 14 inches. The heaviest rainfall is recorded in the Pilbara and drops off as one proceeds towards the south, and increases again in the extreme south. In seasonal distribution, a transition occurs from a summer rainfall in the north to a winter rainfall in the south. The North-West has the highest rainfall variability in any area in Australia, mainly because of the erratic tropical cyclones which hit the north-western coast from time to time. Rainfall intensity can also be very high. Thus there is an unreliable rainfall of high variability coupled with a high rainfall intensity, and this accounts for the droughts and floods in this area.

Temperatures vary considerably more than is the case in the Kimberley, and the area has the town with the highest mean maximum temperature in Australia. The average daily range is from 15 degrees to 35 degrees. The hottest days occur in the summer, with temperatures in the 90's and 100's and the coldest in the winter, with temperatures in the 40's and 50's. Because of the evaporation rate of from 11 to 14 inches a month in the summer, agriculture in the region is restricted to river valleys, as at Carnarvon, where irrigation may be practised. Relative humidity is lower than in the Kimberley and working conditions somewhat better.

This area, as far as pressure and winds are concerned, is characterized by the tropical cyclone, or willy-willy. These originate in northern waters and travel south-west sometimes recurving to cross the coast whence they proceed in a south-casterly direction bringing high winds, sometimes more than 120 m.p.h., and heavy rainfall. They occur mainly in summer and autumn. Thunderstorms also occur in the early summer.

The dry interior has a severe and forbidding climate, the main characteristic of which as the name implies, is dryness. The prevailing winds are the dry south-east trades coming from central Australia. In the north the rainfall occurs mostly in the summer and autumn and, like the rainfall pattern of the North-West area, this changes, as one moves southwards, to a winter maximum. The annual rainfall may vary from 3 inches to 4 inches in a dry year to 10 inches to 12 inches in a wet year.

As might be expected, in this continental land mass far removed from the sea, the outstanding features of the temperatures are their great annual range, with summer heat in the 90's and 100's and with frosts in July. This area is also believed to be the sunniest in Australia with up to 80 per cent of the possible hours of sunshine.

Thus it can be seen that the vast region that is Northwestern Australia has several different and fairly distinct types of climate. It is, in many respects, a land where, despite technological progress in many fields, the climate, together with some of the region's physical characteristics, still broadly defines the limits of human endeavour in terms of time and space.

The development of any given region is partly limited by the nature of its climate. In an area where the factors governing climate are as variable as they are in Northwestern Australia, the simple study of climatic averages may be misleading when examining the potential of the land. Knowledge of the daily and seasonal interaction of the elements controlling weather is an essential prerequisite for the successful pursuit of agricultural and pastoral activities. It must be noted that the region suffers several climatic disabilities: it is subject to a prolonged seasonal drought; it has, in the coastal areas, only a light to moderate rainfall which in the North-West is particularly erratic; it suffers at all times, by virtue of its tropical location, a high evaporation rate. Precipitation, though at times abnormally high, is nowhere near as uniform in its distribution as in south coastal regions. For this reason rainfall cannot be so readily absorbed by the soil and be as useful to plant life. Runoff is greater, and flooding is an ever present menace. Added to these factors is the important influence that the hot and humid climate, as in the north, has on human comfort and bodily well-being.

Such are the features of the climate of Northwestern Australia which must be taken into account when considering possible limitations upon further development. Much of the land of the interior offers no hope of utilization and even in the North-West zone, pastoralism has been so far developed only on an extensive pattern. It is in the better-watered areas of the Kimberley, which present a challenge to the scientist who may contribute much by careful research and planning, that there is most likelihood of economic expansion at the present.

It must not be thought, however, that the climatic picture is a gloomy one as regards development prospects. One of the factors which stands out in this area is the lavishness of nature, at different times of the year, in dispensing bounties. As indicated elsewhere in this work, there exist vast water resources in this region the harnessing of which could change the character of production. The growing season is much longer here than in the south of the state and this makes possible the cultivation of two crops in one year.

Within the broad limits set by climatic and other factors, man will continue to develop his technology and to make greater and greater use of what natural resources there are. The application of this principle to Northwestern Australia would seem to spell vigorous future growth, since, up to the present, the governments and the settlers have tended to devote their attentions more to the combatting of nature than the turning of its gifts to their advantage.

BIBLIOGRAPHY

COMMONWEALTH BUREAU OF METEOROLOGY. *Results of Rainfall Observations made in Western Australia.* Melbourne, 1929.
—— *Climatic Averages of Australia.* Melbourne, 1956.
—— *Average Annual Rainfall Map of Australia.* Melbourne, 1957.

—— *Fifty Years of Weather in Western Australia, 1908-1957.* Melbourne, 1957.

—— 'Proceedings of the Tropical Cyclone Symposium', held in Brisbane in 1955.

COMMONWEALTH DEPARTMENT OF NATIONAL DEVELOPMENT. Atlas of Australian Resources, 1st series, with commentaries. *Rainfall*, 1952; *Temperatures*, 1953; *Climatic Regions*, 1954. Canberra.

COMMONWEALTH SCIENTIFIC AND INDUSTRIAL RESEARCH ORGANISATION. *Lands and Pastoral Resources of the North Kimberley Area, Western Australia.* Land Research Series, no. 4. Melbourne, 1960.

—— *Lands of the Wiluna-Meekatharra Area, Western Australia, 1958.* Land Research Series, no. 7. Melbourne, 1963.

—— *General Report on Lands of the West Kimberley Area, Western Australia.* Land Research Series, no. 9. Melbourne, 1964.

GAFFNEY, D. O. 'The Economic Development of the Kimberleys with Particular Reference to Climate.' Unpublished M.A. thesis, 1957. Library of the University of Western Australia. This thesis contains a detailed discussion of the economic potential of the Kimberleys and points out the limits which the present climatic conditions have imposed on such development.

GARDNER, C. A. 'The Vegetation of Western Australia', *Journal of the Royal Society of Western Australia*, vol. 28. 1942.

GENTILLI, J. *Climatic Discomfort in Western Australia.* Research Report no. 24, Geography Laboratory, University of Western Australia. An attempt to find an objective criterion for the determination of wage allowances and other considerations in country areas of Western Australia. This essay deals primarily with the climatic discomfort suffered in tropical and arid regions (see also Gaffney, D. O. 'The Economic Development of the Kimberleys with particular reference to Climate', ch. 111).

—— *Die Klimate Australiens, Die Erde*, vols. 3-4. Berlin, 1955. References from typescript copy in English, Geography Laboratory, University of Western Australia. This reference deals with the climate of Australia by regions discussing the distinguishing climatic elements of each area and pointing to comparisons from overseas.

—— 'Tropical Cyclones as Bioclimatic Activators.' *The Western Australian Naturalist*, vol. 5. no. 4. Although the bias of this article is towards the effects tropical cyclones have on animal and plant life, the important aspects of cyclone development and influence are discussed fully.

—— *Weather and Climate in Western Australia.* Perth, 1963. This survey, for the Western Australian Government Tourist and Publicity Bureau, separates Western Australia into regions and discusses their salient climatic features.

ROYAL AUSTRALIAN AIR FORCE. *Weather on the Australian Station.* Publication no. 252, vol. 11. Melbourne, 1942.

TEAKLE, L. H. J. *The Kimberley Project.* Western Australian Department of Agriculture, Bulletin no. 2174. 1944. Commencing from the early historical development, this survey contains a study of climate, soils and vegetation and land usage in the Kimberleys. Teakle urges the application of science to the further development of the region.

TABLE 1

KIMBERLEY AREA

Monthly and yearly rainfall averages

(inches)

	Anna Plains	Broome	Derby	Halls Creek	Wyndham
January	3.82	7.35	7.65	5.37	6.79
February	2.45	5.38	4.91	4.16	6.30
March	3.39	4.12	4.76	2.77	5.22
April	1.04	.93	1.16	.54	.50
May	.80	.65	.50	.24	.14
June	.68	.70	.34	.18	.20
July	.30	.15	.26	.24	.08
August	.11	.15	.06	.07	.02
September	.02	.03	.01	.15	.05
October	.04	.02	.10	.49	.38
November	.19	.27	.51	1.36	1.55
December	1.67	3.12	3.70	3.15	3.92
Year	14.51	22.87	23.96	18.72	25.15

Source: Commonwealth Bureau of Meteorology, *Climatic Averages of Australia.*
Melbourne, 1956.

TABLE 2

WYNDHAM AND DERBY

Actual rainfall – random years

(inches)

	Wyndham (Average Annual 25.15")				Derby (Average Annual 23.96")			
	1896	1900	1905	1915	1895	1899	1917	1924
January	19.29	.51	4.49	13.94	5.03	6.15	31.65	2.55
February	10.90	4.88	4.76	2.56	5.79	6.35	2.80	.70
March	2.93	4.97	1.17	1.28	.81	6.79	3.98	—
April	—	1.18	.38	.49	—	1.50	1-89	—
May	.08	.59	—	.14	6.39	1.11	.04	—
June	—	.25	—	—	.58	2.06	.04	—
July	.48	.26	—	—	2.05	—	.02	—
August	—	—	.01	—	—	—	—	—
September	.29	—	—	—	—	—	—	—
October	—	.58	.34	—	.03	—	.40	—
November	2.18	3.47	1.33	.40	—	2.02	1.56	.01
December	6.87	.99	1.92	1.51	1.81	31.03	7.47	1.13
Year	43.02	17.48	14.40	20.32	22.49	57.01	49.85	4.39

Source: Commonwealth Bureau of Meteorology, *Results of Rainfall Observations
made in Western Australia.* Melbourne, 1929.

TABLE 3

KIMBERLEY AREA

Temperature statistics – recordings in degrees Fahrenheit

	Av. Daily Max. Temp.	Av. Daily Min. Temp.	Av. Daily Range Temp.	Av. Daily Mean Temp.
ANNA PLAINS 19° 15' S Lat; 121° 30' E Long. 10 ft. above sea level.				
January	94.7	77.7	17.0	86.2
February	95.4	77.1	18.3	86.3
March	97.1	75.3	21.8	86.2
April	95.7	67.8	27.9	81.7
May	89.7	60.5	29.2	75.1
June	82.8	55.4	27.4	69.1
July	82.1	52.3	29.8	67.2
August	87.0	55.2	31.8	71.1
September	91.9	59.9	32.0	75.9
October	93.2	66.8	27.5	80.5
November	97.4	71.7	25.7	84.5
December	97.6	76.0	21.6	86.8
Year	92.1	66.3	25.8	79.2
BROOME 17° 57' S Lat; 122° 15' E Long. 37 ft. above sea level.				
January	91.3	79.2	12.1	85.3
February	91.8	79.1	12.7	85.5
March	93.1	77.7	15.4	85.4
April	93.3	71.6	21.7	82.5
May	88.0	64.8	23.2	76.4
June	82.5	59.5	23.0	71.0
July	81.8	57.0	24.8	69.4
August	85.0	60.0	25.0	72.5
September	88.8	65.1	23.7	77.0
October	90.5	72.1	18.4	81.3
November	92.7	76.7	16.0	84.7
December	93.2	79.4	13.8	86.3
Year	89.3	70.2	19.2	79.8
DERBY 17° 18' S Lat; 123° 40' E Long. 53 ft above sea level.				
January	94.0	79.1	14.9	86.5
February	94.7	79.0	15.7	86.8
March	94.9	78.3	16.6	86.5
April	94.6	72.6	22.0	83.6
May	89.6	66.6	23.0	78.1
June	85.0	60.9	24.1	73.0
July	84.2	58.3	25.9	71.3
August	88.0	61.5	26.5	74.8
September	82.6	66.7	25.9	79.6
October	85.7	73.8	21.9	84.8
November	100.5	74.2	26.3	87.3
December	96.7	80.0	16.7	88.3
Year	92.2	71.3	21.0	81.7

TABLE 3 – *continued*

	Av. Daily Max. Temp.	Av. Daily Min. Temp.	Av. Daily Range Temp.	Av. Daily Mean Temp.
HALLS CREEK 18° 13' S Lat; 127° 46' E Long. 1,225 ft. above sea level.				
January	97.6	75.4	22.2	86.5
February	97.0	74.2	22.8	85.6
March	95.6	71.2	24.4	83.4
April	92.3	63.0	29.3	77.6
May	85.7	56.0	29.7	70.8
June	80.6	50.5	30.1	65.6
July	80.1	47.6	32.5	63.8
August	85.9	52.1	33.8	69.0
September	98.3	59.0	33.7	75.8
October	98.3	69.5	28.8	83.9
November	100.5	74.2	26.3	87.3
December	99.5	75.5	24.0	87.5
Year	92.2	64.0	28.1	78.1
WYNDHAM 15° 27' S Lat; 128° 07' E Long. 23 ft. above sea level.				
January	95.9	80.2	15.7	88.1
February	95.5	70.7	15.8	87.4
March	95.3	79.5	15.8	87.4
April	94.7	77.2	17.5	85.9
May	90.1	72.4	17.7	81.2
June	85.8	68.0	17.8	76.9
July	85.0	66.2	18.8	75.6
August	88.5	69.5	19.0	79.0
September	93.5	74.8	18.7	84.2
October	96.9	79.7	17.2	88.3
November	98.5	81.4	17.1	90.0
December	97.6	81.2	16.4	89.4
Year	93.1	75.8	17.1	84.4

Source: Commonwealth Bureau of Meteorology, *Climatic Averages of Australia*. Melbourne, 1956.

TABLE 4

KIMBERLEY AREA

Mean relative humidity

(Expressed as a percentage of saturation humidity)

Location	J	F	M	A	M	J	J	A	S	O	N	D	Year
Anna Plains	65	65	59	43	39	44	45	38	44	45	51	57	51
Broome	75	76	73	56	54	53	52	54	56	64	66	70	63
Derby	71	71	68	56	49	50	49	51	52	54	60	65	59
Halls Creek	54	54	50	40	41	44	42	39	35	38	38	46	46
Wyndham	66	67	63	46	41	40	38	40	44	52	55	60	51

Source: Commonwealth Bureau of Meteorology, *Climatic Averages of Australia*. Melbourne, 1956.

TABLE 5

NORTH-WEST AREA

Monthly and yearly rainfall averages

(inches)

Location	J	F	M	A	M	J	J	A	S	O	N	D	Year
Carnarvon	.51	.78	.85	.68	1.61	1.94	1.32	.72	.19	.17	.02	.22	9.01
Hamelin Pool	.33	.43	.74	.47	1.17	1.91	1.40	.68	.31	.17	.20	.10	7.91
Marble Bar	3.13	2.40	1.77	.87	.67	.91	.20	.16	.05	.31	.32	1.54	12.33
Nullagine	3.26	2.34	2.01	.68	.69	.79	.24	.20	.06	.26	.61	.84	12.98
Onslow	.84	1.44	2.46	.97	1.19	1.37	.44	.41	.03	.04	.05	.14	9.38
Peak Hill	1.30	1.14	1.65	.88	1.03	1.11	.54	.38	.16	.14	.33	.67	9.33
Port Hedland	1.86	2.07	3.07	.95	.98	.96	.24	.38	.05	.09	.02	.34	11.01
Roebourne	1.66	1.85	3.38	.97	1.09	.86	.22	.20	.08	.06	.06	.55	10.98
Winning Pool	1.20	1.78	1.56	.52	1.30	1.18	.53	.38	.03	.09	.08	.25	8.90

Source: Commonwealth Bureau of Meteorology, *Climatic Averages of Australia*. Melbourne, 1956.

TABLE 6

ONSLOW

Actual rainfall* – random years

	J	F	M	A	M	J	J	A	S	O	N	D	Year
1900	—	.03	2.54	11.00	10.20	2.04	1.05	.08	.01	—	—	—	26.96
1912	.04	.03	.04	—	.10	—	.36	—	—	—	—	—	0.57
1920	.47	.03	2.21	.63	.03	2.79	.29	.35	.49	—	—	—	7.29
1925	.76	.81	.82	—	4.11	6.20	—	.32	.03	—	—	—	13.05

* Annual average 9.38 inches.

Source: Commonwealth Bureau of Meteorology, *Results of Rainfall Observations made in Western Australia*. Melbourne, 1929.

TABLE 7

NORTH-WEST AREA

Temperature statistics – recordings in degrees Fahrenheit

	Av. Daily Max. Temp.	Av. Daily Min. Temp.	Av. Daily Range Temp.	Av. Daily Mean Temp.
CARNARVON 24° 54' S Lat; 113° 39' E Long. 15 ft. above sea level.				
January	87.2	72.1	15.1	79.7
February	88.1	72.4	15.7	80.2
March	86.9	71.6	15.3	79.3
April	84.4	65.8	18.6	75.1
May	78.3	58.8	19.5	68.6
June	73.7	54.0	19.7	63.8
July	71.7	51.6	20.1	61.7
August	73.1	53.4	19.7	63.2
September	75.4	57.2	18.2	66.5
October	77.4	61.1	16.3	69.5
November	81.4	65.8	15.6	73.6
December	84.2	69.2	15.0	76.7
Year	80.2	62.7	17.5	71.5
HAMELIN POOL 26° 24' S Lat; 114° 12' E Long. 14 ft. above sea level.				
January	97.8	68.5	29.3	83.1
February	97.5	69.1	28.4	83.3
March	93.6	68.0	25.6	80.8
April	87.0	62.2	24.8	74.6
May	77.2	55.2	22.0	66.2
June	70.9	50.4	20.5	60.6
July	69.2	48.2	21.0	58.7
August	71.8	48.8	23.0	60.3
September	78.0	51.6	26.4	64.8
October	82.2	54.7	27.5	68.4
November	89.2	60.5	28.7	74.8
December	94.3	64.6	29.7	79.5
Year	84.1	58.5	25.6	71.3
MARBLE BAR 21° 11' S Lat; 119° 42' E Long. 595 ft. above sea level.				
January	106.2	78.9	27.3	92.6
February	105.5	78.6	26.9	92.0
March	102.9	76.8	26.1	89.8
April	97.0	69.5	27.5	83.3
May	88.0	61.3	26.7	74.6
June	80.9	54.7	26.2	67.8
July	80.6	52.4	28.2	66.5
August	85.8	55.7	30.1	70.8
September	93.8	61.7	32.1	77.7
October	100.1	68.7	31.4	84.4
November	105.9	75.2	30.7	90.5
December	107.5	78.1	29.4	92.8
Year	96.2	67.6	28.6	81.9

TABLE 7 – *continued*

	Av. Daily Max. Temp.	Av. Daily Min. Temp.	Av. Daily Range Temp.	Av. Daily Mean Temp.
NULLAGINE 21° 53' S Lat; 120° 05' E Long. 1265 ft. above sea level.				
January	102.1	75.3	26.8	88.7
February	101.1	74.4	26.7	87.8
March	97.9	71.1	26.8	84.5
April	91.2	62.1	29.1	76.6
May	82.4	53.4	29.0	67.9
June	75.3	47.0	28.3	61.1
July	75.2	44.7	30.5	59.9
August	79.9	47.8	32.1	63.9
September	88.3	54.3	34.0	71.3
October	95.0	62.7	32.3	78.8
November	100.9	70.4	30.5	85.6
December	103.1	73.9	29.2	88.5
Year	91.0	61.4	29.6	76.2
ONSLOW 21° 43' S Lat; 114° 57' E Long. 14 ft. above sea level.				
January	96.4	74.2	22.2	85.3
February	96.4	74.7	21.7	85.5
March	95.4	73.5	21.9	84.4
April	91.9	67.1	24.8	79.5
May	84.3	60.3	24.0	72.3
June	78.0	54.5	23.5	66.2
July	77.3	51.5	25.8	64.4
August	80.0	53.5	26.5	66.8
September	85.1	56.8	28.3	70.9
October	88.9	61.0	27.9	74.9
November	93.5	66.3	27.2	79.9
December	95.4	70.5	24.9	82.9
Year	88.5	63.7	24.8	76.1
PEAK HILL 25° 38' S Lat; 118° 43' E Long. 1930 ft. above sea level.				
January	99.5	74.4	25.1	86.9
February	98.0	73.9	24.1	85.9
March	94.2	70.2	24.0	82.2
April	85.3	62.5	22.8	73.9
May	74.5	53.6	20.9	64.1
June	67.3	47.6	19.7	57.5
July	66.0	45.5	20.5	55.7
August	70.2	47.6	22.6	58.9
September	78.2	52.9	25.3	65.5
October	85.1	58.6	26.5	71.8
November	93.6	66.5	27.1	80.1
December	99.2	72.7	26.5	85.9
Year	84.3	60.5	23.8	72.4

TABLE 7 – *continued*

	Av. Daily Max. Temp.	Av. Daily Min. Temp.	Av. Daily Range Temp.	Av. Daily Mean Temp.
PORT HEDLAND 20° 19' S Lat; 118° 24' E Long. 25 ft. above sea level.				
January	94.3	79.4	14.9	86.9
February	94.6	79.1	14.5	86.9
March	95.3	77.6	17.7	86.5
April	93.3	71.2	22.1	82.3
May	86.1	63.7	22.4	74.9
June	80.2	57.9	22.3	69.1
July	79.3	55.6	23.7	67.5
August	82.3	58.4	23.9	70.3
September	86.9	62.5	24.4	74.7
October	89.7	68.1	21.6	78.9
November	93.2	73.5	19.7	83.3
December	94.2	77.5	16.7	85.9
Year	89.1	68.7	20.4	78.9
ROEBOURNE 20° 46' S Lat; 117° 09' E Long. 40 ft above sea level.				
January	100.8	79.2	21.6	90.0
February	100.9	79.3	21.6	90.1
March	98.5	77.4	21.1	87.9
April	93.9	70.6	23.3	82.3
May	86.2	64.0	22.2	75.1
June	79.4	58.2	21.2	68.8
July	79.0	55.4	23.6	67.2
August	82.9	57.5	25.4	70.2
September	89.6	61.5	28.1	75.5
October	94.4	66.6	27.8	80.5
November	100.5	73.2	27.3	86.9
December	101.7	76.7	25.0	89.2
Year	92.3	68.3	24.0	80.3
WINNING POOL 23° 08' S Lat; 114° 33' E Long. 280 ft. above sea level.				
January	104.5	73.1	31.4	88.8
February	102.5	73.6	28.9	88.1
March	99.5	71.7	27.8	85.6
April	93.8	66.0	27.8	79.9
May	84.3	58.1	26.2	71.2
June	77.2	52.6	24.6	64.9
July	76.2	50.4	25.8	63.3
August	79.1	51.5	27.6	65.3
September	85.7	54.9	30.8	70.3
October	90.8	59.2	31.6	74.5
November	97.2	64.2	33.0	80.7
December	102.4	69.0	33.4	85.7
Year	91.1	62.0	29.1	76.5

Source: J. Gentilli, *Weather and Climate in Western Australia.*

TABLE 8

NORTH-WEST AREA

Mean relative humidity

(Expressed as a percentage of saturation humidity)

Location	J	F	M	A	M	J	J	A	S	O	N	D	Year
Carnarvon	64	64	64	60	63	61	66	66	62	61	62	64	64
Hamelin Pool ..	46	47	49	53	63	71	70	67	59	63	49	48	55
Marble Bar ..	42	44	35	38	44	48	42	38	34	31	31	36	39
Nullagine	40	40	41	40	46	49	49	43	35	31	30	35	39
Onslow	57	59	58	56	58	60	58	55	51	50	52	55	56
Peak Hill	31	34	34	40	48	55	53	48	37	32	29	31	37
Port Hedland ..	67	63	60	48	50	49	49	50	49	53	56	61	55
Roebourne	52	53	55	46	48	51	47	48	41	43	42	47	48
Winning Pool ..	43	46	46	45	52	56	54	51	42	41	39	39	46

Source: Commonwealth Bureau of Meteorology, *Climatic Averages of Australia.* Melbourne, 1956.

TABLE 9

NORTHWESTERN AUSTRALIA

Mean effective temperatures above 69 degrees Fahrenheit

Location	J	F	M	A	M	J	J	A	S	O	N	D	Total day deg. in year
Wyndham	16	15	14	11	8	4	3	5	9	13	15	14	3,870
Halls Creek	12	11	11	5	—	—	—	—	3	8	10	12	2,160
Broome	13	14	13	10	5	1	—	2	5	8	12	14	2,910
Derby	14	14	13	10	5	2	—	3	7	11	13	14	3,180
Marble Bar	16	15	13	9	3	—	—	1	4	8	12	14	2,820
Nullagine	12	12	9	4	—	—	—	—	—	9	4	11	1,830
Port Hedland	13	13	12	8	3	—	—	—	2	5	9	11	2,280
Roebourne	15	15	13	8	3	—	—	—	3	6	11	13	2,610
Onslow	12	12	11	8	2	—	—	—	—	3	7	9	1,920
Carnarvon	7	8	7	3	—	—	—	—	—	—	2	5	960
Hamelin Pool	9	9	8	4	—	—	—	—	—	—	3	6	1,170
Mundiwindi	9	9	6	1	—	—	—	—	—	—	5	8	1,140
Peak Hill	10	9	7	2	—	—	—	—	—	—	5	9	1,260

Source: J. Gentilli, *Climatic Discomfort in Western Australia.* Research Report no. 24, Geography Laboratory, University of Western Australia.

APPENDIX 4

SOILS AND NATURAL VEGETATION

1. Soils - Introduction

The material dealing with soils has mainly been taken from publications by the Soils Division of the Commonwealth Scientific and Industrial Research Organisation. As would be expected, information in detail about such a vast area as Northwestern Australia is scanty. This appendix has therefore been divided into two main parts: the first gives a *resume* of the great soil groups found in Northwestern Australia (after Stephens),[1] the second is a pedological study in greater detail of those soils which have been subject to closer examination, with a view to their irrigability, by the officers of the C.S.I.R.O. Soil erosion has been discussed under a separate heading as the susceptibility of northern soils to this hazard constitutes a serious problem for all those interested in the development of the region.

2. The Great Soil Groups of Northwestern Australia

Although the representative great soil groups of Northwestern Australia number approximately half of those found in the entire continent, their range is not wide for, on the whole, they have been formed in an area where soil moisture conditions can be considered deficient. Rainfall in this area is seasonal and continually high temperatures during the day cause maximum evapotranspiration. Under these conditions soils suffer little leaching, retain iron and aluminium oxides and accumulate lime or gypsum or both. They are in fact of the soil order of Pedocals. Pedalfers (those soils retaining silicates and losing oxides through leaching) are rare in this region and are represented north of the twenty-sixth parallel only on Dirk Hartog Island. For this reason they will not be discussed below.

Of the twelve great soil groups which do have a wide distribution in Northwestern Australia only six could be considered arable whether under

[1] C. G. Stephens, *The Soil Landscapes of Australia*.

the conditions of dry-land farming or under irrigation. Desert sandplain soils, solonchak and skeletal soils, which cover approximately five-eighths of the area, must at present be ruled out as soils of agricultural potential. The distribution of the remaining soils – calcareous desert soils, solonized brown soils, brown soils of light texture, grey and brown soils of heavy texture, arid red earths and alluvial soils – is severely limited and, due to the exigencies of climate, their agricultural potential is entirely dependent upon their proximity to the larger river courses. In this regard alluvial soils assume a position of importance.

Soils of the Arid Interior

The soils of this arid central region of Northwestern Australia are comprised of desert sandhills, stony desert tableland soils, red earths and skeletal soils. This is perhaps the least known of any of the inland areas of Australia and, as a consequence, the soil data has been interpreted from information supplied by aerial reconnaissance and verbal report rather than from detailed surface surveys.

The soils of the arid interior are essentially the product of the weathering of the residual desert landscape; arid red earths and stony desert tableland soils are found in the valleys between the residual hills and ranges, skeletal soils cover the hill slopes and crests, and desert sandhills mark the deposition of windborne desert detritus in the less protected arid plainlands away from the ranges.

DESERT SANDHILLS

These soils of desert detritus are found over a wide area extending from the Great Sandy Desert in the Canning basin across to the Western Australian border in a south-easterly direction, and occur in a broad arc to the south of Lake Disappointment. They are found in the characteristic form of red parallel dunes composed of sands which are deep and coarse-textured on the ridges with fine-textured and often coherent loamy sands in the depressions. They have a high porosity, and wet deeply during the occasional heavy rains when myriads of ephemeral plants colonize the ridges. Although the average rainfall is only between 5 and 10 inches per annum, the dune corridors and slopes support a sparse but permanent vegetation cover. Mostly the crests of the dunes are unstable, and under the influence of prevailing winds they maintain a seif or linear form. They have no agricultural or pastoral potential.

STONY DESERT TABLELAND SOILS

Most of the stony desert tableland soils of Western Australia lie within the 8 inch rainfall isohyet. A small area of these soils occurs around and to the south of the Percival Lakes in the Canning basin, but they may perhaps best be observed in the vicinity of the Gibson Desert. As their name suggests these soils have been formed on part of the ancient denuded

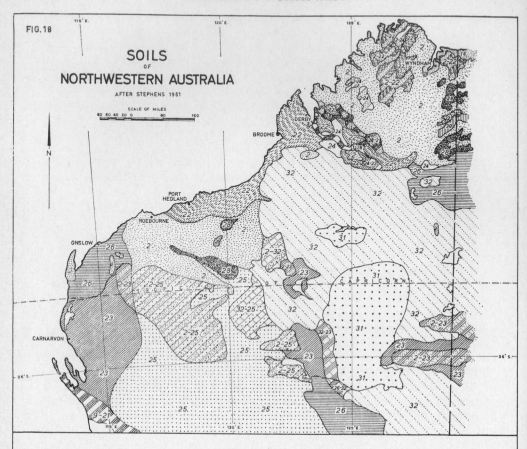

KEY

1 ALLUVIAL SOILS	22 BROWN SOILS OF LIGHT TEXTURE	28 GREY & BROWN SOILS OF HEAVY TEXTURE
2 SKELETAL SOILS	23 ARID RED EARTHS	30 CALCAREOUS DESERT SOILS
9 LATERITIC PODZOLIC SOILS	24 LATERITIC RED EARTHS	31 STONY DESERT TABLELAND SOILS
16 SOLONCHAK	25 RED & BROWN HARDPAN SOILS	32 DESERT SANDHILLS
21 SOLONIZED BROWN SOILS	26 DESERT SAND PLAIN SOILS	

tableland of central Australia, and are not confined solely to Western Australia. Characteristically they consist of a pavement of wind-polished siliceous stones above a deep soil of varying texture. In composition these soils may be calcareous, gypseous or saline, but they exhibit only slight profile differentiation. The stones of the surface pavement have probably been derived from the mechanical breakdown and redistribution of siliceous cap-rock of the surrounding hills and ranges. The soils below are generally red in color and of low fertility.

ARID RED EARTHS

Arid red earths are found in small patches in this central region in the vicinity of Lake Disappointment. They also occur to the north and east of Lake Carnegie and in an area stretching from the Warburton Ranges to the junction of the Northern Territory, South Australian and Western Australian borders.

In general, arid red earths are deep soils of a medium to coarse texture which usually becomes finer with increasing depth. These reddish coloured soils are massive but have a vesicular structure and a completely porous profile. They occur over transported or sedentary material and are essentially soils of pediments. Like the stony desert soils, they are found in the vicinity of higher rugged land, the detrital from which has built up the plains and ground of low relief over which these non-sedentary members have their origin. Arid red earths occur with marked uniformity over wide areas but also exist in pockets within areas of skeletal soil and desert sandhills where conditions for their formation are favourable.

In view of their porous profiles and gentle relief, these soils offer the greatest prospect of any desert soils for agricultural purposes. Their location in this central area however is at present a bar to their utilization.

SKELETAL SOILS

Skeletal soils, as the name suggests, are comprised of an undifferentiated assortment of mineral material produced by the recent breakdown of local landforms. They may be stony or gravelly, but show no profile development other than organic matter accumulation in the surface. They are shallow and of coarse texture and, although the fragmented rock particles may show some degree of weathering, any fine-textured soil material is removed by the natural forces of erosion.

Skeletal soils are usually found where the topography is rugged and the natural processes of erosion are active enough to remove soil. These conditions are found on the eastern extension of the Pilbara block and in a region eastward from the Warburton Ranges to the Western Australian border. In both these localities soils are a complex of skeletal soils, desert sandhills and arid red earths, the former being found mainly on the crests and slopes of weathering outcrops, the latter being situated on valley floors and in open plainlands surrounding residual hills and ranges. These skeletal soils are produced from siliceous mother-rock and are essentially non-arable.

Soils of the North-West

In addition to the soils of the interior which are common to the North-West – arid red earths and skeletal soils – the following soils also occur in this region : desert sandplain soils, brown soils of light texture, grey and brown soils of heavy texture and alluvial soils. The latter are not shown on the map since their occurrence is not widespread.

The groups described above are found in a semi-arid region with an 8-14 inch rainfall where moisture is deficient except within a short humid period during the summer months.

ARID RED EARTHS AND SKELETAL SOILS

These soils occupy more than half of the soil surface of the North-West. Arid red earths have been developed over the sediments of the Carnarvon basin south of the twenty-third parallel and encroach upon the granites composing the western margin of the plateau to the east of the basin. They are traversed by the Minilya, Wooramel and lower Gascoyne rivers. Although these soils are suitable for agricultural development, the lack of abundant surface water in the North-West is a bar to their extensive utilization.

Skeletal soils are common throughout the Pilbara block and Hamersley plateau where they have been produced from the breakdown of Precambrian granites and greenstones and Nullagine sandstones respectively. Skeletal soils also occur over the dissected sedimentary rocks of North-West Cape. They are non-arable. The arid red earths and skeletal soils of the North-West support a natural vegetation suitable for sheep pasture.

DESERT SANDPLAIN SOILS

Desert sandplain soils are found at the northern end of the Carnarvon basin and extend along the coast to the mouth of the Fortescue River. They are composed of brown to red loose surface sands underlain by a horizon of lateritic gravel, at a depth of about three feet, below which is a mottled zone. The coarse texture of these soils at the surface is probably due to the removal of the upper profile by wind under the present semi-arid conditions. The presence of laterite (ironstone concretions) would however indicate that this soil was possibly the product of a former, more humid climatic era. Sand dunes are a feature of this soil group and are found to the east of Exmouth Gulf. The natural vegetation of the desert sandplain soils provides grazing for sheep but the carrying capacity is low.

BROWN SOILS OF LIGHT TEXTURE

The brown soils of light texture of the North-West are a continuation of those soils of the Pindan country of the West Kimberley. They are located along the coast around the lower reaches of the Yule and De Grey rivers and stretch northward in a thin belt skirting the Eighty Mile Beach. Their profile shows little differentiation and, at the surface, they are characterized by coarse brown sands or sandy loam containing only a slight accumulation of organic matter. Some lime is usually present at depth, but the acid reaction of the upper horizon would indicate that these soils have been subject to stronger leaching than is at present experienced. These soils are used exclusively for sheep grazing in this area.

GREY AND BROWN SOILS OF HEAVY TEXTURE

Within the area commonly known as the Fortescue sunkland, grey and brown soils of heavy texture have been formed over a dominantly alluvial parent material. Both these soils are characterized by the fine texture of the profile which varies between a loam, clay-loam and clay. The soil surface is frequently leached due to periodic river flooding – the grey soils mostly occupying areas of seasonal inundation. Because of the clay fraction, these soils tend to dry out in the summer months when they are traversed by cracks which are more pronounced in the finer grey soils.

Because of the slow permeability of the upper horizon, these soils are not well suited to irrigation except for the cultivation of rice as has been found in the Riverina of New South Wales. However, they can support a richer natural pasture than soils elsewhere in the same climatic region. In the North-West they are used for grazing; the small pocket of grey and brown soils of heavy texture coincides with the station properties of Roy Hill and Ethel Creek.

ALLUVIAL SOILS

See below.

Soils of the Kimberley

In view of certain other natural advantages the Kimberley possesses for agricultural development, the soils of this region have been the subject of closer study than those elsewhere in Northwestern Australia. The climate although humid allows but a short growing period, for the rainfall is seasonal; it is received mainly between the months of November and December, and March and April. Whereas dryland farming is unlikely under these conditions, the water resources of the Kimberleys are by far the best in the state, and water conservation and irrigation schemes have been developed to provide the basis for closer agricultural settlement in the future, and for extended growing seasons. As yet, there has been no comprehensive soil survey of the Kimberley but attention has been paid to potentially irrigable soils which will be described in greater detail below in this Appendix.

The soil groups of the Kimberley include all the groups previously discussed, with the exception of arid red earths and red and brown hard-pan soils, added to which are the calcareous desert soils, lateritic red earths and solonchaks. On the whole they are essentially soils of the humid to semi-arid group. Humid soils occur in the gorges and around the sources of the Charnley and Prince Regent rivers.

DESERT SANDHILLS AND DESERT SANDPLAIN SOILS

The South Kimberley region is bordered by desert sandhills and desert sandplain soils which form a continuation of the soils of the arid interior. Only sparsely vegetated, they mark the southern limit of pastoral extension.

CALCAREOUS DESERT SOILS

Calcareous desert soils occur in a small area flanking the right bank of the Ord River below its confluence within the Elvire River. They are commonly formed over limestone (c.f. Nullabor Plain soils) and here overlie the Cambrian flaggy limestones of the Ord basin. These soils consist of powdery grey-brown to red calcareous loams having little profile differentiation. Calcareous desert soils are useful for light grazing but their fine powdery nature makes them very susceptible to deflation. Dust storms are frequently generated on these soils.

SKELETAL SOILS AND BROWN SOILS OF LIGHT TEXTURE

The great bulk of the Kimberley region is occupied by the skeletal soils of the plateau and ranges and the deep sandy brown soils of light texture, such as the Cockatoo sands of the East Kimberley, and the Pindan sands of the West Kimberley.

Rough stony skeletal soils are formed over a wide variety of parent material and are typical of the Kimberley range country and the Hann plateau. They are the most extensive of the Kimberley soil groups and occur on hilly outcrops of sandstones, shales, quartzites and basic volcanics — the immature soil matrix surrounding the stony fragments varying from a sand to a loam depending on the parent source. The widespread occurrence of these skeletal soils largely limits the development of the Kimberley as they are low in fertility and support a vegetation of low pastoral value.

The brown soils of light texture occur extensively in the Fitzroy valley. There are patches of these soils scattered throughout the Hann plateau, and in the east Kimberley, while the soils of Dampier Land, commonly called 'Pindan sands', form a continuation of those brown soils of light texture of the North-West. The Pindan sands are typical of these brown soils of light texture. They form a sandy upland in the West Kimberley where they are marked by east-west oriented stabilized sand dunes. Investigation of these soils in the Derby and Pt. Torment areas shows that because of their low water-holding capacity they have no potential for dry-land farming. In patches where the soil is more clayey in character, they may prove suitable for sprinkler irrigation. At present the brown soils of light texture support a light pasture vegetation.

LATERITIC RED EARTH

Lateritic red earths occur over a variety of materials scattered in pockets throughout the Hann plateau and in the Fitzroy basin. They are red to light red soils of deep profile containing a horizon of laterite beneath which is a mottled and pallid zone. The surface soil is commonly sandy to loamy in texture with a little organic matter contained. The depth of the laterite horizon varies. However its occurrence would indicate that these soils are a remnant of an old land surface.

Lateritic red earths support a pasture of natural grasses and edible plants which are readily grazed for sheep in the Fitzroy valley. These soils have been found useful for horticultural purposes in Darwin and Brisbane where, with the use of irrigation and the application of artificial manures, they have proved quite productive.

GREY AND BROWN SOILS OF HEAVY TEXTURE

In the Kimberley grey and brown soils of heavy texture are predominantly associated with alluvial parent material, hence their location in the valleys of the Ord, Fitzroy and Lennard rivers. They are not confined to riverain sites, however, and are also found to the south of the King Leopold Ranges and in the border area to the east of Hall's Creek. As mentioned previously, these soils are suitable for irrigation particularly when the crop requires inundation. Grey and brown soils of heavy texture carry a good pasture of long grasses and support sheep and cattle grazing in the west and east respectively.

ALLUVIAL SOILS

Because alluvial soils occur on deposits of juvenile alluvium, soil-forming processes have had no time to function. These soils may show a surface accumulation of organic matter and give evidence of sedimentary layering, but they have no fully developed soil profile.

Alluvial soils of the Kimberley are mostly associated with river deposits where they occur as level banks and low-level terraces in valleys of any size. Their colour varies from brown to black and they normally support a good vegetation cover where well watered. Pockets of these soils in the gorges of the plateau country are very fertile but have limited agricultural value. Investigations by the C.S.I.R.O. have shown that more extensive areas of alluvial soil along the major water courses, are admirably suited to irrigation for a wide variety of tropical crops.

SOLONCHAK

Solonchak is a term used to denote saline soil. In the Kimberley solonchaks coincide with the areas of tidal marsh and deltaic formations, principally those found at the mouths of the Fitzroy, Lennard and Meda rivers in the west, and the Ord, Durack and Chamberlain rivers in the east. In fact there are many pockets of solonchak along the coast where soils accumulate soluble salts from the ocean as a result of tidal inundation. But, generally speaking, solonchaks of the Kimberley have been produced by the deposition of river-transported material. They are heavy-textured, show little horizon differentiation and are rich in salt. In most cases they support a mangrove vegetation association. There is little likelihood of their utilization.

3. Soils of Agricultural Potential

Dry-Land Farming or Irrigation

The nature of the climatic regime of Northwestern Australia precludes dry-land farming on a commerical basis. Even given a sufficiency of water-retentive soils in this area, such agriculture could be carried out only on a limited scale and would provide only a limited range of products. High temperatures preclude all but tropical crops which, in the main, need a higher rainfall than Northwestern Australia experiences. The rainfall pattern, with its concentration of precipitation within the summer months, gives a variable growing season, and high temperatures during this time lead to maximum water loss due to evapotranspiration. Further to this, the generally high rainfall variability and incidence of drought would make farming a very hazardous business. Added to these factors are the high rainfall intensity during the wet which increases the danger of flooding, and the other climatic disturbances which are a hazard to crops.

On the other hand, where water conservation schemes are combined with irrigation projects, the growing season can be extended, water losses through evapotranspiration lessened, and the flood menace controlled. By means of irrigation, an area unsuited to dry-land agriculture can become highly productive.

Such is the case in Northwestern Australia, particularly in the Kimberley, where water resources and suitable topography for the construction of dams and weirs may in the future prove the basis of a thriving tropical agriculture. However, in so far as irrigation can overcome the unfavourable aspects of the climate by providing adequate moisture throughout the year, it is just this constant reticulation of agricultural lands which severely restricts the types of soils which may be used. Whereas dry-land farming calls for water-retentive soils, irrigable soils must have the ability to absorb moisture and, at the same time, permit adequate drainage.

Although there are many thousands of acres of land which could be adequately irrigated by virtue of the suitable composition and structure of the soils, their utilization greatly depends upon their location.

Location of Irrigable Soils

Proximity to the water supply is an important pre-requisite for potentially irrigable soils. Where the damming of irrigation waters has occurred at some point along a river valley, the most accessible agricultural soils are usually those which have been formed over the river's alluvium. Generally these soils are of two types : the light, reddish, sandy soils of the river levee, and the heavier, dark-coloured soils of the river flood-plains and terraces. The former allow free drainage and are admirably suited to irrigation, while the latter, having a higher clay content, offer greater problems in regard to drainage. Both soils however maintain their structure under irrigation and can be utilized according to the particular drainage requirements of given crops.

There are many localities in Northwestern Australia where such soils are to be found, but lack of adequate water supplies has been a bar to their utilization. This is particularly true of the North-West where rainfall is unreliable and river flow intermittent. A notable exception occurs at Carnarvon where terrace soils of the lower Gascoyne valley are irrigated by water pumped from the river bed. Irrigated crops have been successfully grown here on a commercial basis for several decades. In isolated instances pockets of river soil are utilized for horticultural purposes, and pastures may be irrigated in order to supplement natural grasses. Such is the case at Boolaloo station in the Ashburton River valley where water pumped from a river pool supports a small-scale irrigation experiment.

However the region where irrigation offers most and where water could be readily dammed, rather than pumped from river beds, is the Kimberley. Two projects have been developed in this region, one on the Ord River and the other on the Fitzroy, for the commercial production of irrigated tropical crops. Pilot farms at Kimberley Research Station on the Ord River and at Liveringa on the Fitzroy, have already established the suitability of some of these soils for irrigation. Officers of the Soils Division of the C.S.I.R.O. in 1952 surveyed other soils along the valleys of the Lennard and Barker rivers and the Margaret and Fitzroy rivers.[2] They pointed to the possible location of dam sites in these areas and the favourable location of many acres of alluvial soil which are potentially irrigable. Similar alluvial soils occur along the lower reaches of, at least, the Drysdale and the Meda rivers and possibly many more.

Irrigated Soils of Northwestern Australia

IRRIGATED SOILS OF THE LOWER GASCOYNE RIVER

Irrigation is carried out on alluvial soils at Carnarvon in the lower Gascoyne River valley. These soils principally occur on a recent river terrace situated 12-30 feet above the present bed of the river, and are up to 20 feet above the normal flood level although flooding in bad years still presents problems. The river terrace consists of recent deposits of brown sands, brown micaceous loams and sandy loams, the latter two soils generally exhibiting a calcareous sub-soil. Because of their coarse texture, the

[2]C. S. Christian and G. A. Stewart, 'Report on Preliminary Examination of Several Areas in the West Kimberley Division of Western Australia'.

brown sands respond less satisfactorily than the loamy soils which work
into a good tilth with vigorous cultivation.

All three soil types drain well, but the loamy soils with their calcareous
sub-soil are better suited to the Gascoyne water as the calcium carbonate
counteracts its solonizing effect.[3] Irrigation waters pumped from the dry
bed of the Gascoyne River contain from 43 to 77 G.P.G. principally of
sodium chloride. The irrigable soils of the Gascoyne are well supplied with
the plant food constituents of phosphate and potash, although they are not so
well endowed with nitrogen. However, the presence of calcium augers well
for the permanent irrigation of these soils because calcium soils generally
maintain their structure.

They have been cultivated since 1922 when the Gascoyne Research
Station was established. Since that time they have proved their suitability
for the growing of tropical fruits, especially bananas, and vegetables.

IRRIGATED SOILS OF THE ORD RIVER

The largest present known area of irrigable soils in the Kimberley corresponds to the flood-plains of the lower reaches of the Ord River. These
flood-plains have been laid down in a previous cycle of erosion when the
river ponded over a wide area between Wyndham and the Northern Territory border. Over the alluvial deposits of these plains, the product of
the weathering of the basalts, limestones and mudstones of the Ord basin,
the darker soils of heavier texture have been developed, while along the
river banks are found the reddish sandy levee soils.

It is estimated that some 200,000 acres of irrigable soils are available in
the Western Australian portion of the lower Ord valley, while many more
acres of similar soils extend across the Northern Territory border. At
present, in conjunction with the C.S.I.R.O., the state Department of Agriculture is conducting research into the value of the flood-plain soils of the
Ord, namely the Kununurra clay.

The darker soils of heavier texture and their counterparts elsewhere in
the Kimberley have been locally called 'black soil' or 'black clay'. In the
vicinity of the Kimberley Research Station, this so-called black soil is known
as 'Kununurra clay', after the native name for the Ord River.

The Kununurra clay is a dark-brown to dark-grey, crumbly clay soil.
The surface layer contains a mixture of clay, silt and fine sand with an
accumulation of organic matter derived from its grassland vegetation cover.
In the dry season the clayey surface soil cracks into massive blocks which
are difficult to work but when broken down produce clods which weather
to give a good structure. Wet working, on the other hand, is no less
difficult and produces a glazed surface which does not readily break down
when the soil dries out.

[3]'Solonization' is the term used to denote the accumulation of sodium in the
replaceable base fraction of the soil.

The fine texture of the Kununurra clay imposes other disabilities on this soil when irrigated. The heavy clay nature of the soil makes it prone to water-logging after rains and thus restricts the range of crops that can be grown. Likewise the impermeability of the soil sub-surfaces renders drainage measures difficult and expensive. However, the low permeability of the Kununurra clay once the soil is wetted, allows the cutting of conducting channels straight from the soil, and there is no need for costly concrete lining.

Although these black soils are deficient in phosphate and nitrogen, and hence require artificial fertilizers, they have proved a satisfactory soil for irrigation, and at the Kimberley Research Station they have successfully supported crops as described in Chapter 6.

IRRIGATED SOILS OF THE FITZROY RIVER

At Liveringa, 120 miles from Derby along the valley of the Fitzroy River, are found soils of the so-called black type which roughly correspond to the Kununurra clays of the Ord. They are dark-coloured soils of heavier texture formed over the alluvial deposits of the Fitzroy. They exhibit similar characteristics to the irrigated Ord River clays; their finer texture leads to marked shrinkage and cracking when dry and stickiness when wet. Despite the engineering problems that such features present, this soil is an excellent agricultural soil.

As is most often the case in the Kimberley, these black soils in the Fitzroy are flanked by the reddish sandy levee soils which line the innumerable billabongs and anna-branches of the old river. It is along one such channel, namely Uralla Creek, that the waters of the Fitzroy are pumped for irrigation purposes – they are diverted from a weir built across the Fitzroy 17 miles from the irrigation project.

Until a major dam can be built, flooding creates a problem and, at present, because of the seasonal flow of the river, only wet-season crops can be cultivated. These soils have so far proved their suitability for the cropping of rice, safflower, sudan grass and linseed.

4. Soil Erosion

The decimation of pastoral land due to soil erosion constitutes a grave problem in Northwestern Australia; many thousands of acres of good pastoral land have been denuded of surface soil and vegetation cover by gullying and sheet erosion and by the process of deflation. Undoubtedly much of this has been due to overstocking, but man alone cannot be held entirely to blame. The exigencies of climate, the nature of the soil surface and the increasing number of grazing native fauna have frequently combined to create dust bowl conditions; overstocking has often merely aggravated these conditions.

The wholesale wastage of surface soil cover has repercussions upon the pastoralist and the agriculturalist, for a serious problem in the region is the silting up of the dams and reservoirs which are essential to conserve water in these seasonally dry areas. The silt load of northern rivers is high because of the high rainfall intensity, but it is increasing where vegetation cover has been removed and is creating engineering problems especially in such undertakings as the Ord River project. Perhaps an even more serious aspect of the threat of erosion is the fact that the loss of vegetation cover of a river's drainage basin will not only aid the process of erosion but will diminish the soil's capacity to hold moisture, and thus the river's drainage basin will no longer act efficiently as a natural reservoir.

The implications of this for development programmes based on water conservation are obvious. It is vital to preserve natural vegetation both along the main course of the river and its upper reaches, and to reclaim areas that are at present suffering from the removal of the vegetation cover.

Factors Influencing Soil Erosion.

CLIMATE

Whenever rainfall is restricted to a limited period of the year there is always the danger of soil erosion. In Northwestern Australia where rainfall occurs roughly between the months of November and April, water erosion is at a maximum. As noted in Appendix 3, this factor combined with a high intensity, creates a condition where rainfall has not sufficient time to soak into the soil, and the subsequent runoff leads to the widespread removal of the soil surface through rainwash. The most common forms of this are gullying and sheet erosion. This occurs mostly in previously dry soils.

Gullying is common in areas where the soil has a marked slope and it is particularly in evidence along river levees. Unfortunately, on pastoral holdings where cattle and sheep gather along river frontages, the process of erosion is accelerated by the natural vegetation surrounding common watering places being trampled down and eaten out. Thus constant herding along river frontages results in the loss of the natural vegetation which is essential to regulate the sub-surface flow of water into the river bed. Such conditions exist in the valleys of the Ord and Fitzroy rivers where along the banks of the Ord, Fitzroy and Margaret rivers and Christmas Creek drastic measures will have to be taken to prevent further degradation of levee soils.

Sheet erosion occurs principally on the flood-plains of the major northern rivers and causes damage to extensive tracts of good pastoral lands. Surface soil is removed with the consequent loss of pasture. When such is the case, exposed soil surfaces are prone to deflation during the period of drought. Sheet and gully erosion have reached their maximum intensity on the Ord River catchment area where over 1,100 square miles of pasture lands are affected. Degradation ranges from partial to complete denudation. It also extends along the Fitzroy flood-plain.

SOILS

In the case mentioned above, where erosion is so rife, the nature of the soil has been a major contributing factor. In the Ord River catchment area the Upper Cambrian flaggy limestones and mudstones have weathered into fine powdery soils, the surface of which is readily removed by both wind and water. The present natural grass cover, an inferior annual species, has been overgrazed and the combined result is a badly dissected landscape almost devoid of tree cover except along stream lines. Instead of an undulating grassland, this region is one of bare, exposed sub-soils where wide shallow channels and the 'perched' roots of dead trees bear witness to the severity of both gullying and sheet erosion. The whole region is prone to severe dust storms.

A further example of the soil factor and its influence upon erosion can be seen along the river flood-plains where the finer grey and brown soils of heavier texture are reduced to powdery claypans under conditions of alternate flooding, overgrazing and stock trampling. They are particularly troublesome in the West Kimberleys and in small areas on station properties in the North-West Division. Such soils are normally water-retentive and support a moderate to good pasture but when overgrazed they become 'scalded'; they are denuded of vegetation cover which has little chance of natural regeneration. In the North-West Division observation of such claypans shows that natural grasses are being encroached upon at an alarming rate, and that early reclamation is essential. In Chapter 3 there is a more detailed discussion of the attempts to overcome this problem.

OVERSTOCKING

As can be seen from the comments above, it is impossible to isolate the factors contributing to the degradation of the soil, for they are interactive. Usually in the process of soil erosion one factor may act as a trigger, and there can be little doubt that, in the case of the pastoral lands of North-western Australia, overstocking has played an initiatory role in the past. Overstocking results in the eating out of the natural pasture cover, edible bushes and trees, and exposes the soil to the elements of climate which lead to erosion. Some soils are more prone to erosion than others, but once the vegetation cover is removed – and so many of the northern plant species show little tendency towards natural regeneration – the outcome is always the same : soil erosion.

Overstocking may take two forms. The most obvious occurs where the numbers of cattle or sheep pastured are greater than the safe carrying capacity of the whole station run. In areas where rainfall is seasonal and drought common the carrying capacities are low and the limits easily over-reached.

The second form occurs when animals are left on a given pasture as long as they continue to do well. In this case the grasses have little or no opportunity to set seed or establish root reserves, with the result that the more palatable and usually more nutritious species have only a limited opportunity for natural regeneration, and the quality of the pasture deteriorates. The less palatable, and usually less nutritious, grass varieties take the place of better pasture grasses and this leads to a decline in the carrying capacity. This is particularly in evidence in the North-West Division where, for instance, soft spinifex takes over when the better woollybutt grass is eaten out. Particularly in the case of sheep, the decline in the quality of pasture has grave repercussions, for lambing percentages are seriously affected. The nutritional value of spinifex is low and, while it will sustain dry sheep, better pastures are needed for pregnant or lactating ewes.

Overstocking may be intentional or it may be accidental. The question of immediate returns has often prompted pastoralists to overstock their holdings by choice whereas in bad seasons, when surplus stock is not readily saleable due to distance from markets, station managers are often forced to retain stock in numbers beyond the carrying capacity of the available pasture. Whatever the reason for overstocking, the outcome in terms of erosion is always the same : soil deterioration and the silting up of waterways.

Overstocking is a universal problem throughout the pastoral areas of the region but the grasslands of the so-called black soils – the better quality Mitchell and Flinders grasses – are most subject to overgrazing. If this process continues the whole nature of the pasture will eventually change but, as outlined in Chapter 3, attempts are now being made to halt the general deterioration which has become manifest. Likewise, edible shrubs and trees are suffering a similar fate, and such trees as the Kimberley camel tree, which produces edible beans, show no sign of regeneration. On the whole, woody vegetation tends to collapse under heavy grazing with the resultant loss of shade trees in addition to the effect which their collapse has on soil erosion.

Lighter pastures, such as those found on the coarse sandy pindan soils, do not escape the fate of their richer counterparts. These grasses are over-eaten and, in places in the West Kimberley, have left exposed dune sands which quickly shift and envelope relatively good lands. Such is the case in the marginal rainfall areas bordering on the desert to the south of the Fitzroy basin. Here bores and natural springs attract a concentration of stock, light pastures are eaten out and the removal of the original sparse vegetation cover assists in the encroachment of sands to the north. Many similar examples could be cited in the North-West Division.

OTHER FACTORS

In addition to the overstocking of natural pastures with cattle and sheep, great numbers of animals classed as vermin add to the drain on the vegetation resources of the region. Kangaroos, wild dogs, wild goats, and donkeys compete with sheep and cattle for available feed and water. The vermin in the region have, of course, a direct and adverse effect on the pastoral industry. The attempts to combat vermin are examined in Chapter 3.

A further factor affecting soil erosion is the bushfire, but it may be said that, in general, its regenerative effects on native plant species outweigh its destructive effects. The burning out of old culms of spinifex to activate new growth is often undertaken.

Gardner also draws attention to insolation as a factor in soil erosion.[4] As top cover is removed for one reason or another, its natural insulating effect is reduced and larger species then die until, finally, even the bigger trees are lost and the area becomes completely denuded.

Soil Conservation and Erosion Control Measures

The Soil Conservation Branch of the Western Australian Department of Agriculture has in recent years been devoting much time and attention to the problem of soil erosion in Northwestern Australia. They cannot succeed in their programmes of conservation and reclamation unless given full co-operation by station owners and managers. In many cases this co-operation has been forthcoming, in many others economic expediency has been a bar to costly conservation programmes. Where attempts have been made to improve pasture and re-establish vegetation the results have been very promising.

Control measures as adopted by the Department of Agriculture have one feature in common; they are all directed towards the re-establishment of natural and introduced pasture vegetation. In attempting to regenerate eaten-out and degraded country, the department hopes to reduce rainfall runoff, and increase water penetration of the soil, and so reduce soil erosion.

Erosion control measures serve a twofold purpose in that, if they are successful, they inhibit soil erosion while at the same time improving the value of pasture. Most control measures involve the re-seeding of fenced paddocks coupled with the deferred grazing of cattle or sheep. The reclamation process usually involves the ploughing and seeding of scalded patches of soil after the first rains, commonly in a checkerboard pattern. The seeded paddock is fenced and the grazing of stock is deferred until such time as the pasture sets seed. The animals are then turned into the treated paddock at heavy stocking rate so that the seed will be trampled into the earth and spread. By such means buffel and birdwood grasses and kapok bush have been introduced to station properties in the region. Buffel grass, brought to the region by accident, has proved of great value and the active spreading of it took place as early as 1927 and 1928. Buffel grass has taken well in the coastal areas on soils originally occupied by native grasses such as weeping grass and bundle-bundle, rather than in the spinifex

[4]C. A. Gardner, *Flora of Western Australia,* vol. 1, part 1.

areas, but birdwood is more palatable and permanent.

Recently, pasture regeneration has been practised with remarkable success in station properties along the Margaret River frontage near Fitzroy Crossing. Soil erosion has been inhibited in all cases and the better pasture cover has assisted in the process of building up the soil. Water spreading and contour ripping have also proved of value in re-establishing pasture along river frontage properties. At the time of re-seeding, creek water is dammed and allowed to spill over the countryside to moisten the ground. Such methods have proved successful east of Derby along the banks of the Fitzroy River.

Conservation and control methods are not widely accepted as yet, but small-scale experiments prove that results are worthwhile. Such grasses as buffel and birdwood, because of their tussock-forming habits and their massive rooting systems, have proved ideal for the control of soil erosion. Their introduction in the north has done much to halt soil deterioration. The same degree of success cannot be claimed for the large-scale regeneration trials which require a marked degree of station co-operation. The Ord River catchment area remains a most serious erosion problem. In order to reduce siltation, the government has attempted to introduce a large-scale regeneration programme. Proposals call for fencing, re-seeding and deferred rotational grazing, and the adoption of contour methods. It is hoped that the introduction of buffel and birdwood grasses and kapok bush will be successful in reclaiming this area in the near future.

5. NATURAL VEGETATION – INTRODUCTION

The natural vegetation of any area consists of a complex integrated cover of plants of many different types which depends for its constitution and stability upon such factors as climate, geology and soils, topography, and the influence of man and animals.

In origin the vegetation of Northwestern Australia is most closely related to the flora of Malaya and the tropical islands of Indonesia and Melanesia. The major plant forms have spread southward from the Kimberley adapting themselves to increasingly arid conditions. Gardner postulates that this Indo-Malayan element is strong in the Kimberley region and can be traced to the North-West Division, linking these two areas via the vegetated corridor fringing the arid interior along the Eighty Mile Beach.[5] However, there are no true rain forests which are usually considered so characteristic of the tropics, and the Indo-Malayan element gives a distinct physiognomy only where representative plants are concentrated in special habitats, as along stream lines and scarps in the far north.

From the Cretaceous era onwards the Australian bush developed in isolation and it is believed that many of the old luxuriant plant forms from the

[5]C. A. Gardner, 'The Vegetation of Western Australia', p.38.

north developed numerous xerophytic species in response to the harsher climatic environment. The xerophytes or 'dry living' plants have evolved means of conserving water and can thus maintain their stability in arid areas, during periods of drought, or over porous soils. As evidence of this adaptation Gardner cites the *Acacia* spp., which he believes were originally tropical plants. Whether Australian or Indo-Malayan in origin most species occurring in Northwestern Australia are hard-leaved (sclerophyllous) and xerophytic.

Vegetation types have been variously categorized into forms and sub-forms which exhibit a set of communal characteristics unique to each group. In Northwestern Australia the dominant forms are woodlands, shrub communities, savannahs, and grasslands, added to which is a miscellaneous grouping including sandhill desert, stony desert, and the littoral complex.

One of the features of the vegetation of the vast surface area of this region is the prominent place grasses take as an important ground flora. Except in the riverain forest and mangrove formations of the littoral complex, grass occurs almost everywhere. Grasses range from the long tussock-forming species of the northern and western parts of the region, to the spiney tussock-forming species of the southern part and the interior. It is not surprising, therefore, that land usage in Northwestern Australia has been primarily devoted to pastoralism.

In view of the strong influence exerted upon natural vegetation both by the climatic and edaphic factors, the major vegetation associations of Northwestern Australia have been grouped according to their location in the Kimberley, the North-West Division and the arid interior respectively. In both the text, the chart (p. 422), and the map (Fig. 19), the terminology relating to sub-forms follows that of Williams.[6] His grouping of associations is based on the structure of the vegetation, i.e., the spatial relationships of the various growth forms and the seasonal charateristics of the component species.

6. Natural Vegetation of the Kimberley

Three major vegetation forms are represented in the Kimberley, namely : woodlands, savannah and grasslands. Miscellaneous forms include the littoral complex of the coastal lowlands and the sandhill desert fringing the southern edge of the Fitzroy basin.

It is virtually impossible to establish any strict latitudinal (climatic) division between the major forms, for frequently topography and soils exert a strong determining influence on their location. However, broadly speaking, woodlands are found in a wide arc bordering the north coast from Dampier Land in the west, across the Gardner plateau and across the Ord valley in the east where they form a continuation with the woodlands of the Northern Territory. Savannah vegetation is found in a wide belt corresponding to

[6]Commonwealth Department of National Development, Atlas of Australian Resources, 1st series, with commentaries, *Vegetation Regions*.

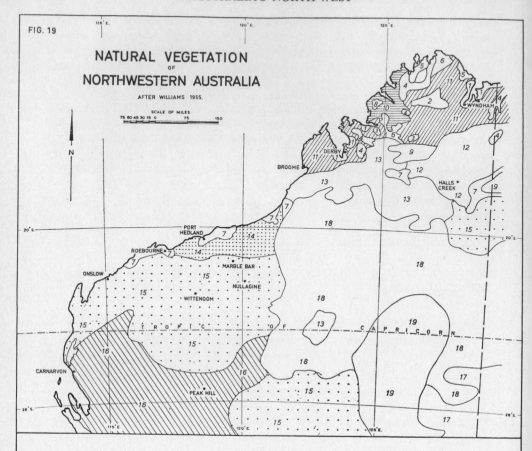

FIG. 19

NATURAL VEGETATION
OF
NORTHWESTERN AUSTRALIA

AFTER WILLIAMS 1955.

SCALE OF MILES
75 60 45 30 15 0   75   150

KEY

WOODLAND.
5 TROPICAL DECIDUOUS WOODLAND
11 TROPICAL WOODLAND (MIXED)
SAVANNAH.
4 TROPICAL TREE SAVANNAH
13 SCLEROPHYLL SHRUB SAVANNAH
14 SCLEROPHYLL LOW TREE SAVANNAH
GRASSLAND.
7 SEMI ARID TUSSOCK GRASSLAND
8 TROPICAL TUSSOCK GRASSLAND
MISCELLANEOUS.
18 SANDHILL DESERT
19 STONY DESERT

COMPLEXES.
1 LITTORAL COMPLEX
2 TROPICAL TUSSOCK GRASSLAND AND TROPICAL WOODLAND (MIXED)
3 TROPICAL TUSSOCK GRASSLAND AND TROPICAL TREE SAVANNAH
6 TROPICAL WOODLAND (MIXED) AND TROPICAL TREE SAVANNAH
9 SEMI-ARID TUSSOCK GRASSLAND AND LOW ARID WOODLAND
10 TROPICAL DECIDUOUS WOODLAND AND TROPICAL WOODLAND (MIXED)
12 LOW ARID WOODLAND AND SCLEROPHYLL LOW TREE SAVANNAH
15 SCLEROPHYLL SHRUB SAVANNAH AND SCLEROPHYLL HUMMOCK GRASS
16 ARID SCRUB AND SCLEROPHYLL SHRUB SAVANNAH
17 SCLEROPHYLL SHRUB SAVANNAH, LOW ARID WOODLAND AND ARID SCRUB

the Fitzroy valley and sweeping eastward to the Northern Territory border where it is intermingled with the woodland form. Pockets of both savannah and grassland occur where conditions are less favourable for woodlands in various localities throughout the entire area.

Woodland Form

The sub-forms represented in the Kimberley woodlands include tropical woodland (mixed), tropical deciduous woodland and low arid woodland. There are no true forests in the Kimberley although Gardner speaks of the riverain or corridor forests which fringe such northern-flowing rivers as the Drysdale. Even within the woodland formation, trees are usually sparsely distributed and the formation may be more readily described as open woodland.

TROPICAL WOODLAND (mixed)

This is an artificial group brought together for the purposes of mapping. It includes a variety of woodland type which has been variously named by different authors. In structure it is not unlike the temperate woodlands of southern Australia, but in the north the growing season is restricted to the few hot wet summer months.

TROPICAL SAVANNAH WOODLAND

The dominant sub-form of the tropical woodland is characterized by sclerophyllous *Eucalyptus* spp. However, communities having Indo-Malayan affinities are frequently found where moisture conditions favour lush growth. Generally speaking the tropical woodlands are open and, due to the high light intensity and adequate moisture, develop a fairly dense ground stratum of grasses. They are most commonly called tropical savannah woodland.

This sub-form closely reflects the influence of the underlying soils. Tree density increases where the soils become lighter or rocky where, as also on steep slopes, the ground layer is often sparse. Grass species under such conditions lose their nutritional value and palatability and their carrying capacity is low. On the other hand, where soils are of heavier quality and are moisture-retentive, the grass layer becomes more dense and the better quality species give rise to a good pasture.

In the plateau region two types of savannah woodland have been distinguished. The first may be called basaltic savannah woodland which occurs over the basalt soils of this region. *Eucalyptus* spp. (e.g., greybox, coolibah and bloodwoods) are characteristic and deciduous trees such as rosewoods are not uncommon. Apart from *Eucalyptus* spp., the only prevalent evergreen trees are species of *Hakea* and *Grevillea*. Species present, which provide cattle top-feed, include mimosa *(Acacia* sp.) cameltree and konkerberry. There are few shrubs and the ground is densely covered with perennial grasses, notably Flinders and blue grasses and kangaroo grass. The pastures are good but, where scattered over small areas within the plateau region, lose their economic value due to inaccessibility.

The sandstone savannah woodland is largely restricted to the steep escarpments and ranges of the plateau. This country carries a denser tree vegetation with a good deal of shrubbery undergrowth and, in consequence, the grass understorey suffers and species are of the coarser, poorer type.

Whereas there is a uniformity about the vegetation of the basaltic savannah woodland, the sandstone savannah woodland, because of the deeply eroded nature of the country, is remarkably diversified.

Floristically it is much richer than its basaltic counterpart and shows a more marked intrusion of the Indo-Malayan element. The more common *Eucalyptus* spp. include messmate and woollybutt and species of *Grevillea, Hakea* and *Banksia* are well represented. The tropical groups that give this woodland its distinctive character include *Ficus* and cyprus pine, rosewood and konkenberry and the distinctive baobab tree. Sub-shrubby plants such as the hibiscus lend colour to the woodland because of their flowering habits.

Grasses of the savannah woodland are dominated by annual *Sorghum* spp. – one of which attains a height of 6 to 8 feet – and soft spinifex *(Plectrachne pungens)*. These grasses are less attractive as pasture and of a poorer quality than those found in the basaltic savannah woodland. Sugar grass is common and many genera of the family *Cyperaceae* are found in swampy areas.

RIVERAIN OR CORRIDOR FORESTS

It has been previously stated that rain forests are not represented in Northwestern Australia. Nevertheless, where the environment is conducive to tree growth, a woody association predominates which is not strictly woodland but is classified under this heading as its occurrence is restricted.

Riverain or corridor forests, so named after their location, are found in pockets in the canyons and gorges of the sandstone plateau of the North Kimberleys and along the black swampy soils of the lower Brockman and Drysdale rivers.[7] Whereas at plateau level the period of winter drought restricts the plant population to the xerophytic Australian species, mesophytic and hydrophytic elements of the Indo-Malayan flora find a suitable habitat in the deep river gorges. Here telluric water supplies their greater moisture requirements and provides a microclimate suitable for the development of a forest association. Moisture persists throughout the dry period and a dense forest practically devoid of *Eucalyptus* spp. has become established. Such locations carry a profusion of broad-leaved trees whose canopy is more dense than previous sub-forms. Shrubs form a second storey and the ground flora is commonly composed of ferns, but no grasses. The Leichardt trees, banyan, cadjiput and species of *Ficus, Calythrix* and *Solanum*

[7]C. A. Gardner, 'The Vegetation of Western Australia'.

are characteristic and, where the riverain forest occurs in the lower reaches of northern rivers, this association merges with the mangroves of the littoral complex.

SCLEROPHYLL WOODLAND

A type of woodland closely resembling the jarrah forests of the South-West has established itself in the lateritic and skeletal soils of the North-West Kimberley and must be considered under this heading of mixed tropical woodland.[8] It is particularly prominent in the Drysdale region away from the water-course. The tree association is dominated by the hard-leaved ever-green *Eucalyptus* spp. and such trees as messmate, iron bark, stringy bark and woollybutt are characteristic. Shrubby plants such as pindan wattle and species of *Jacksonia* and *Grevillea* are found with the more tropical *Pandanus* and *Livistona* (fan palm). A ground flora of grasses is dominated by soft spinifex and *Sorghum*.

TROPICAL DECIDUOUS WOODLAND

The woodland community of this sub-form is dominated by deciduous (in the dry winter season) or semi-deciduous trees. The leafless period depends greatly upon the length and severity of the dry period and in many species is very short. Tropical deciduous woodland is usually found on stony soils on the higher rainfall areas of the plateau where soils are shallow or skeletal, and thus this association is found in suitable habitats scattered throughout the north-western plateau region.

Dominants are either low deciduous *Eucalyptus* spp. or those with Indo-Malayan affinities including the camel tree, rosewood, supplejack, and whitewood. Several species of *Hakea* are also present. The tropical element is particularly prominent on soils overlying the limestone formations. A discontinuous understorey of sclerophyllous shrubs is found in this sub-form. A sparse herb stratum composed chiefly of annual and perennial grasses provides only a limited pasture of low carrying capacity.

LOW ARID WOODLAND

This sub-form is dominated by a layer of low trees usually less than 30 feet high with an open to almost continuous canopy. A sub-strata of shrubs and under-shrubs may be found and the herbaceous layer where present is composed of a high proportion of short-lived annuals and spinifex *(Triodia)*.

Low arid woodland occurs in the less well watered areas of the Kimber-ley, particularly over the stony skeletal soils of the ranges and the porous sandy soils such as the Cockatoo Sands of the East Kimberley. Although this association occurs in a lighter rainfall area, the soil characteristics affect moisture availability and, as a result, carry a woodland of smaller trees. Evergreen *Eucalyptus* spp. are dominant species. This is commonly known as savannah steppe.

[8]C. A. Gardner, 'The Vegetation of Western Australia'.

This sub-form occurs in the East Kimberley over a wide area stretching from the Fitzroy River, east of Fitzroy Crossing, to the Northern Territory border and encompasses the Ord River catchment area. Here the low arid woodland grades into the sclerophyll low tree savannah. Its pastoral potential has been severely limited due to overgrazing.

Savannah Form

Three sub-forms of savannah vegetation are found in the Kimberley, namely the tropical tree savannah, the sclerophyll shrub savannah and the sclerophyll low tree savannah. They are dominated by a herbaceous ground layer with hummock grasses dominating the first two sub-forms, and tall grasses being characteristic of the third. Despite the better quality of the grasses of the tropical tree savannah, they are of the least economic value in view of their location in inaccessible areas along the north and western sectors of the sandstone plateau.

TROPICAL TREE SAVANNAH

Tropical tree savannah is found over a variety of soils in the Kimberley but is usually restricted to patches within the boundaries of the woodland formation. Thus sub-form occurs over a wide area in the vicinity of the King Edward River in the north, the Lennard, Meda and Robinson rivers in the west, and in limited patches to the north of the King Leopold Range. It is also represented in the East Kimberley to the east of the Ord River.

Tropical tree savannah is typified by a ground flora of tall grasses having a summer growing season. These may be stratified into two or more layers and the dominant species are varied both in location and nutritional value. They include beard grass, silky brown top, kerosene grass, wire grass, bundle-bundle and plume sorghum. The latter grasses provide the better quality pastures. Plume sorghum, which thrives on skeletal volcanic soils, is a grass particularly valuable by virtue of its palatability during its growing period, and by its provision of edible fodder during the dry season. Bundle-bundle, a blue grass species, which grows on soils of heavier texture, is perhaps the better fodder grass as it has a high nutritive value. Its occurrence is usually limited, however, to the better watered river valleys.

In the tree layer of this sub-form the eucalypts are represented predominantly by bloodwood. Shrubby trees, such as konkerberry and ironwood, typify the tropical element. Pastoral usage of the tropical tree savannah is restricted due to the relatively small area covered by this association and its discontinuous nature.

SCLEROPHYLL LOW-TREE SAVANNAH

Whereas the previous sub-form is dominated by tall grasses, the grass layer of the sclerophyll low-tree savannah is mainly composed of sclerophyllous hummock-forming grasses such as the spinifexes. This sub-form is found in the eastern Kimberleys mixed as a complex with the low arid woodland formation.

Several species of hard and soft spinifex are typical of this association. Spinifex is characteristic of skeletal and sandy soils where the rainfall is generally less than 30 inches per annum and usually restricted to about three months of the year or less. For most of the year the land surface grassed by spinifex gives the appearance of semi-desert as, because of the hummock-forming habit of this grass, much bare ground is exposed. However, after rains numerous ephemerals appear.

The hard needle-like nature of the dominant grasses reduces the danger of over-grazing to some degree. However, this means that better-quality grasses established in depressions and along river beds are usually eaten out while the spinifex re-generates and so reduces the overall quality of pastures. Although spinifex pastures provide useful feed for a few months, they are only useful for extensive grazing.

The tree layer in the sclerophyll low-tree savannah is dominated by species of *Eucalyptus*, *Grevillea* and *Hakea*, and it is in this sub-form that *Acacia aneura*, commonly known as mulga, is found.

SCLEROPHYLL SHRUB SAVANNAH

This is found over a wide area of the West Kimberley sweeping in an arc from La Grange, across the Fitzroy valley to the Leopold Ranges and south-eastward across Margaret River and Christmas and Sturt creeks to the Northern Territory border. Between the headwaters of Christmas Creek and the border, this savannah is mixed in a complex with the sclerophyll hummock grassland. It is one of the most widespread of the vegetation sub-forms in the Kimberley and certainly one of the most economically significant. It is commonly known as pindan.

The sclerophyll shrub savannah is dominated by grasses of various forms according to location. Hummock grasses of the spinifex variety are most common but in the better-watered river valleys over the soils of heavier texture, tall tussock grasses are frequently found. The grasslands are dotted with a variety of sclerophyllous shrubs, particularly *Acacia* spp. Where trees occur they are predominantly *Eucalyptus* spp. Some shrubby plants, such as the camel tree, provide top feed, but they occur in limited quantities where the soil is rich and well-watered.

Grasses of the Fitzroy River may be taken as representative of those occurring over the better soils, in contrast to the spinifex of the sandy and skeletal soils. They include Flinders and blue grass, Mitchell, button, kangaroo, sugar, rice grasses and *Sorghum* spp. Of these grasses the first three provide the most nutritious and palatable pasture though they are restricted to the heavier soil regions. Spinifex species are the most abundant grass type and cover wide areas of higher ground. As in other areas where better-quality pasture grasses are overgrazed, the spinifex spreads and so the general quality of the pasture deteriorates. Pastures along river frontages are often overgrazed with the result that soil erosion is a major problem.

Grassland Form

In the Kimberley, three sub-forms represent the pure grassland form. They are the tropical tussock grassland, the semi-arid tussock grassland and the sclerophyll hummock grassland. Generally speaking, they are of limited extent and do not provide as good a pasture as that found in the savannah sub-form.

TROPICAL TUSSOCK GRASSLAND

This sub-form is found in isolated pockets on the plateau in a mixed complex either with the tropical woodland (mixed) or the tropical tree savannah. It is typified by tall perennial tussock grasses having a marked wet (summer) season growing period. Characteristic of tropical grass communities, the representative types – kangaroo and wanderrie grass, plume sorghum and wild rice – show a pronounced decline in nutritional status after maturity. Due to their limited distribution within the plateau, their economic potential is not great.

SEMI-ARID TUSSOCK GRASSLAND

In an area around Glenroy Station the semi-arid tussock grassland is found in a mixed complex with the low arid woodland formation. A similar complex is found along the Northern Territory border to the south-east of Hall's Creek. Other small areas of this grassland type occur along Sturt Creek, north of Fitzroy Crossing, and in pockets along the Eighty Mile Beach from Anna Plains southwards.

Once again the grasses are of tussock form and are dominated by species of Mitchell grass, particularly where soil moisture conditions are favourable. Bundle-bundle is also found in damp areas and along the coast, where this sub-form occurs, the introduced buffel grass has replaced many of the native grass species.

SCLEROPHYLL HUMMOCK GRASSLAND

This sub-form, which is so typical of the north, is found as a mixed complex with the sclerophyll shrub savannah in the South-East Kimberley along the Northern Territory border. Spinifex species dominate the sub-form which is found in the drier area bordering on the desert. The grasses form an open community, but between the isolated grass hummocks societies of short-lived annuals may develop after heavy rains. These grasses are adapted to an arid habitat and are found over desert sandplain soils. They are of limited pastoral value as there are no richer grasses in this sub-form to supplement them. This is steppe vegetation.

Miscellaneous Forms

The miscellaneous vegetation forms in the Kimberley occur at the two climatic extremes. The former, the littoral complex, is found in the well-watered marshy coastal areas and the latter, the sandhill desert, is found along the southern fringe of the Fitzroy valley where the sclerophyll shrub savannah merges into the desert proper.

LITTORAL COMPLEX

This is found in the delta regions of the Ord, Chamberlain, Isdell, Lennard and Fitzroy rivers and other low-lying coastal areas which remain unmapped. The complex is composed of more than just the commonly known mangroves and contains areas of salt flats, coastal dunes, narrow grassland bands, mangroves, lagoon swamps and swampy grasslands. The salt flats are frequently bare but may be vegetated by a cover or fringing of halophytic (salt-loving) herbs and grasses. In the soils bordering these, a narrow band of salt-tolerant grasses may become established, and in seasonally flooded areas sedges and grasses of the swamp grassland thrive. The dune vegetation is more scrubby with low trees or tall shrubs found on the old dunes. Mangroves occur over a thick muddy soil along the tidal flats; in lagoons subject to periodic flooding, waterlilies are characteristic. This is an estaurine formation. The complex is of little economic signifance.

SANDHILL DESERT

Along the southern fringe of the Fitzroy valley lies the northern edge of the Canning desert. It is sparsely vegetated in the inter-dune corridors with hummock grass (spinifex) and a seasonal cover of herbs. Small shrubs, including species of *Hakea, Grevillea* and *Eremophila,* occur on the lower slopes of the characteristic dunes. Their crests are usually unstable. Along this fringe of the pastoral Fitzroy valley, where grasses have been overgrazed, dune sands are spreading northward and soil erosion poses an urgent problem. Further to the south the true desert is practically waterless and the vegetation too sparse for pastoral pursuits.

7. NATURAL VEGETATION OF THE NORTH-WEST

As previously mentioned, the natural vegetation of the North-West retains a close link with that of the Kimberley via the connecting corridor along the Eighty Mile Beach. The Indo-Malayan element is present though representative species may be in a more stunted form due to the increasing aridity of the climate. An essentially low rainfall is supplemented by the occurrence of cyclones between November and March and the incidence of plant species is surprisingly varied because of this. Plant life is adapted to the pattern of seasonal drought and xerophytic species are most abundant. Due to the reduction in available moisture, woodland communities are no longer in evidence and the characteristic sub-forms are hummock grasslands and shrub savannahs. The entire area is devoted to sheep grazing.

Grassland Form

The semi-arid tussock grassland and the sclerophyll hummock grassland are the representative associations of the grassland form found in the North-West.

SEMI-ARID TUSSOCK GRASSLAND

Patches of this grassland are found along the North-West coast from Exmouth Gulf to Anna Plains. This sub-form is essentially coastal and vegetation varies according to the nature of the underlying soil, be it coastal sand dune, loam flat or salt marsh. Hummock-forming grasses, such as spinifex, occupy the old sand hills and stony ridges but are not found on the loamy soils. Here the tussock-forming grasses predominate and species of Mitchell grass are important. Other species include woollybutt grass, salt grass, bundle-bundle and the introduced buffel grass. These pastures are of greater nutritive value than the spinifex but they are often over-grazed and the soils underlying them eventually reduced to dry clay-pans. Moves towards their reclamation are being made by some pastoralists. As a rule the grass flats are treeless but species of *Melaleuca,* especially the cadjiput tree, are found and on the sand ridges away from the coast, the camel tree and *Acacia* spp. are not uncommon.

Samphire flats and claypans occur where drainage is poor and accumulation of mineral salts in the soil is higher than elsewhere. Stunted acacias usually surround these flats while salt grass is the dominant grass form. Samphire species locally known as yellow, red or black samphire, ring the inner edges of the salt flats. Because of the mixed nature of this sub-form its grazing value is limited. However the tussock grasses do provide some of the better quality pasture of the North-West.

SCLEROPHYLL HUMMOCK GRASSLAND

This sub-form occurs over wide areas of the North-West and its occurrence coincides almost entirely with the upland area of the Pilbara block. It forms a complex with the sclerophyll shrub savannah in a wide band stretching from North-West Cape to the eastern edge of the block where the complex merges into the sandhill vegetation of the arid interior.

Sclerophyll hummock grassland, otherwise known as Triodia steppe[9], is found over the skeletal soils of the plateau in the North-West and is typified by spinifex species. Because of the dissected nature of the plateau in this region, the complex of hummock grassland and savannah is understandable. Where soils are poorer and drier, as on the rugged slopes, the hummock grass sub-form predominates, while in the better-watered valleys, grasslands are dotted with trees in the typical savannah formation.

Spinifex of this sub-form provides a pasture the value of which lies in its resistance to drought. It is a supplement to the better grasses of the savannah and in a bad season is often the only available pasture.

[9]C. A. Gardner, 'The Vegetation of Western Australia'.

Of the shrubs found in association with this grassland, species of *Acacia* such as kanji, and snakewood are found in the north with an increasing predominance of mulga to the south.

Savannah Form

Of the two savannah sub-forms found in the North-West only the northern savannah is a tree form. The sclerophyll low-tree savannah reflects the increasingly arid climate southward of the Kimberley, for the trees are of a more stunted type. In the sclerophyll shrub savannah, found to the south of the low tree savannah, the woody layer is further reduced to shrub form.

SCLEROPHYLL LOW-TREE SAVANNAH

As with its northern counterpart, the sclerophyll low-tree savannah of the North-West is dominated by a spinifex grass layer. This sub-form is restricted to the area of brown soils of light texture which occur across the northern fringe of the Pilbara block and northward along the Eighty Mile Beach. Other grasses of the sclerophyll low-tree savannah include wire and weeping grass, and along the river flats the tussock grasses such as Mitchell, Flinders and weeping grasses predominate. The occurrence of soft spinifex improves the quality of the hummock grassland, and in all this region provides a pasture of good feeding value.

On hill slopes the tree layer of the savannah is composed of the tropical white-wood and camel tree (locally called warralong) and the ubiquitous kanji. Other shrubby plants include species of *Acacia, Melaleuca, Grevillea* and *Hakea*. Where the soil conditions are better, particularly along river flood plains, a woodland characterized by *Eucalyptus* spp. is found.

SCLEROPHYLL SHRUB SAVANNAH

South of the sclerophyll low-tree savannah the vegetation of the North-West is typified by the complex association of the sclerophyll shrub savannah and the schlerophyll hummock grassland. The dominant species are hard-leaved and, whereas spinifex hummock grasses are characteristic of the plateau skeletal soils, the shrub savannah occupies the valley regions where moisture conditions are more favourable to the development of better quality grasses and shrubs.

On alluvial soils the predominant grasses of the savannah are Mitchell, Flinders, wire, beard, and spear grasses, silky browntop and *Sorghum* spp. Such grasses are more nutritious than the spinifex of the skeletal soils and supplement it for grazing. These grasses occur along the main river valleys and are found over a wider area in the Fortescue sunkland. Tropical trees occur also along the rivers where valleys are steep and in the declivities of the ranges. They include fig species, rosewoods and the camel or warralong tree. *Eucalyptus* spp., such as flood-gums and coolibah, are also present.

In the savannah of the open range country the shrub species are characterized by *Acacia* spp., and these include kanji, snakewood, curara and the occasional mulga. The bloodwood Eucalypt is representative of the scattered small trees of the savannah while *Cassia, Hakea* and *Grevillea* spp. are common shrubs. There is little variation in the vegetation towards the coast so that the Cape Range area has a similar ecology to that of the plateau. Old coastal and ridge dunes are fixed with spinifex and the rough stony hills carry spinifex and scrubby *Acacia* spp. including kanji and snakewood.

Shrub Communities

The only shrub community found in the North-West is that of the arid shrub which is found to the south of the Pilbara block within the 10 inch rainfall isohyet. The arid scrub is found as a complex with the sclerophyll shrub savannah, the latter being the characteristic sub-form of the North-West area.

ARID SCRUB

Arid scrub is dominated by a layer of tall shrubs or low trees branching close to the ground. In view of the characteristic *Acacia* sp. commonly called mulga, this sub-form is otherwise known as mulga bush.[10] It is most commonly developed over soils with a hard sub-soil close to the surface and in the North-West overlies arid red earths and red and brown hard pan soils. Where soils are lighter and deeper the mulga becomes scarce or its place is taken by another *Acacia* sp., the bowgada bush.

Arid scrub is typical of the Minilya, Gascoyne and Murchison areas. The topography of these areas is more gently undulating and less rugged than that to the north. Over large areas the dull green-leaved acacias of the lower hill slope provide a uniformity of colour and physiognomy which is characteristic. Where the topography is broken by rocky outcrops, a more varied flora occurs and along breakaways and escarpments scrubby plants such as *Hibiscus, Grevillea, Melaleuca* spp., and native fuchsias are found. Where the scrub is more scattered a remarkable growth of ephemeral flora is witnessed after good rains and the whole area is carpeted with annual herbs whose floral wealth is unexcelled in any other sub-form.

Along what may be called the channel country of the arid scrub region, where the heavier textured soils are found, the sclerophyll shrub savannah sub-form is located. The vegetation reflects the wetter conditions and, although *Acacia* spp. are present, *Eucalyptus* spp. mostly form a savannah with Mitchell, wire and kangaroo grasses, native vetches and native lucernes. It is the occurrence of this sub-form, in suitable localities throughout the area covered by arid scrub, which enhances the region's pastoral value. It is however the vegetational region which is most prone to drought and one where pastoralism is most hazardous.

[10]C. A. Gardner, 'The Vegetation of Western Australia'.

8. Natural Vegetation of the Arid Interior

Over most of the surface area of the arid interior vegetation is sparse, the characteristic sub-forms being the Sandhill Desert and the Stony Desert. On the outer fringes of the Great Sandy Desert and the Gibson Desert which roughly underly the above sub-forms, sclerophyll shrub savannah, sclerophyll hummock grassland, arid scrub and low arid woodland communities are found. These latter are usually transitional types where the rainfall is a little higher.

The central region of the arid interior is a true desert incapable of supporting man or his animals. It is unoccupied and has little or no economic potential. The Great Western Desert is at least of equal aridity to the Simpson Desert in Central Australia which ranks fifth on a vegetational basis of aridity amongst the world's hot deserts.[11] The only source of information concerning the vegetation of the region has been garnered from reports of the area's explorers, for no botanical investigations have been carried out here.

Within the boundaries of the arid interior the climate is capricious. Rainfall is low and of uncertain regularity and temperatures are extreme. The elements composing the vegetation of this region are derived both from northern and southern origins and, with few exceptions, the tropical types are confined to loamy or alluvial soils while species of southern origin are found over sandy soils. In this hostile environment the permanent element is sclerophyllous; the herbaceous plants are ephemeral or markedly xerophytic in structure. Most woody plants have a covering of hairs, or a protective layer of resin, their leaf surface is reduced and their seeds are noted for their longevity. The characteristic grass is spinifex.

Woodland Form

The only representative of the woodland form is the low arid woodland which occurs in a mixed complex with arid scrub and sclerophyll shrub savannah in the hilly region surrounding the Rawlinson and Warburton ranges near the Western Australian border. This complex is characteristic of the mountain and range country of Central Australia and forms a continuation of it. Trees of this sub-form are low, but where moisture conditions are favourable as on drainage flats, they form a woodland formation. *Acacia* spp. predominate, especially mulga, and *Casuarina* spp. are common.

Shrub Communities

Arid scrub forms part of the above complex and it may be seen as an opening out of the low arid woodland, for its dominant elements are *Acacia* and *Casuarina* spp.. It is found over the gently undulating hills of this area. However, where the topography is broken by escarpments, native fuchsias,

[11]Commonwealth Department of National Development, 1st series, with commentaries, *Vegetation Regions*.

needle bushes and species of *Cassia* and *Grevillea* break the monotony of the dull green *Acacia* community.

Savannah Form

The third element in the complex vegetation found about the hilly border country is the sclerophyll shrub savannah. Here it occupies loam flats and the occurrence of tussock grasses indicate better soil moisture conditions. Acacias are prominent in this sub-form but *eucalypts* are found in drainage channels where the cork tree and desert she-oak may also be found.

The sclerophyll shrub savannah is also found in a complex with a sclerophyll hummock grassland in the area surrounding Lake Carnegie and in a small area around the shores of Lake Disappointment.

Grassland Form

In all cases where the grassland form borders on the arid interior, it is represented by the sclerophyll hummock grassland and is in a complex with the sclerophyll shrub savannah. This sub-form borders the desert in the north-east in the vicinity of the Gregory Salt Sea, in the west along the drainage basin of the Oakover River and in the south-west between Lake Carnegie and the Gibson Desert.

The sclerophyll hummock grassland is here typified by an open layer of grasses such as spinifex which are adapted to an arid habitat. Between the isolated grass hummocks, societies of short-lived annuals may thrive after precipitation. Whereas spinifex occupies sandy or rocky slopes, low-lying land is vegetated by a savannah sub-form where tussock grasses and *Acacia* spp. are located.

Miscellaneous Forms

The greater part of the arid interior is occupied by the vegetation species typical of the Sandhill and Stony deserts. The area is marked by the extensive development of red sand which prevails either in the form of undulating country or parallel sand ridges. Low cliffs or escarpments mark the edge of plateaux which may be sand or gibber plains, the depressions between may be sandy or loamy. The dunes are either devoid of vegetation or populated by widely spaced hummocks of spinifex and isolated xerophytic shrubs which have been stunted by the harsh environment. The stony table lands or gibber plains are often bare or grassy in patches and the herbage of these plains is ephemeral.

Sandhill Desert

The vegetation of the Sandhill Desert is typified by those species which inhabit the inter-ridge depressions and lower slopes of the sandhills. The cover is sparse and consists of xeromorphic grasses, seasonal herbs and low shrubs. The dune crests are often bare and unstable but sometimes they are populated with clumps of spinifex, cane and wanderrie grasses and small half-woody shrubs. The lower slopes of the dunes are scantily grassed with spinifex and shrubby plants such as native fuchsias and species of *Crotalaria, Newcastlia, Duboisia* and *Grevillea*. The *Hakea* sp. commonly known as needlewood is found in depressions between the dunes. Where such shrubs abound they give shelter to semi-succulents including species of *Euphorbia*.

It must be remembered that although the number of plant species found in the Sandhill Desert is considerable, a list of them may imply a greater vegetation cover than exists. The Sandhill Desert remains a true desert and one which threatens to encroach upon the richer formations around its borders. This is particularly so along its northern and north-western fringes where careful pastoral management is necessary to check erosion and the threatened invasion by this impoverished sub-form.

Stony Desert

In the centre of the arid interior are extensive undulating areas of bare wind-eroded sand and gibber plains known as the Gibson Desert. The vegetation sub-form here is that of the Stony Desert and it is represented by a very sparse cover of low shrubs, which inhabit depression areas, and a seasonal cover of short-lived annuals when moisture conditions are most propitious.

The only trees found in the Stony Desert are located in drainage depressions or where seepage provides soil water at the foot of escarpments. The most common of these are the desert she-oak, the cork tree, a few mulga bushes and stunted *Eucalyptus* spp. On heavy soils isolated patches of blue bush and saltbush occur. Ephemeral flora resembling that of the savannah formations, is in evidence after heavy rains but it quickly dies after completing a short life cycle.

9. SUMMARY

The vegetation of Northwestern Australia strongly reflects both climatic and edaphic factors. Upon this basis the area has been divided into the Kimberley, the North-West and the arid interior, and the representative forms and sub-forms of each discussed.

Plant species over this vast region represent both indigenous and imported types, the major outside element being Indo-Malayan. Tropical species have spread southward from the Kimberley and provide a bridge between the vegetation of the Kimberley and the North-West. In no case is the climate moist enough to support tropical forests, but woodland sub-forms are characteristic of the North Kimberley. These woodlands grade into savannah formations, then to grassland and eventually to desert associations as climatic and edaphic factors become increasingly harsh. There is however no complete merging from one form to another according to climatic pattern as soils and topography exert a strong influence upon the natural flora.

Apart from the woodlands of the north, savannah and grassland sub-forms are characteristic and even the central desert region is typified by a sparse

MAJOR VEGETATION FORMS AND SUB-FORMS OF NORTHWESTERN AUSTRALIA

Trees dominant *Sclerophyllous*	Sclerophyll Woodland		Dominants deciduous	Summer Growth: Tall grass layer 'Tropical Woodland' Mixed (K)	TROPICAL DECIDUOUS WOODLAND (K)
			Trees low; subordinate layers sparse and seasonal	Sparse Semi-arid to arid communities	LOW ARID WOODLAND (K)
Shrubs dominant	Shrubs medium to tall	Dominants without Mallee habit	Ground flora sparse; growth after spasmodic rain	Only one developed tall shrub stratum	ARID SCRUB (A.I.)
	Scattered trees Tree Savannah	Trees medium, grass strata dense		Grasses tall, summer growing	TROPICAL TREE SAVANNAH (K)
		Trees low, grasses of hummock form			SCLEROPHYLL LOW-TREE SAVANNAH (K. and N.W.)
Grasses dominant	Scattered shrubs Shrub Savannah	Grasses of hummock form			SCLEROPHYLL SHRUB SAVANNAH (K., N.W. and A.I.)
	Trees or tall shrubs absent or nearly so.	Grasses tall, summer growing			TROPICAL TUSSOCK GRASSLAND (K)
		Grasses short to medium; open strata with many annuals			SEMI-ARID TUSSOCK GRASSLAND (K. and N.W.)
	Grassland	Grasses low to medium; open hummock form			SCLEROPHYLL HUMMOCK GRASSLAND (K., N.W.)
Deserts	A very sparse complex of annual herbs, zerophytic medium shrubs and hummock form grasses	Sandy dune soils			SANDHILL DESERT (K. and A.I.)
		Stony pavement soils			STONY DESERT (A.I.)

After Commonwealth Department of National Development, Atlas of Australian Resources, 1st series, with commentaries, *Vegetation Regions*, 1955. Canberra.
K. Kimberley, N.W. North-West, A.I. Arid Interior.

cover of hummock grasses. For this reason the natural vegetation of Northwestern Australia forms the basis of a large pastoral industry. In view of the unreliability of rainfall over the entire region there are strict limits to the pastoral areas which border the arid interior. Serious soil erosion problems have been created when this limit has been over-reached and natural pasture has become impoverished as a result.

BIBLIOGRAPHY

BEATTIE, W. A. *A Survey of the Beef Cattle Industry of Australia.* Commonwealth Scientific and Industrial Research Organisation Bulletin no. 278. Melbourne, 1956.

BURVILL, G. H. 'Soil Surveys and Related Investigations in the Ord River Area, East Kimberley, 1944.' Report of the Department of Agriculture, Western Australia. Mimeographed paper, 1945.

CHRISTIAN, C. S. and STEWART, G. A. 'Report on Preliminary Examination of Several Areas in the West Kimberley Division of Western Australia.' Commonwealth Scientific and Industrial Research Organisation Land Research and Regional Survey Section. Reference from unpublished records no. 52/1, held at the Public Works Department, Perth. Contains a detailed survey of selected river soils in the West Kimberley and points to their agricultural potential.

CHURCHWARD, H. M. and BETTENAY, E. *The Soils of Portion of the Fitzroy River Valley at Liveringa Station, Western Australia.* Melbourne, 1962.

COMMONWEALTH DEPARTMENT OF NATIONAL DEVELOPMENT. Atlas of Australian Resources, 1st series, with commentaries. *Soils,* 1953; *Vegetation Regions,* 1955. Canberra.

COMMONWEALTH SCIENTIFIC AND INDUSTRIAL RESEARCH ORGANISA- TION. *Lands and Pastoral Resources of the North Kimberley Area, Western Australia.* Land Research Series, no. 4. Melbourne, 1960.

—— *Lands of the Wiluna-Meekatharra Area, Western Australia.* Land Research Series, no. 7. Melbourne, 1963.

—— *General Report on Lands of the West Kimberley Area, Western Australia.* Land Research Series, no. 9. Melbourne, 1964.

FITZGERALD, K. 'Soil Conversion in the Kimberley Area of Western Australia.' *Journal of Agriculture,* vol. 1, no. 11. 1960. Deals with soil erosion problems, with suggested schemes of conservation and results of present experiments.

GAFFNEY, D. O. 'The Economic Development of the Kimberleys with particular reference to Climate.' Unpublished M.A. thesis, 1957. Library of the University of Western Australia. Contains comments relating to soils and natural vegetation.

GARDNER, C. A. 'The Vegetation of Western Australia.' *Journal of the Royal Society of Western Australia,* vol. 28. 1942. This publication has particular reference to the relationship of vegetation to climate and soils. Basic reference for vegetation distribution.

—— *Flora of Western Australia,* vol. 1, part 1. Perth, 1952. Contains comment on isolation as an erosion factor.

GASCOYNE RESEARCH STATION. 'Gascoyne Research Station Report.' *Journal of Agriculture,* vol. 4. 1955. Describes the development of irrigation agriculture. Some comments on soils.

GENTILLI, J. 'The Survival of the National Environment in Western Australia.' *The Western Australian Naturalist,* vol. 7, no. 7. Observations concerning the survival of species of flora and fauna in Western Australia. Special reference to pastoral grasses of the north.

GUPPY, D. J., LINDNER, A. W., RATTIGAN, J. H. and CASEY, J. N. *The Geology of the Fitzroy Basin, Western Australia.* Bureau of Mineral Resources Bulletin no. 36. 1958.

KIMBERLEY RESEARCH STATION. 'Kimberley Research Station Progress Report, 1958.' *Journal of Agriculture,* vol. 7, no. 2. 1958. Detailed report of agricultural experimentation as at that date. Information concerning how soils of the Ord (c. clay) stand up to irrigation.

MARSHALL, T. J. *Physical Properties of Ord River Soils.* Commonwealth Scientific and Industrial Research Organisation Division of Soils Divisional Report no. 15. 1944.

STEPHENS, C. G. *The Soil Landscapes of Australia.* Commonwealth Scientific and Industrial Research Organisation Soil Publication no. 18. Melbourne, 1961.

WESTERN AUSTRALIA FORESTS DEPARTMENT. 'Visit of the Conservator and Party to the Kimberleys, 17th October, 1958.' Forests Department Record 671. 1958. Information on some aspects of Kimberley vegetation. Comments on soil erosion and soil conservation.

INDEX

INDEX

288; and climate, 380; and industry groupings, 220; and mineral resources, 331; and mining, 93; and pastoral industry, 74-79; and population growth, 28; and power resources, 213; and secondary industry, 223; and structural change, 287; and tertiary industry, 224; and transport, 246, 270-273; and water resources, 186-187

Development pattern to 1950, 288-291; agriculture, 289; fishing 289; mining, 288-289; pastoral industry, 288; secondary industry, 289; tertiary industry, 289

Development pattern 1950-1965, 291-295; agriculture, 293-294; cattle industry, 291, 293; fishing, 293; mining, 293; sheep industry, 291

Development 1965-1975, 295-301; administrative aspects, 302-304; agriculture, 299; basic problems, 300; fishing, 299; government and private development, 301-302; mining, 298; pastoral industry, 297-298; proposals for policy, 307-315; research and planning, 304-307; secondary industry, 300

Dirk Hartog Island, 359, 367, 390
Durack, Kim, 161, 190, 197
Durack River, 321, 397
Drysdale River, 189, 200, 201-202, 321, 399

East Kimberley, 6, 19, 50, 59, 61, 312, 361; capital investment, 72; goldfield, 350; health services, 232; minerals, 336, 345; Ord River Project, 166, 178, 195, 203; pastoral settlement, 43-46 pass., 196-197; road transport, 67-68, 247, 248, 254-255

Education, 3, 22, 230-231
Education Department, 17, 22, 230-231
Eighty Mile Beach: climate, 358, 373; natural vegetation, 406, 414; pearling, 135-136; physiography, 327-328, 329; soils, 395

Employment, 12-23; Carnarvon agriculture, 150; effect of climatic discomfort on, 377-378; effect of working conditions on, 308; fishing industry, 134; future development, 300; and industrial development, 221; of natives, 16-22, 27; pastoral industry, 42, 49-50, 77; seasonal nature of, 13-14, 27; wages and earnings, 14-16, 27

Exmouth: health services, 231; housing, 228; port, 247, 266; town water supply, 207; townsite established, 233; transport, 257

Exmouth Gulf, 12, 14, 136, 326, 328, 394, 416; fishing, 138, 142; oil search, 96; temperatures, 370; and tropical cyclones, 372

Felspar, 332, 335, 337, 350, 351
Fisheries and Fauna, Department of, 143, 144, 225, 312
Fishing industry, 7, 8, 134-145; aboriginal labour, 16, 19; changes since 1950, 293; crustaceans and shellfish, 141-142, 144, 293; early history, 135-137, 289, 373; employment, 11-12, 134; fish resources, 142-144; future prospects, 134-135, 138-139, 144-145, 297, 299; offshore fishery development, 142-144; pearl culture, 140-141, 144, 293, 299; pearling, 135-137, 139-141, 221, 289, 293, 299; policy proposals, 311-312, 313; prawns, 141-142, 293, 299; scalefish, 137-139, 144, 293; tuna, 143; whaling, 134, 137, 144, 289, 293

Fitzgerald, K., 56
Fitzroy basin: artesian water, 212; oil exploration, 121-122, 351; physiography, 325, 344; soils, 397
Fitzroy Crossing: government administrative agencies, 225; and rainfall, 361; and transport, 23, 47, 56, 67, 71, 248, 250, 254
Fitzroy River, 254-259 pass., 415; agriculture, 161-163, 256; climate, 355, 361; damsites, 197-198; hydrology, 199; pastoral settlement, 42-46; physiography and geology, 321, 325; road transport, 248; soils, 396, 397, 401, 402, 403, 406; water

percentages, 50, 56, 77; lease conditions, 42-43, 45, 46, 51-53, 74, 310-311; markets, 68-70, 74; mechanization, 48-49; and mining, 95, 331; and natural vegetation, 408-416; and Ord River Project, 178-179; Pastoral Leases Committee, 52; pasture development, 53-59; and physiography, 321, 322; policy proposals, 310-311; present characteristics, 47-53; production trends, 50-51; property size, 51-53; rural holdings and land utilization, 48; soils, 395, 396; soil erosion, 401-406; transport, 64-68, 252-256, 261-264, pass., 270-271; vermin, 3, 45, 59-64, 71-72, 288, 310

Peak Hill, 336, 343, 370

Peak Hill Goldfield, 323, 336, 338, 350, 342-343

Pearling, 139-141; early history, 135-137, 289, 373; future prospects, 299; pearl culture, 140-141, 144; recent developments, 293

Pentecost River basin, 200, 202

Perloff, H. S., Dunn, E. S., Lampard, E. E., Muth, R. F., 220

Physiography and Geology, 288, 317-329; Bonaparte Gulf plain, 327; Canning basin, 324; Carnarvon basin, 326; Carnarvon coastal plain, 328, 329; coastal plains, 326; Drysdale River basin, 201; Eighty Mile Beach, 327-328, 329; Fitzroy River, 199; Gulf Basin, 324; Isdell River basin, 200-201; King Edward River basin, 201, Kimberley block, 321-322, 317-329 pass.; Lennard River basin, 200; Nullagine platform, 322-323; Onslow coastal plain, 328, 329; Precambrian shield, 317, 319-323; Prince Regent River basin, 201; and secondary industry, 223; sedimentary basins, 324-326; and transport, 246, 267, 270, 271; and underground water, 211-212; Yilgarn block, 323

Pilbara, 3, 4; air transport, 259; asbestos, 95, 334; climate, 358, 368, 369-370; copper, 94, 261; future prospects for mining, 126-129, 298; goldfield, 94-95, 336, 337, 346, 347-350; impact

of iron ore development, 108-115; iron ore, 307, 338-341; iron ore mining, 106-108, 257, 293, 302; lead, 345; living conditions, 25; manganese, 115, 257, 342-343; mining, 93-129 pass., 287, 303, 332; mineral production, 99; mining workforce, 98; native labour, 17, 19; other minerals, 96, 261, 347-350; pasture development, 54, 77; population, 12; postal facilities, 227; public capital, 71-72, 78; rural holdings and land utilization, 48; secondary industry, 222; stock numbers, 47-48; telephone and telegraph facilities, 227; transport of livestock, 255, 256, 263; transport of minerals, 257-258; vermin, 59-64, 77; water resources, 186-190, 203-204, 206, 216

Pilbara block: and minerals, 332, 338, 340-341, 342, 346, 348; natural vegetation, 417; physiography, 322; and rainfall, 367; soils, 393, 394

Pindan, 19-21

Pindan country, 46, 162, 325, 394, 396, 413

Planet Fisheries Ltd. 139, 142

Point Cloates, 134, 137

Point Samson, 323, 334-335; port, 247, 257, 268; town water consumption and supply, 206, 208; transport, 257, 261

Policy proposals: for agriculture, 312; costs of proposed measures, 309-310; for fishing industry, 311-312; for government, 307; to improve native conditions, 308-309; to increase available real income, 308; to increase disposable income, 308; for mining development, 311; for pastoral lease conditions, 310-311; for town planning, 313; for using revenues for reinvestment, 309-310

Population, 2, 10-29, 287; aboriginal, 16-22; demographic characteristics, 10-11; density, 2, 10, 246; effect of working and living conditions on, 308; employment, 13-16; growth, 11-12, 27-28; 295; and mining, 97; and transport 270